BY **KIRKMAN**
& **AZACETA**

BOOK ONE

CREATED BY **ROBERT KIRKMAN**

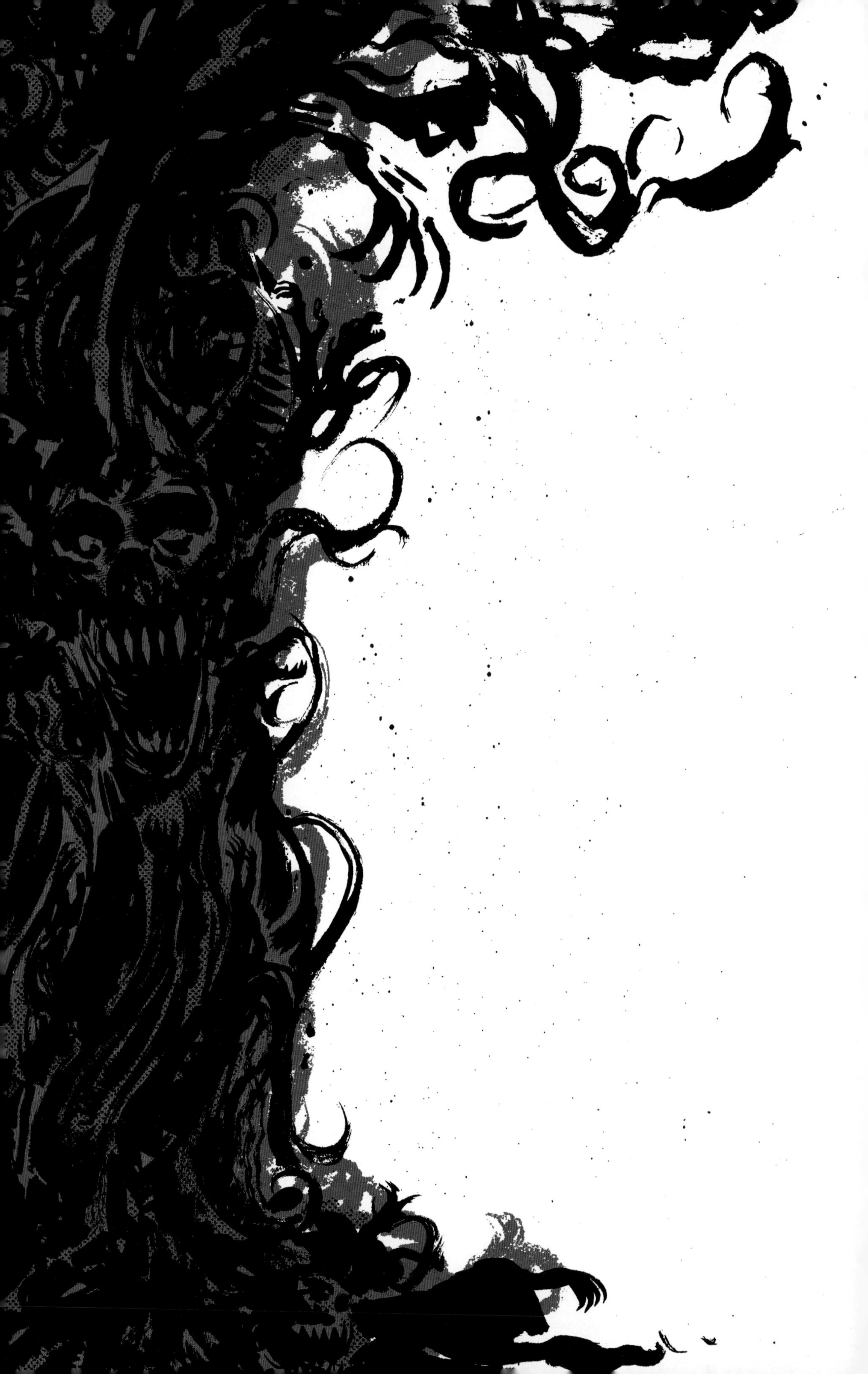

Robert Kirkman
Creator, Writer

Paul Azaceta
Artist

Elizabeth Breitweiser
Colorist

Rus Wooton
Letterer

Paul Azaceta
Elizabeth Breitweiser
Cover

Arielle Basich
Assistant Editor

Sean Mackiewicz
Editor

Rian Hughes
Logo Design

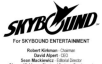

For SKYBOUND ENTERTAINMENT

Robert Kirkman - Chairman
David Alpert - CEO
Sean Mackiewicz - Editorial Director
Shawn Kirkham - Director of Business Development
Brian Huntington - Online Editorial Director
June Alian - Publicity Director
Jon Moisan - Editor
Arielle Basich - Assistant Editor
Andres Juarez - Graphic Designer
Stephan Murillo - Business Development Assistant
Johnny O'Dell - Online Editorial Assistant
Dan Petersen - Operations Manager
Nick Palmer - Operations Coordinator

International inquiries: ag@sequentialrights.com
Licensing inquiries: contact@skybound.com

WWW.SKYBOUND.COM

IMAGE COMICS, INC.
Robert Kirkman – Chief Operating Officer
Erik Larsen – Chief Financial Officer
Todd McFarlane – President
Marc Silvestri – Chief Executive Officer
Jim Valentino – Vice-President

Eric Stephenson – Publisher
Corey Murphy – Director of Sales
Jeff Boison – Director of Publishing Planning & Book Trade Sales
Jeremy Sullivan – Director of Digital Sales
Kat Salazar – Director of PR & Marketing
Branwyn Bigglestone – Controller
Drew Gill – Art Director
Jonathan Chan – Production Manager
Meredith Wallace – Print Manager
Briah Skelly – Publicist
Sasha Head – Sales & Marketing Production Designer
Randy Okamura – Digital Production Designer
David Brothers – Branding Manager
Olivia Ngai – Content Manager
Addison Duke – Production Artist
Vincent Kukua – Production Artist
Tricia Ramos – Production Artist
Jeff Stang – Direct Market Sales Representative
Emilio Bautista – Digital Sales Associate
Leanna Caunter – Accounting Assistant
Chloe Ramos-Peterson – Library Market Sales Representative
IMAGECOMICS.COM

Outcast By Kirkman & Azaceta™ Book One. First Printing. Published by Image Comics, Inc., Office of publication: 2001 Center Street, 6th Floor, Berkeley, California 94704.

PRINTED IN CANADA. Regular Edition: 978-1-5343-0091-0, LCSD Edition: 978-1-5343-0121-4

CHAPTER 1:
A DARKNESS SURROUNDS HIM

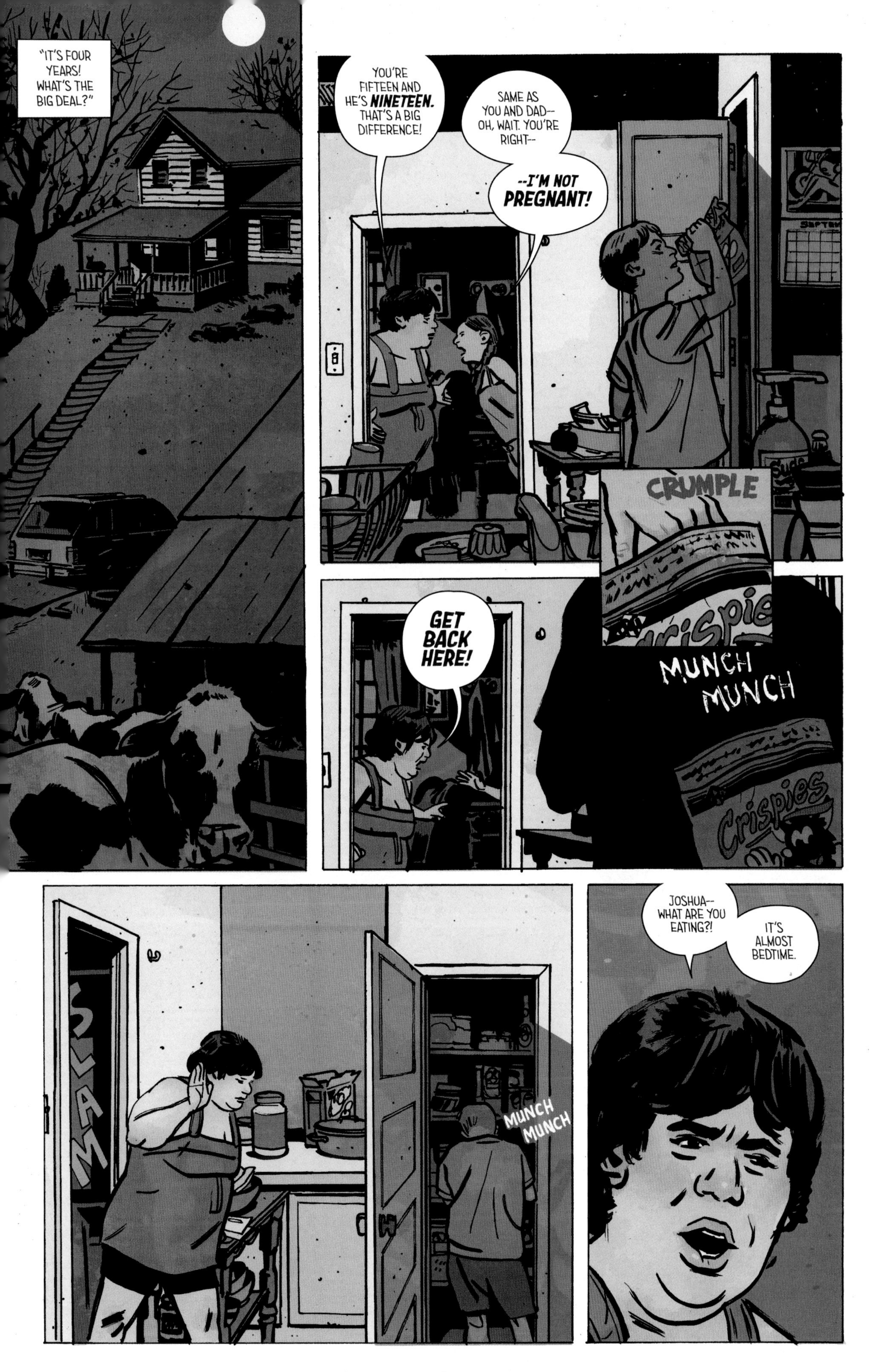
"IT'S FOUR YEARS! WHAT'S THE BIG DEAL?"
YOU'RE FIFTEEN AND HE'S NINETEEN. THAT'S A BIG DIFFERENCE!
SAME AS YOU AND DAD-- OH, WAIT. YOU'RE RIGHT--
--I'M NOT PREGNANT!
CRUMPLE
Crispies
GET BACK HERE!
MUNCH MUNCH
Crispies
SLAM
MUNCH MUNCH
JOSHUA-- WHAT ARE YOU EATING?!
IT'S ALMOST BEDTIME.

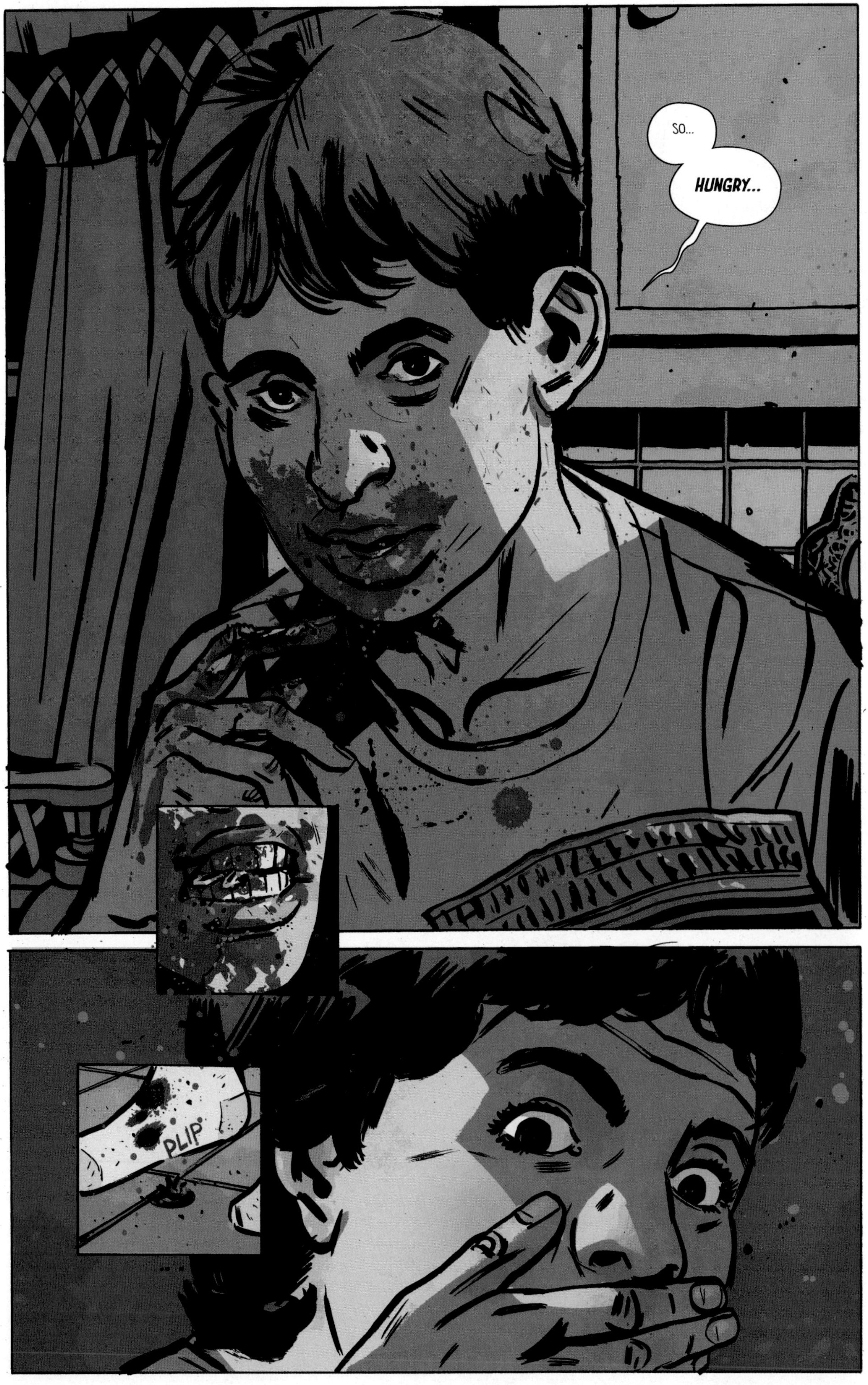
SO...
HUNGRY...
PLIP

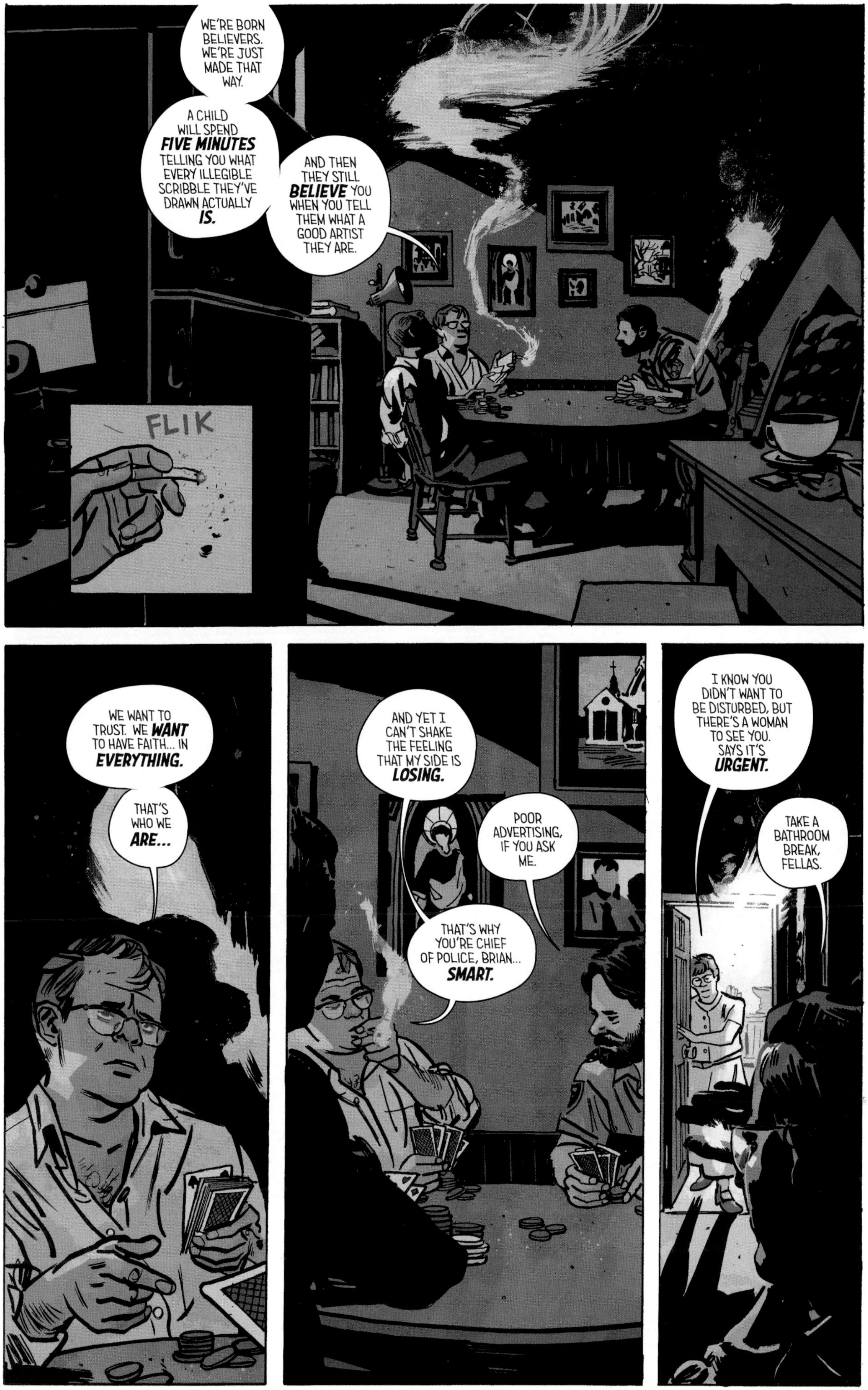
WE'RE BORN BELIEVERS. WE'RE JUST MADE THAT WAY.
A CHILD WILL SPEND FIVE MINUTES TELLING YOU WHAT EVERY ILLEGIBLE SCRIBBLE THEY'VE DRAWN ACTUALLY IS.
AND THEN THEY STILL BELIEVE YOU WHEN YOU TELL THEM WHAT A GOOD ARTIST THEY ARE.
FLIK
WE WANT TO TRUST. WE WANT TO HAVE FAITH... IN EVERYTHING.
THAT'S WHO WE ARE...
AND YET I CAN'T SHAKE THE FEELING THAT MY SIDE IS LOSING.
POOR ADVERTISING, IF YOU ASK ME.
THAT'S WHY YOU'RE CHIEF OF POLICE, BRIAN... SMART.
I KNOW YOU DIDN'T WANT TO BE DISTURBED, BUT THERE'S A WOMAN TO SEE YOU. SAYS IT'S URGENT.
TAKE A BATHROOM BREAK, FELLAS.

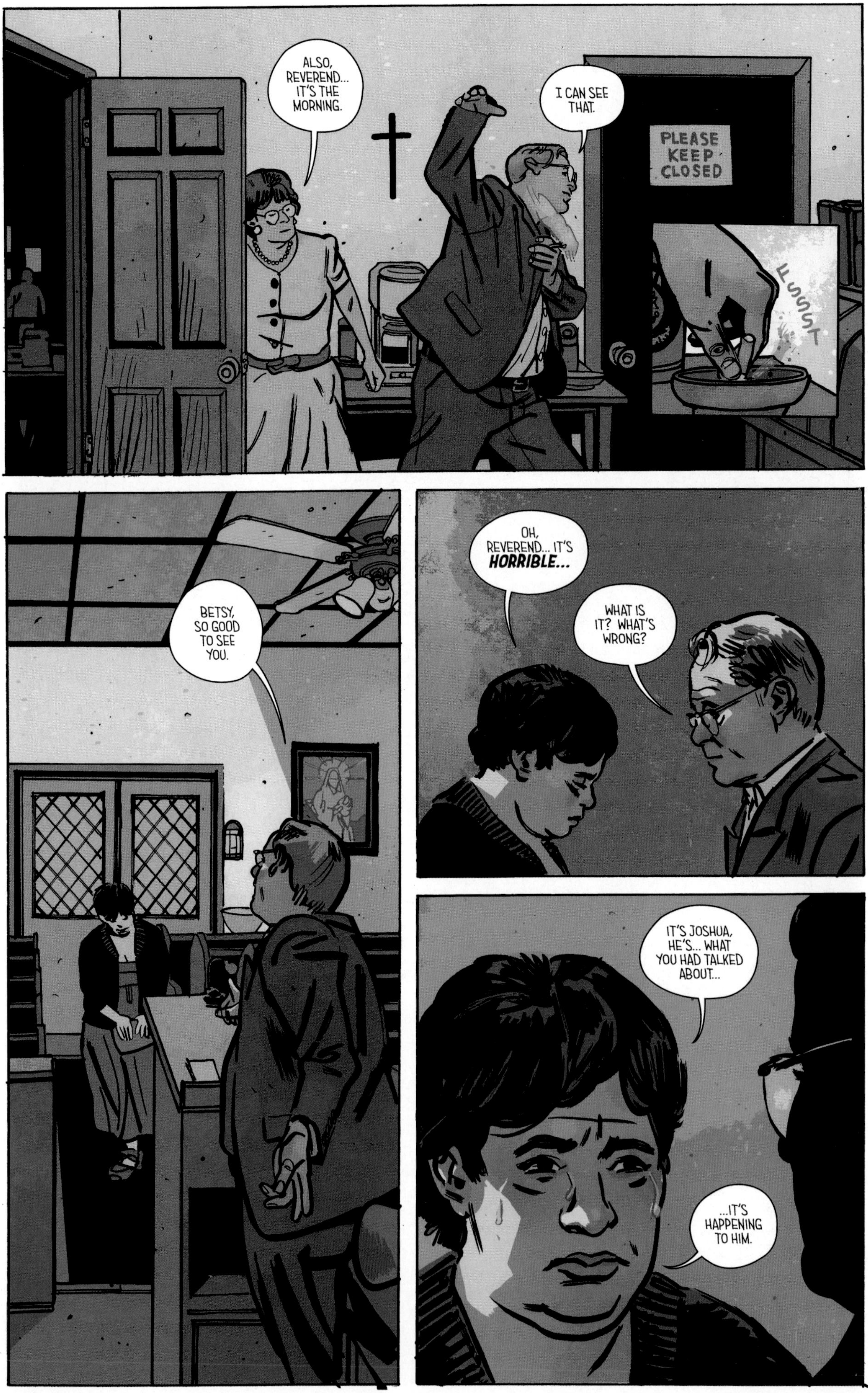
ALSO, REVEREND... IT'S THE MORNING.
I CAN SEE THAT.
PLEASE KEEP CLOSED
FSSST
BETSY, SO GOOD TO SEE YOU.
OH, REVEREND... IT'S HORRIBLE...
WHAT IS IT? WHAT'S WRONG?
IT'S JOSHUA, HE'S... WHAT YOU HAD TALKED ABOUT...
...IT'S HAPPENING TO HIM.

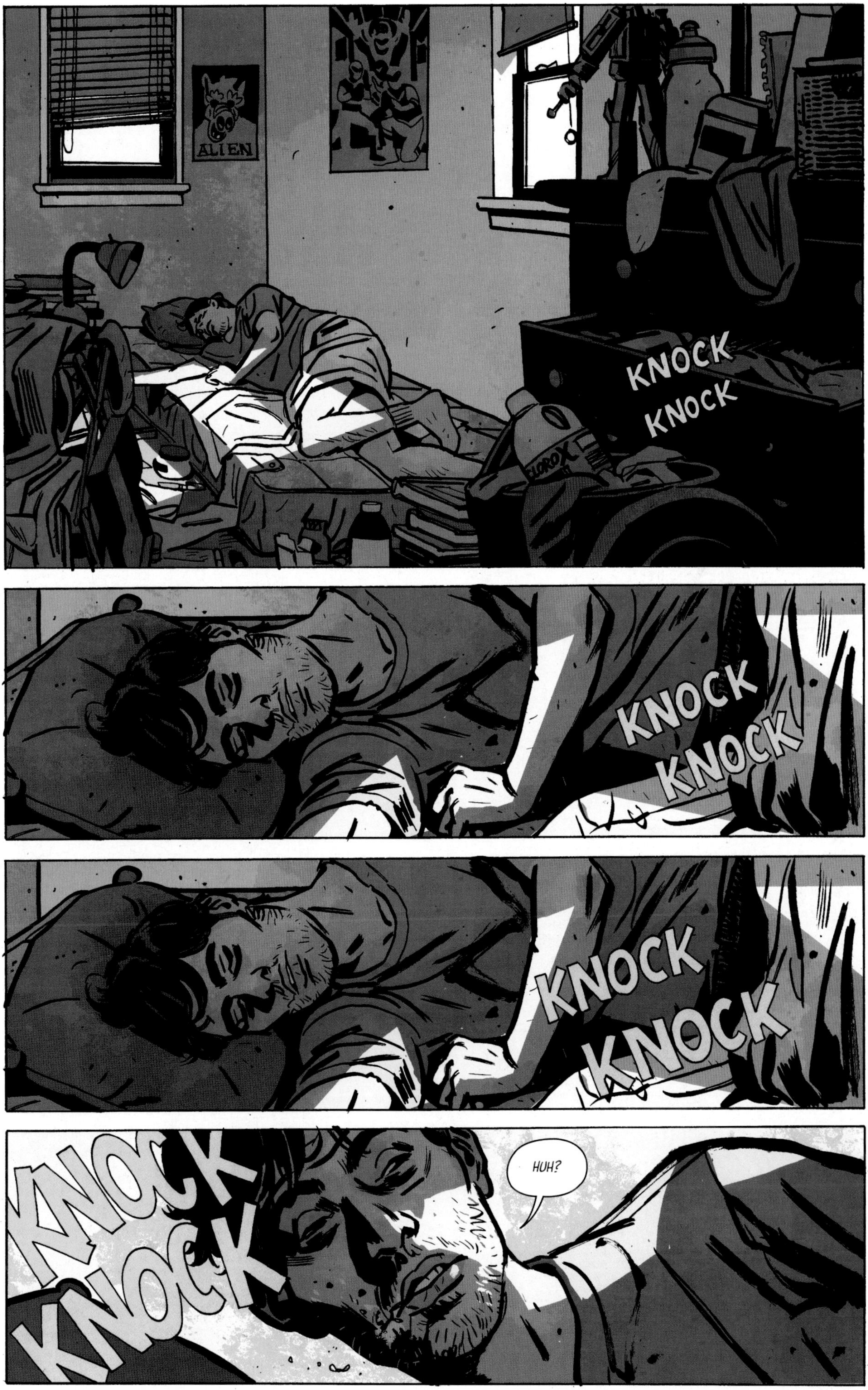
ALIEN
CLOROX
KNOCK
KNOCK
KNOCK
KNOCK
KNOCK
KNOCK
KNOCK
KNOCK
HUH?

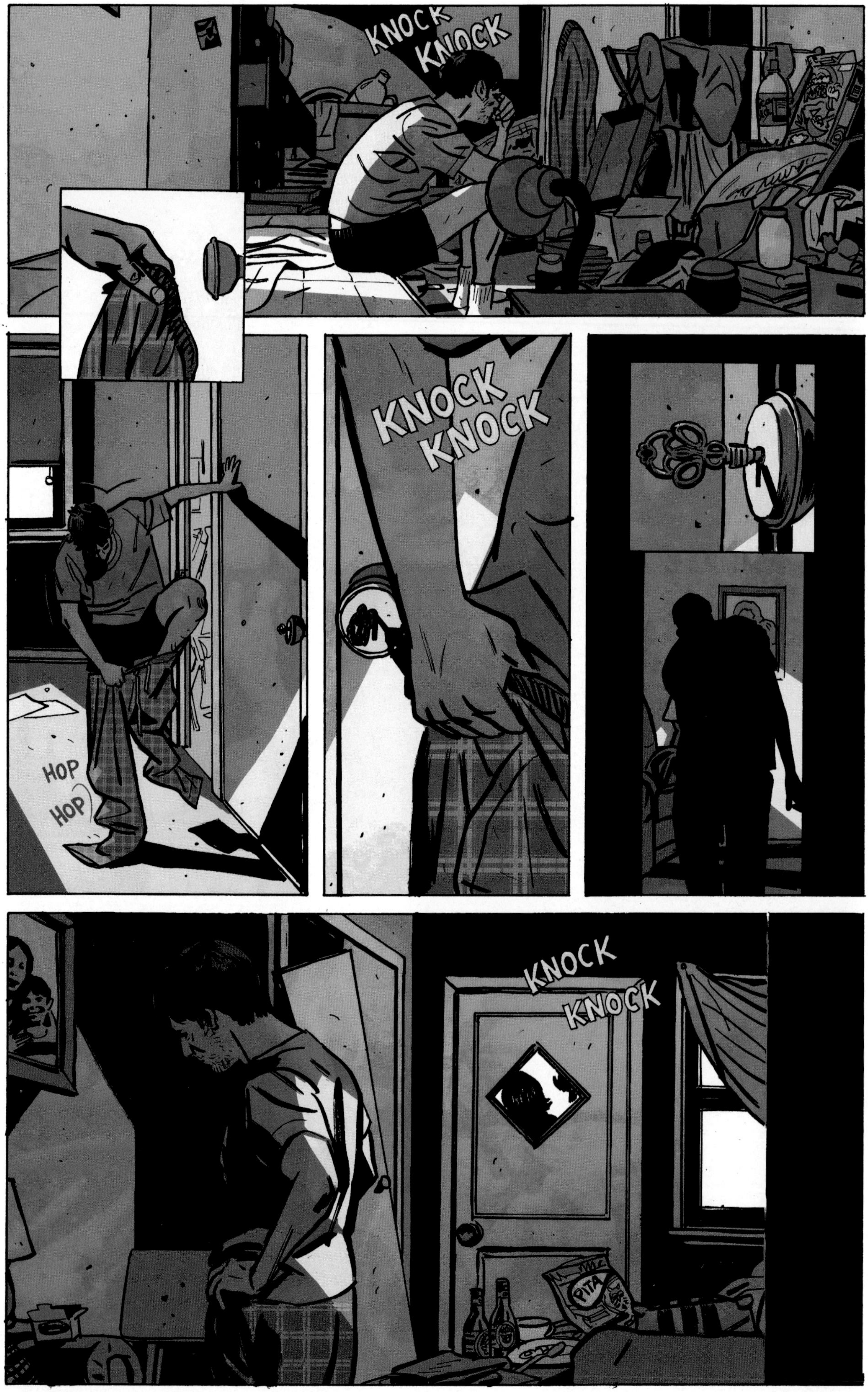
KNOCK
KNOCK
HOP
HOP
KNOCK
KNOCK
KNOCK
KNOCK
PITA

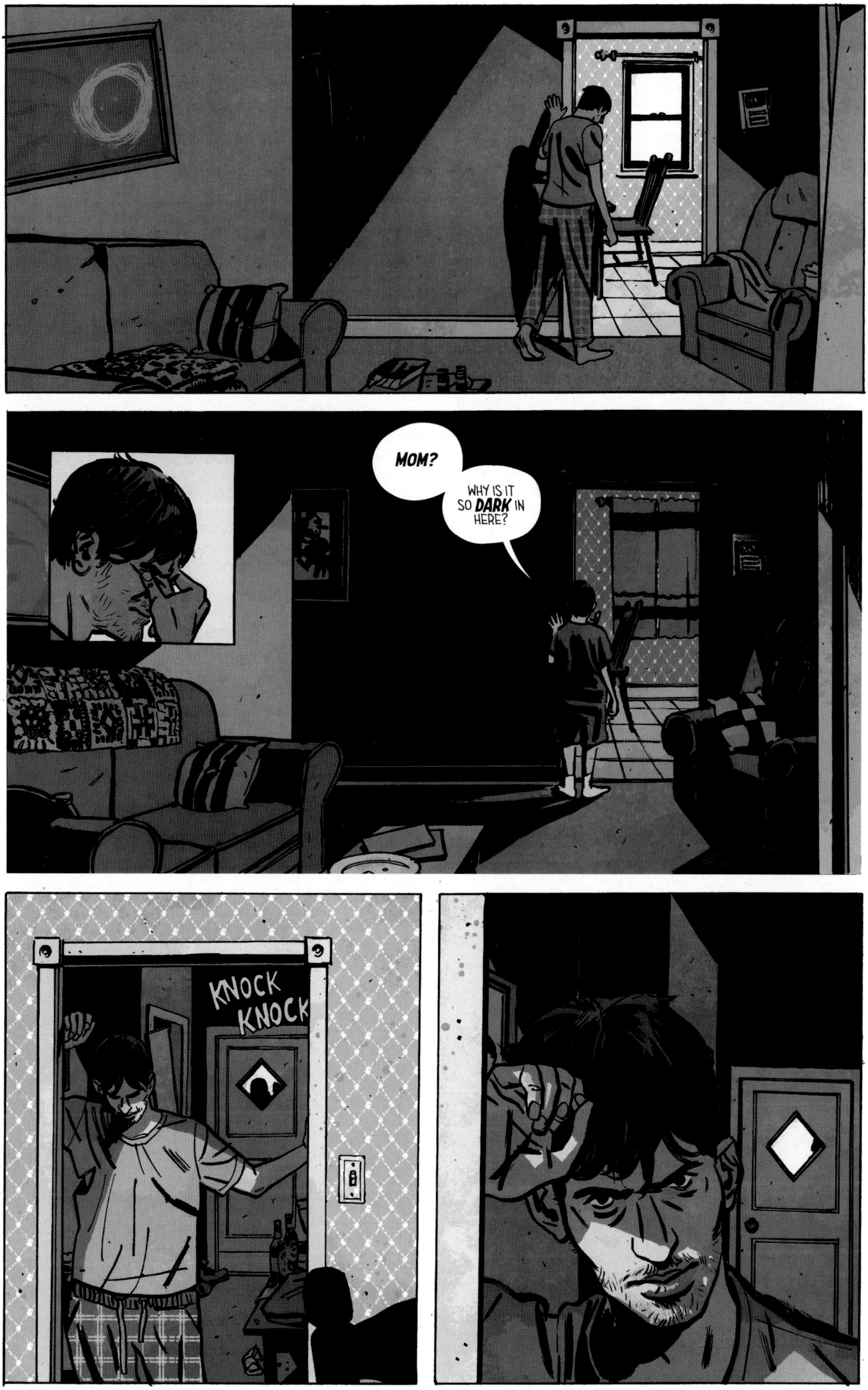
MOM?
WHY IS IT SO DARK IN HERE?
KNOCK KNOCK

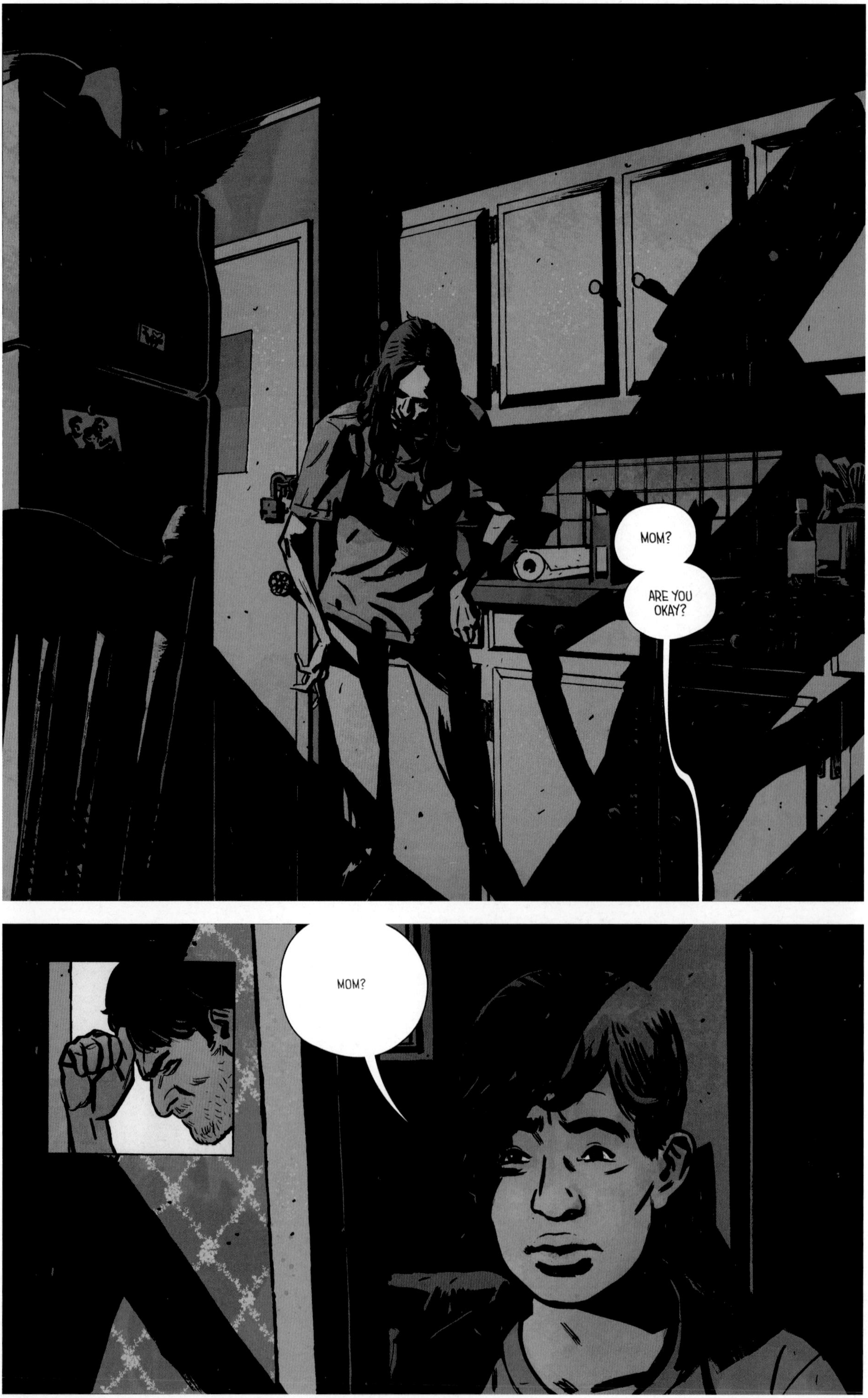
MOM?
ARE YOU OKAY?
MOM?

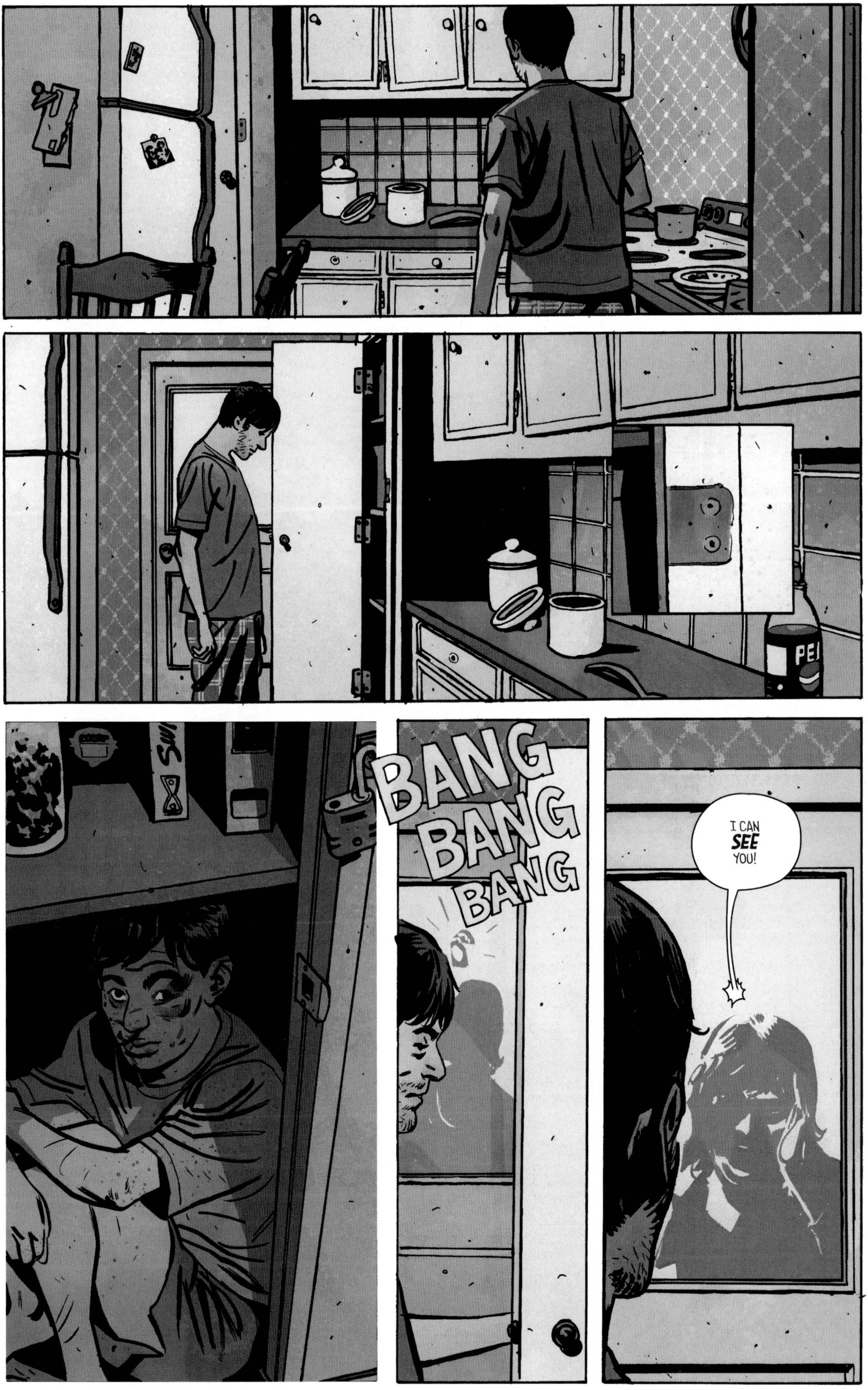
BANG
BANG
BANG
I CAN **SEE** YOU!

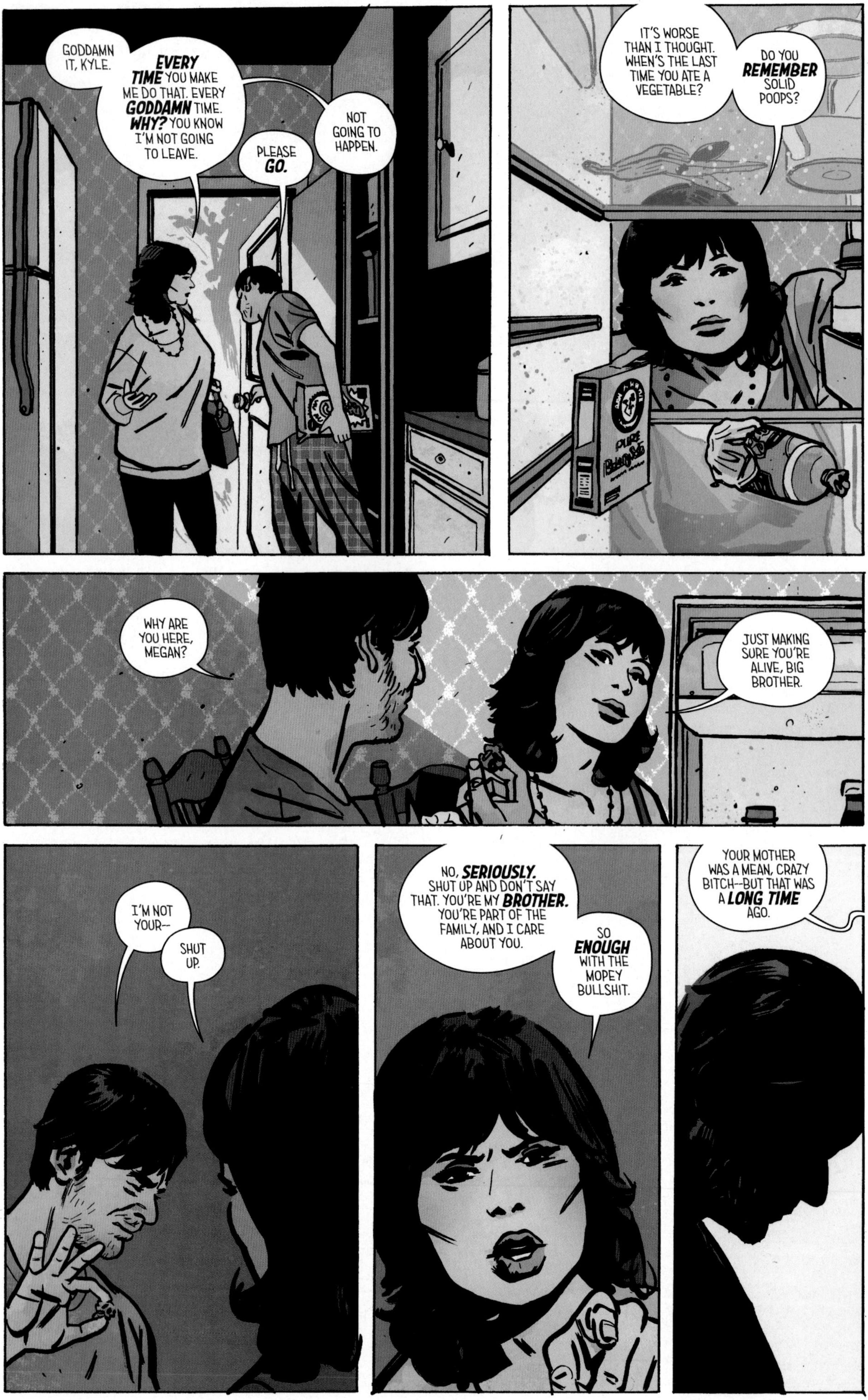
GODDAMN IT, KYLE.
EVERY TIME YOU MAKE ME DO THAT. EVERY GODDAMN TIME. WHY? YOU KNOW I'M NOT GOING TO LEAVE.
PLEASE GO.
NOT GOING TO HAPPEN.
IT'S WORSE THAN I THOUGHT. WHEN'S THE LAST TIME YOU ATE A VEGETABLE?
DO YOU REMEMBER SOLID POOPS?
PURE
WHY ARE YOU HERE, MEGAN?
JUST MAKING SURE YOU'RE ALIVE, BIG BROTHER.
I'M NOT YOUR--
SHUT UP.
NO, SERIOUSLY. SHUT UP AND DON'T SAY THAT. YOU'RE MY BROTHER. YOU'RE PART OF THE FAMILY, AND I CARE ABOUT YOU.
SO ENOUGH WITH THE MOPEY BULLSHIT.
YOUR MOTHER WAS A MEAN, CRAZY BITCH--BUT THAT WAS A LONG TIME AGO.

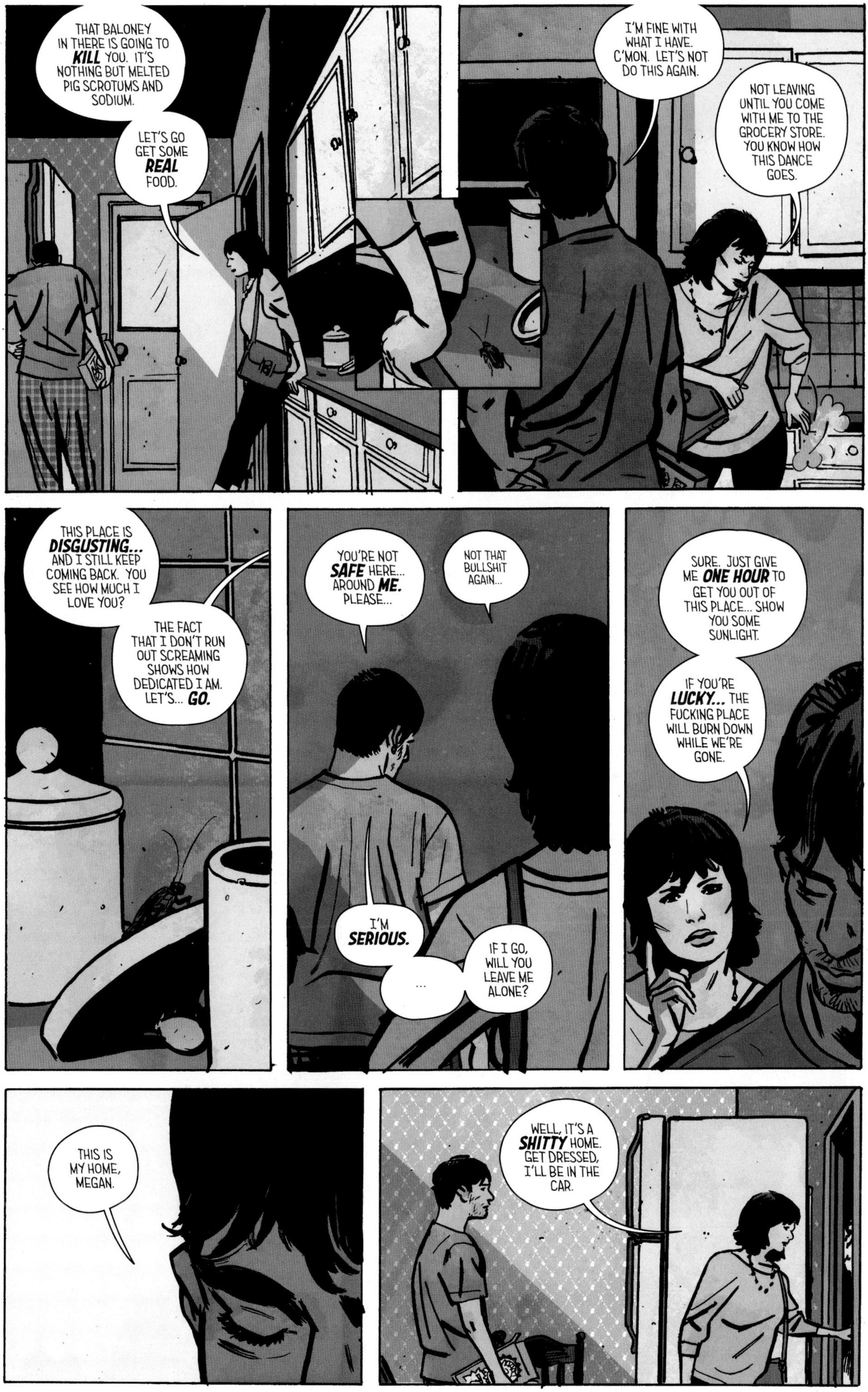
THAT BALONEY IN THERE IS GOING TO KILL YOU. IT'S NOTHING BUT MELTED PIG SCROTUMS AND SODIUM.
LET'S GO GET SOME REAL FOOD.
I'M FINE WITH WHAT I HAVE. C'MON. LET'S NOT DO THIS AGAIN.
NOT LEAVING UNTIL YOU COME WITH ME TO THE GROCERY STORE. YOU KNOW HOW THIS DANCE GOES.
THIS PLACE IS DISGUSTING... AND I STILL KEEP COMING BACK. YOU SEE HOW MUCH I LOVE YOU?
THE FACT THAT I DON'T RUN OUT SCREAMING SHOWS HOW DEDICATED I AM. LET'S... GO.
YOU'RE NOT SAFE HERE... AROUND ME. PLEASE...
NOT THAT BULLSHIT AGAIN...
I'M SERIOUS.
...
IF I GO, WILL YOU LEAVE ME ALONE?
SURE. JUST GIVE ME ONE HOUR TO GET YOU OUT OF THIS PLACE... SHOW YOU SOME SUNLIGHT.
IF YOU'RE LUCKY... THE FUCKING PLACE WILL BURN DOWN WHILE WE'RE GONE.
THIS IS MY HOME, MEGAN.
WELL, IT'S A SHITTY HOME. GET DRESSED, I'LL BE IN THE CAR.

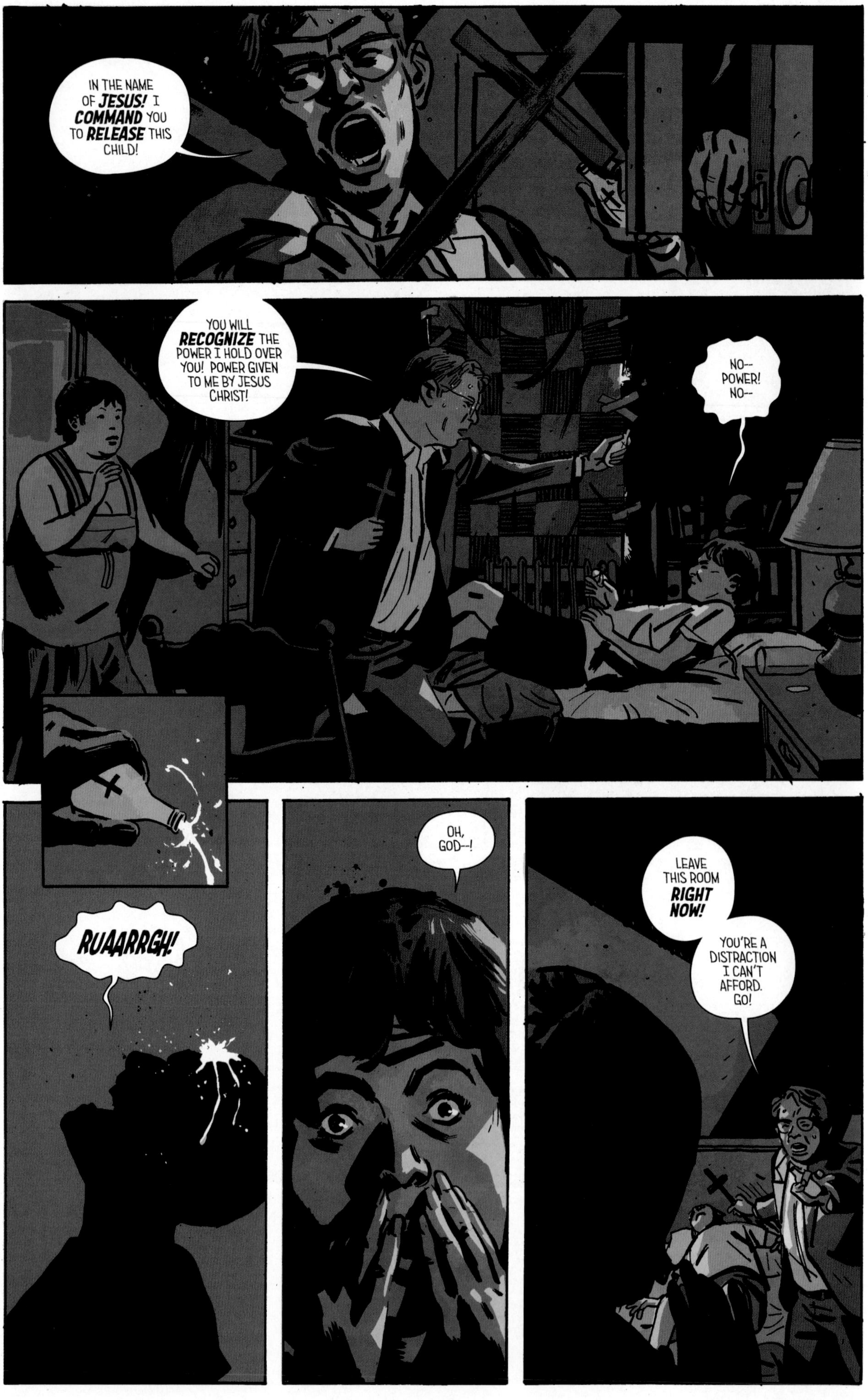
IN THE NAME OF JESUS! I COMMAND YOU TO RELEASE THIS CHILD!
YOU WILL RECOGNIZE THE POWER I HOLD OVER YOU! POWER GIVEN TO ME BY JESUS CHRIST!
NO-- POWER! NO--
RUAARRGH!
OH, GOD--!
LEAVE THIS ROOM RIGHT NOW!
YOU'RE A DISTRACTION I CAN'T AFFORD. GO!

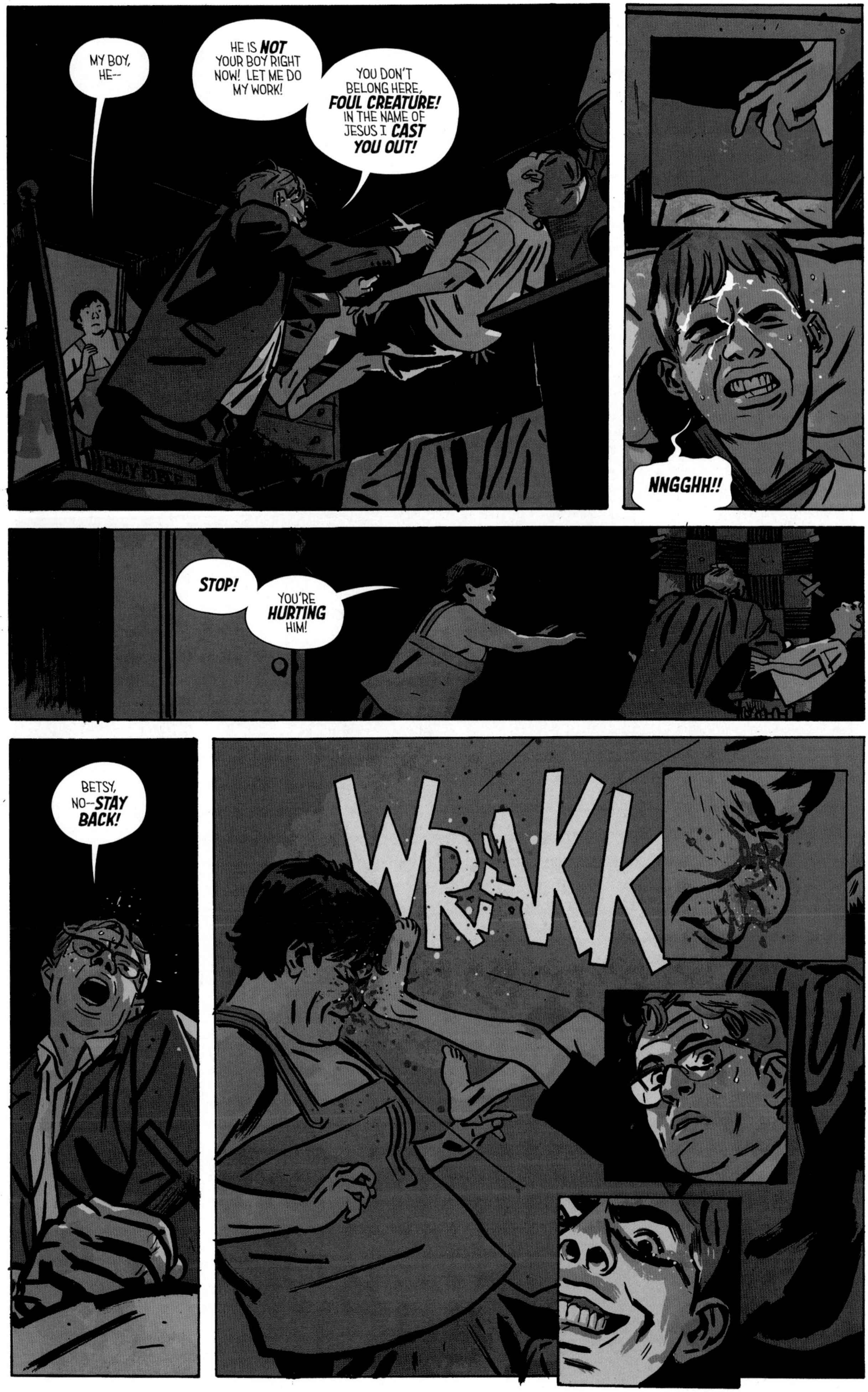
MY BOY, HE--
HE IS NOT YOUR BOY RIGHT NOW! LET ME DO MY WORK!
YOU DON'T BELONG HERE, FOUL CREATURE! IN THE NAME OF JESUS I CAST YOU OUT!
NNGGHH!!
STOP!
YOU'RE HURTING HIM!
BETSY, NO--STAY BACK!
WRAKK

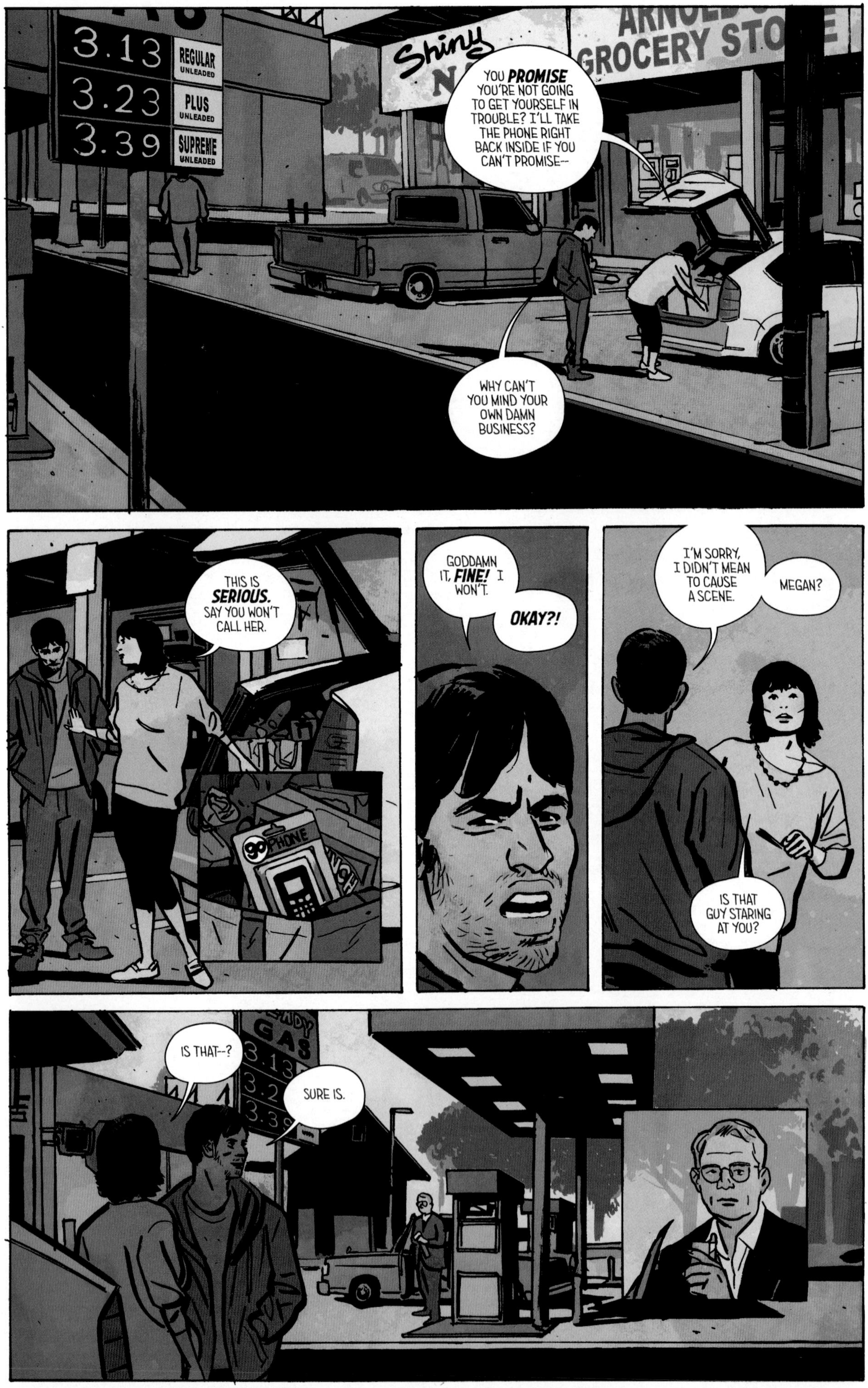
3.13 REGULAR UNLEADED
3.23 PLUS UNLEADED
3.39 SUPREME UNLEADED
GROCERY STORE
YOU **PROMISE** YOU'RE NOT GOING TO GET YOURSELF IN TROUBLE? I'LL TAKE THE PHONE RIGHT BACK INSIDE IF YOU CAN'T PROMISE--
WHY CAN'T YOU MIND YOUR OWN DAMN BUSINESS?
THIS IS **SERIOUS.** SAY YOU WON'T CALL HER.
PHONE
GODDAMN IT, **FINE!** I WON'T.
OKAY?!
I'M SORRY, I DIDN'T MEAN TO CAUSE A SCENE.
MEGAN?
IS THAT GUY STARING AT YOU?
GAS
IS THAT--?
SURE IS.

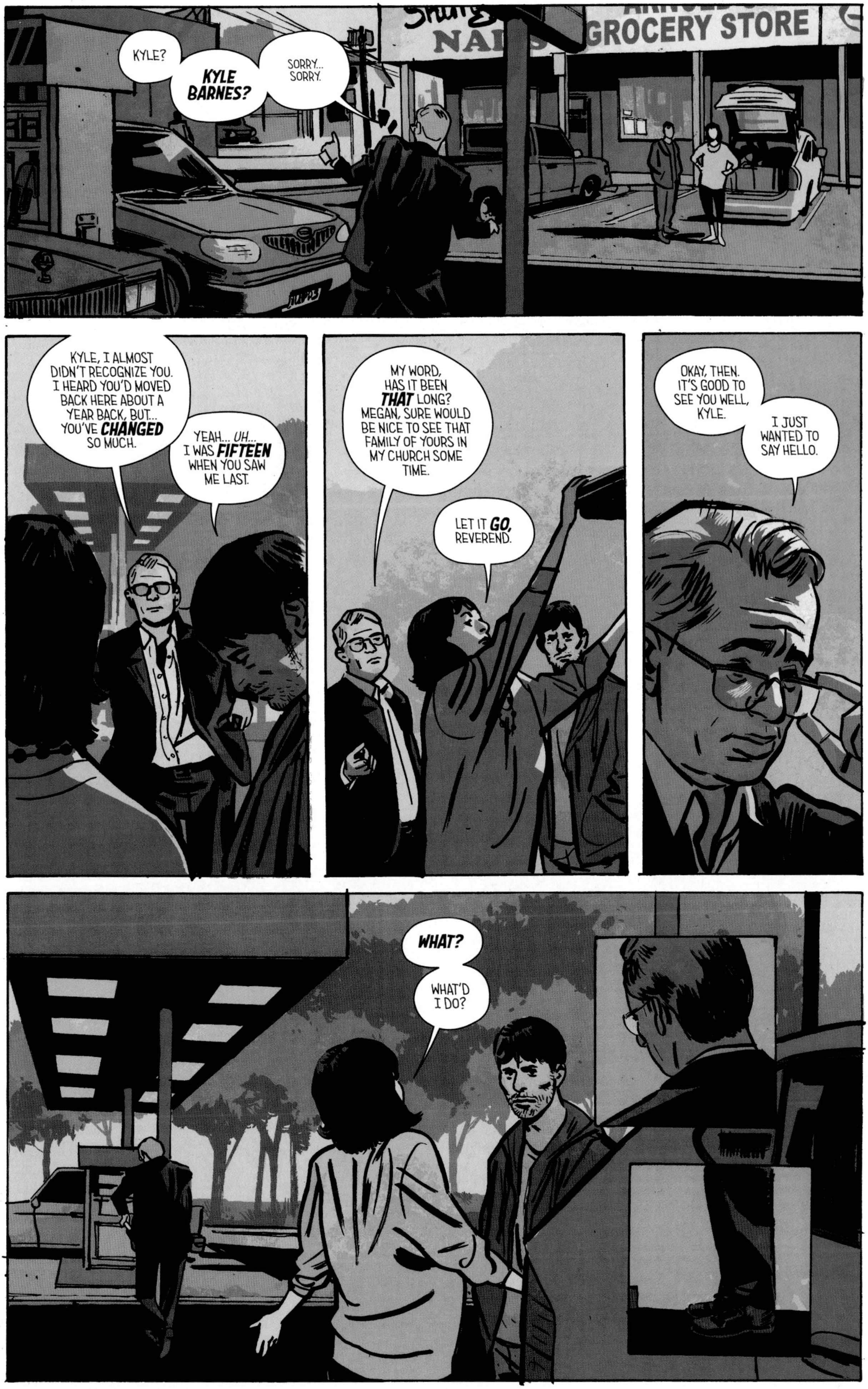

NAILS
GROCERY STORE
KYLE?
KYLE BARNES?
SORRY... SORRY.
KYLE, I ALMOST DIDN'T RECOGNIZE YOU. I HEARD YOU'D MOVED BACK HERE ABOUT A YEAR BACK, BUT... YOU'VE CHANGED SO MUCH.
YEAH... UH... I WAS FIFTEEN WHEN YOU SAW ME LAST.
MY WORD, HAS IT BEEN THAT LONG? MEGAN, SURE WOULD BE NICE TO SEE THAT FAMILY OF YOURS IN MY CHURCH SOME TIME.
LET IT GO, REVEREND.
OKAY, THEN. IT'S GOOD TO SEE YOU WELL, KYLE.
I JUST WANTED TO SAY HELLO.
WHAT?
WHAT'D I DO?

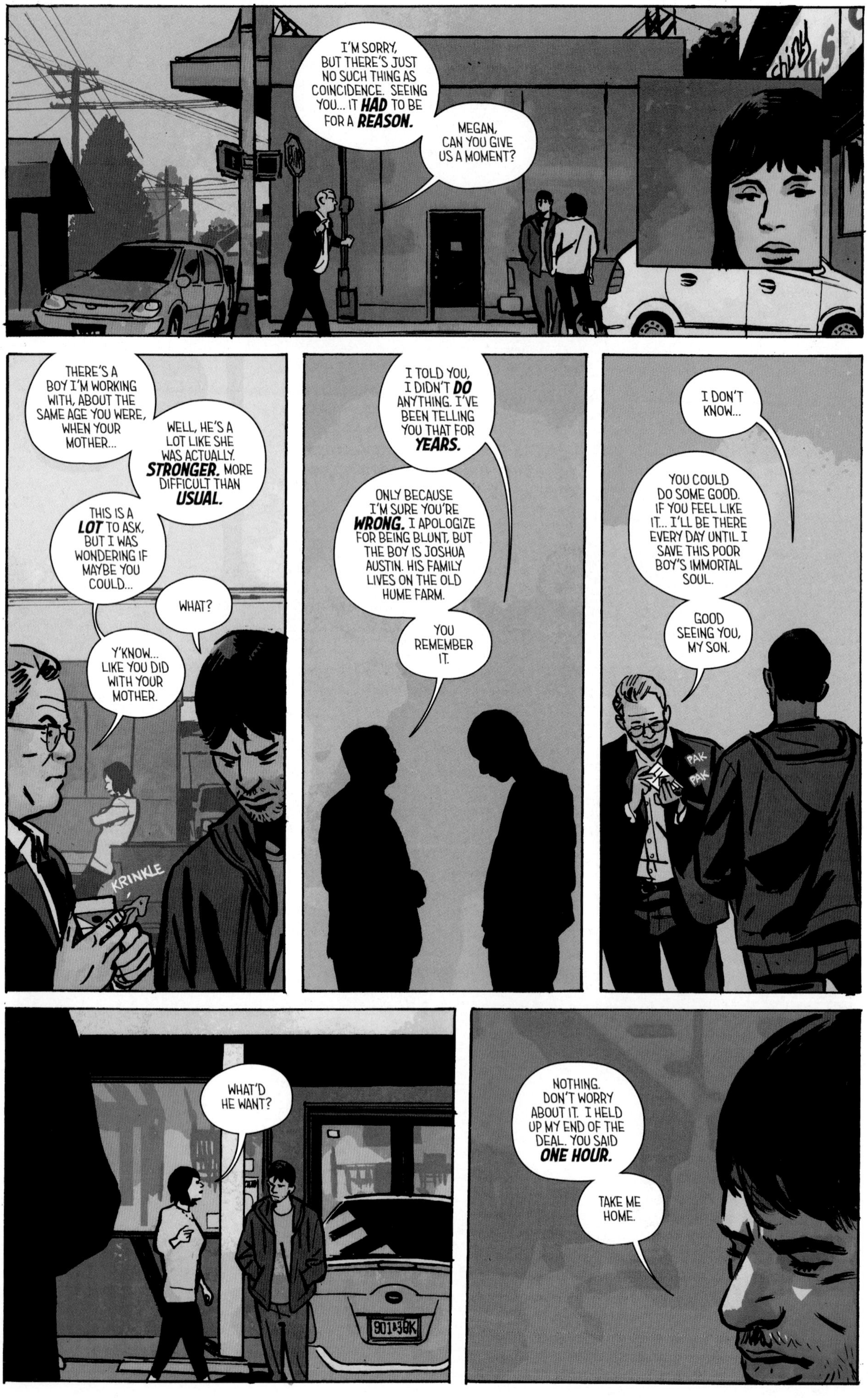
I'M SORRY, BUT THERE'S JUST NO SUCH THING AS COINCIDENCE. SEEING YOU... IT **HAD** TO BE FOR A **REASON.**
MEGAN, CAN YOU GIVE US A MOMENT?
THERE'S A BOY I'M WORKING WITH, ABOUT THE SAME AGE YOU WERE, WHEN YOUR MOTHER...
WELL, HE'S A LOT LIKE SHE WAS ACTUALLY. **STRONGER.** MORE DIFFICULT THAN **USUAL.**
THIS IS A **LOT** TO ASK, BUT I WAS WONDERING IF MAYBE YOU COULD...
WHAT?
Y'KNOW... LIKE YOU DID WITH YOUR MOTHER.
KRINKLE
I TOLD YOU, I DIDN'T **DO** ANYTHING. I'VE BEEN TELLING YOU THAT FOR **YEARS.**
ONLY BECAUSE I'M SURE YOU'RE **WRONG.** I APOLOGIZE FOR BEING BLUNT, BUT THE BOY IS JOSHUA AUSTIN. HIS FAMILY LIVES ON THE OLD HUME FARM.
YOU REMEMBER IT.
I DON'T KNOW...
YOU COULD DO SOME GOOD. IF YOU FEEL LIKE IT... I'LL BE THERE EVERY DAY UNTIL I SAVE THIS POOR BOY'S IMMORTAL SOUL.
GOOD SEEING YOU, MY SON.
PAK
PAK
WHAT'D HE WANT?
NOTHING. DON'T WORRY ABOUT IT. I HELD UP MY END OF THE DEAL. YOU SAID **ONE HOUR.**
TAKE ME HOME.

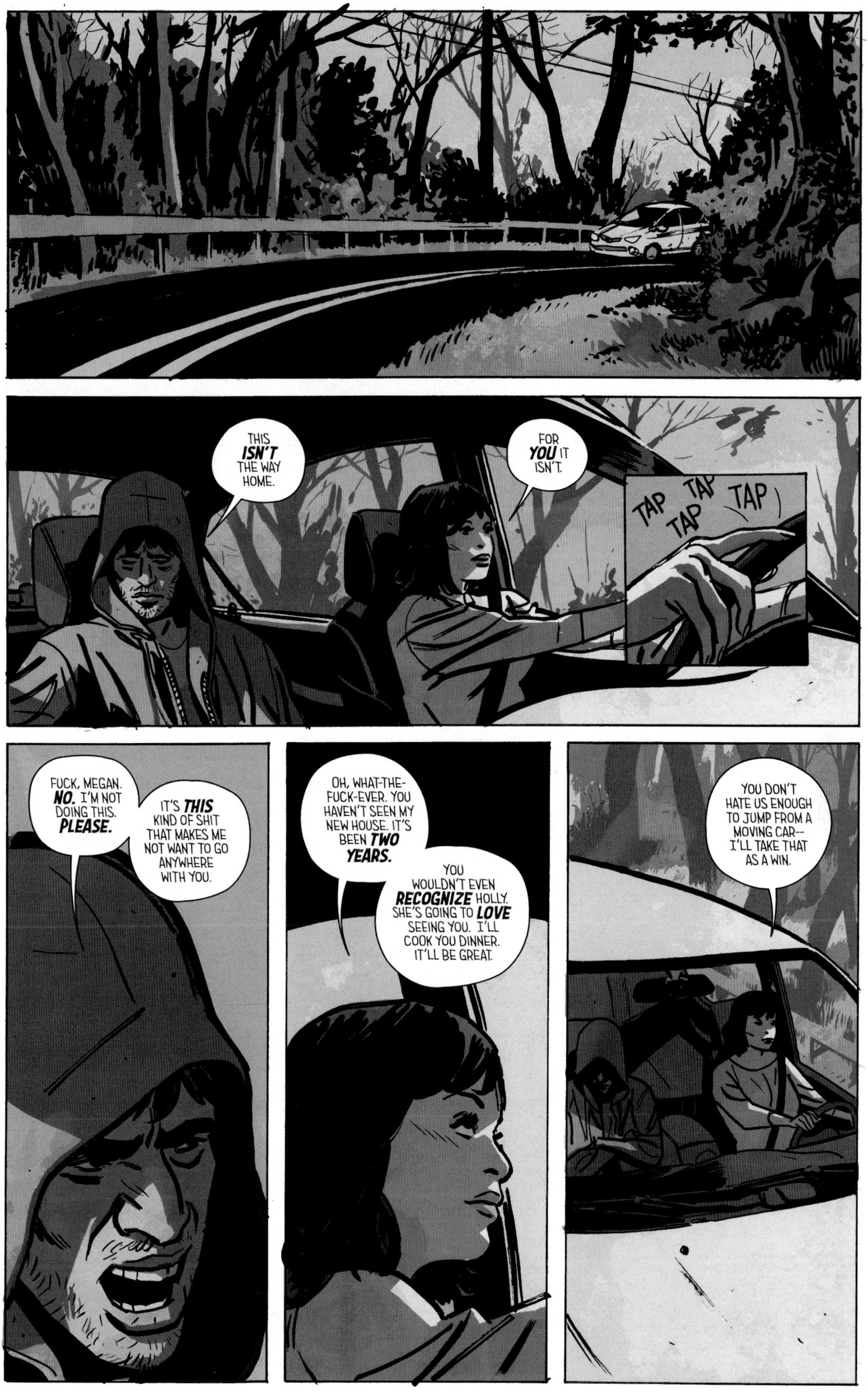
THIS ISN'T THE WAY HOME.
FOR YOU IT ISN'T.
TAP TAP TAP TAP
FUCK, MEGAN. NO. I'M NOT DOING THIS. PLEASE.
IT'S THIS KIND OF SHIT THAT MAKES ME NOT WANT TO GO ANYWHERE WITH YOU.
OH, WHAT-THE-FUCK-EVER. YOU HAVEN'T SEEN MY NEW HOUSE. IT'S BEEN TWO YEARS.
YOU WOULDN'T EVEN RECOGNIZE HOLLY. SHE'S GOING TO LOVE SEEING YOU. I'LL COOK YOU DINNER. IT'LL BE GREAT.
YOU DON'T HATE US ENOUGH TO JUMP FROM A MOVING CAR-- I'LL TAKE THAT AS A WIN.

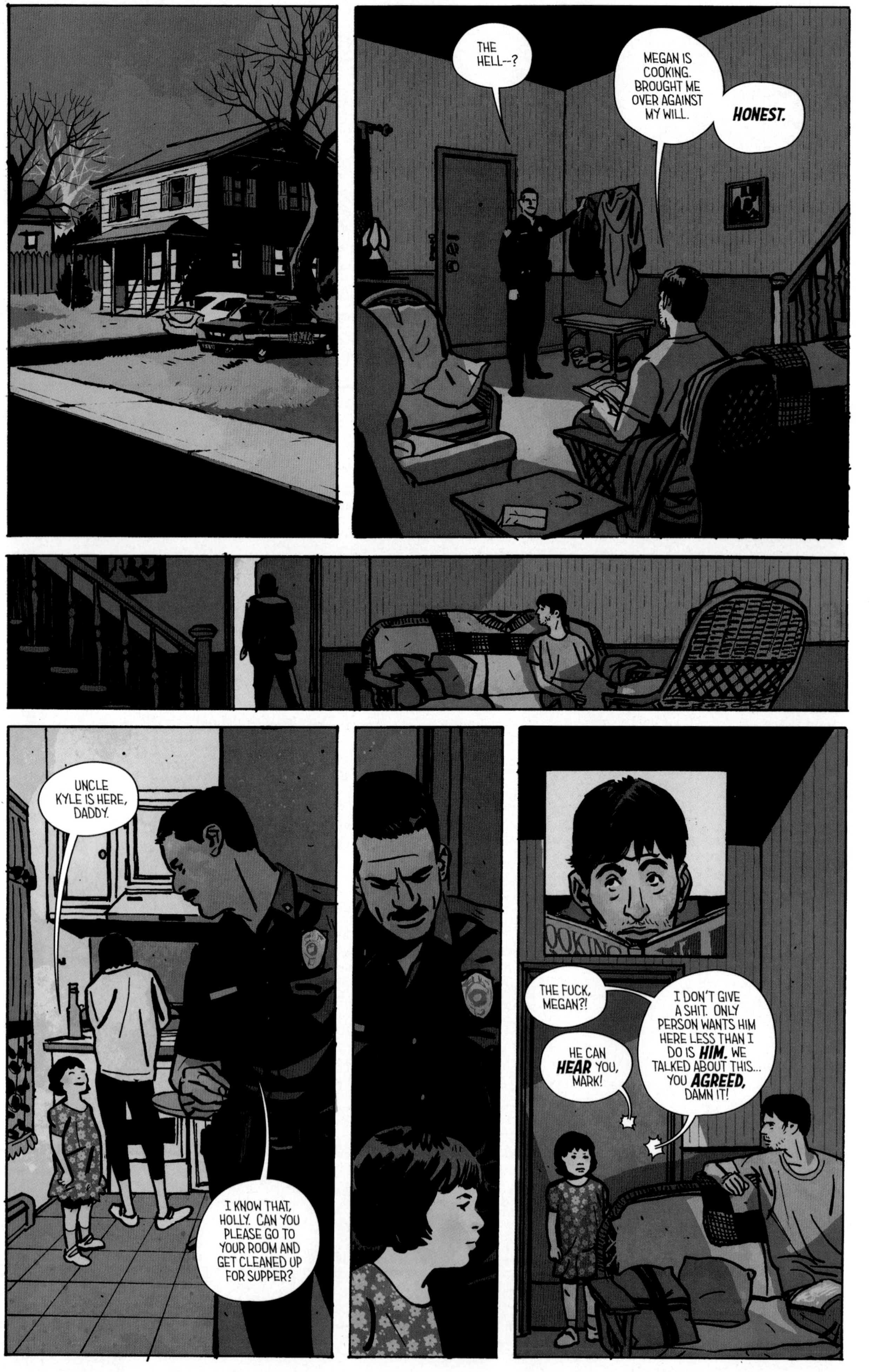
THE HELL--?
MEGAN IS COOKING. BROUGHT ME OVER AGAINST MY WILL.
HONEST.
UNCLE KYLE IS HERE, DADDY.
I KNOW THAT, HOLLY. CAN YOU PLEASE GO TO YOUR ROOM AND GET CLEANED UP FOR SUPPER?
THE FUCK, MEGAN?!
I DON'T GIVE A SHIT. ONLY PERSON WANTS HIM HERE LESS THAN I DO IS HIM. WE TALKED ABOUT THIS... YOU AGREED, DAMN IT!
HE CAN HEAR YOU, MARK!

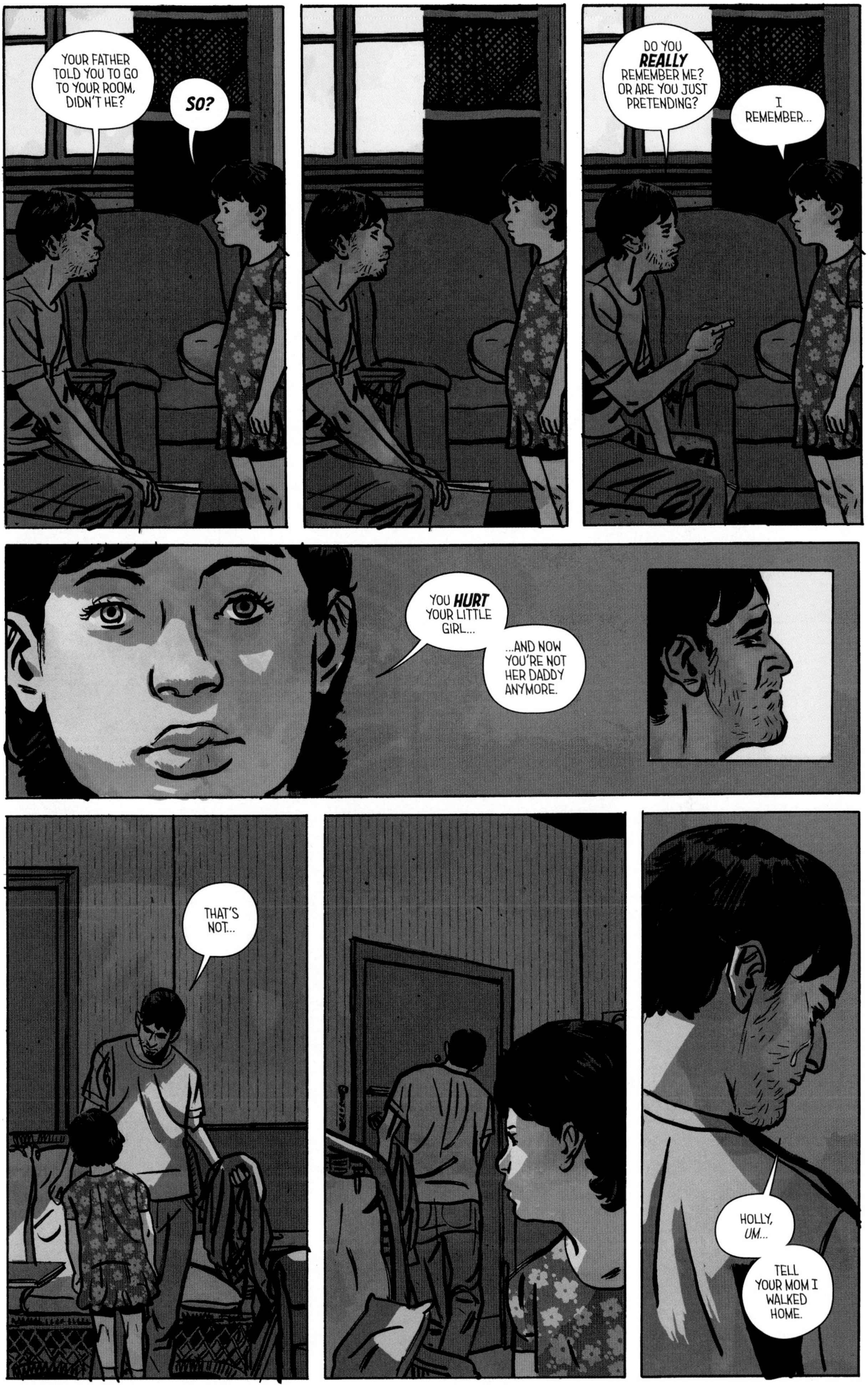
YOUR FATHER TOLD YOU TO GO TO YOUR ROOM, DIDN'T HE?
SO?
DO YOU REALLY REMEMBER ME? OR ARE YOU JUST PRETENDING?
I REMEMBER...
YOU HURT YOUR LITTLE GIRL...
...AND NOW YOU'RE NOT HER DADDY ANYMORE.
THAT'S NOT...
HOLLY, UM...
TELL YOUR MOM I WALKED HOME.

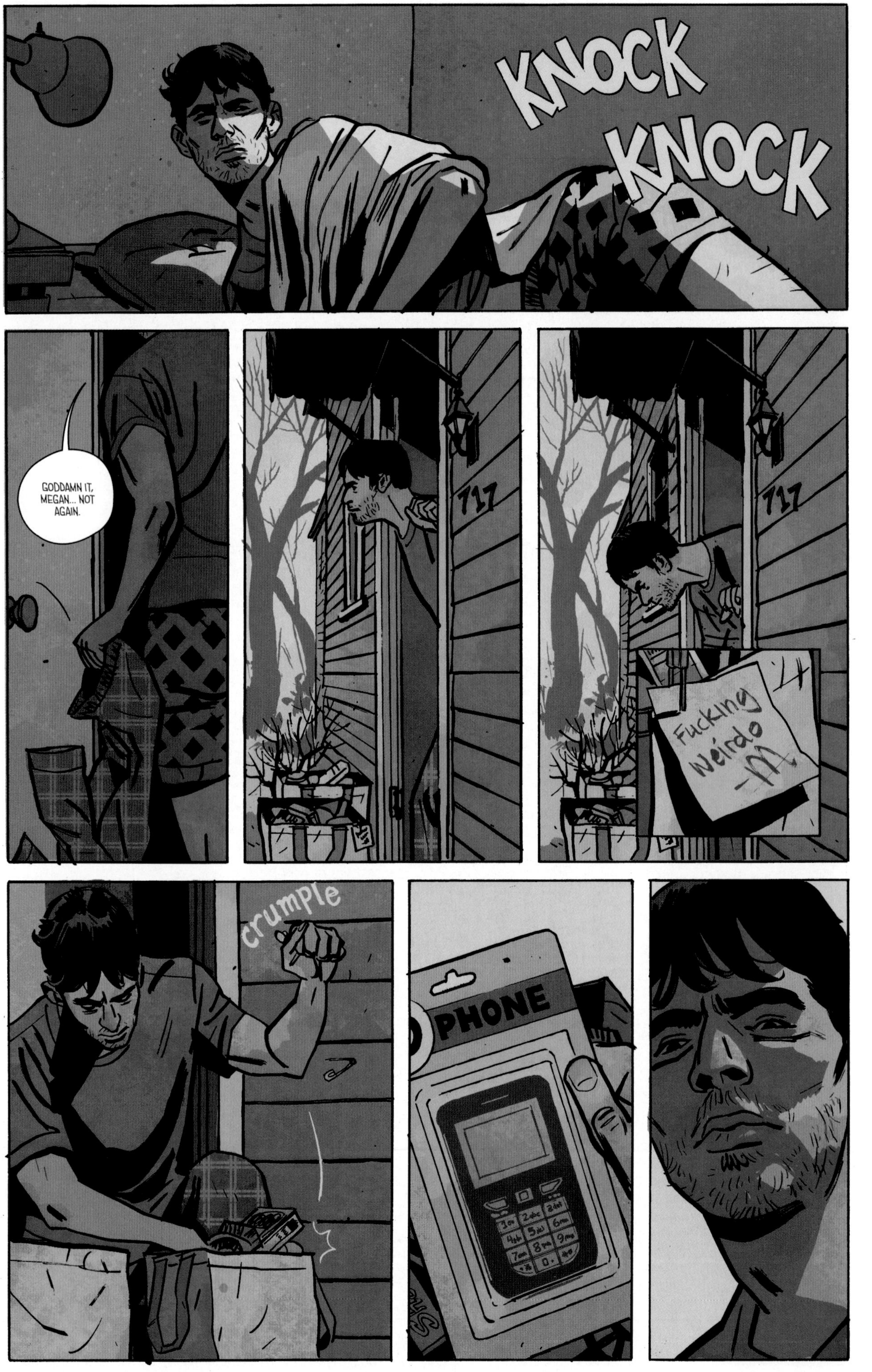

KNOCK
KNOCK
GODDAMN IT, MEGAN... NOT AGAIN.
717
717
Fucking Weirdo -M
crumple
PHONE

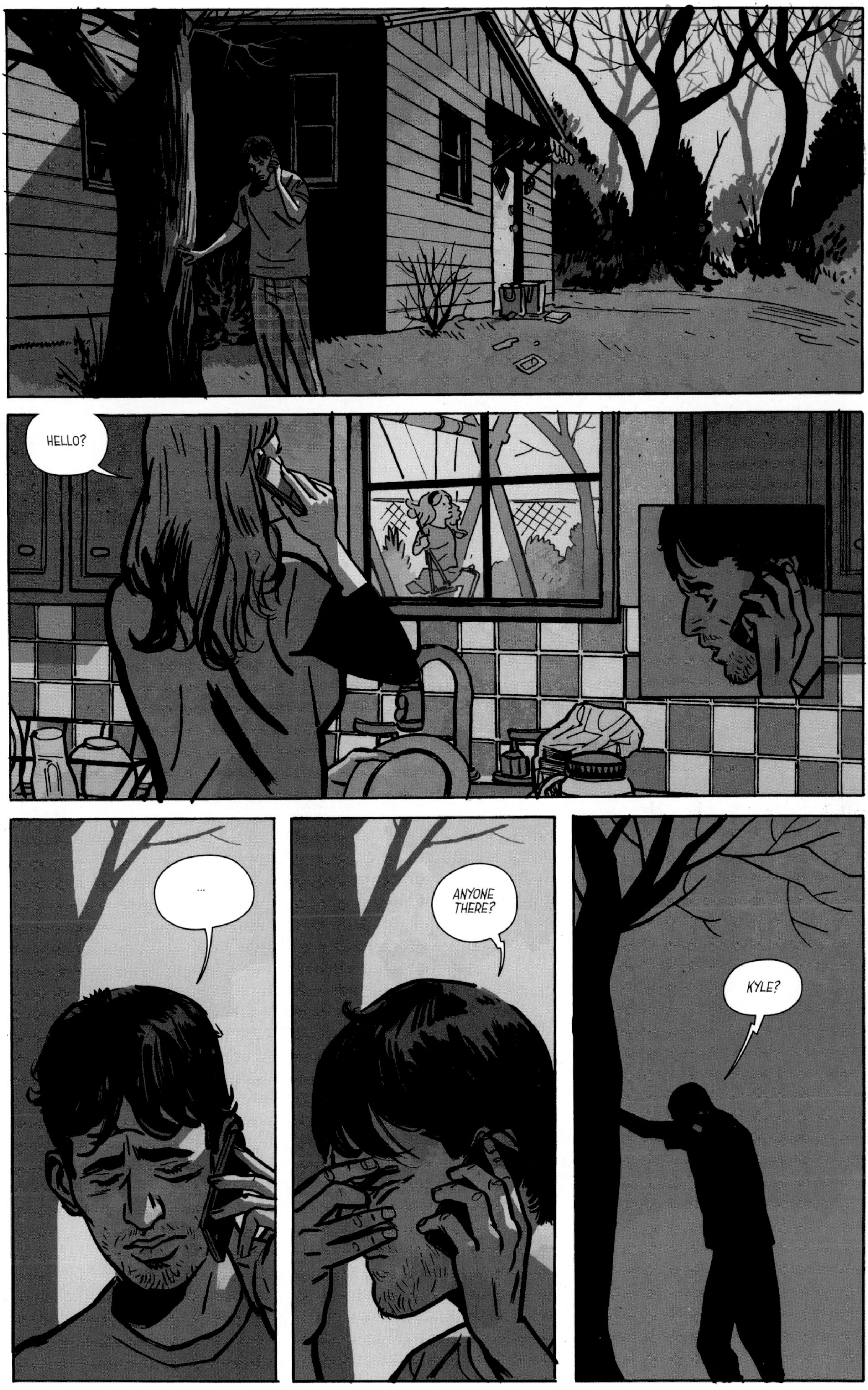
HELLO?
...
ANYONE THERE?
KYLE?

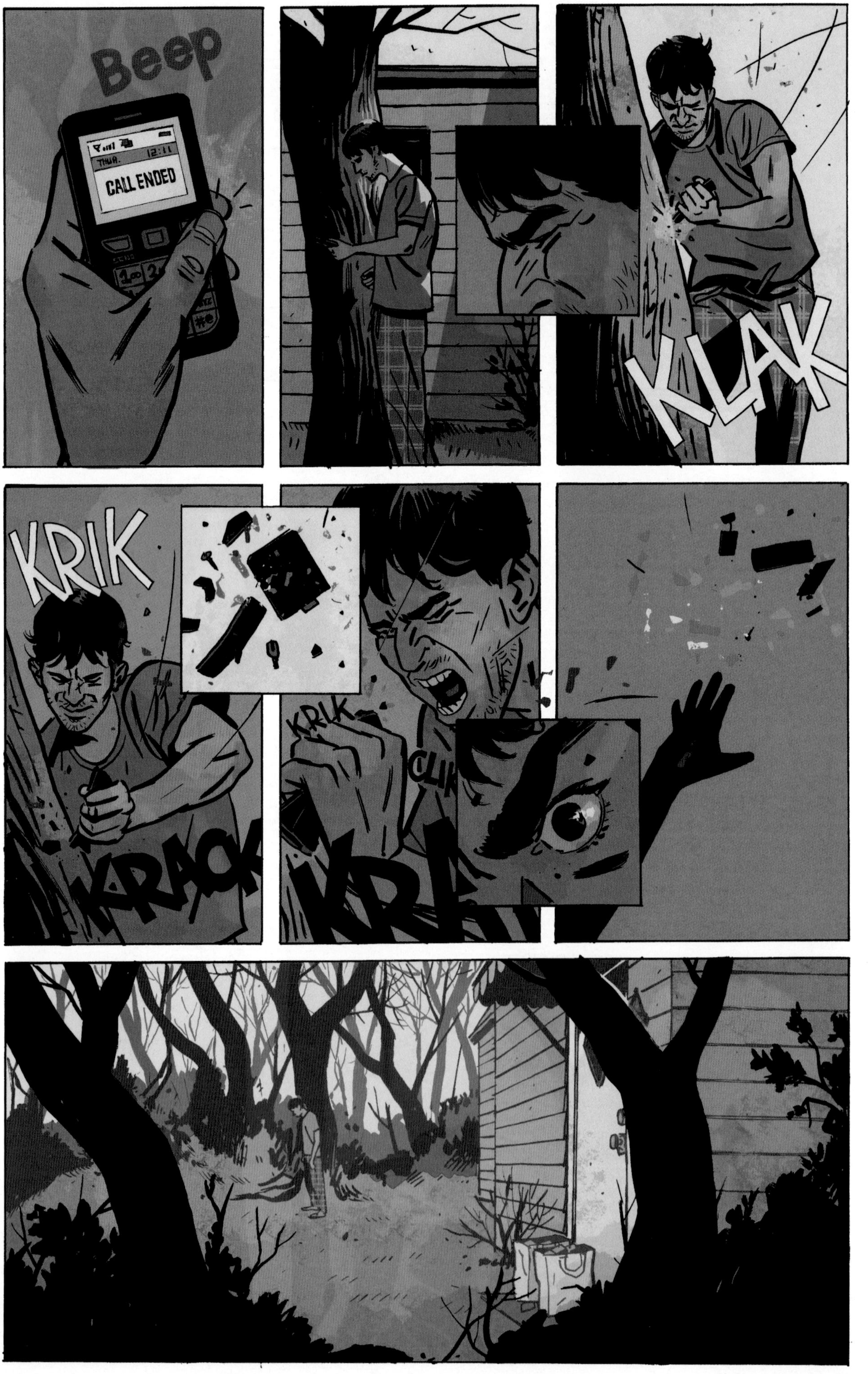
Beep
THUR. 12:11
CALL ENDED
KLAK
KRIK
KRACK
KRIK
CLIK
KRI

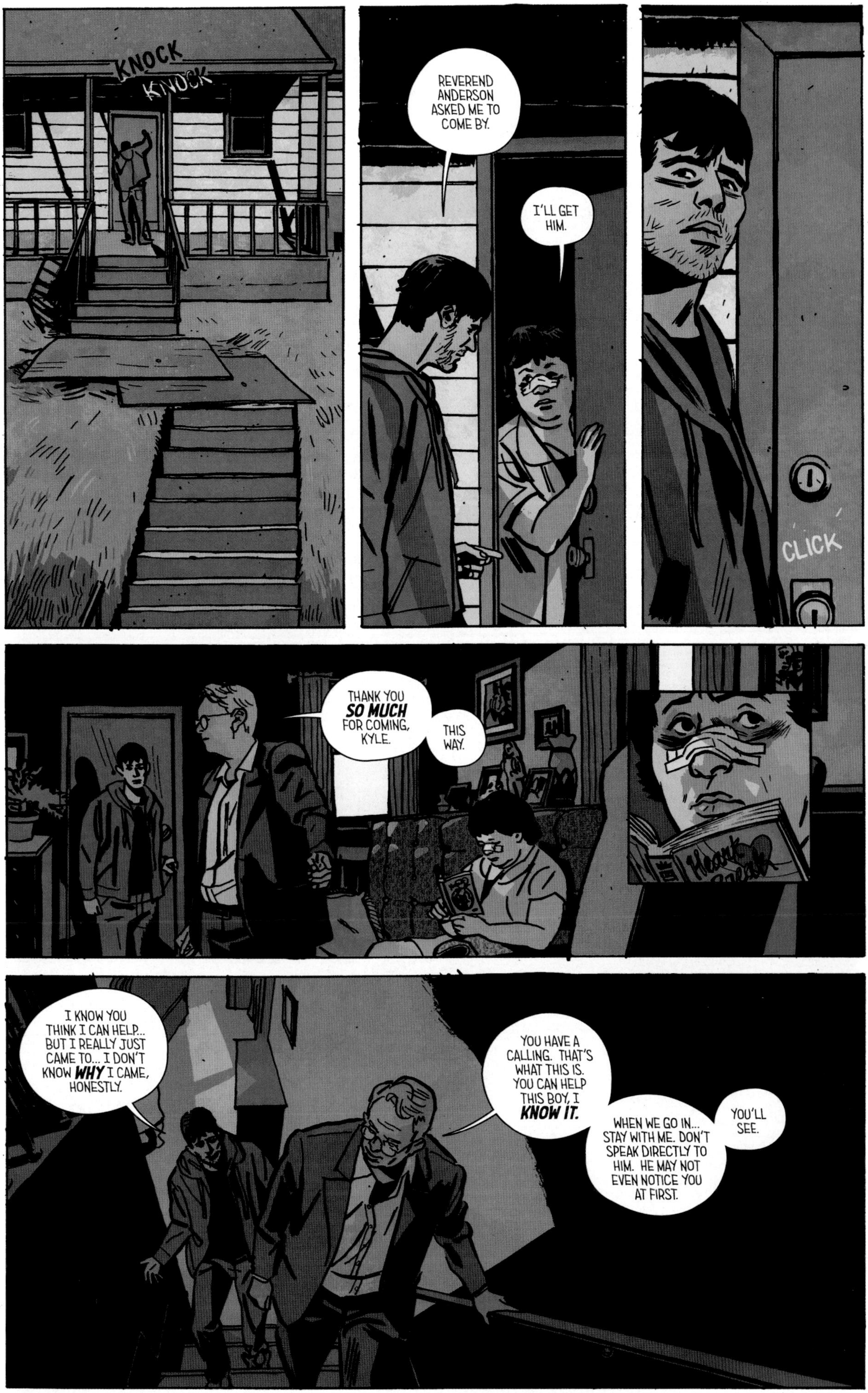
KNOCK
KNOCK
REVEREND ANDERSON ASKED ME TO COME BY.
I'LL GET HIM.
CLICK
THANK YOU SO MUCH FOR COMING, KYLE.
THIS WAY.
I KNOW YOU THINK I CAN HELP... BUT I REALLY JUST CAME TO... I DON'T KNOW WHY I CAME, HONESTLY.
YOU HAVE A CALLING. THAT'S WHAT THIS IS. YOU CAN HELP THIS BOY, I KNOW IT.
WHEN WE GO IN... STAY WITH ME. DON'T SPEAK DIRECTLY TO HIM. HE MAY NOT EVEN NOTICE YOU AT FIRST.
YOU'LL SEE.

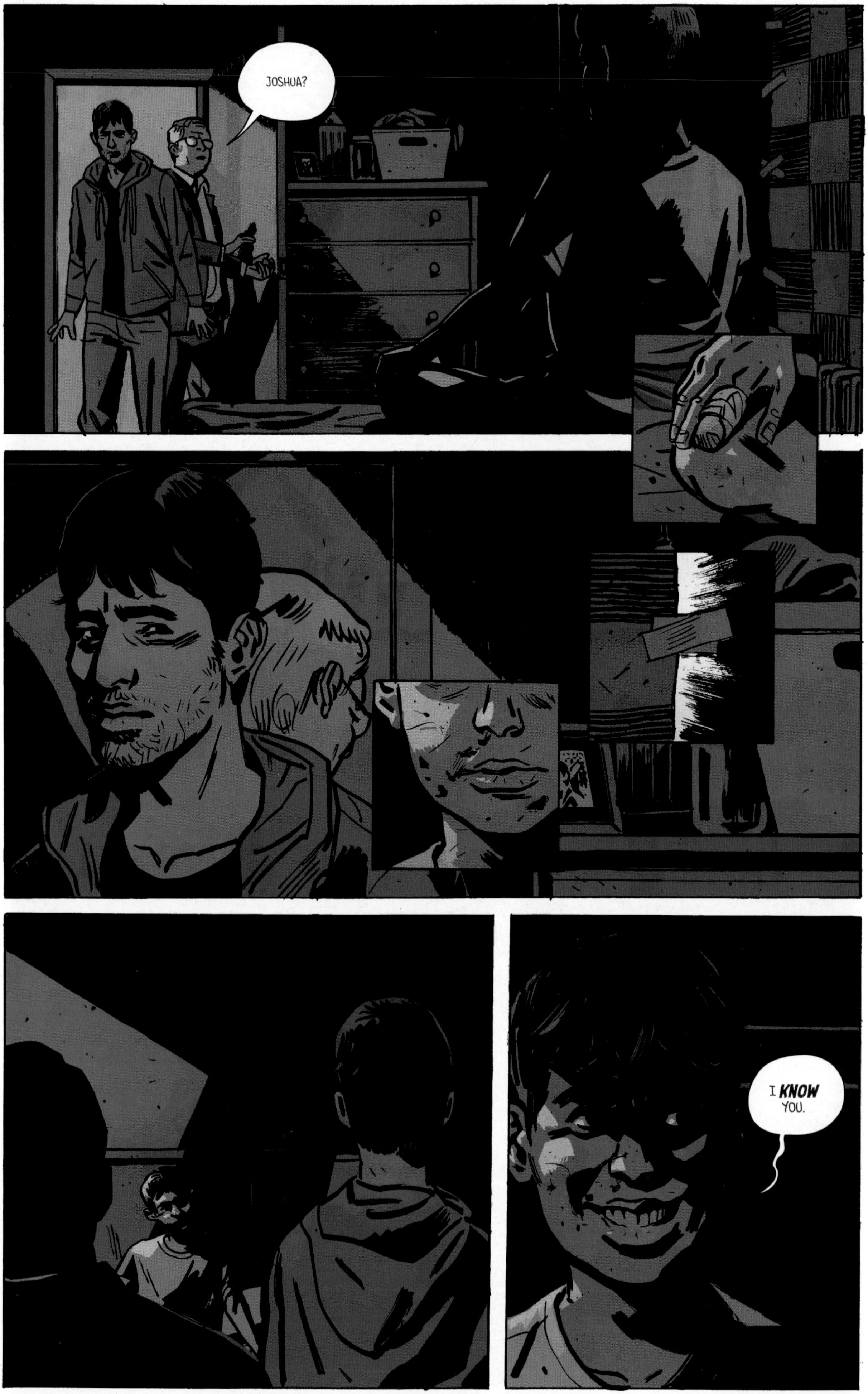
JOSHUA?
I KNOW YOU.

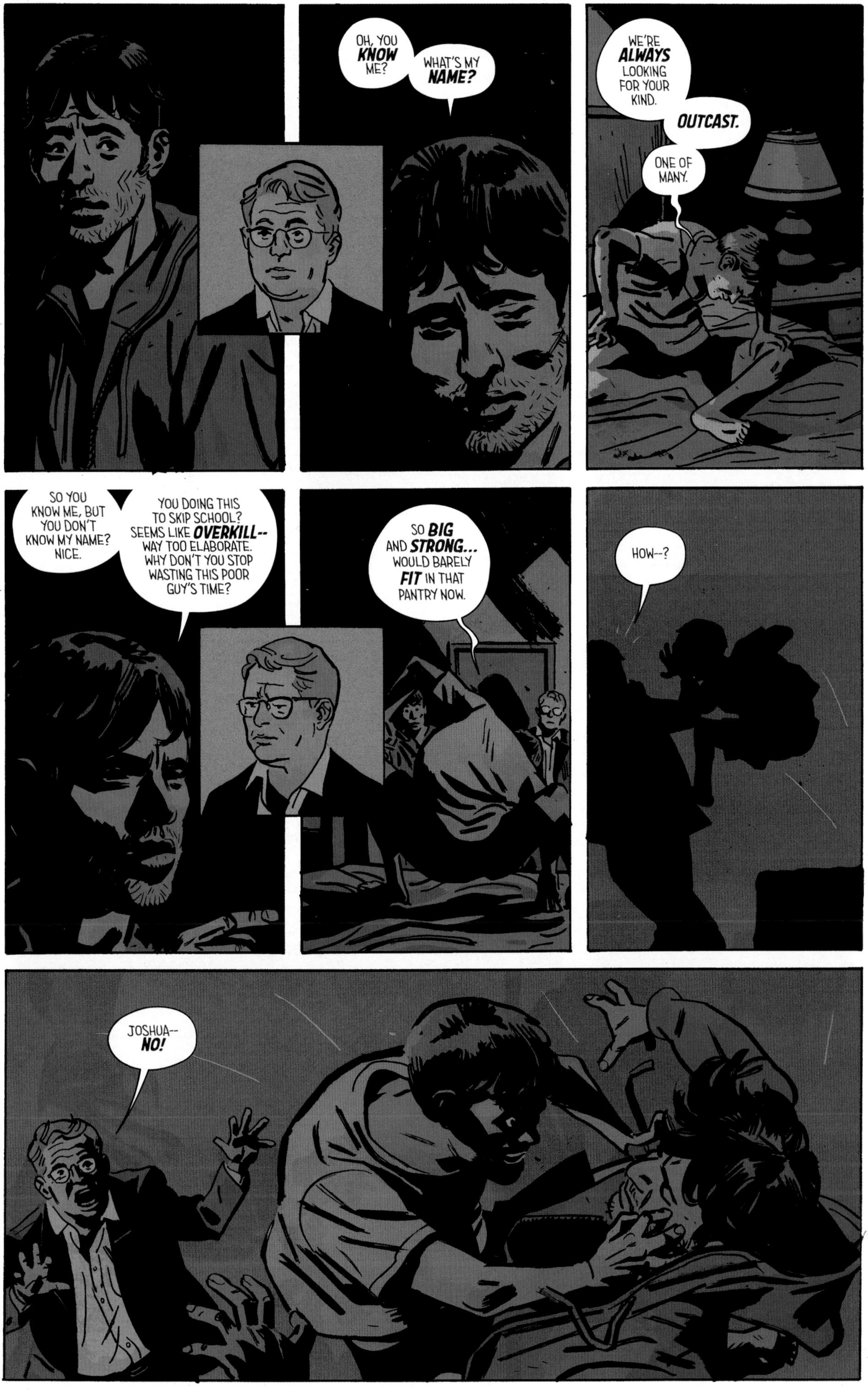

OH, YOU KNOW ME?
WHAT'S MY NAME?
WE'RE ALWAYS LOOKING FOR YOUR KIND.
OUTCAST.
ONE OF MANY.
SO YOU KNOW ME, BUT YOU DON'T KNOW MY NAME? NICE.
YOU DOING THIS TO SKIP SCHOOL? SEEMS LIKE OVERKILL-- WAY TOO ELABORATE. WHY DON'T YOU STOP WASTING THIS POOR GUY'S TIME?
SO BIG AND STRONG... WOULD BARELY FIT IN THAT PANTRY NOW.
HOW--?
JOSHUA-- NO!

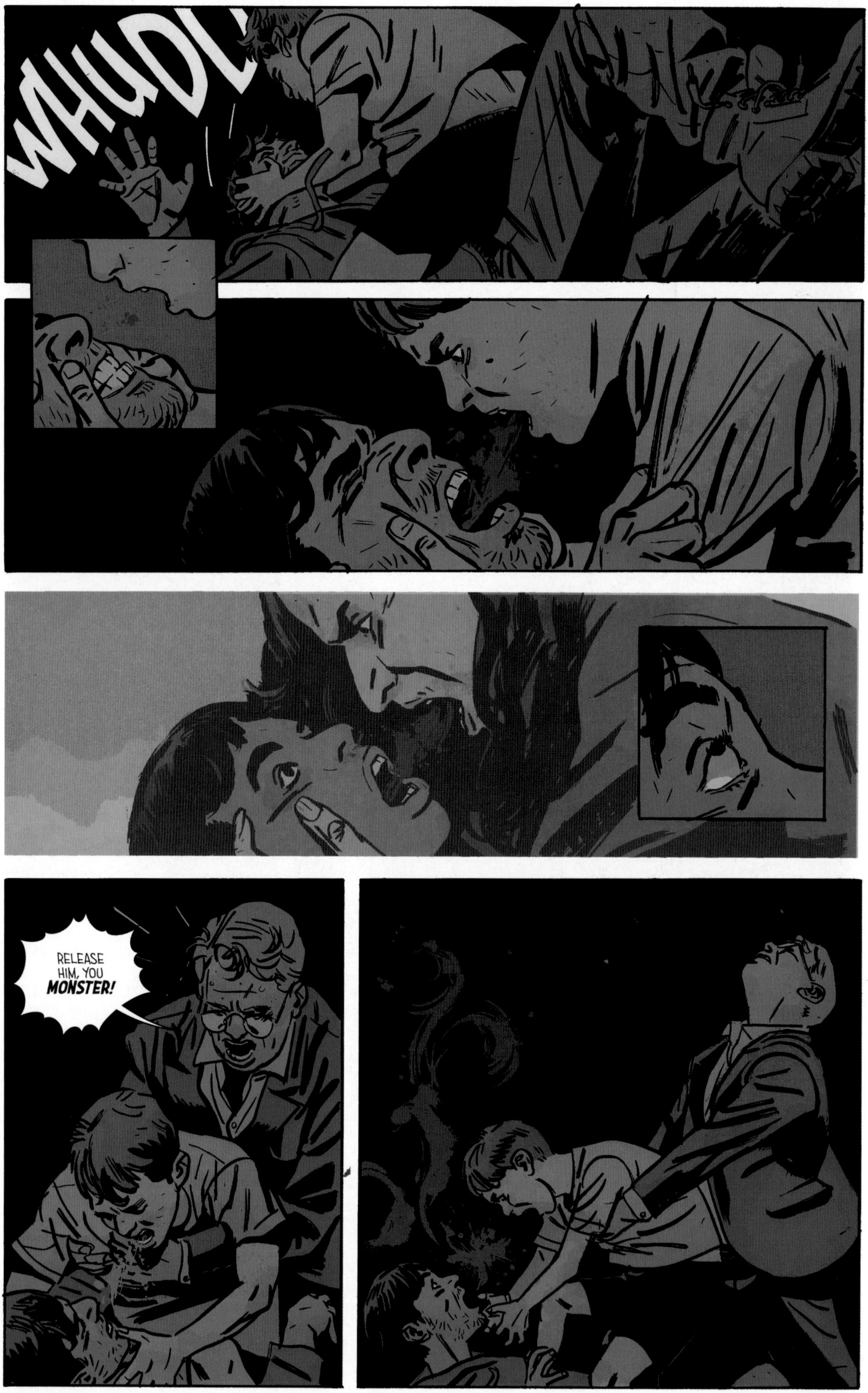
WHUDD
RELEASE HIM, YOU MONSTER!

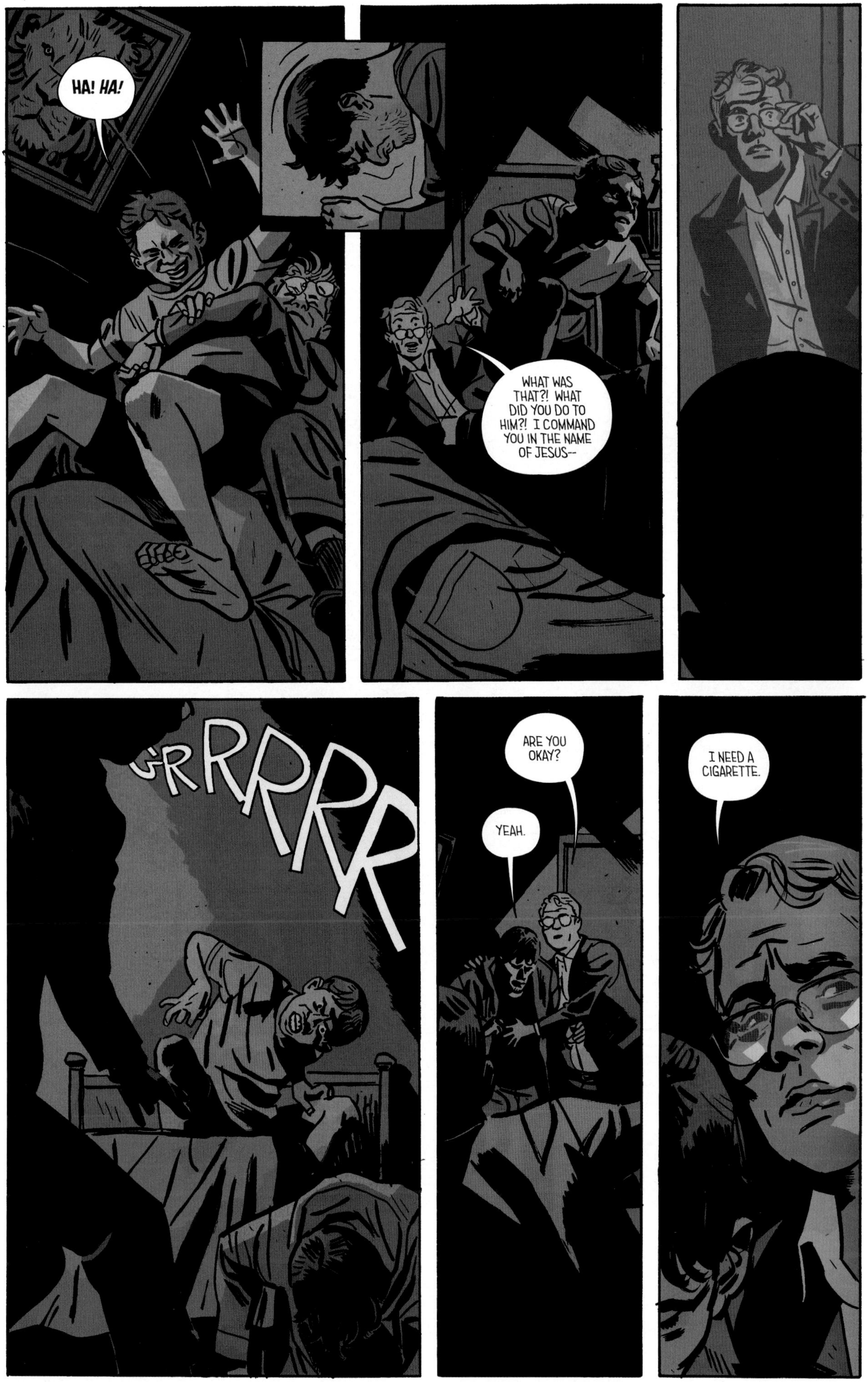
HA! HA!
WHAT WAS THAT?! WHAT DID YOU DO TO HIM?! I COMMAND YOU IN THE NAME OF JESUS--
GRRRRRR
ARE YOU OKAY?
YEAH.
I NEED A CIGARETTE.

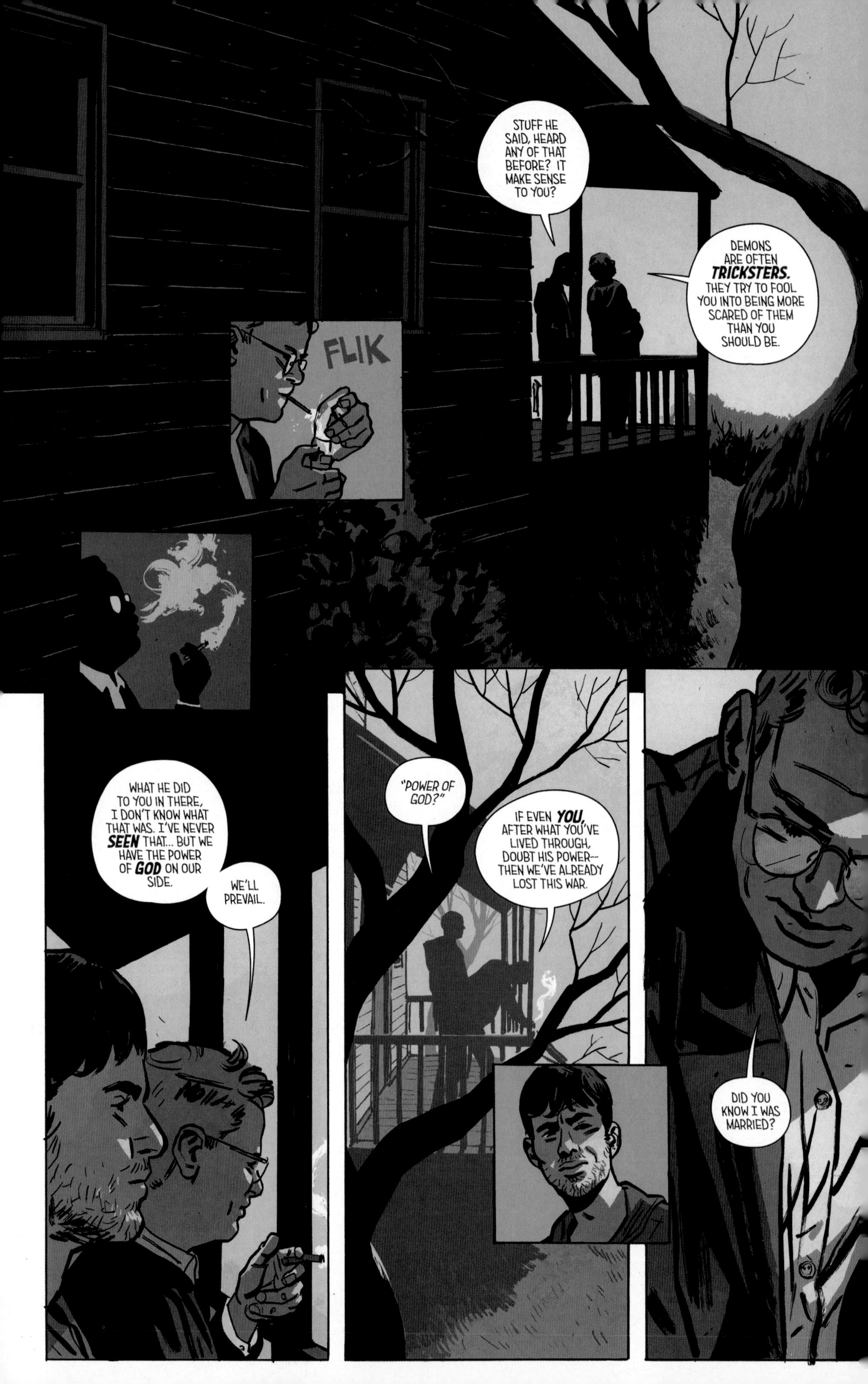

STUFF HE SAID, HEARD ANY OF THAT BEFORE? IT MAKE SENSE TO YOU?
DEMONS ARE OFTEN TRICKSTERS. THEY TRY TO FOOL YOU INTO BEING MORE SCARED OF THEM THAN YOU SHOULD BE.
FLIK
WHAT HE DID TO YOU IN THERE, I DON'T KNOW WHAT THAT WAS. I'VE NEVER SEEN THAT... BUT WE HAVE THE POWER OF GOD ON OUR SIDE.
WE'LL PREVAIL.
"POWER OF GOD?"
IF EVEN YOU, AFTER WHAT YOU'VE LIVED THROUGH, DOUBT HIS POWER-- THEN WE'VE ALREADY LOST THIS WAR.
DID YOU KNOW I WAS MARRIED?

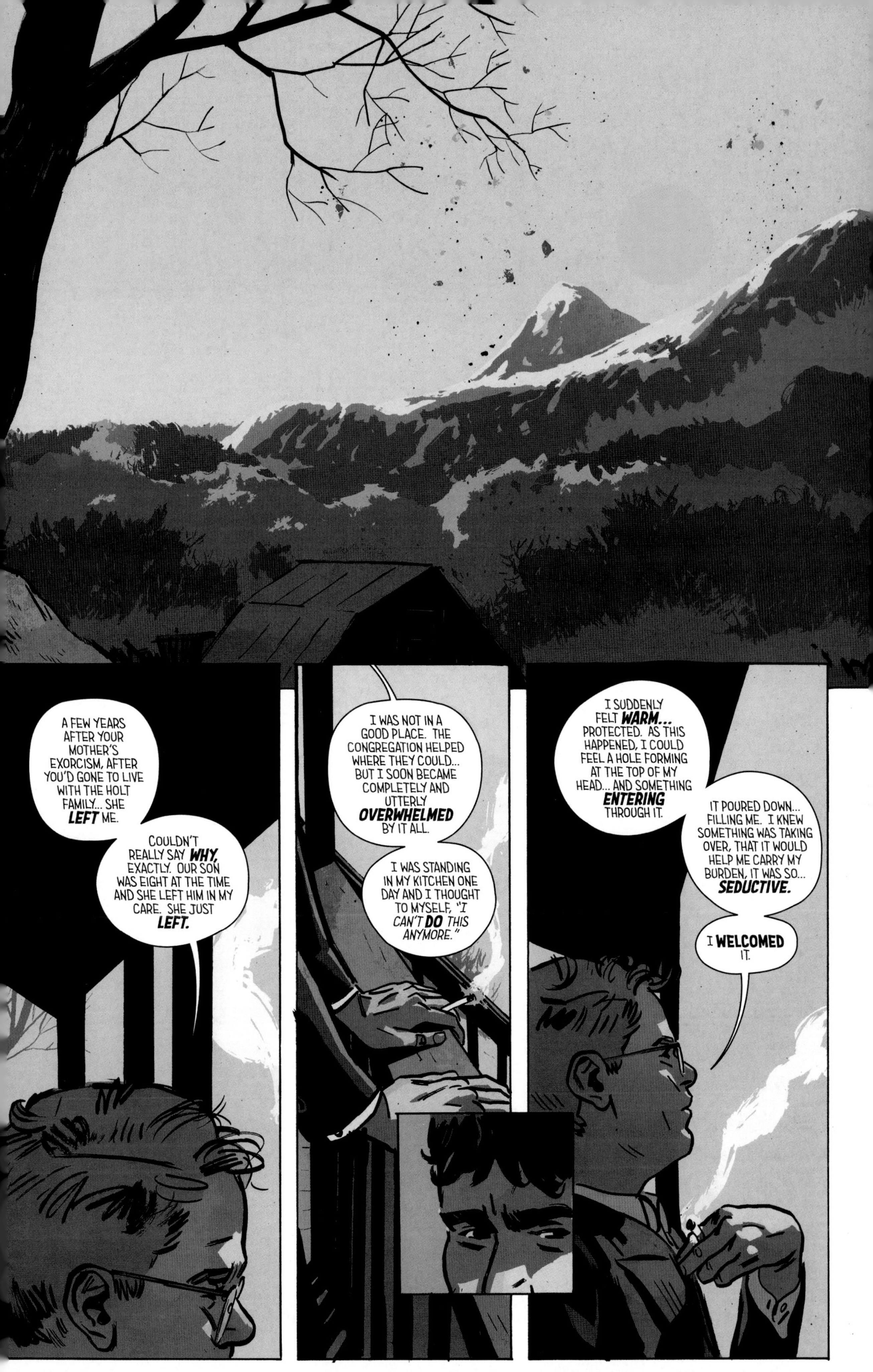
A FEW YEARS AFTER YOUR MOTHER'S EXORCISM, AFTER YOU'D GONE TO LIVE WITH THE HOLT FAMILY... SHE **LEFT** ME.
COULDN'T REALLY SAY **WHY,** EXACTLY. OUR SON WAS EIGHT AT THE TIME AND SHE LEFT HIM IN MY CARE. SHE JUST **LEFT.**
I WAS NOT IN A GOOD PLACE. THE CONGREGATION HELPED WHERE THEY COULD... BUT I SOON BECAME COMPLETELY AND UTTERLY **OVERWHELMED** BY IT ALL.
I WAS STANDING IN MY KITCHEN ONE DAY AND I THOUGHT TO MYSELF, *"I CAN'T **DO** THIS ANYMORE."*
I SUDDENLY FELT **WARM...** PROTECTED. AS THIS HAPPENED, I COULD FEEL A HOLE FORMING AT THE TOP OF MY HEAD... AND SOMETHING **ENTERING** THROUGH IT.
IT POURED DOWN... FILLING ME. I KNEW SOMETHING WAS TAKING OVER, THAT IT WOULD HELP ME CARRY MY BURDEN, IT WAS SO... **SEDUCTIVE.**
I **WELCOMED** IT.

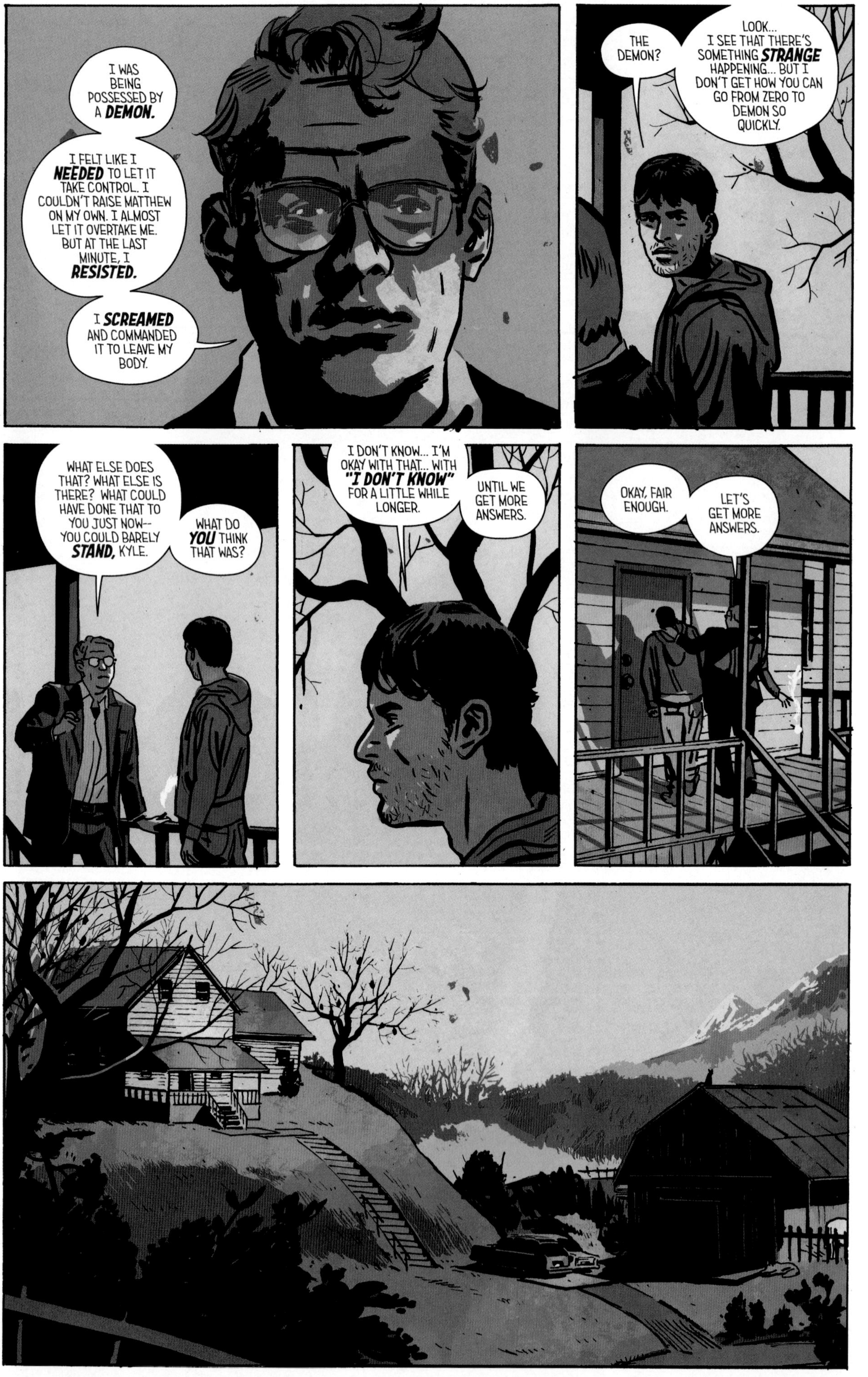
I WAS BEING POSSESSED BY A DEMON.
I FELT LIKE I NEEDED TO LET IT TAKE CONTROL. I COULDN'T RAISE MATTHEW ON MY OWN. I ALMOST LET IT OVERTAKE ME. BUT AT THE LAST MINUTE, I RESISTED.
I SCREAMED AND COMMANDED IT TO LEAVE MY BODY.
THE DEMON?
LOOK... I SEE THAT THERE'S SOMETHING STRANGE HAPPENING... BUT I DON'T GET HOW YOU CAN GO FROM ZERO TO DEMON SO QUICKLY.
WHAT ELSE DOES THAT? WHAT ELSE IS THERE? WHAT COULD HAVE DONE THAT TO YOU JUST NOW-- YOU COULD BARELY STAND, KYLE.
WHAT DO YOU THINK THAT WAS?
I DON'T KNOW... I'M OKAY WITH THAT... WITH "I DON'T KNOW" FOR A LITTLE WHILE LONGER.
UNTIL WE GET MORE ANSWERS.
OKAY, FAIR ENOUGH.
LET'S GET MORE ANSWERS.

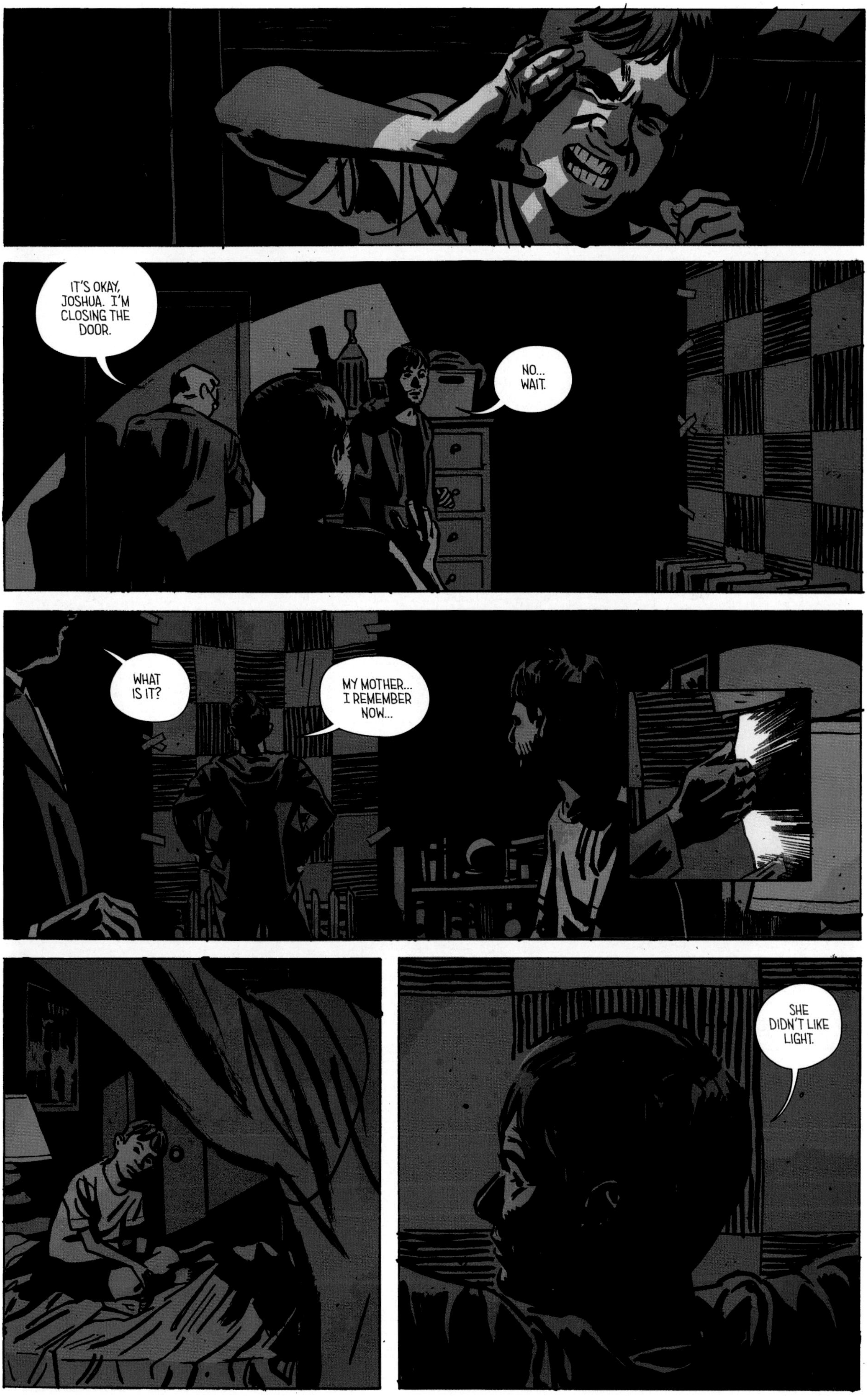
IT'S OKAY, JOSHUA. I'M CLOSING THE DOOR.
NO... WAIT.
WHAT IS IT?
MY MOTHER... I REMEMBER NOW...
SHE DIDN'T LIKE LIGHT.

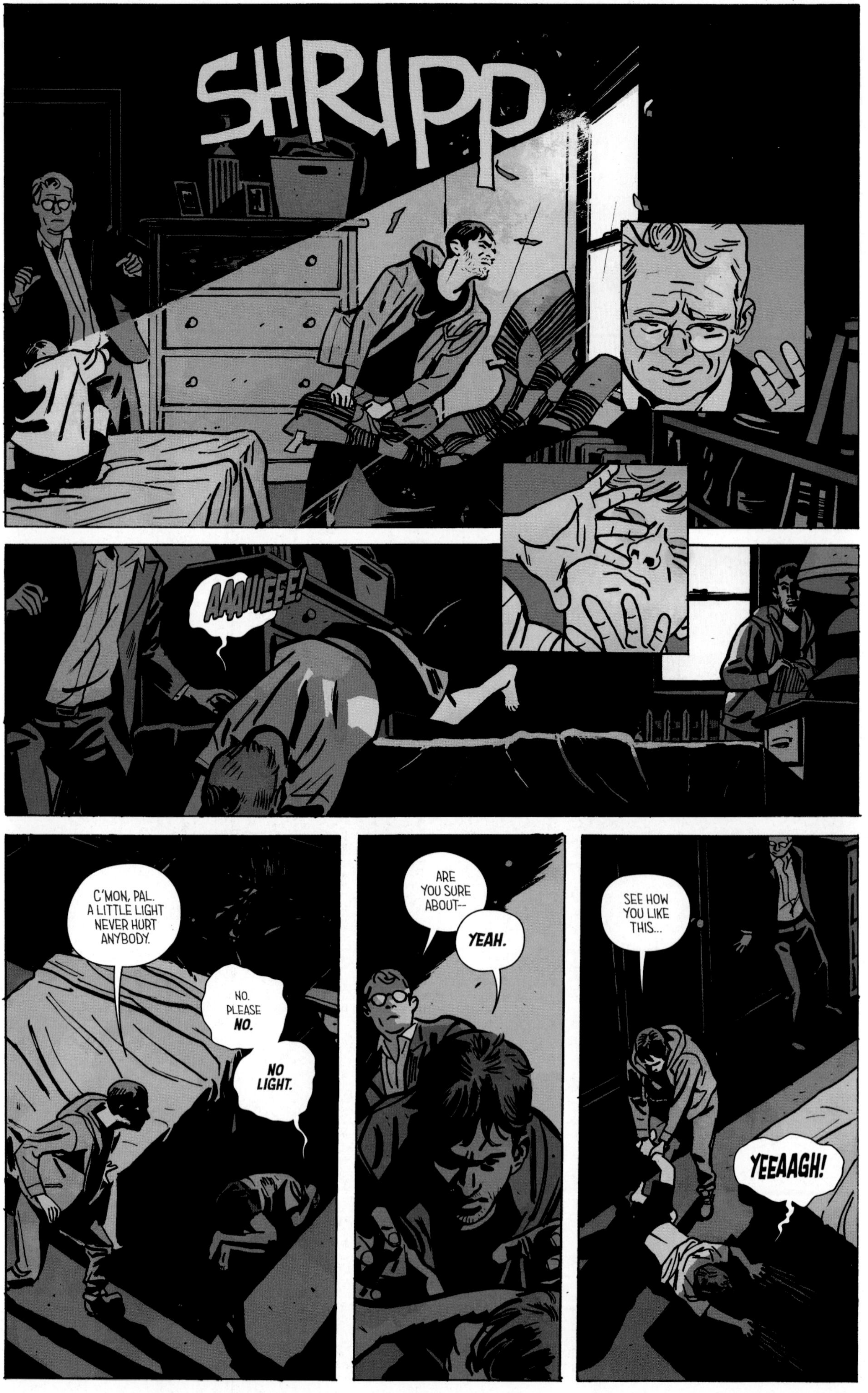
SHRIPP
AAAIIEEE!
C'MON, PAL. A LITTLE LIGHT NEVER HURT ANYBODY.
NO. PLEASE NO.
NO LIGHT.
ARE YOU SURE ABOUT--
YEAH.
SEE HOW YOU LIKE THIS...
YEEAAGH!

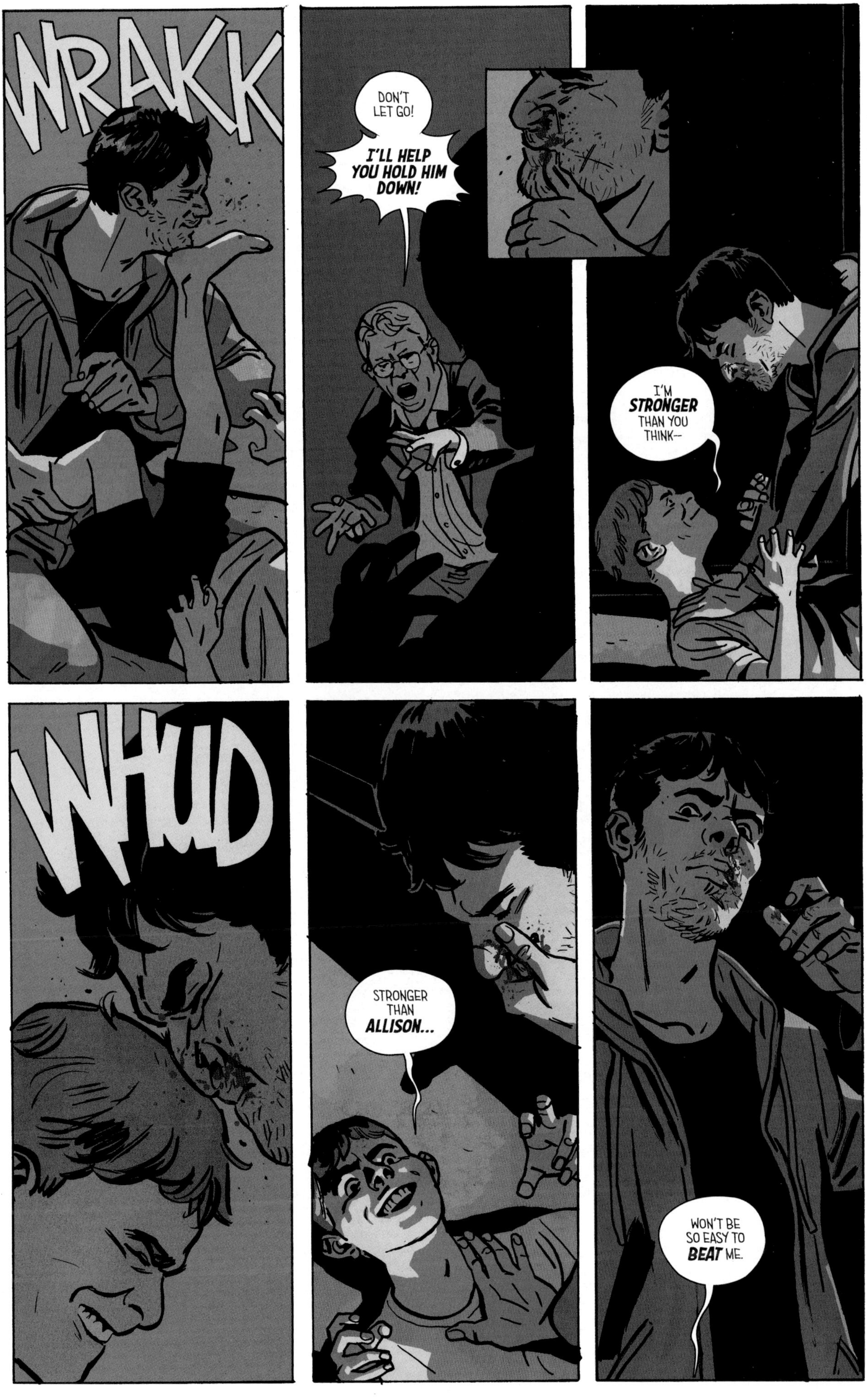
WRAKK
DON'T LET GO!
I'LL HELP YOU HOLD HIM DOWN!
I'M STRONGER THAN YOU THINK--
WHUD
STRONGER THAN ALLISON...
WON'T BE SO EASY TO BEAT ME.

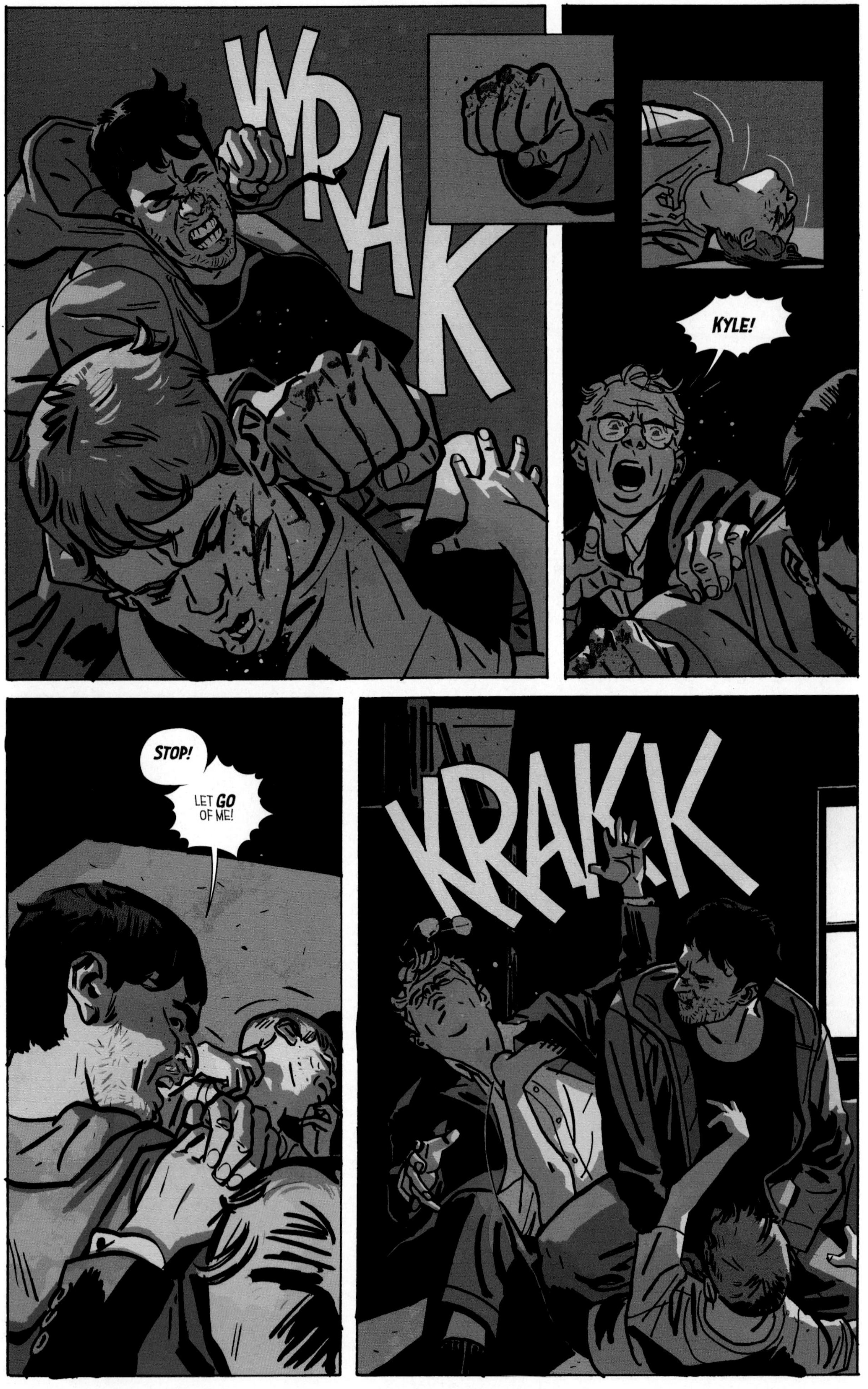
WRAK
KYLE!
STOP!
LET GO OF ME!
KRAKK

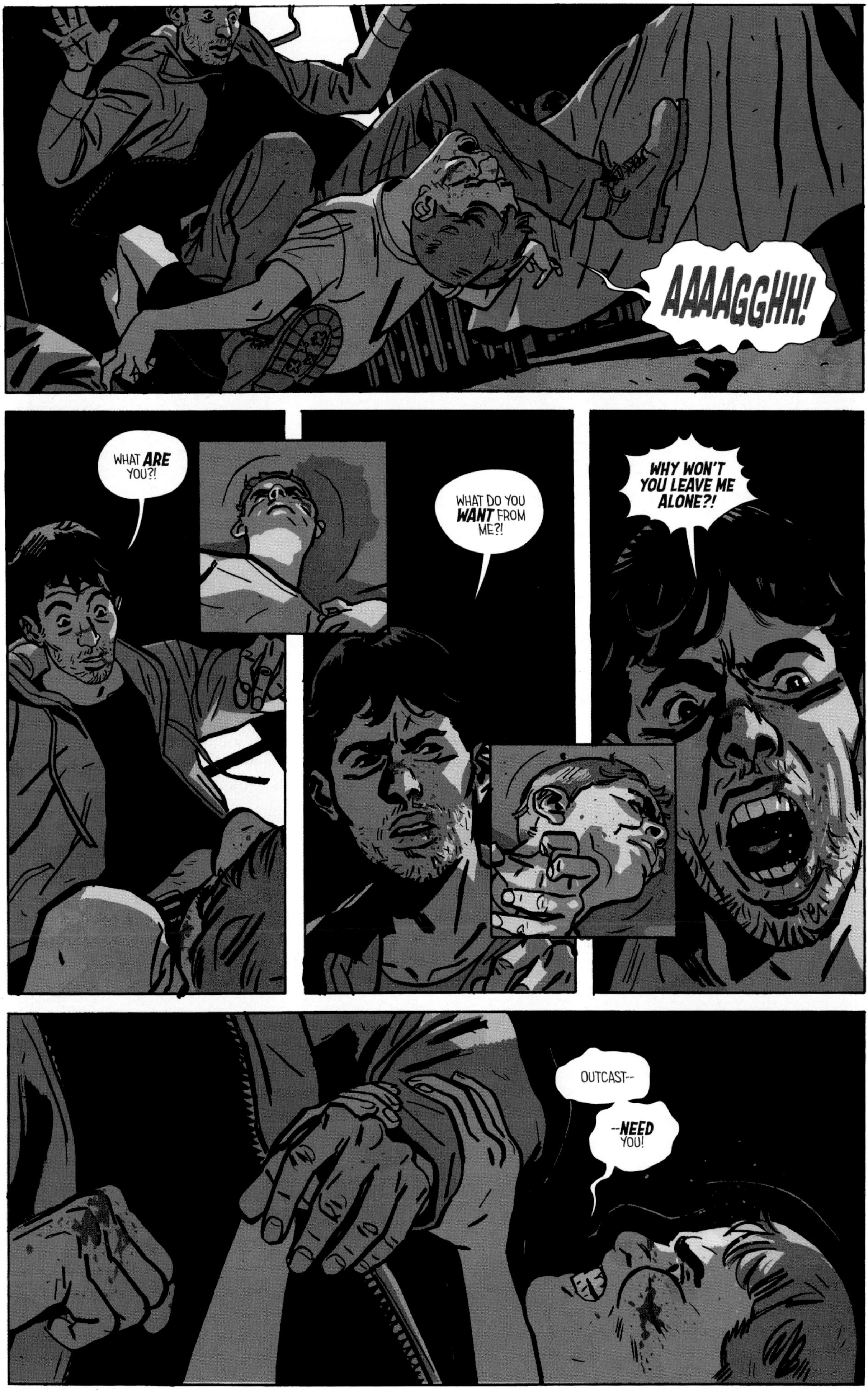
AAAAGGHH!
WHAT ARE YOU?!
WHAT DO YOU WANT FROM ME?!
WHY WON'T YOU LEAVE ME ALONE?!
OUTCAST--
--NEED YOU!

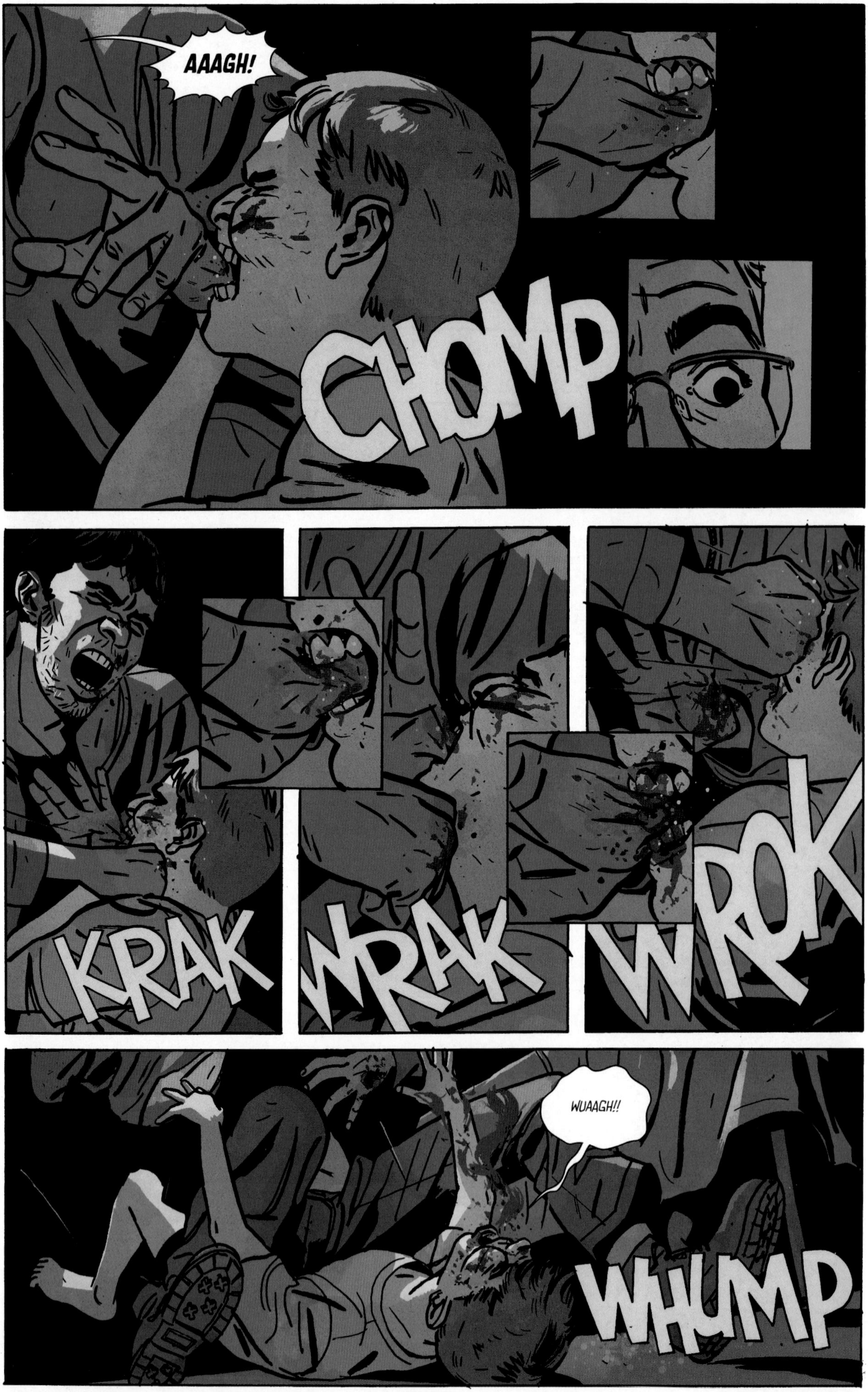
AAAGH!
CHOMP
KRAK
WRAK
WROK
WUAAGH!!
WHUMP

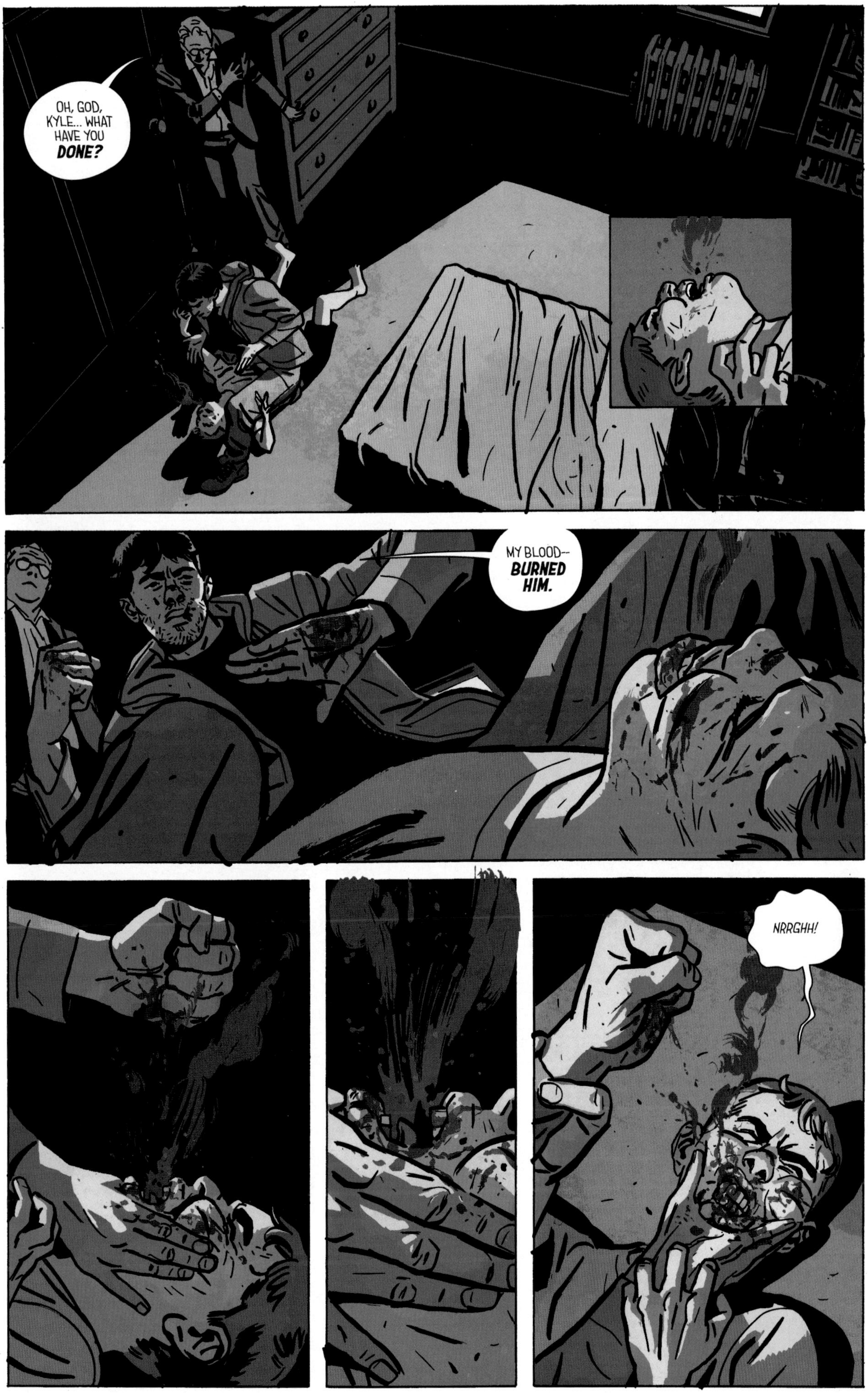

OH, GOD, KYLE... WHAT HAVE YOU DONE?
MY BLOOD-- BURNED HIM.
NRRGHH!

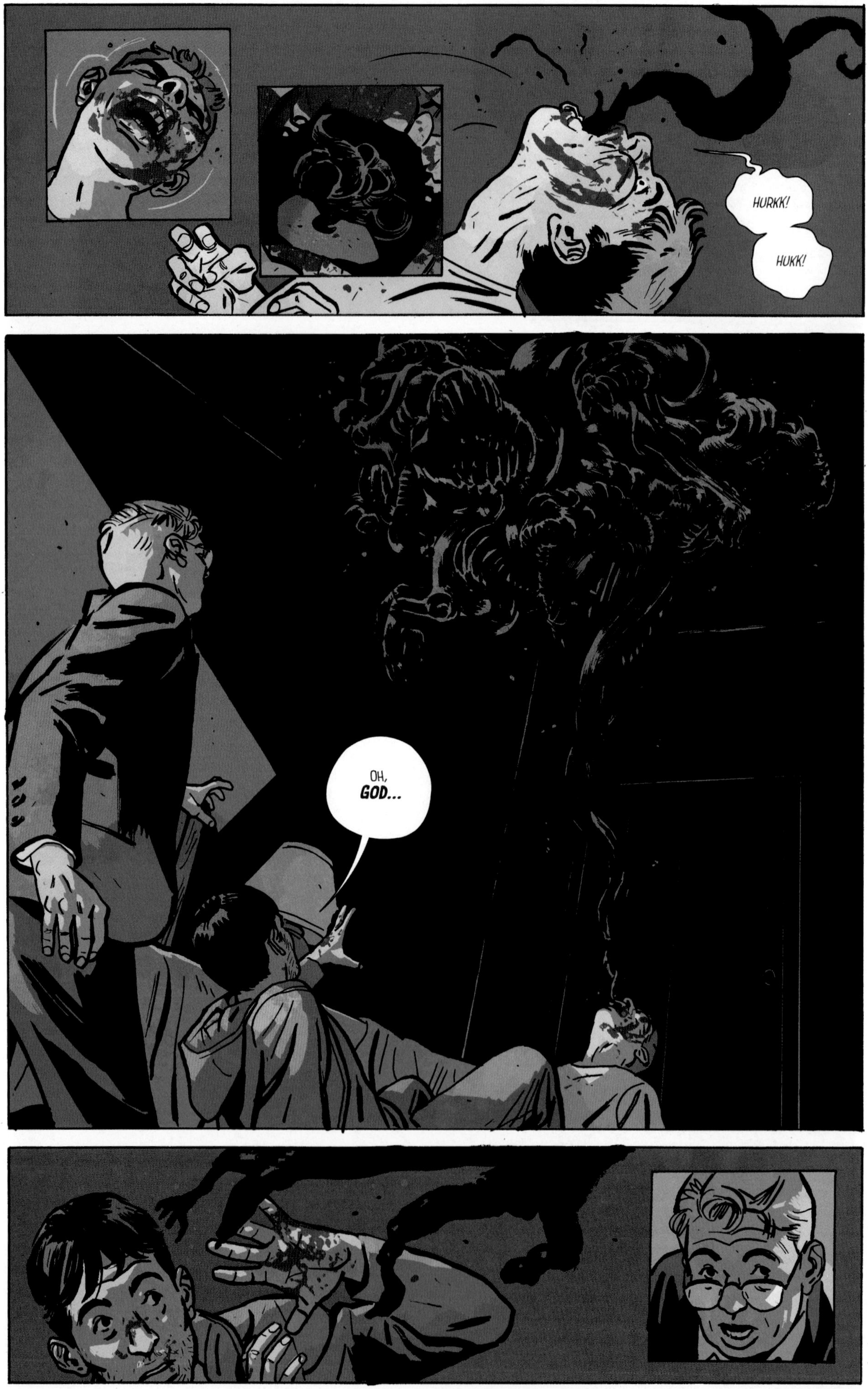
HURKK!
HUKK!
OH, GOD...

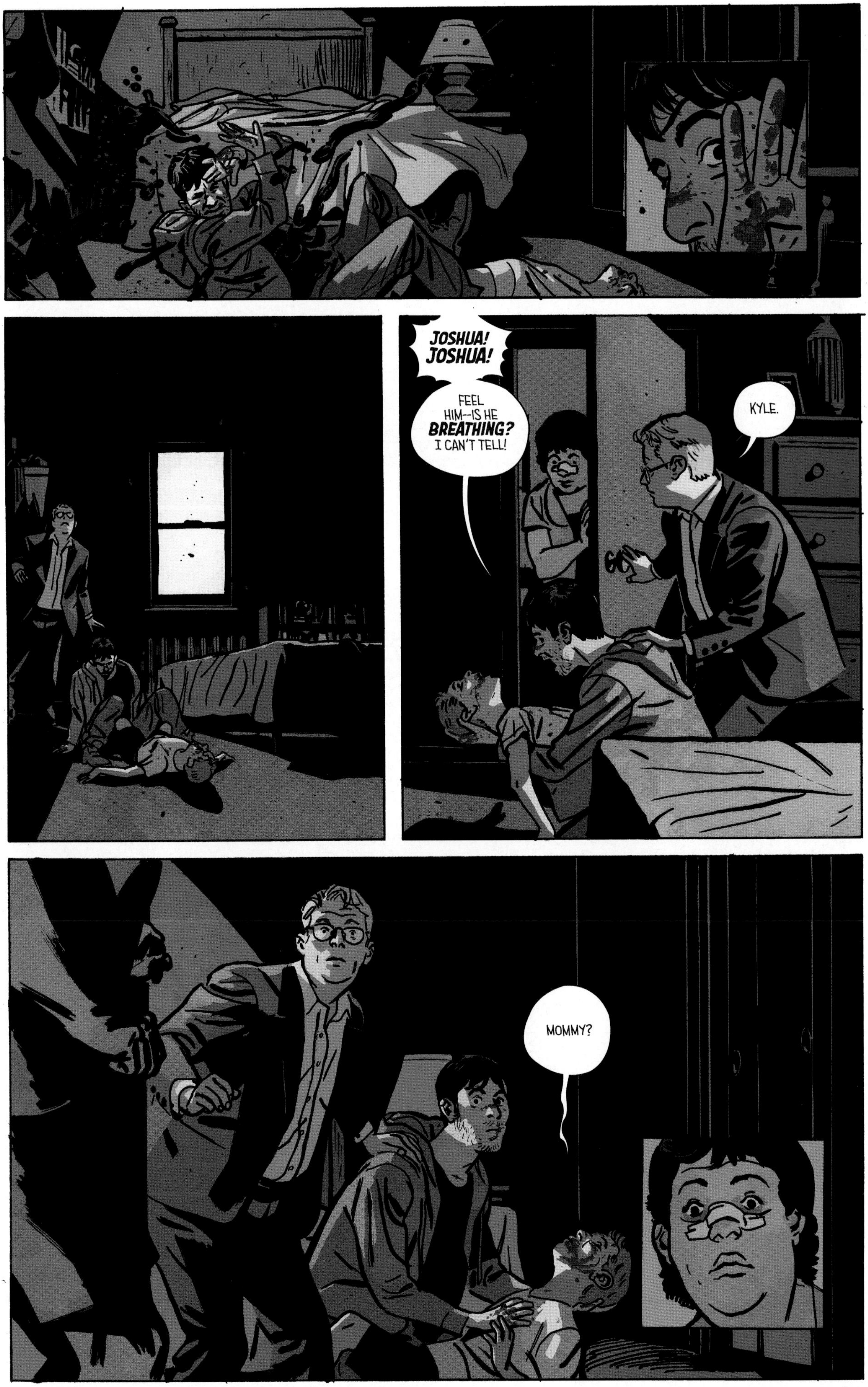
JOSHUA! JOSHUA!
FEEL HIM--IS HE **BREATHING?** I CAN'T TELL!
KYLE.
MOMMY?

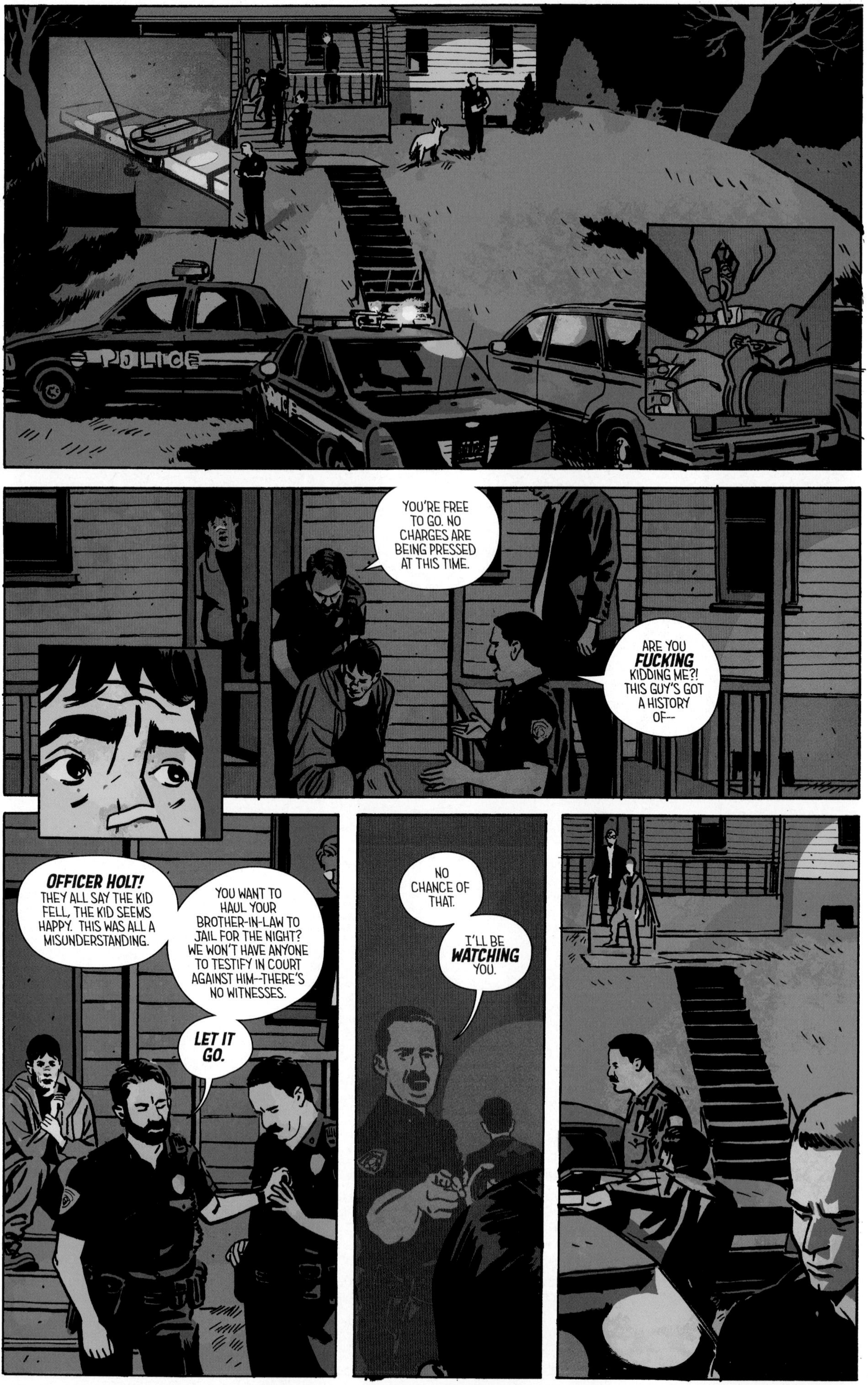

POLICE
YOU'RE FREE TO GO. NO CHARGES ARE BEING PRESSED AT THIS TIME.
ARE YOU **FUCKING** KIDDING ME?! THIS GUY'S GOT A HISTORY OF--
OFFICER HOLT! THEY ALL SAY THE KID FELL, THE KID SEEMS HAPPY. THIS WAS ALL A MISUNDERSTANDING.
YOU WANT TO HAUL YOUR BROTHER-IN-LAW TO JAIL FOR THE NIGHT? WE WON'T HAVE ANYONE TO TESTIFY IN COURT AGAINST HIM--THERE'S NO WITNESSES.
LET IT GO.
NO CHANCE OF THAT.
I'LL BE **WATCHING** YOU.

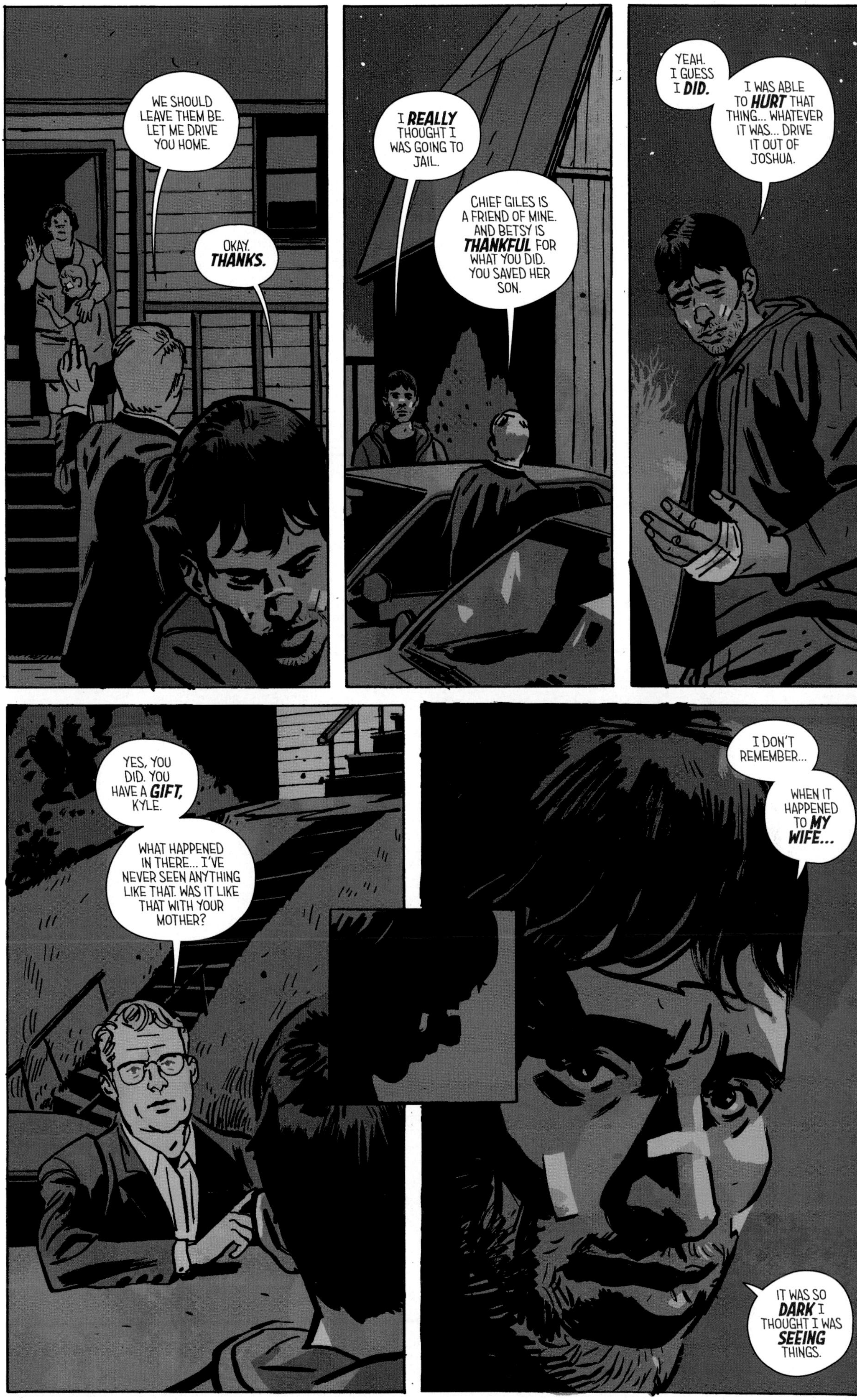
WE SHOULD LEAVE THEM BE. LET ME DRIVE YOU HOME.
OKAY. THANKS.
I REALLY THOUGHT I WAS GOING TO JAIL.
CHIEF GILES IS A FRIEND OF MINE. AND BETSY IS THANKFUL FOR WHAT YOU DID. YOU SAVED HER SON.
YEAH. I GUESS I DID.
I WAS ABLE TO HURT THAT THING... WHATEVER IT WAS... DRIVE IT OUT OF JOSHUA.
YES, YOU DID. YOU HAVE A GIFT, KYLE.
WHAT HAPPENED IN THERE... I'VE NEVER SEEN ANYTHING LIKE THAT. WAS IT LIKE THAT WITH YOUR MOTHER?
I DON'T REMEMBER...
WHEN IT HAPPENED TO MY WIFE...
IT WAS SO DARK I THOUGHT I WAS SEEING THINGS.

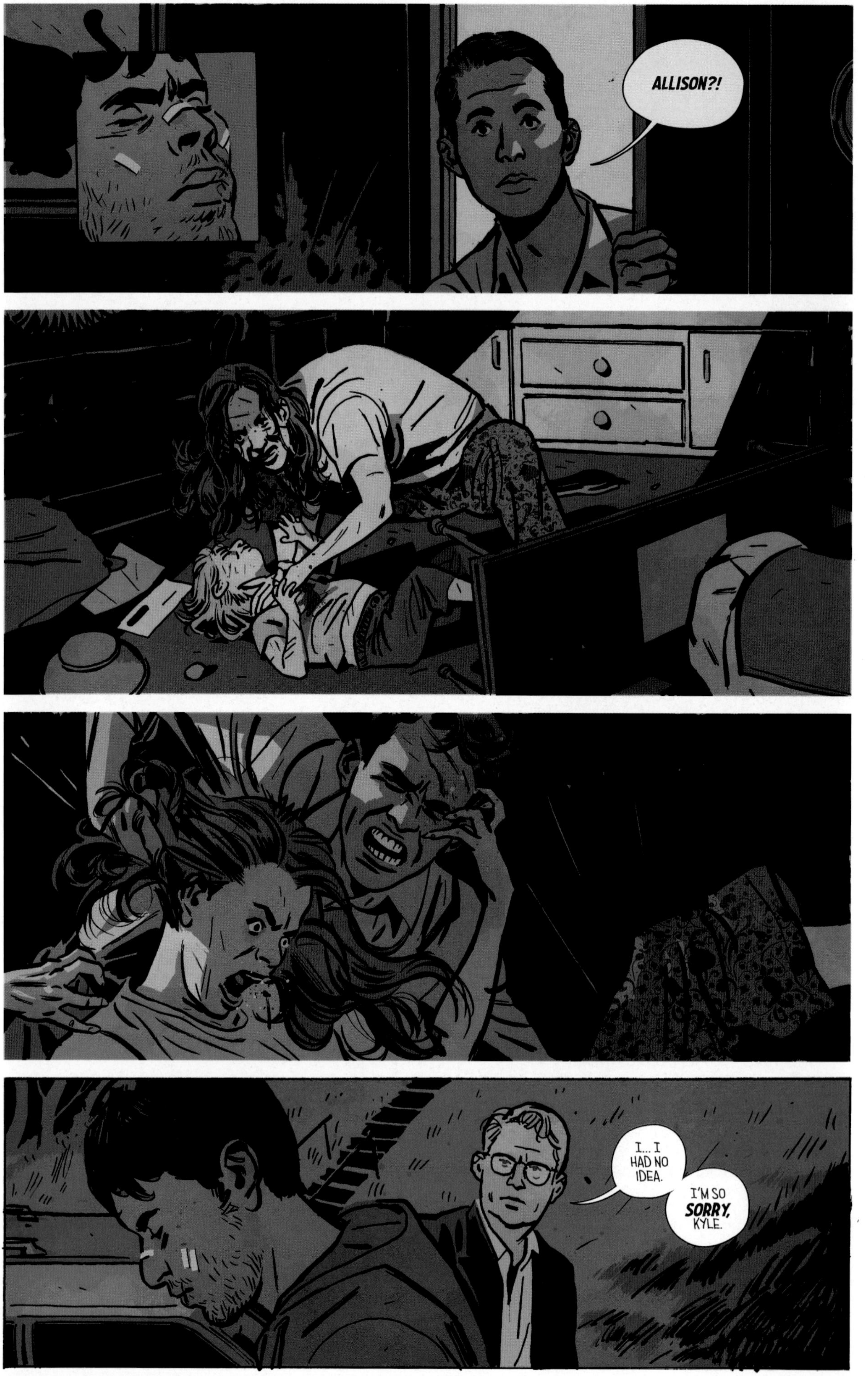
ALLISON?!
I... I HAD NO IDEA.
I'M SO SORRY, KYLE.

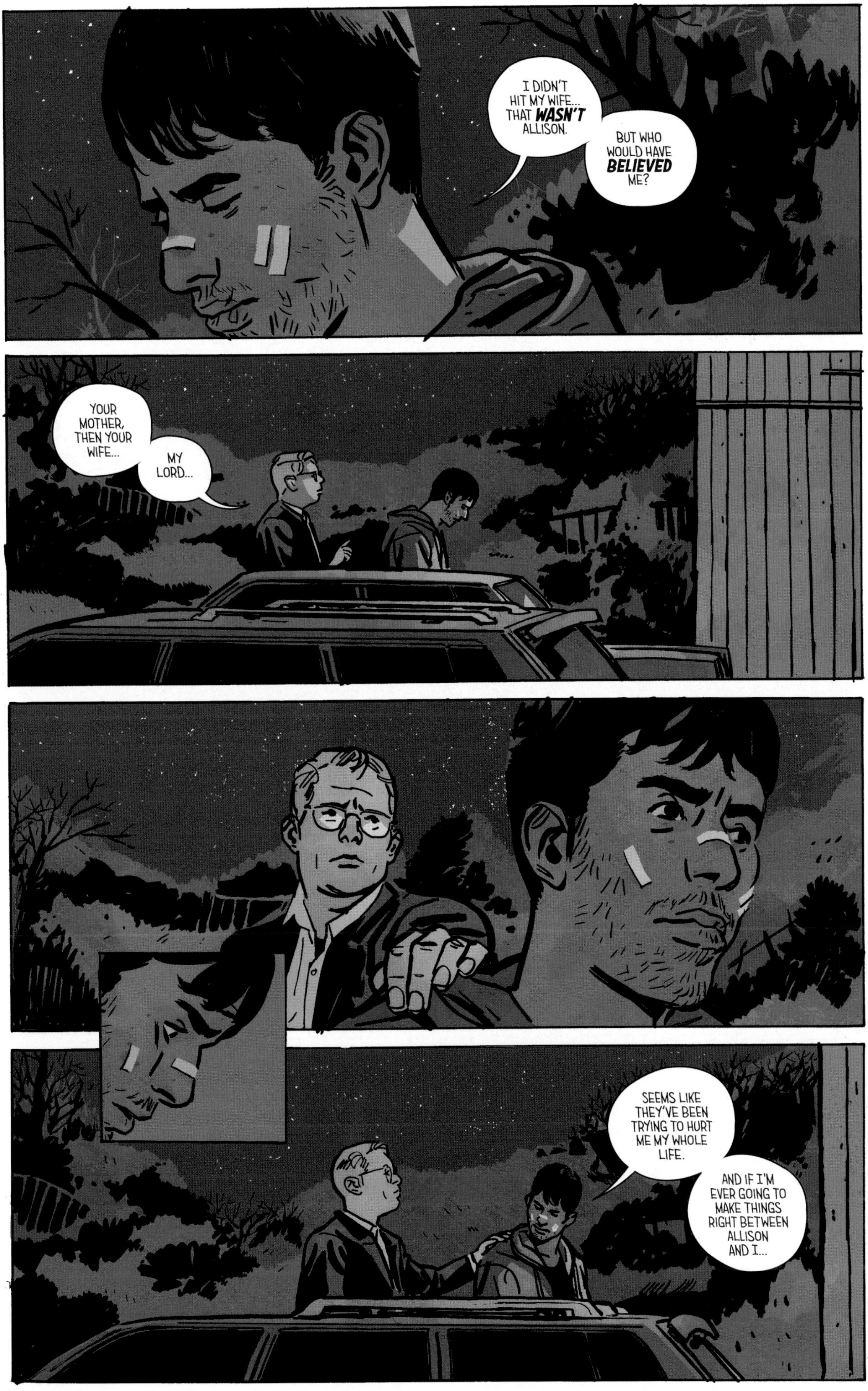
I DIDN'T HIT MY WIFE... THAT WASN'T ALLISON.
BUT WHO WOULD HAVE BELIEVED ME?
YOUR MOTHER, THEN YOUR WIFE...
MY LORD...
SEEMS LIKE THEY'VE BEEN TRYING TO HURT ME MY WHOLE LIFE.
AND IF I'M EVER GOING TO MAKE THINGS RIGHT BETWEEN ALLISON AND I...

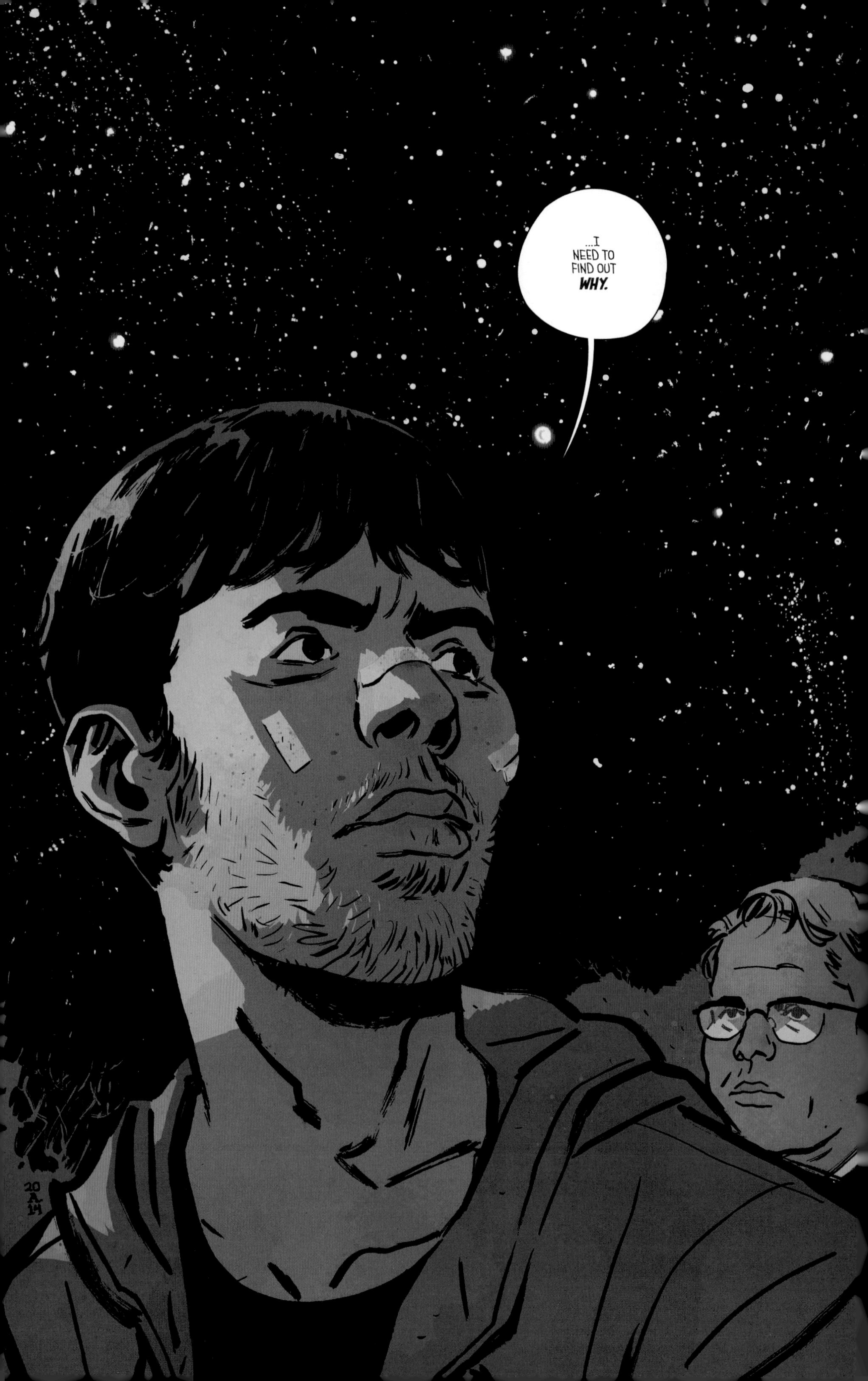
...I NEED TO FIND OUT **WHY.**
20 A. 14

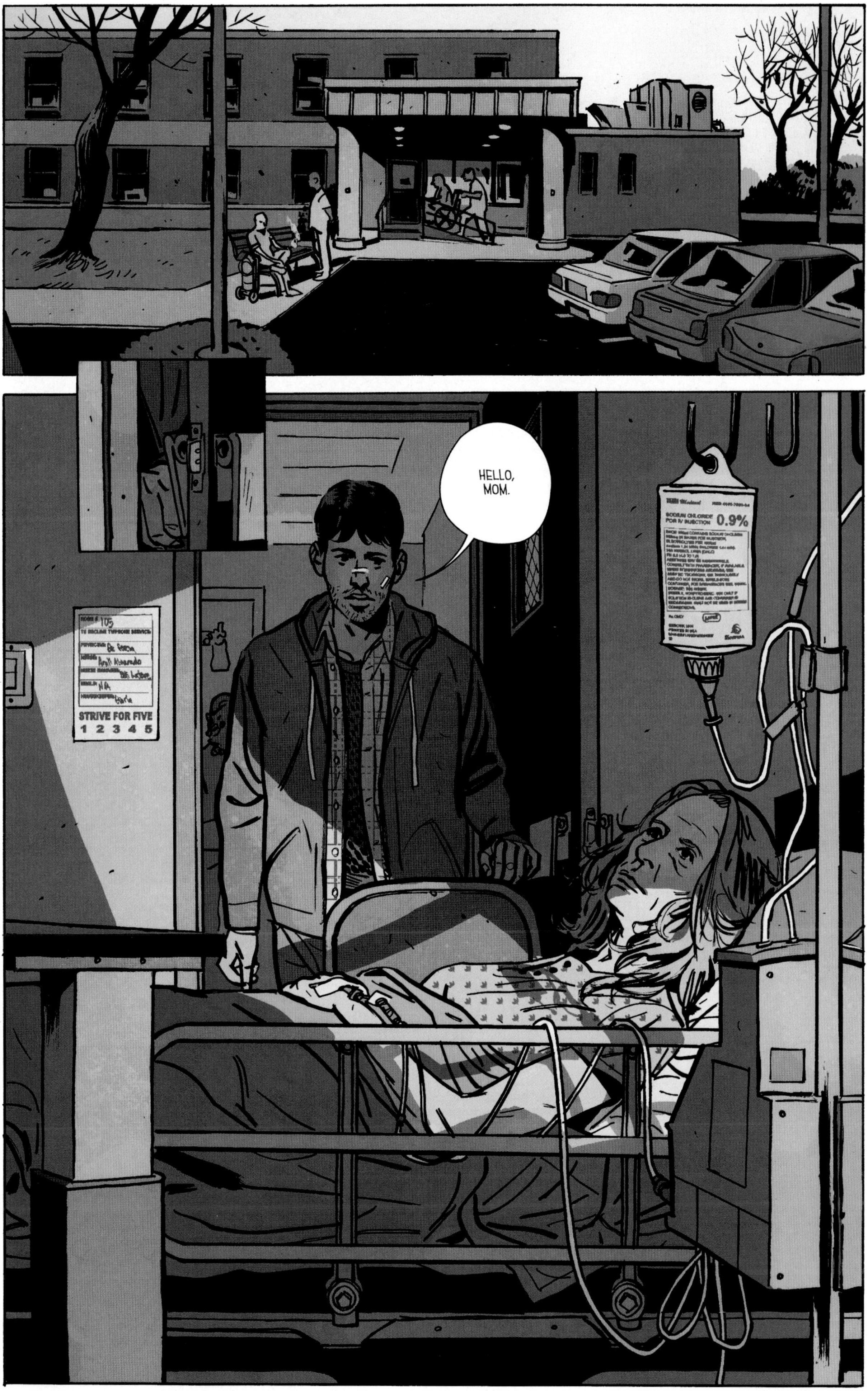
STRIVE FOR FIVE
1 2 3 4 5
0.9%
HELLO, MOM.

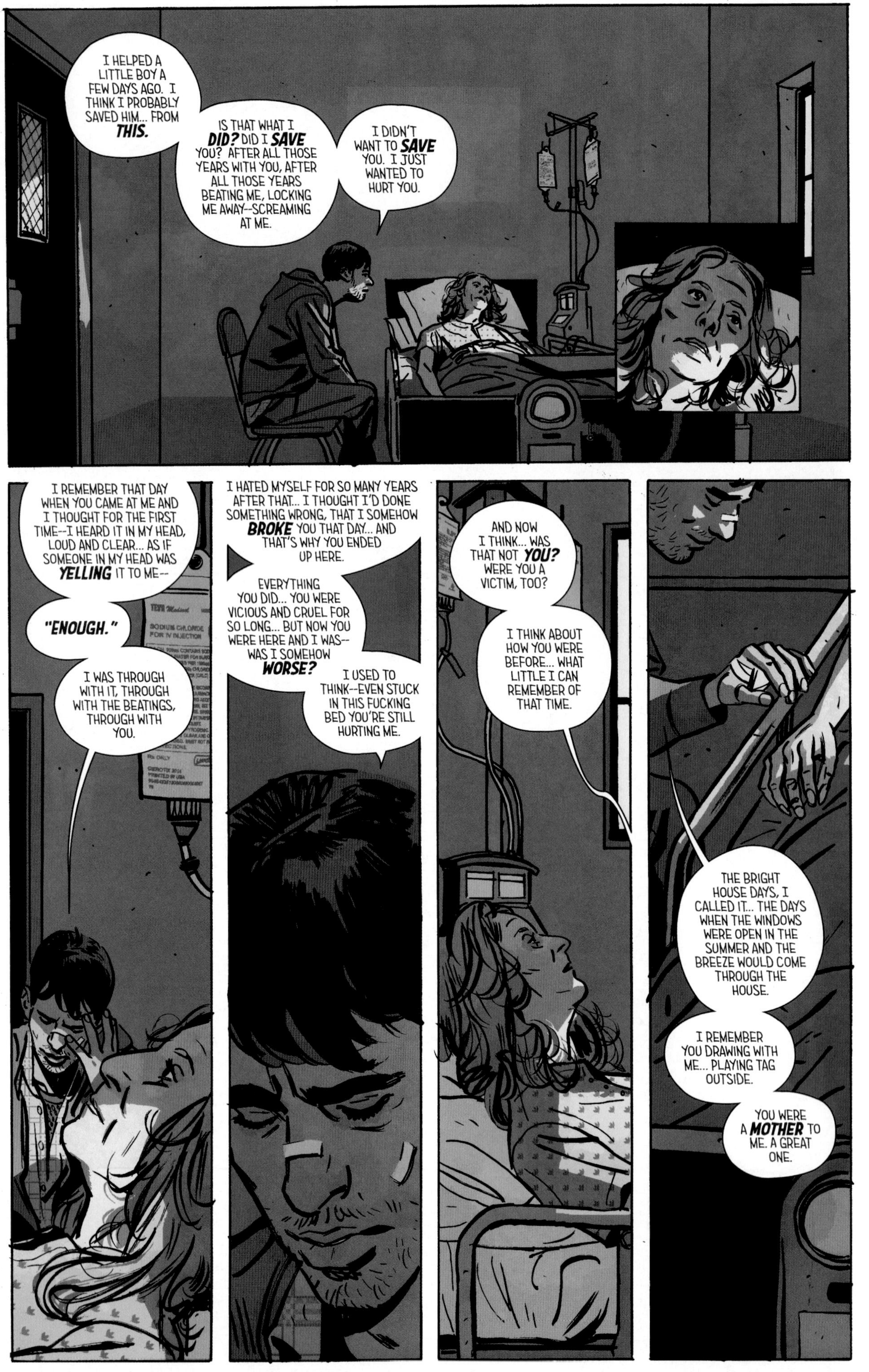
I HELPED A LITTLE BOY A FEW DAYS AGO. I THINK I PROBABLY SAVED HIM... FROM **THIS.**
IS THAT WHAT I ***DID?*** DID I ***SAVE*** YOU? AFTER ALL THOSE YEARS WITH YOU, AFTER ALL THOSE YEARS BEATING ME, LOCKING ME AWAY--SCREAMING AT ME.
I DIDN'T WANT TO ***SAVE*** YOU. I JUST WANTED TO HURT YOU.
I REMEMBER THAT DAY WHEN YOU CAME AT ME AND I THOUGHT FOR THE FIRST TIME--I HEARD IT IN MY HEAD, LOUD AND CLEAR... AS IF SOMEONE IN MY HEAD WAS ***YELLING*** IT TO ME--
"ENOUGH."
I WAS THROUGH WITH IT, THROUGH WITH THE BEATINGS, THROUGH WITH YOU.
SODIUM CHLORIDE FOR IV INJECTION
I HATED MYSELF FOR SO MANY YEARS AFTER THAT... I THOUGHT I'D DONE SOMETHING WRONG, THAT I SOMEHOW ***BROKE*** YOU THAT DAY... AND THAT'S WHY YOU ENDED UP HERE.
EVERYTHING YOU DID... YOU WERE VICIOUS AND CRUEL FOR SO LONG... BUT NOW YOU WERE HERE AND I WAS--WAS I SOMEHOW ***WORSE?***
I USED TO THINK--EVEN STUCK IN THIS FUCKING BED YOU'RE STILL HURTING ME.
AND NOW I THINK... WAS THAT NOT ***YOU?*** WERE YOU A VICTIM, TOO?
I THINK ABOUT HOW YOU WERE BEFORE... WHAT LITTLE I CAN REMEMBER OF THAT TIME.
THE BRIGHT HOUSE DAYS, I CALLED IT... THE DAYS WHEN THE WINDOWS WERE OPEN IN THE SUMMER AND THE BREEZE WOULD COME THROUGH THE HOUSE.
I REMEMBER YOU DRAWING WITH ME... PLAYING TAG OUTSIDE.
YOU WERE A ***MOTHER*** TO ME. A GREAT ONE.

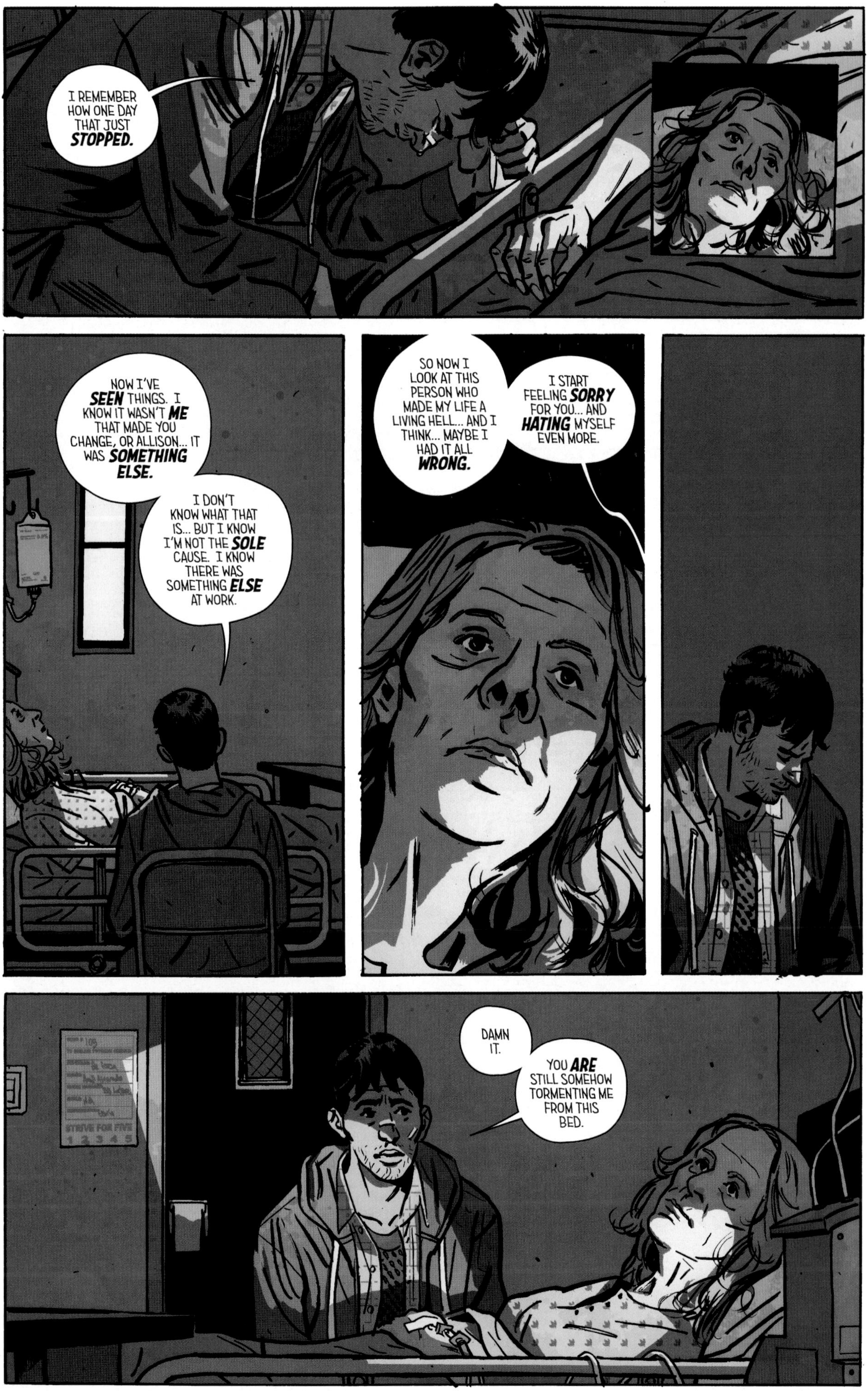
I REMEMBER HOW ONE DAY THAT JUST STOPPED.
NOW I'VE SEEN THINGS. I KNOW IT WASN'T ME THAT MADE YOU CHANGE, OR ALLISON... IT WAS SOMETHING ELSE.
I DON'T KNOW WHAT THAT IS... BUT I KNOW I'M NOT THE SOLE CAUSE. I KNOW THERE WAS SOMETHING ELSE AT WORK.
SO NOW I LOOK AT THIS PERSON WHO MADE MY LIFE A LIVING HELL... AND I THINK... MAYBE I HAD IT ALL WRONG.
I START FEELING SORRY FOR YOU... AND HATING MYSELF EVEN MORE.
STRIVE FOR FIVE
1 2 3 4 5
DAMN IT.
YOU ARE STILL SOMEHOW TORMENTING ME FROM THIS BED.

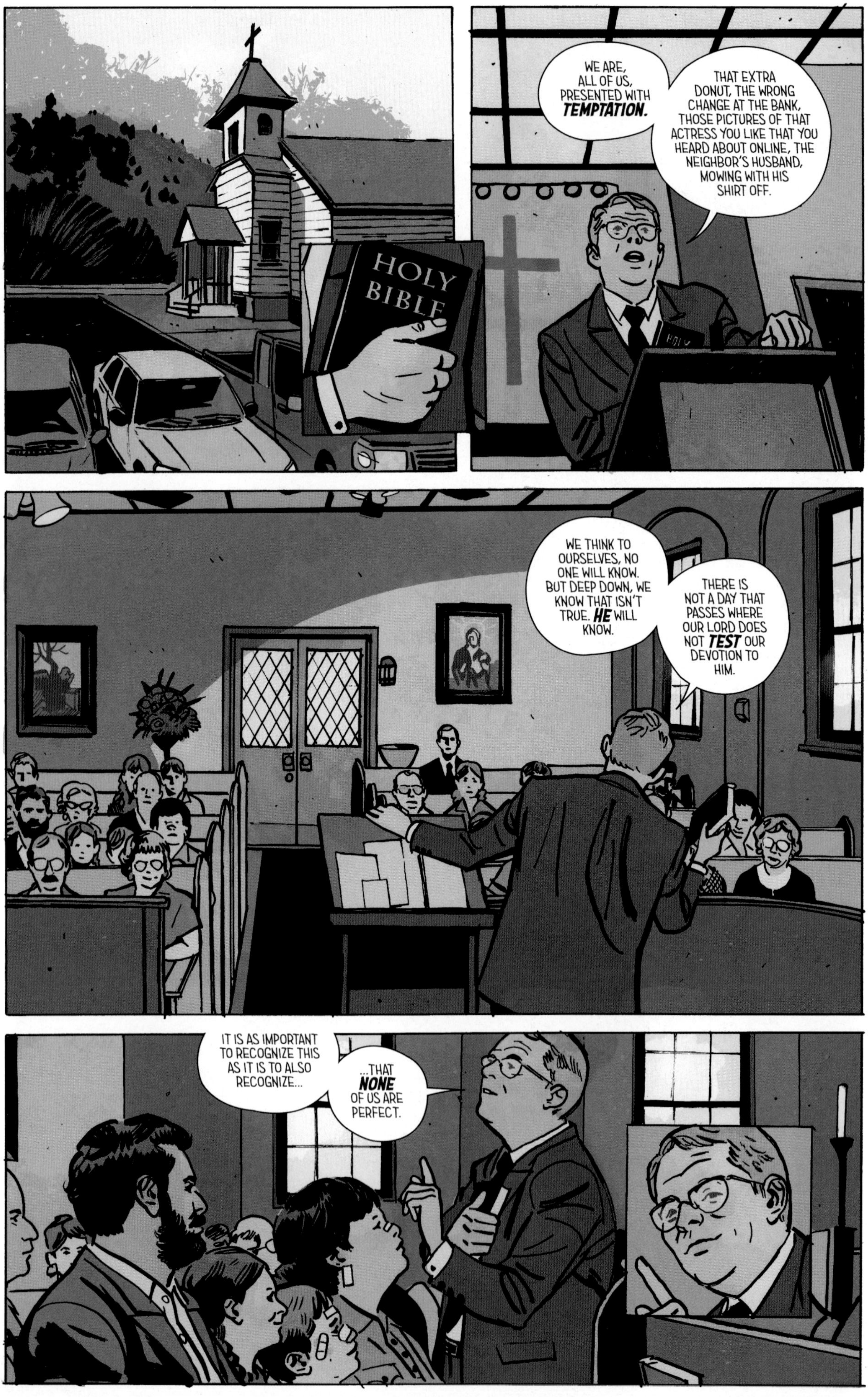
HOLY BIBLE
WE ARE, ALL OF US, PRESENTED WITH *TEMPTATION.*
THAT EXTRA DONUT, THE WRONG CHANGE AT THE BANK, THOSE PICTURES OF THAT ACTRESS YOU LIKE THAT YOU HEARD ABOUT ONLINE, THE NEIGHBOR'S HUSBAND, MOWING WITH HIS SHIRT OFF.
WE THINK TO OURSELVES, NO ONE WILL KNOW. BUT DEEP DOWN, WE KNOW THAT ISN'T TRUE. *HE* WILL KNOW.
THERE IS NOT A DAY THAT PASSES WHERE OUR LORD DOES NOT *TEST* OUR DEVOTION TO HIM.
IT IS AS IMPORTANT TO RECOGNIZE THIS AS IT IS TO ALSO RECOGNIZE...
...THAT *NONE* OF US ARE PERFECT.

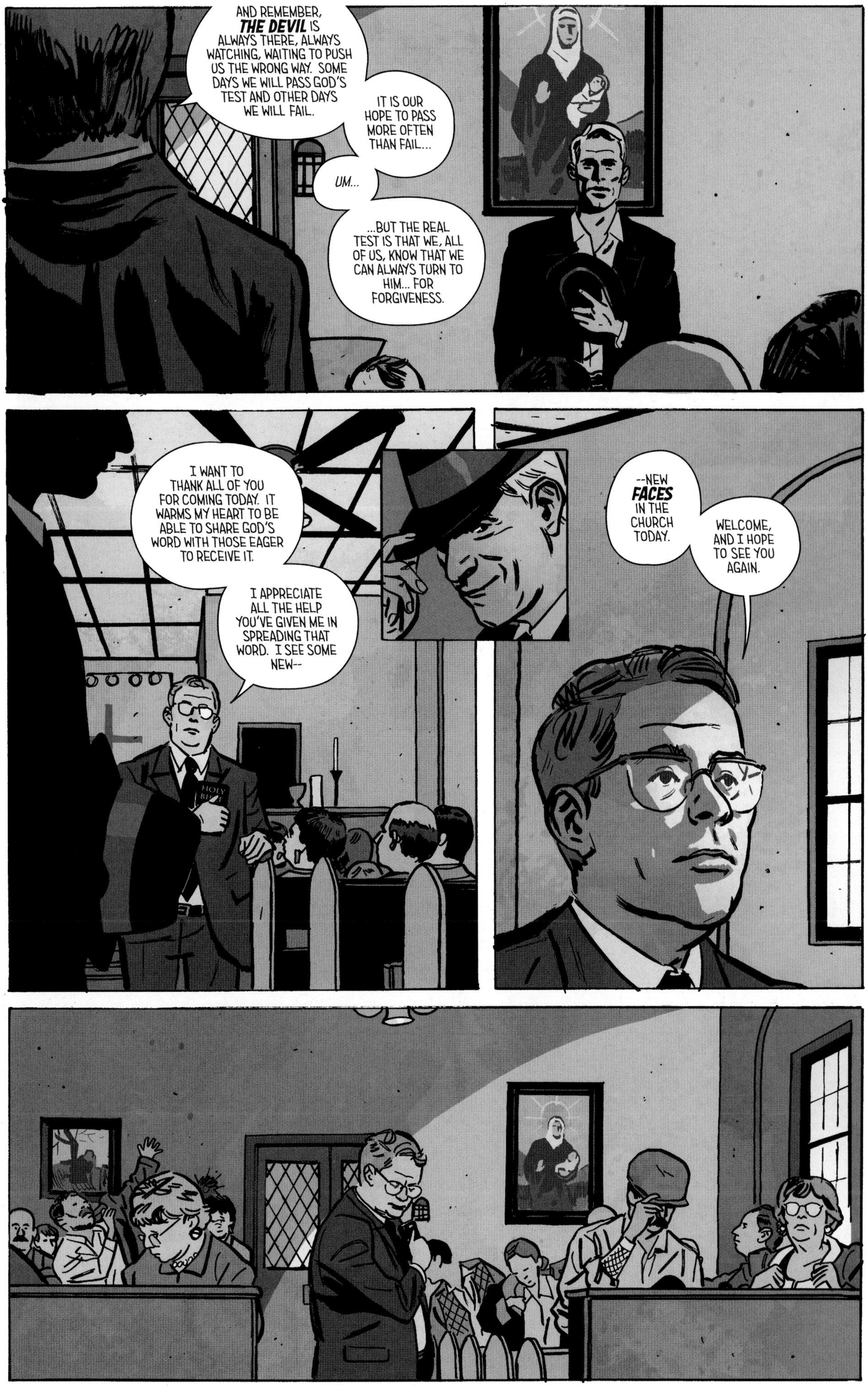
AND REMEMBER, THE DEVIL IS ALWAYS THERE, ALWAYS WATCHING, WAITING TO PUSH US THE WRONG WAY. SOME DAYS WE WILL PASS GOD'S TEST AND OTHER DAYS WE WILL FAIL.
IT IS OUR HOPE TO PASS MORE OFTEN THAN FAIL...
UM...
...BUT THE REAL TEST IS THAT WE, ALL OF US, KNOW THAT WE CAN ALWAYS TURN TO HIM... FOR FORGIVENESS.
I WANT TO THANK ALL OF YOU FOR COMING TODAY. IT WARMS MY HEART TO BE ABLE TO SHARE GOD'S WORD WITH THOSE EAGER TO RECEIVE IT.
I APPRECIATE ALL THE HELP YOU'VE GIVEN ME IN SPREADING THAT WORD. I SEE SOME NEW--
HOLY BIBLE
--NEW FACES IN THE CHURCH TODAY.
WELCOME, AND I HOPE TO SEE YOU AGAIN.

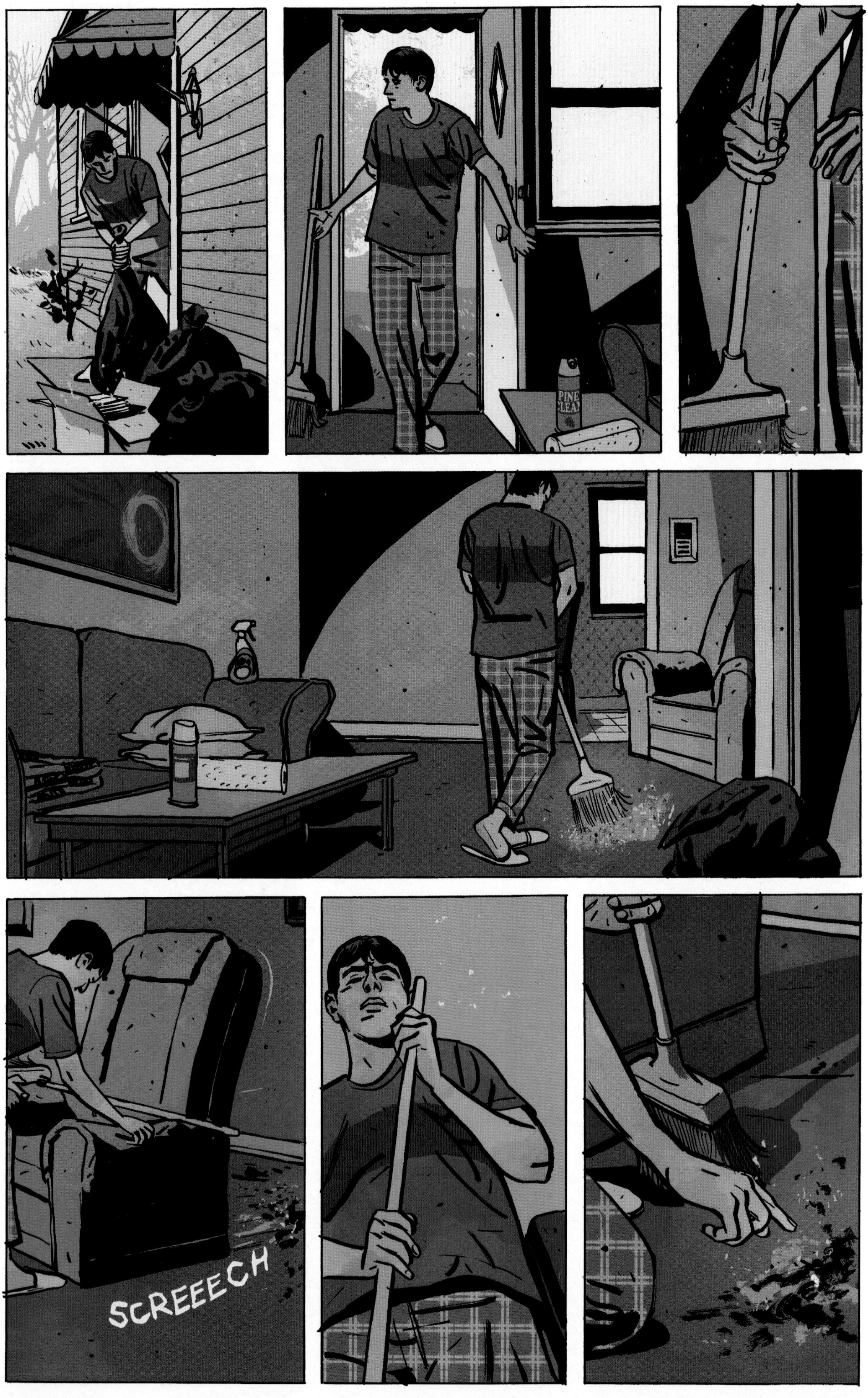
PINE CLEAN
SCREEECH

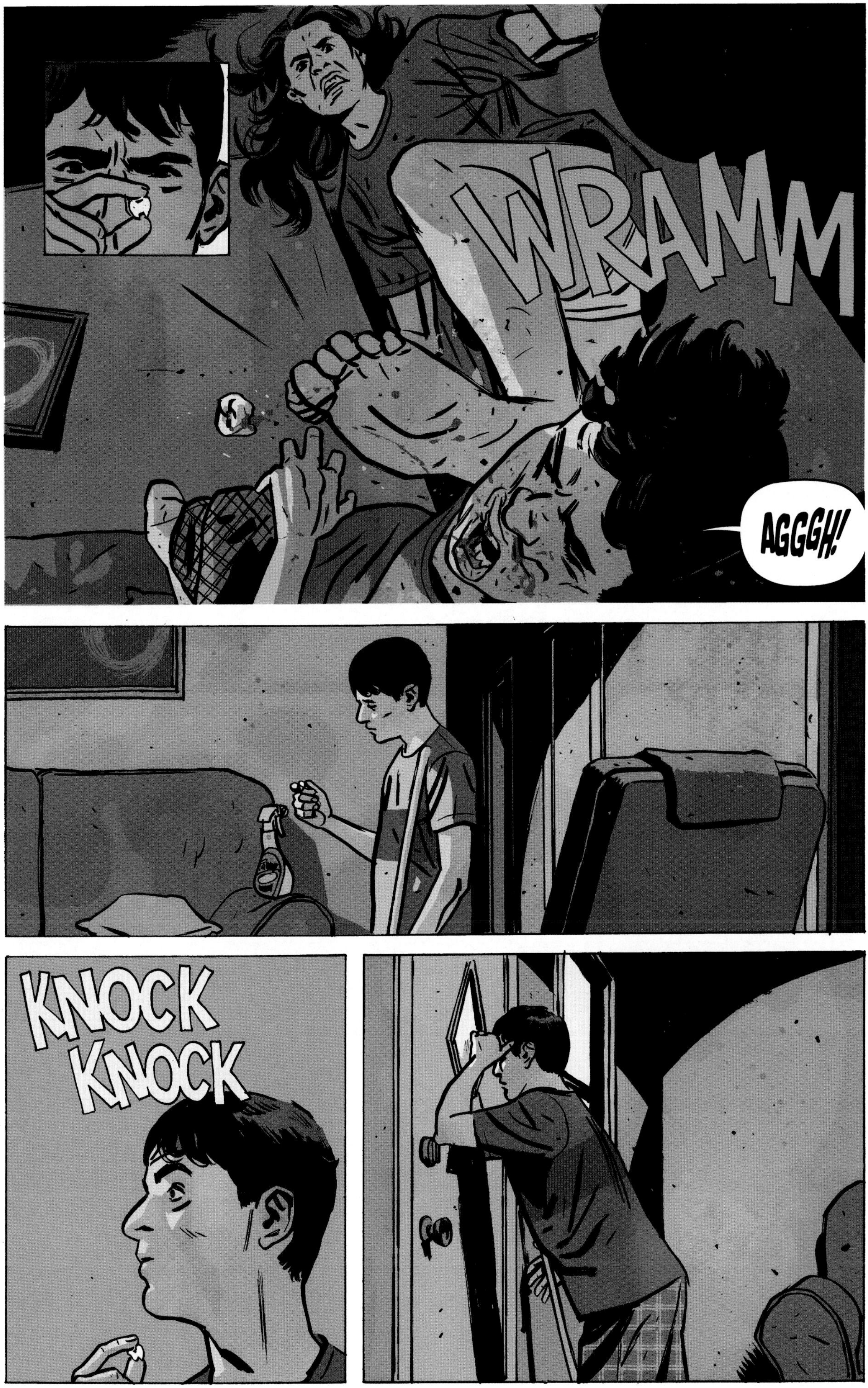
WRAMM
AGGGH!
KNOCK
KNOCK

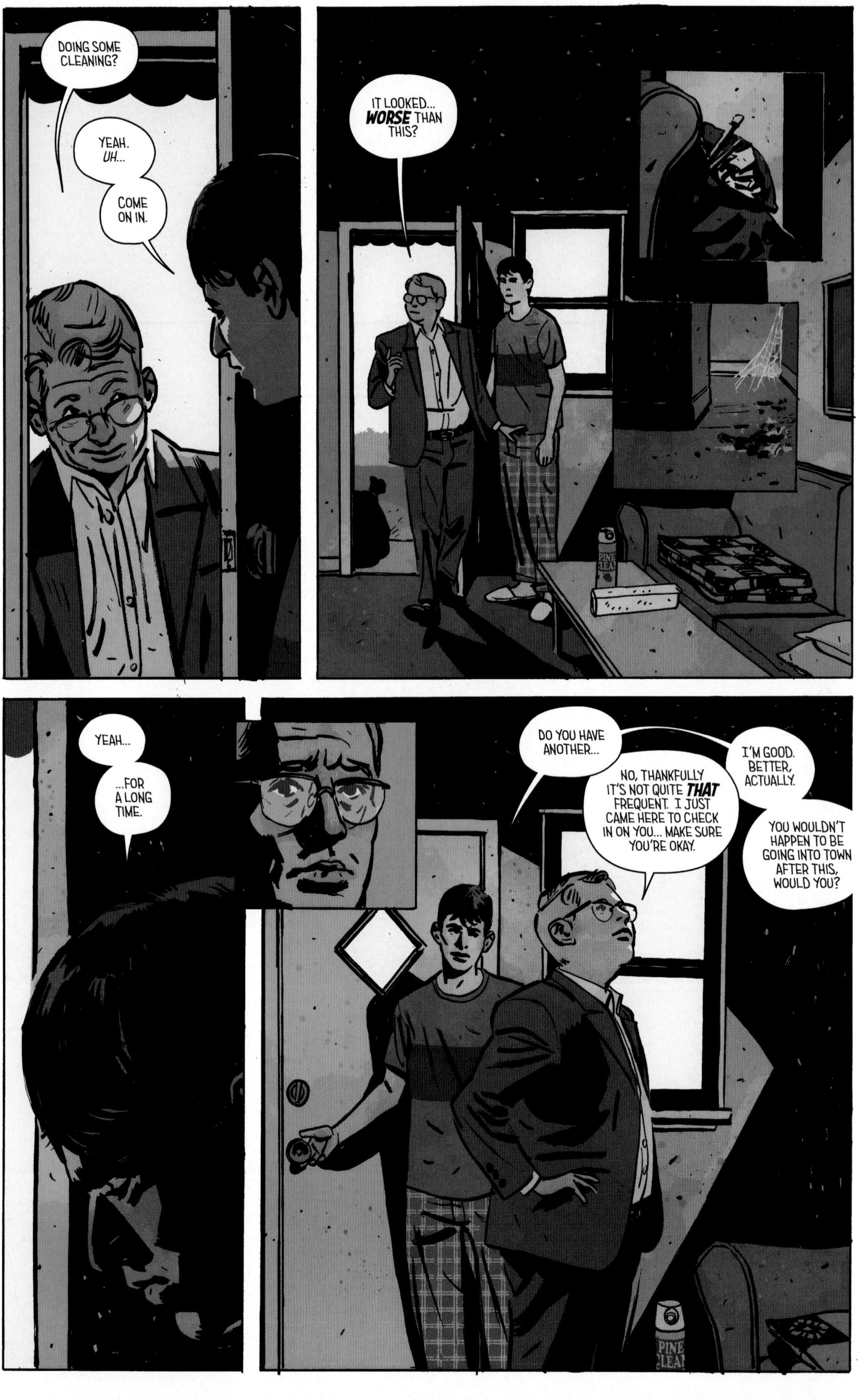
DOING SOME CLEANING?
YEAH. UH...
COME ON IN.
IT LOOKED... WORSE THAN THIS?
YEAH...
...FOR A LONG TIME.
DO YOU HAVE ANOTHER...
NO, THANKFULLY IT'S NOT QUITE THAT FREQUENT. I JUST CAME HERE TO CHECK IN ON YOU... MAKE SURE YOU'RE OKAY.
I'M GOOD. BETTER, ACTUALLY.
YOU WOULDN'T HAPPEN TO BE GOING INTO TOWN AFTER THIS, WOULD YOU?

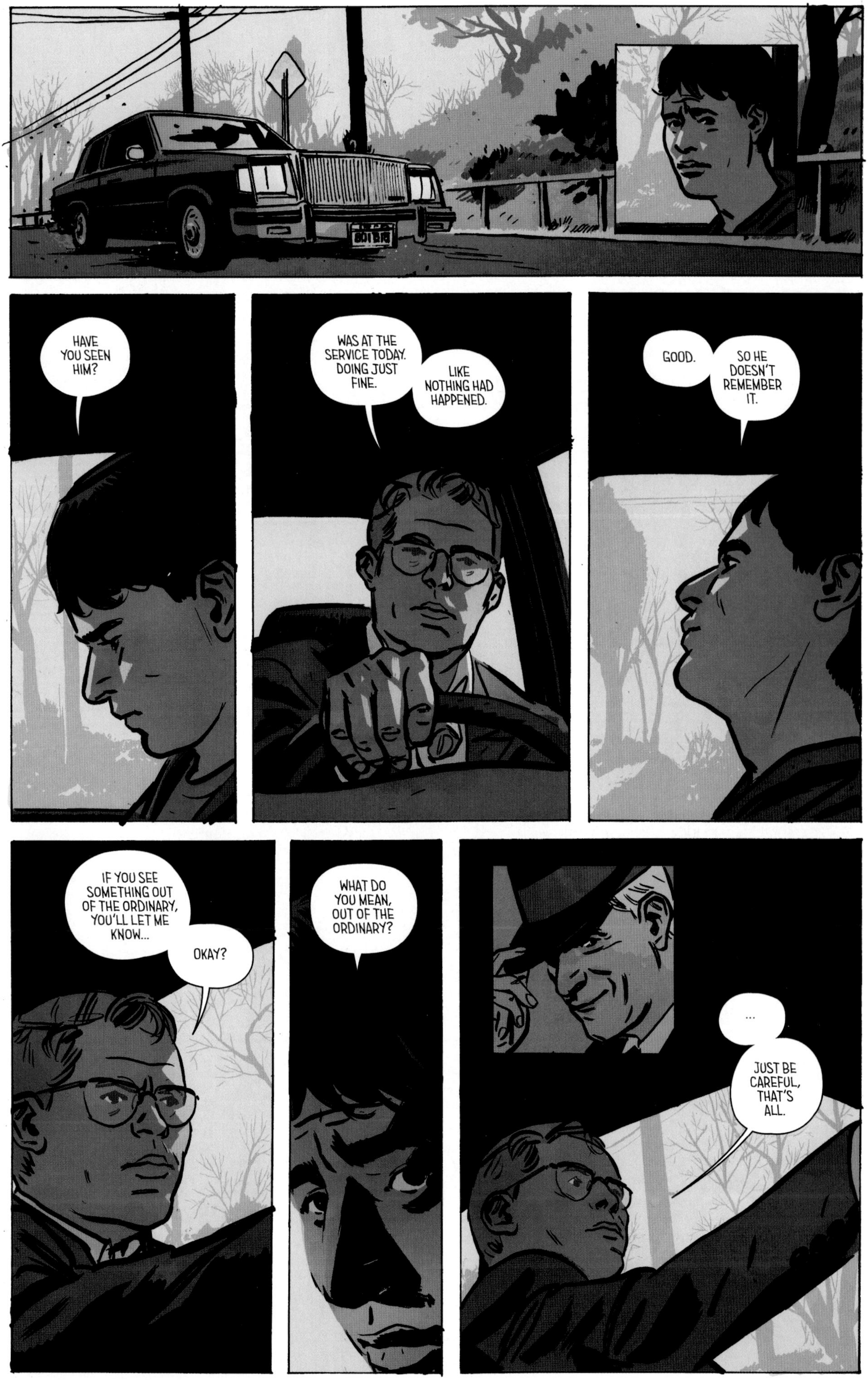
HAVE YOU SEEN HIM?
WAS AT THE SERVICE TODAY. DOING JUST FINE.
LIKE NOTHING HAD HAPPENED.
GOOD.
SO HE DOESN'T REMEMBER IT.
IF YOU SEE SOMETHING OUT OF THE ORDINARY, YOU'LL LET ME KNOW...
OKAY?
WHAT DO YOU MEAN, OUT OF THE ORDINARY?
...
JUST BE CAREFUL, THAT'S ALL.

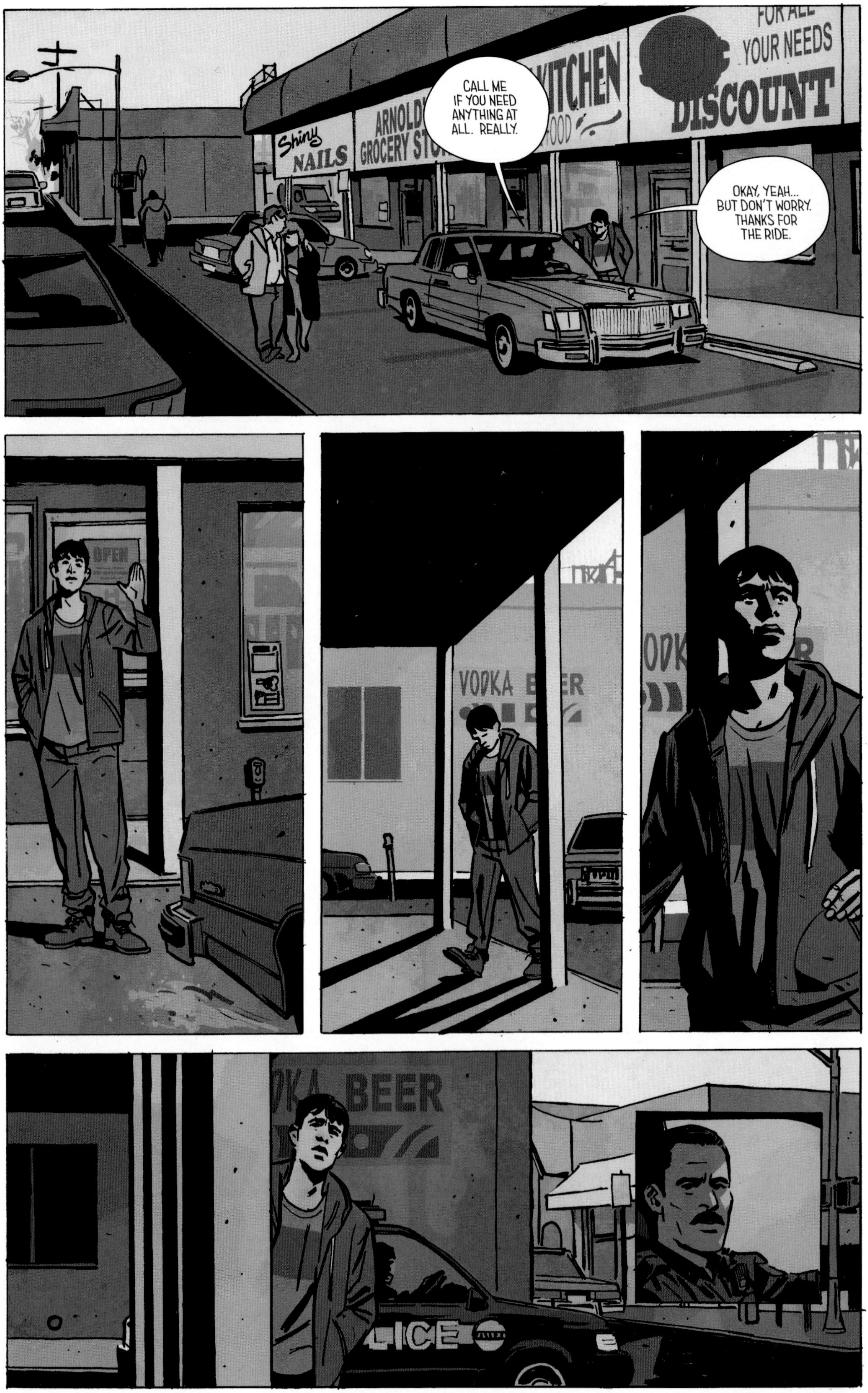
FOR ALL YOUR NEEDS
DISCOUNT
KITCHEN
Shiny NAILS
CALL ME IF YOU NEED ANYTHING AT ALL. REALLY.
OKAY, YEAH... BUT DON'T WORRY. THANKS FOR THE RIDE.
OPEN
VODKA BEER
BEER
LICE

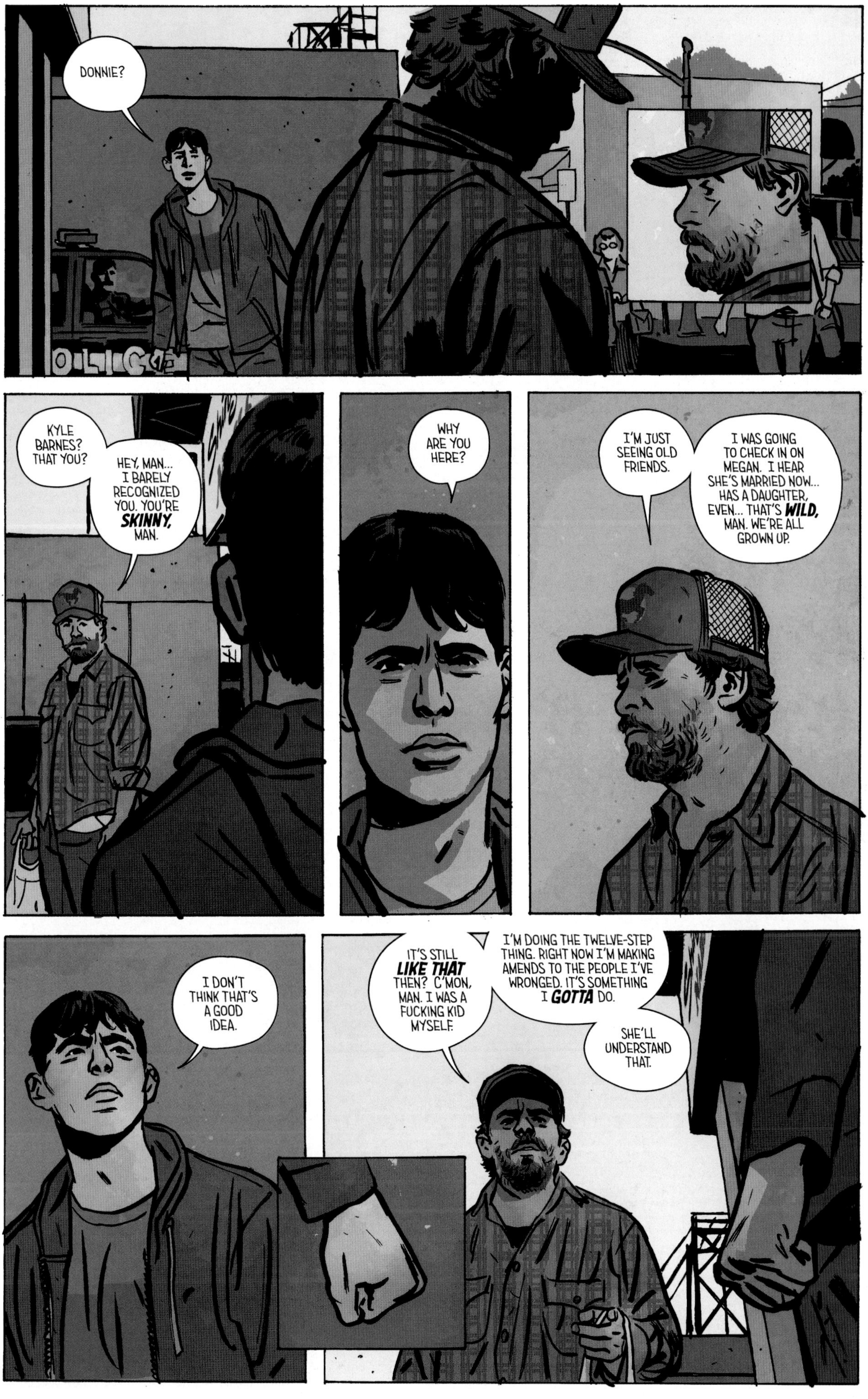
DONNIE?
KYLE BARNES? THAT YOU?
HEY, MAN... I BARELY RECOGNIZED YOU. YOU'RE **SKINNY,** MAN.
WHY ARE YOU HERE?
I'M JUST SEEING OLD FRIENDS.
I WAS GOING TO CHECK IN ON MEGAN. I HEAR SHE'S MARRIED NOW... HAS A DAUGHTER, EVEN... THAT'S **WILD,** MAN. WE'RE ALL GROWN UP.
I DON'T THINK THAT'S A GOOD IDEA.
IT'S STILL **LIKE THAT** THEN? C'MON, MAN. I WAS A FUCKING KID MYSELF.
I'M DOING THE TWELVE-STEP THING. RIGHT NOW I'M MAKING AMENDS TO THE PEOPLE I'VE WRONGED. IT'S SOMETHING I **GOTTA** DO.
SHE'LL UNDERSTAND THAT.

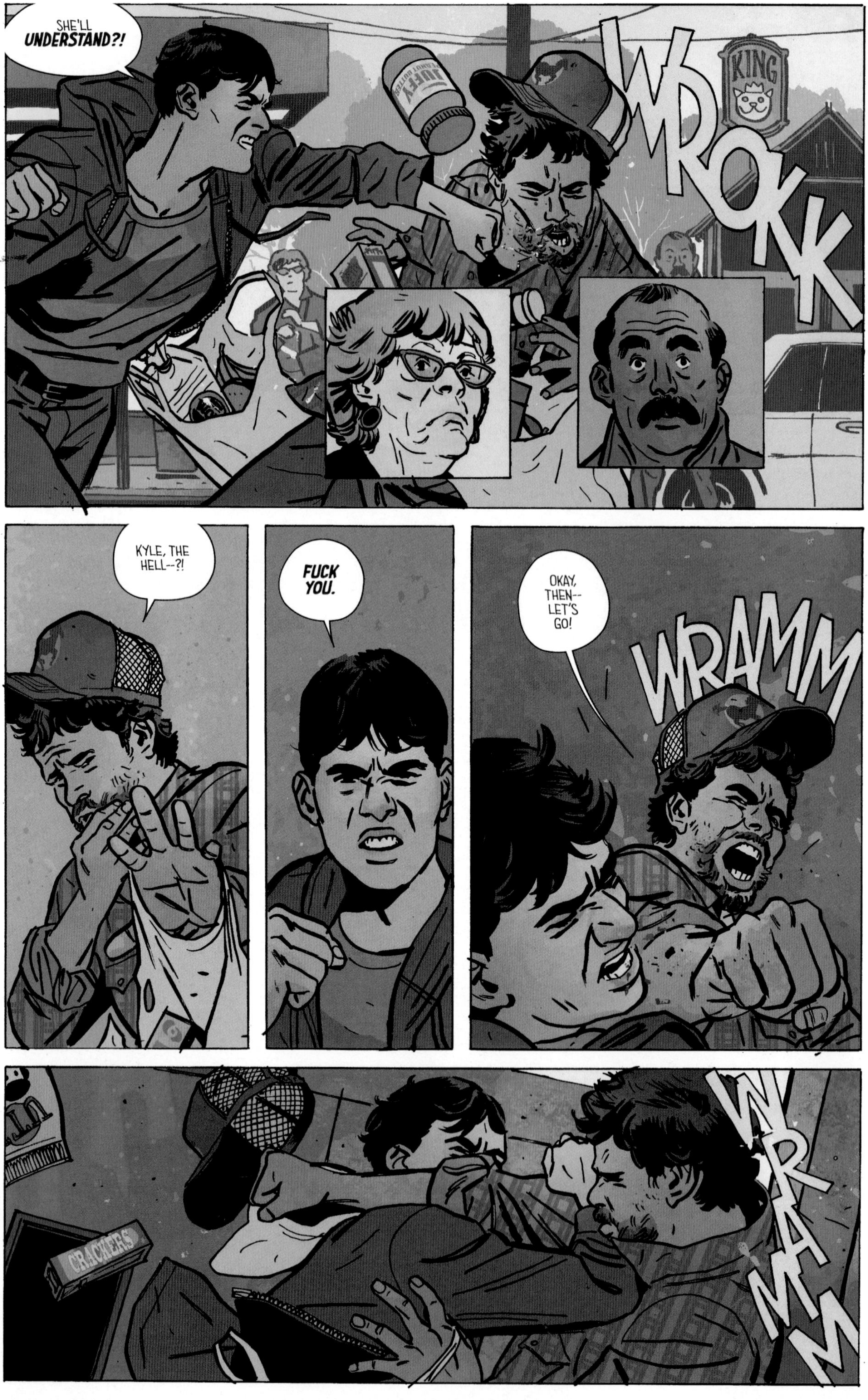
SHE'LL UNDERSTAND?!
JUFFY PEANUT BUTTER
WROKK
KING
KYLE, THE HELL--?!
FUCK YOU.
OKAY, THEN-- LET'S GO!
WRAMM
CRACKERS
WRAMM

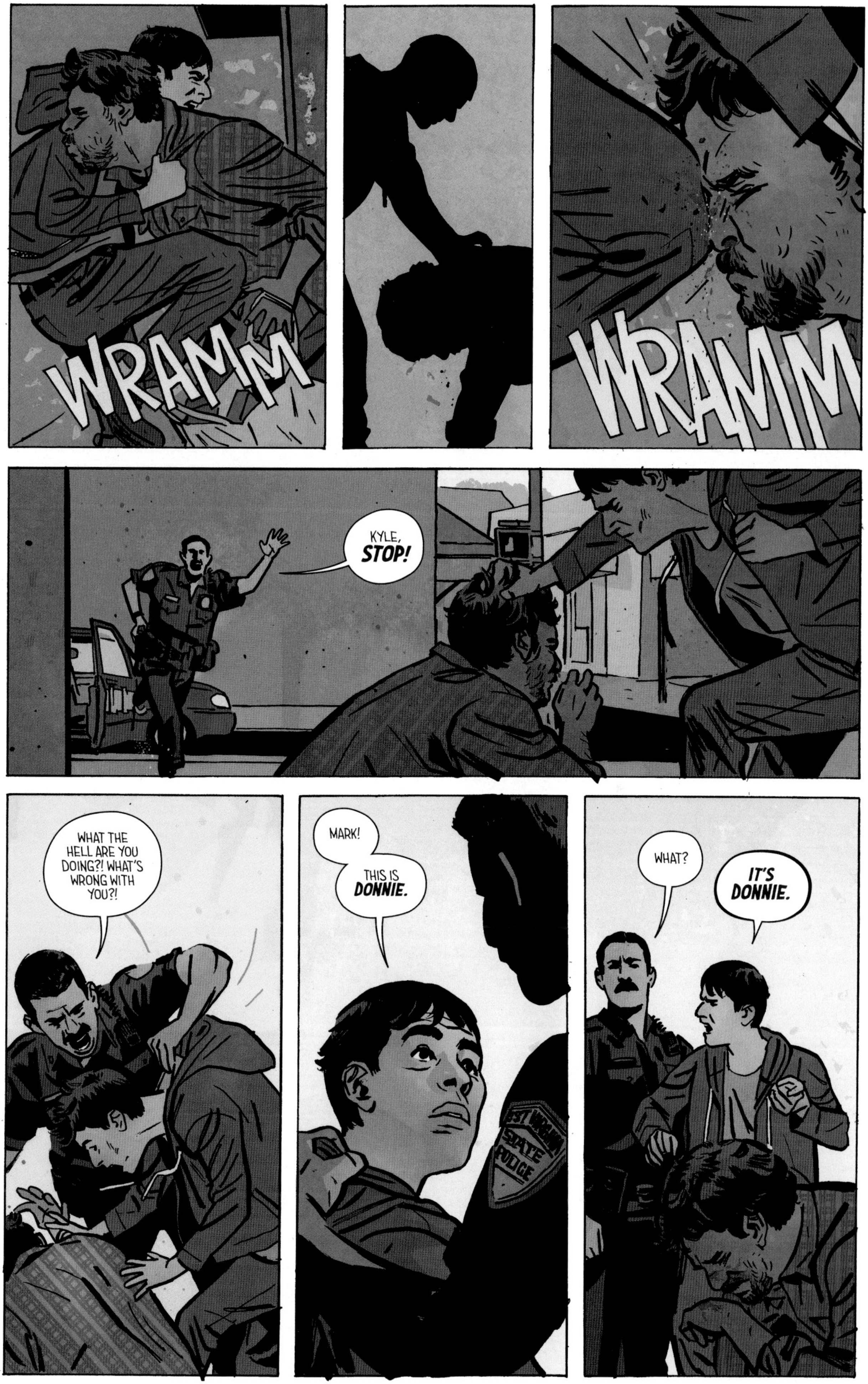
WRAMM
WRAMM
KYLE, STOP!
WHAT THE HELL ARE YOU DOING?! WHAT'S WRONG WITH YOU?!
MARK!
THIS IS DONNIE.
WHAT?
IT'S DONNIE.

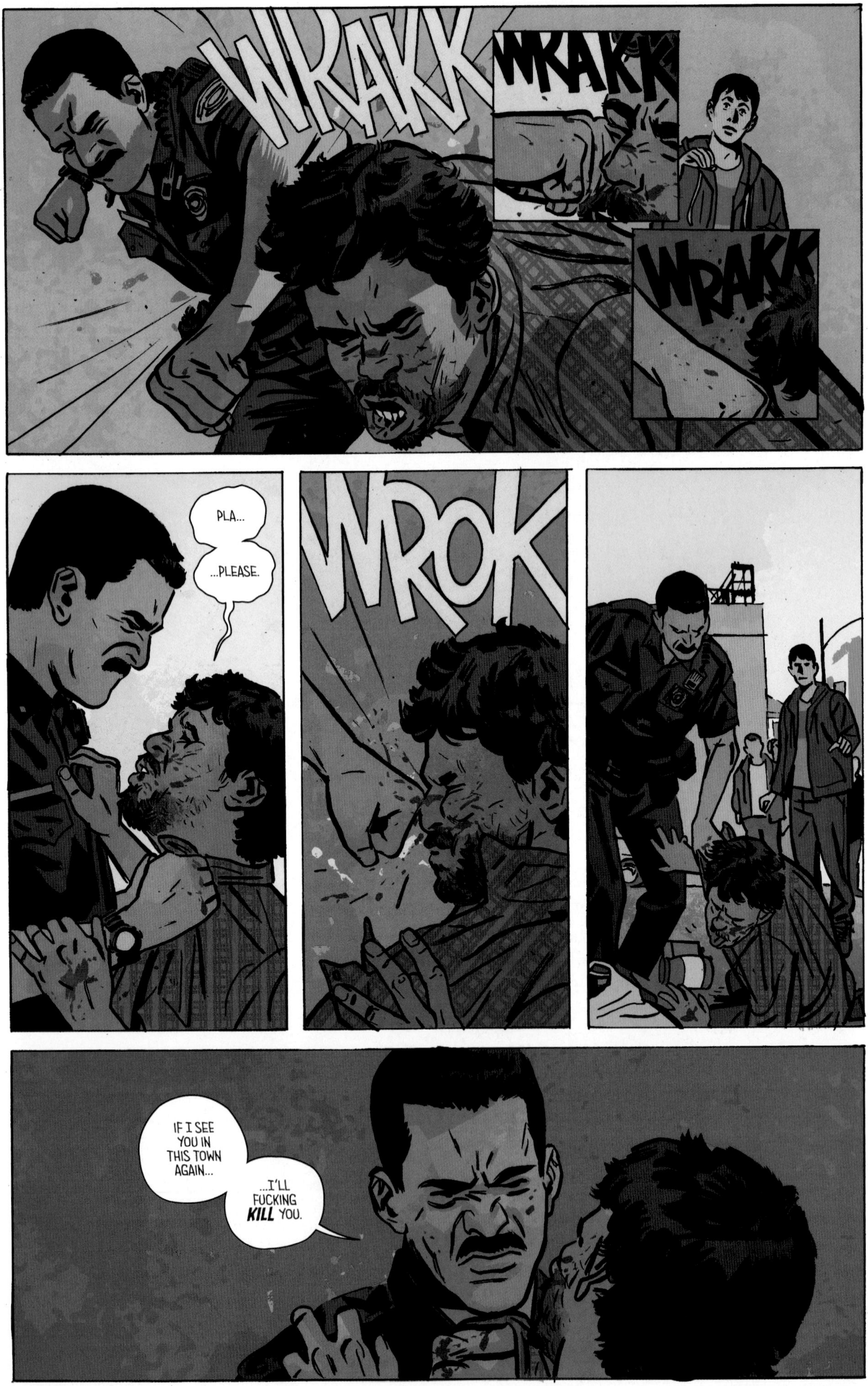
WRAKK
WRAKK
WRAKK
PLA...
...PLEASE.
WROK
IF I SEE YOU IN THIS TOWN AGAIN...
...I'LL FUCKING KILL YOU.

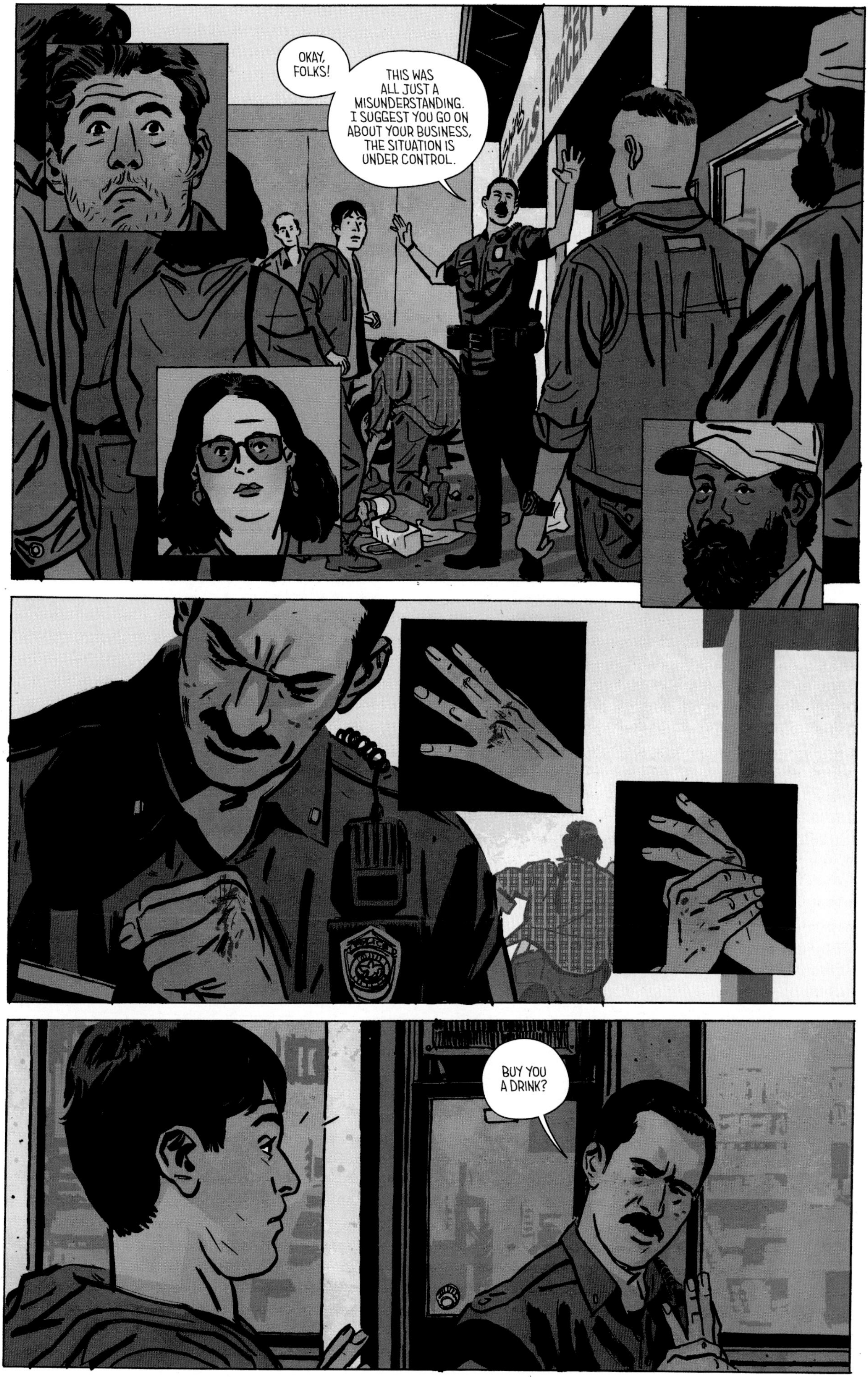
OKAY, FOLKS!
THIS WAS ALL JUST A MISUNDERSTANDING. I SUGGEST YOU GO ON ABOUT YOUR BUSINESS, THE SITUATION IS UNDER CONTROL.
BUY YOU A DRINK?

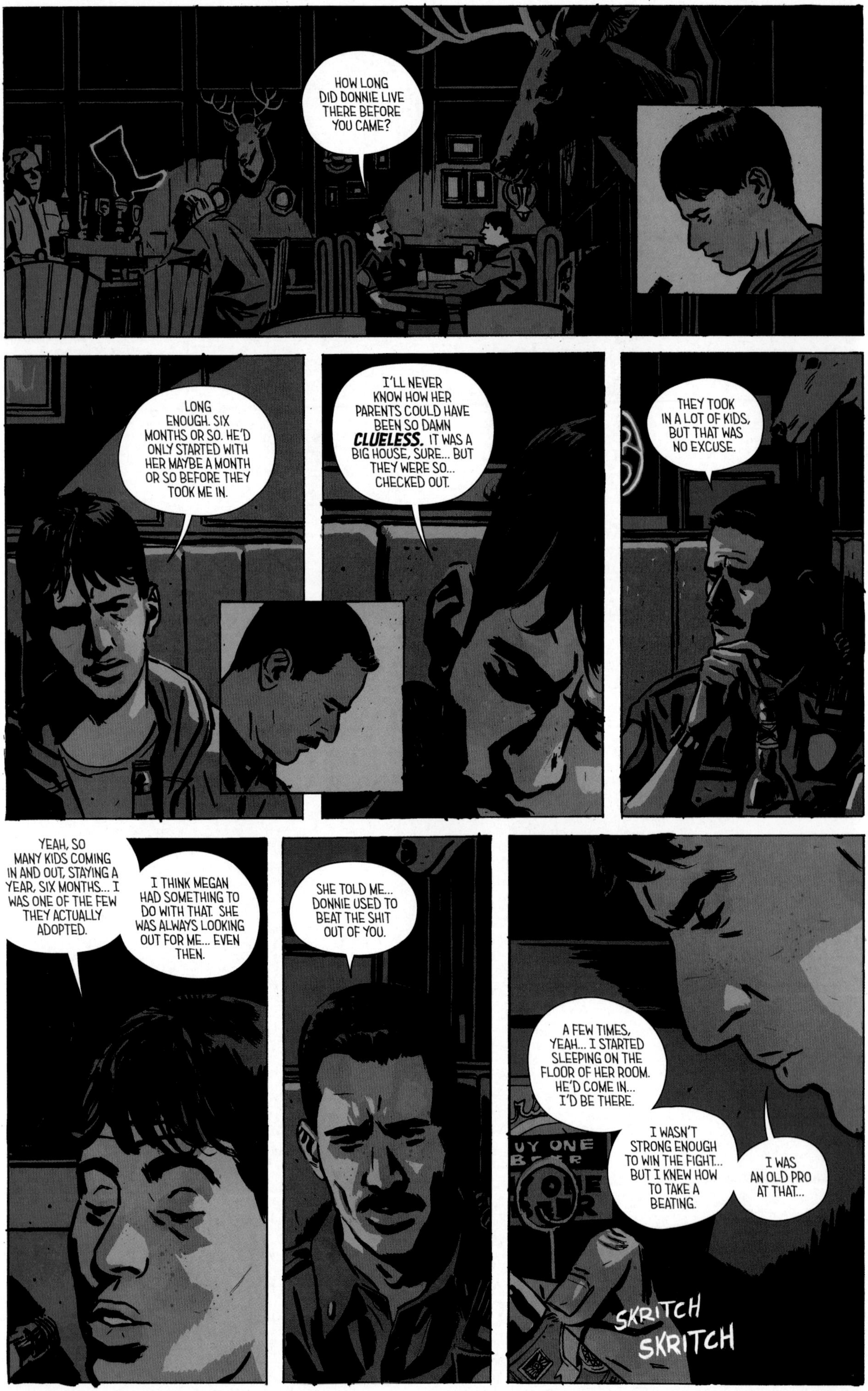
HOW LONG DID DONNIE LIVE THERE BEFORE YOU CAME?
LONG ENOUGH. SIX MONTHS OR SO. HE'D ONLY STARTED WITH HER MAYBE A MONTH OR SO BEFORE THEY TOOK ME IN.
I'LL NEVER KNOW HOW HER PARENTS COULD HAVE BEEN SO DAMN CLUELESS. IT WAS A BIG HOUSE, SURE... BUT THEY WERE SO... CHECKED OUT.
THEY TOOK IN A LOT OF KIDS, BUT THAT WAS NO EXCUSE.
YEAH, SO MANY KIDS COMING IN AND OUT, STAYING A YEAR, SIX MONTHS... I WAS ONE OF THE FEW THEY ACTUALLY ADOPTED.
I THINK MEGAN HAD SOMETHING TO DO WITH THAT. SHE WAS ALWAYS LOOKING OUT FOR ME... EVEN THEN.
SHE TOLD ME... DONNIE USED TO BEAT THE SHIT OUT OF YOU.
A FEW TIMES, YEAH... I STARTED SLEEPING ON THE FLOOR OF HER ROOM. HE'D COME IN... I'D BE THERE.
I WASN'T STRONG ENOUGH TO WIN THE FIGHT... BUT I KNEW HOW TO TAKE A BEATING.
I WAS AN OLD PRO AT THAT...
SKRITCH
SKRITCH

EVENTUALLY... HE GAVE UP AND STOPPED COMING AROUND. THEN HE FINALLY MOVED ON TO ANOTHER HOME.

NEVER KNEW WHERE THAT WAS... NEVER *CARED.*

Y'KNOW... I STILL CAN'T FIGURE IT OUT.

WHAT?

MAN LIKE YOU, EVERYTHING MEGAN TOLD ME ABOUT YOU... THEN YOU GO AND BEAT *YOUR DAUGHTER* UP?

SHE WAS IN THE HOSPITAL FOR A WEEK. SHE ALMOST *DIED.*

MEGAN AND I... WE *SAW* ALLISON... WHAT YOU DID TO HER.

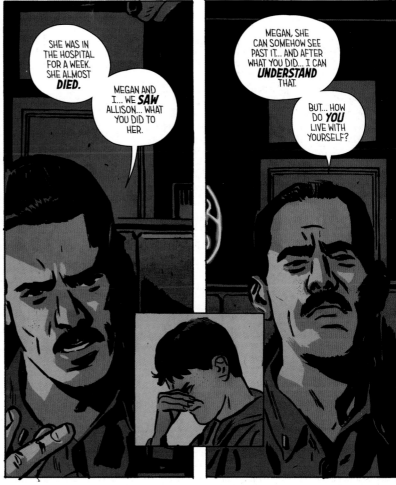

MEGAN, SHE CAN SOMEHOW SEE PAST IT... AND AFTER WHAT YOU DID... I CAN *UNDERSTAND* THAT.

BUT... HOW DO *YOU* LIVE WITH YOURSELF?

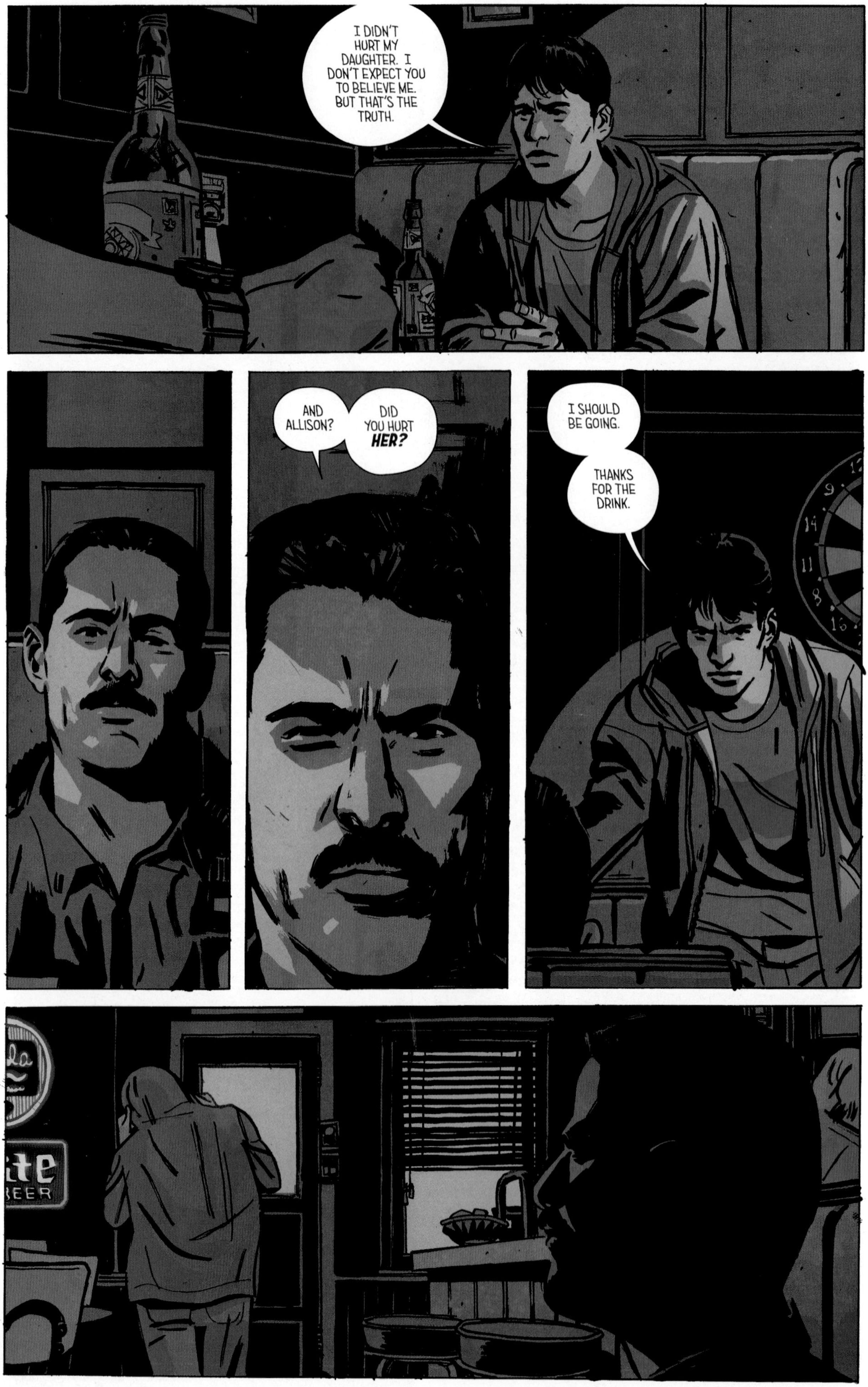
I DIDN'T HURT MY DAUGHTER. I DON'T EXPECT YOU TO BELIEVE ME. BUT THAT'S THE TRUTH.
AND ALLISON?
DID YOU HURT **HER?**
I SHOULD BE GOING.
THANKS FOR THE DRINK.

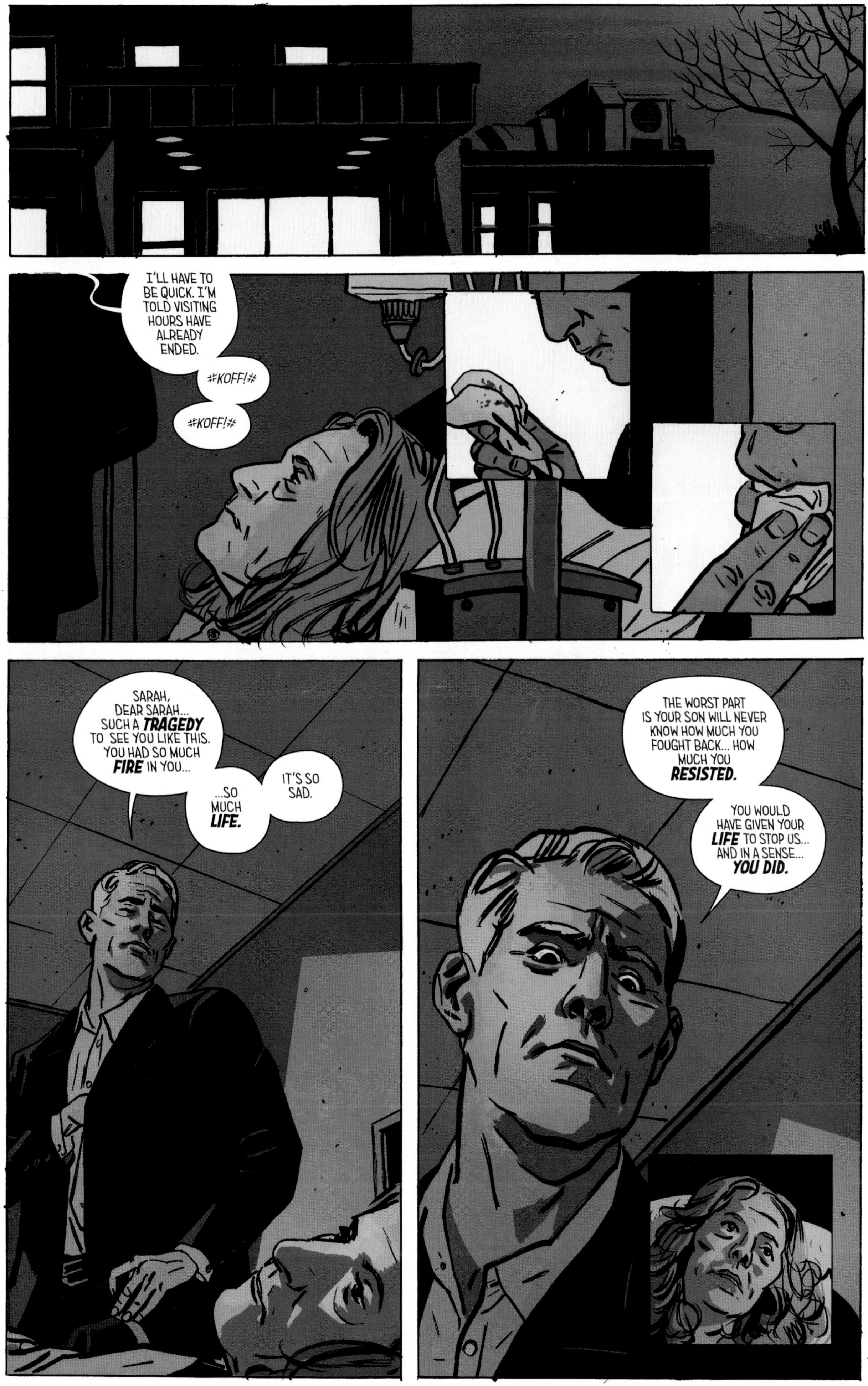
I'LL HAVE TO BE QUICK. I'M TOLD VISITING HOURS HAVE ALREADY ENDED.
#KOFF!#
#KOFF!#
SARAH, DEAR SARAH... SUCH A TRAGEDY TO SEE YOU LIKE THIS. YOU HAD SO MUCH FIRE IN YOU...
...SO MUCH LIFE.
IT'S SO SAD.
THE WORST PART IS YOUR SON WILL NEVER KNOW HOW MUCH YOU FOUGHT BACK... HOW MUCH YOU RESISTED.
YOU WOULD HAVE GIVEN YOUR LIFE TO STOP US... AND IN A SENSE... YOU DID.

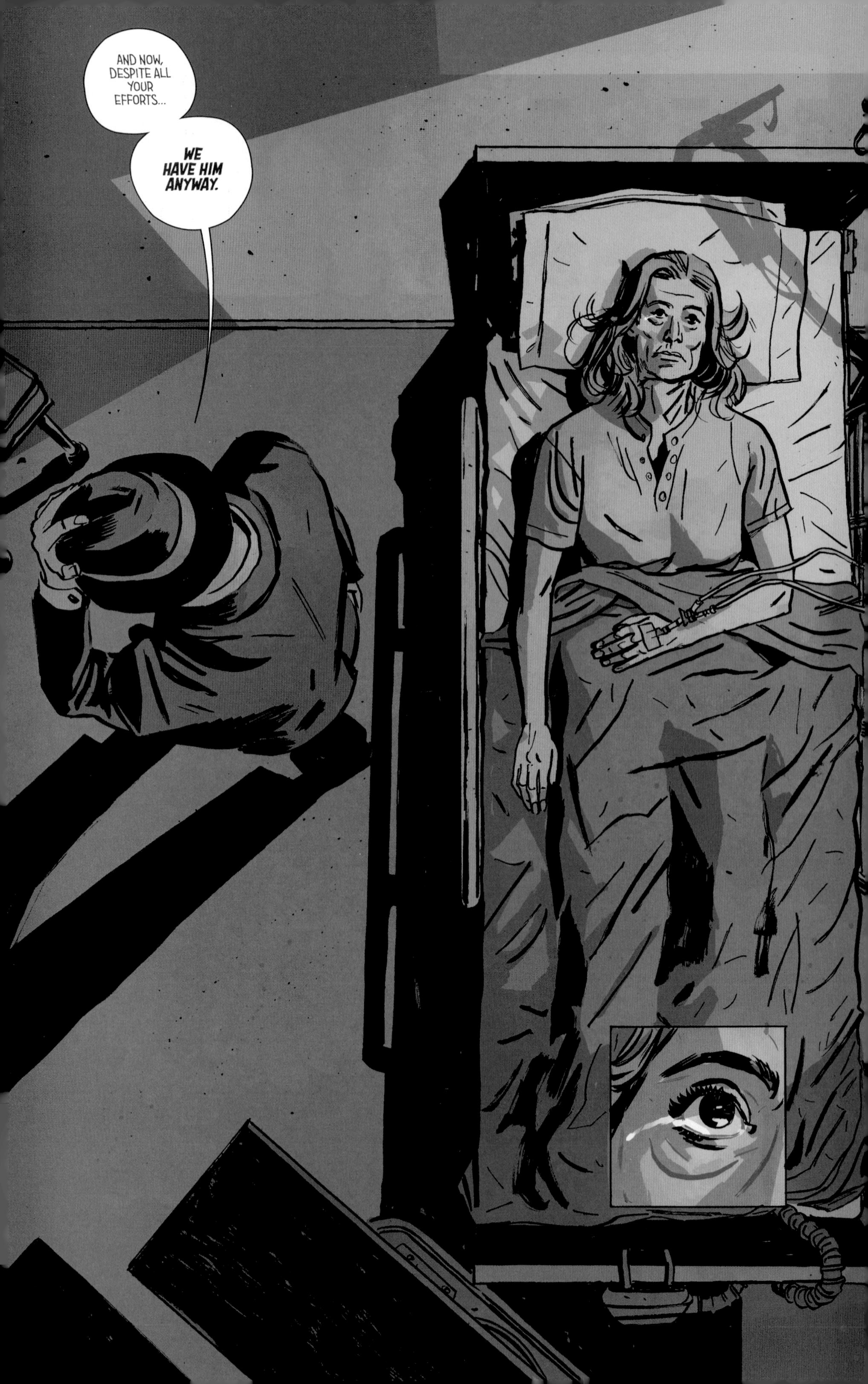
AND NOW, DESPITE ALL YOUR EFFORTS...
WE HAVE HIM ANYWAY.

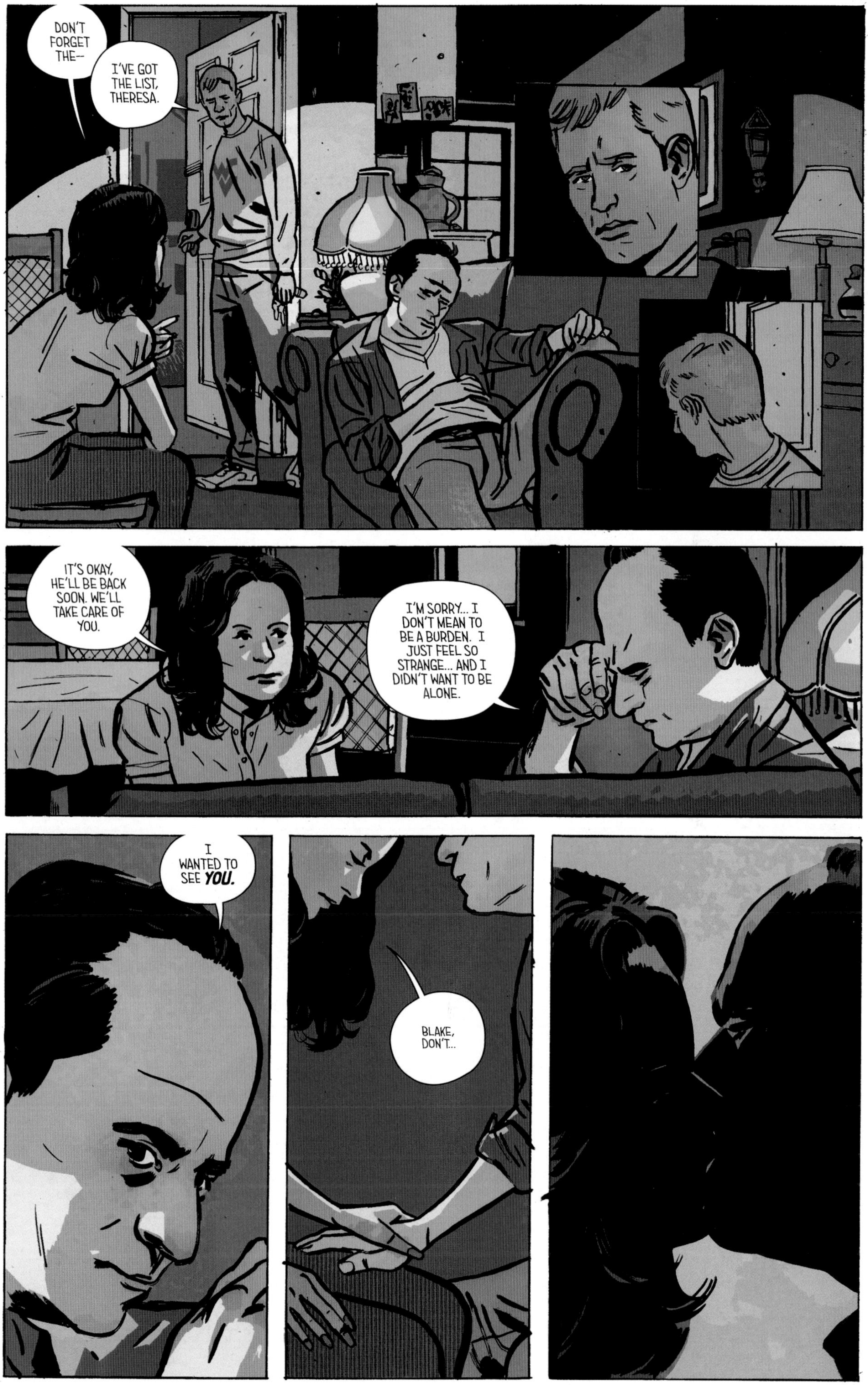
DON'T FORGET THE--
I'VE GOT THE LIST, THERESA.
IT'S OKAY, HE'LL BE BACK SOON. WE'LL TAKE CARE OF YOU.
I'M SORRY... I DON'T MEAN TO BE A BURDEN. I JUST FEEL SO STRANGE... AND I DIDN'T WANT TO BE ALONE.
I WANTED TO SEE YOU.
BLAKE, DON'T...

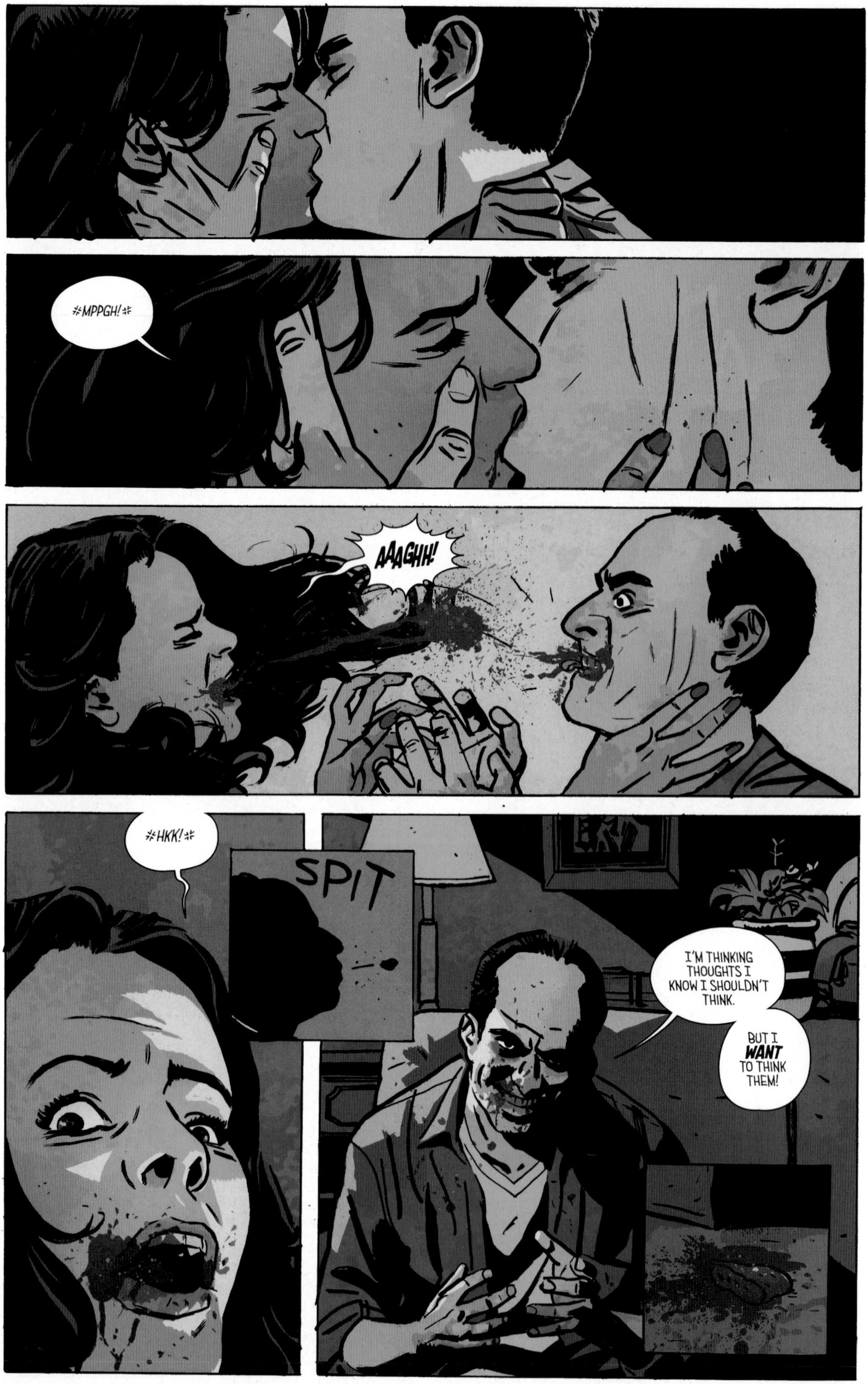

#MPPGH!#
AAAGHH!
#HKK!#
SPIT
I'M THINKING THOUGHTS I KNOW I SHOULDN'T THINK.
BUT I **WANT** TO THINK THEM!

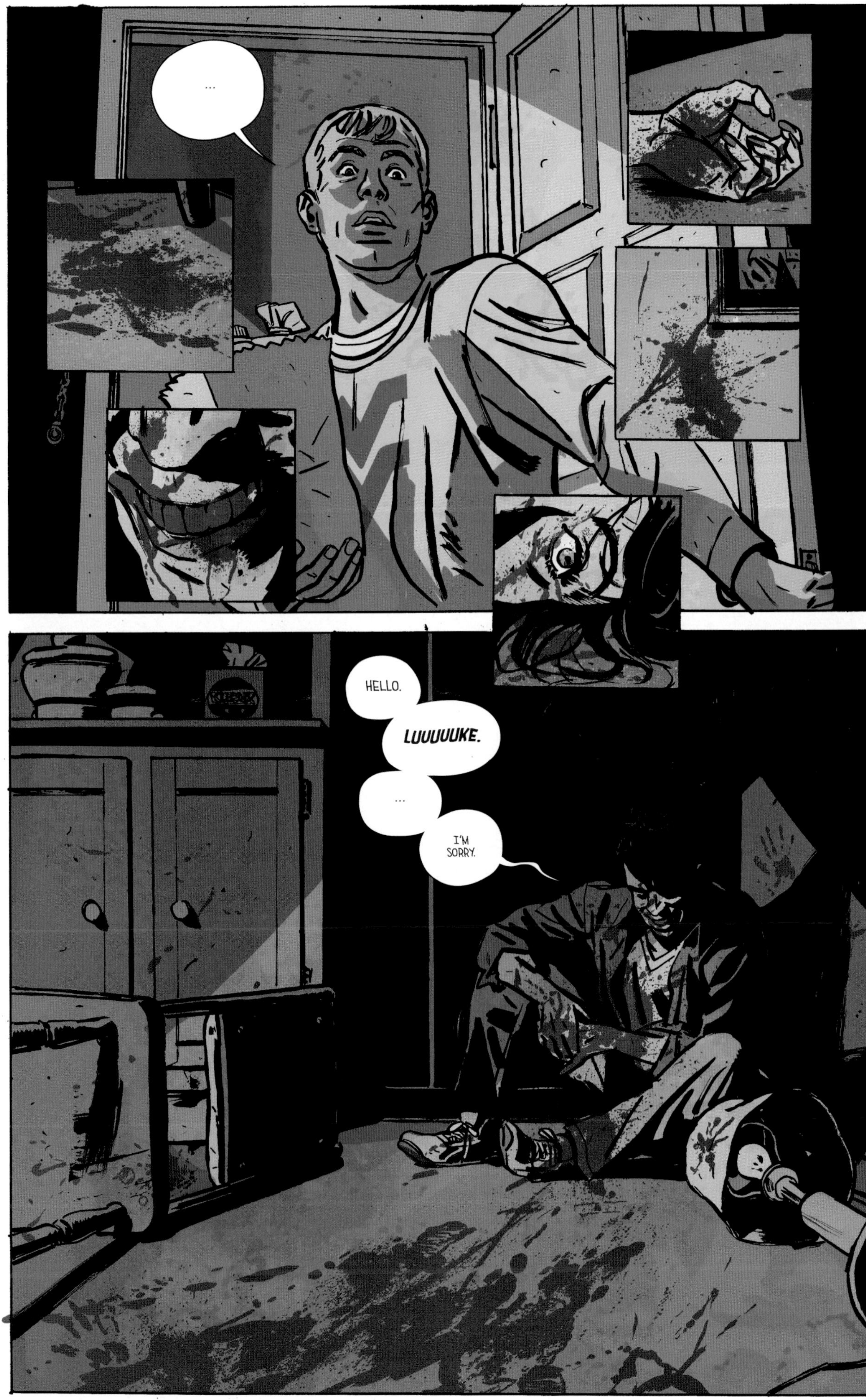
...
HELLO.
LUUUUUKE.
...
I'M SORRY.

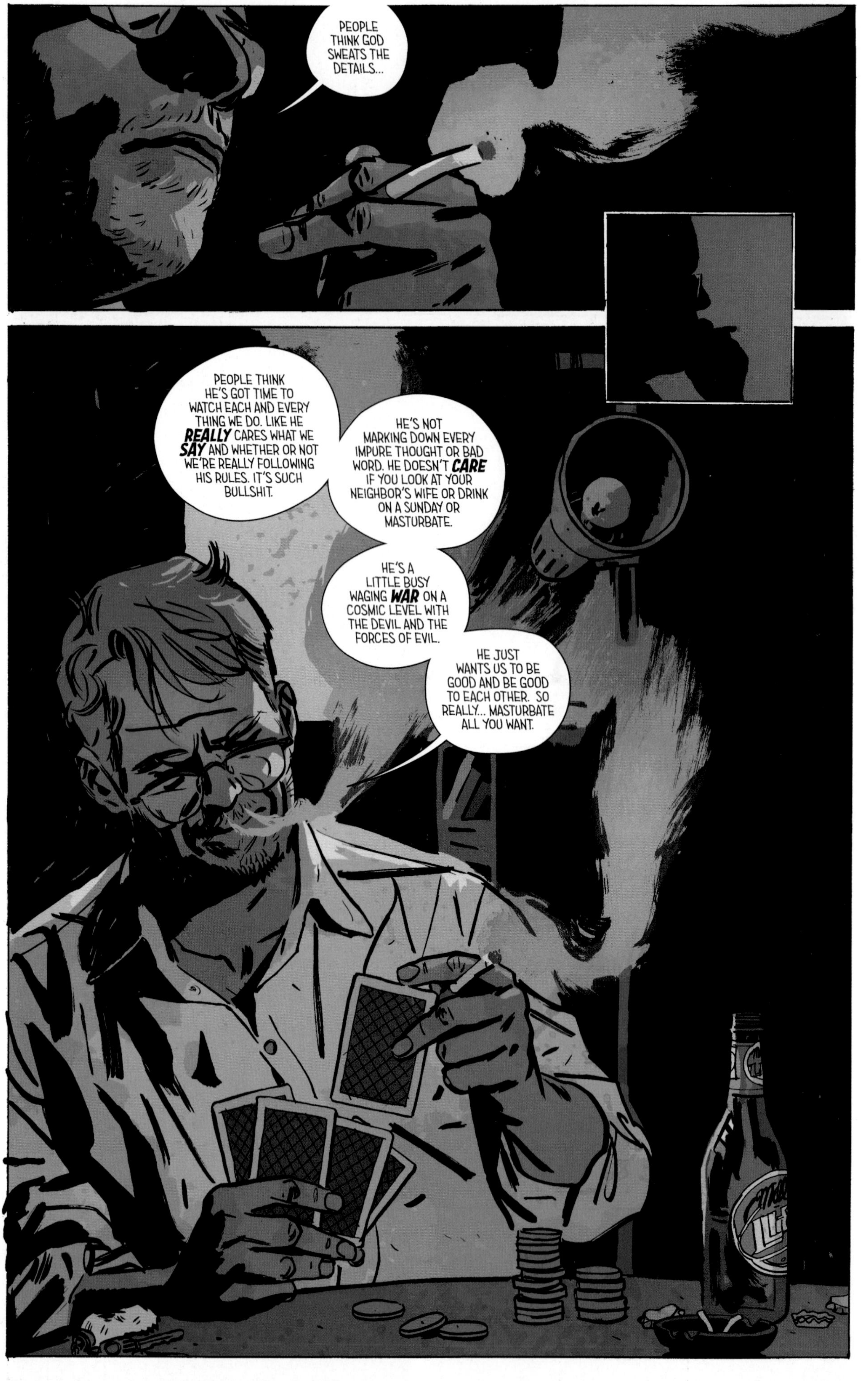
PEOPLE THINK GOD SWEATS THE DETAILS...
PEOPLE THINK HE'S GOT TIME TO WATCH EACH AND EVERY THING WE DO. LIKE HE REALLY CARES WHAT WE SAY AND WHETHER OR NOT WE'RE REALLY FOLLOWING HIS RULES. IT'S SUCH BULLSHIT.
HE'S NOT MARKING DOWN EVERY IMPURE THOUGHT OR BAD WORD. HE DOESN'T CARE IF YOU LOOK AT YOUR NEIGHBOR'S WIFE OR DRINK ON A SUNDAY OR MASTURBATE.
HE'S A LITTLE BUSY WAGING WAR ON A COSMIC LEVEL WITH THE DEVIL AND THE FORCES OF EVIL.
HE JUST WANTS US TO BE GOOD AND BE GOOD TO EACH OTHER. SO REALLY... MASTURBATE ALL YOU WANT.

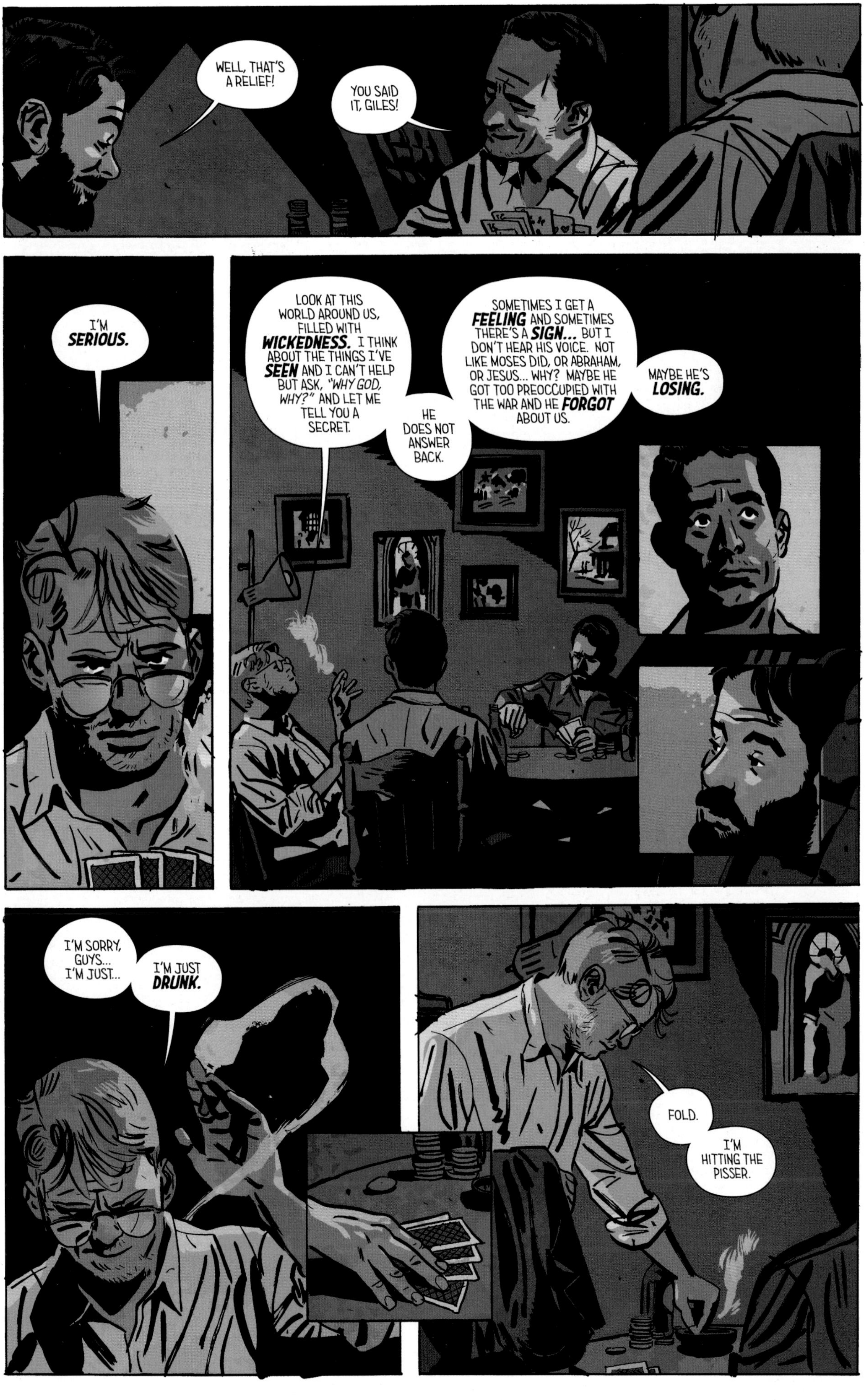

WELL, THAT'S A RELIEF!
YOU SAID IT, GILES!
I'M **SERIOUS.**
LOOK AT THIS WORLD AROUND US, FILLED WITH **WICKEDNESS.** I THINK ABOUT THE THINGS I'VE **SEEN** AND I CAN'T HELP BUT ASK, *"WHY GOD, WHY?"* AND LET ME TELL YOU A SECRET.
HE DOES NOT ANSWER BACK.
SOMETIMES I GET A **FEELING** AND SOMETIMES THERE'S A **SIGN...** BUT I DON'T HEAR HIS VOICE. NOT LIKE MOSES DID, OR ABRAHAM, OR JESUS... WHY? MAYBE HE GOT TOO PREOCCUPIED WITH THE WAR AND HE **FORGOT** ABOUT US.
MAYBE HE'S **LOSING.**
I'M SORRY, GUYS... I'M JUST...
I'M JUST **DRUNK.**
FOLD.
I'M HITTING THE PISSER.

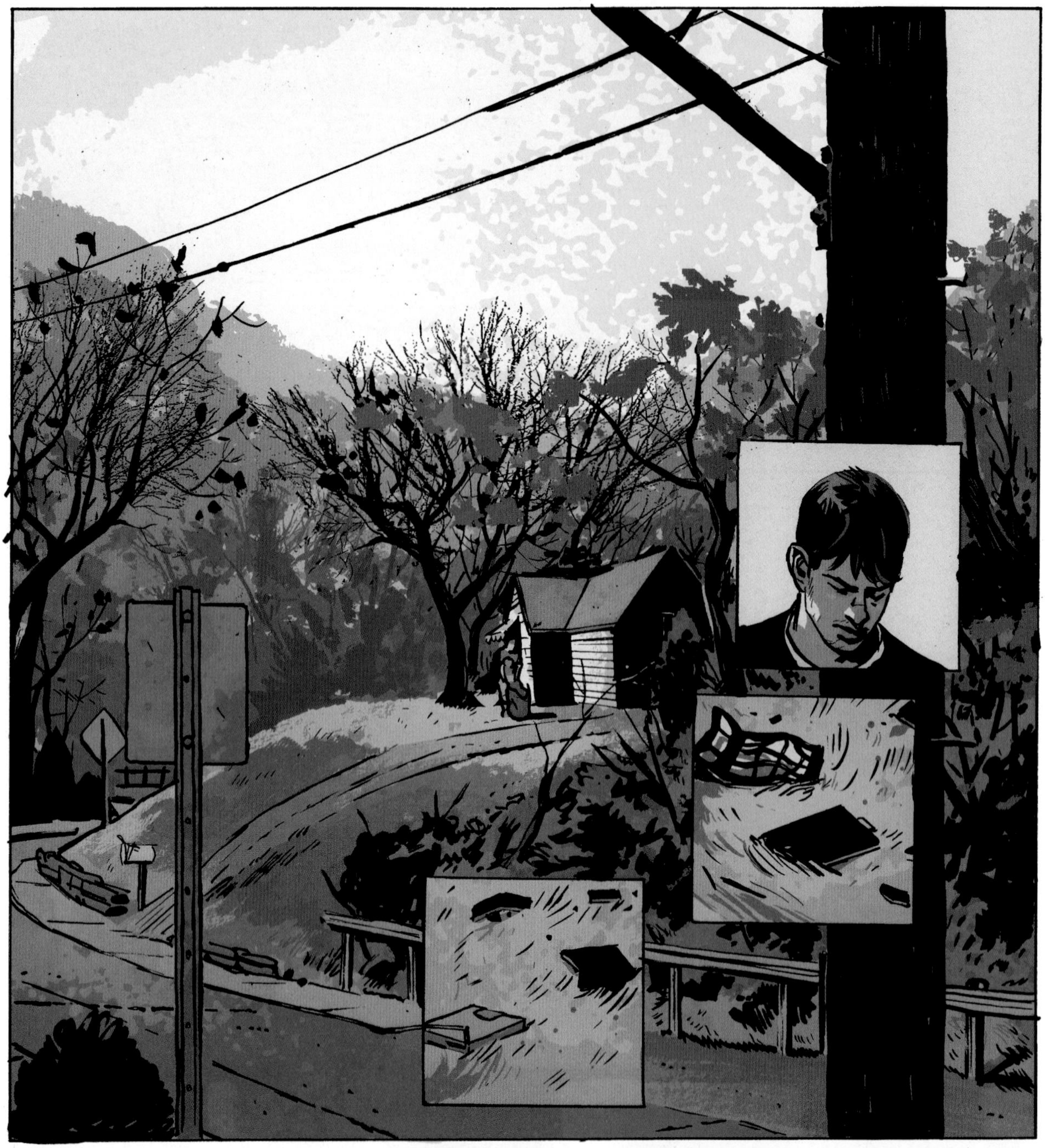

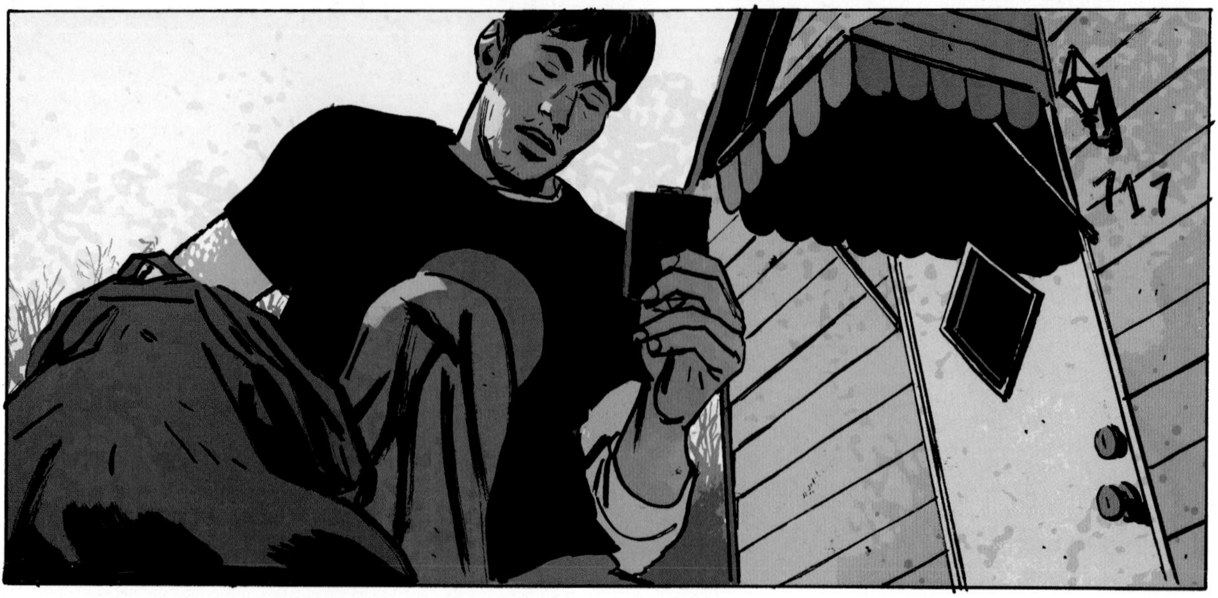
717

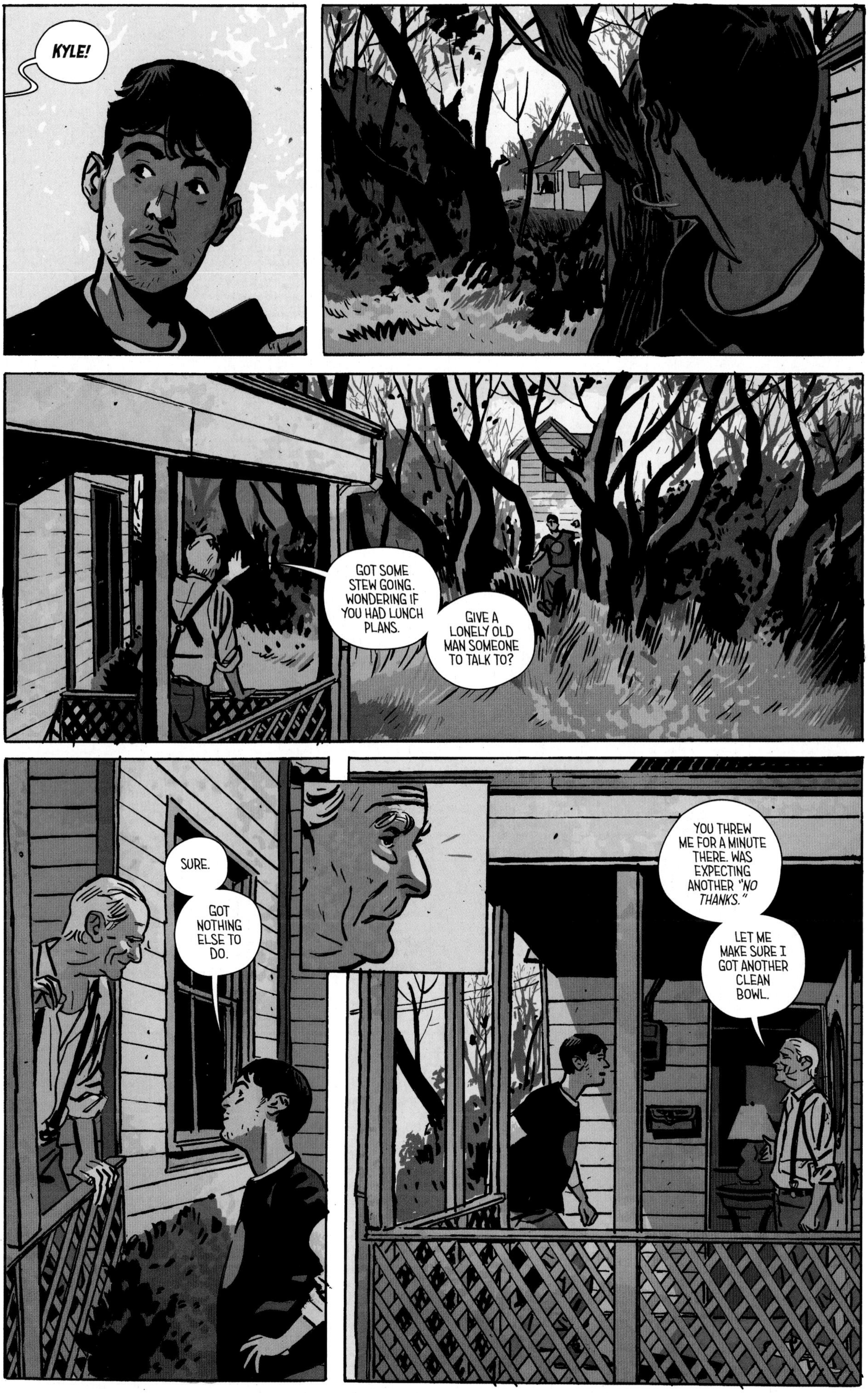
KYLE!
GOT SOME STEW GOING. WONDERING IF YOU HAD LUNCH PLANS.
GIVE A LONELY OLD MAN SOMEONE TO TALK TO?
SURE.
GOT NOTHING ELSE TO DO.
YOU THREW ME FOR A MINUTE THERE. WAS EXPECTING ANOTHER *"NO THANKS."*
LET ME MAKE SURE I GOT ANOTHER CLEAN BOWL.

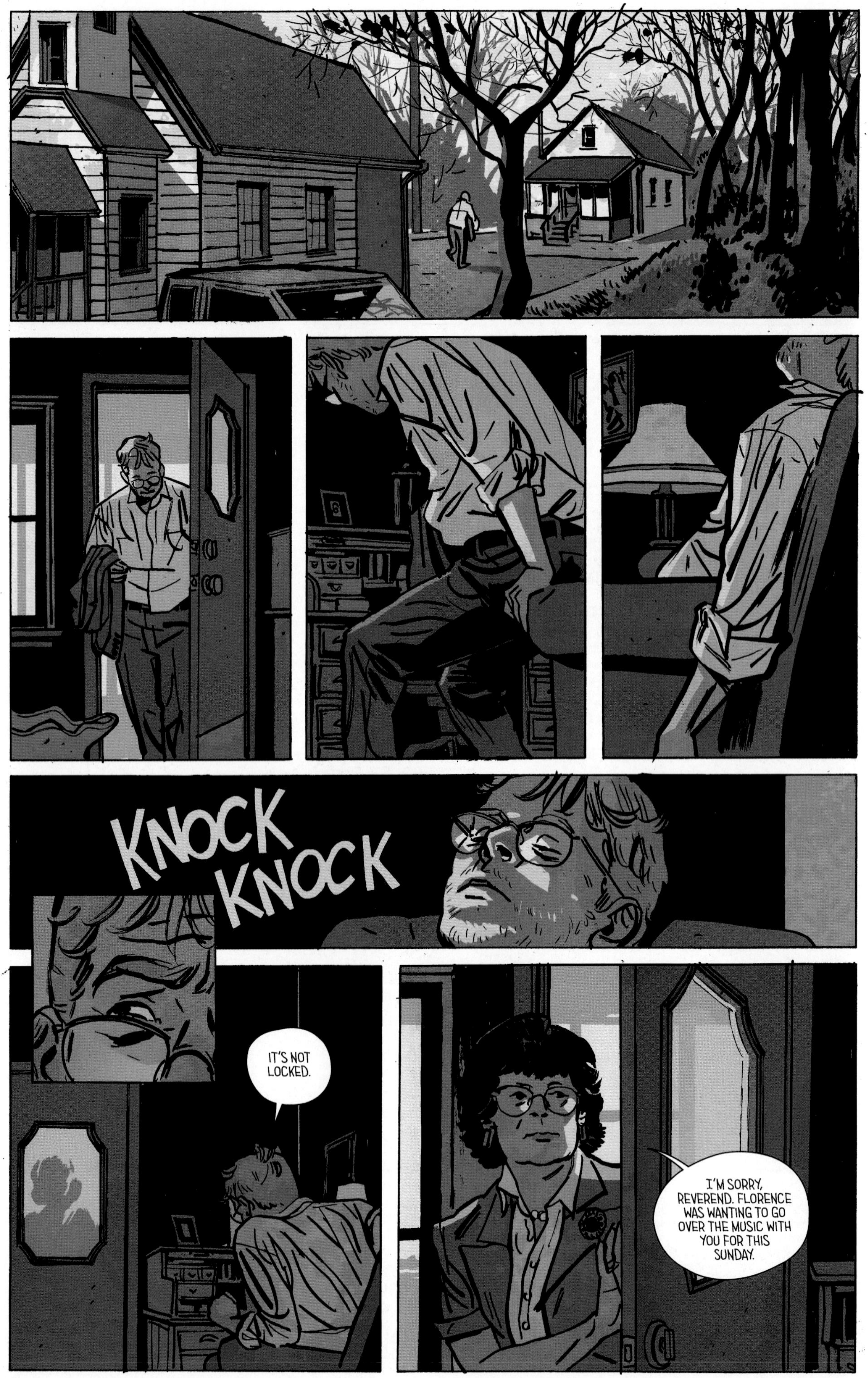
KNOCK KNOCK
IT'S NOT LOCKED.
I'M SORRY, REVEREND. FLORENCE WAS WANTING TO GO OVER THE MUSIC WITH YOU FOR THIS SUNDAY.

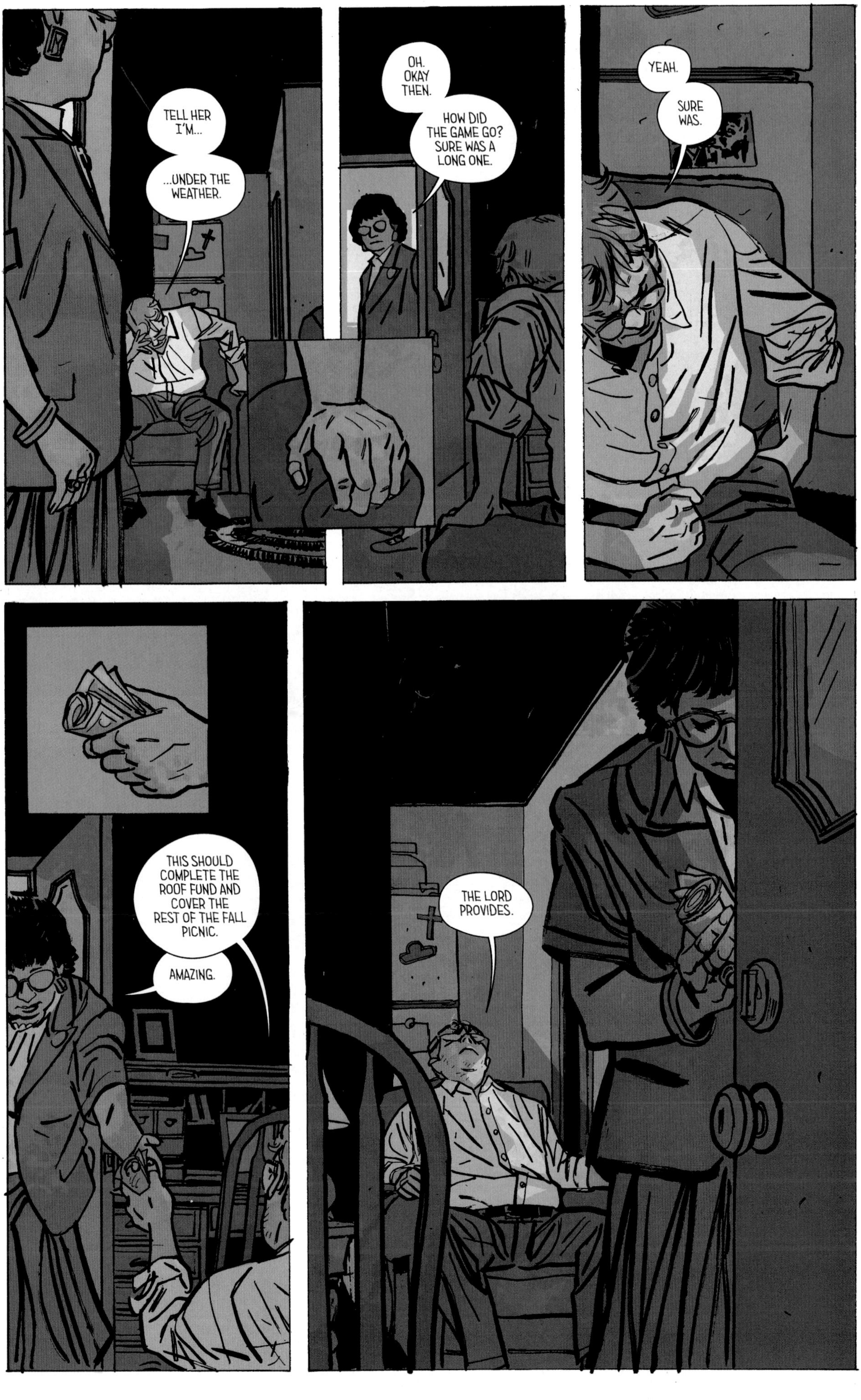
TELL HER I'M...
...UNDER THE WEATHER.
OH. OKAY THEN.
HOW DID THE GAME GO? SURE WAS A LONG ONE.
YEAH.
SURE WAS.
THIS SHOULD COMPLETE THE ROOF FUND AND COVER THE REST OF THE FALL PICNIC.
AMAZING.
THE LORD PROVIDES.

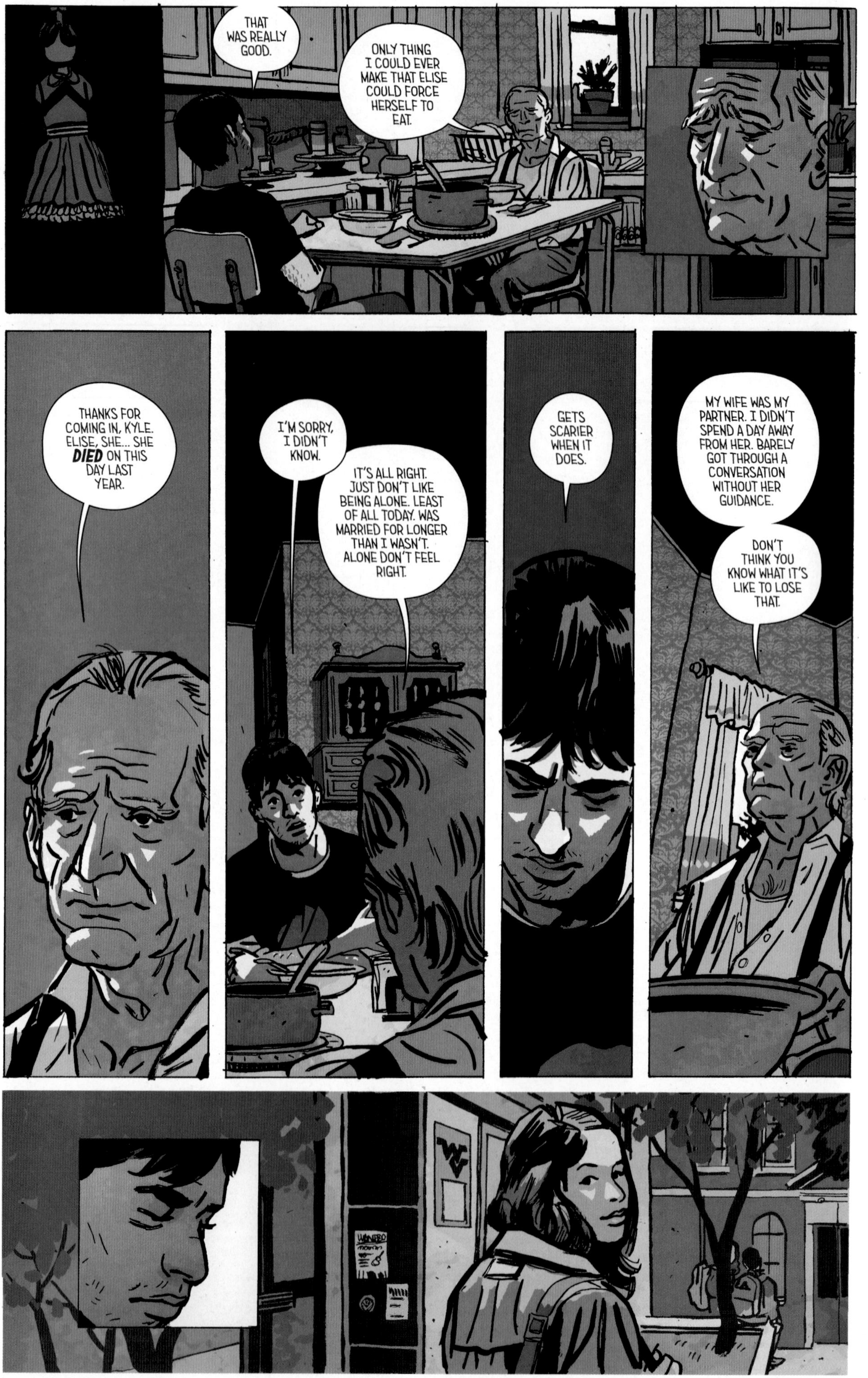

THAT WAS REALLY GOOD.
ONLY THING I COULD EVER MAKE THAT ELISE COULD FORCE HERSELF TO EAT.
THANKS FOR COMING IN, KYLE. ELISE, SHE... SHE **DIED** ON THIS DAY LAST YEAR.
I'M SORRY, I DIDN'T KNOW.
IT'S ALL RIGHT. JUST DON'T LIKE BEING ALONE. LEAST OF ALL TODAY. WAS MARRIED FOR LONGER THAN I WASN'T. ALONE DON'T FEEL RIGHT.
GETS SCARIER WHEN IT DOES.
MY WIFE WAS MY PARTNER. I DIDN'T SPEND A DAY AWAY FROM HER. BARELY GOT THROUGH A CONVERSATION WITHOUT HER GUIDANCE.
DON'T THINK YOU KNOW WHAT IT'S LIKE TO LOSE THAT.

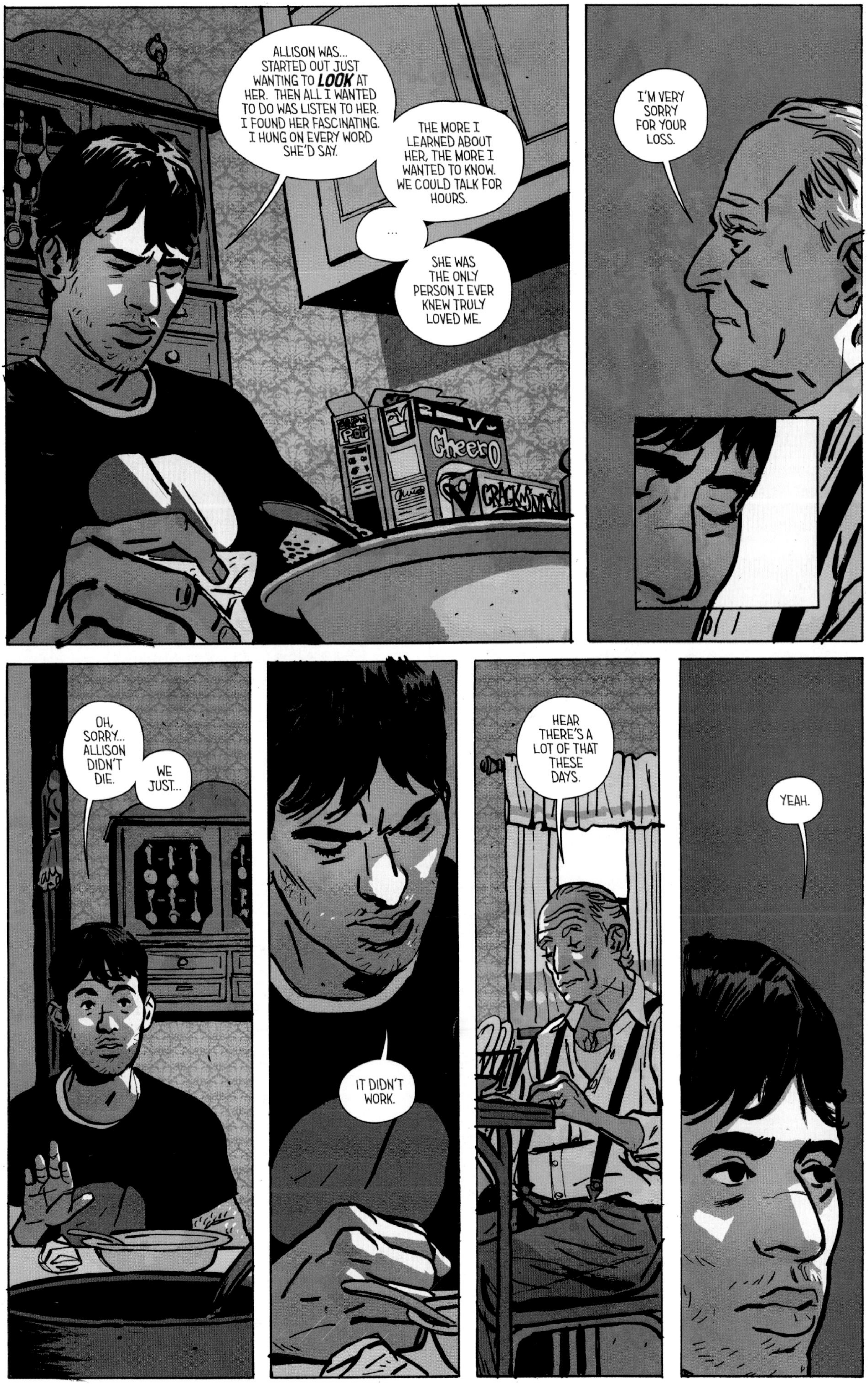
ALLISON WAS... STARTED OUT JUST WANTING TO **LOOK** AT HER. THEN ALL I WANTED TO DO WAS LISTEN TO HER. I FOUND HER FASCINATING. I HUNG ON EVERY WORD SHE'D SAY.
THE MORE I LEARNED ABOUT HER, THE MORE I WANTED TO KNOW. WE COULD TALK FOR HOURS.
...
SHE WAS THE ONLY PERSON I EVER KNEW TRULY LOVED ME.
I'M VERY SORRY FOR YOUR LOSS.
OH, SORRY... ALLISON DIDN'T DIE.
WE JUST...
IT DIDN'T WORK.
HEAR THERE'S A LOT OF THAT THESE DAYS.
YEAH.

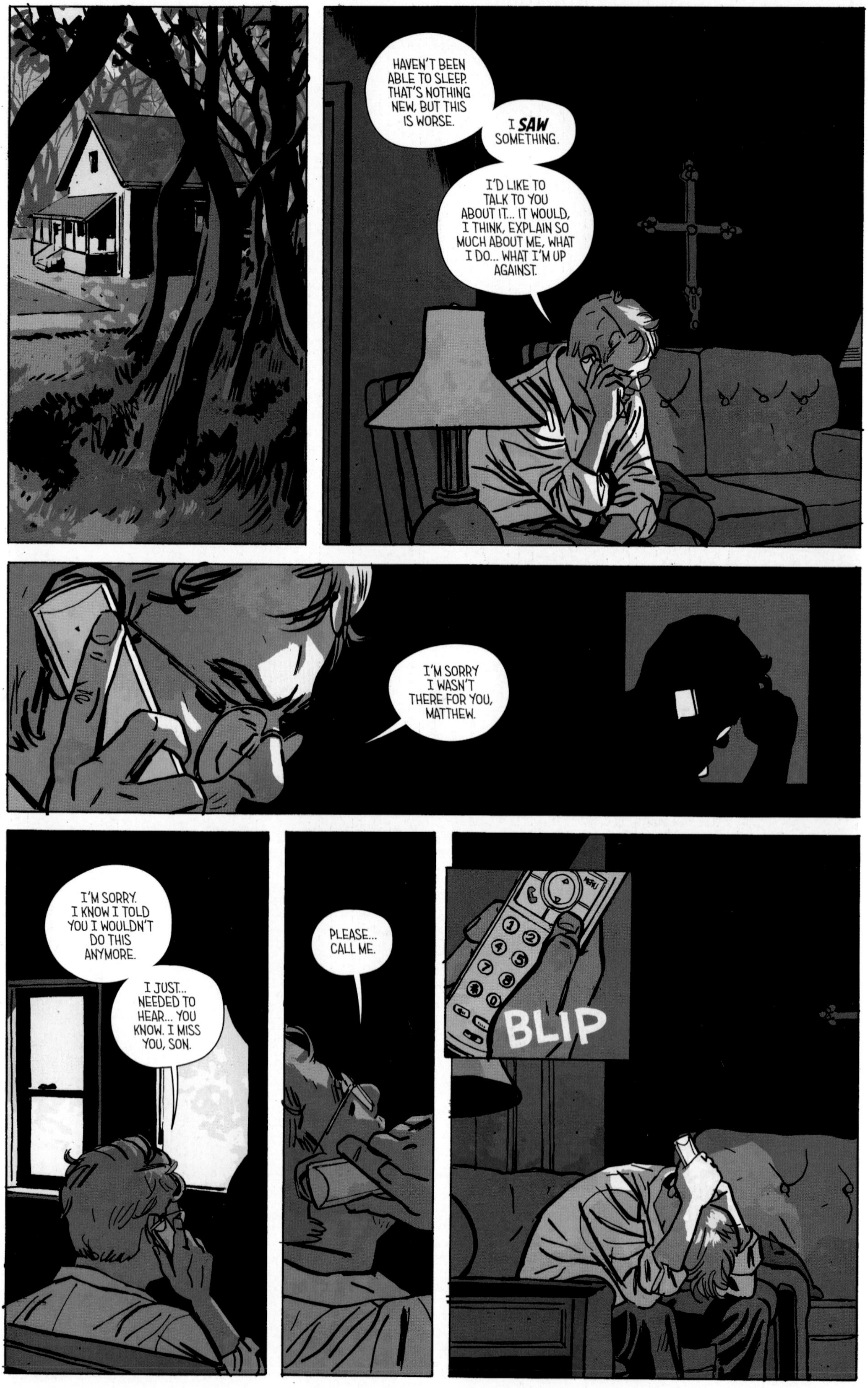

HAVEN'T BEEN ABLE TO SLEEP. THAT'S NOTHING NEW, BUT THIS IS WORSE.
I SAW SOMETHING.
I'D LIKE TO TALK TO YOU ABOUT IT... IT WOULD, I THINK, EXPLAIN SO MUCH ABOUT ME, WHAT I DO... WHAT I'M UP AGAINST.
I'M SORRY I WASN'T THERE FOR YOU, MATTHEW.
I'M SORRY. I KNOW I TOLD YOU I WOULDN'T DO THIS ANYMORE.
I JUST... NEEDED TO HEAR... YOU KNOW. I MISS YOU, SON.
PLEASE... CALL ME.
MENU
BLIP

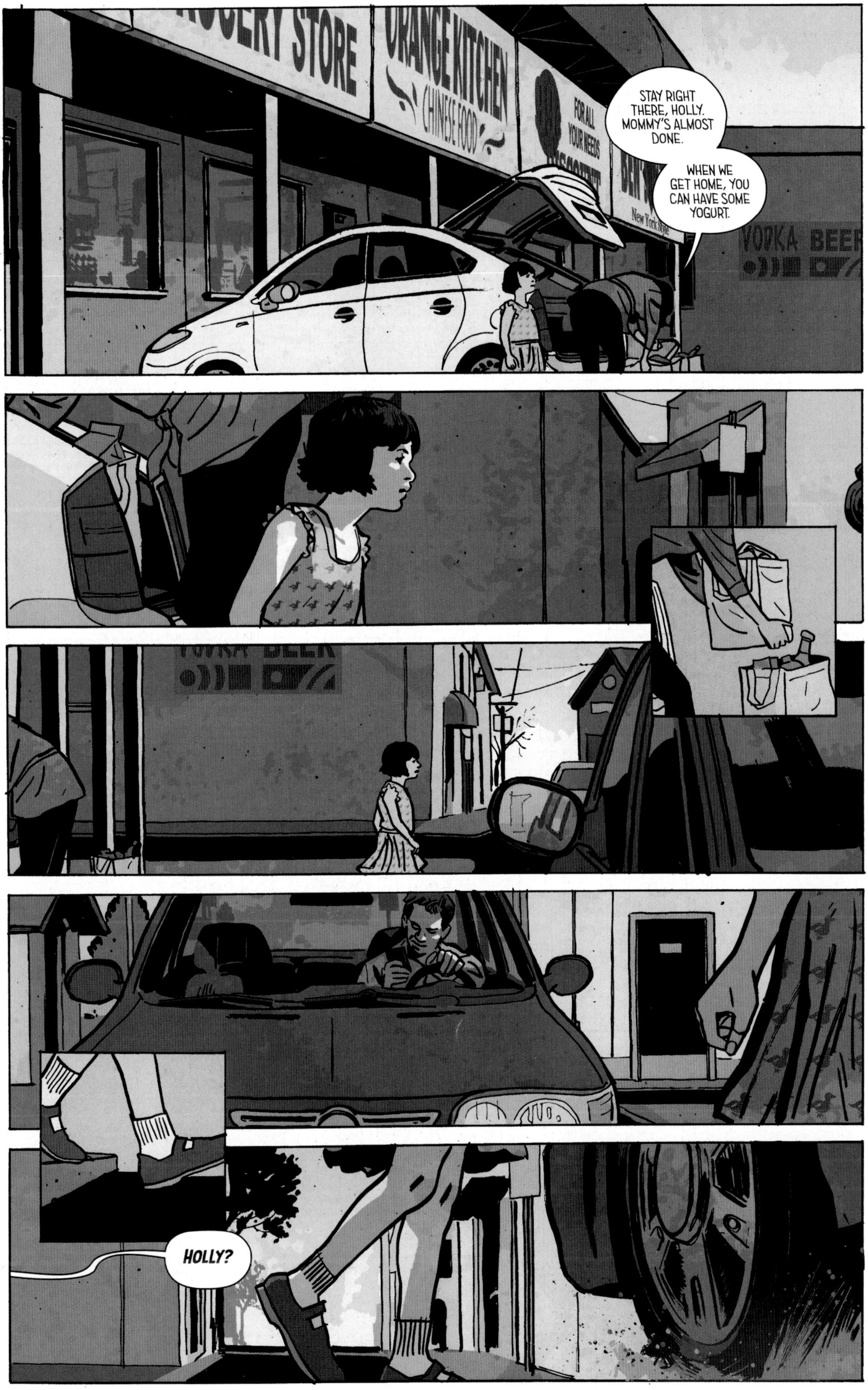
GROCERY STORE
ORANGE KITCHEN
CHINESE FOOD
FOR ALL YOUR NEEDS
New York Style
STAY RIGHT THERE, HOLLY. MOMMY'S ALMOST DONE.
WHEN WE GET HOME, YOU CAN HAVE SOME YOGURT.
VODKA BEER
VODKA BEER
HOLLY?

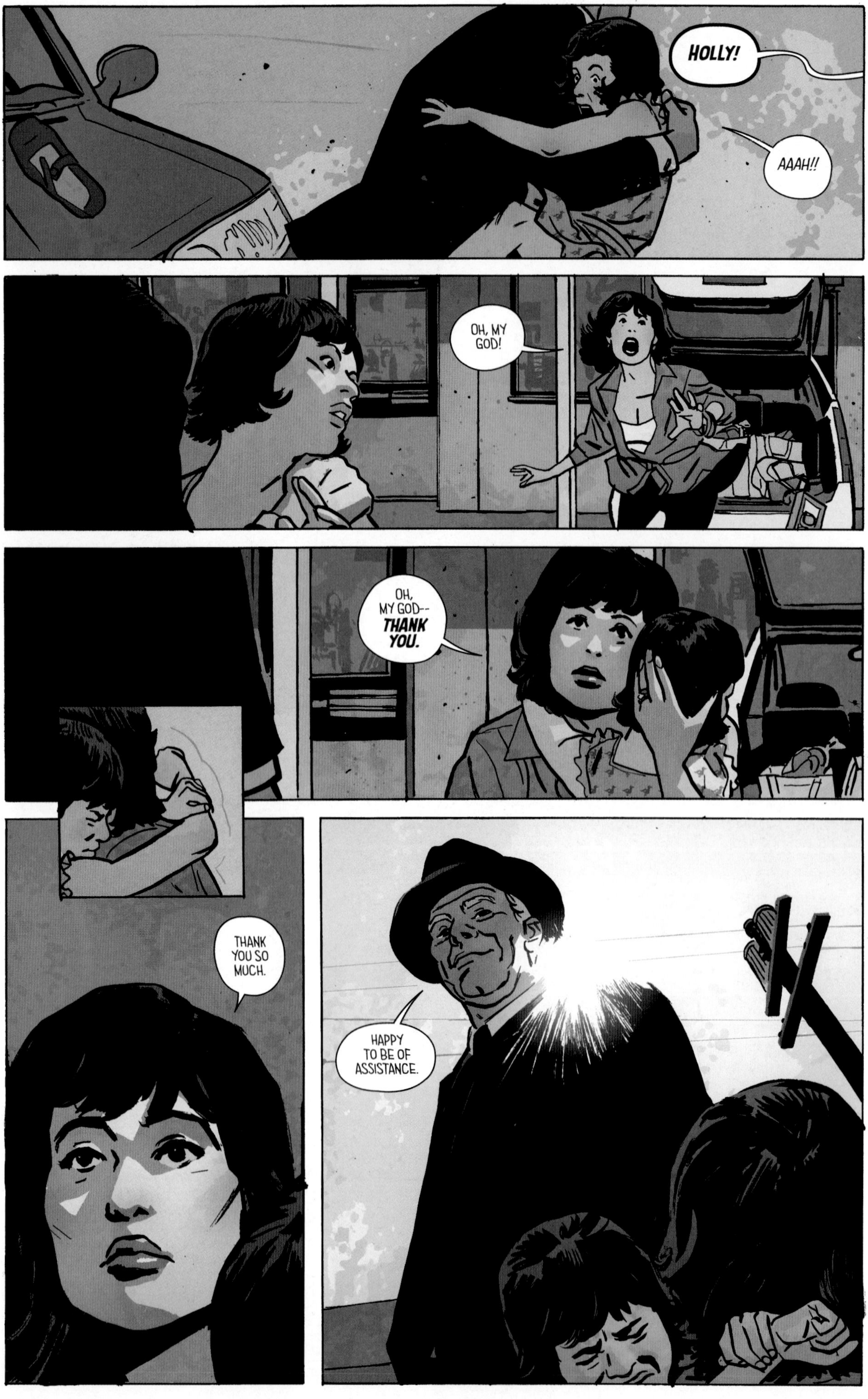
HOLLY!
AAAH!!
OH, MY GOD!
OH, MY GOD-- THANK YOU.
THANK YOU SO MUCH.
HAPPY TO BE OF ASSISTANCE.

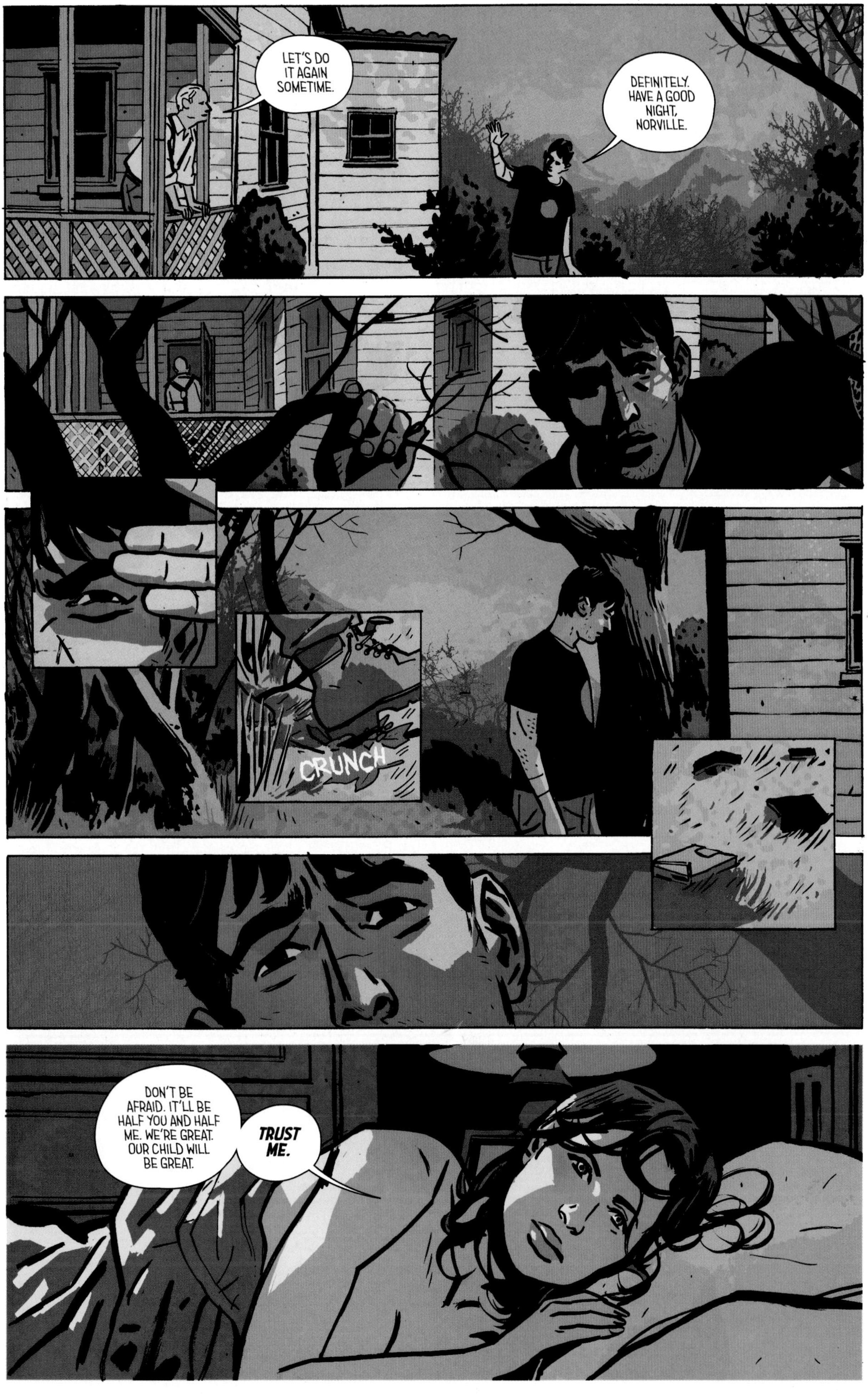
LET'S DO IT AGAIN SOMETIME.
DEFINITELY. HAVE A GOOD NIGHT, NORVILLE.
CRUNCH
DON'T BE AFRAID. IT'LL BE HALF YOU AND HALF ME. WE'RE GREAT. OUR CHILD WILL BE GREAT.
TRUST ME.

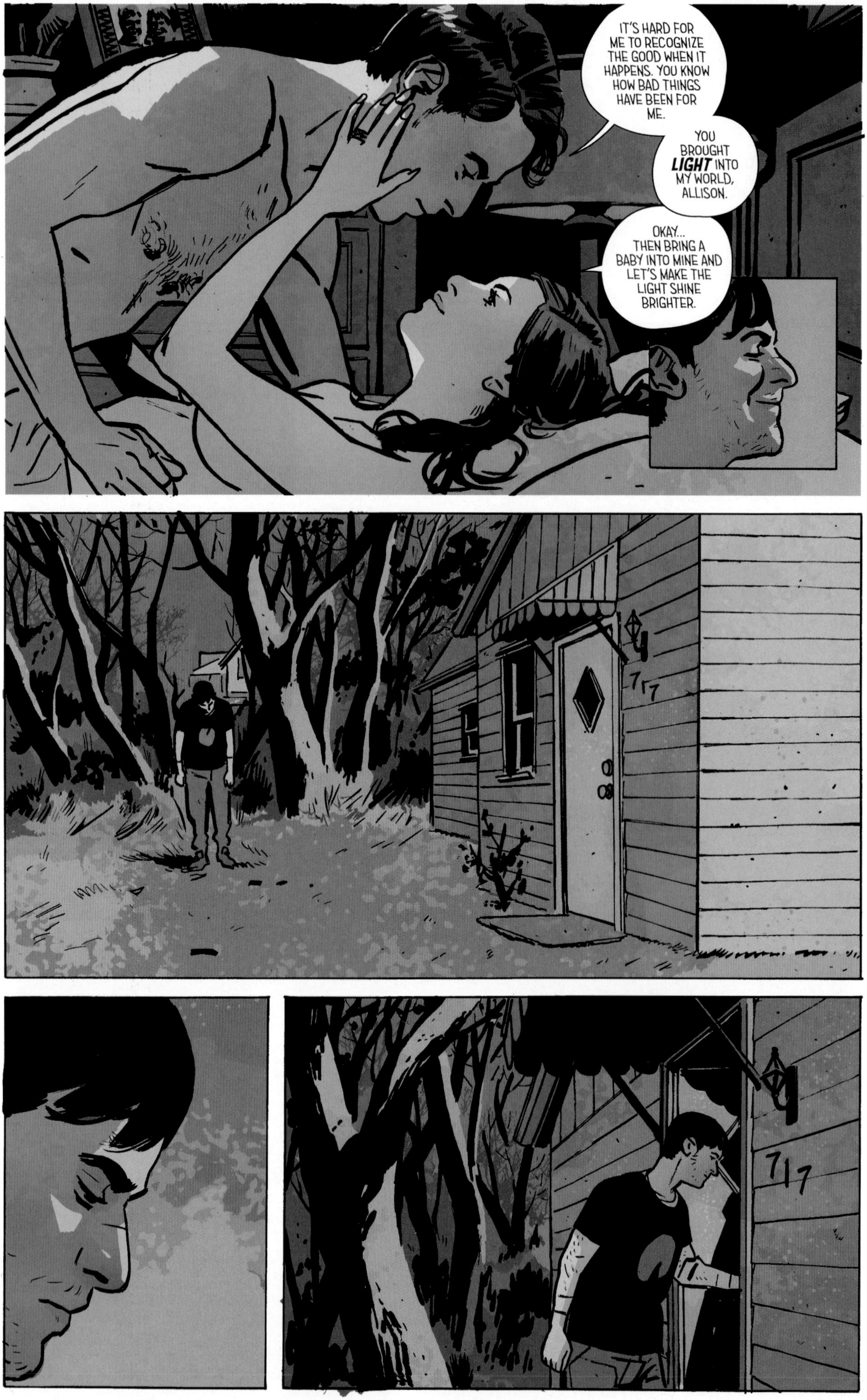
IT'S HARD FOR ME TO RECOGNIZE THE GOOD WHEN IT HAPPENS. YOU KNOW HOW BAD THINGS HAVE BEEN FOR ME.
YOU BROUGHT **LIGHT** INTO MY WORLD, ALLISON.
OKAY... THEN BRING A BABY INTO MINE AND LET'S MAKE THE LIGHT SHINE BRIGHTER.
717
717

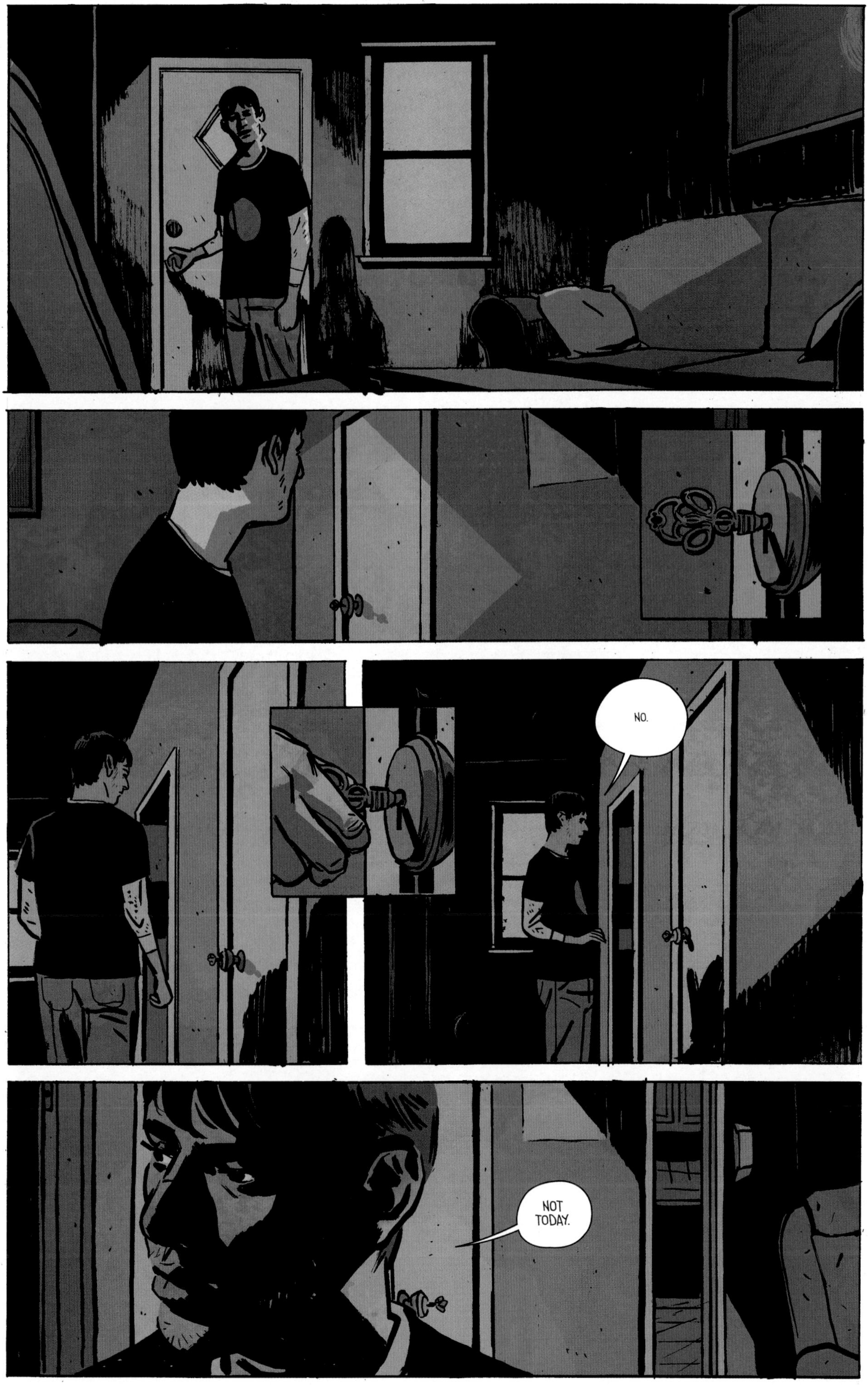
NO.
NOT TODAY.

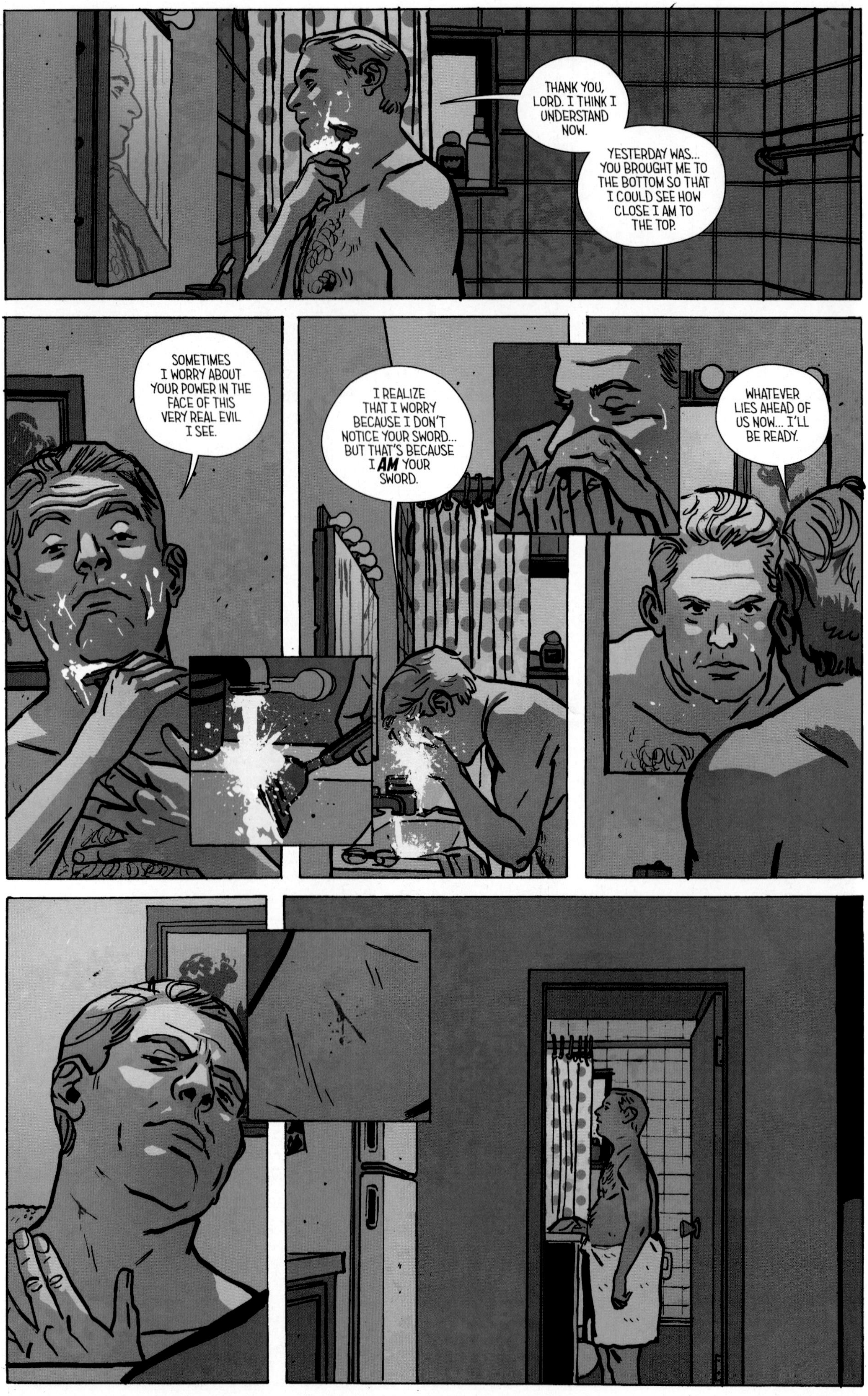
THANK YOU, LORD. I THINK I UNDERSTAND NOW.
YESTERDAY WAS... YOU BROUGHT ME TO THE BOTTOM SO THAT I COULD SEE HOW CLOSE I AM TO THE TOP.
SOMETIMES I WORRY ABOUT YOUR POWER IN THE FACE OF THIS VERY REAL EVIL I SEE.
I REALIZE THAT I WORRY BECAUSE I DON'T NOTICE YOUR SWORD... BUT THAT'S BECAUSE I **AM** YOUR SWORD.
WHATEVER LIES AHEAD OF US NOW... I'LL BE READY.

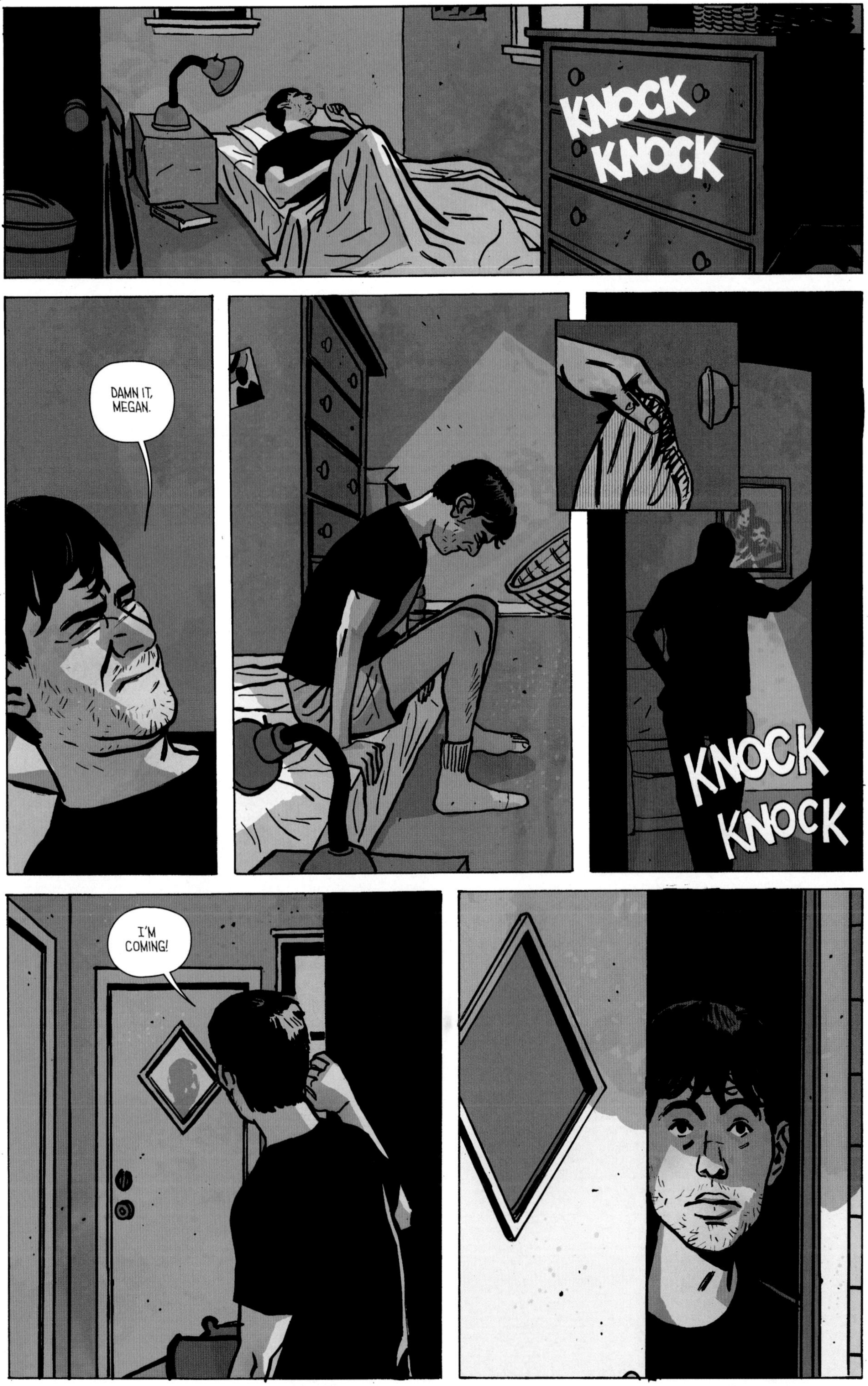
KNOCK
KNOCK
DAMN IT, MEGAN.
KNOCK
KNOCK
I'M COMING!

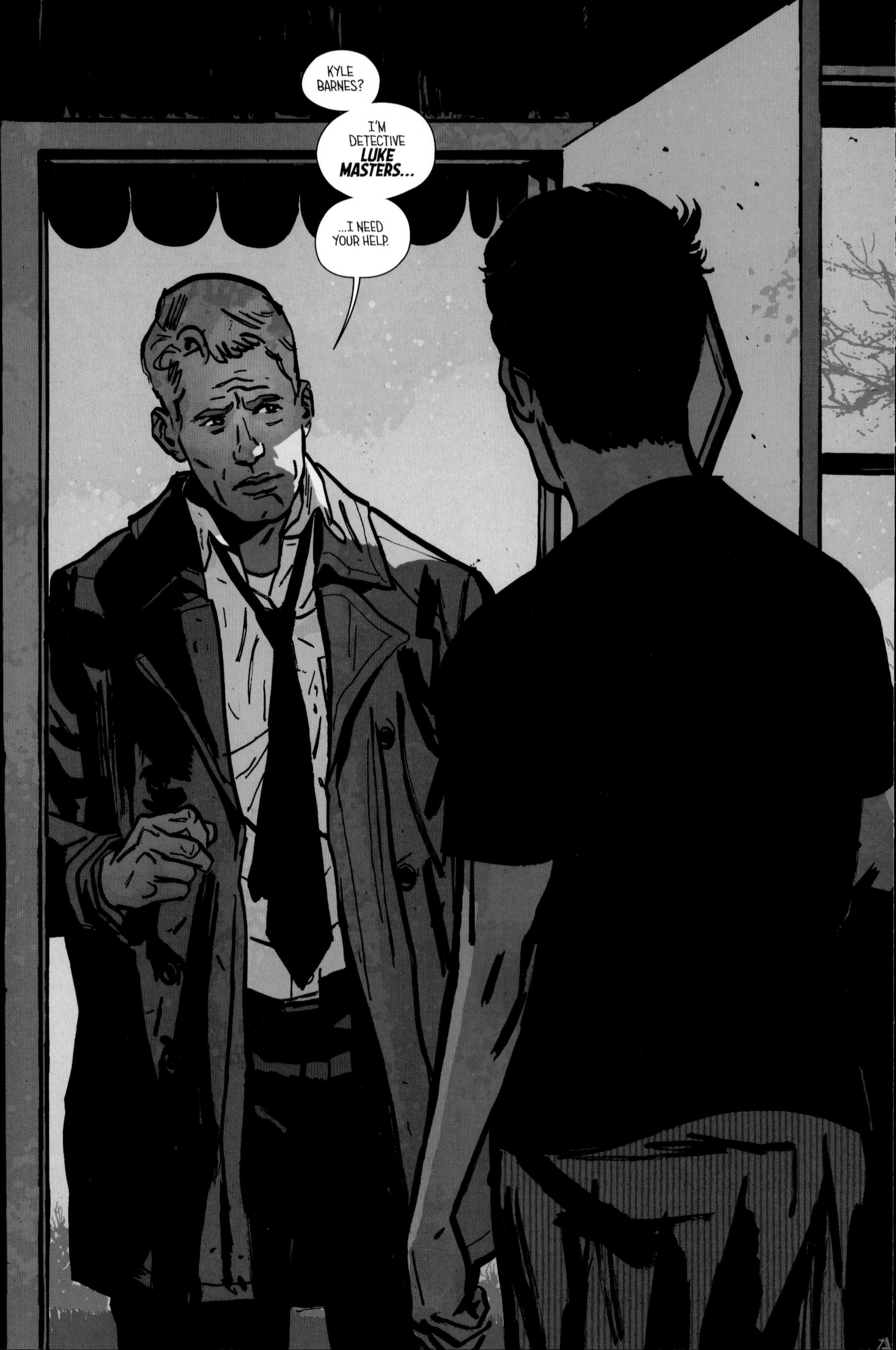
KYLE BARNES?
I'M DETECTIVE LUKE MASTERS...
...I NEED YOUR HELP.

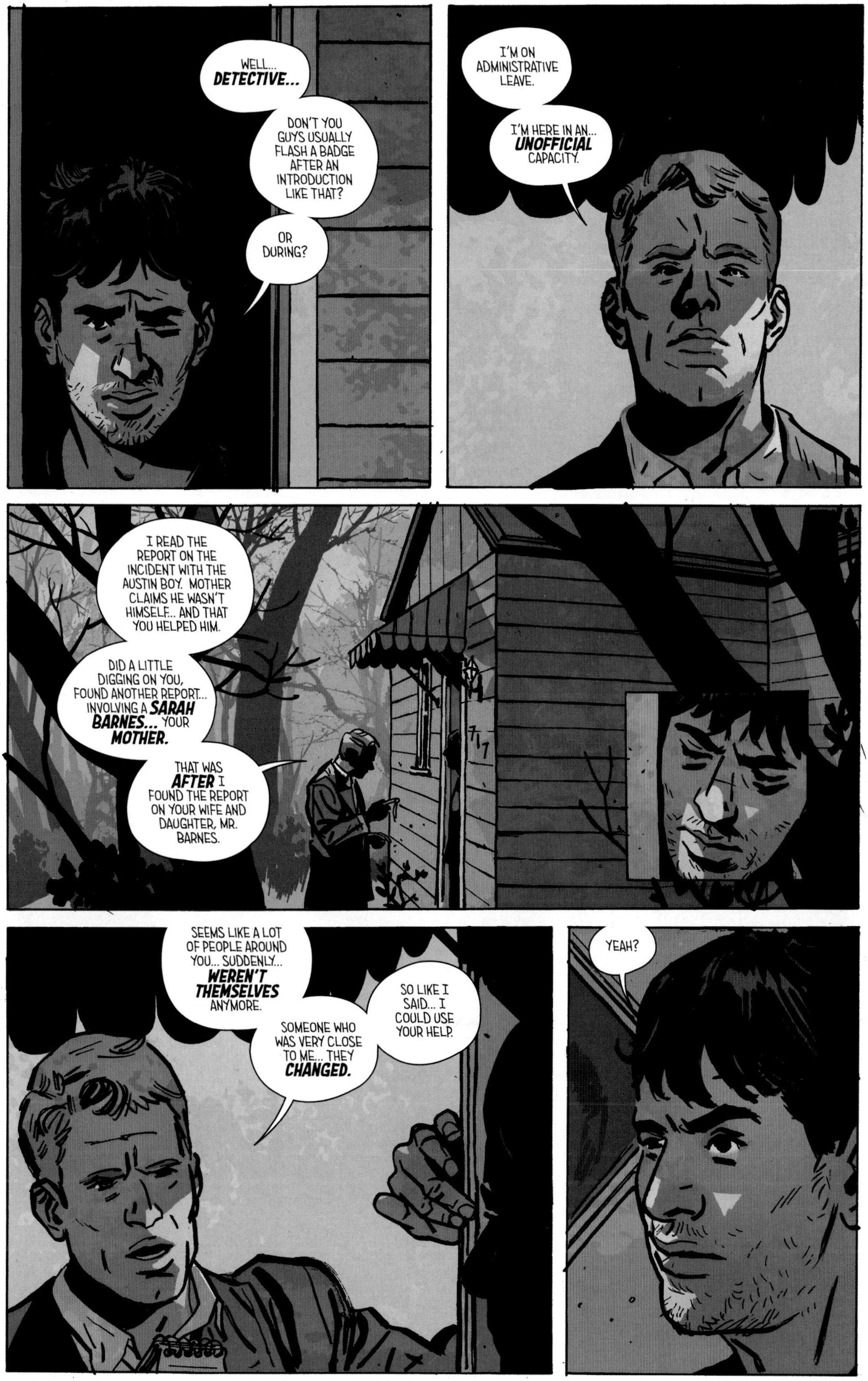
WELL... DETECTIVE...
DON'T YOU GUYS USUALLY FLASH A BADGE AFTER AN INTRODUCTION LIKE THAT?
OR DURING?
I'M ON ADMINISTRATIVE LEAVE.
I'M HERE IN AN... UNOFFICIAL CAPACITY.
I READ THE REPORT ON THE INCIDENT WITH THE AUSTIN BOY. MOTHER CLAIMS HE WASN'T HIMSELF... AND THAT YOU HELPED HIM.
DID A LITTLE DIGGING ON YOU, FOUND ANOTHER REPORT... INVOLVING A SARAH BARNES... YOUR MOTHER.
THAT WAS AFTER I FOUND THE REPORT ON YOUR WIFE AND DAUGHTER, MR. BARNES.
SEEMS LIKE A LOT OF PEOPLE AROUND YOU... SUDDENLY... WEREN'T THEMSELVES ANYMORE.
SOMEONE WHO WAS VERY CLOSE TO ME... THEY CHANGED.
SO LIKE I SAID... I COULD USE YOUR HELP.
YEAH?

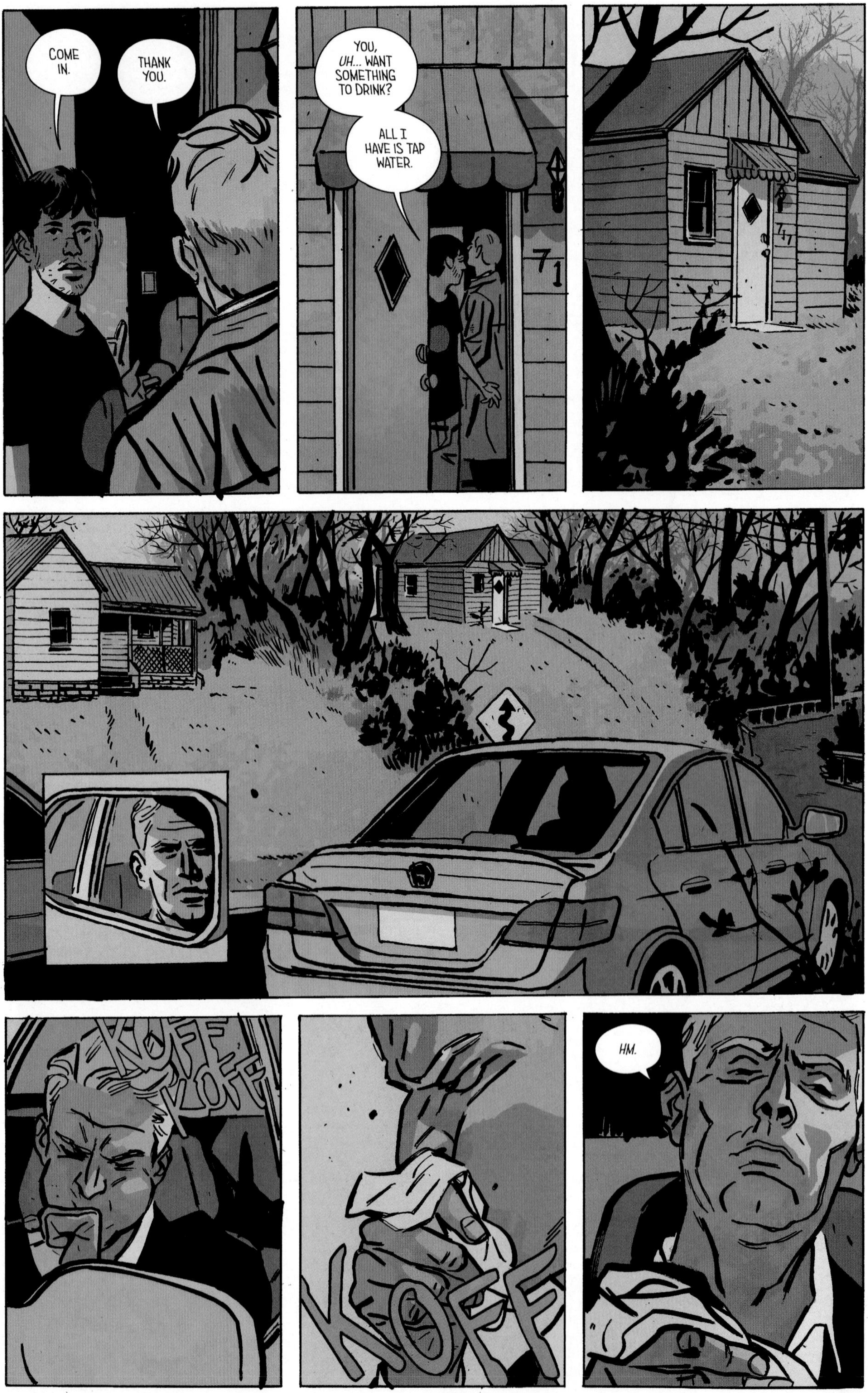
COME IN.
THANK YOU.
YOU, UH... WANT SOMETHING TO DRINK?
ALL I HAVE IS TAP WATER.
KOFF
KOFF
KOFF
HM.

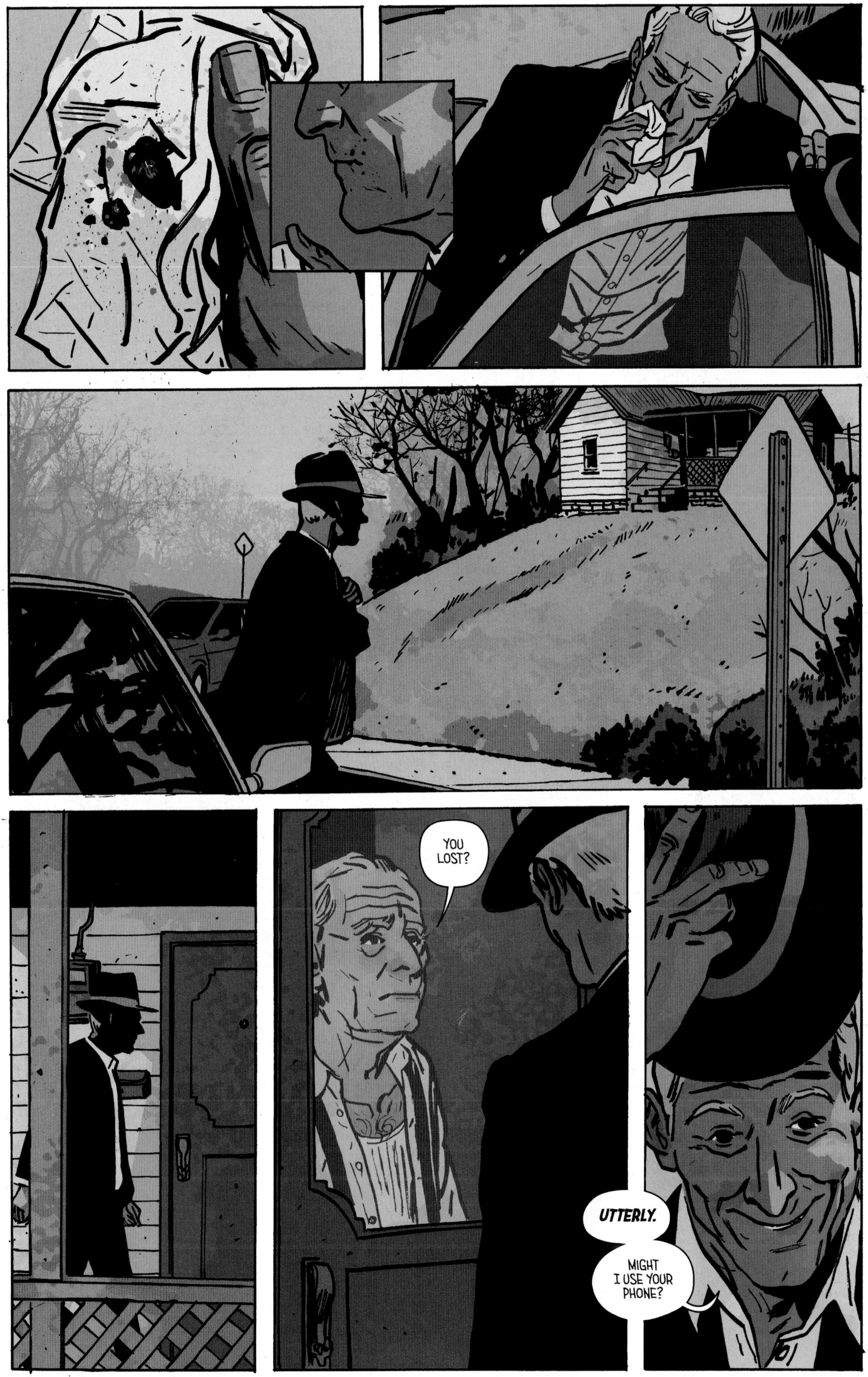
YOU LOST?
UTTERLY.
MIGHT I USE YOUR PHONE?

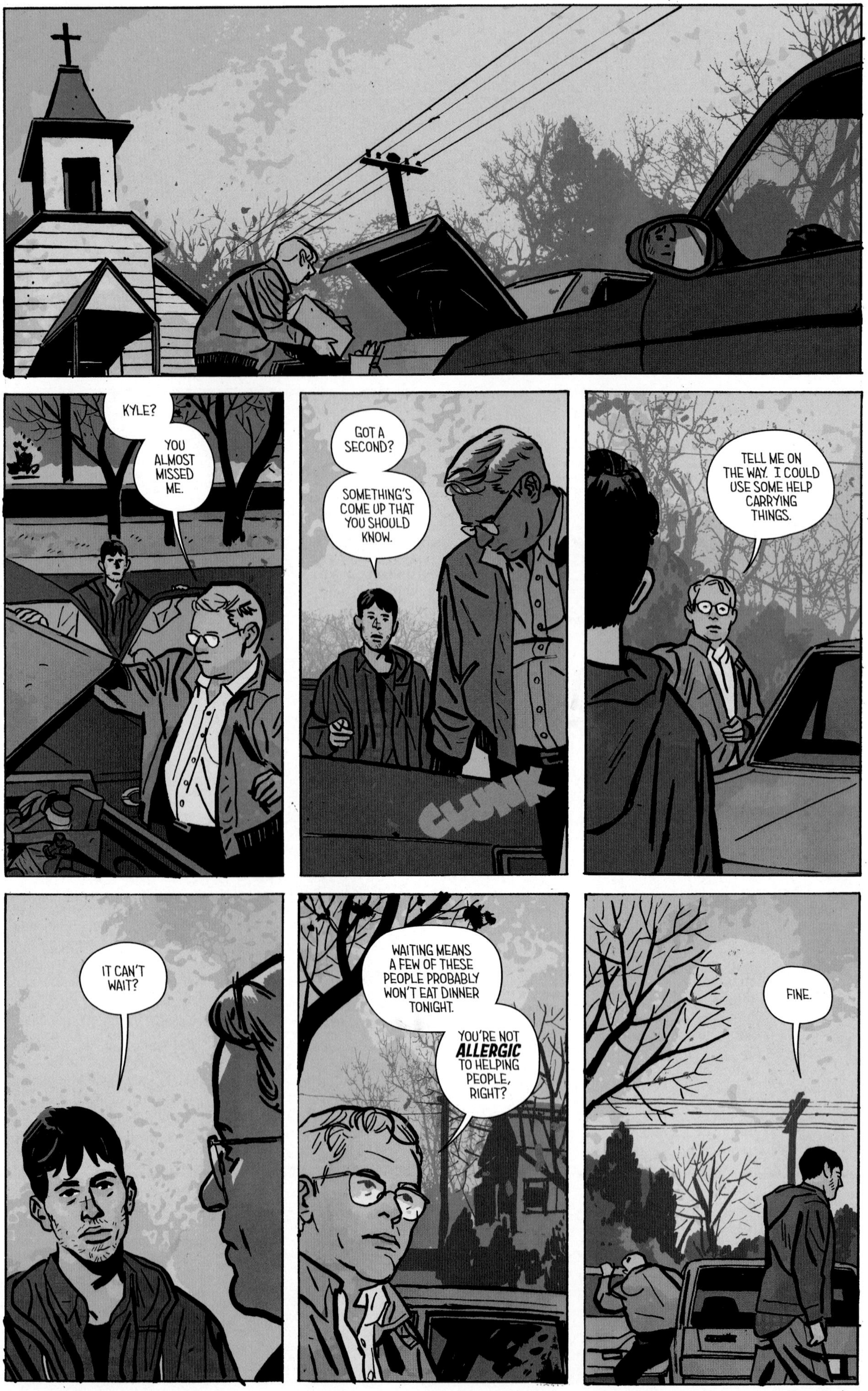
KYLE?
YOU ALMOST MISSED ME.
GOT A SECOND?
SOMETHING'S COME UP THAT YOU SHOULD KNOW.
CLUNK
TELL ME ON THE WAY. I COULD USE SOME HELP CARRYING THINGS.
IT CAN'T WAIT?
WAITING MEANS A FEW OF THESE PEOPLE PROBABLY WON'T EAT DINNER TONIGHT.
YOU'RE NOT ALLERGIC TO HELPING PEOPLE, RIGHT?
FINE.

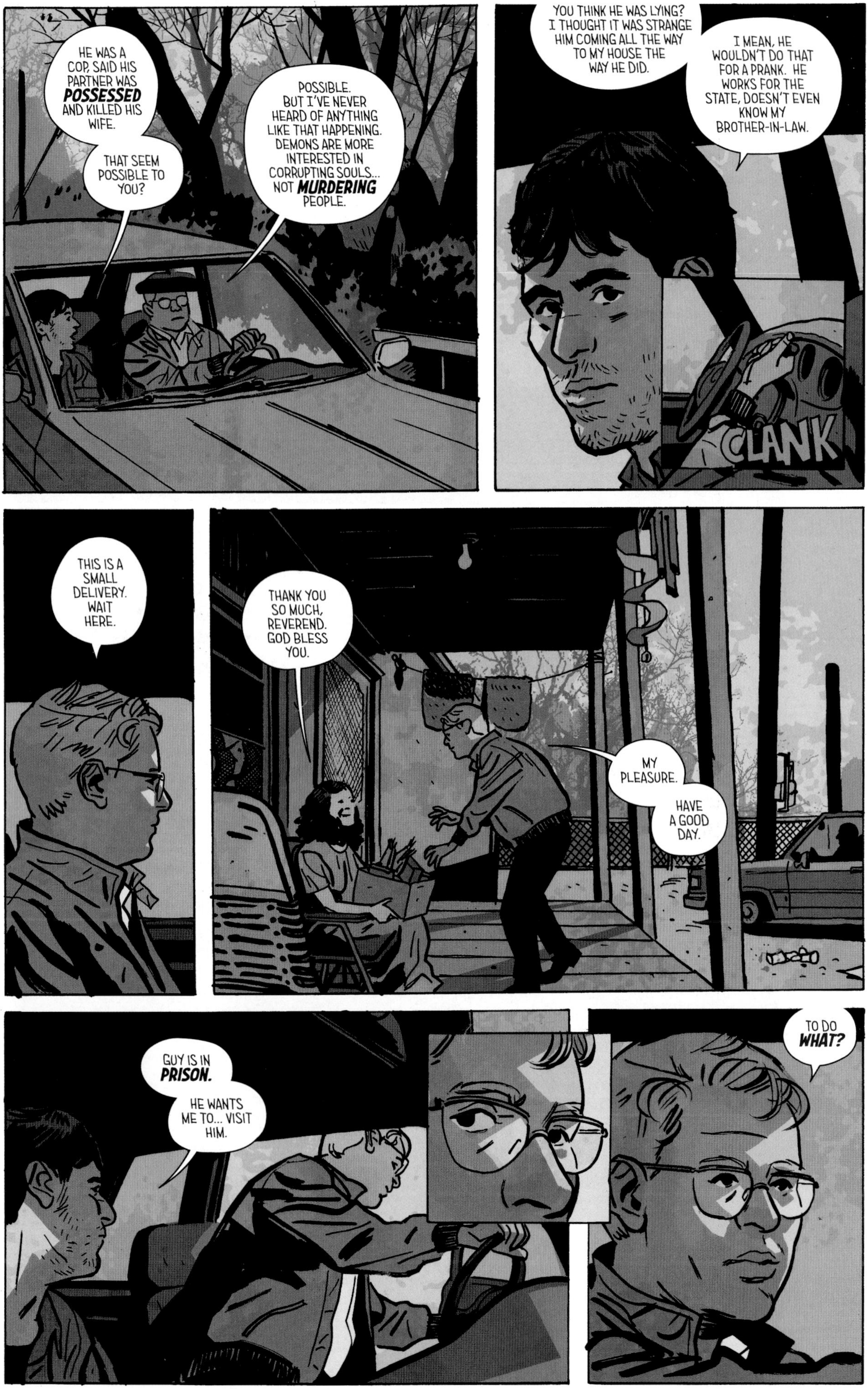
HE WAS A COP, SAID HIS PARTNER WAS **POSSESSED** AND KILLED HIS WIFE.
THAT SEEM POSSIBLE TO YOU?
POSSIBLE. BUT I'VE NEVER HEARD OF ANYTHING LIKE THAT HAPPENING. DEMONS ARE MORE INTERESTED IN CORRUPTING SOULS... NOT **MURDERING** PEOPLE.
YOU THINK HE WAS LYING? I THOUGHT IT WAS STRANGE HIM COMING ALL THE WAY TO MY HOUSE THE WAY HE DID.
I MEAN, HE WOULDN'T DO THAT FOR A PRANK. HE WORKS FOR THE STATE, DOESN'T EVEN KNOW MY BROTHER-IN-LAW.
CLANK
THIS IS A SMALL DELIVERY. WAIT HERE.
THANK YOU SO MUCH, REVEREND. GOD BLESS YOU.
MY PLEASURE.
HAVE A GOOD DAY.
GUY IS IN **PRISON.**
HE WANTS ME TO... VISIT HIM.
TO DO **WHAT?**

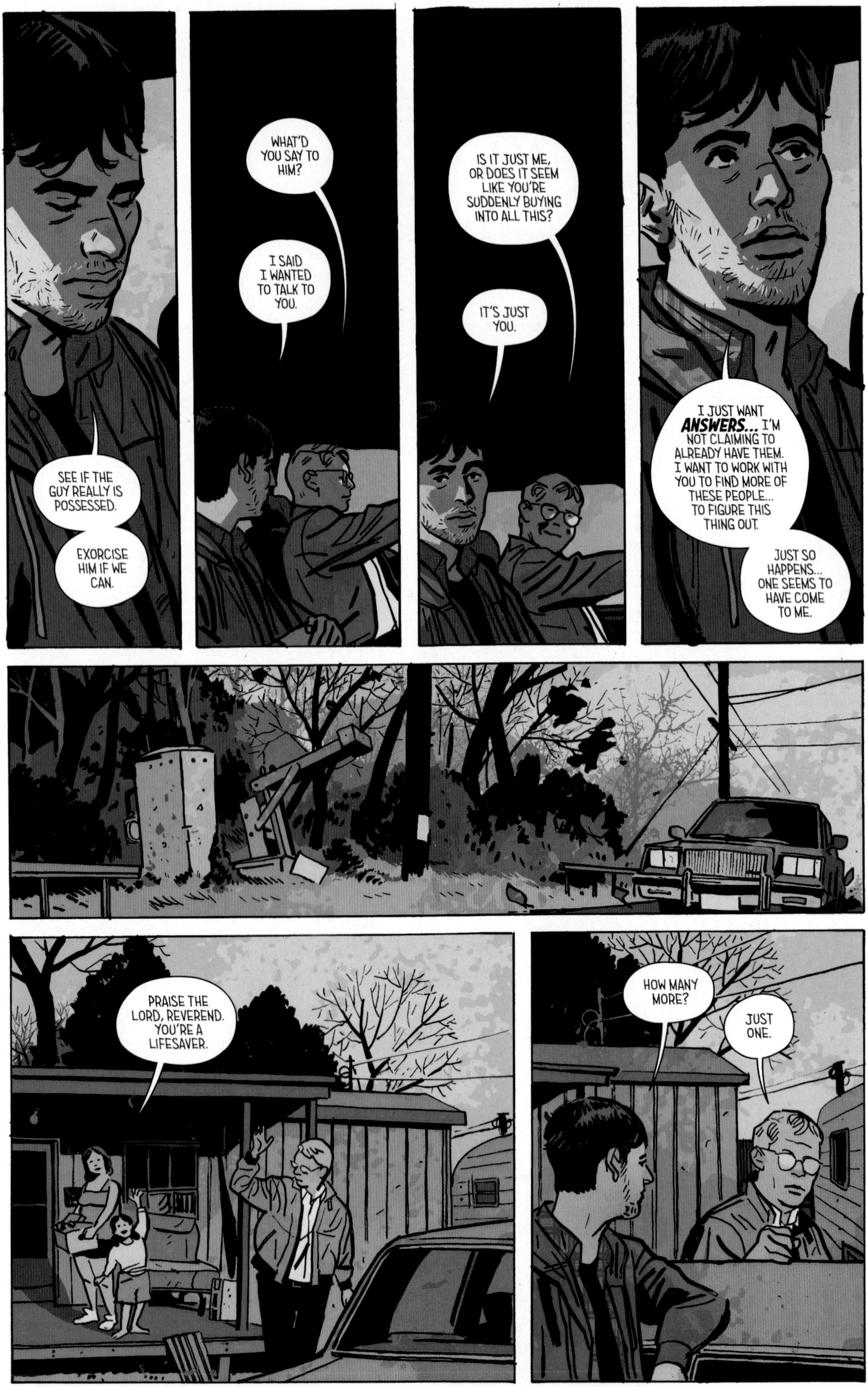
SEE IF THE GUY REALLY IS POSSESSED.
EXORCISE HIM IF WE CAN.
WHAT'D YOU SAY TO HIM?
I SAID I WANTED TO TALK TO YOU.
IS IT JUST ME, OR DOES IT SEEM LIKE YOU'RE SUDDENLY BUYING INTO ALL THIS?
IT'S JUST YOU.
I JUST WANT ANSWERS... I'M NOT CLAIMING TO ALREADY HAVE THEM. I WANT TO WORK WITH YOU TO FIND MORE OF THESE PEOPLE... TO FIGURE THIS THING OUT.
JUST SO HAPPENS... ONE SEEMS TO HAVE COME TO ME.
PRAISE THE LORD, REVEREND. YOU'RE A LIFESAVER.
HOW MANY MORE?
JUST ONE.

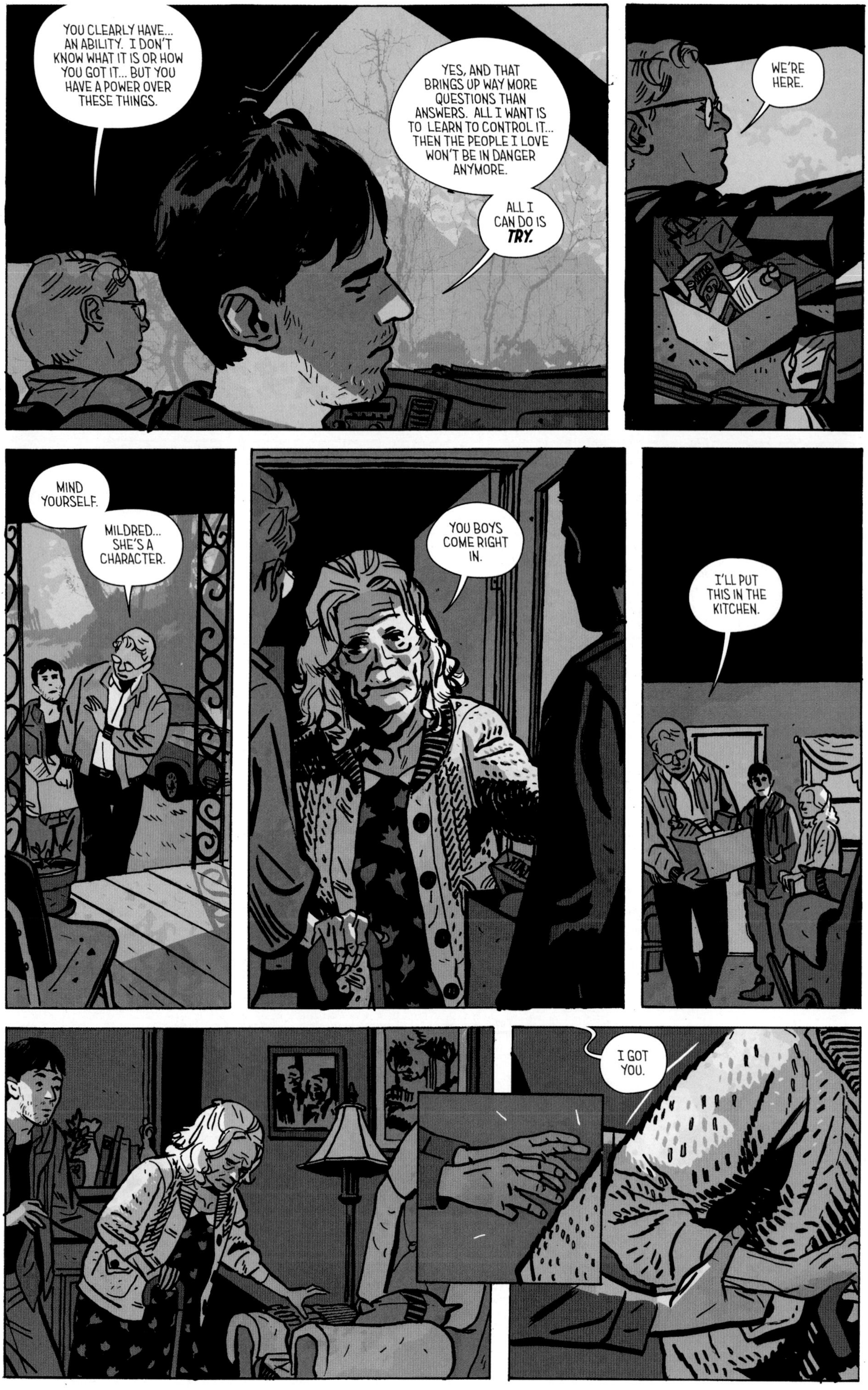
YOU CLEARLY HAVE... AN ABILITY. I DON'T KNOW WHAT IT IS OR HOW YOU GOT IT... BUT YOU HAVE A POWER OVER THESE THINGS.
YES, AND THAT BRINGS UP WAY MORE QUESTIONS THAN ANSWERS. ALL I WANT IS TO LEARN TO CONTROL IT... THEN THE PEOPLE I LOVE WON'T BE IN DANGER ANYMORE.
ALL I CAN DO IS *TRY.*
WE'RE HERE.
MIND YOURSELF.
MILDRED... SHE'S A CHARACTER.
YOU BOYS COME RIGHT IN.
I'LL PUT THIS IN THE KITCHEN.
I GOT YOU.

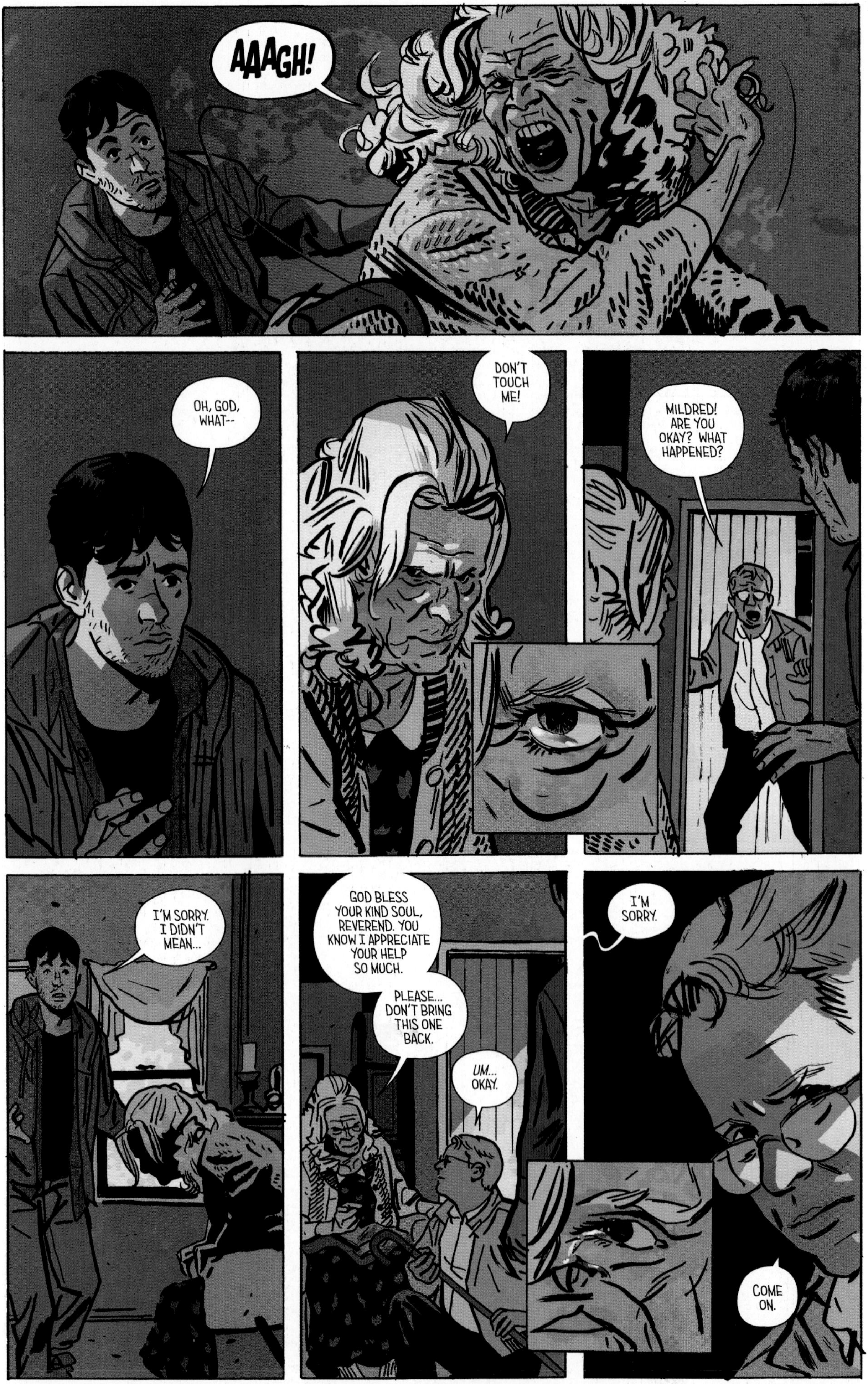
AAAGH!
OH, GOD, WHAT--
DON'T TOUCH ME!
MILDRED! ARE YOU OKAY? WHAT HAPPENED?
I'M SORRY. I DIDN'T MEAN...
GOD BLESS YOUR KIND SOUL, REVEREND. YOU KNOW I APPRECIATE YOUR HELP SO MUCH.
PLEASE... DON'T BRING THIS ONE BACK.
UM... OKAY.
I'M SORRY.
COME ON.

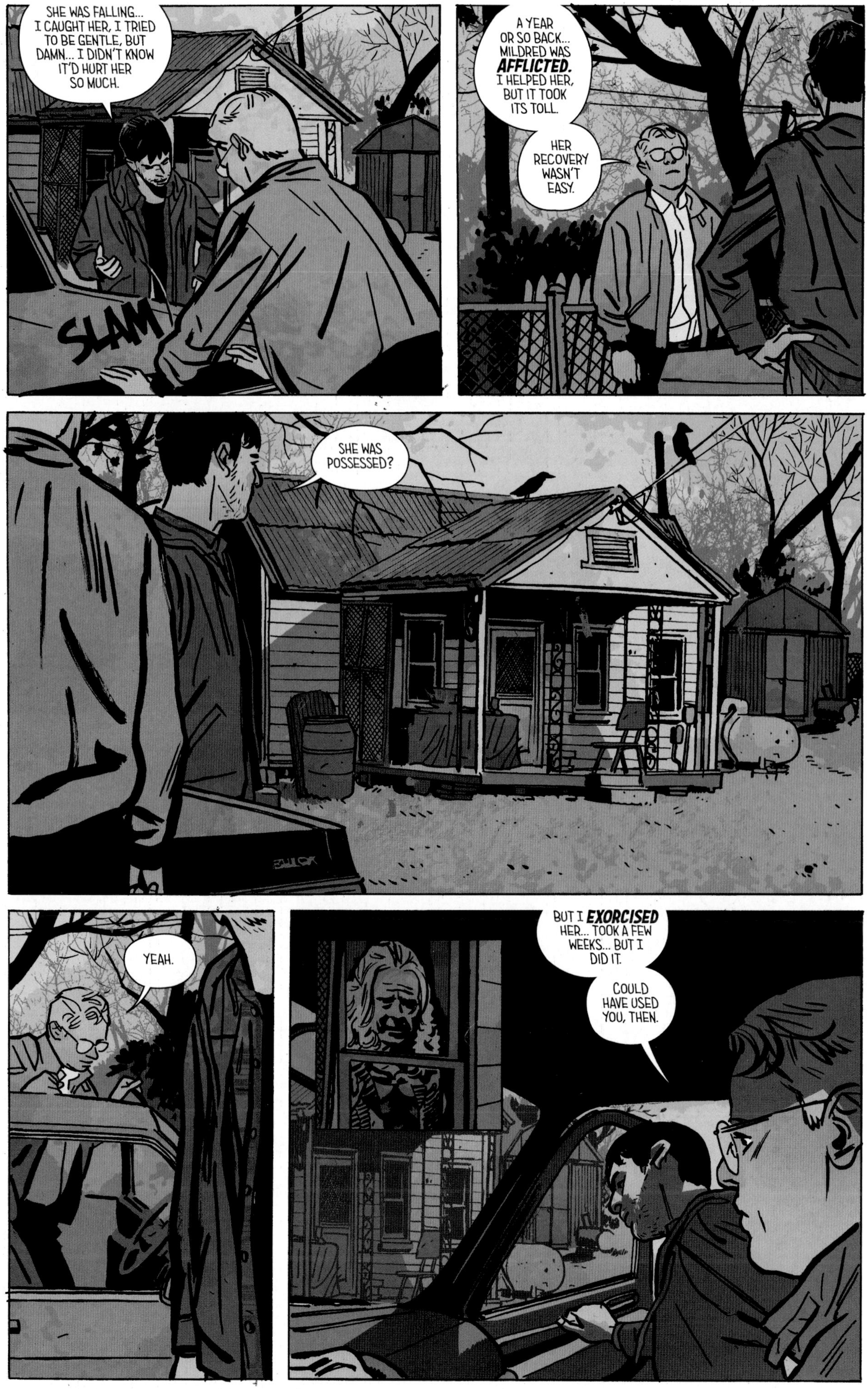
SHE WAS FALLING... I CAUGHT HER, I TRIED TO BE GENTLE, BUT DAMN... I DIDN'T KNOW IT'D HURT HER SO MUCH.
SLAM
A YEAR OR SO BACK... MILDRED WAS AFFLICTED. I HELPED HER, BUT IT TOOK ITS TOLL.
HER RECOVERY WASN'T EASY.
SHE WAS POSSESSED?
YEAH.
BUT I EXORCISED HER... TOOK A FEW WEEKS... BUT I DID IT.
COULD HAVE USED YOU, THEN.

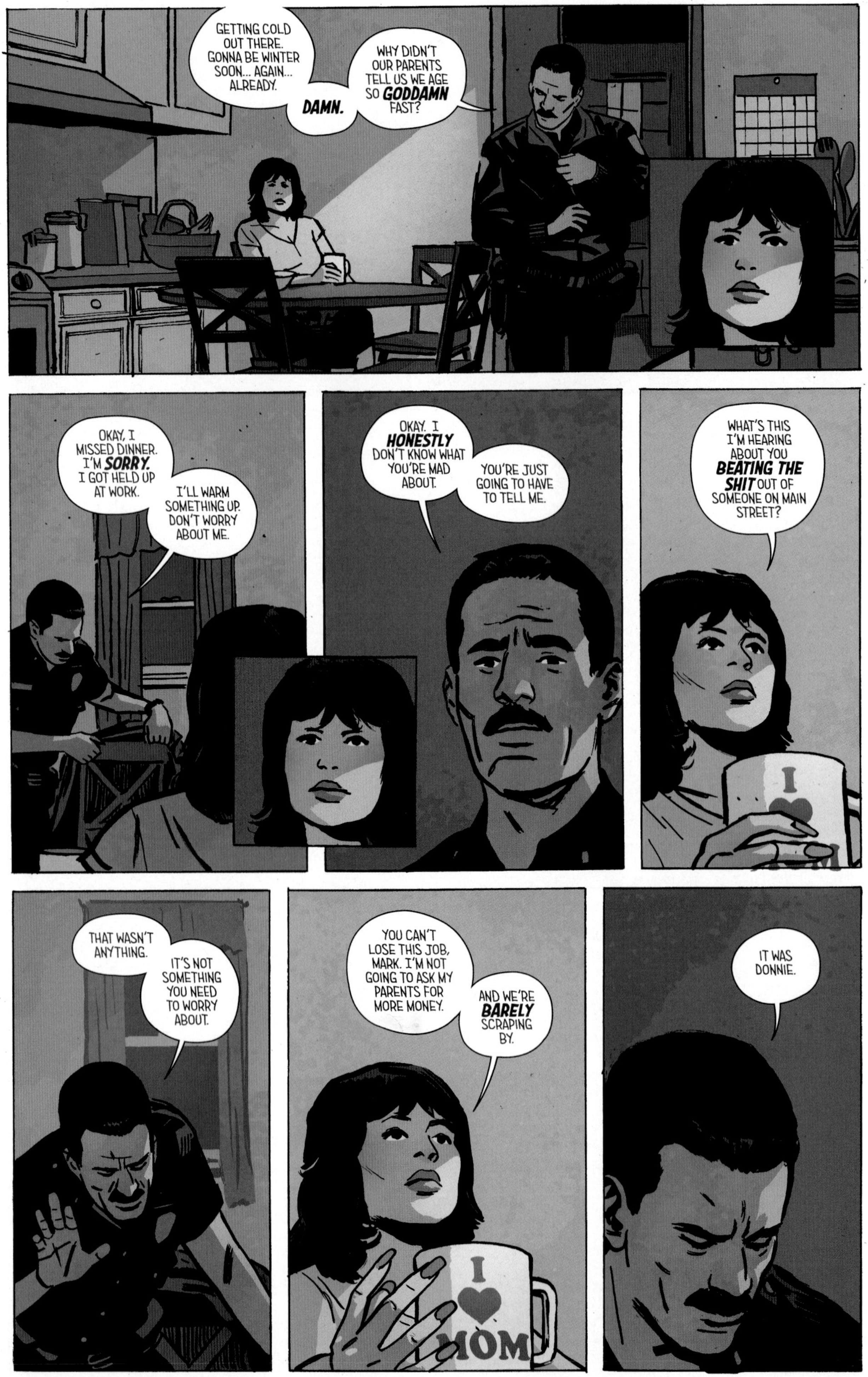
GETTING COLD OUT THERE. GONNA BE WINTER SOON... AGAIN... ALREADY.
DAMN.
WHY DIDN'T OUR PARENTS TELL US WE AGE SO GODDAMN FAST?
OKAY, I MISSED DINNER. I'M SORRY. I GOT HELD UP AT WORK.
I'LL WARM SOMETHING UP. DON'T WORRY ABOUT ME.
OKAY. I HONESTLY DON'T KNOW WHAT YOU'RE MAD ABOUT.
YOU'RE JUST GOING TO HAVE TO TELL ME.
WHAT'S THIS I'M HEARING ABOUT YOU BEATING THE SHIT OUT OF SOMEONE ON MAIN STREET?
THAT WASN'T ANYTHING.
IT'S NOT SOMETHING YOU NEED TO WORRY ABOUT.
YOU CAN'T LOSE THIS JOB, MARK. I'M NOT GOING TO ASK MY PARENTS FOR MORE MONEY.
AND WE'RE BARELY SCRAPING BY.
I ♥ MOM
IT WAS DONNIE.

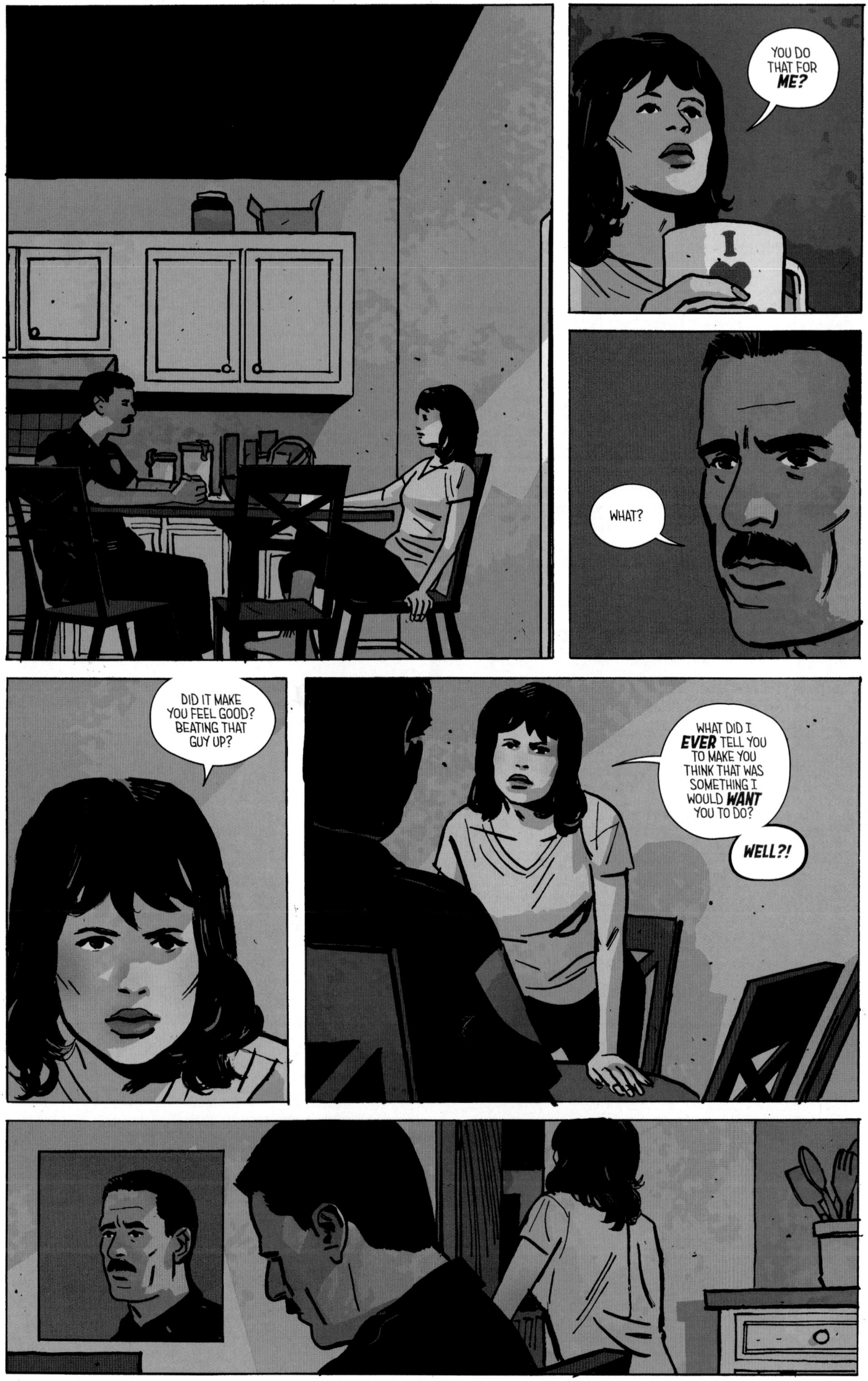
YOU DO THAT FOR ME?
WHAT?
DID IT MAKE YOU FEEL GOOD? BEATING THAT GUY UP?
WHAT DID I EVER TELL YOU TO MAKE YOU THINK THAT WAS SOMETHING I WOULD WANT YOU TO DO?
WELL?!

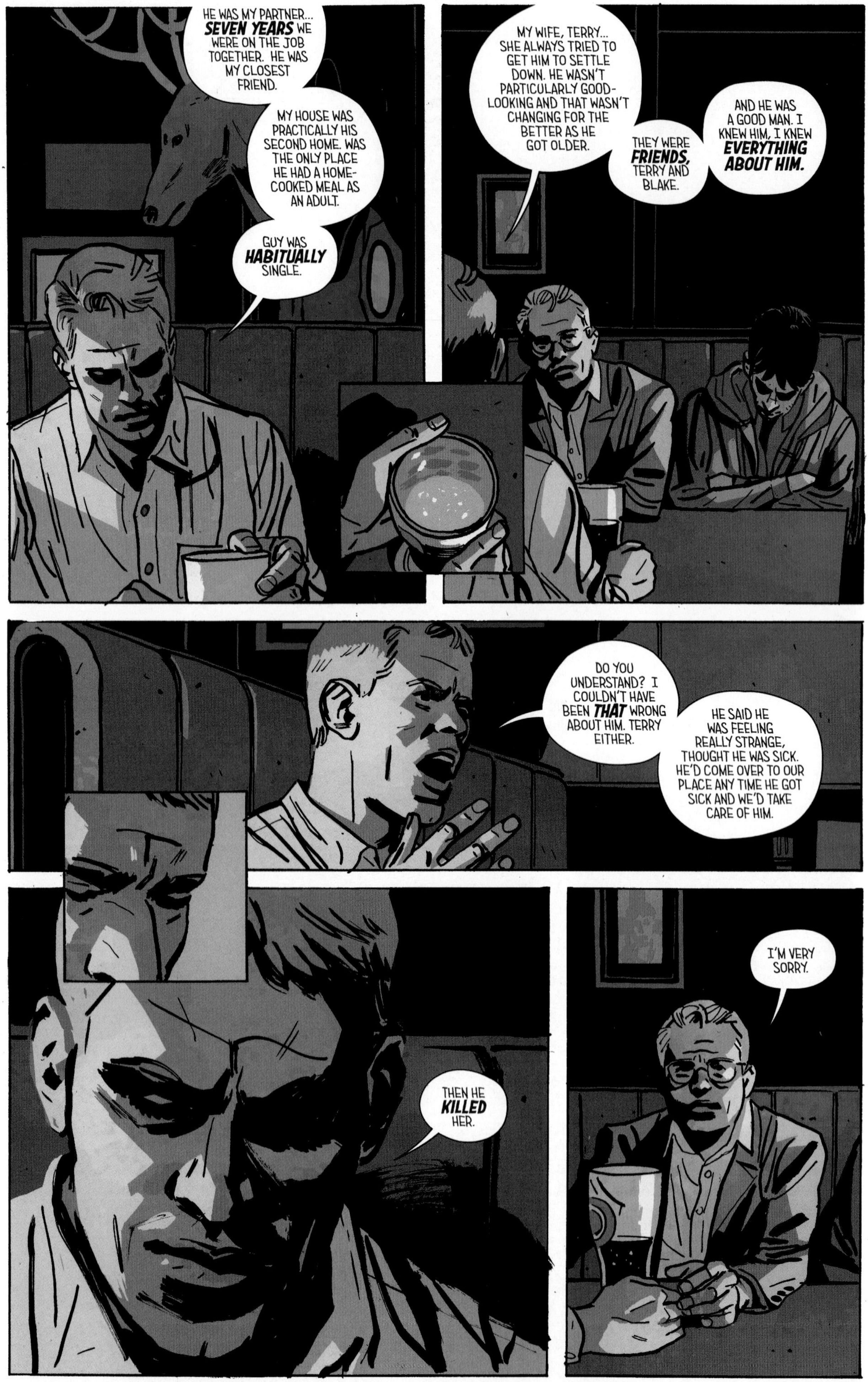
HE WAS MY PARTNER... SEVEN YEARS WE WERE ON THE JOB TOGETHER. HE WAS MY CLOSEST FRIEND.
MY HOUSE WAS PRACTICALLY HIS SECOND HOME. WAS THE ONLY PLACE HE HAD A HOME-COOKED MEAL AS AN ADULT.
GUY WAS HABITUALLY SINGLE.
MY WIFE, TERRY... SHE ALWAYS TRIED TO GET HIM TO SETTLE DOWN. HE WASN'T PARTICULARLY GOOD-LOOKING AND THAT WASN'T CHANGING FOR THE BETTER AS HE GOT OLDER.
THEY WERE FRIENDS, TERRY AND BLAKE.
AND HE WAS A GOOD MAN. I KNEW HIM, I KNEW EVERYTHING ABOUT HIM.
DO YOU UNDERSTAND? I COULDN'T HAVE BEEN THAT WRONG ABOUT HIM. TERRY EITHER.
HE SAID HE WAS FEELING REALLY STRANGE, THOUGHT HE WAS SICK. HE'D COME OVER TO OUR PLACE ANY TIME HE GOT SICK AND WE'D TAKE CARE OF HIM.
THEN HE KILLED HER.
I'M VERY SORRY.

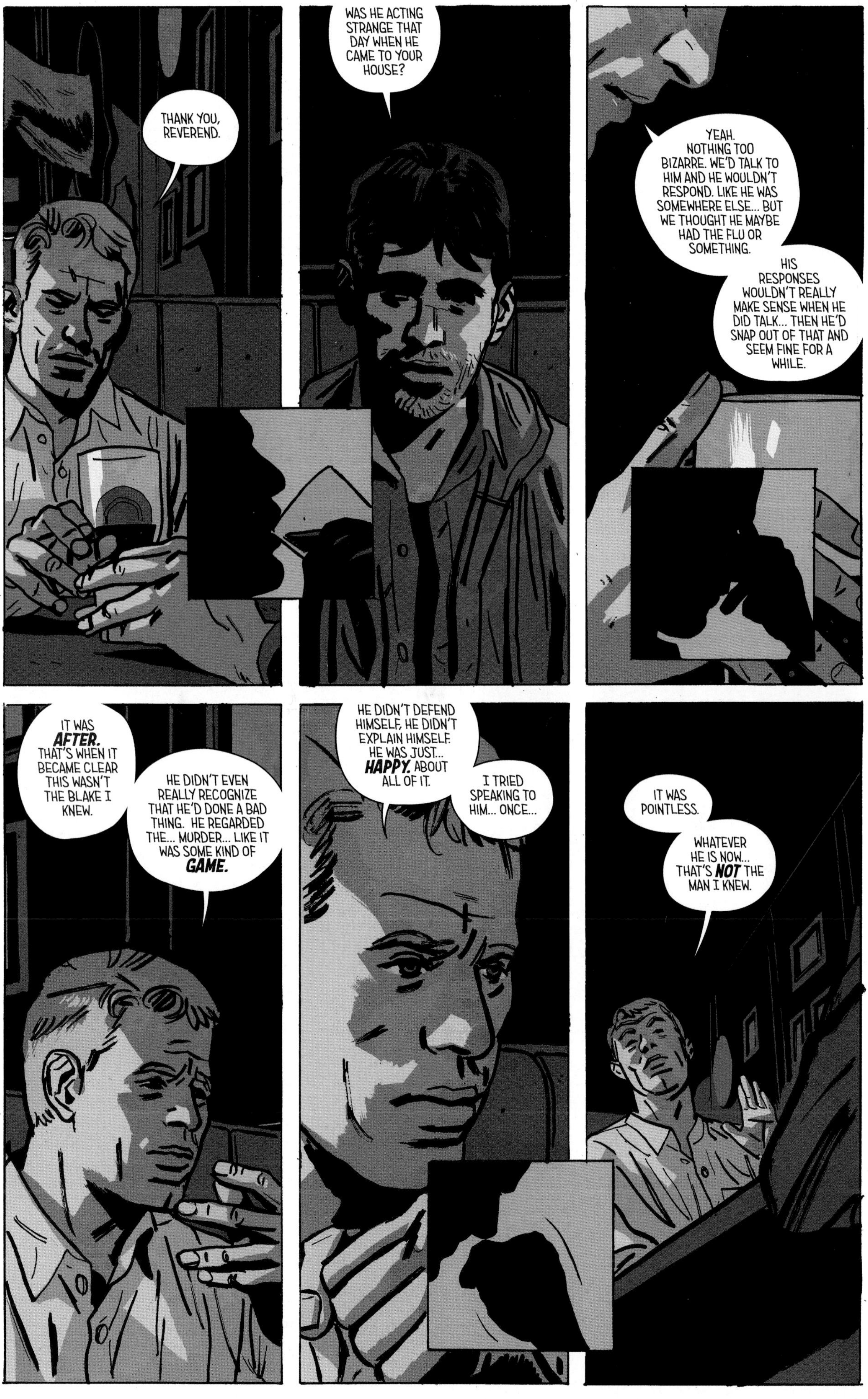
THANK YOU, REVEREND.
WAS HE ACTING STRANGE THAT DAY WHEN HE CAME TO YOUR HOUSE?
YEAH. NOTHING TOO BIZARRE. WE'D TALK TO HIM AND HE WOULDN'T RESPOND. LIKE HE WAS SOMEWHERE ELSE... BUT WE THOUGHT HE MAYBE HAD THE FLU OR SOMETHING.
HIS RESPONSES WOULDN'T REALLY MAKE SENSE WHEN HE DID TALK... THEN HE'D SNAP OUT OF THAT AND SEEM FINE FOR A WHILE.
IT WAS **AFTER.** THAT'S WHEN IT BECAME CLEAR THIS WASN'T THE BLAKE I KNEW.
HE DIDN'T EVEN REALLY RECOGNIZE THAT HE'D DONE A BAD THING. HE REGARDED THE... MURDER... LIKE IT WAS SOME KIND OF **GAME.**
HE DIDN'T DEFEND HIMSELF, HE DIDN'T EXPLAIN HIMSELF. HE WAS JUST... **HAPPY.** ABOUT ALL OF IT.
I TRIED SPEAKING TO HIM... ONCE...
IT WAS POINTLESS.
WHATEVER HE IS NOW... THAT'S **NOT** THE MAN I KNEW.

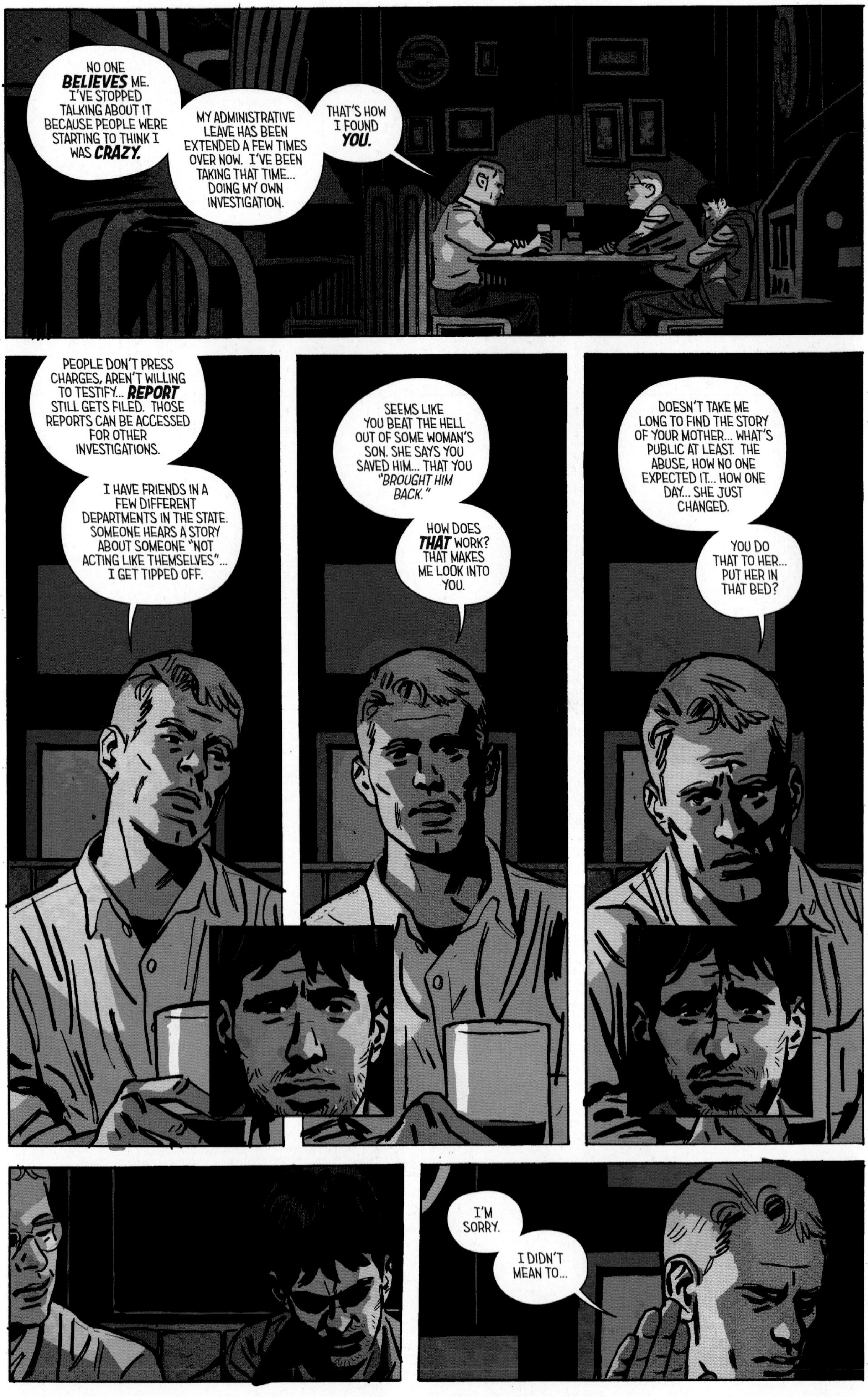
NO ONE BELIEVES ME. I'VE STOPPED TALKING ABOUT IT BECAUSE PEOPLE WERE STARTING TO THINK I WAS CRAZY.
MY ADMINISTRATIVE LEAVE HAS BEEN EXTENDED A FEW TIMES OVER NOW. I'VE BEEN TAKING THAT TIME... DOING MY OWN INVESTIGATION.
THAT'S HOW I FOUND YOU.
PEOPLE DON'T PRESS CHARGES, AREN'T WILLING TO TESTIFY... REPORT STILL GETS FILED. THOSE REPORTS CAN BE ACCESSED FOR OTHER INVESTIGATIONS.
I HAVE FRIENDS IN A FEW DIFFERENT DEPARTMENTS IN THE STATE. SOMEONE HEARS A STORY ABOUT SOMEONE "NOT ACTING LIKE THEMSELVES"... I GET TIPPED OFF.
SEEMS LIKE YOU BEAT THE HELL OUT OF SOME WOMAN'S SON. SHE SAYS YOU SAVED HIM... THAT YOU "BROUGHT HIM BACK."
HOW DOES THAT WORK? THAT MAKES ME LOOK INTO YOU.
DOESN'T TAKE ME LONG TO FIND THE STORY OF YOUR MOTHER... WHAT'S PUBLIC AT LEAST. THE ABUSE, HOW NO ONE EXPECTED IT... HOW ONE DAY... SHE JUST CHANGED.
YOU DO THAT TO HER... PUT HER IN THAT BED?
I'M SORRY.
I DIDN'T MEAN TO...

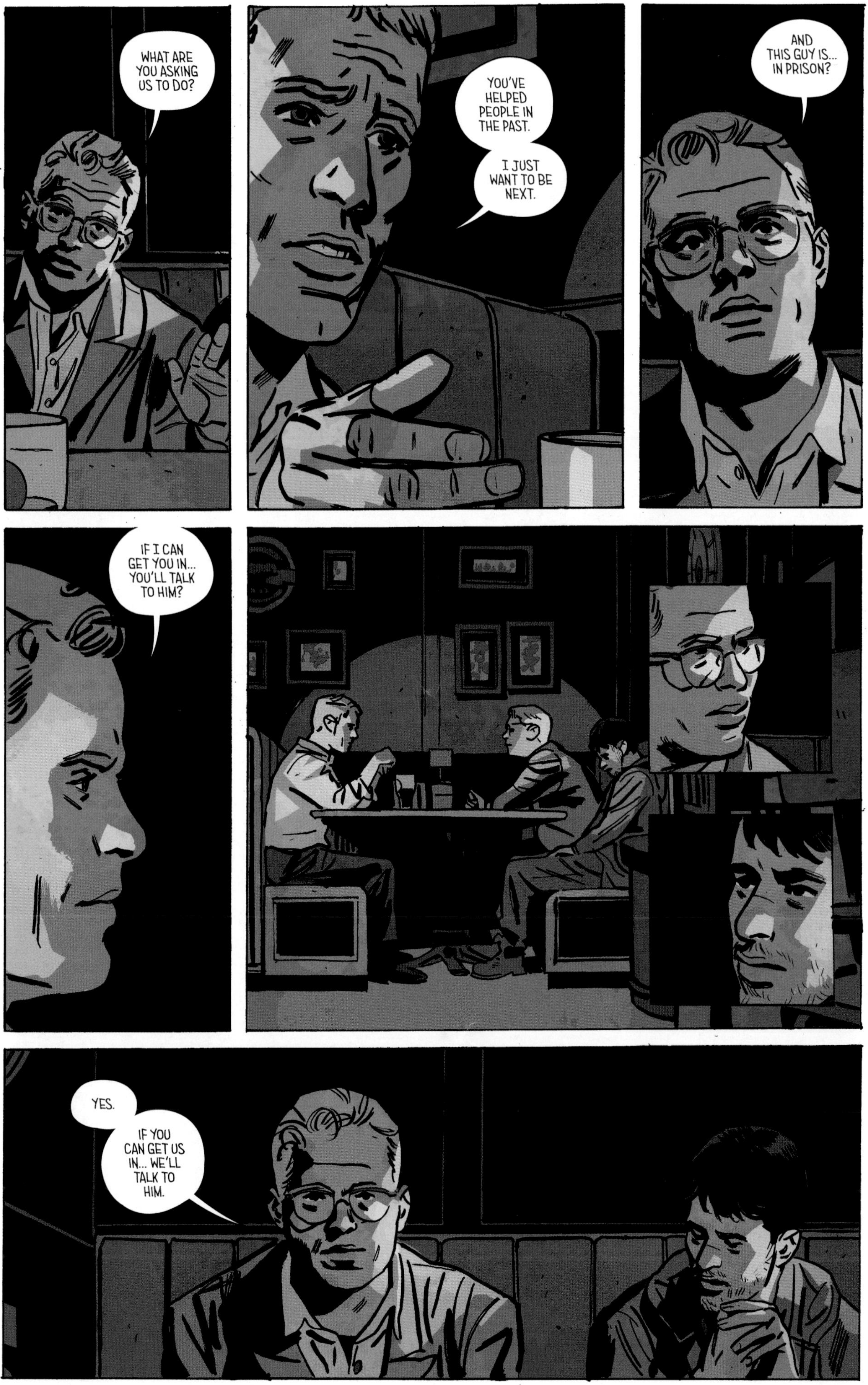
WHAT ARE YOU ASKING US TO DO?
YOU'VE HELPED PEOPLE IN THE PAST.
I JUST WANT TO BE NEXT.
AND THIS GUY IS... IN PRISON?
IF I CAN GET YOU IN... YOU'LL TALK TO HIM?
YES.
IF YOU CAN GET US IN... WE'LL TALK TO HIM.

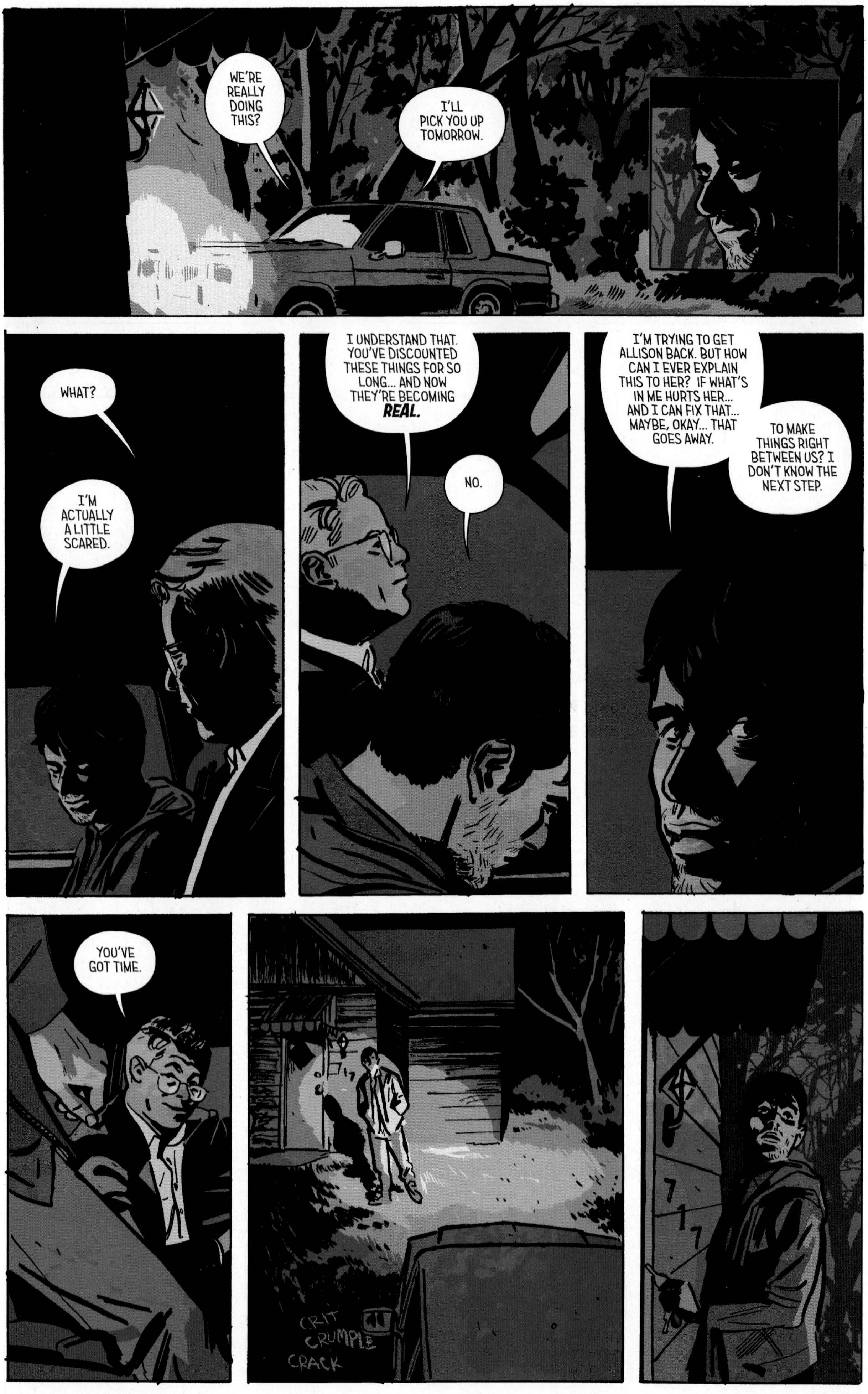
WE'RE REALLY DOING THIS?
I'LL PICK YOU UP TOMORROW.
WHAT?
I'M ACTUALLY A LITTLE SCARED.
I UNDERSTAND THAT. YOU'VE DISCOUNTED THESE THINGS FOR SO LONG... AND NOW THEY'RE BECOMING **REAL.**
NO.
I'M TRYING TO GET ALLISON BACK. BUT HOW CAN I EVER EXPLAIN THIS TO HER? IF WHAT'S IN ME HURTS HER... AND I CAN FIX THAT... MAYBE, OKAY... THAT GOES AWAY.
TO MAKE THINGS RIGHT BETWEEN US? I DON'T KNOW THE NEXT STEP.
YOU'VE GOT TIME.
CRIT
CRUMPLE
CRACK

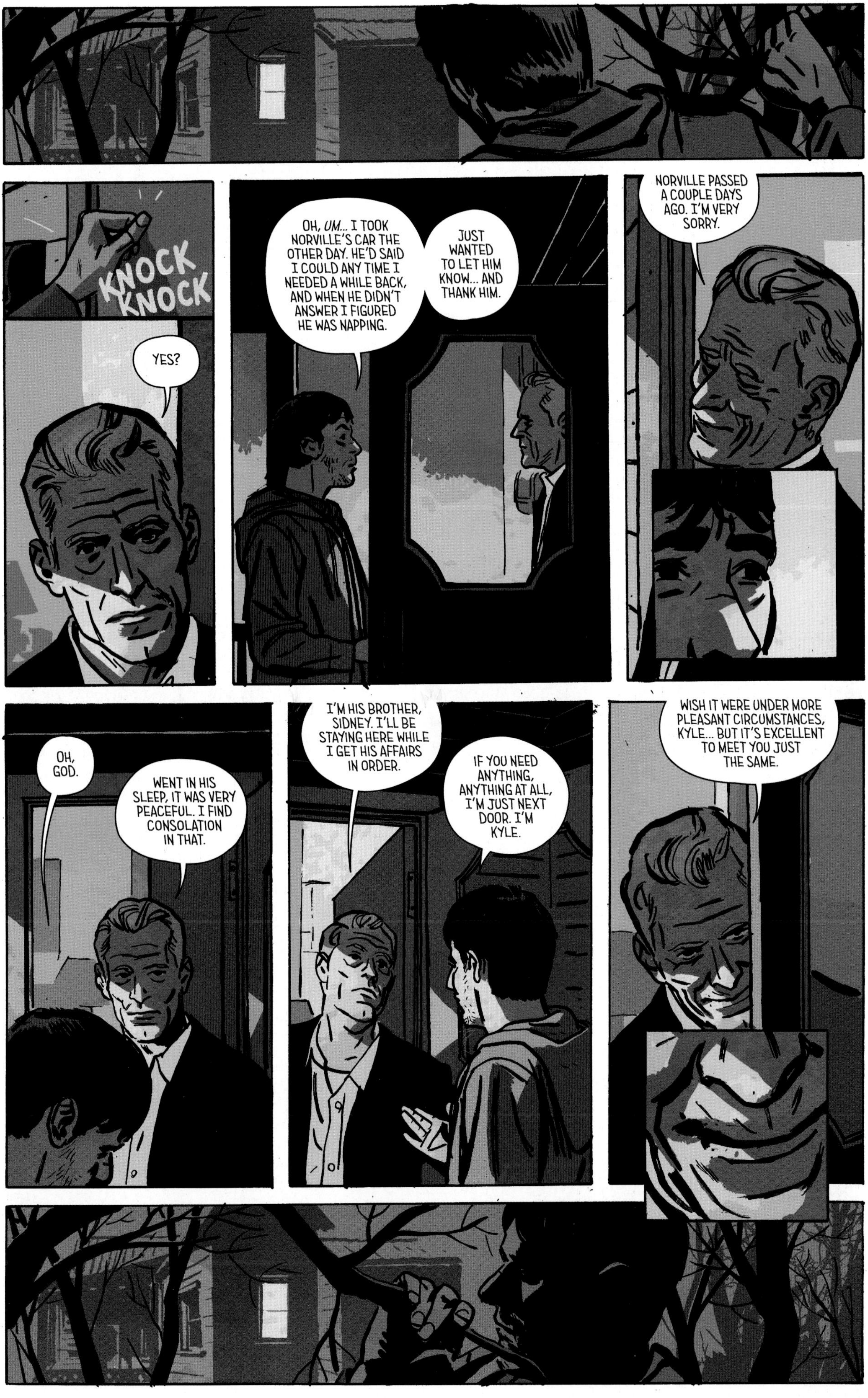
KNOCK KNOCK
YES?
OH, UM... I TOOK NORVILLE'S CAR THE OTHER DAY. HE'D SAID I COULD ANY TIME I NEEDED A WHILE BACK, AND WHEN HE DIDN'T ANSWER I FIGURED HE WAS NAPPING.
JUST WANTED TO LET HIM KNOW... AND THANK HIM.
NORVILLE PASSED A COUPLE DAYS AGO. I'M VERY SORRY.
OH, GOD.
WENT IN HIS SLEEP, IT WAS VERY PEACEFUL. I FIND CONSOLATION IN THAT.
I'M HIS BROTHER, SIDNEY. I'LL BE STAYING HERE WHILE I GET HIS AFFAIRS IN ORDER.
IF YOU NEED ANYTHING, ANYTHING AT ALL, I'M JUST NEXT DOOR. I'M KYLE.
WISH IT WERE UNDER MORE PLEASANT CIRCUMSTANCES, KYLE... BUT IT'S EXCELLENT TO MEET YOU JUST THE SAME.

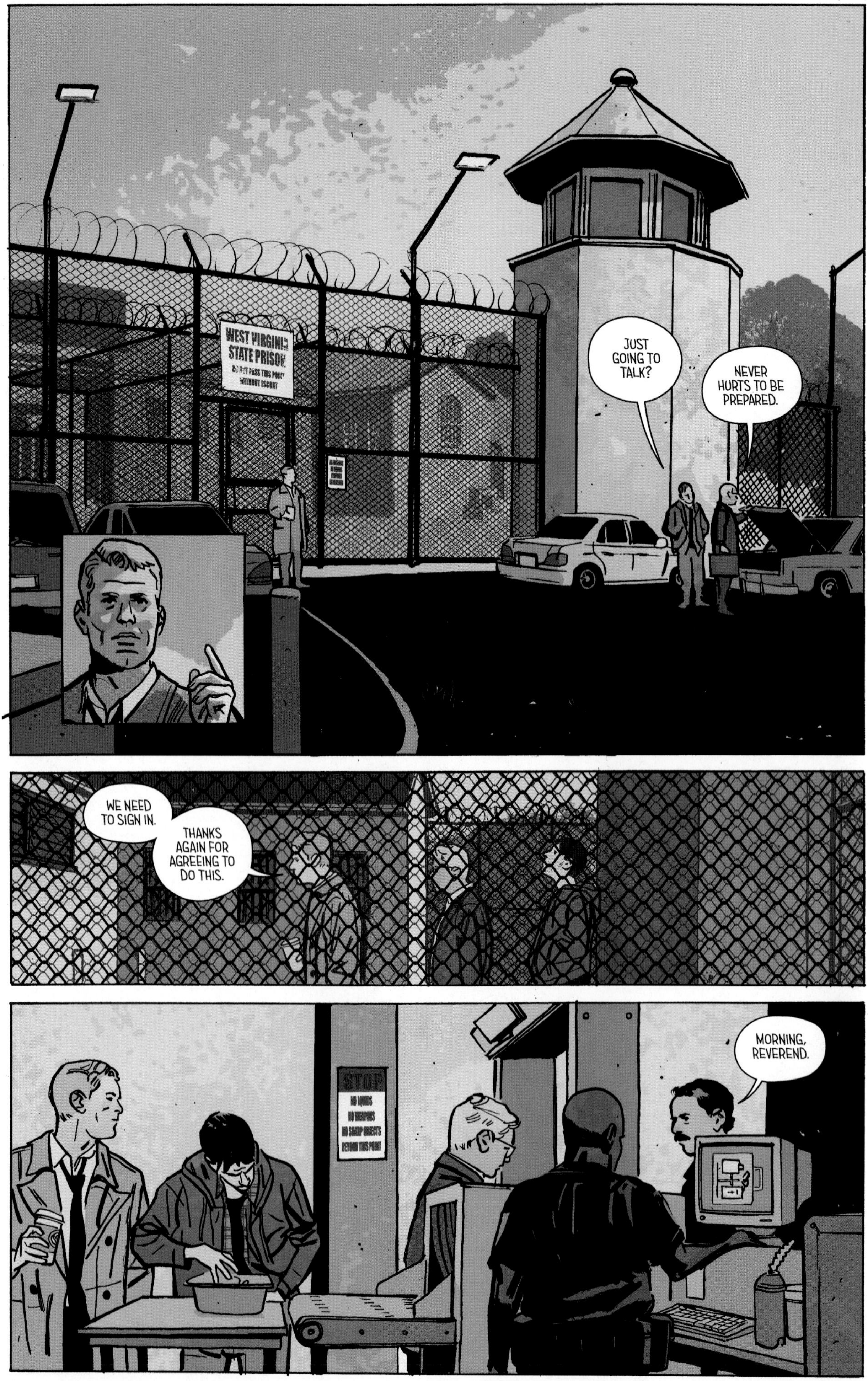
JUST GOING TO TALK?
NEVER HURTS TO BE PREPARED.
WE NEED TO SIGN IN.
THANKS AGAIN FOR AGREEING TO DO THIS.
STOP
NO LIQUIDS
NO WEAPONS
NO SHARP OBJECTS
BEYOND THIS POINT
MORNING, REVEREND.

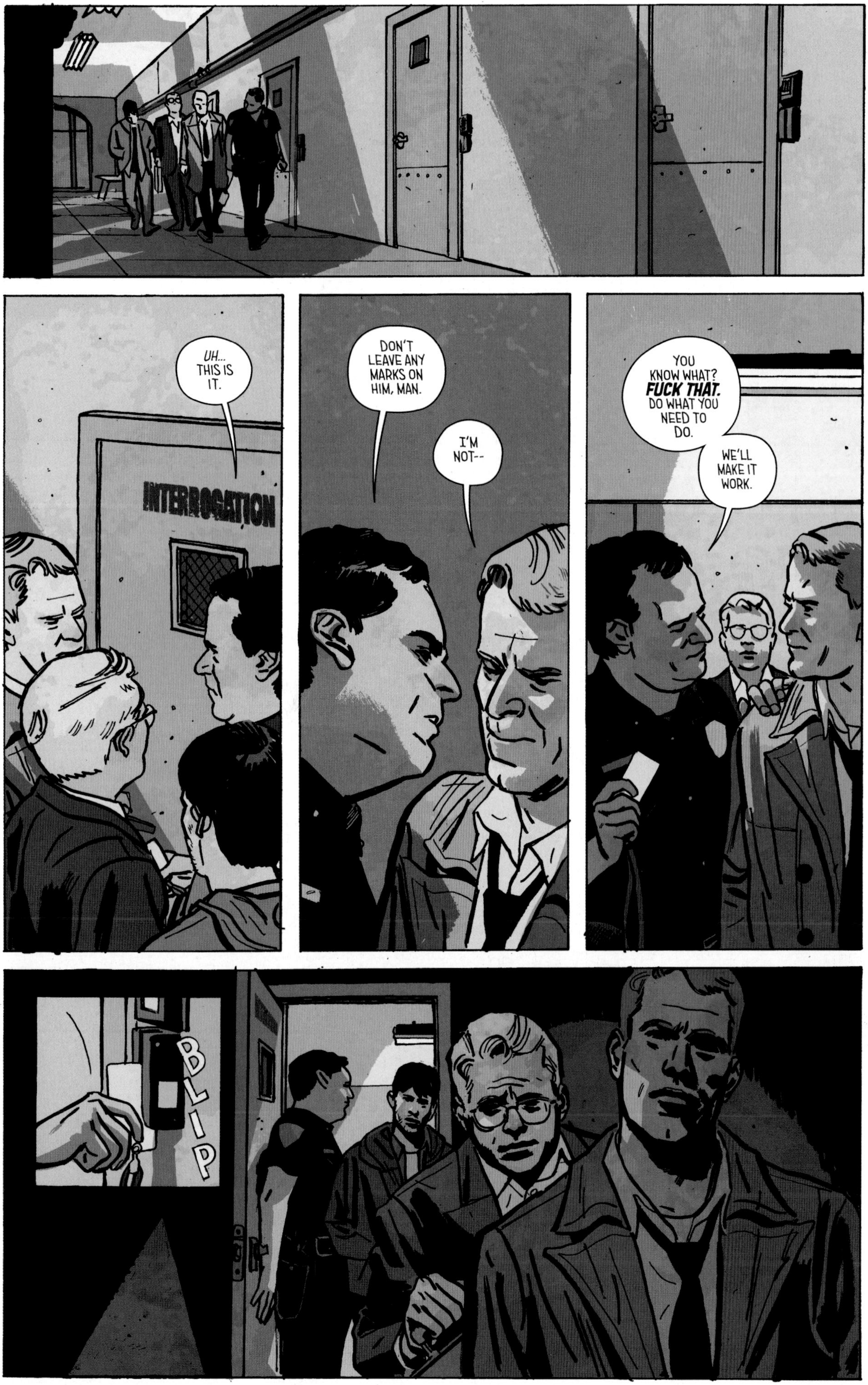
UH... THIS IS IT.
INTERROGATION
DON'T LEAVE ANY MARKS ON HIM, MAN.
I'M NOT--
YOU KNOW WHAT? **FUCK THAT.** DO WHAT YOU NEED TO DO.
WE'LL MAKE IT WORK.
BLIP

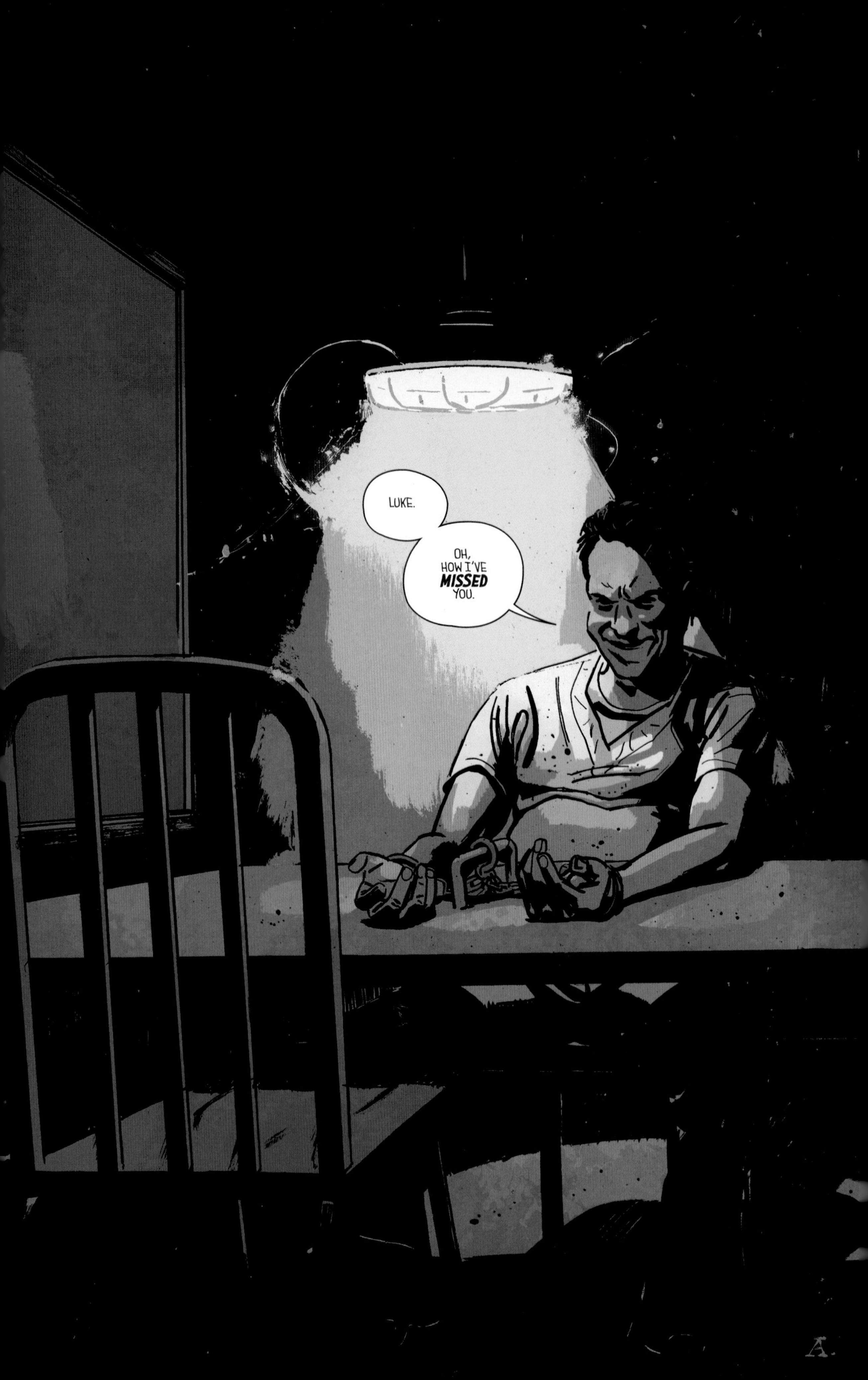
LUKE.
OH, HOW I'VE **MISSED** YOU.

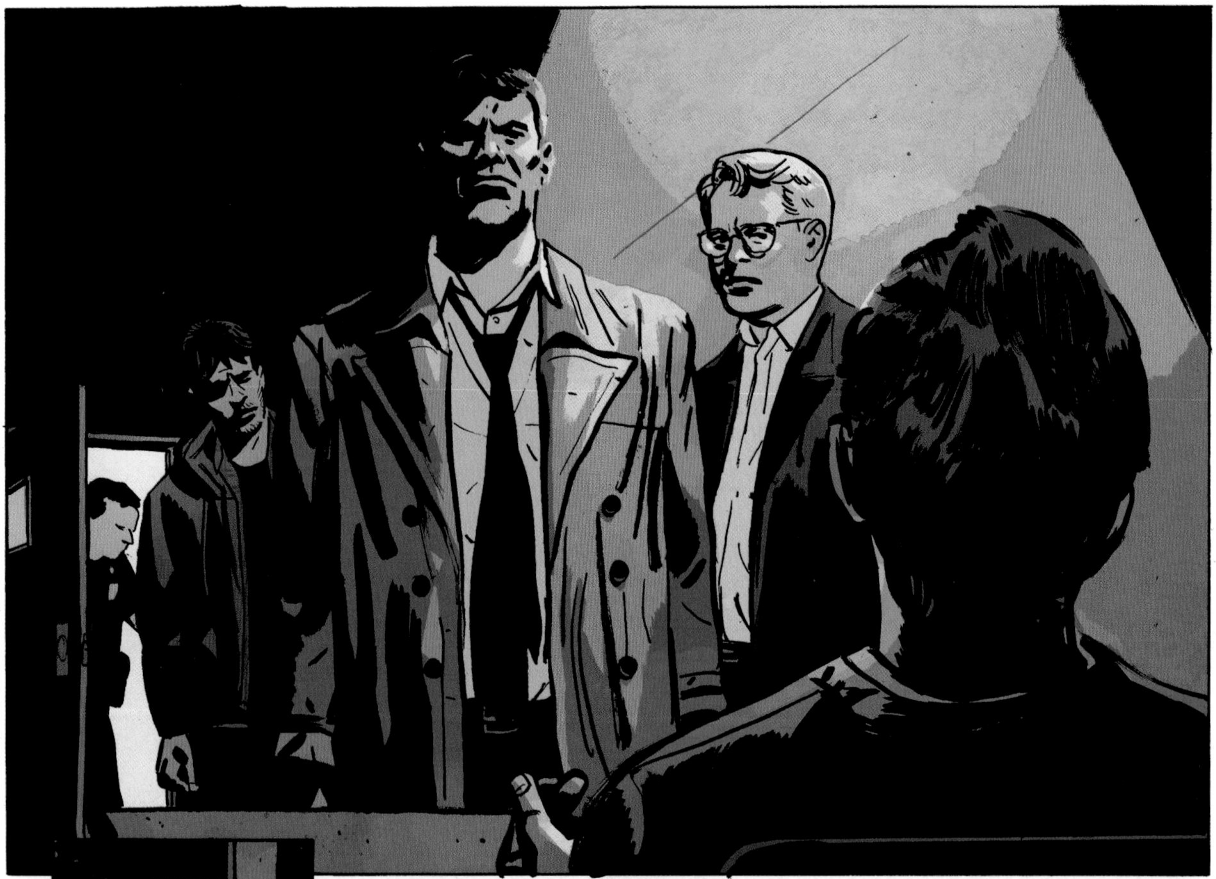

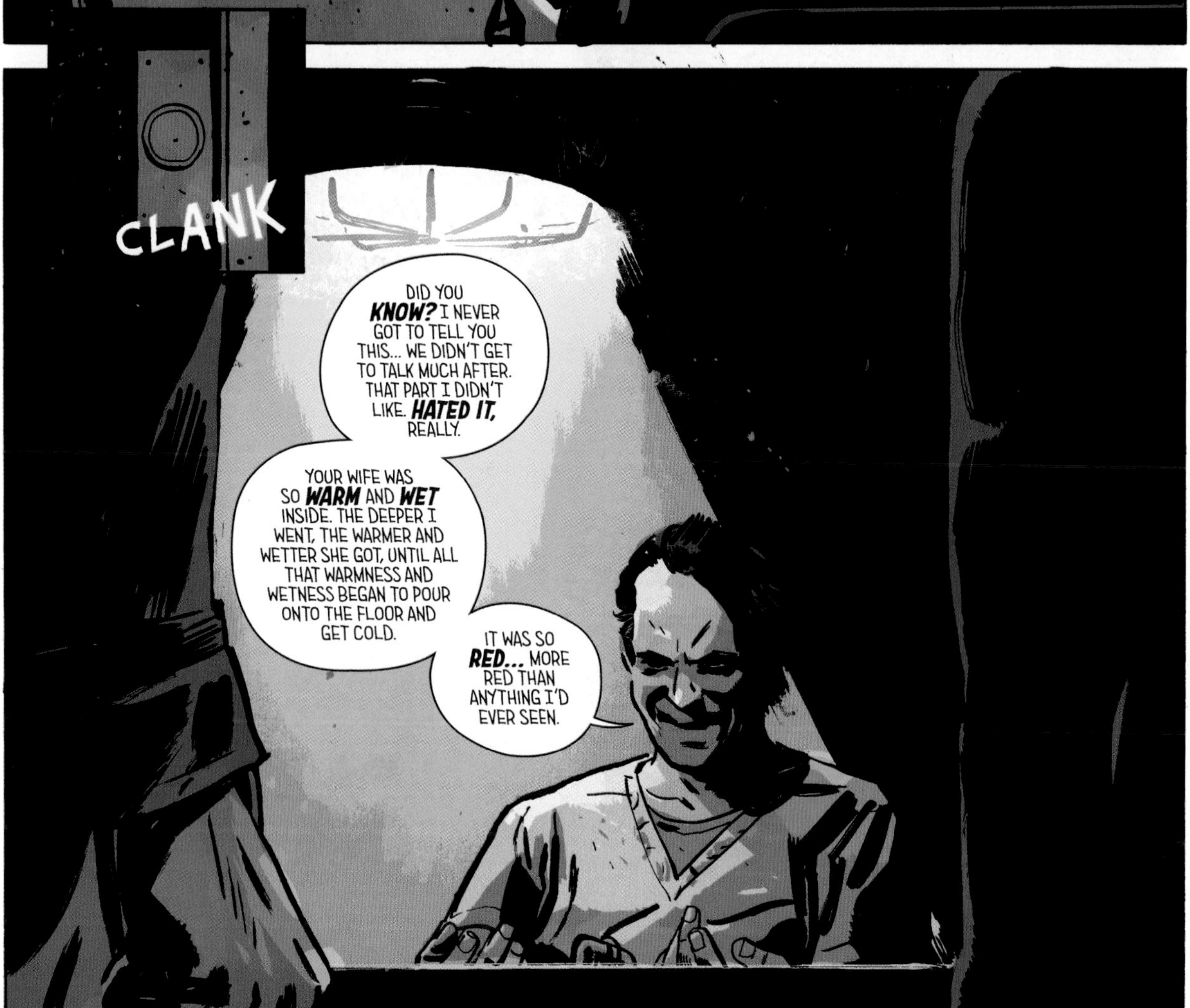
CLANK
DID YOU KNOW? I NEVER GOT TO TELL YOU THIS... WE DIDN'T GET TO TALK MUCH AFTER. THAT PART I DIDN'T LIKE. HATED IT, REALLY.
YOUR WIFE WAS SO WARM AND WET INSIDE. THE DEEPER I WENT, THE WARMER AND WETTER SHE GOT, UNTIL ALL THAT WARMNESS AND WETNESS BEGAN TO POUR ONTO THE FLOOR AND GET COLD.
IT WAS SO RED... MORE RED THAN ANYTHING I'D EVER SEEN.

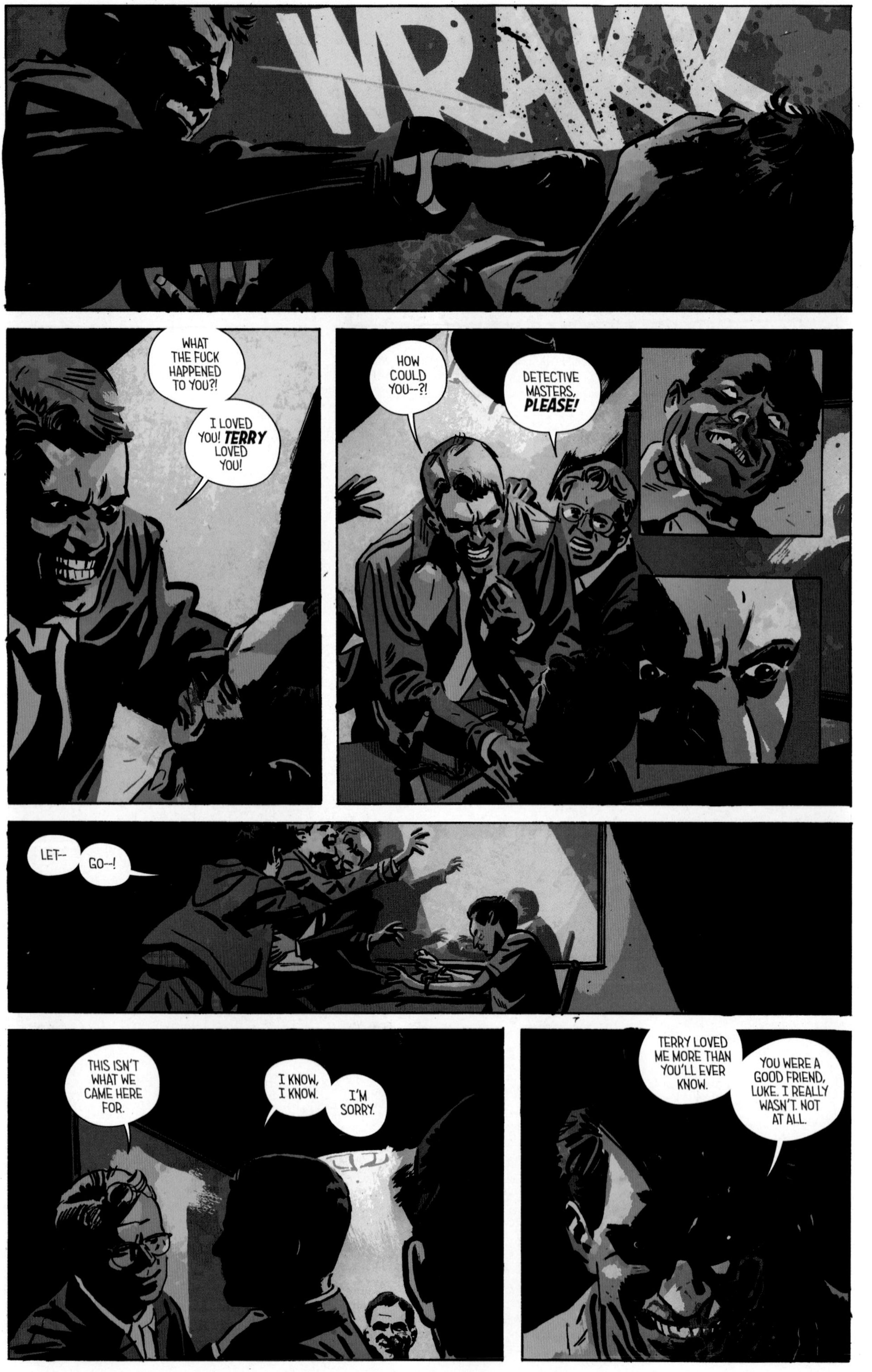
WRAKK
WHAT THE FUCK HAPPENED TO YOU?!
I LOVED YOU! TERRY LOVED YOU!
HOW COULD YOU--?!
DETECTIVE MASTERS, PLEASE!
LET--
GO--!
THIS ISN'T WHAT WE CAME HERE FOR.
I KNOW, I KNOW.
I'M SORRY.
TERRY LOVED ME MORE THAN YOU'LL EVER KNOW.
YOU WERE A GOOD FRIEND, LUKE. I REALLY WASN'T. NOT AT ALL.

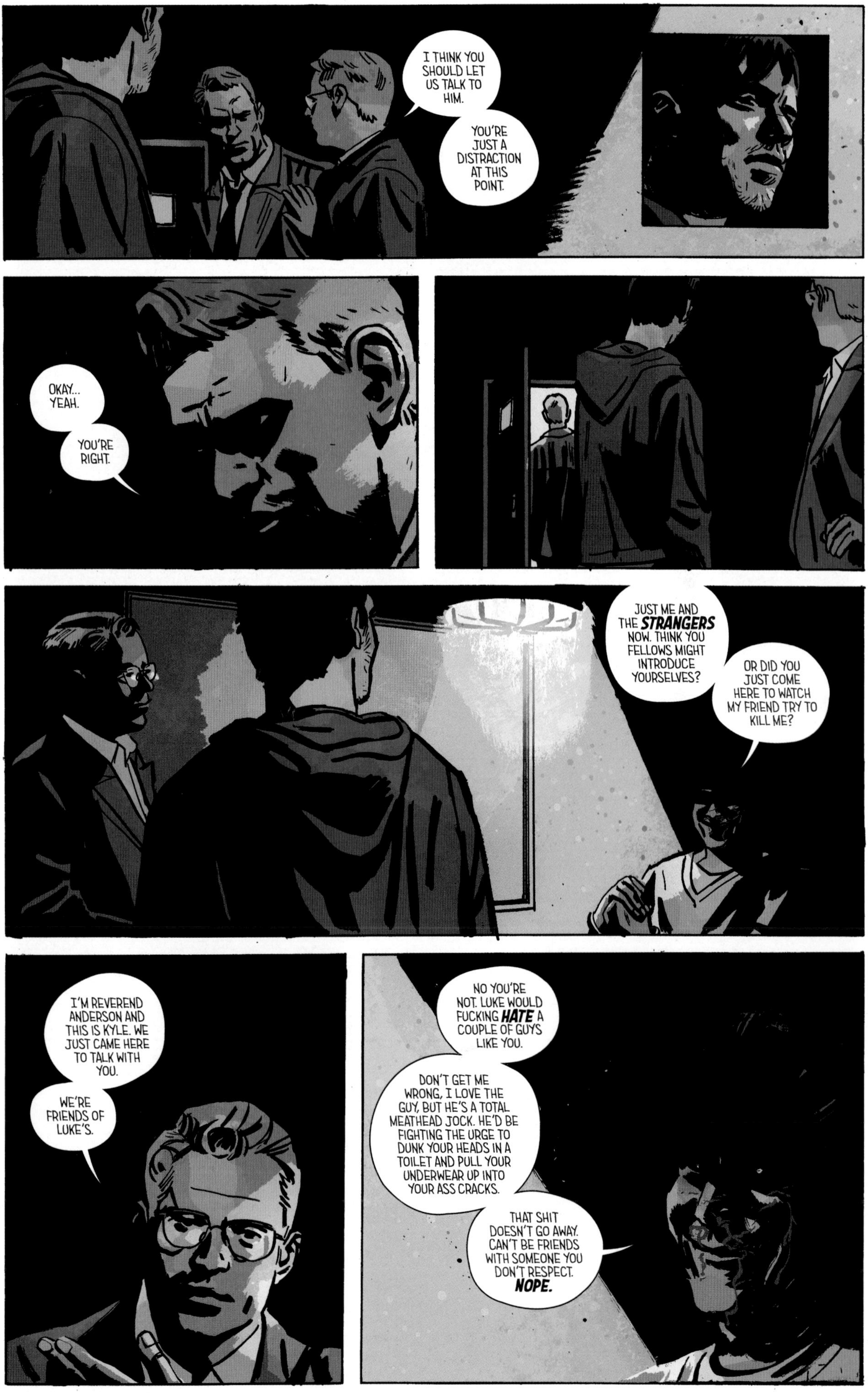
I THINK YOU SHOULD LET US TALK TO HIM.
YOU'RE JUST A DISTRACTION AT THIS POINT.
OKAY... YEAH.
YOU'RE RIGHT.
JUST ME AND THE ***STRANGERS*** NOW. THINK YOU FELLOWS MIGHT INTRODUCE YOURSELVES?
OR DID YOU JUST COME HERE TO WATCH MY FRIEND TRY TO KILL ME?
I'M REVEREND ANDERSON AND THIS IS KYLE. WE JUST CAME HERE TO TALK WITH YOU.
WE'RE FRIENDS OF LUKE'S.
NO YOU'RE NOT. LUKE WOULD FUCKING ***HATE*** A COUPLE OF GUYS LIKE YOU.
DON'T GET ME WRONG, I LOVE THE GUY, BUT HE'S A TOTAL MEATHEAD JOCK. HE'D BE FIGHTING THE URGE TO DUNK YOUR HEADS IN A TOILET AND PULL YOUR UNDERWEAR UP INTO YOUR ASS CRACKS.
THAT SHIT DOESN'T GO AWAY. CAN'T BE FRIENDS WITH SOMEONE YOU DON'T RESPECT. ***NOPE.***

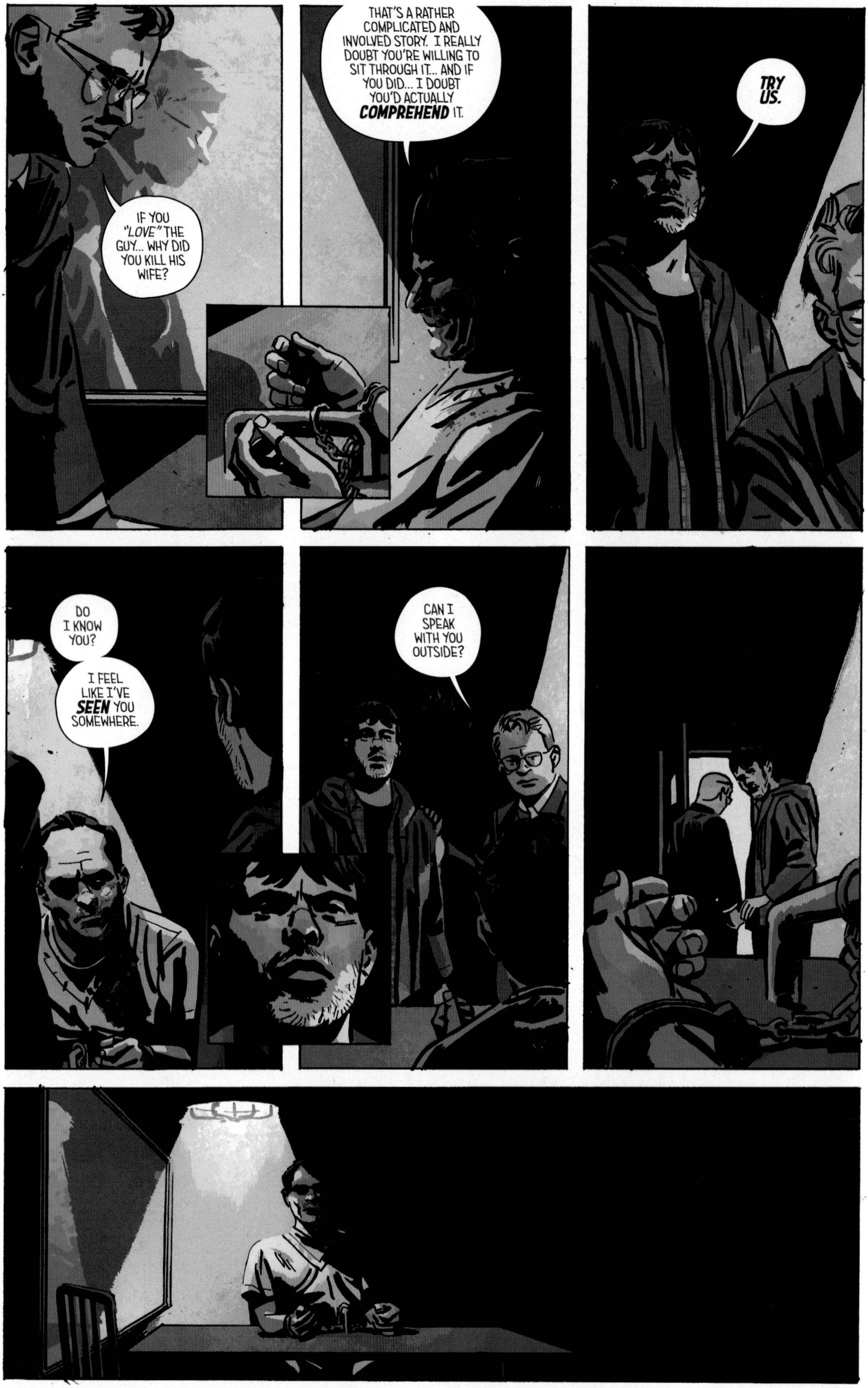
IF YOU "LOVE" THE GUY... WHY DID YOU KILL HIS WIFE?
THAT'S A RATHER COMPLICATED AND INVOLVED STORY. I REALLY DOUBT YOU'RE WILLING TO SIT THROUGH IT... AND IF YOU DID... I DOUBT YOU'D ACTUALLY COMPREHEND IT.
TRY US.
DO I KNOW YOU?
I FEEL LIKE I'VE SEEN YOU SOMEWHERE.
CAN I SPEAK WITH YOU OUTSIDE?

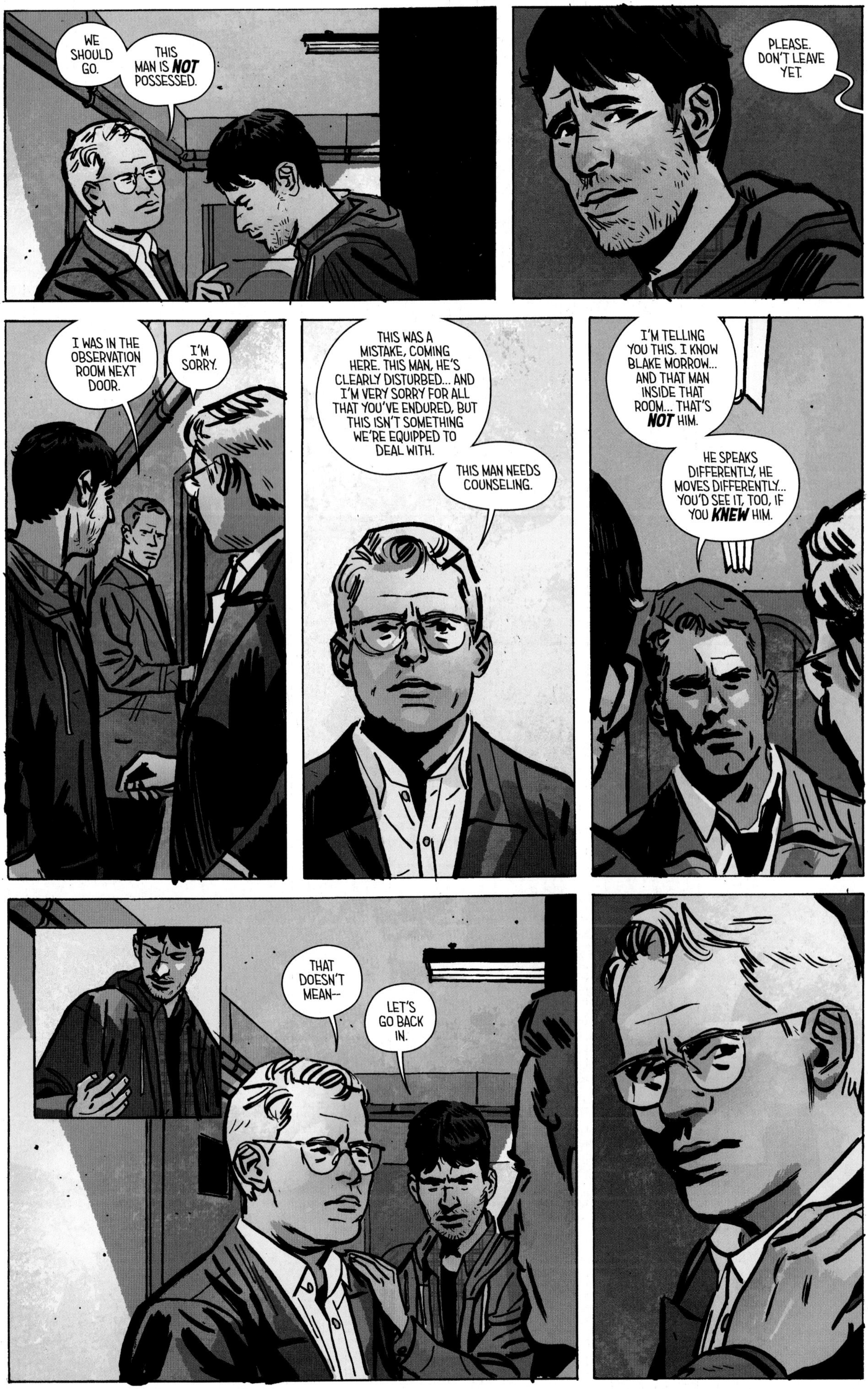
WE SHOULD GO.
THIS MAN IS **NOT** POSSESSED.
PLEASE. DON'T LEAVE YET.
I WAS IN THE OBSERVATION ROOM NEXT DOOR.
I'M SORRY.
THIS WAS A MISTAKE, COMING HERE. THIS MAN, HE'S CLEARLY DISTURBED... AND I'M VERY SORRY FOR ALL THAT YOU'VE ENDURED, BUT THIS ISN'T SOMETHING WE'RE EQUIPPED TO DEAL WITH.
THIS MAN NEEDS COUNSELING.
I'M TELLING YOU THIS. I KNOW BLAKE MORROW... AND THAT MAN INSIDE THAT ROOM... THAT'S **NOT** HIM.
HE SPEAKS DIFFERENTLY, HE MOVES DIFFERENTLY... YOU'D SEE IT, TOO, IF YOU **KNEW** HIM.
THAT DOESN'T MEAN--
LET'S GO BACK IN.

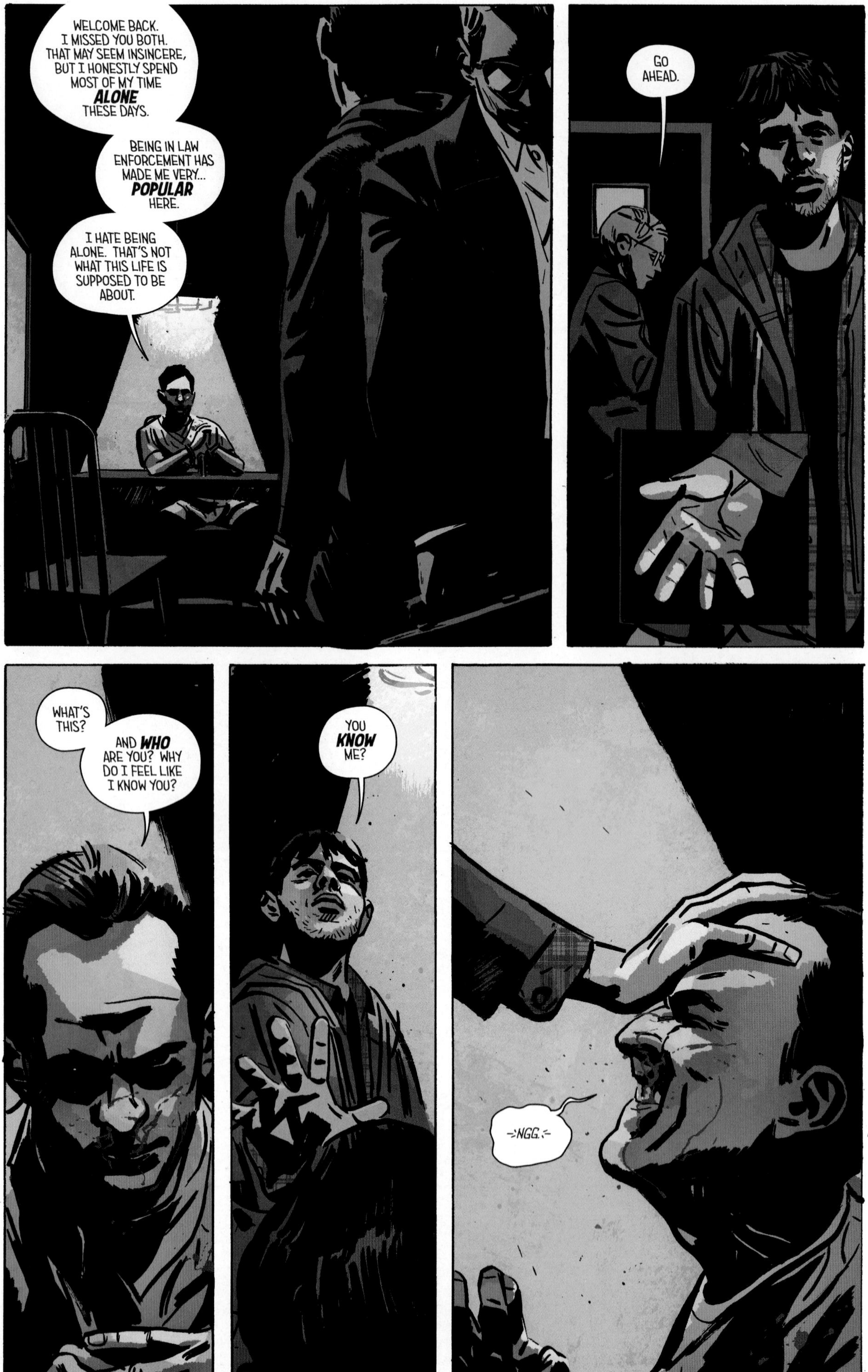
WELCOME BACK. I MISSED YOU BOTH. THAT MAY SEEM INSINCERE, BUT I HONESTLY SPEND MOST OF MY TIME ALONE THESE DAYS.
BEING IN LAW ENFORCEMENT HAS MADE ME VERY... POPULAR HERE.
I HATE BEING ALONE. THAT'S NOT WHAT THIS LIFE IS SUPPOSED TO BE ABOUT.
GO AHEAD.
WHAT'S THIS?
AND WHO ARE YOU? WHY DO I FEEL LIKE I KNOW YOU?
YOU KNOW ME?
-NGG.-

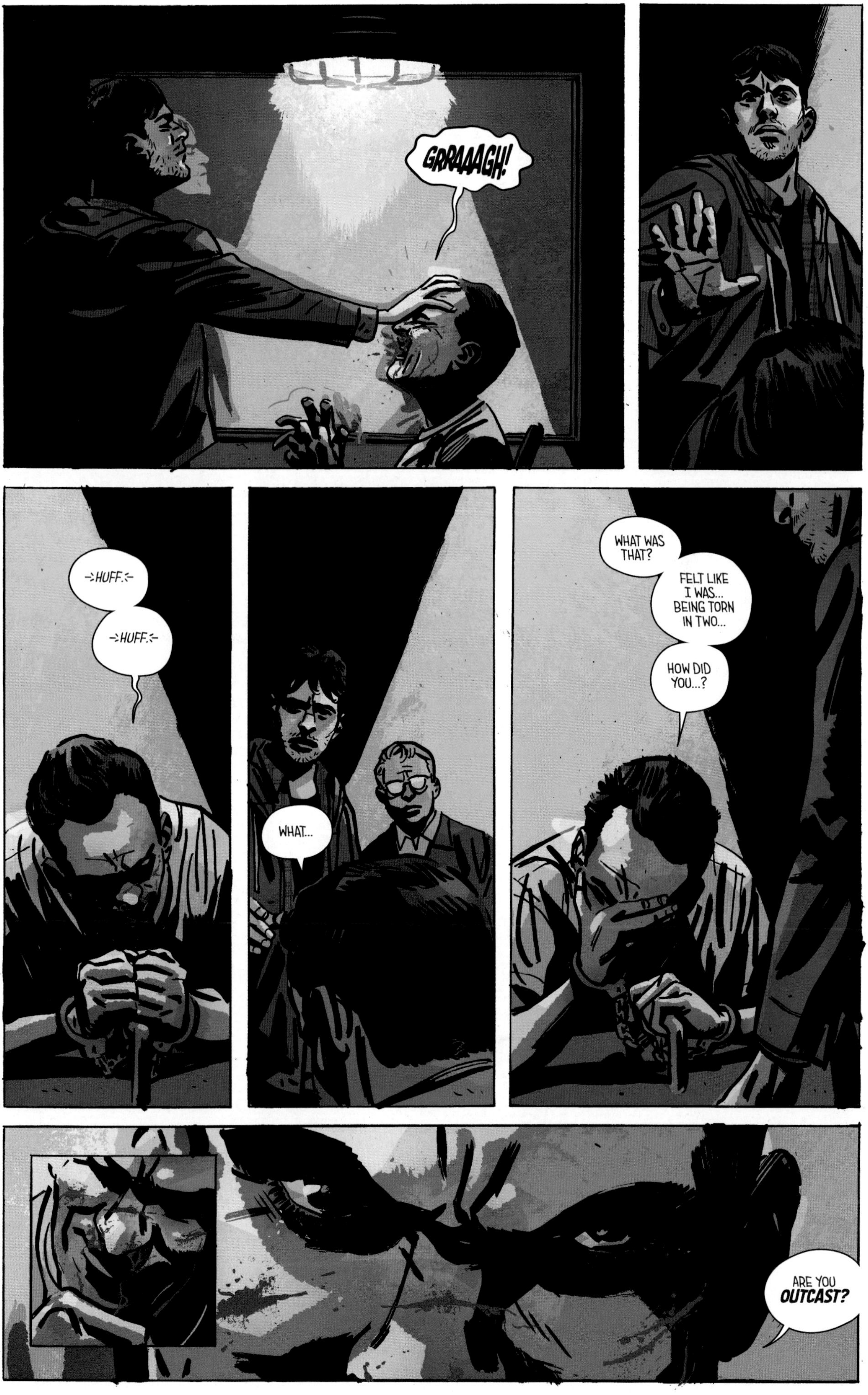
GRRAAAGH!
-HUFF.-
-HUFF.-
WHAT...
WHAT WAS THAT?
FELT LIKE I WAS... BEING TORN IN TWO...
HOW DID YOU...?
ARE YOU OUTCAST?

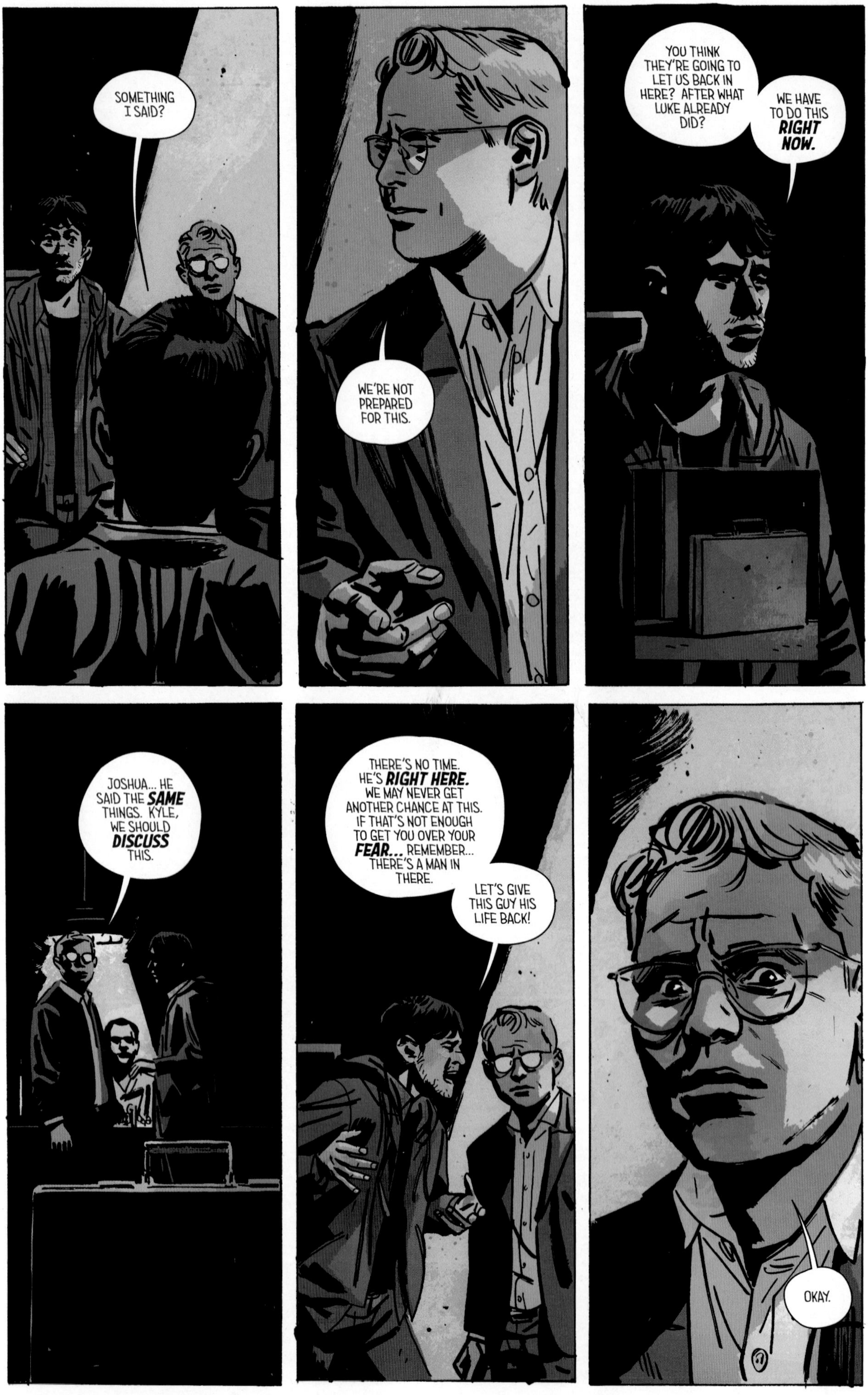
SOMETHING I SAID?
WE'RE NOT PREPARED FOR THIS.
YOU THINK THEY'RE GOING TO LET US BACK IN HERE? AFTER WHAT LUKE ALREADY DID?
WE HAVE TO DO THIS **RIGHT NOW.**
JOSHUA... HE SAID THE **SAME** THINGS. KYLE, WE SHOULD **DISCUSS** THIS.
THERE'S NO TIME. HE'S **RIGHT HERE.** WE MAY NEVER GET ANOTHER CHANCE AT THIS. IF THAT'S NOT ENOUGH TO GET YOU OVER YOUR **FEAR...** REMEMBER... THERE'S A MAN IN THERE.
LET'S GIVE THIS GUY HIS LIFE BACK!
OKAY.

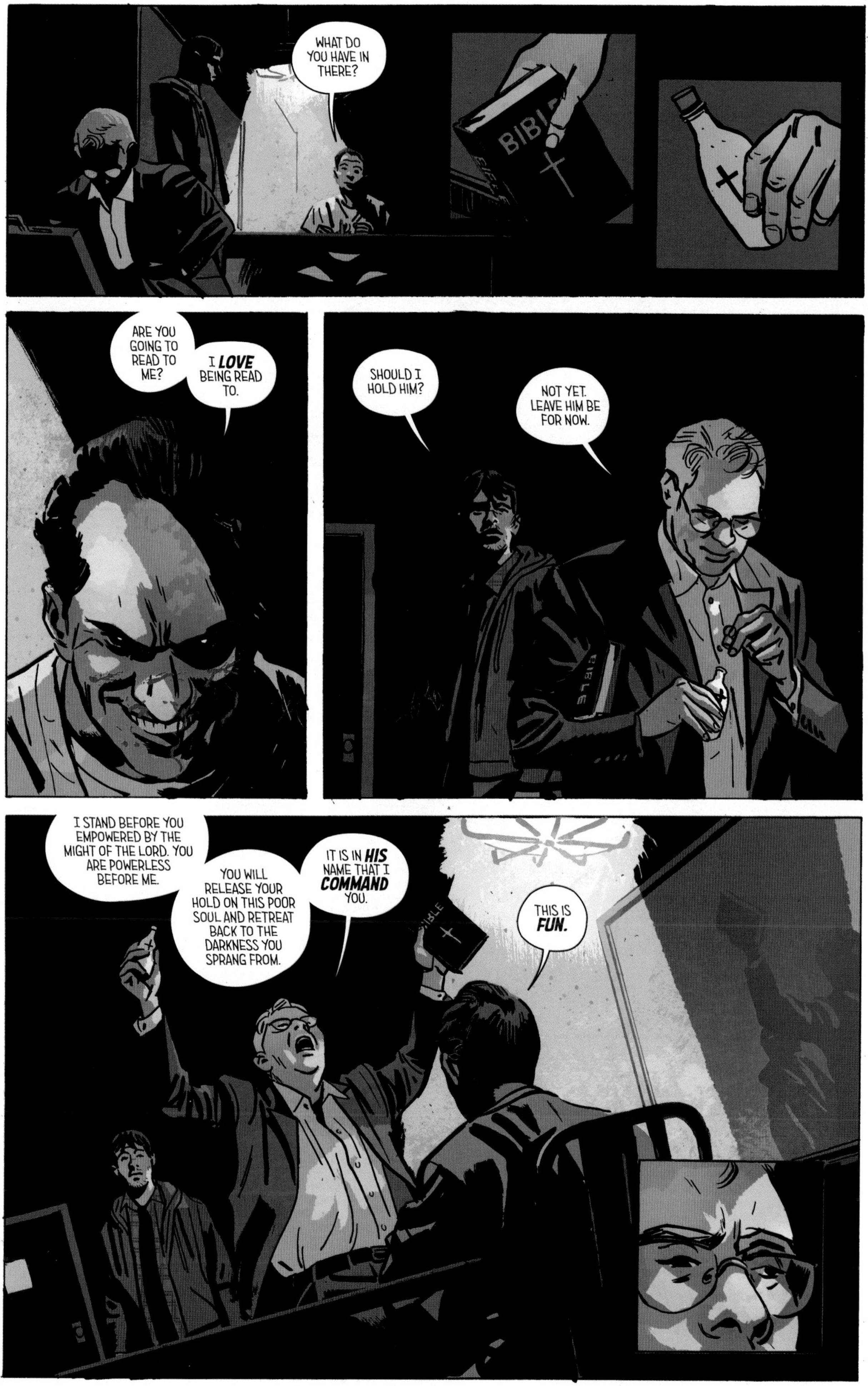
WHAT DO YOU HAVE IN THERE?
BIBLE
ARE YOU GOING TO READ TO ME?
I **LOVE** BEING READ TO.
SHOULD I HOLD HIM?
NOT YET. LEAVE HIM BE FOR NOW.
I STAND BEFORE YOU EMPOWERED BY THE MIGHT OF THE LORD. YOU ARE POWERLESS BEFORE ME.
YOU WILL RELEASE YOUR HOLD ON THIS POOR SOUL AND RETREAT BACK TO THE DARKNESS YOU SPRANG FROM.
IT IS IN **HIS** NAME THAT I **COMMAND** YOU.
THIS IS **FUN.**

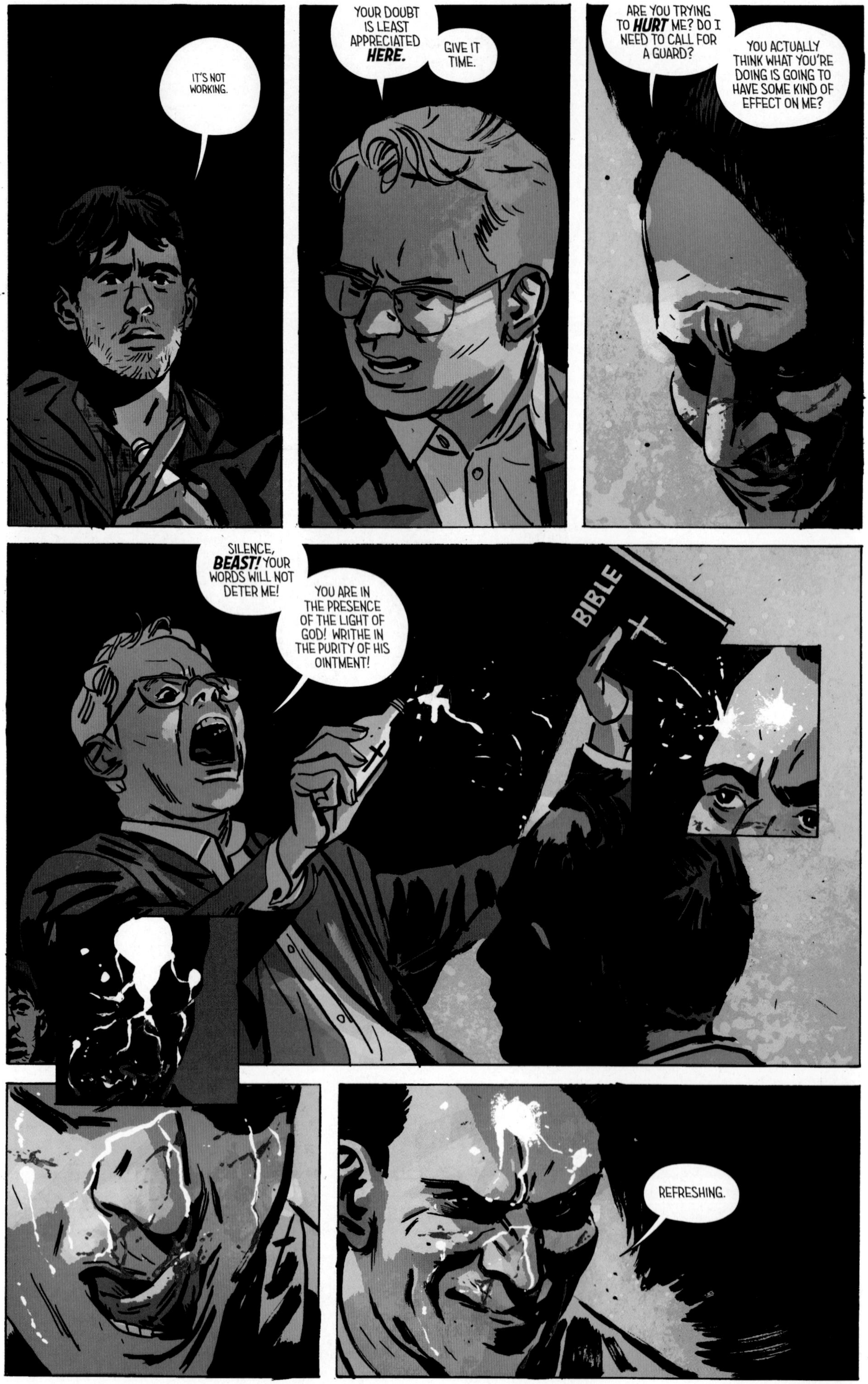
IT'S NOT WORKING.
YOUR DOUBT IS LEAST APPRECIATED HERE.
GIVE IT TIME.
ARE YOU TRYING TO HURT ME? DO I NEED TO CALL FOR A GUARD?
YOU ACTUALLY THINK WHAT YOU'RE DOING IS GOING TO HAVE SOME KIND OF EFFECT ON ME?
SILENCE, BEAST! YOUR WORDS WILL NOT DETER ME!
YOU ARE IN THE PRESENCE OF THE LIGHT OF GOD! WRITHE IN THE PURITY OF HIS OINTMENT!
BIBLE
REFRESHING.

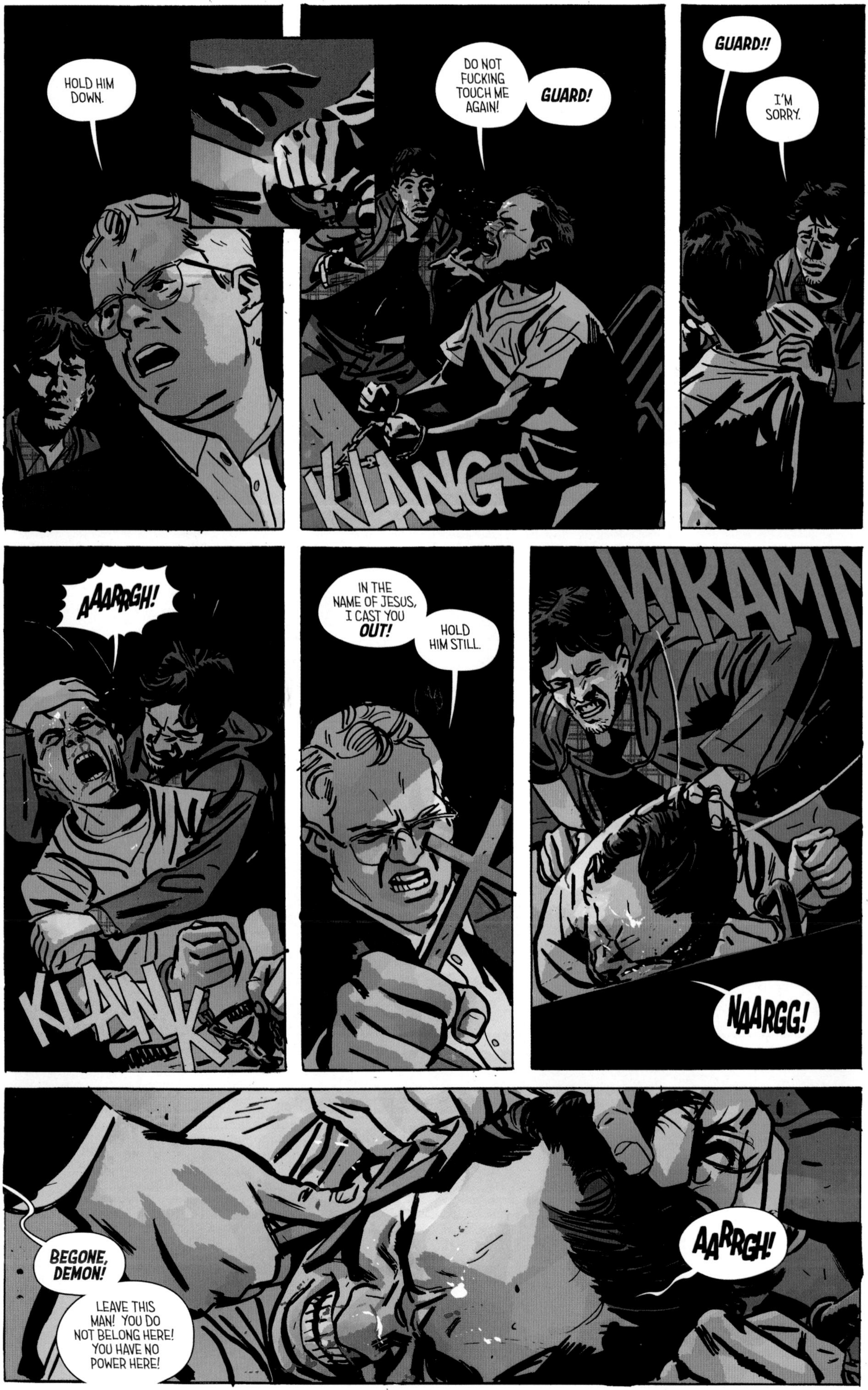
HOLD HIM DOWN.
DO NOT FUCKING TOUCH ME AGAIN!
GUARD!
KLANG
GUARD!!
I'M SORRY.
AAARRGH!
KLANK
IN THE NAME OF JESUS, I CAST YOU OUT!
HOLD HIM STILL.
WRAMM
NAARGG!
BEGONE, DEMON!
LEAVE THIS MAN! YOU DO NOT BELONG HERE! YOU HAVE NO POWER HERE!
AARRGH!

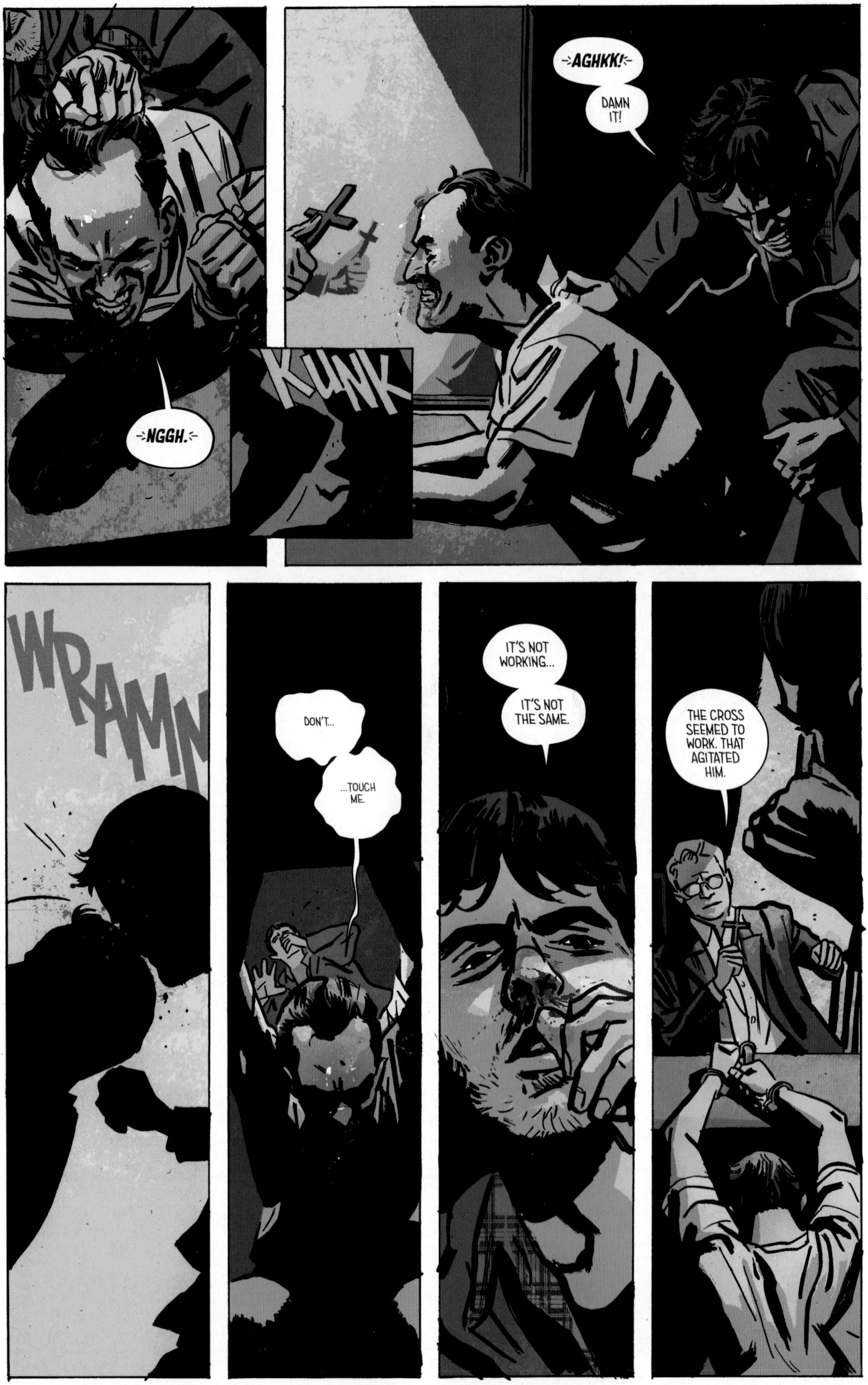
NGGH.
KUNK
AGHKK!
DAMN IT!
WRAMM
DON'T...
...TOUCH ME.
IT'S NOT WORKING...
IT'S NOT THE SAME.
THE CROSS SEEMED TO WORK. THAT AGITATED HIM.

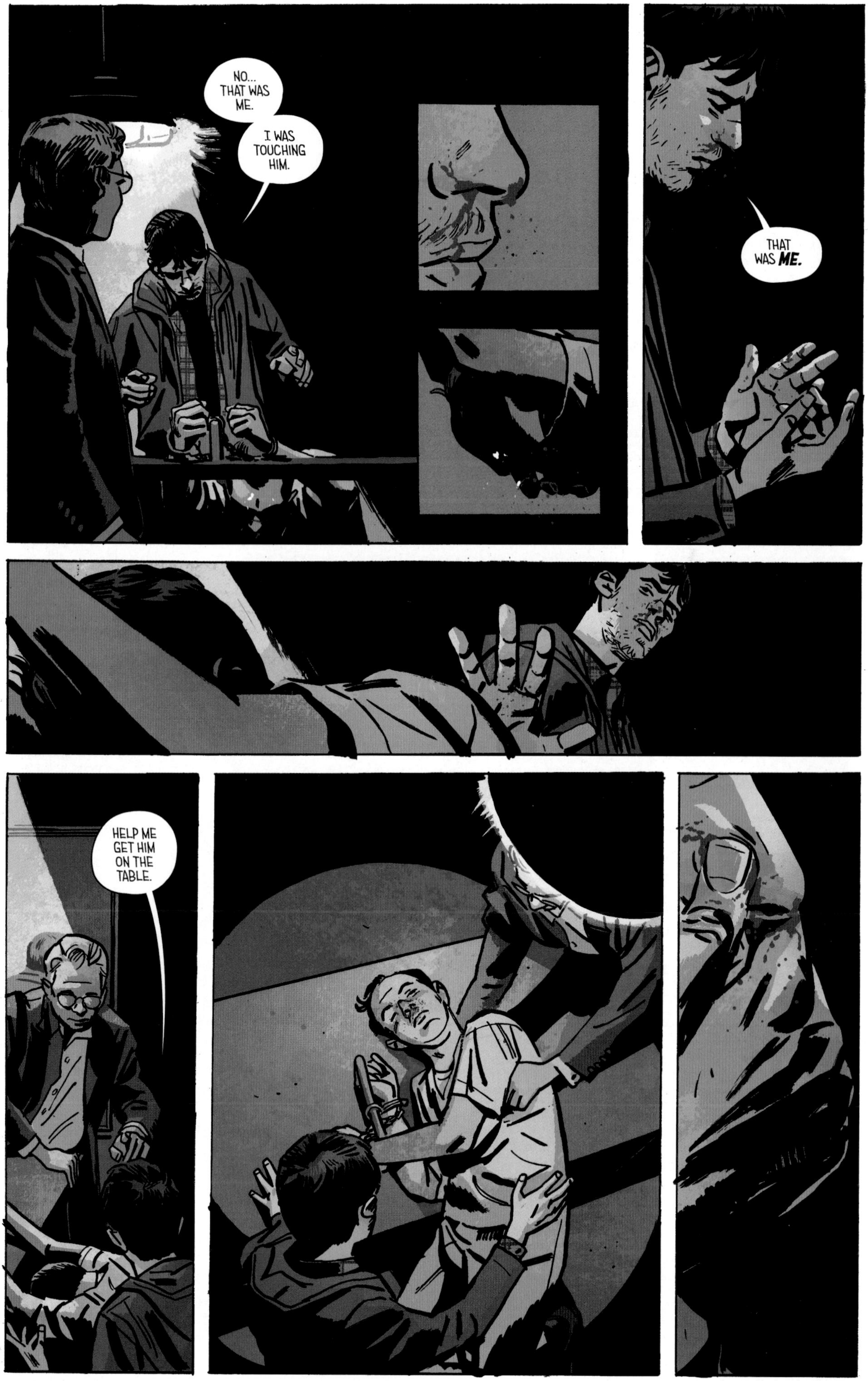
NO... THAT WAS ME.
I WAS TOUCHING HIM.
THAT WAS ME.
HELP ME GET HIM ON THE TABLE.

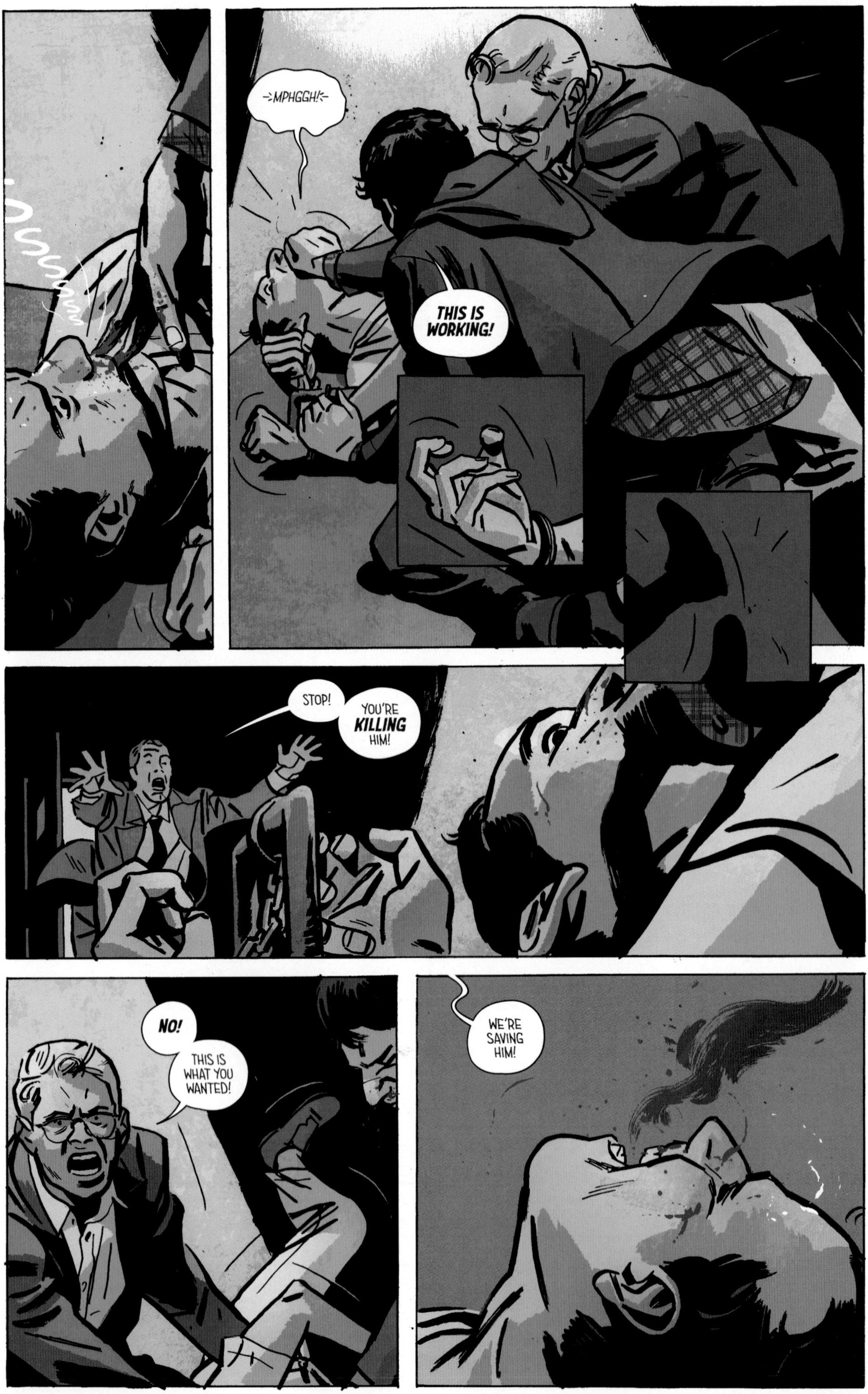
-MPHGGH!-
THIS IS WORKING!
STOP!
YOU'RE KILLING HIM!
NO!
THIS IS WHAT YOU WANTED!
WE'RE SAVING HIM!

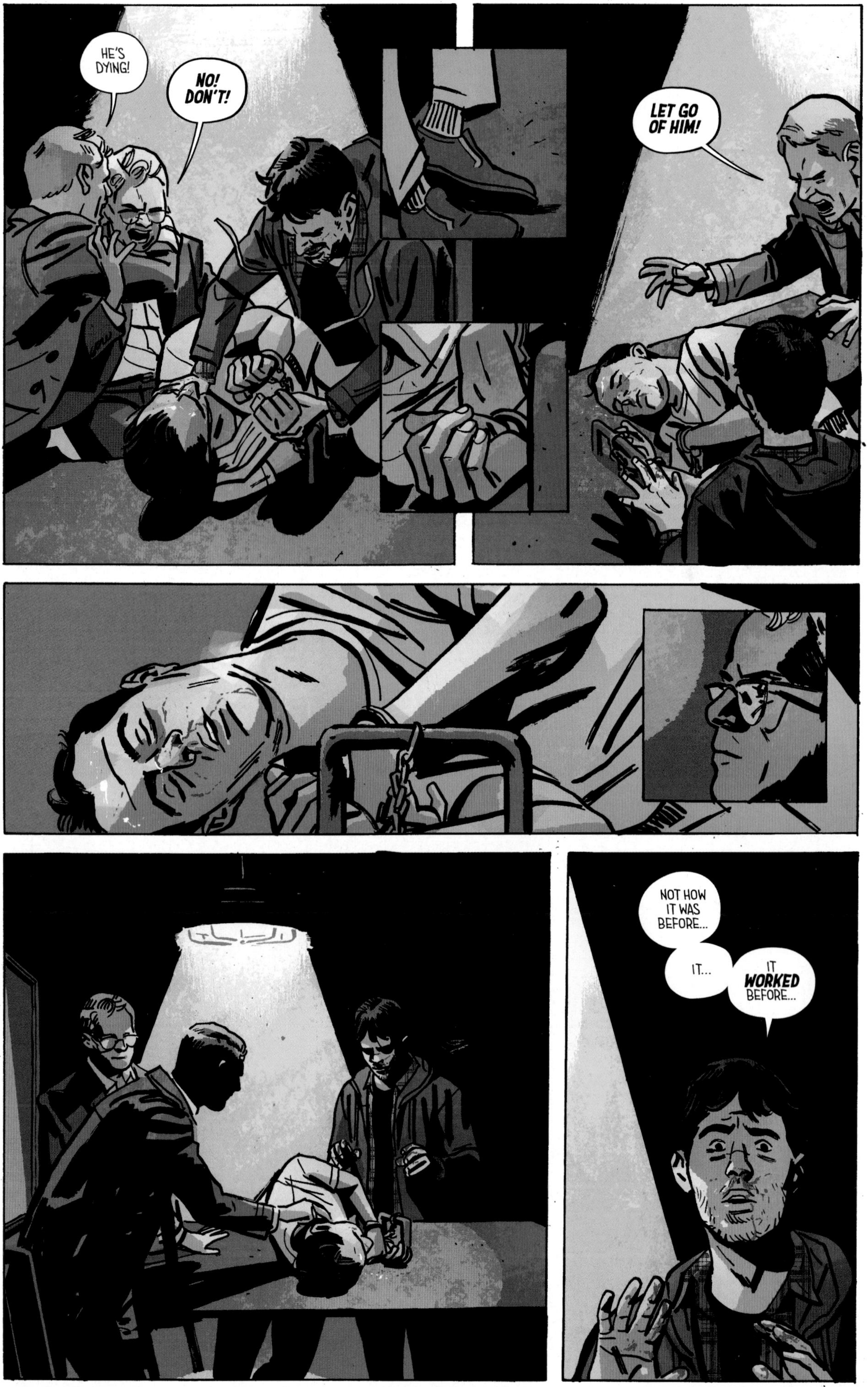
HE'S DYING!
NO! DON'T!
LET GO OF HIM!
NOT HOW IT WAS BEFORE...
IT...
IT WORKED BEFORE...

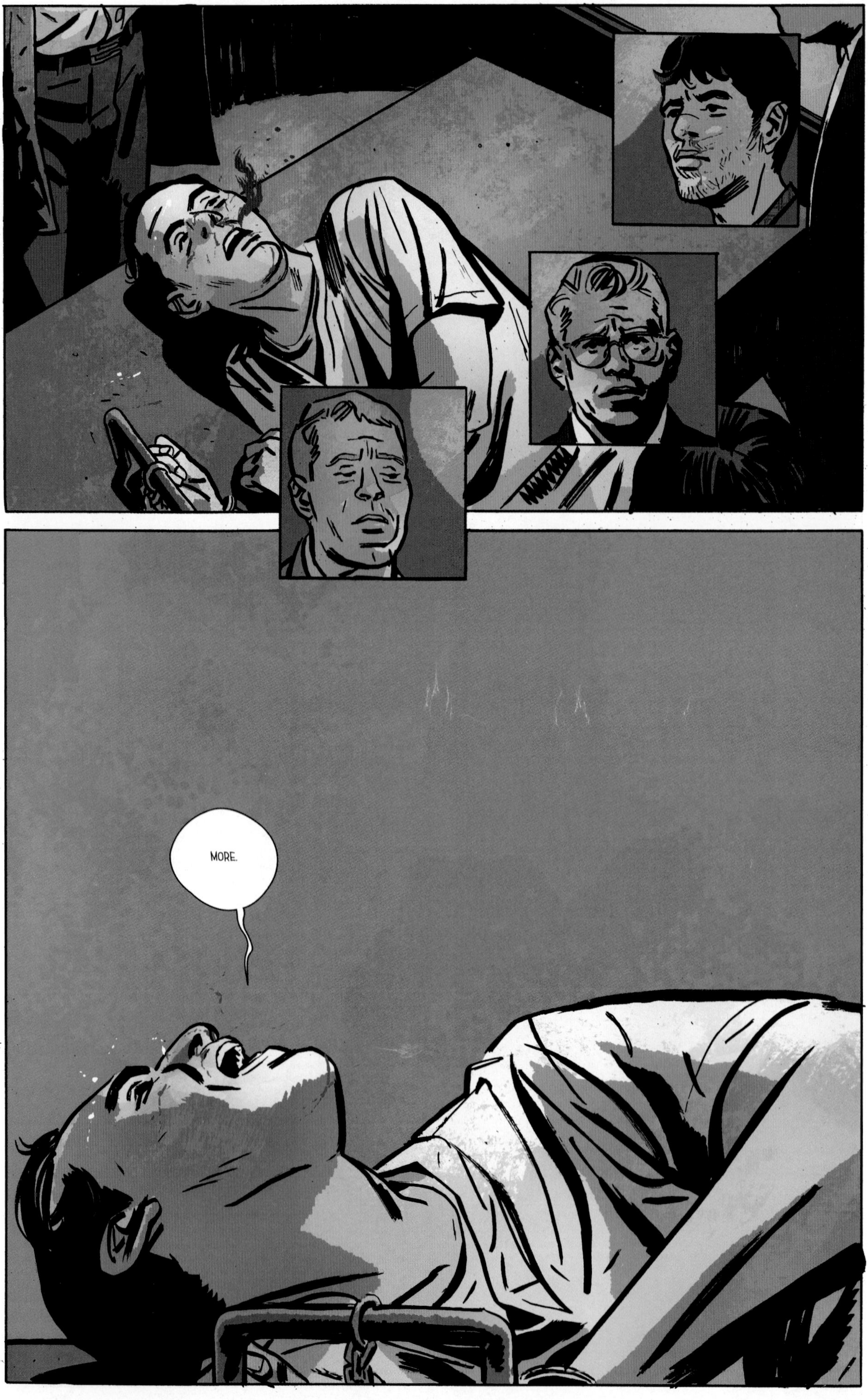
MORE.

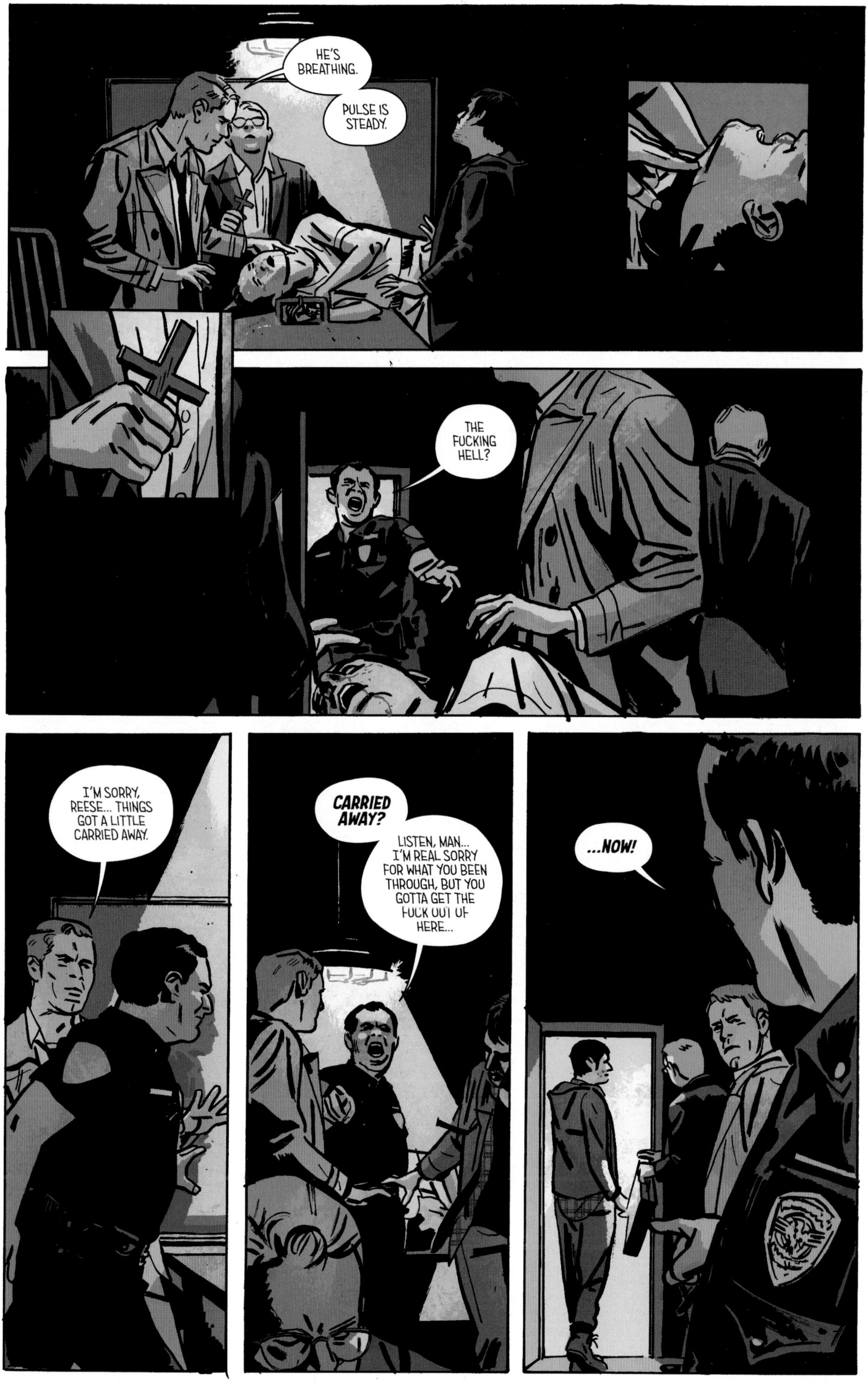
HE'S BREATHING.
PULSE IS STEADY.
THE FUCKING HELL?
I'M SORRY, REESE... THINGS GOT A LITTLE CARRIED AWAY.
CARRIED AWAY?
LISTEN, MAN... I'M REAL SORRY FOR WHAT YOU BEEN THROUGH, BUT YOU GOTTA GET THE FUCK OUT OF HERE...
...NOW!

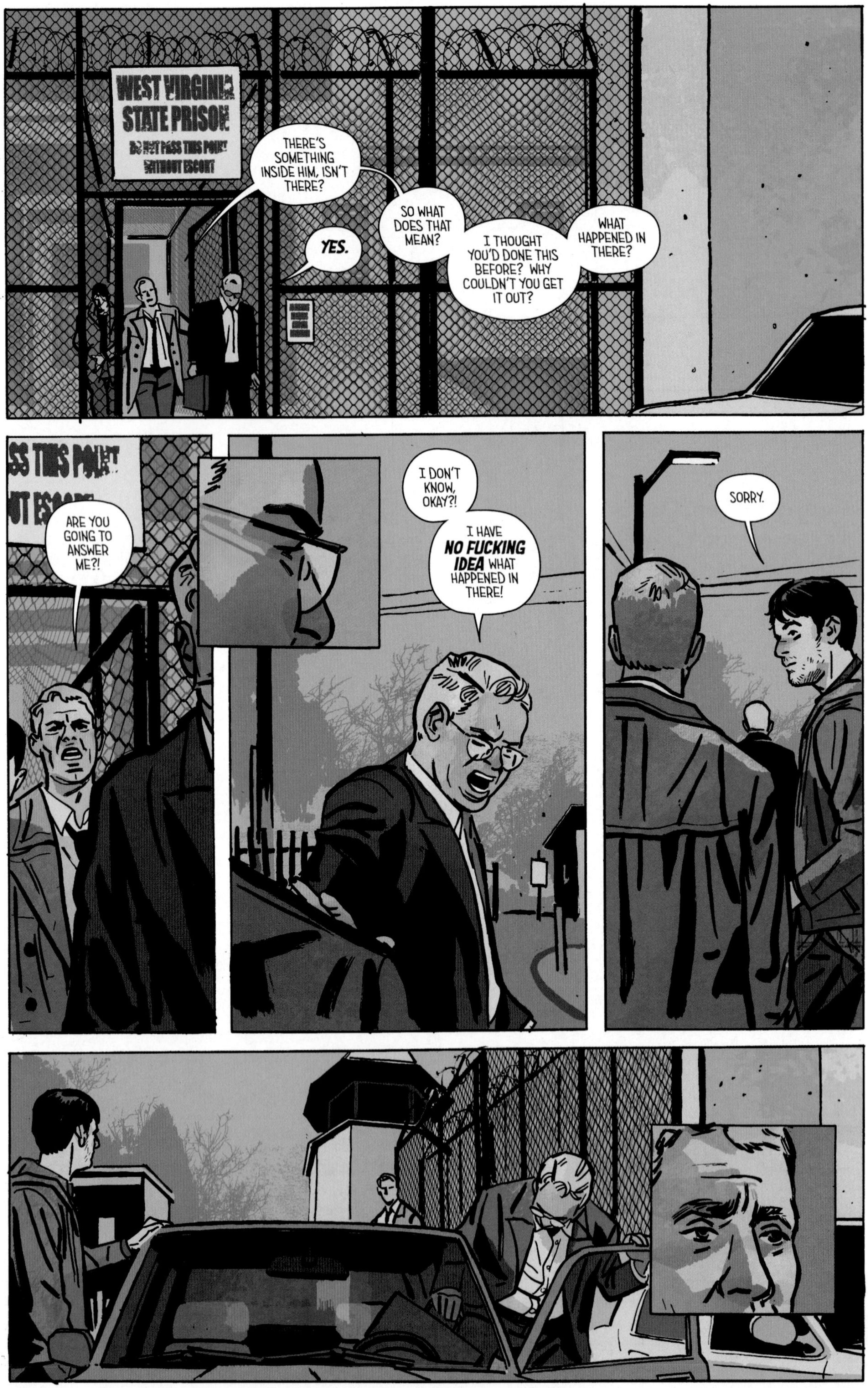
WEST VIRGINIA
STATE PRISON
DO NOT PASS THIS POINT WITHOUT ESCORT
THERE'S SOMETHING INSIDE HIM, ISN'T THERE?
YES.
SO WHAT DOES THAT MEAN?
I THOUGHT YOU'D DONE THIS BEFORE? WHY COULDN'T YOU GET IT OUT?
WHAT HAPPENED IN THERE?
ARE YOU GOING TO ANSWER ME?!
I DON'T KNOW, OKAY?!
I HAVE NO FUCKING IDEA WHAT HAPPENED IN THERE!
SORRY.

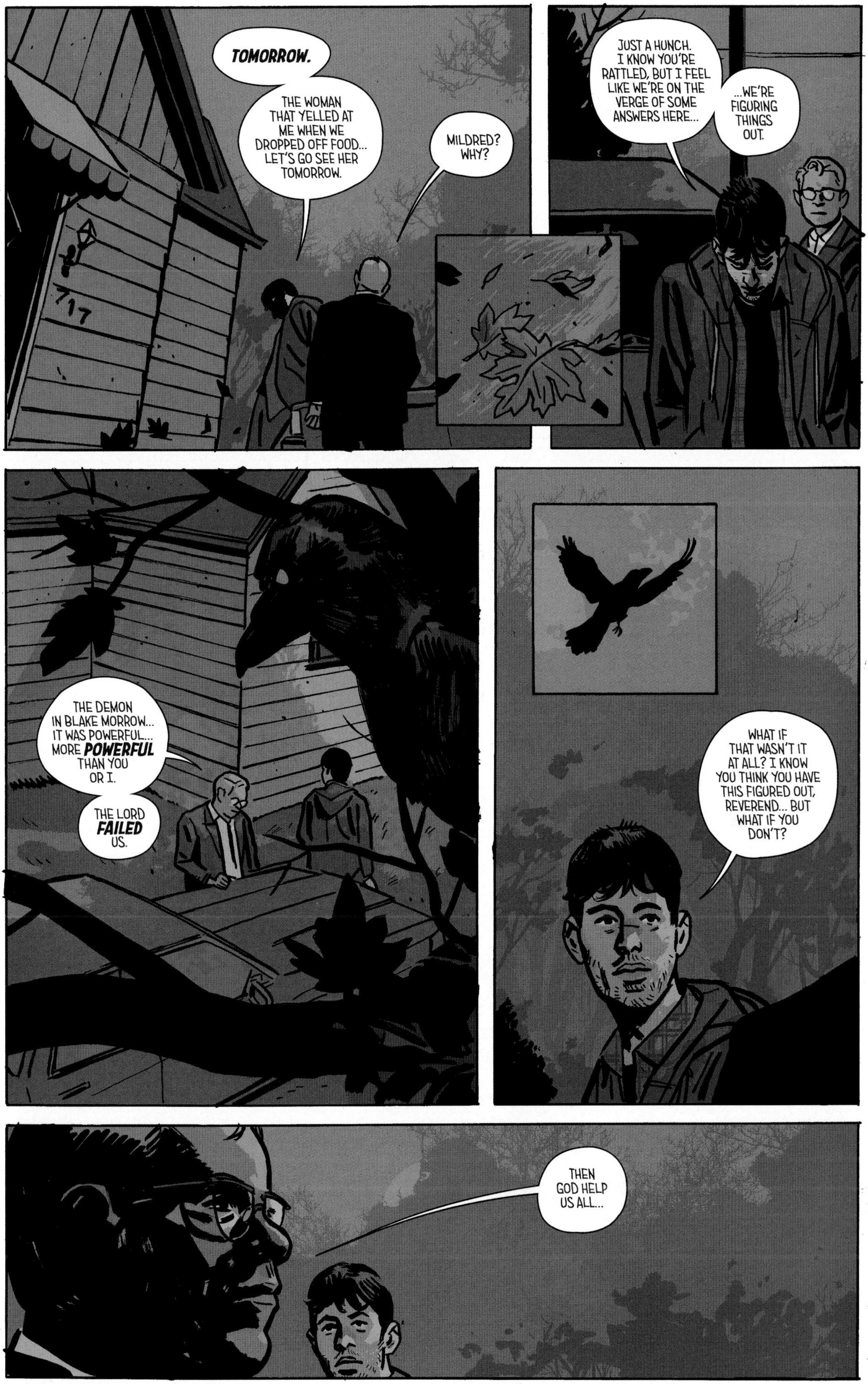
TOMORROW.
THE WOMAN THAT YELLED AT ME WHEN WE DROPPED OFF FOOD... LET'S GO SEE HER TOMORROW.
MILDRED? WHY?
JUST A HUNCH. I KNOW YOU'RE RATTLED, BUT I FEEL LIKE WE'RE ON THE VERGE OF SOME ANSWERS HERE...
...WE'RE FIGURING THINGS OUT.
717
THE DEMON IN BLAKE MORROW... IT WAS POWERFUL... MORE POWERFUL THAN YOU OR I.
THE LORD FAILED US.
WHAT IF THAT WASN'T IT AT ALL? I KNOW YOU THINK YOU HAVE THIS FIGURED OUT, REVEREND... BUT WHAT IF YOU DON'T?
THEN GOD HELP US ALL...

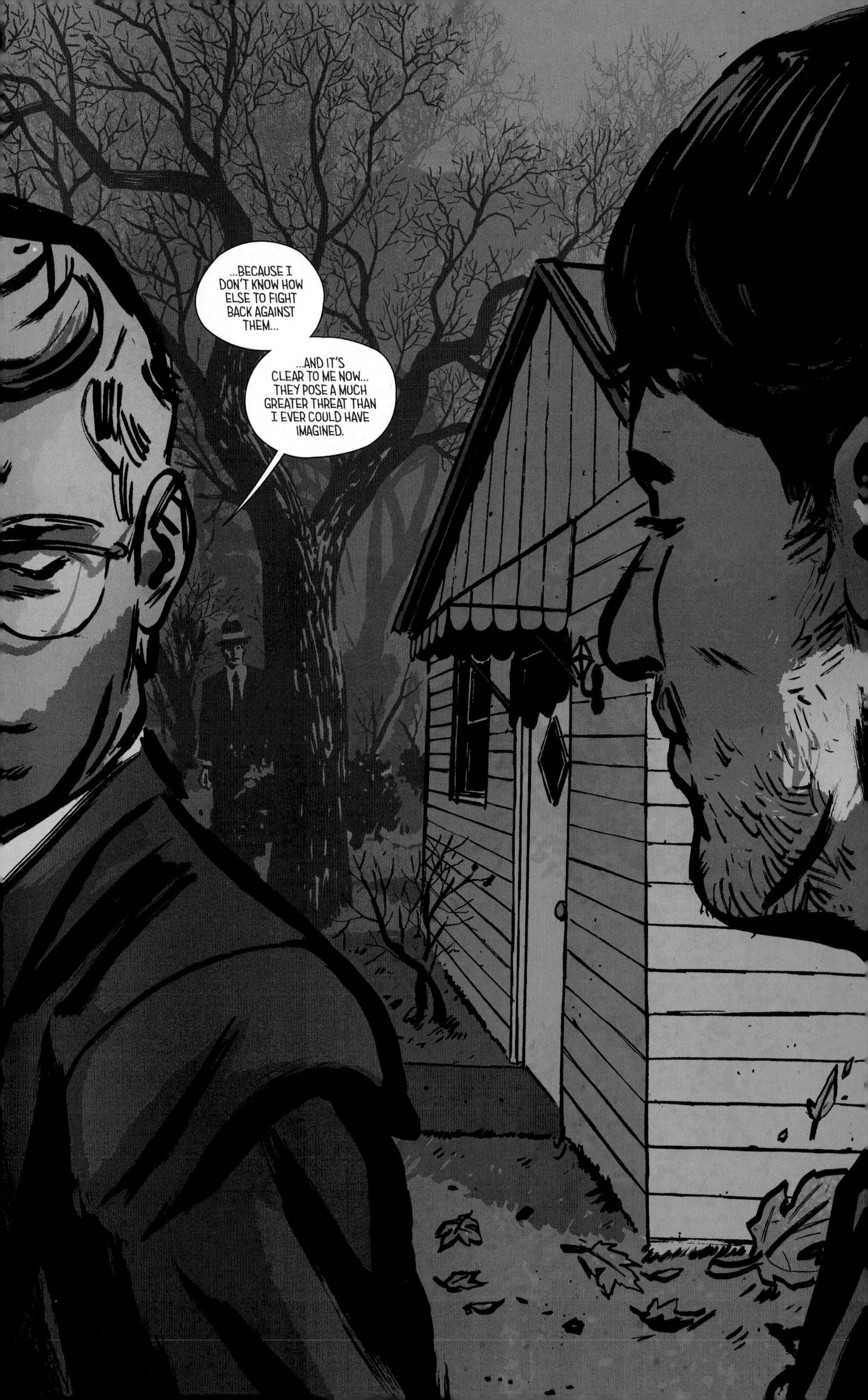
...BECAUSE I DON'T KNOW HOW ELSE TO FIGHT BACK AGAINST THEM...
...AND IT'S CLEAR TO ME NOW... THEY POSE A MUCH GREATER THREAT THAN I EVER COULD HAVE IMAGINED.

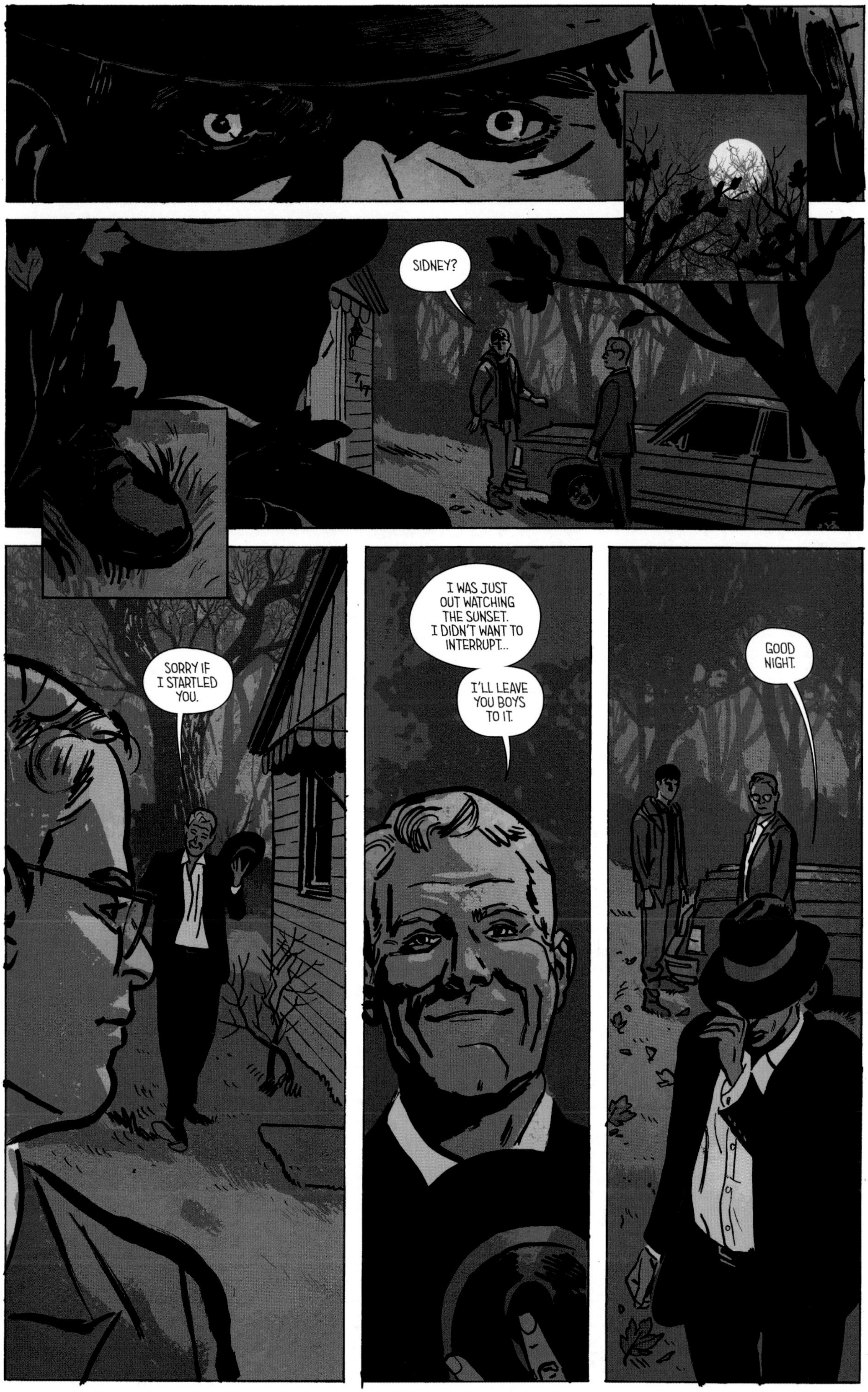
SIDNEY?
SORRY IF I STARTLED YOU.
I WAS JUST OUT WATCHING THE SUNSET. I DIDN'T WANT TO INTERRUPT...
I'LL LEAVE YOU BOYS TO IT.
GOOD NIGHT.

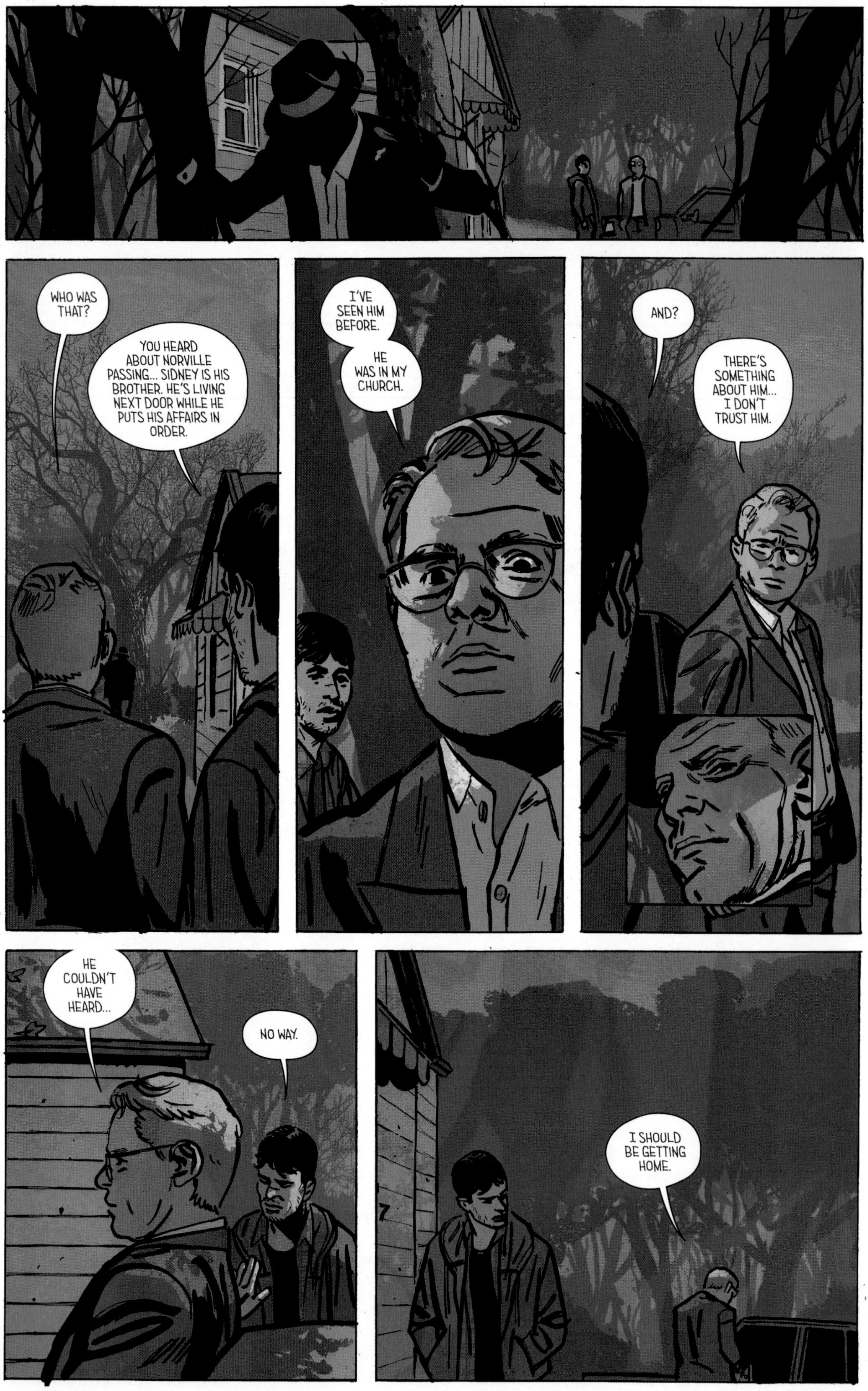
WHO WAS THAT?
YOU HEARD ABOUT NORVILLE PASSING... SIDNEY IS HIS BROTHER. HE'S LIVING NEXT DOOR WHILE HE PUTS HIS AFFAIRS IN ORDER.
I'VE SEEN HIM BEFORE.
HE WAS IN MY CHURCH.
AND?
THERE'S SOMETHING ABOUT HIM... I DON'T TRUST HIM.
HE COULDN'T HAVE HEARD...
NO WAY.
I SHOULD BE GETTING HOME.

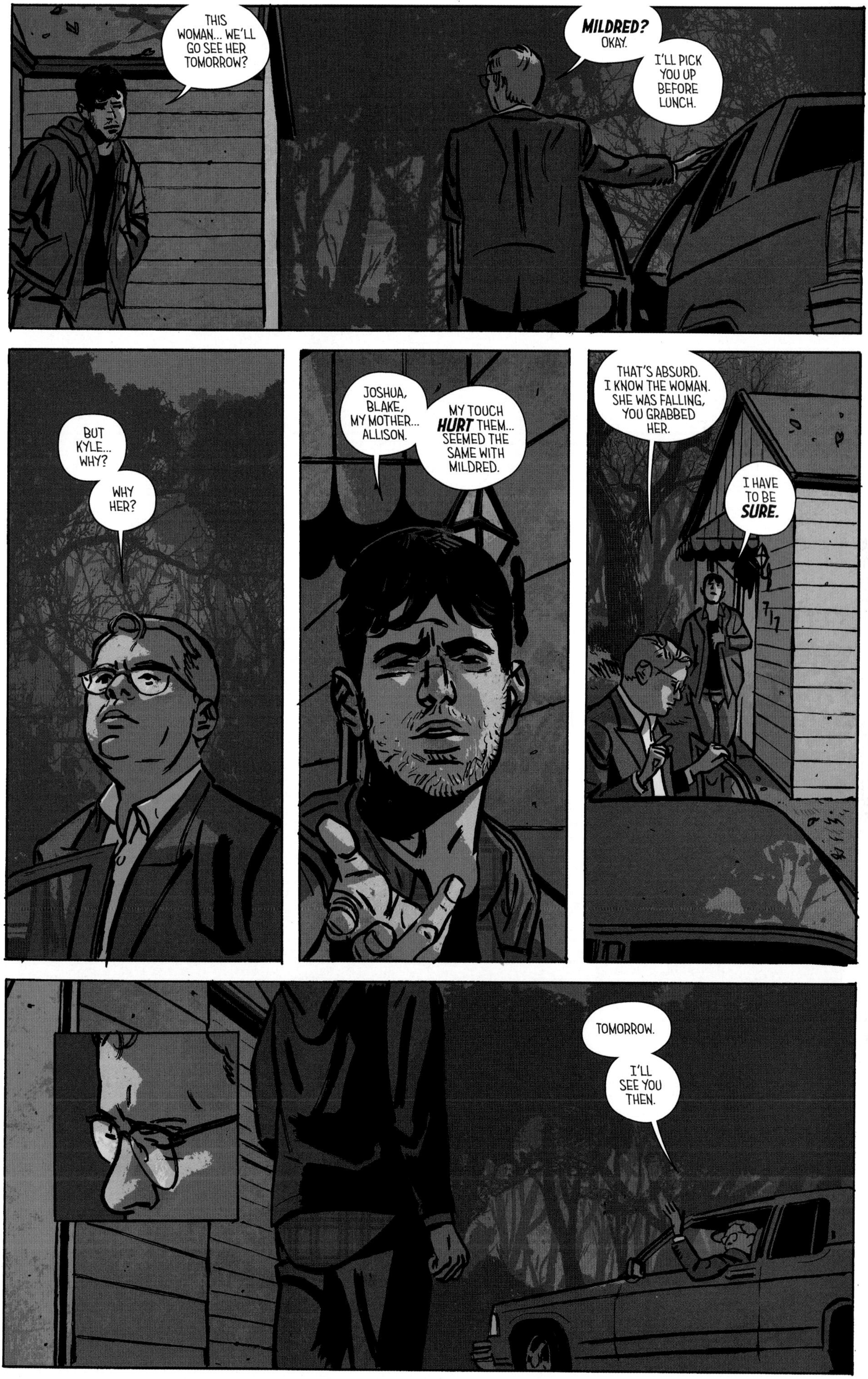
THIS WOMAN... WE'LL GO SEE HER TOMORROW?
MILDRED? OKAY.
I'LL PICK YOU UP BEFORE LUNCH.
BUT KYLE... WHY?
WHY HER?
JOSHUA, BLAKE, MY MOTHER... ALLISON.
MY TOUCH HURT THEM... SEEMED THE SAME WITH MILDRED.
THAT'S ABSURD. I KNOW THE WOMAN. SHE WAS FALLING, YOU GRABBED HER.
I HAVE TO BE SURE.
TOMORROW.
I'LL SEE YOU THEN.

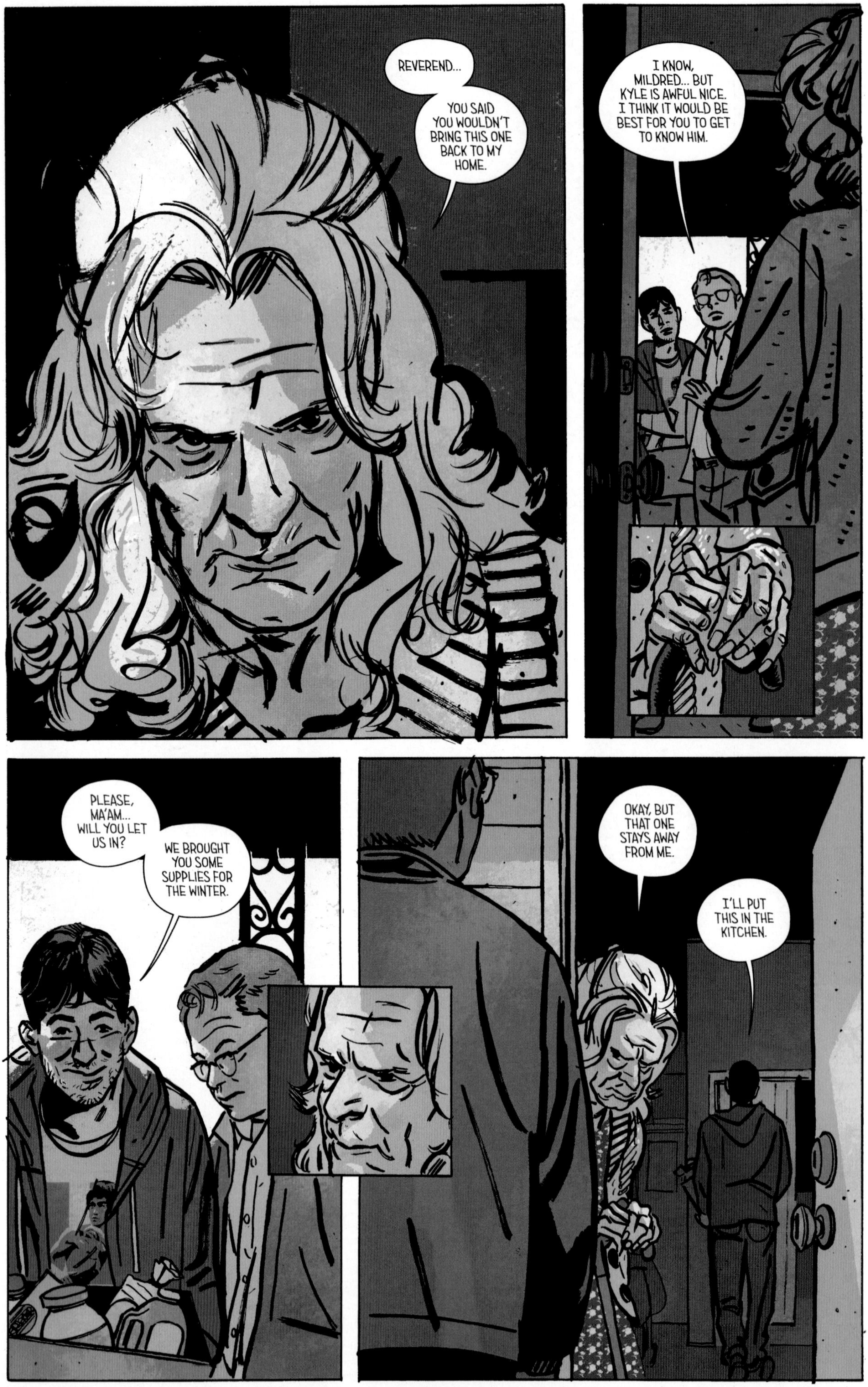
REVEREND...
YOU SAID YOU WOULDN'T BRING THIS ONE BACK TO MY HOME.
I KNOW, MILDRED... BUT KYLE IS AWFUL NICE. I THINK IT WOULD BE BEST FOR YOU TO GET TO KNOW HIM.
PLEASE, MA'AM... WILL YOU LET US IN?
WE BROUGHT YOU SOME SUPPLIES FOR THE WINTER.
OKAY, BUT THAT ONE STAYS AWAY FROM ME.
I'LL PUT THIS IN THE KITCHEN.

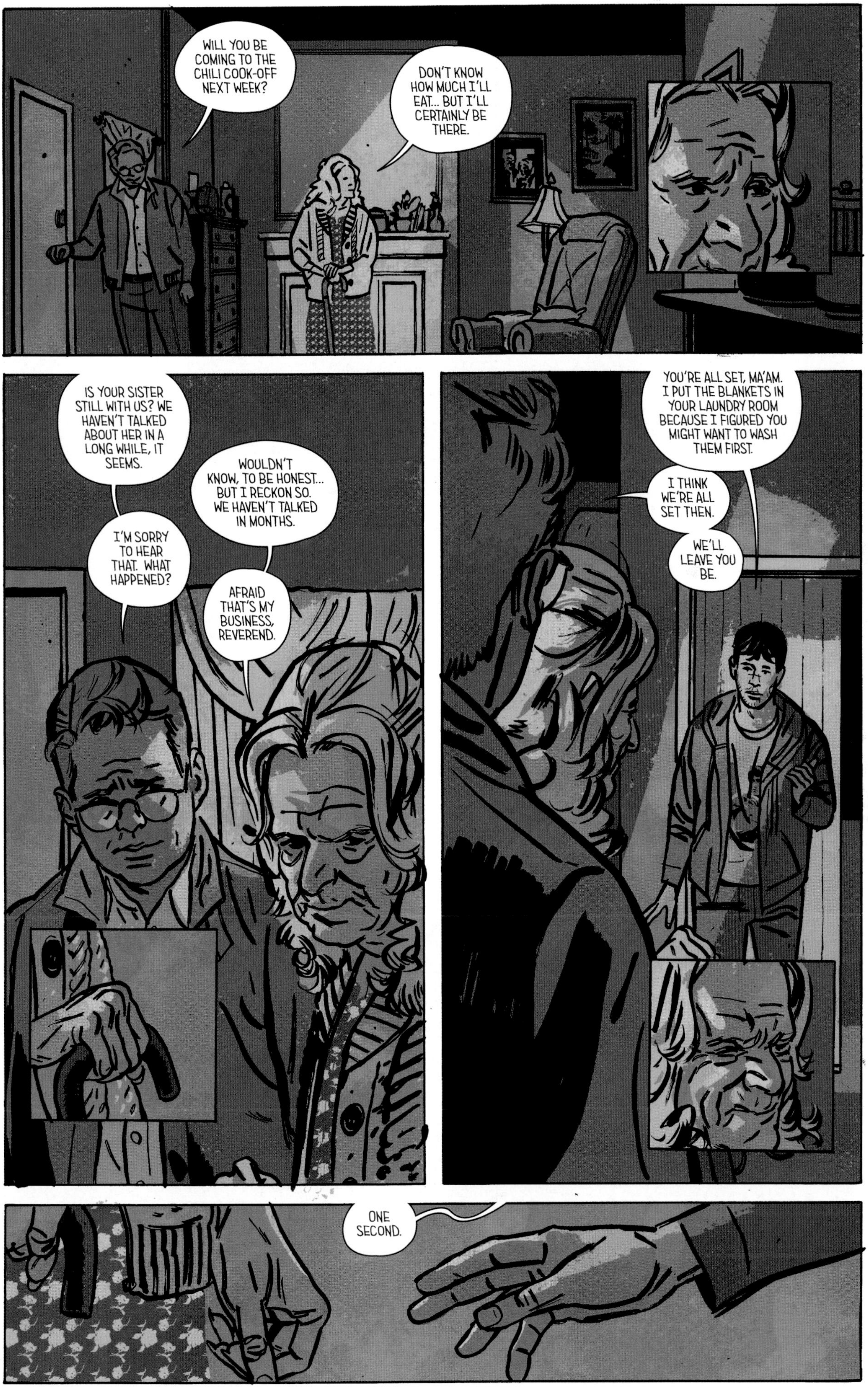
WILL YOU BE COMING TO THE CHILI COOK-OFF NEXT WEEK?
DON'T KNOW HOW MUCH I'LL EAT... BUT I'LL CERTAINLY BE THERE.
IS YOUR SISTER STILL WITH US? WE HAVEN'T TALKED ABOUT HER IN A LONG WHILE, IT SEEMS.
WOULDN'T KNOW, TO BE HONEST... BUT I RECKON SO. WE HAVEN'T TALKED IN MONTHS.
I'M SORRY TO HEAR THAT. WHAT HAPPENED?
AFRAID THAT'S MY BUSINESS, REVEREND.
YOU'RE ALL SET, MA'AM. I PUT THE BLANKETS IN YOUR LAUNDRY ROOM BECAUSE I FIGURED YOU MIGHT WANT TO WASH THEM FIRST.
I THINK WE'RE ALL SET THEN.
WE'LL LEAVE YOU BE.
ONE SECOND.

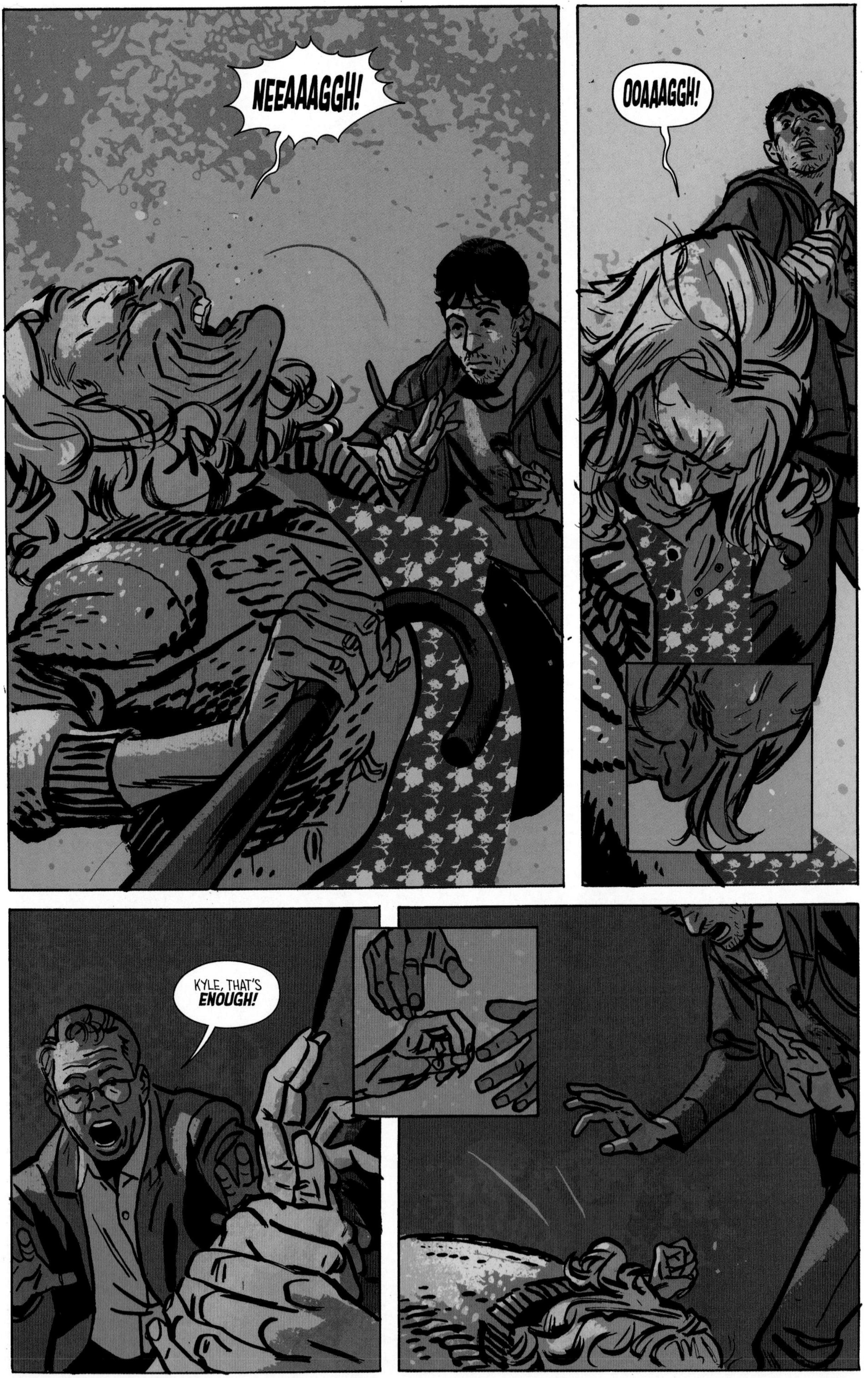
NEEAAAGGH!
OOAAAGGH!
KYLE, THAT'S ENOUGH!

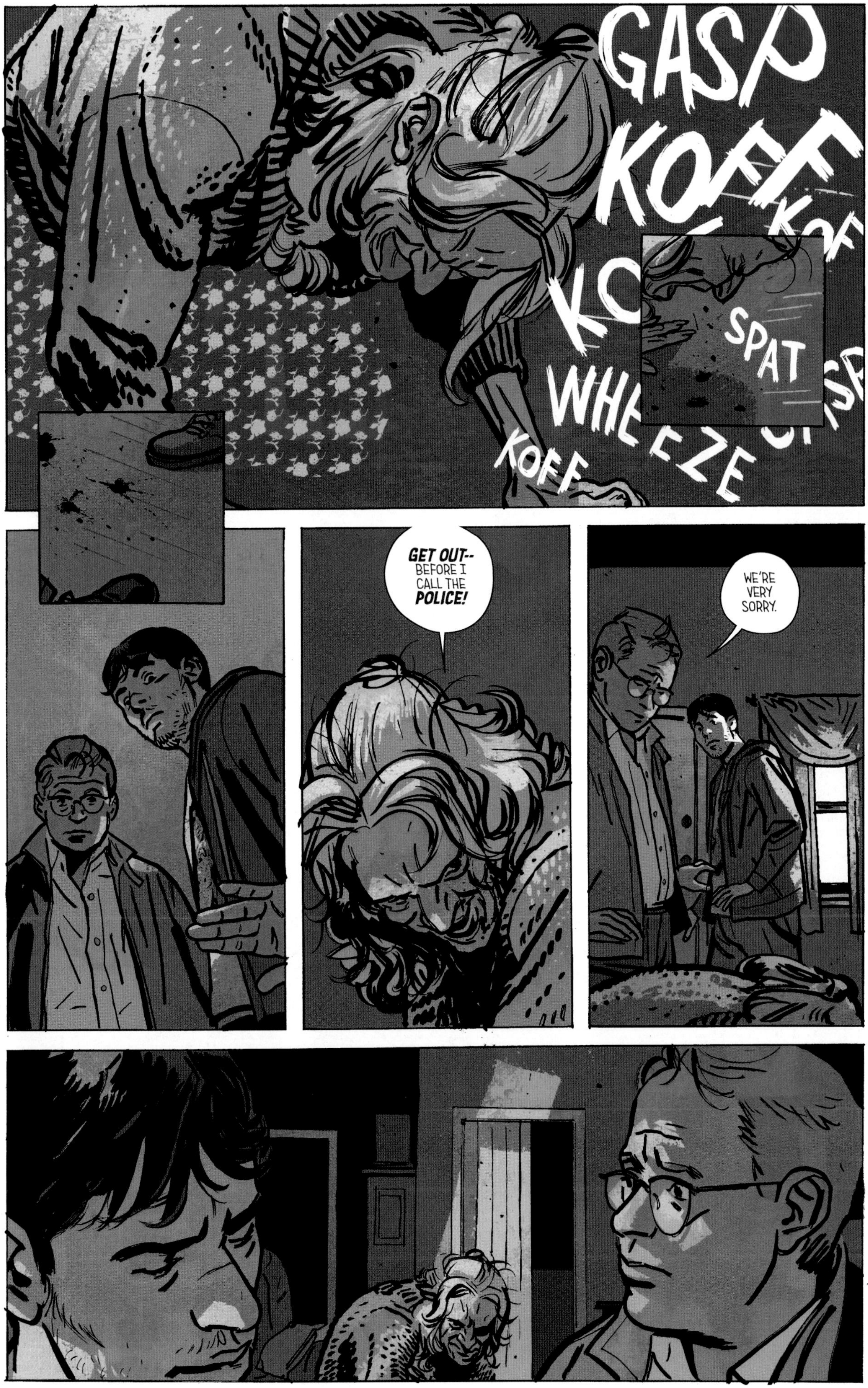
GASP
KOFF
KOFF
SPAT
WHEEZE
KOFF
GET OUT-- BEFORE I CALL THE POLICE!
WE'RE VERY SORRY.

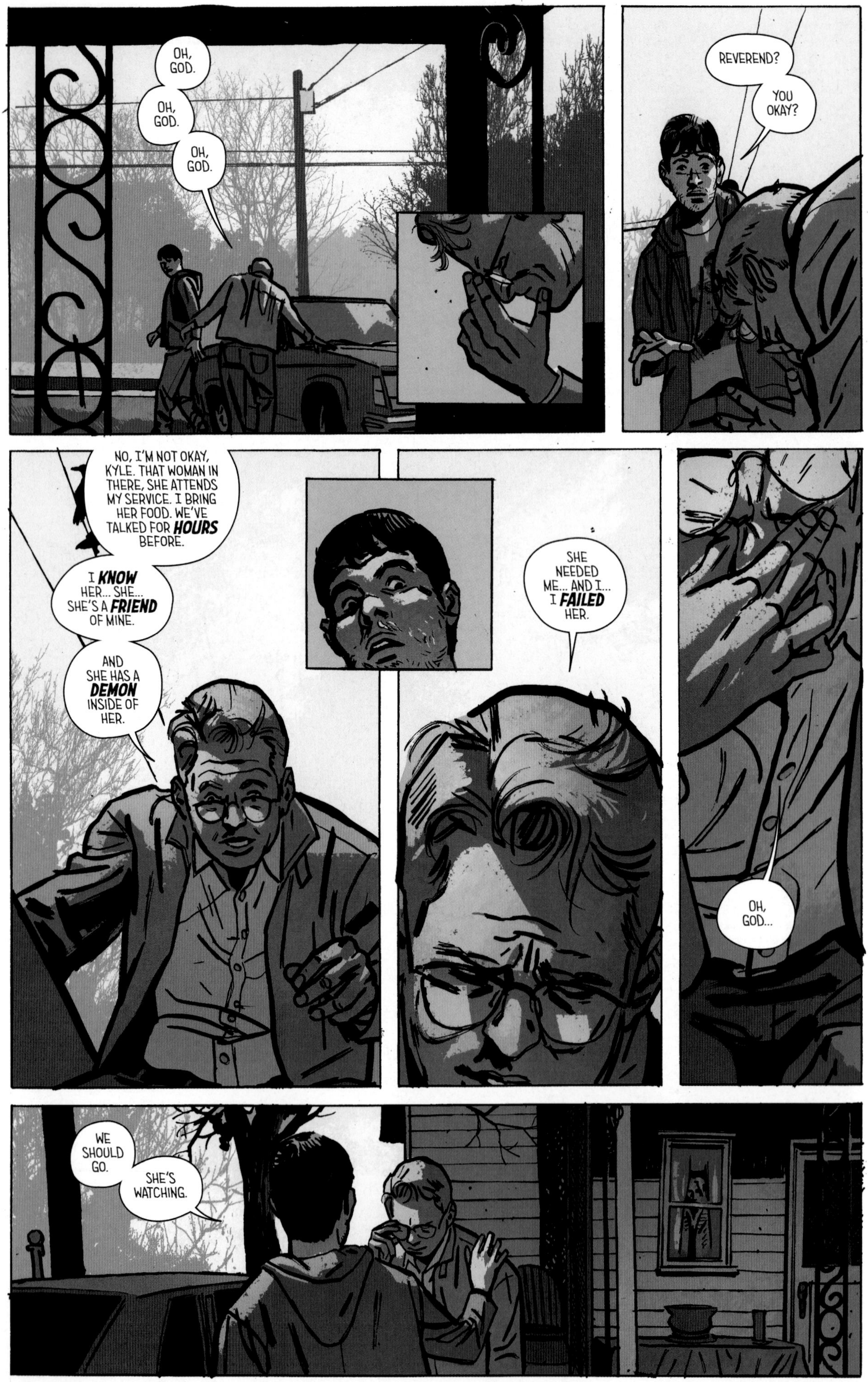
OH, GOD.
OH, GOD.
OH, GOD.
REVEREND?
YOU OKAY?
NO, I'M NOT OKAY, KYLE. THAT WOMAN IN THERE, SHE ATTENDS MY SERVICE. I BRING HER FOOD. WE'VE TALKED FOR HOURS BEFORE.
I KNOW HER... SHE... SHE'S A FRIEND OF MINE.
AND SHE HAS A DEMON INSIDE OF HER.
SHE NEEDED ME... AND I... I FAILED HER.
OH, GOD...
WE SHOULD GO.
SHE'S WATCHING.

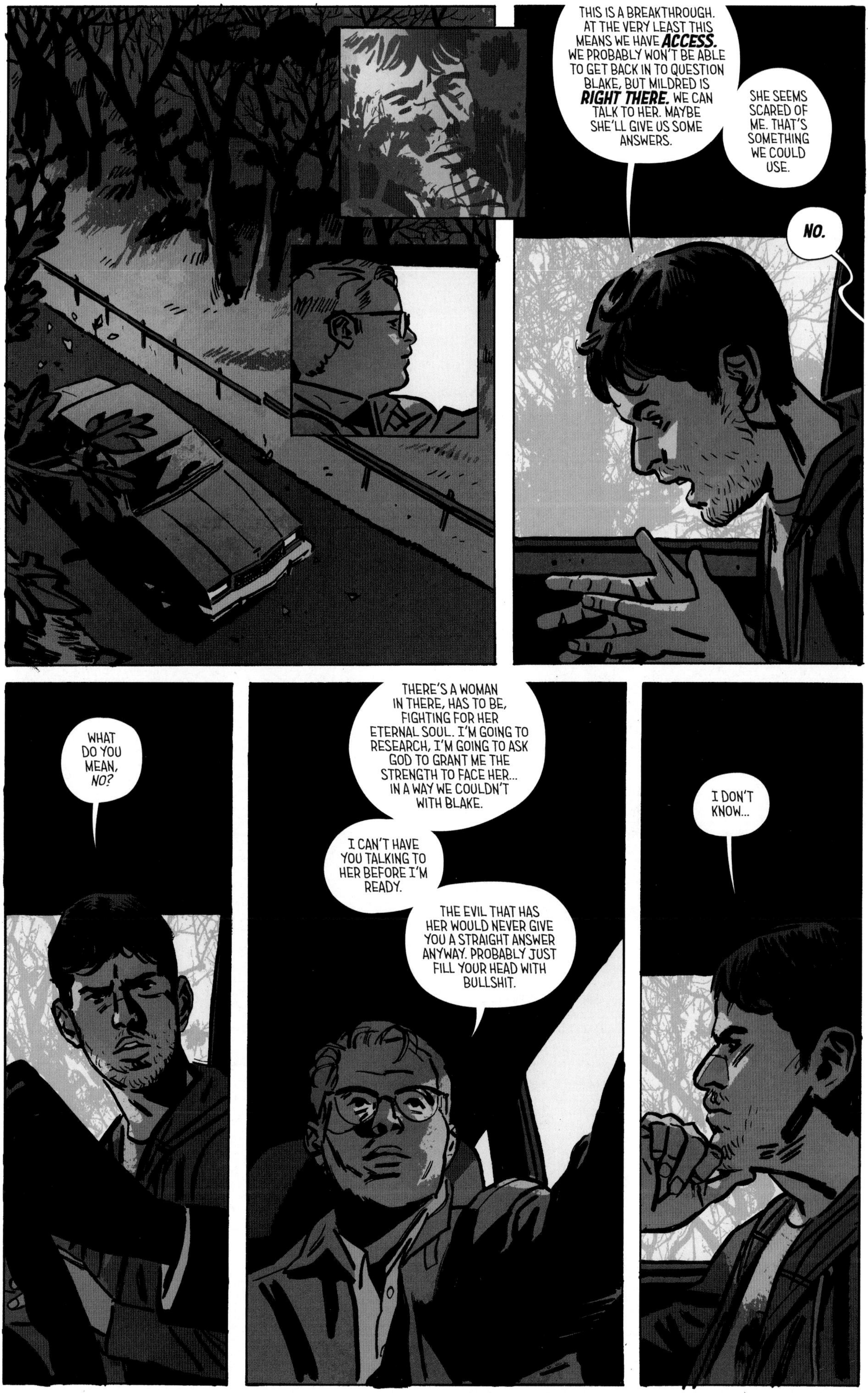
THIS IS A BREAKTHROUGH. AT THE VERY LEAST THIS MEANS WE HAVE ACCESS. WE PROBABLY WON'T BE ABLE TO GET BACK IN TO QUESTION BLAKE, BUT MILDRED IS RIGHT THERE. WE CAN TALK TO HER. MAYBE SHE'LL GIVE US SOME ANSWERS.
SHE SEEMS SCARED OF ME. THAT'S SOMETHING WE COULD USE.
NO.
WHAT DO YOU MEAN, NO?
THERE'S A WOMAN IN THERE, HAS TO BE, FIGHTING FOR HER ETERNAL SOUL. I'M GOING TO RESEARCH, I'M GOING TO ASK GOD TO GRANT ME THE STRENGTH TO FACE HER... IN A WAY WE COULDN'T WITH BLAKE.
I CAN'T HAVE YOU TALKING TO HER BEFORE I'M READY.
THE EVIL THAT HAS HER WOULD NEVER GIVE YOU A STRAIGHT ANSWER ANYWAY. PROBABLY JUST FILL YOUR HEAD WITH BULLSHIT.
I DON'T KNOW...

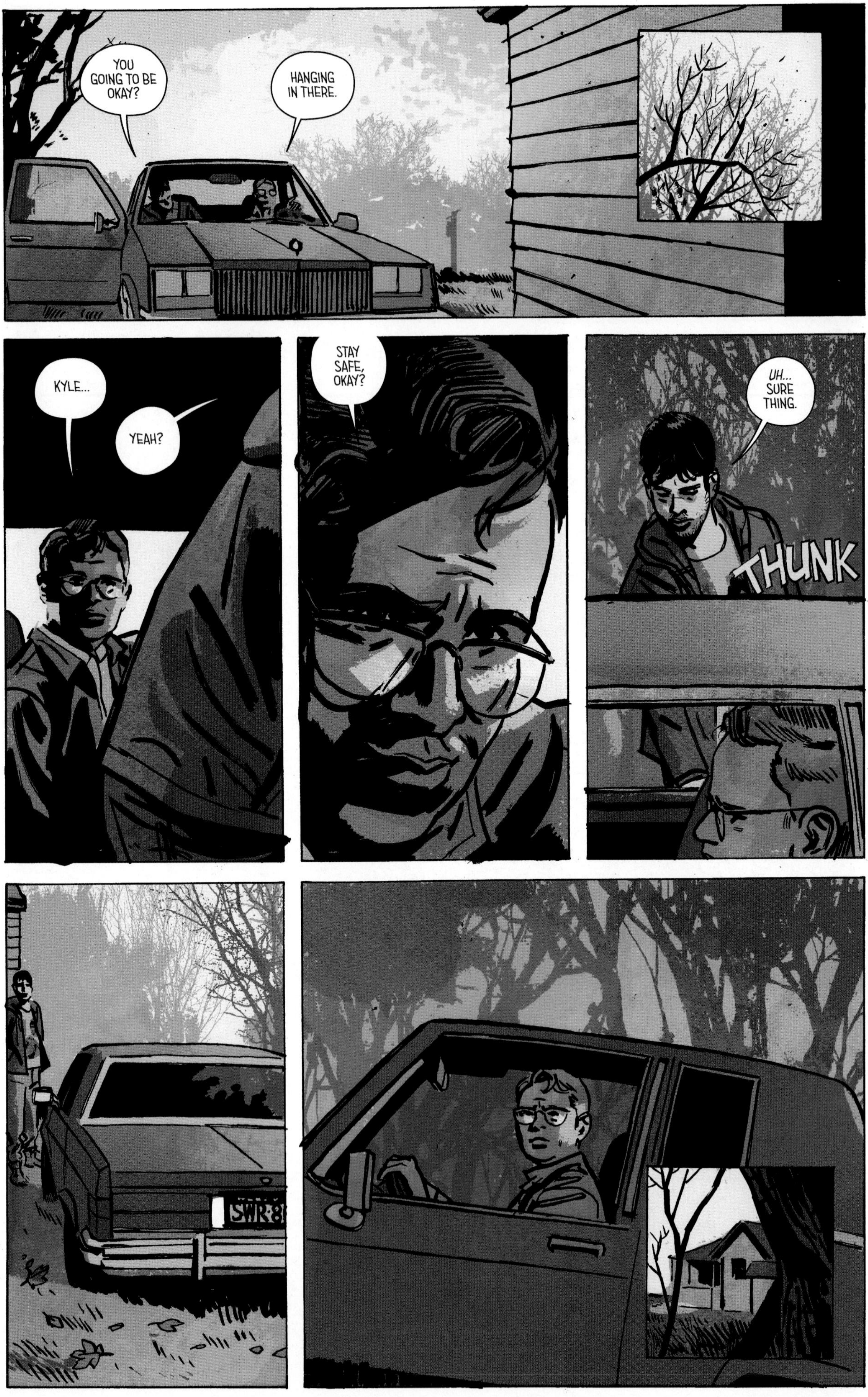
YOU GOING TO BE OKAY?
HANGING IN THERE.
KYLE...
YEAH?
STAY SAFE, OKAY?
UH... SURE THING.
THUNK
SWR-8

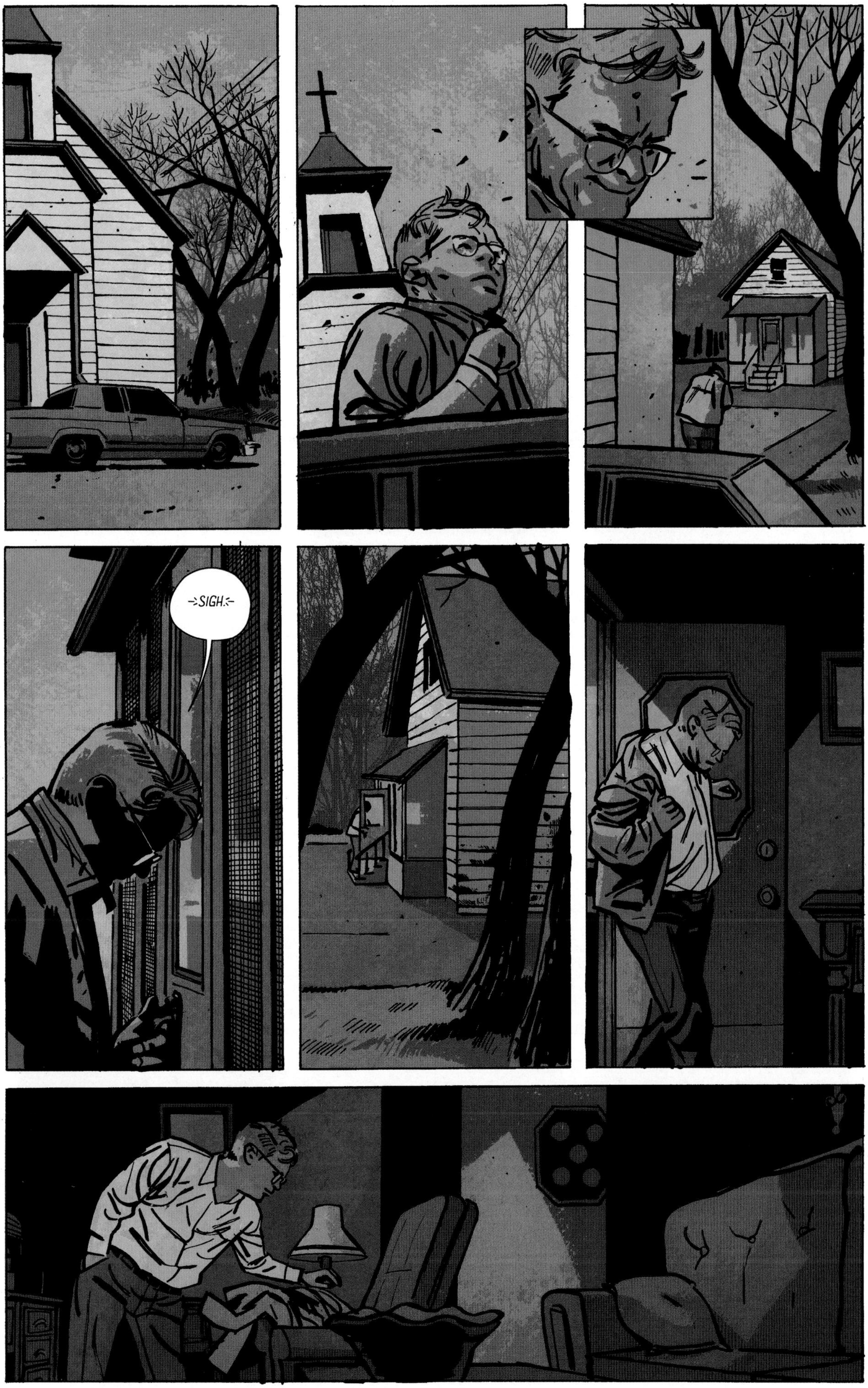
SIGH.

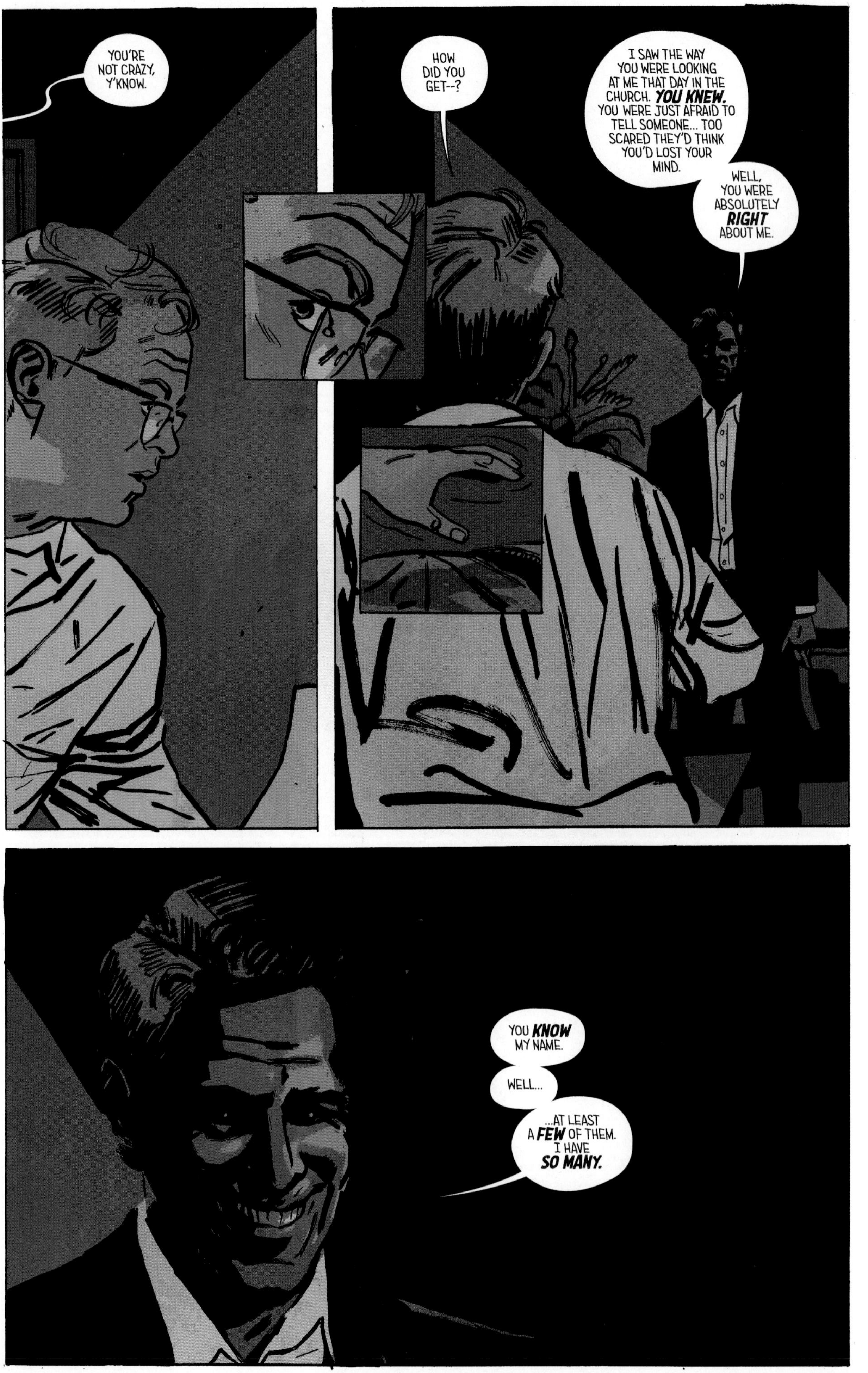
YOU'RE NOT CRAZY, Y'KNOW.
HOW DID YOU GET--?
I SAW THE WAY YOU WERE LOOKING AT ME THAT DAY IN THE CHURCH. YOU KNEW. YOU WERE JUST AFRAID TO TELL SOMEONE... TOO SCARED THEY'D THINK YOU'D LOST YOUR MIND.
WELL, YOU WERE ABSOLUTELY RIGHT ABOUT ME.
YOU KNOW MY NAME.
WELL...
...AT LEAST A FEW OF THEM. I HAVE SO MANY.

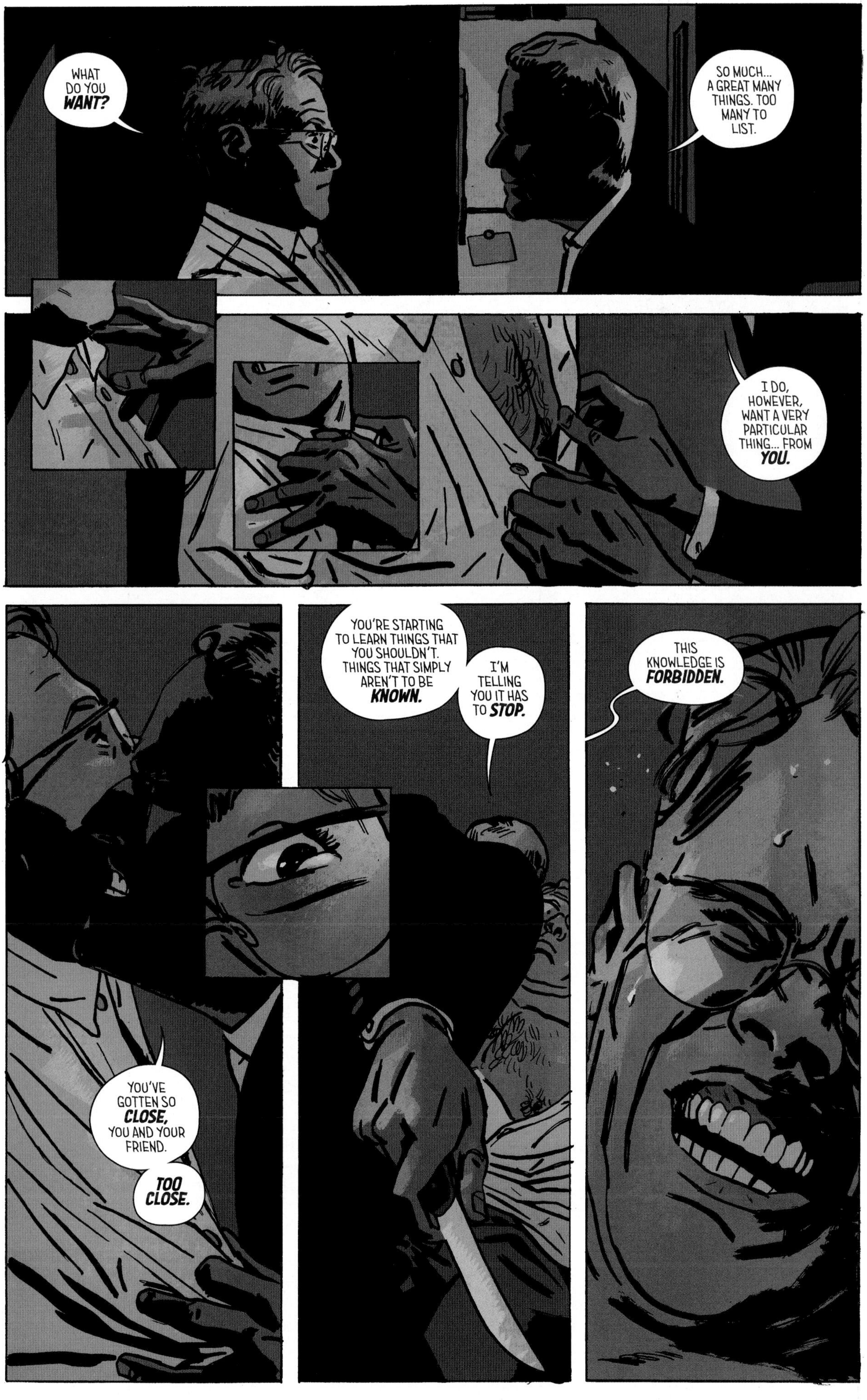
WHAT DO YOU WANT?
SO MUCH... A GREAT MANY THINGS. TOO MANY TO LIST.
I DO, HOWEVER, WANT A VERY PARTICULAR THING... FROM YOU.
YOU'VE GOTTEN SO CLOSE, YOU AND YOUR FRIEND.
TOO CLOSE.
YOU'RE STARTING TO LEARN THINGS THAT YOU SHOULDN'T. THINGS THAT SIMPLY AREN'T TO BE KNOWN.
I'M TELLING YOU IT HAS TO STOP.
THIS KNOWLEDGE IS FORBIDDEN.

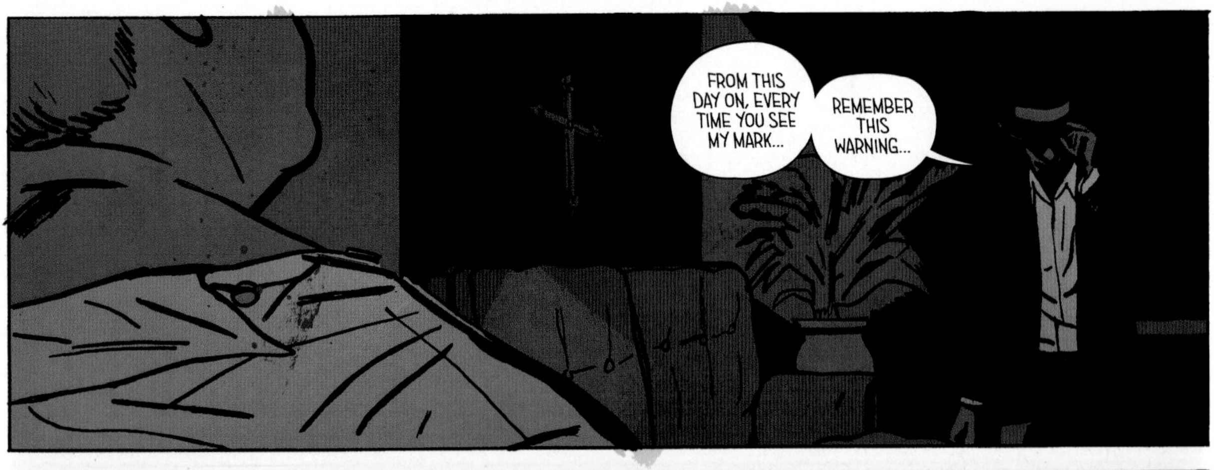
FROM THIS DAY ON, EVERY TIME YOU SEE MY MARK...
REMEMBER THIS WARNING...

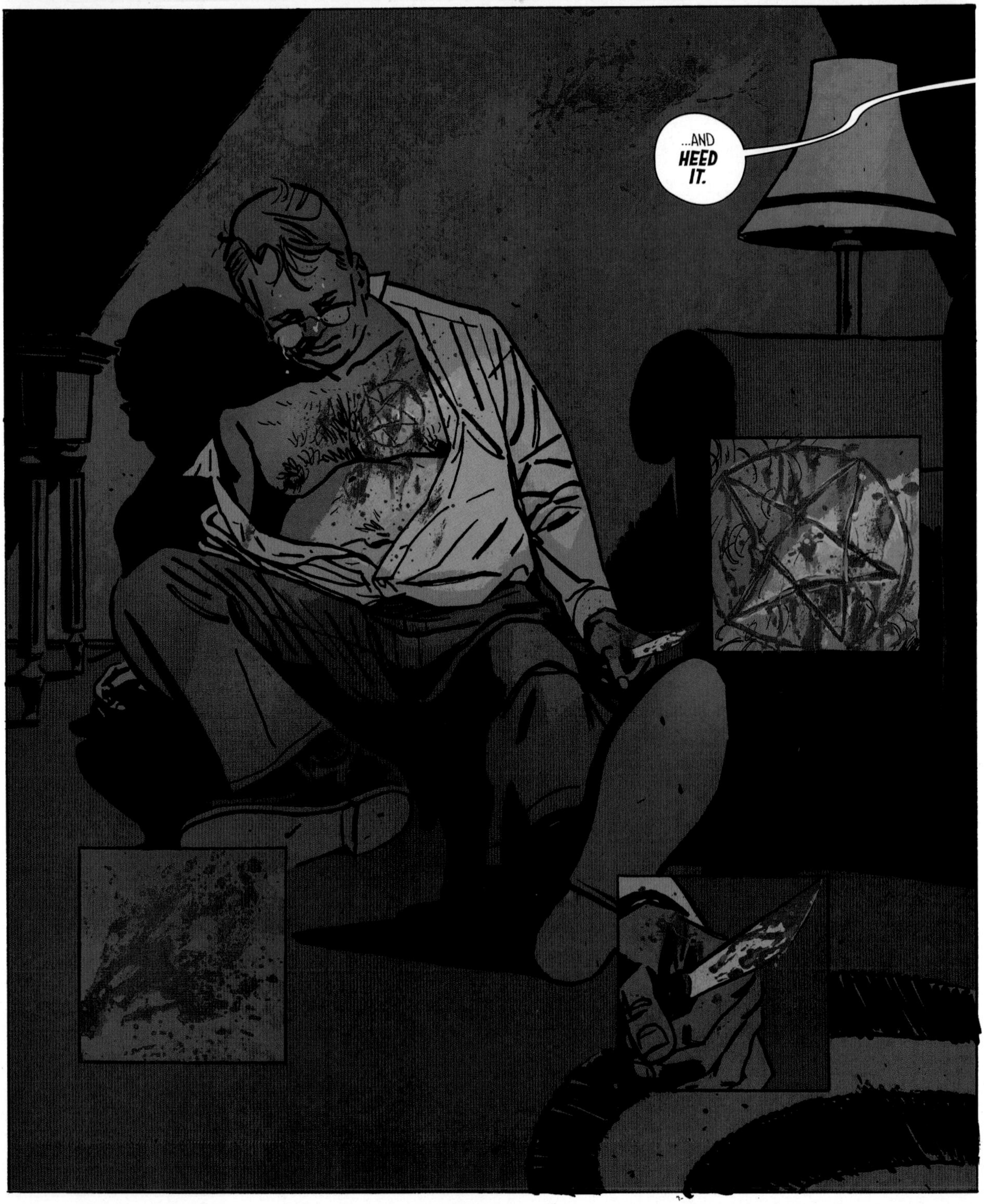
...AND HEED IT.

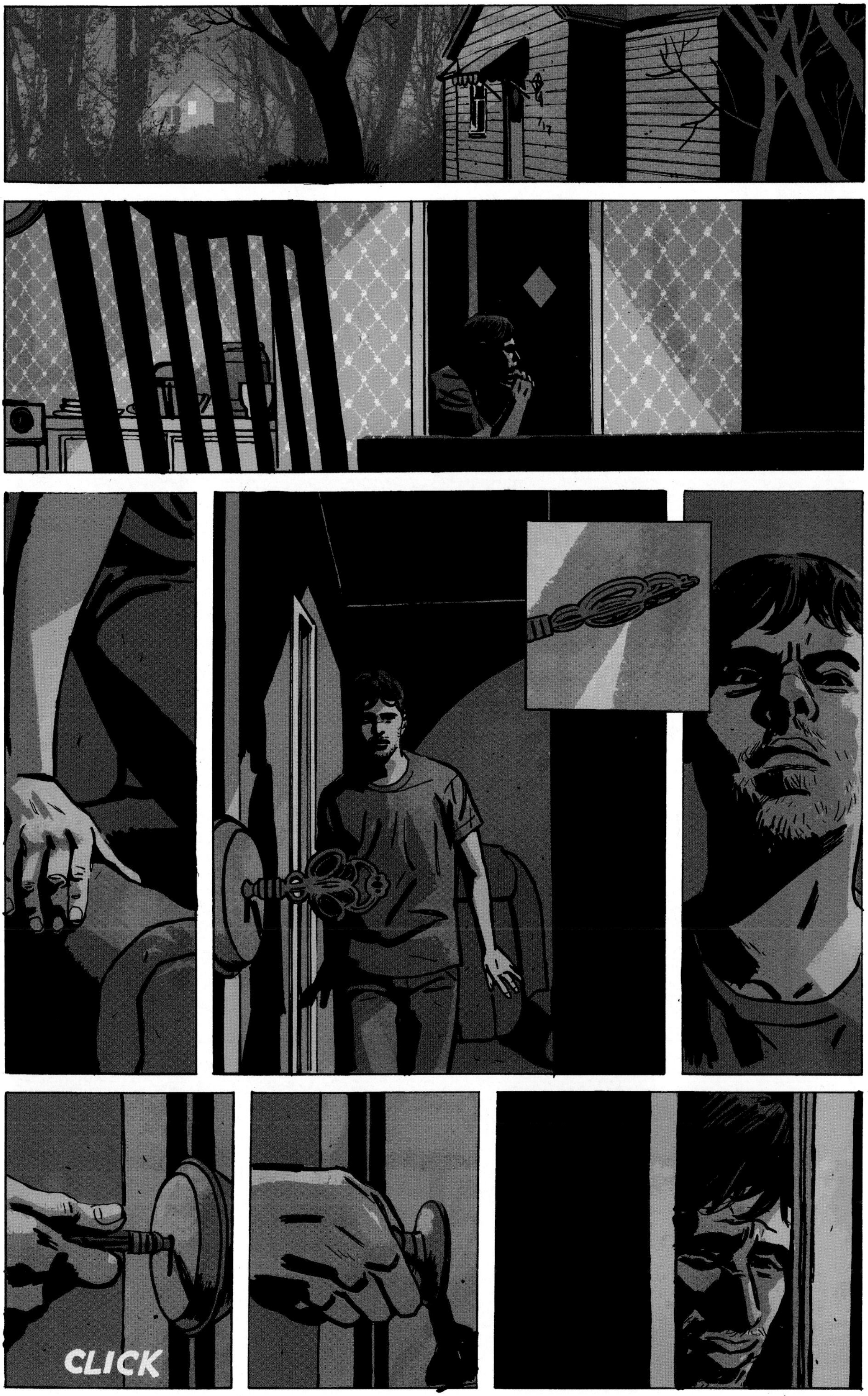
CLICK

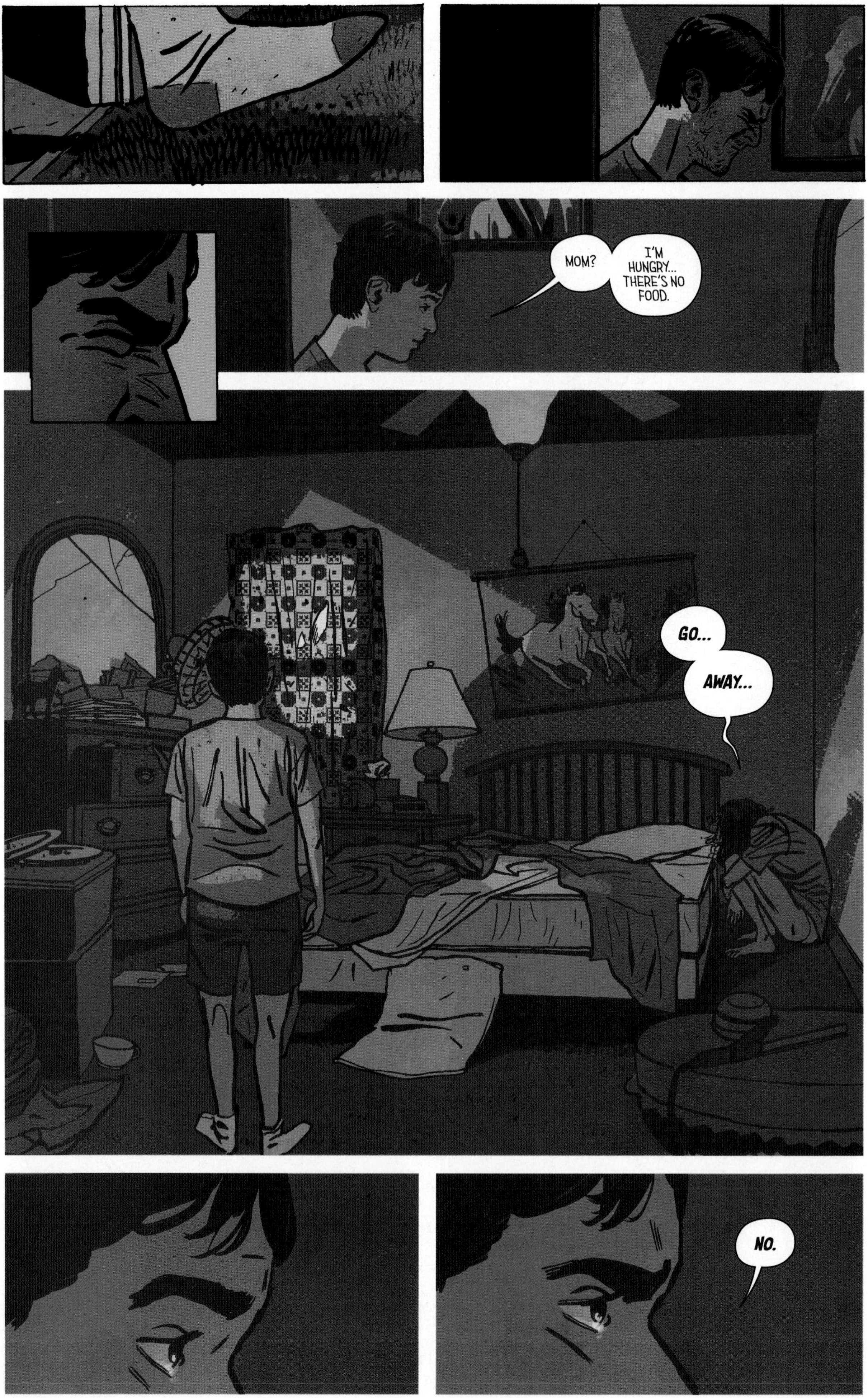
MOM?
I'M HUNGRY... THERE'S NO FOOD.
GO...
AWAY...
NO.

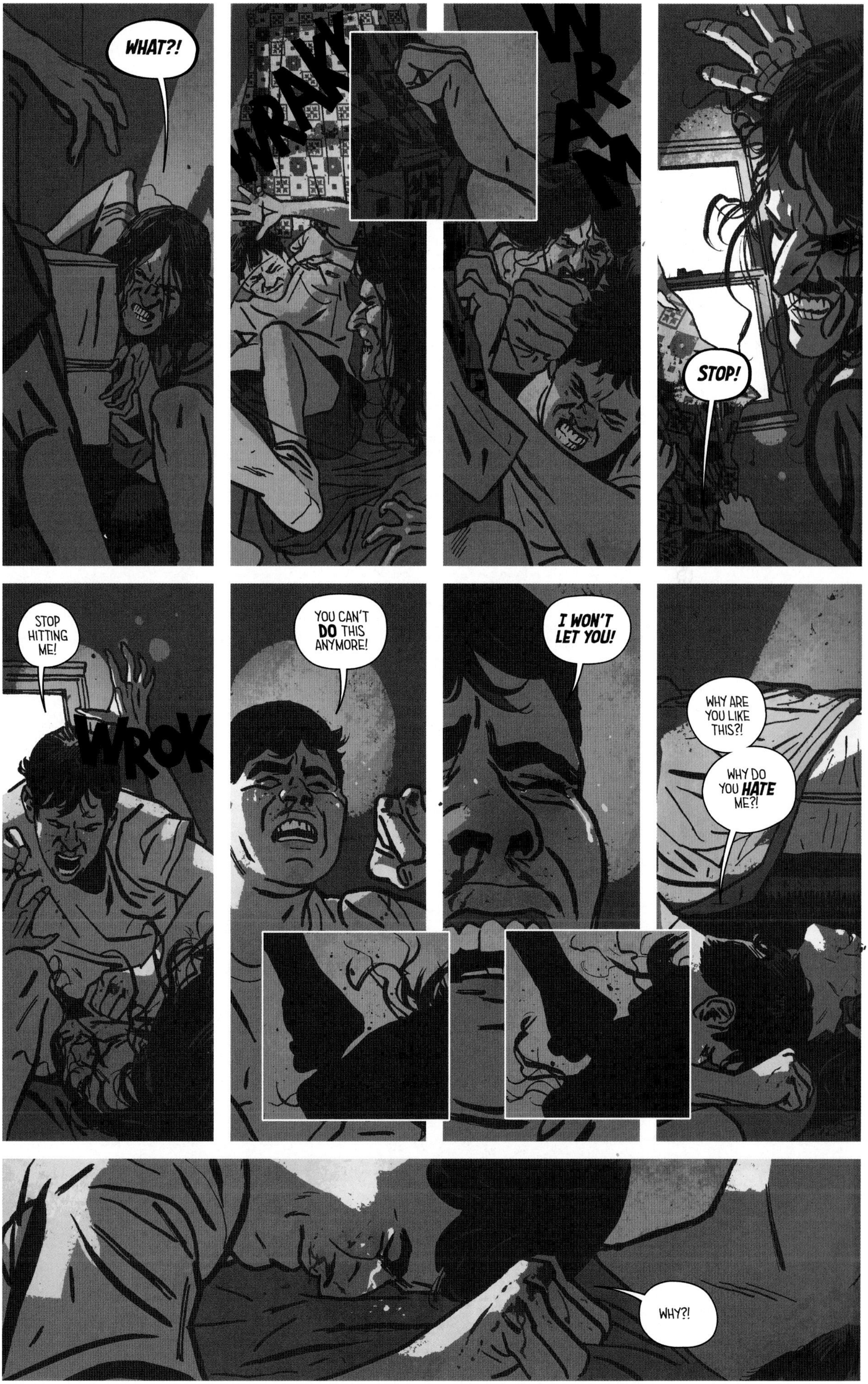
WHAT?!
WRAK
WRAM
STOP!
STOP HITTING ME!
WROK
YOU CAN'T DO THIS ANYMORE!
I WON'T LET YOU!
WHY ARE YOU LIKE THIS?!
WHY DO YOU HATE ME?!
WHY?!

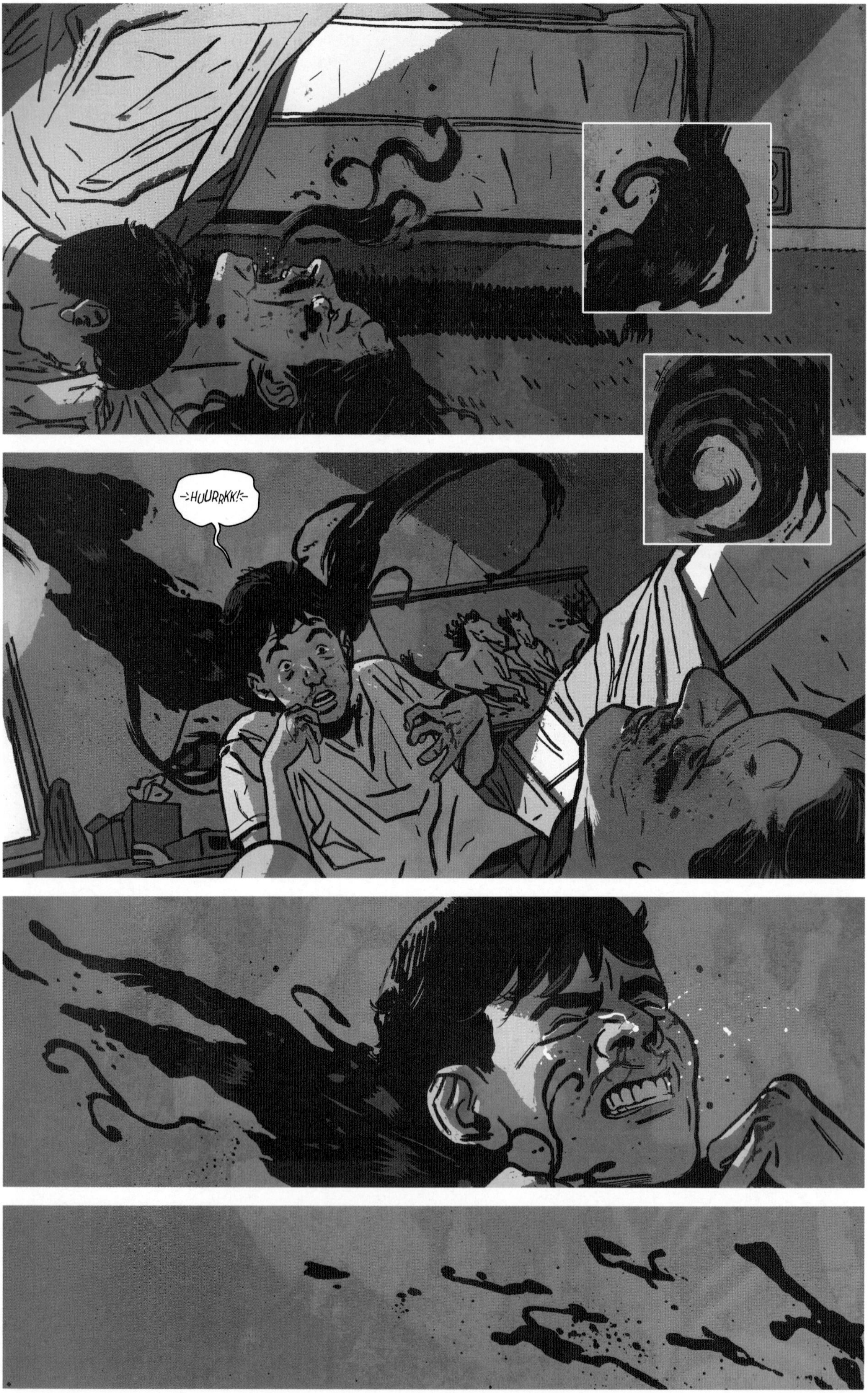

HUURRKK!

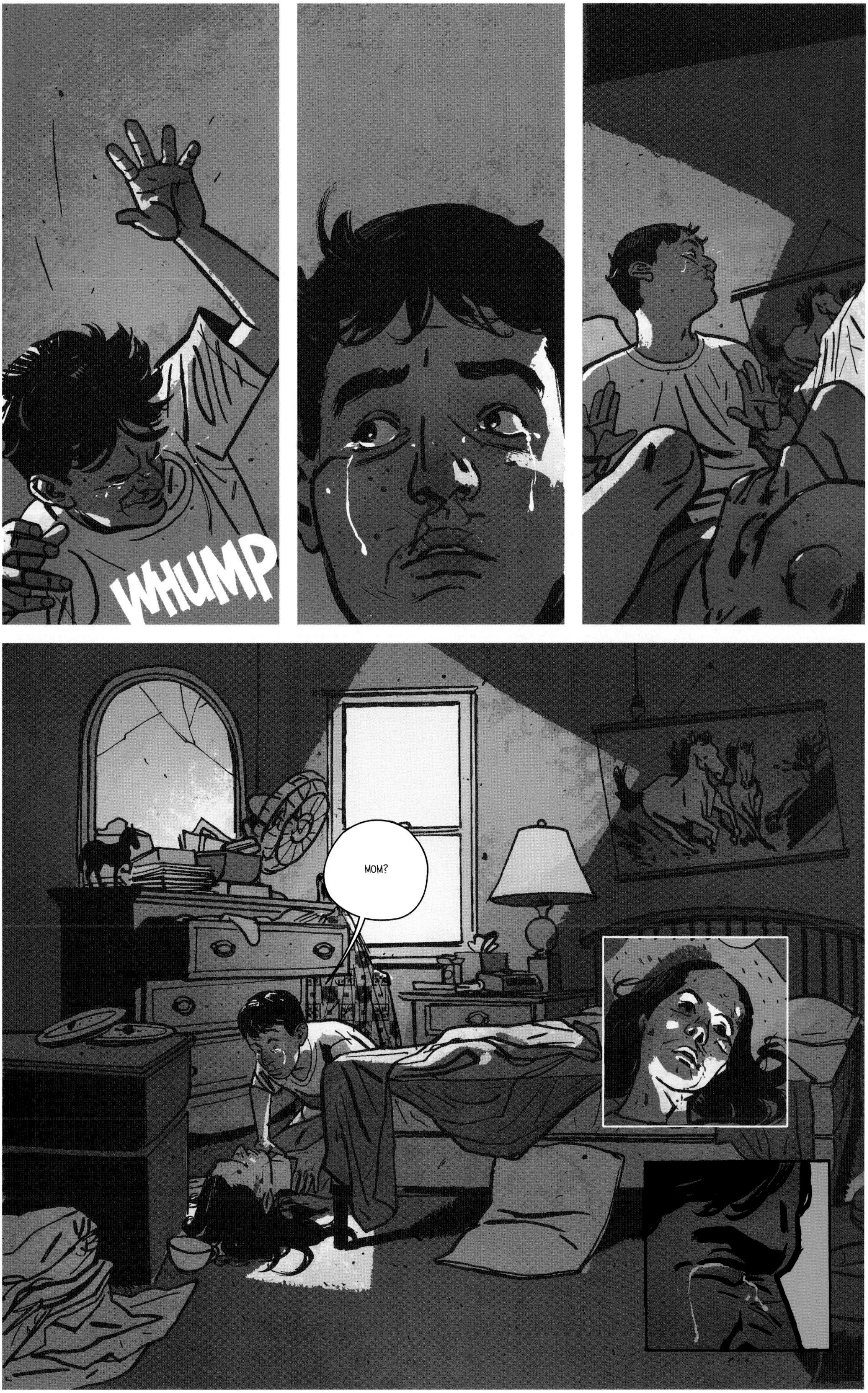
WHUMP
MOM?

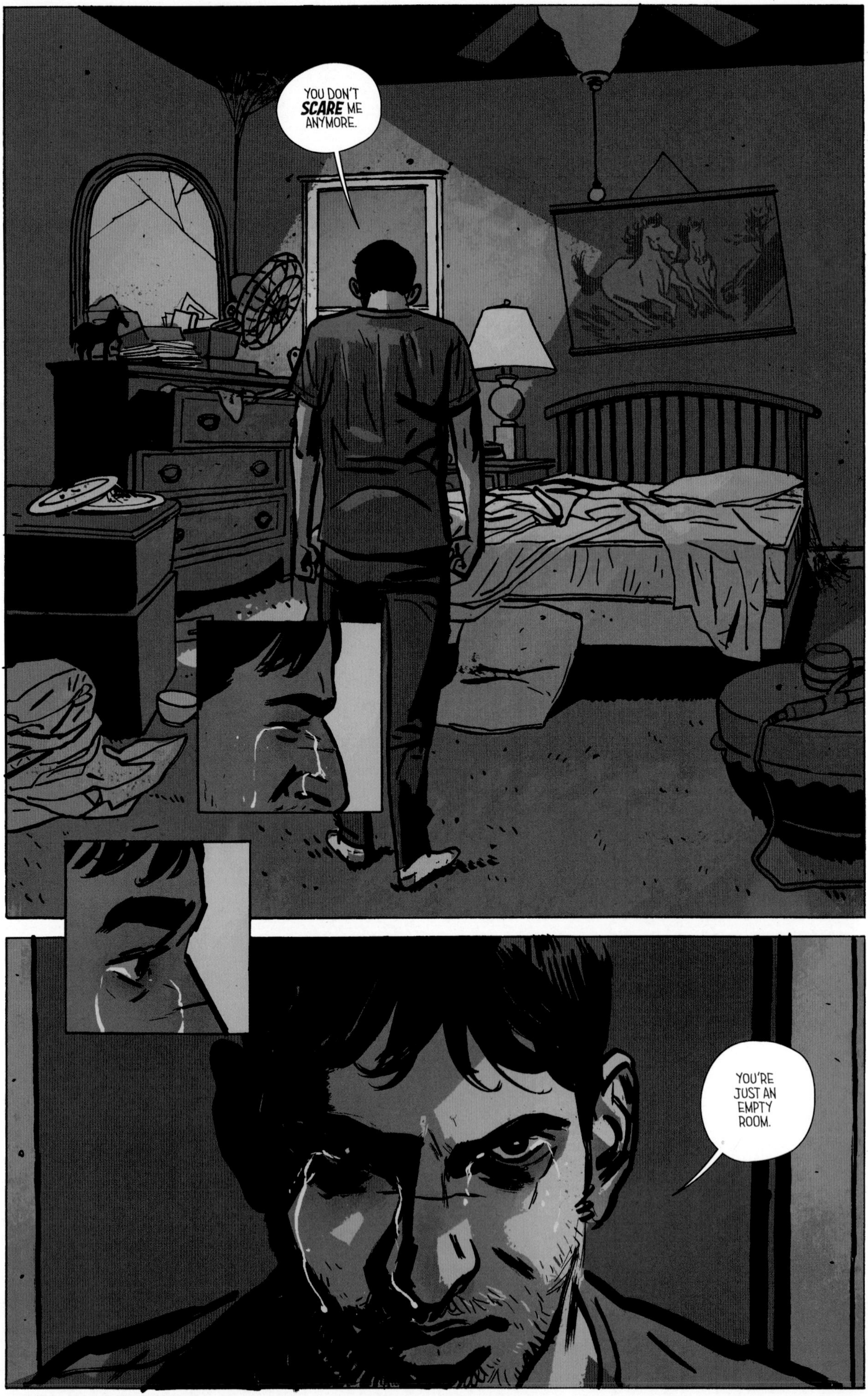
YOU DON'T SCARE ME ANYMORE.
YOU'RE JUST AN EMPTY ROOM.

CHAPTER 2:
A VAST AND UNENDING RUIN

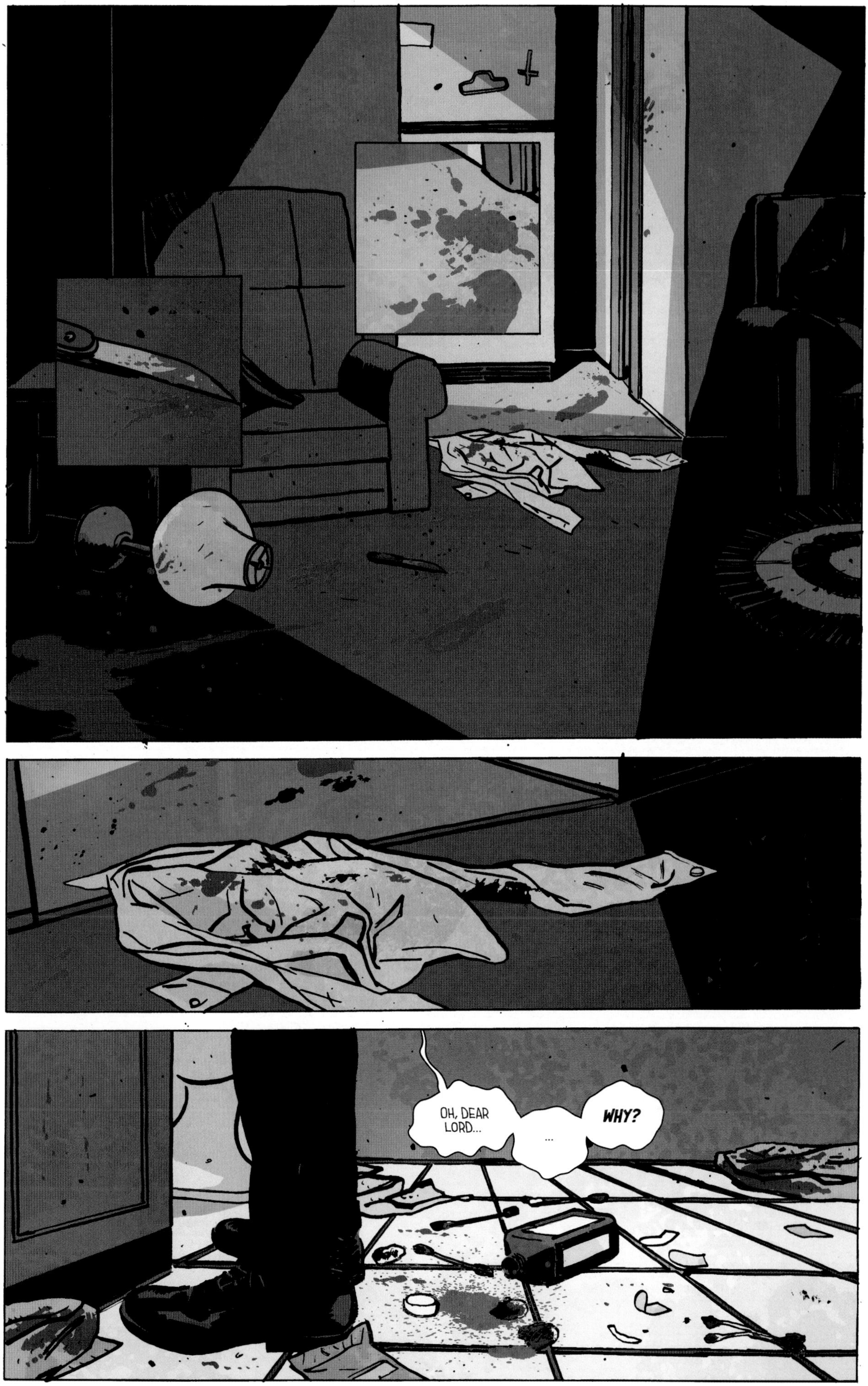
OH, DEAR LORD...
...
WHY?

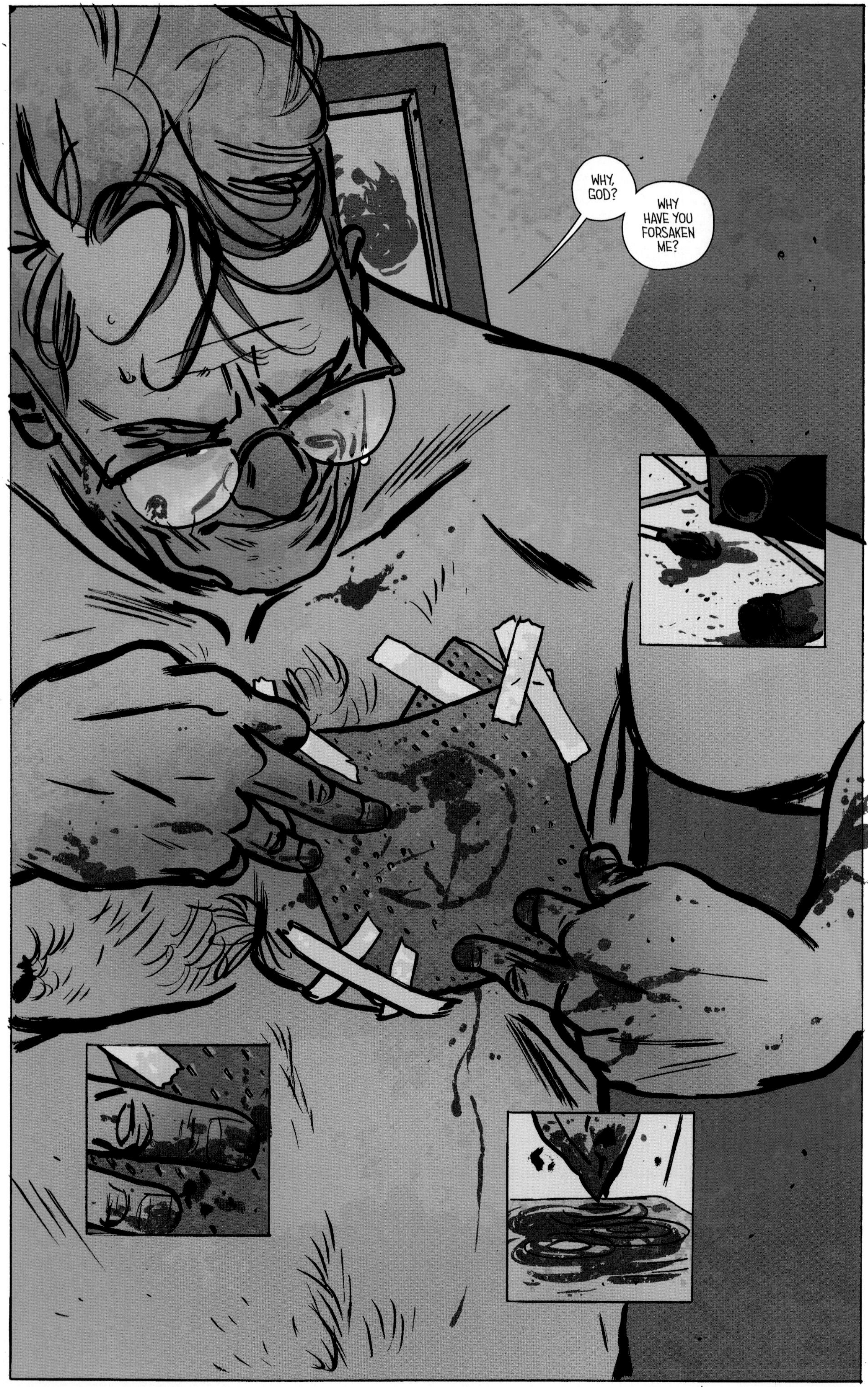
WHY, GOD?
WHY HAVE YOU FORSAKEN ME?

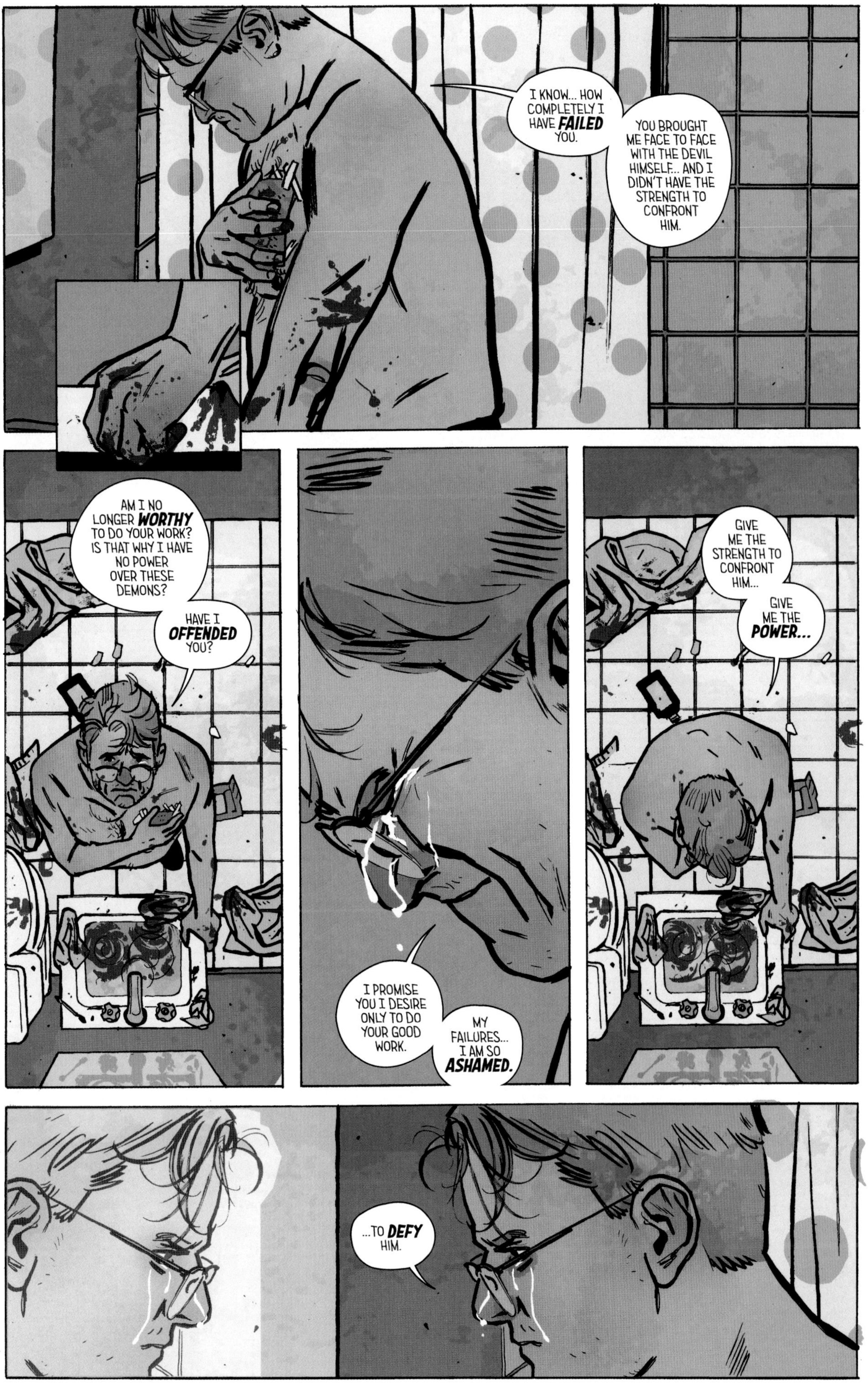
I KNOW... HOW COMPLETELY I HAVE FAILED YOU.
YOU BROUGHT ME FACE TO FACE WITH THE DEVIL HIMSELF... AND I DIDN'T HAVE THE STRENGTH TO CONFRONT HIM.
AM I NO LONGER WORTHY TO DO YOUR WORK? IS THAT WHY I HAVE NO POWER OVER THESE DEMONS?
HAVE I OFFENDED YOU?
I PROMISE YOU I DESIRE ONLY TO DO YOUR GOOD WORK.
MY FAILURES... I AM SO ASHAMED.
GIVE ME THE STRENGTH TO CONFRONT HIM...
GIVE ME THE POWER...
...TO DEFY HIM.

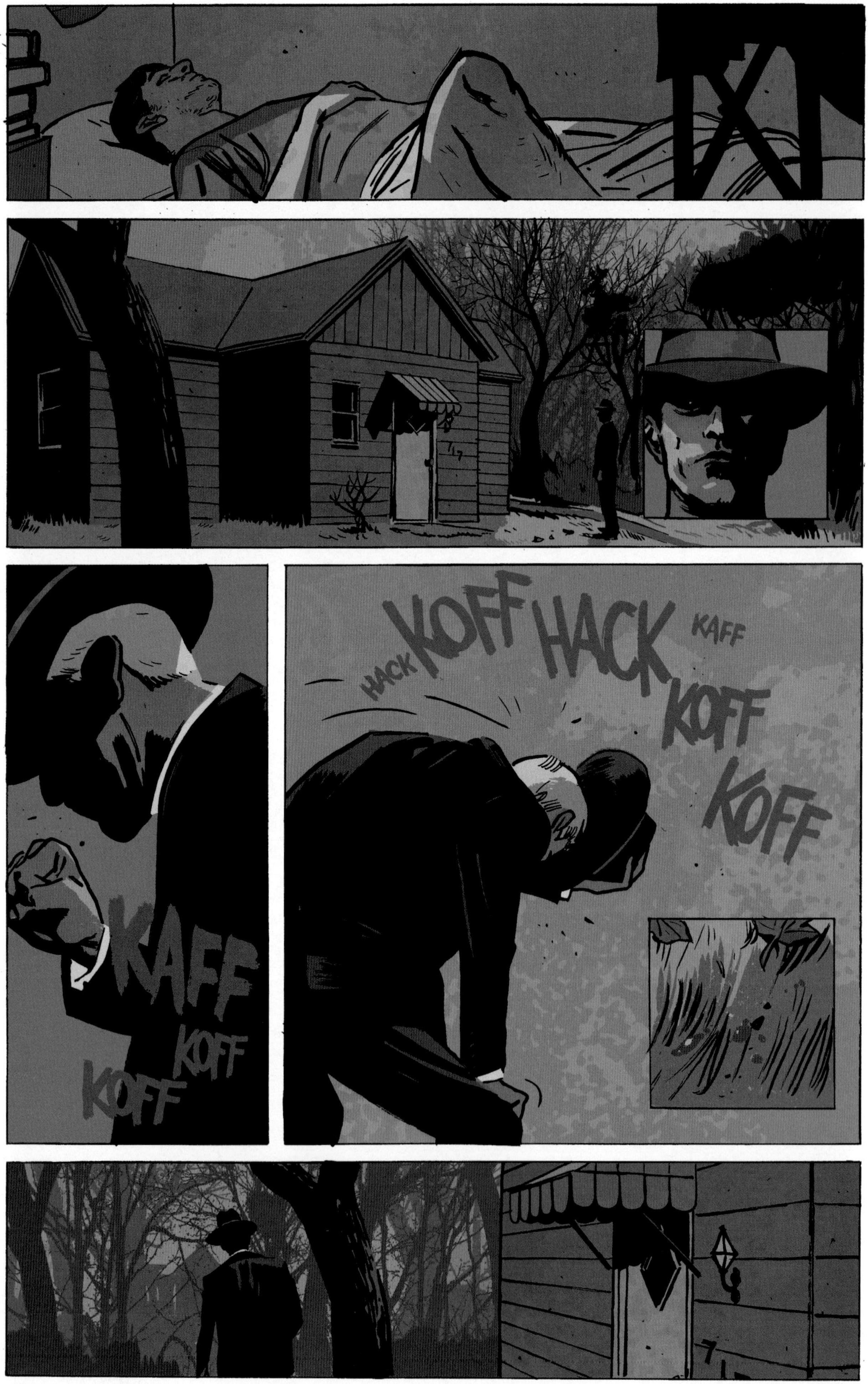

KAFF
KOFF
KOFF
HACK
KOFF
HACK
KAFF
KOFF
KOFF

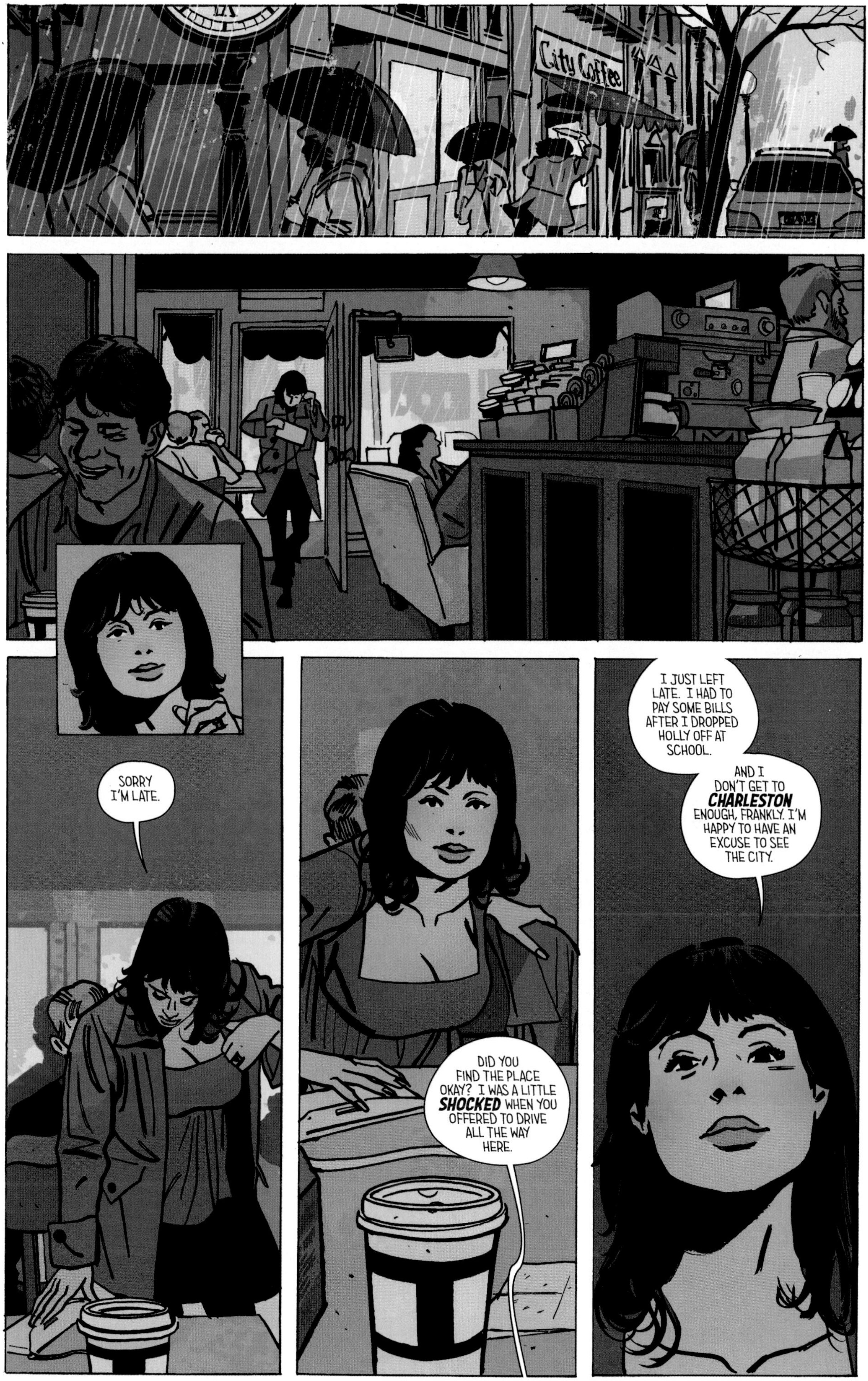
City Coffee
SORRY I'M LATE.
DID YOU FIND THE PLACE OKAY? I WAS A LITTLE **SHOCKED** WHEN YOU OFFERED TO DRIVE ALL THE WAY HERE.
I JUST LEFT LATE. I HAD TO PAY SOME BILLS AFTER I DROPPED HOLLY OFF AT SCHOOL.
AND I DON'T GET TO **CHARLESTON** ENOUGH, FRANKLY. I'M HAPPY TO HAVE AN EXCUSE TO SEE THE CITY.

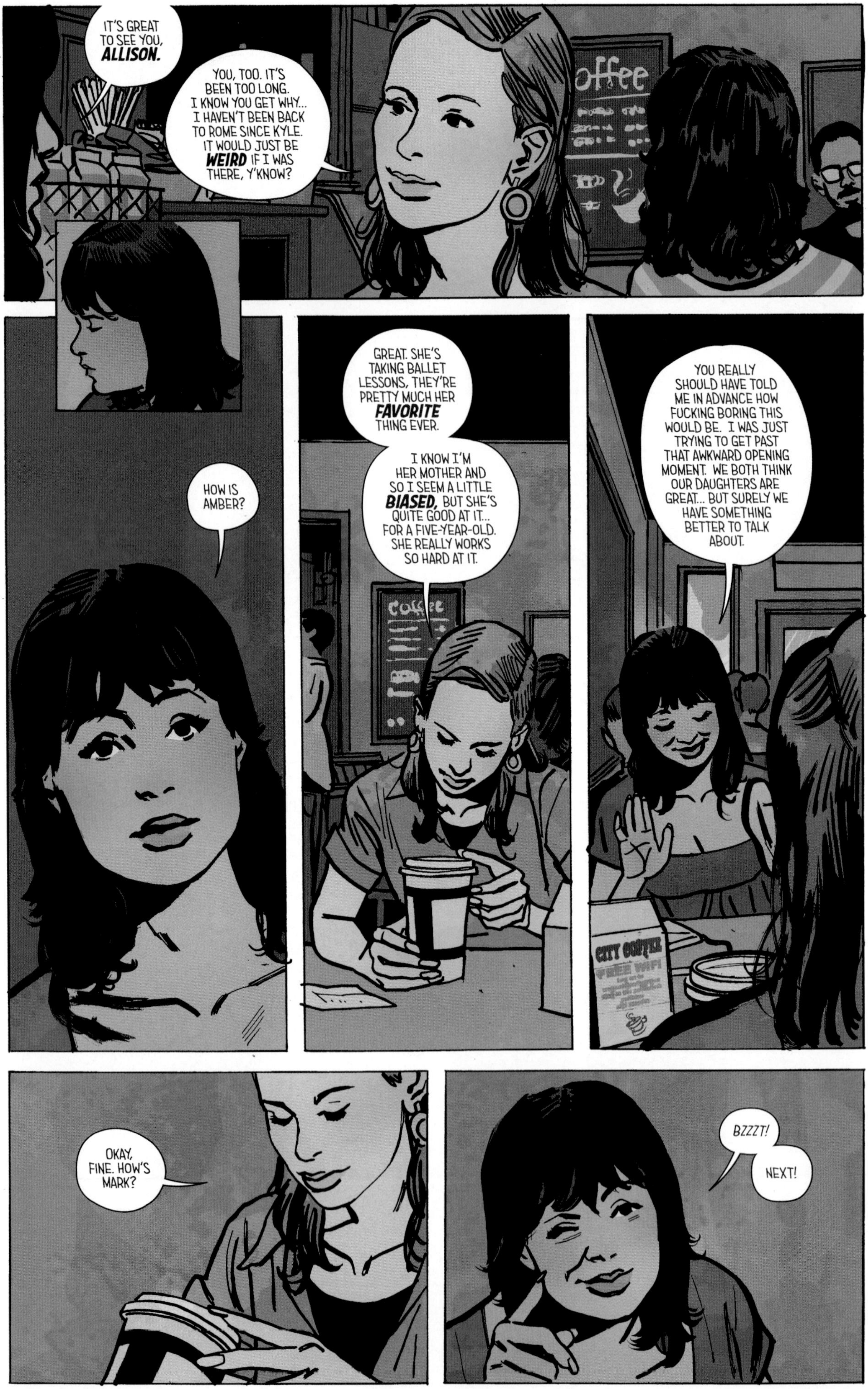
IT'S GREAT TO SEE YOU, ALLISON.
YOU, TOO. IT'S BEEN TOO LONG. I KNOW YOU GET WHY... I HAVEN'T BEEN BACK TO ROME SINCE KYLE. IT WOULD JUST BE WEIRD IF I WAS THERE, Y'KNOW?
offee
HOW IS AMBER?
GREAT. SHE'S TAKING BALLET LESSONS, THEY'RE PRETTY MUCH HER FAVORITE THING EVER.
I KNOW I'M HER MOTHER AND SO I SEEM A LITTLE BIASED, BUT SHE'S QUITE GOOD AT IT... FOR A FIVE-YEAR-OLD. SHE REALLY WORKS SO HARD AT IT.
YOU REALLY SHOULD HAVE TOLD ME IN ADVANCE HOW FUCKING BORING THIS WOULD BE. I WAS JUST TRYING TO GET PAST THAT AWKWARD OPENING MOMENT. WE BOTH THINK OUR DAUGHTERS ARE GREAT... BUT SURELY WE HAVE SOMETHING BETTER TO TALK ABOUT.
CITY COFFEE
FREE WIFI
OKAY, FINE. HOW'S MARK?
BZZZT!
NEXT!

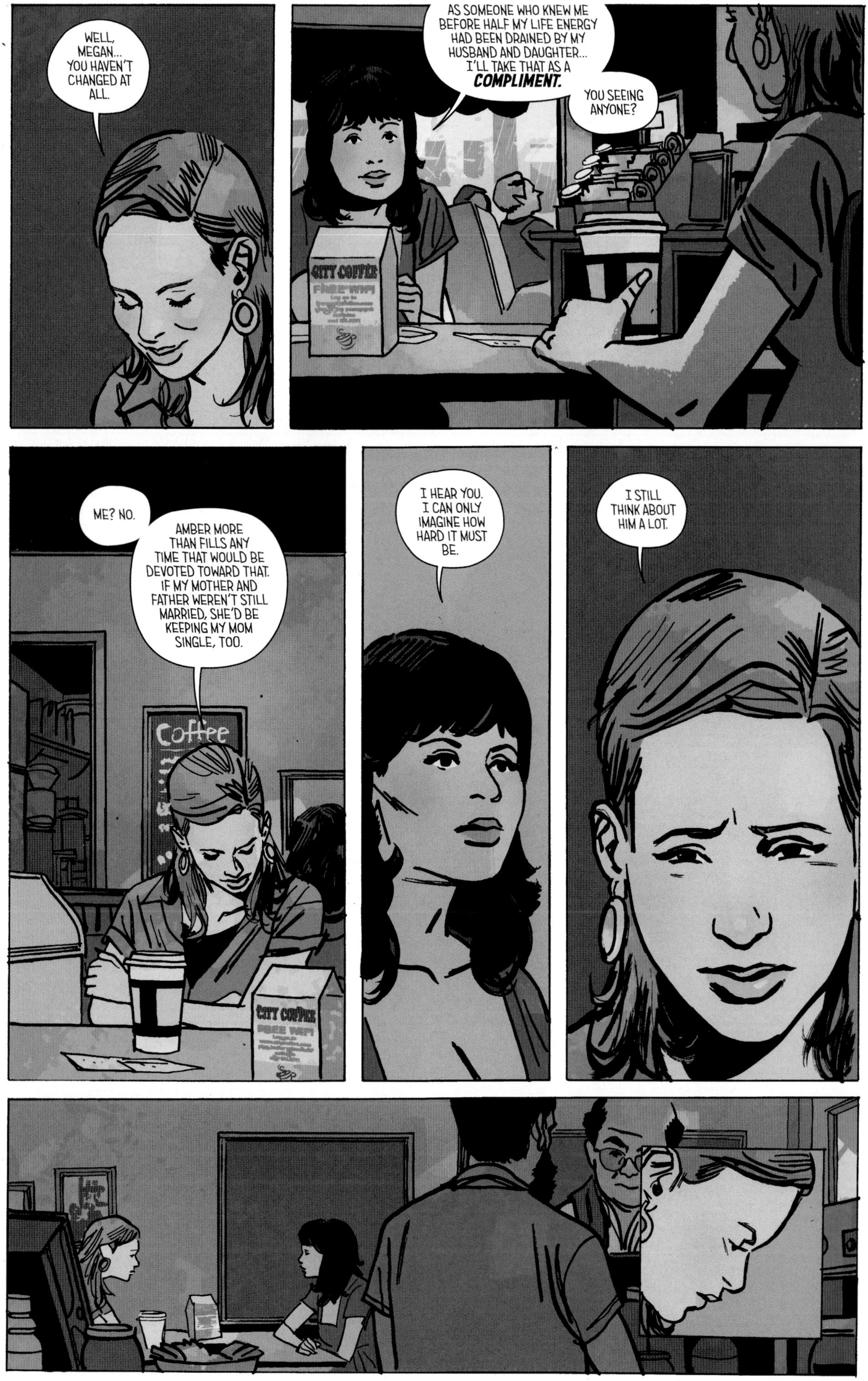
WELL, MEGAN... YOU HAVEN'T CHANGED AT ALL.
AS SOMEONE WHO KNEW ME BEFORE HALF MY LIFE ENERGY HAD BEEN DRAINED BY MY HUSBAND AND DAUGHTER... I'LL TAKE THAT AS A **COMPLIMENT.**
YOU SEEING ANYONE?
CITY COFFEE
ME? NO.
AMBER MORE THAN FILLS ANY TIME THAT WOULD BE DEVOTED TOWARD THAT. IF MY MOTHER AND FATHER WEREN'T STILL MARRIED, SHE'D BE KEEPING MY MOM SINGLE, TOO.
Coffee
CITY COFFEE
I HEAR YOU. I CAN ONLY IMAGINE HOW HARD IT MUST BE.
I STILL THINK ABOUT HIM A LOT.

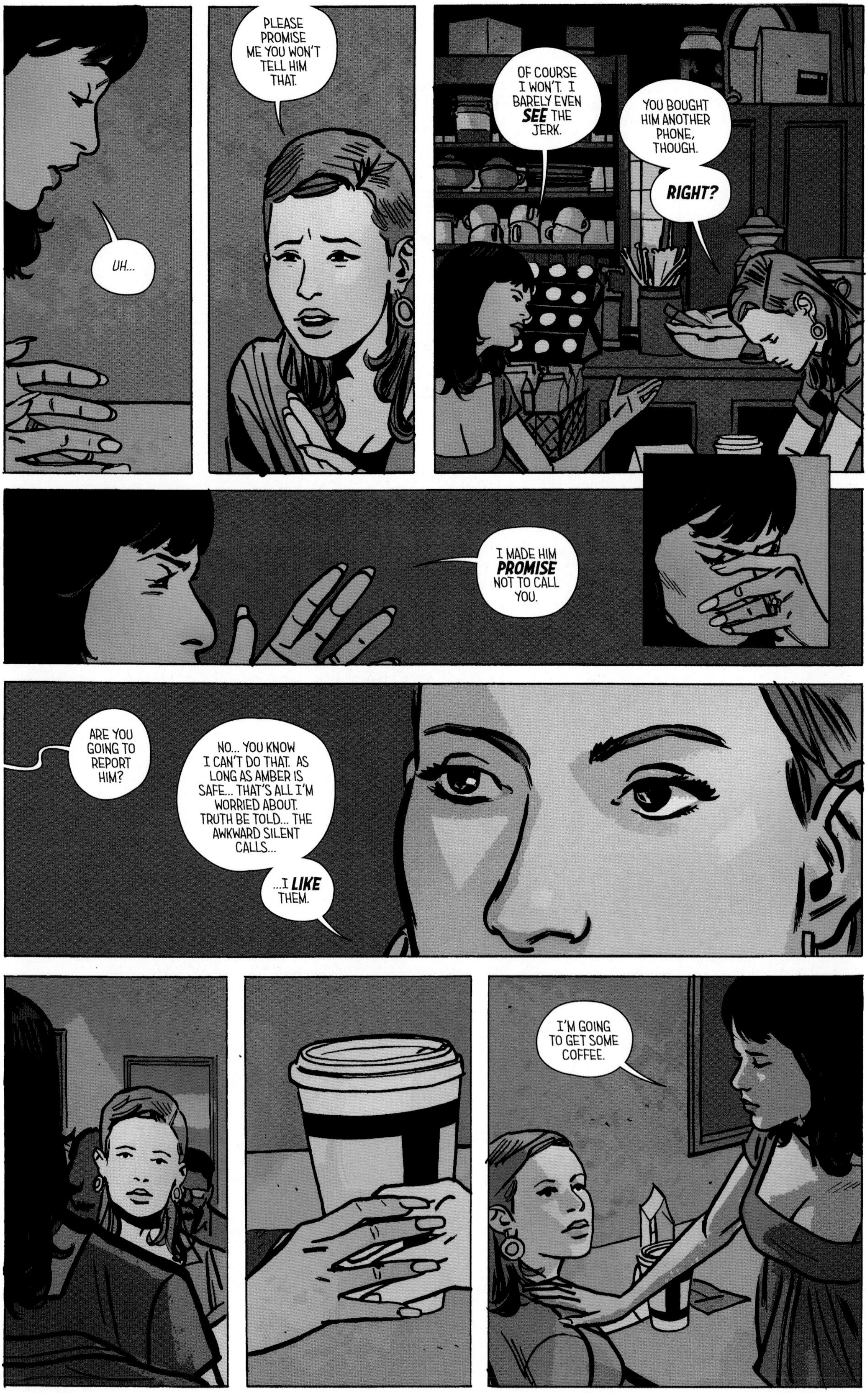
UH...
PLEASE PROMISE ME YOU WON'T TELL HIM THAT.
OF COURSE I WON'T. I BARELY EVEN SEE THE JERK.
YOU BOUGHT HIM ANOTHER PHONE, THOUGH.
RIGHT?
I MADE HIM PROMISE NOT TO CALL YOU.
ARE YOU GOING TO REPORT HIM?
NO... YOU KNOW I CAN'T DO THAT. AS LONG AS AMBER IS SAFE... THAT'S ALL I'M WORRIED ABOUT. TRUTH BE TOLD... THE AWKWARD SILENT CALLS...
...I LIKE THEM.
I'M GOING TO GET SOME COFFEE.

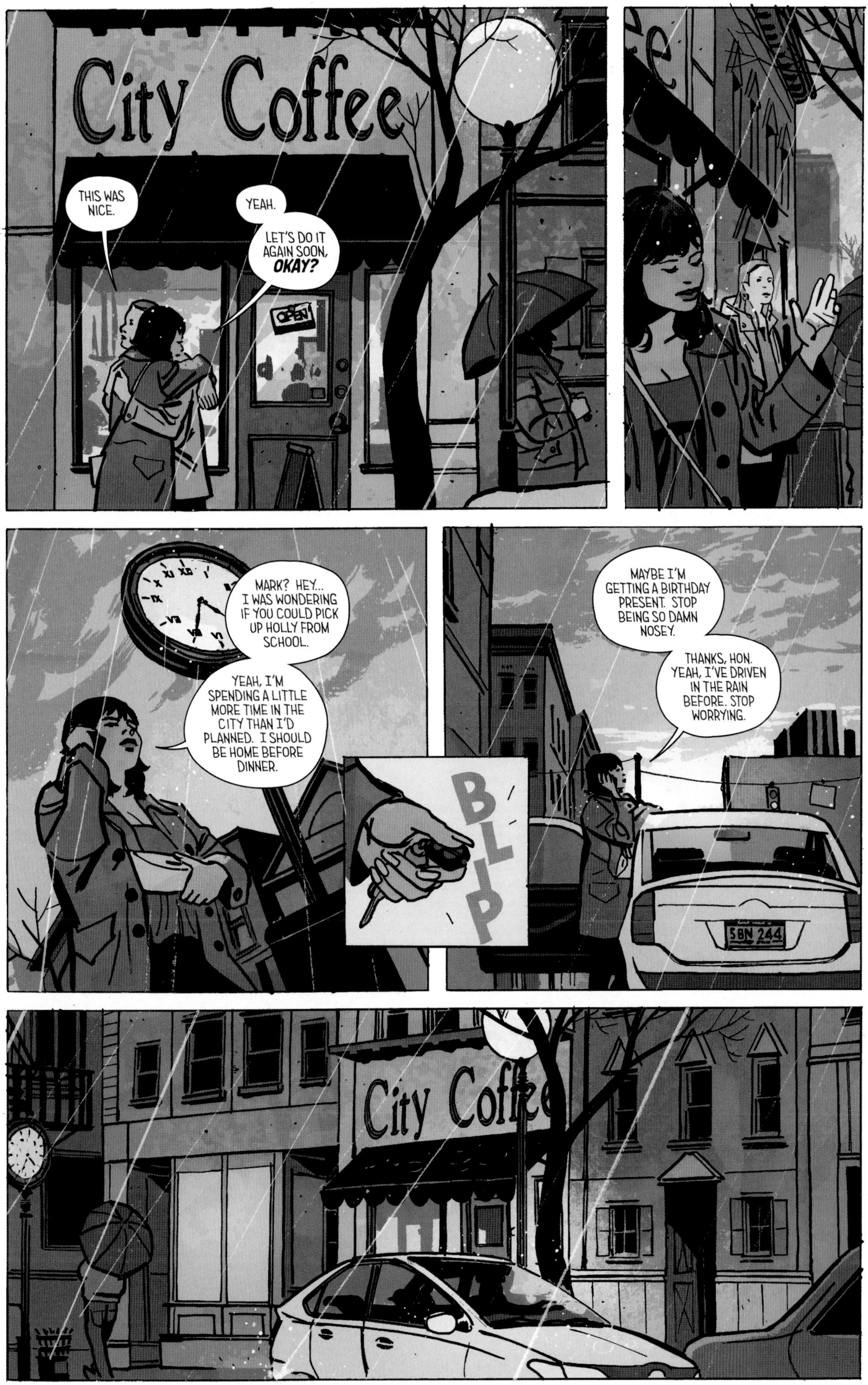
City Coffee
THIS WAS NICE.
YEAH.
LET'S DO IT AGAIN SOON, **OKAY?**
OPEN
MARK? HEY... I WAS WONDERING IF YOU COULD PICK UP HOLLY FROM SCHOOL.
YEAH, I'M SPENDING A LITTLE MORE TIME IN THE CITY THAN I'D PLANNED. I SHOULD BE HOME BEFORE DINNER.
BLIP
MAYBE I'M GETTING A BIRTHDAY PRESENT. STOP BEING SO DAMN NOSEY.
THANKS, HON. YEAH, I'VE DRIVEN IN THE RAIN BEFORE. STOP WORRYING.
SBN 244
City Coffee

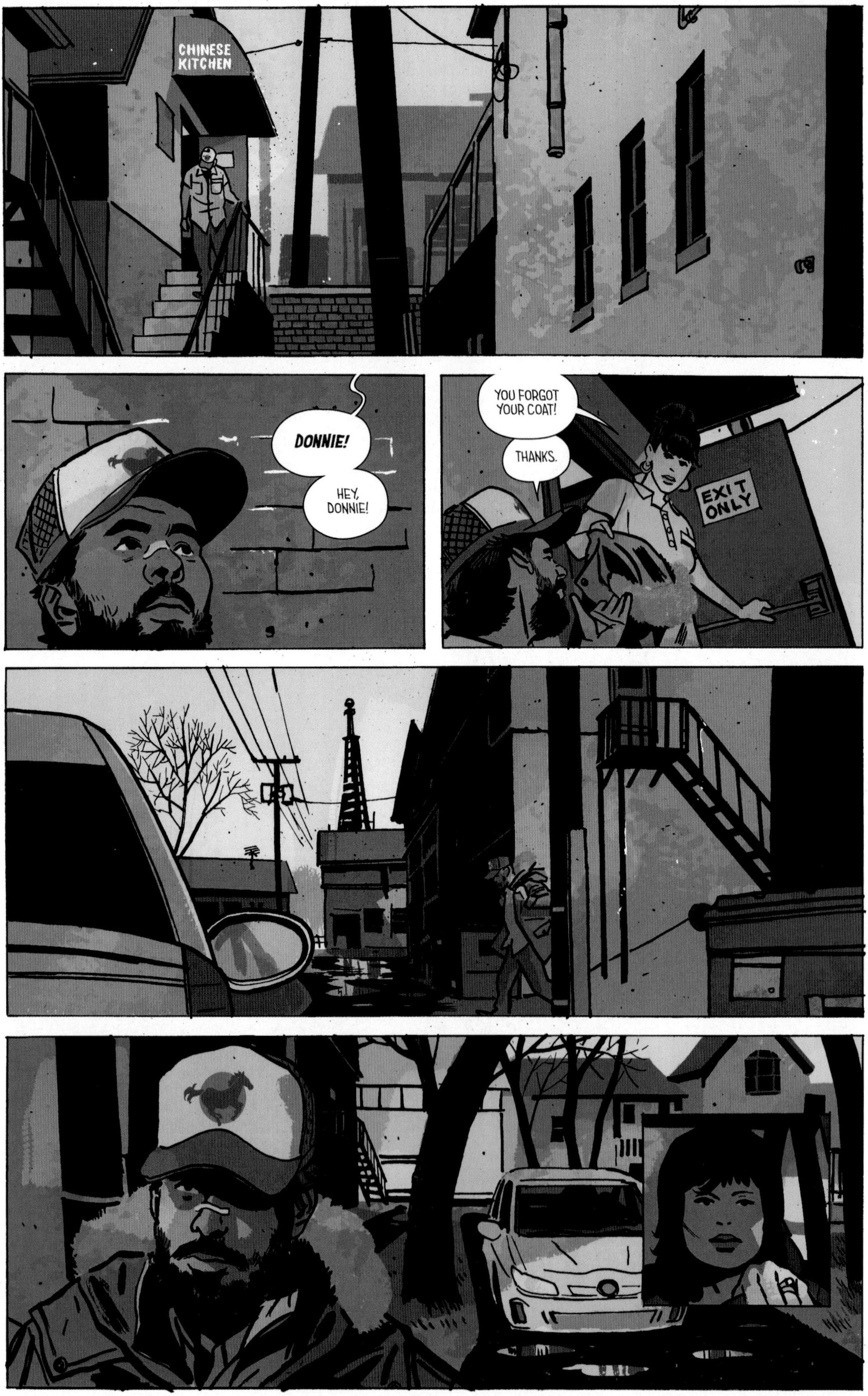
CHINESE KITCHEN
DONNIE!
HEY, DONNIE!
YOU FORGOT YOUR COAT!
THANKS.
EXIT ONLY

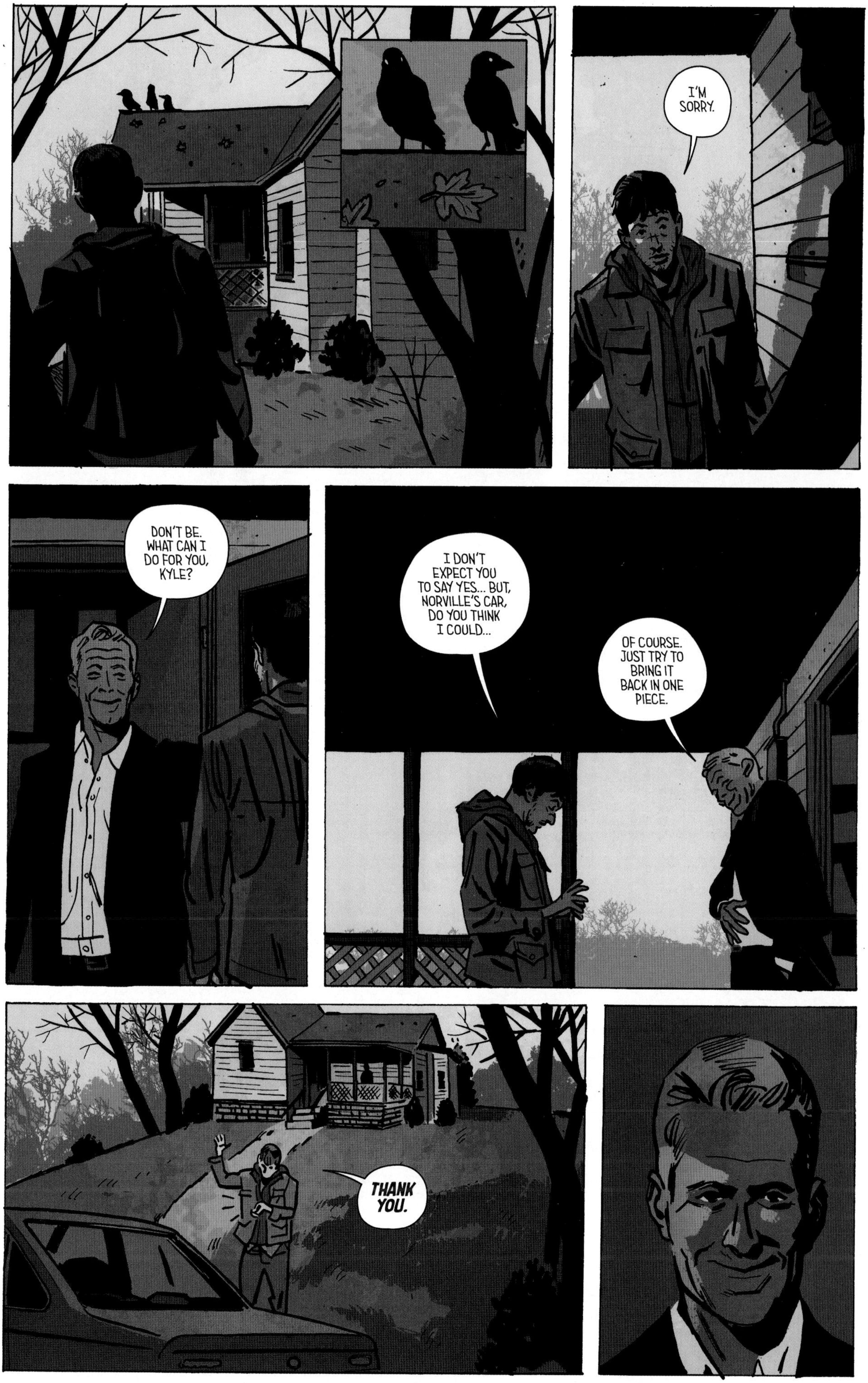
I'M SORRY.
DON'T BE. WHAT CAN I DO FOR YOU, KYLE?
I DON'T EXPECT YOU TO SAY YES... BUT, NORVILLE'S CAR, DO YOU THINK I COULD...
OF COURSE. JUST TRY TO BRING IT BACK IN ONE PIECE.
THANK YOU.

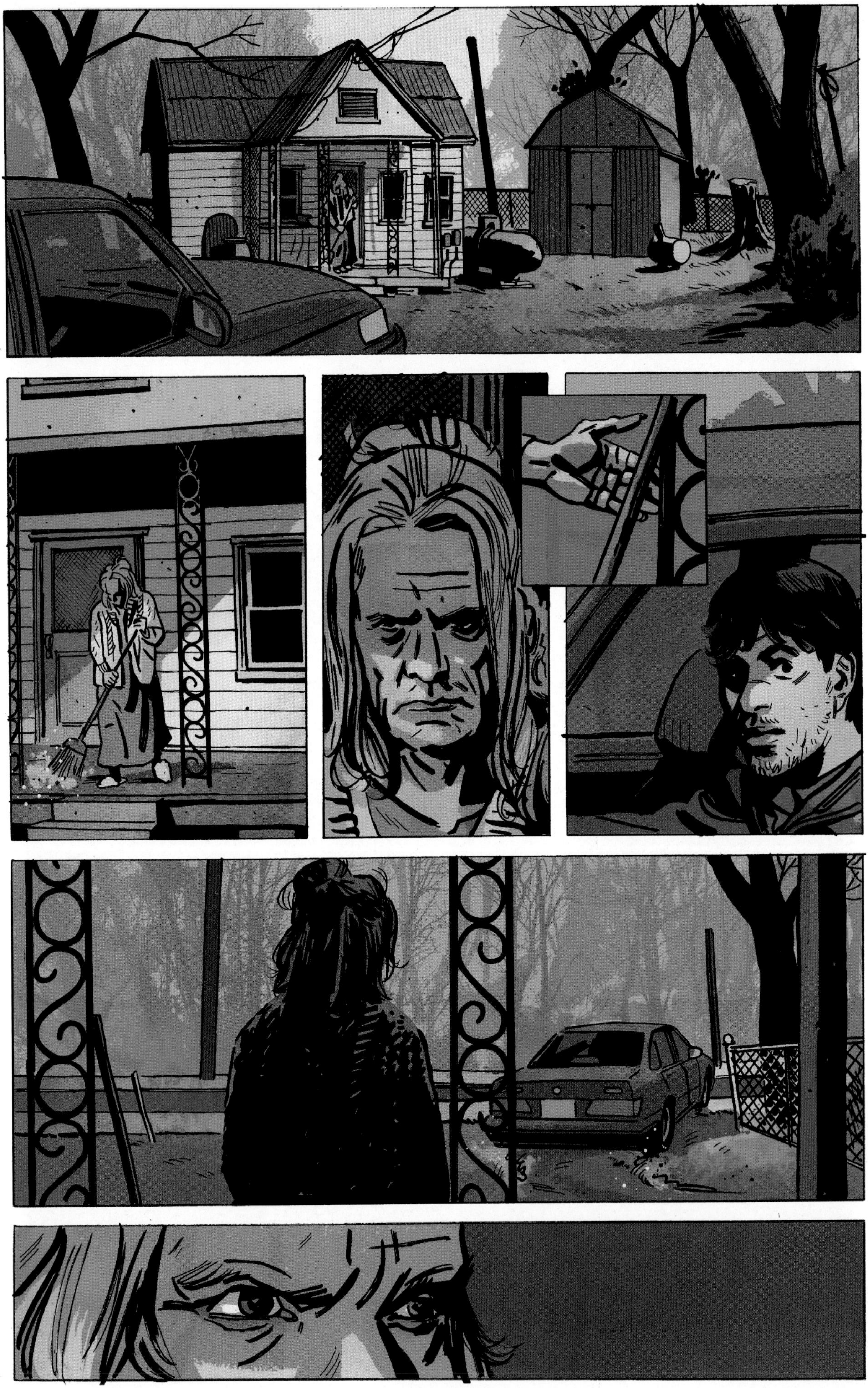

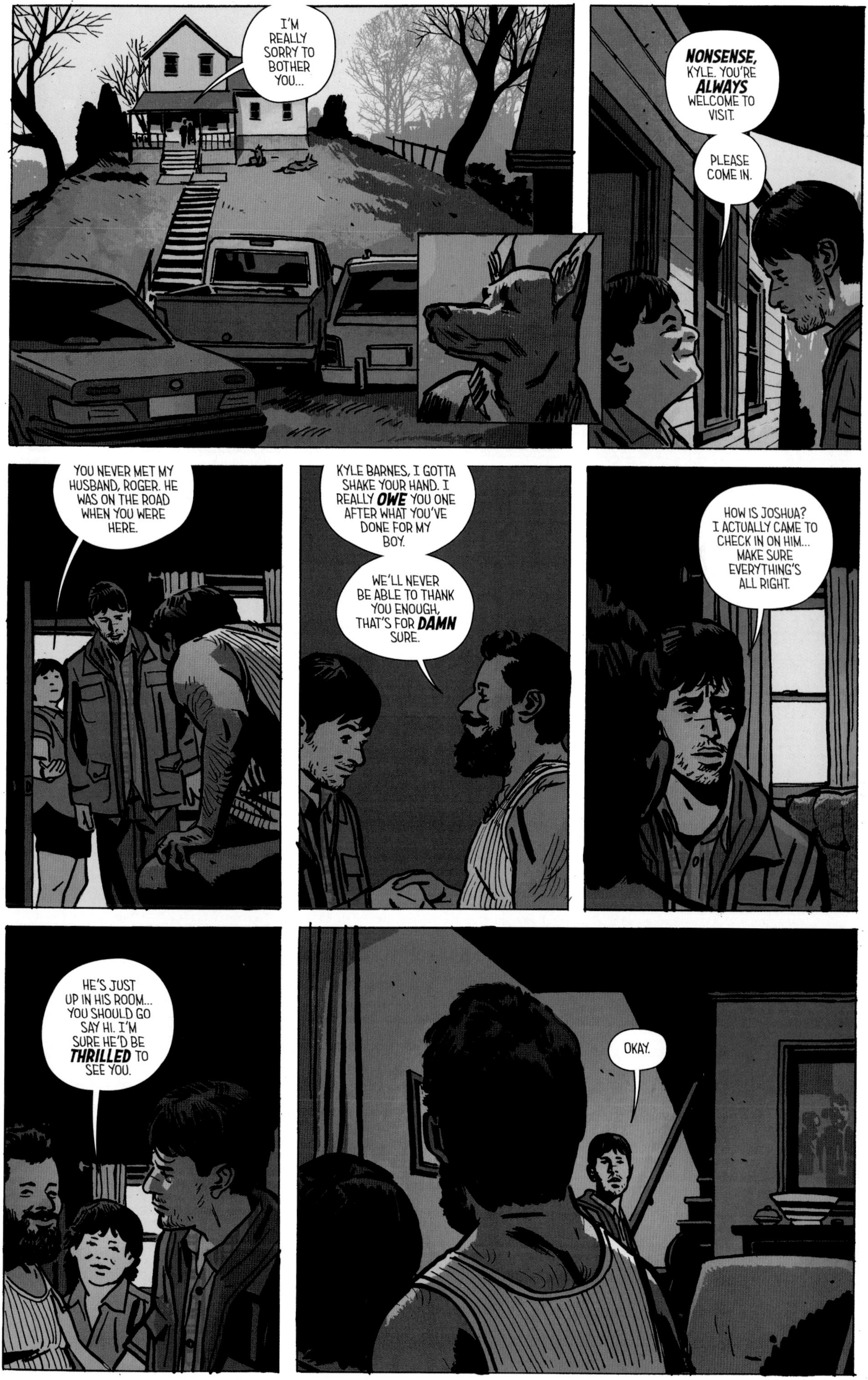
I'M REALLY SORRY TO BOTHER YOU...
NONSENSE, KYLE. YOU'RE ALWAYS WELCOME TO VISIT.
PLEASE COME IN.
YOU NEVER MET MY HUSBAND, ROGER. HE WAS ON THE ROAD WHEN YOU WERE HERE.
KYLE BARNES, I GOTTA SHAKE YOUR HAND. I REALLY OWE YOU ONE AFTER WHAT YOU'VE DONE FOR MY BOY.
WE'LL NEVER BE ABLE TO THANK YOU ENOUGH, THAT'S FOR DAMN SURE.
HOW IS JOSHUA? I ACTUALLY CAME TO CHECK IN ON HIM... MAKE SURE EVERYTHING'S ALL RIGHT.
HE'S JUST UP IN HIS ROOM... YOU SHOULD GO SAY HI. I'M SURE HE'D BE THRILLED TO SEE YOU.
OKAY.

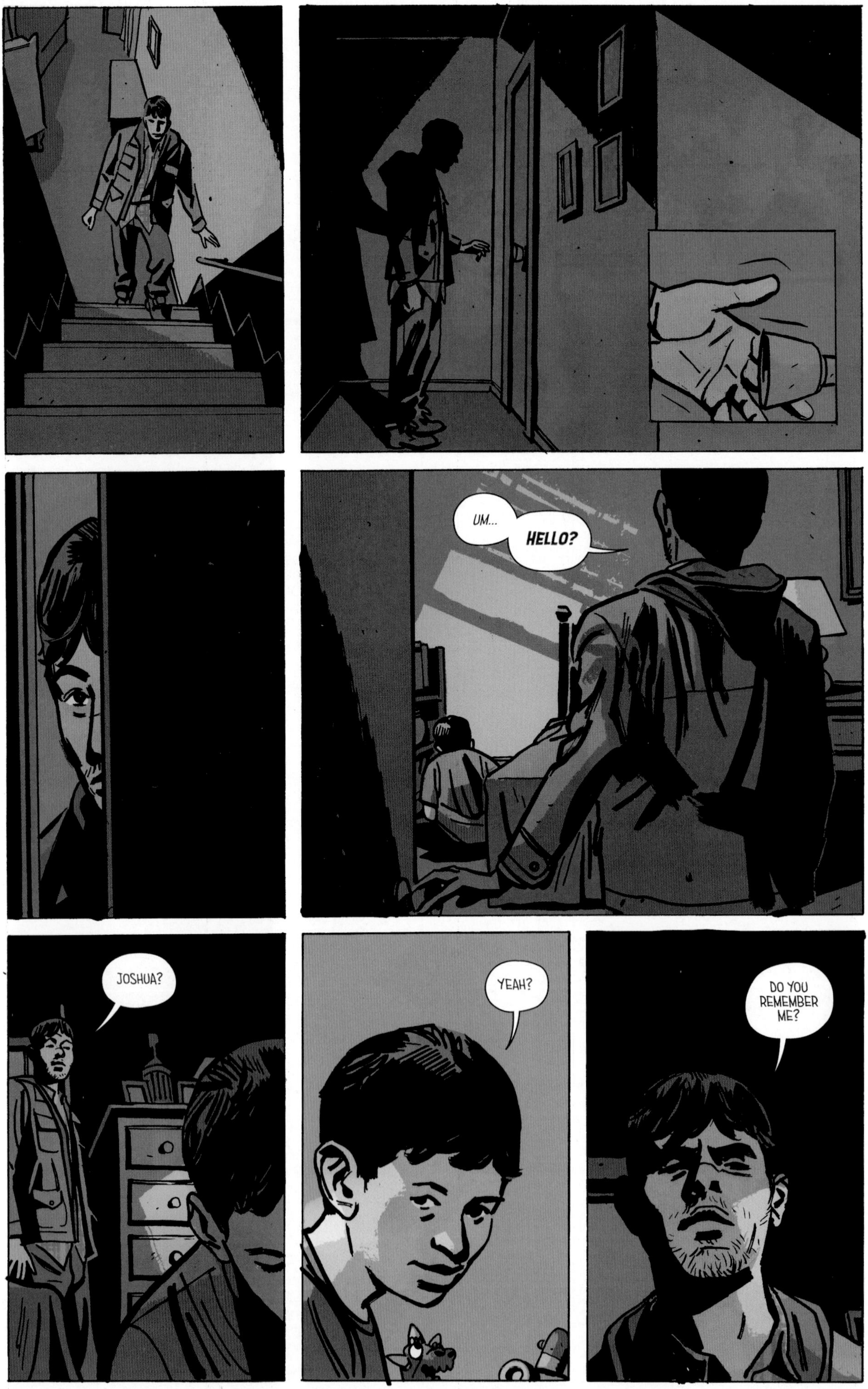
UM...
HELLO?
JOSHUA?
YEAH?
DO YOU REMEMBER ME?

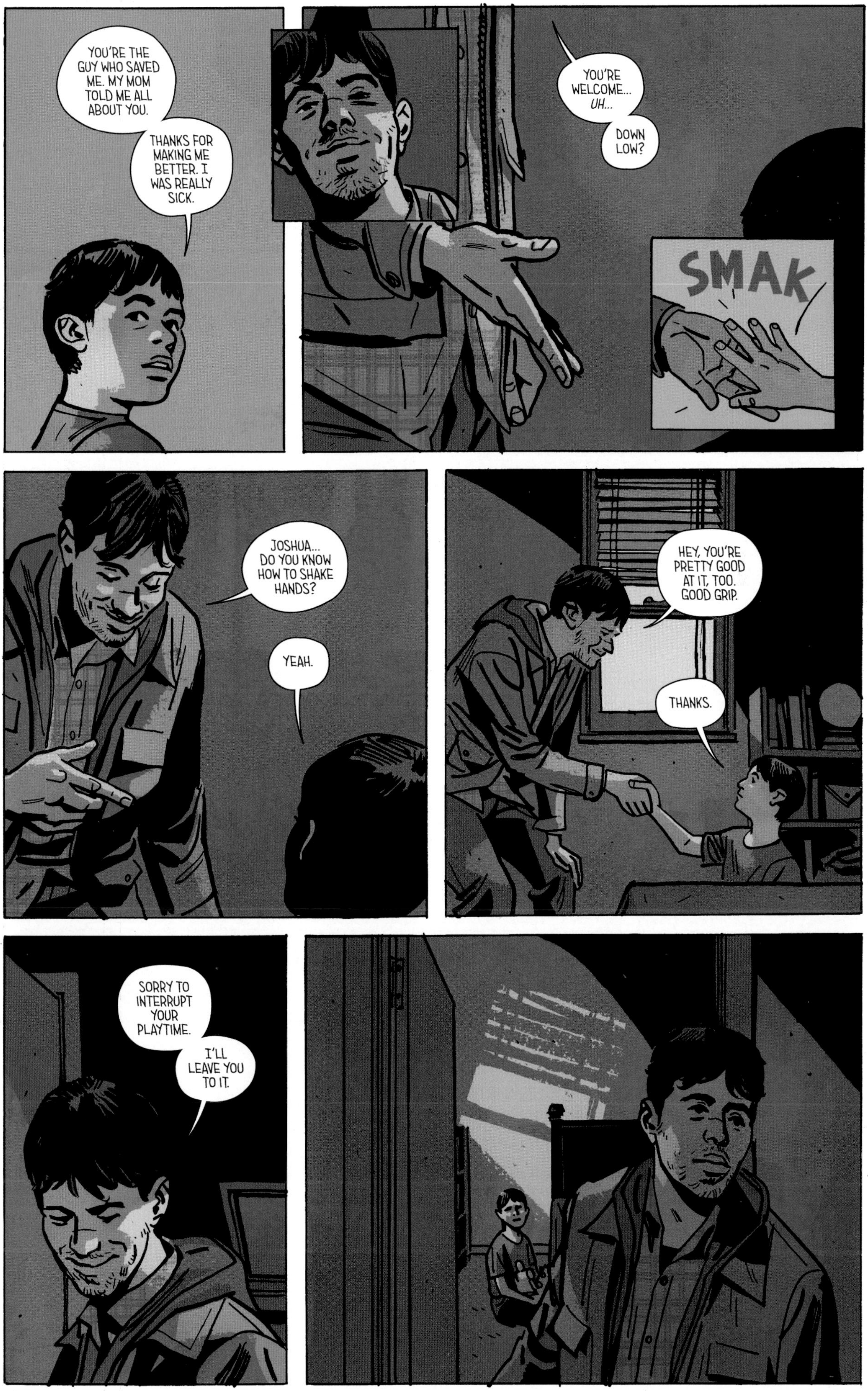

YOU'RE THE GUY WHO SAVED ME. MY MOM TOLD ME ALL ABOUT YOU.
THANKS FOR MAKING ME BETTER. I WAS REALLY SICK.
YOU'RE WELCOME... UH...
DOWN LOW?
SMAK
JOSHUA... DO YOU KNOW HOW TO SHAKE HANDS?
YEAH.
HEY, YOU'RE PRETTY GOOD AT IT, TOO. GOOD GRIP.
THANKS.
SORRY TO INTERRUPT YOUR PLAYTIME.
I'LL LEAVE YOU TO IT.

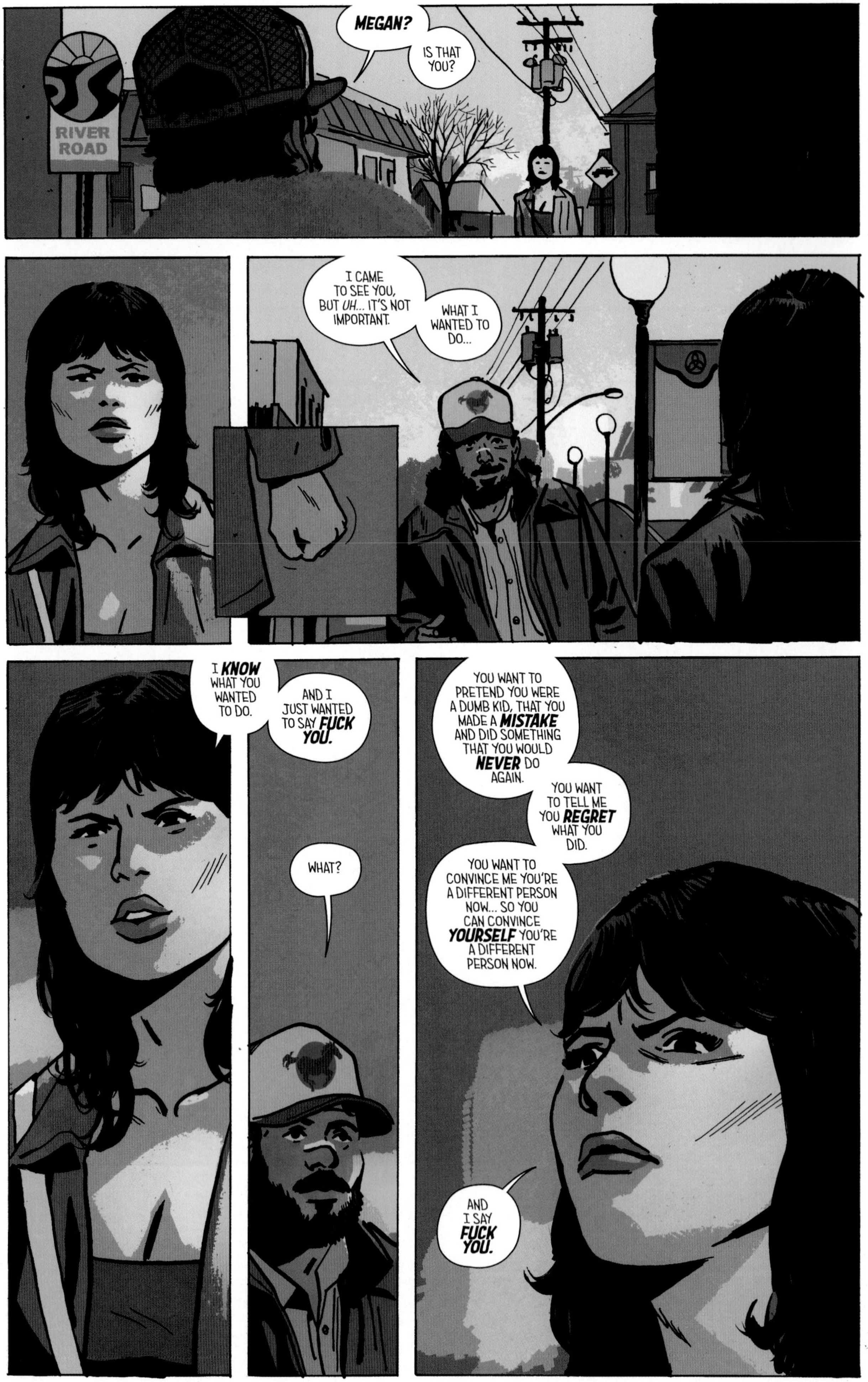
RIVER ROAD
MEGAN?
IS THAT YOU?
I CAME TO SEE YOU, BUT UH... IT'S NOT IMPORTANT.
WHAT I WANTED TO DO...
I KNOW WHAT YOU WANTED TO DO.
AND I JUST WANTED TO SAY FUCK YOU.
WHAT?
YOU WANT TO PRETEND YOU WERE A DUMB KID, THAT YOU MADE A MISTAKE AND DID SOMETHING THAT YOU WOULD NEVER DO AGAIN.
YOU WANT TO TELL ME YOU REGRET WHAT YOU DID.
YOU WANT TO CONVINCE ME YOU'RE A DIFFERENT PERSON NOW... SO YOU CAN CONVINCE YOURSELF YOU'RE A DIFFERENT PERSON NOW.
AND I SAY FUCK YOU.

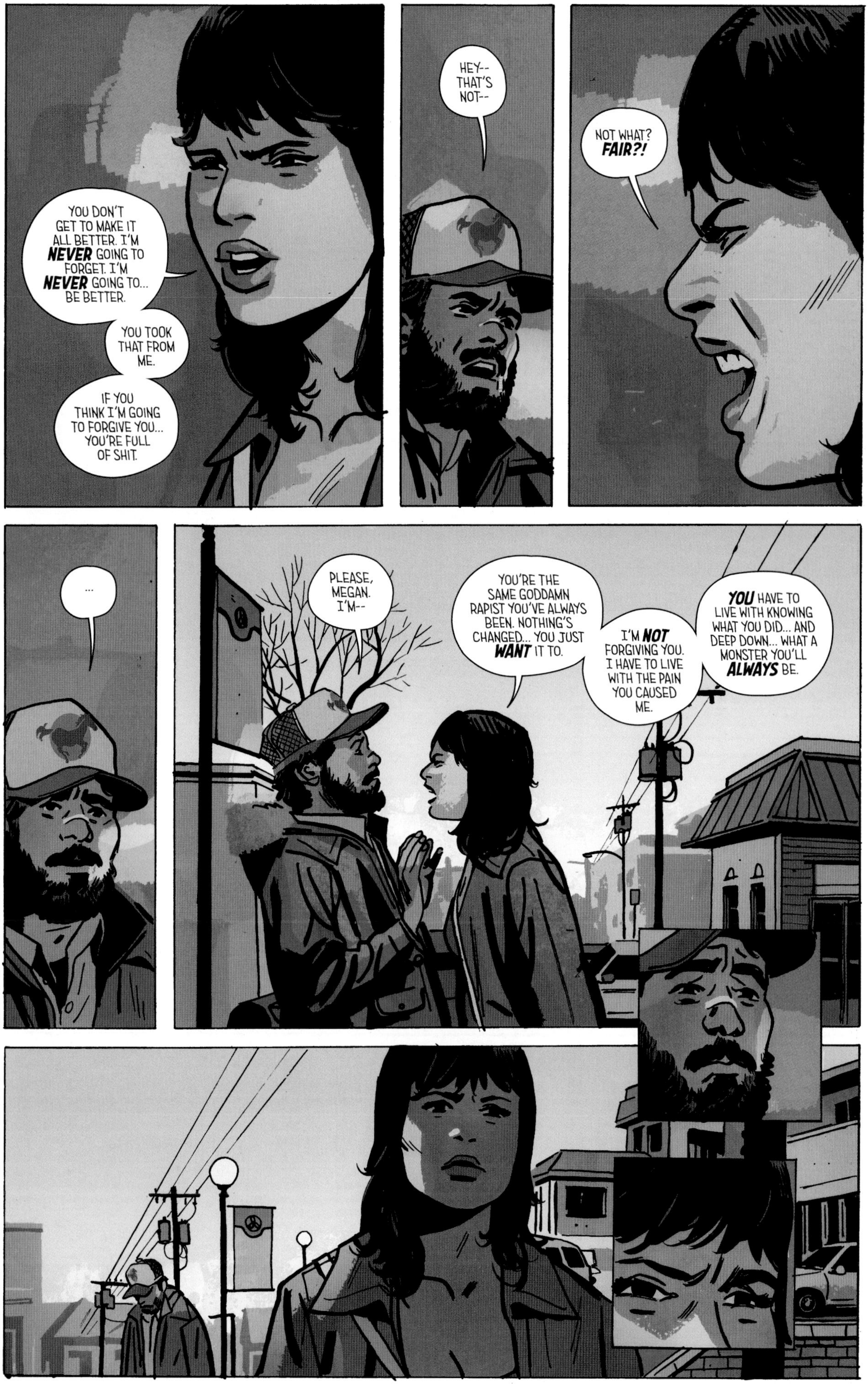
YOU DON'T GET TO MAKE IT ALL BETTER. I'M **NEVER** GOING TO FORGET. I'M **NEVER** GOING TO... BE BETTER.
YOU TOOK THAT FROM ME.
IF YOU THINK I'M GOING TO FORGIVE YOU... YOU'RE FULL OF SHIT.
HEY-- THAT'S NOT--
NOT WHAT? ***FAIR?!***
...
PLEASE, MEGAN. I'M--
YOU'RE THE SAME GODDAMN RAPIST YOU'VE ALWAYS BEEN. NOTHING'S CHANGED... YOU JUST **WANT** IT TO.
I'M **NOT** FORGIVING YOU. I HAVE TO LIVE WITH THE PAIN YOU CAUSED ME.
YOU HAVE TO LIVE WITH KNOWING WHAT YOU DID... AND DEEP DOWN... WHAT A MONSTER YOU'LL **ALWAYS** BE.

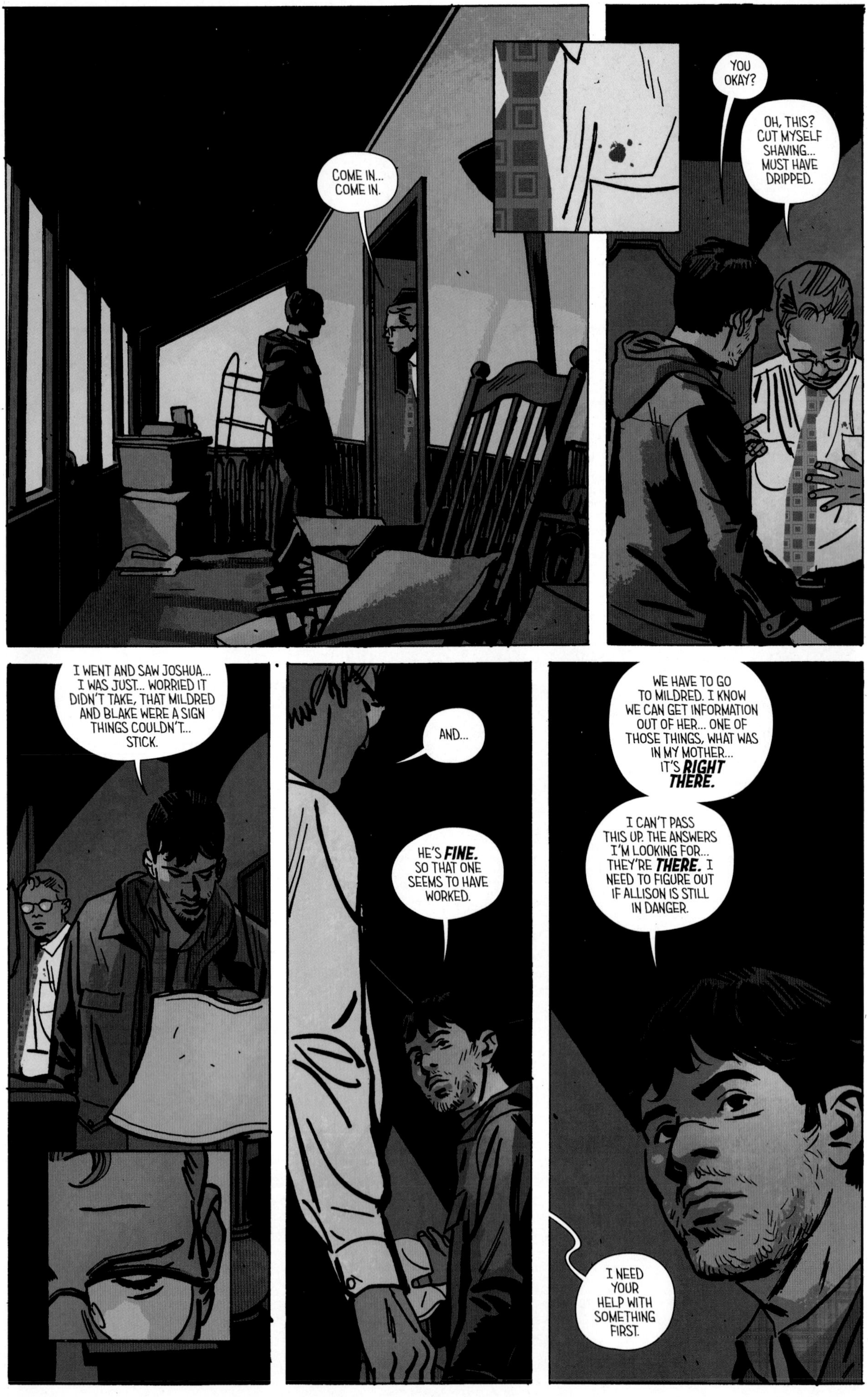
COME IN... COME IN.
YOU OKAY?
OH, THIS? CUT MYSELF SHAVING... MUST HAVE DRIPPED.
I WENT AND SAW JOSHUA... I WAS JUST... WORRIED IT DIDN'T TAKE, THAT MILDRED AND BLAKE WERE A SIGN THINGS COULDN'T... STICK.
AND...
HE'S **FINE.** SO THAT ONE SEEMS TO HAVE WORKED.
WE HAVE TO GO TO MILDRED. I KNOW WE CAN GET INFORMATION OUT OF HER... ONE OF THOSE THINGS, WHAT WAS IN MY MOTHER... IT'S **RIGHT THERE.**
I CAN'T PASS THIS UP. THE ANSWERS I'M LOOKING FOR... THEY'RE **THERE.** I NEED TO FIGURE OUT IF ALLISON IS STILL IN DANGER.
I NEED YOUR HELP WITH SOMETHING FIRST.

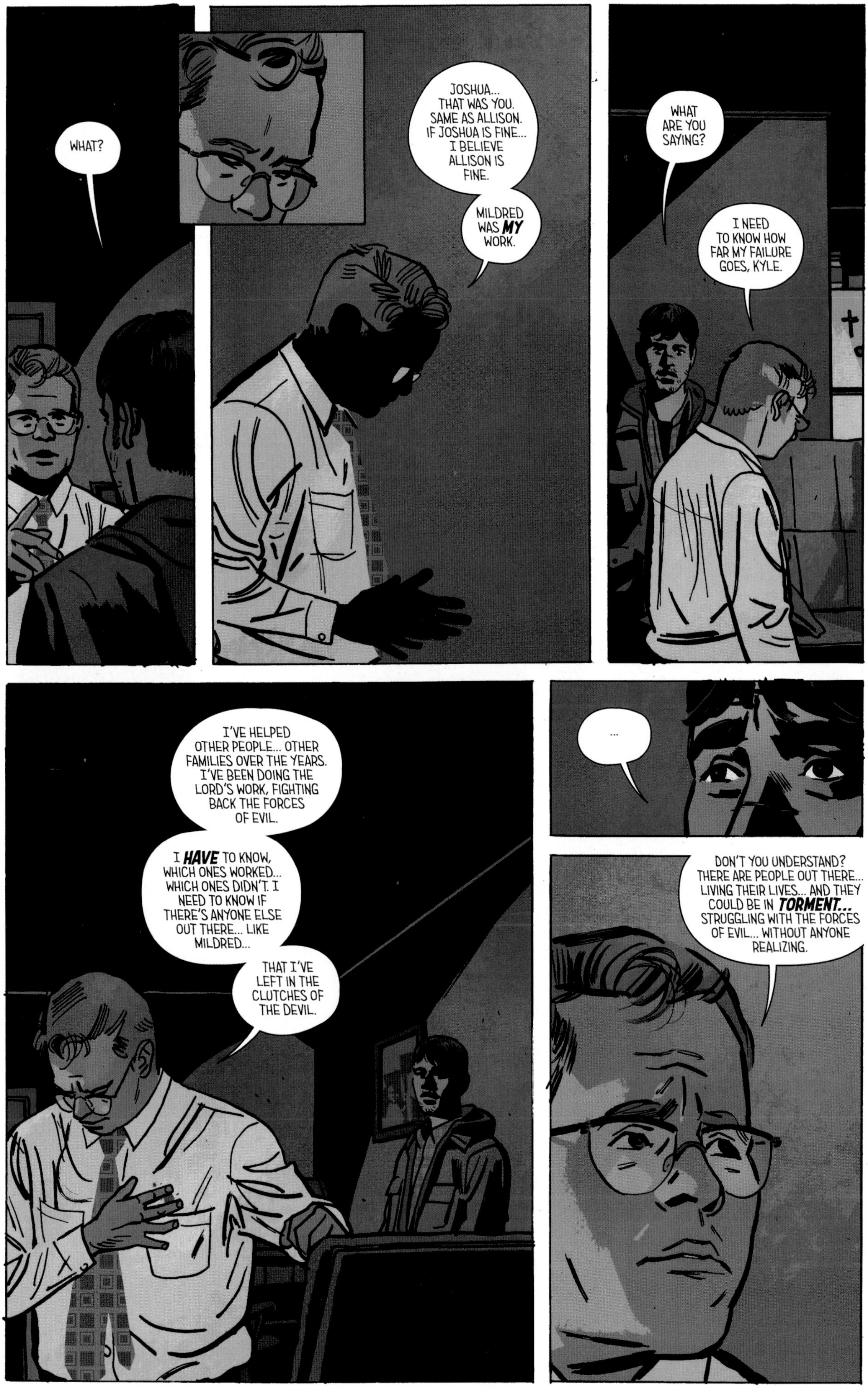
WHAT?
JOSHUA... THAT WAS YOU. SAME AS ALLISON. IF JOSHUA IS FINE... I BELIEVE ALLISON IS FINE.
MILDRED WAS MY WORK.
WHAT ARE YOU SAYING?
I NEED TO KNOW HOW FAR MY FAILURE GOES, KYLE.
I'VE HELPED OTHER PEOPLE... OTHER FAMILIES OVER THE YEARS. I'VE BEEN DOING THE LORD'S WORK, FIGHTING BACK THE FORCES OF EVIL.
I HAVE TO KNOW, WHICH ONES WORKED... WHICH ONES DIDN'T. I NEED TO KNOW IF THERE'S ANYONE ELSE OUT THERE... LIKE MILDRED...
THAT I'VE LEFT IN THE CLUTCHES OF THE DEVIL.
...
DON'T YOU UNDERSTAND? THERE ARE PEOPLE OUT THERE... LIVING THEIR LIVES... AND THEY COULD BE IN TORMENT... STRUGGLING WITH THE FORCES OF EVIL... WITHOUT ANYONE REALIZING.

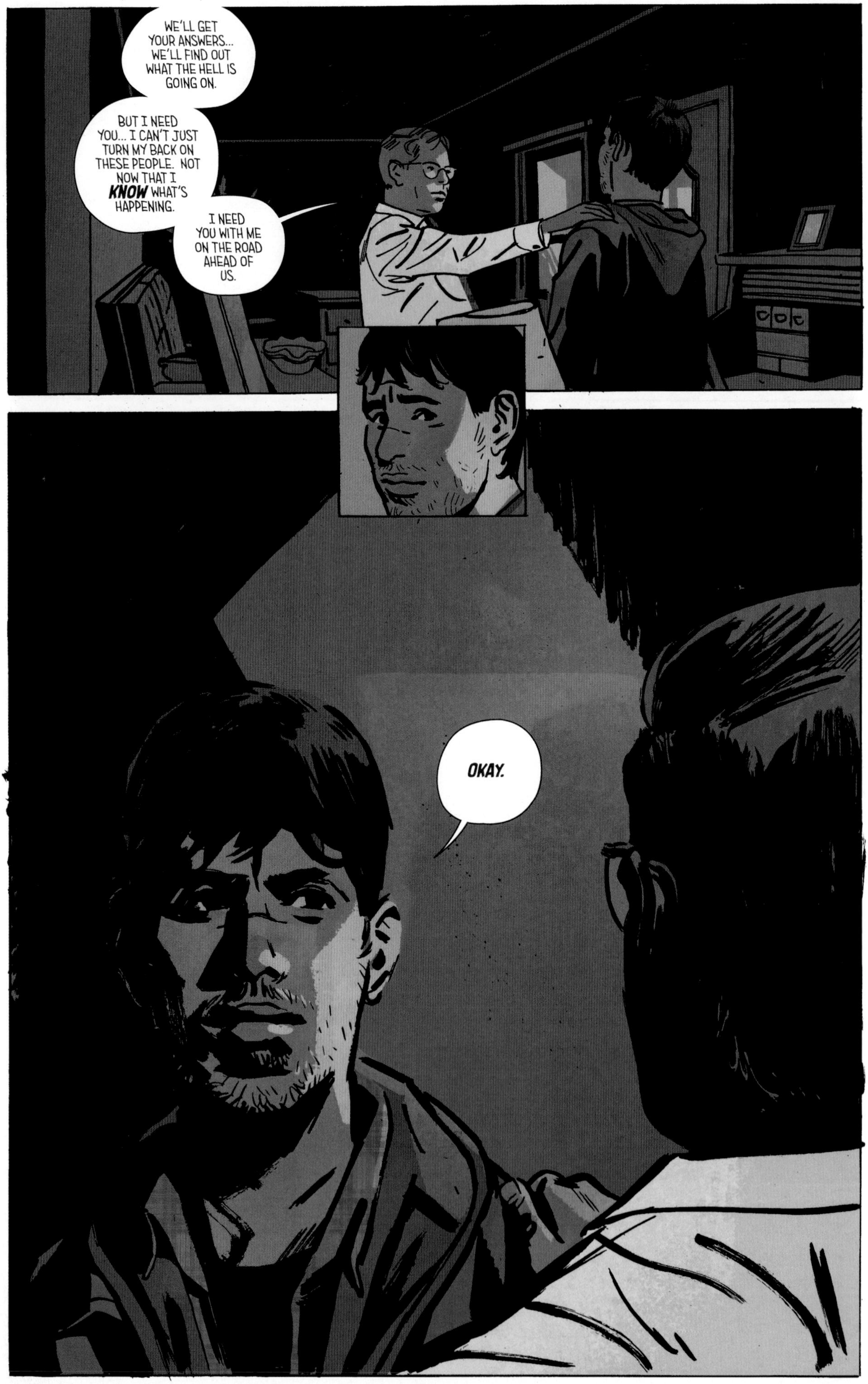
WE'LL GET YOUR ANSWERS... WE'LL FIND OUT WHAT THE HELL IS GOING ON.
BUT I NEED YOU... I CAN'T JUST TURN MY BACK ON THESE PEOPLE. NOT NOW THAT I **KNOW** WHAT'S HAPPENING.
I NEED YOU WITH ME ON THE ROAD AHEAD OF US.
OKAY.

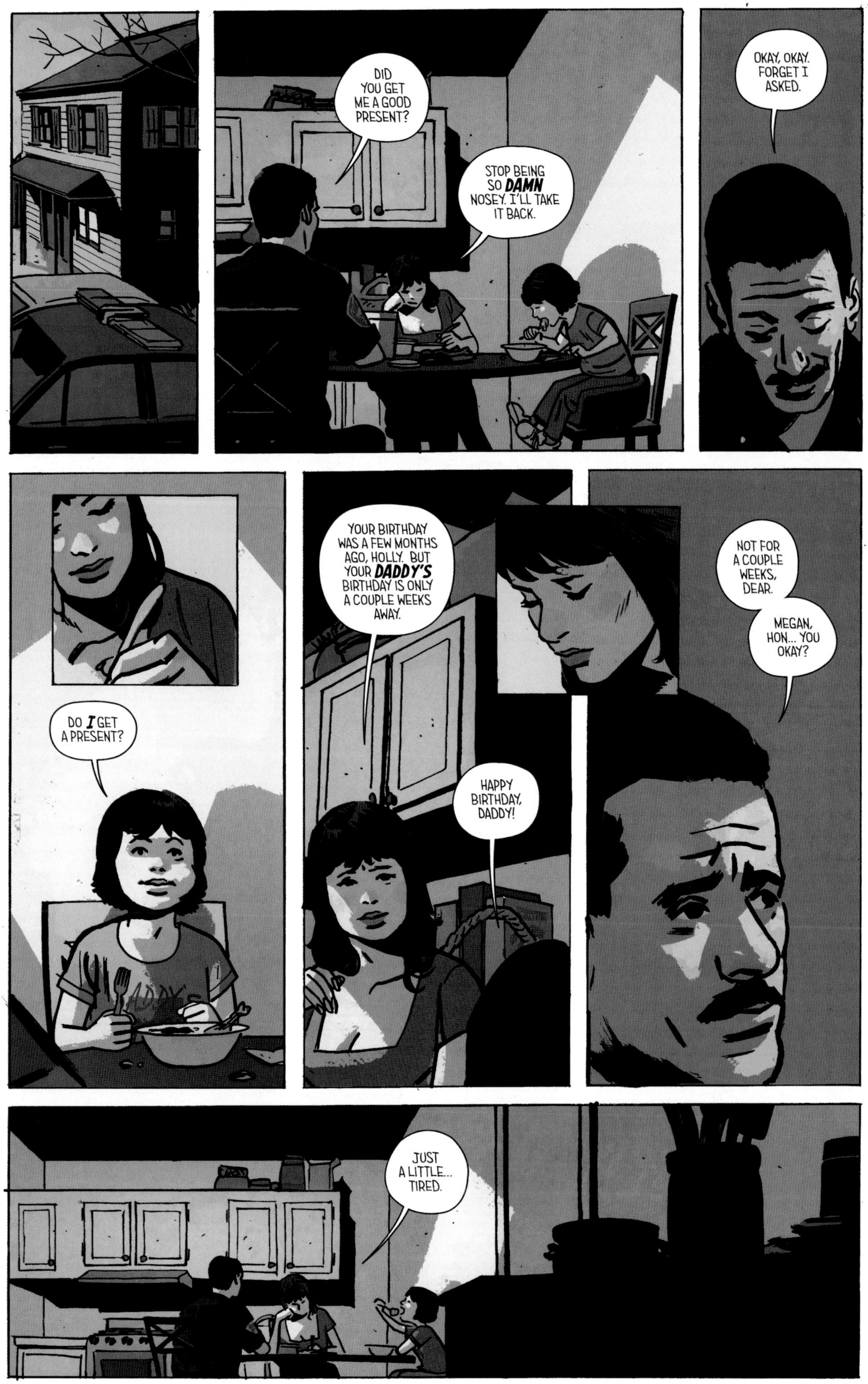
DID YOU GET ME A GOOD PRESENT?
STOP BEING SO **DAMN** NOSEY. I'LL TAKE IT BACK.
OKAY, OKAY. FORGET I ASKED.
DO **I** GET A PRESENT?
YOUR BIRTHDAY WAS A FEW MONTHS AGO, HOLLY. BUT YOUR **DADDY'S** BIRTHDAY IS ONLY A COUPLE WEEKS AWAY.
HAPPY BIRTHDAY, DADDY!
NOT FOR A COUPLE WEEKS, DEAR.
MEGAN, HON... YOU OKAY?
JUST A LITTLE... TIRED.

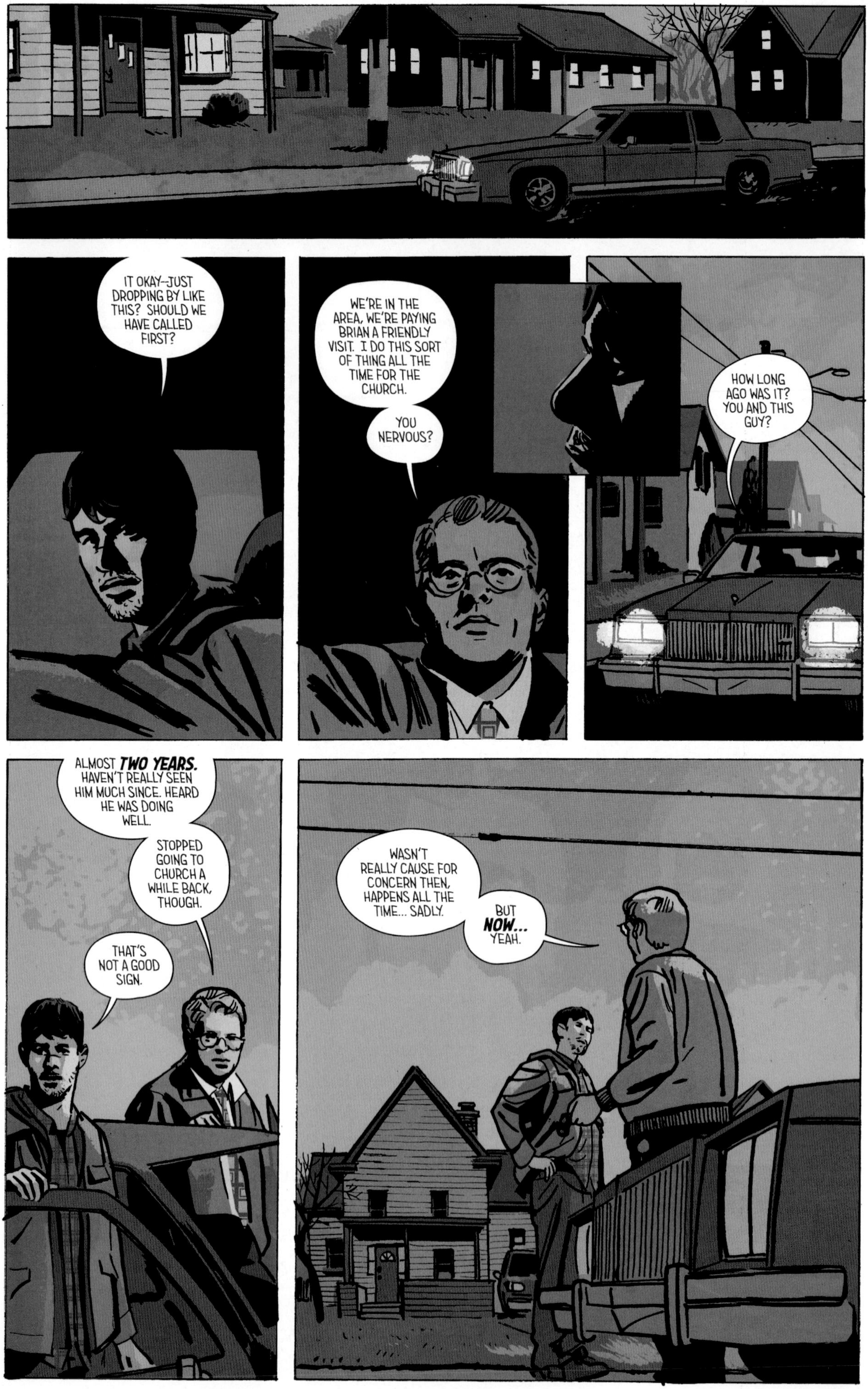
IT OKAY--JUST DROPPING BY LIKE THIS? SHOULD WE HAVE CALLED FIRST?
WE'RE IN THE AREA, WE'RE PAYING BRIAN A FRIENDLY VISIT. I DO THIS SORT OF THING ALL THE TIME FOR THE CHURCH.
YOU NERVOUS?
HOW LONG AGO WAS IT? YOU AND THIS GUY?
ALMOST **TWO YEARS.** HAVEN'T REALLY SEEN HIM MUCH SINCE. HEARD HE WAS DOING WELL.
STOPPED GOING TO CHURCH A WHILE BACK, THOUGH.
THAT'S NOT A GOOD SIGN.
WASN'T REALLY CAUSE FOR CONCERN THEN, HAPPENS ALL THE TIME... SADLY.
BUT **NOW...** YEAH.

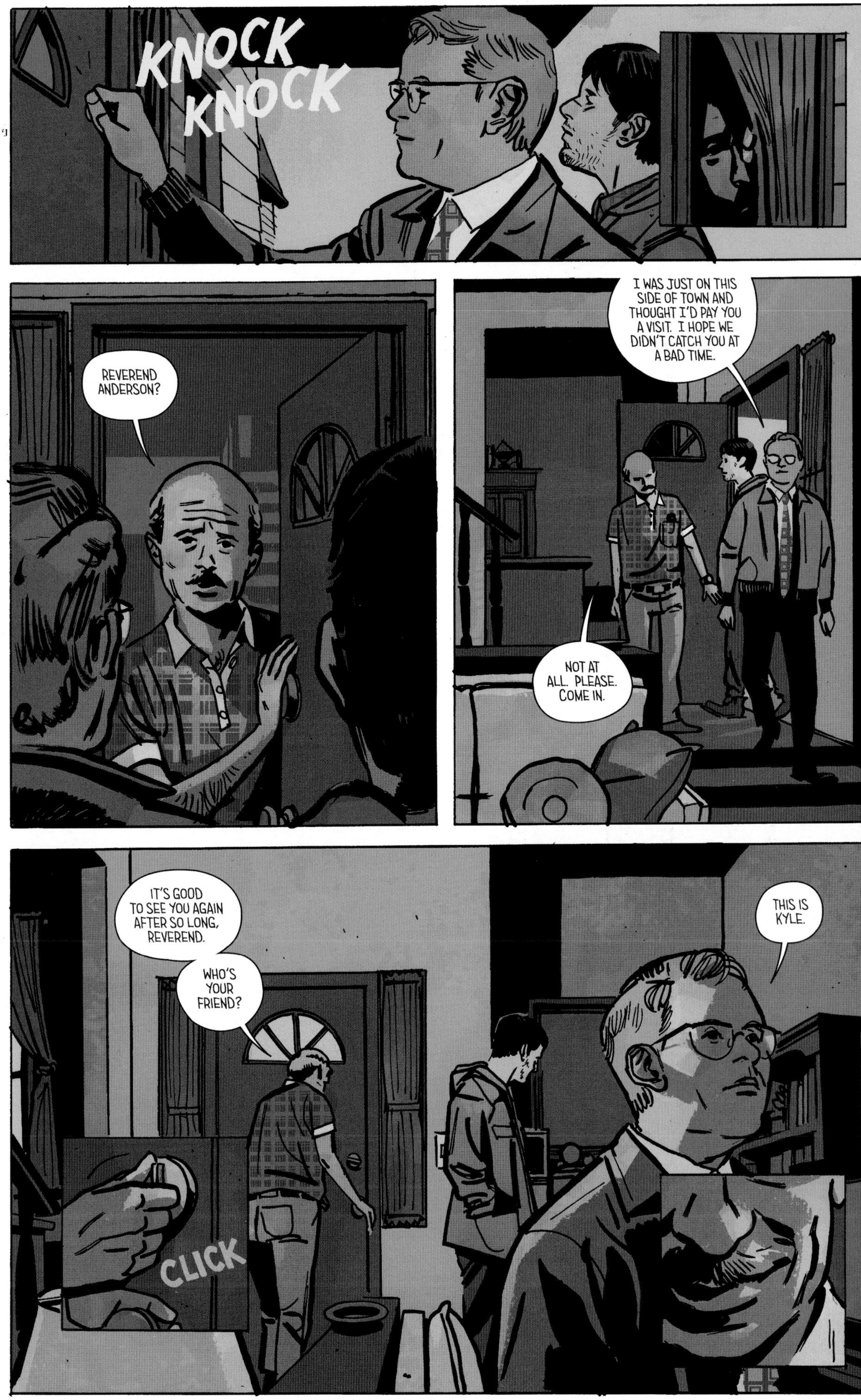
KNOCK KNOCK
REVEREND ANDERSON?
I WAS JUST ON THIS SIDE OF TOWN AND THOUGHT I'D PAY YOU A VISIT. I HOPE WE DIDN'T CATCH YOU AT A BAD TIME.
NOT AT ALL. PLEASE. COME IN.
IT'S GOOD TO SEE YOU AGAIN AFTER SO LONG, REVEREND.
WHO'S YOUR FRIEND?
THIS IS KYLE.
CLICK

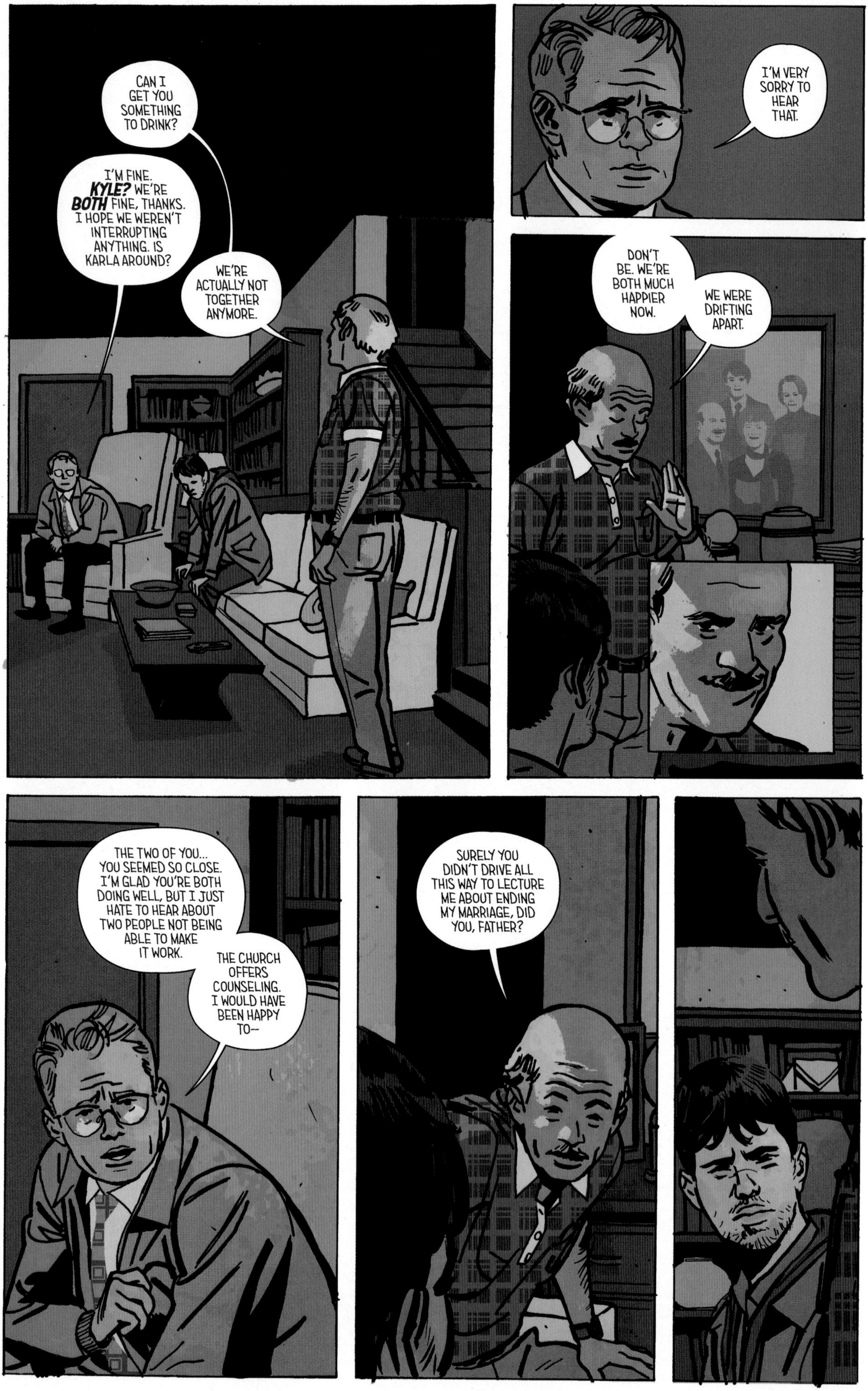
CAN I GET YOU SOMETHING TO DRINK?
I'M FINE. KYLE? WE'RE BOTH FINE, THANKS. I HOPE WE WEREN'T INTERRUPTING ANYTHING. IS KARLA AROUND?
WE'RE ACTUALLY NOT TOGETHER ANYMORE.
I'M VERY SORRY TO HEAR THAT.
DON'T BE. WE'RE BOTH MUCH HAPPIER NOW.
WE WERE DRIFTING APART.
THE TWO OF YOU... YOU SEEMED SO CLOSE. I'M GLAD YOU'RE BOTH DOING WELL, BUT I JUST HATE TO HEAR ABOUT TWO PEOPLE NOT BEING ABLE TO MAKE IT WORK.
THE CHURCH OFFERS COUNSELING. I WOULD HAVE BEEN HAPPY TO--
SURELY YOU DIDN'T DRIVE ALL THIS WAY TO LECTURE ME ABOUT ENDING MY MARRIAGE, DID YOU, FATHER?

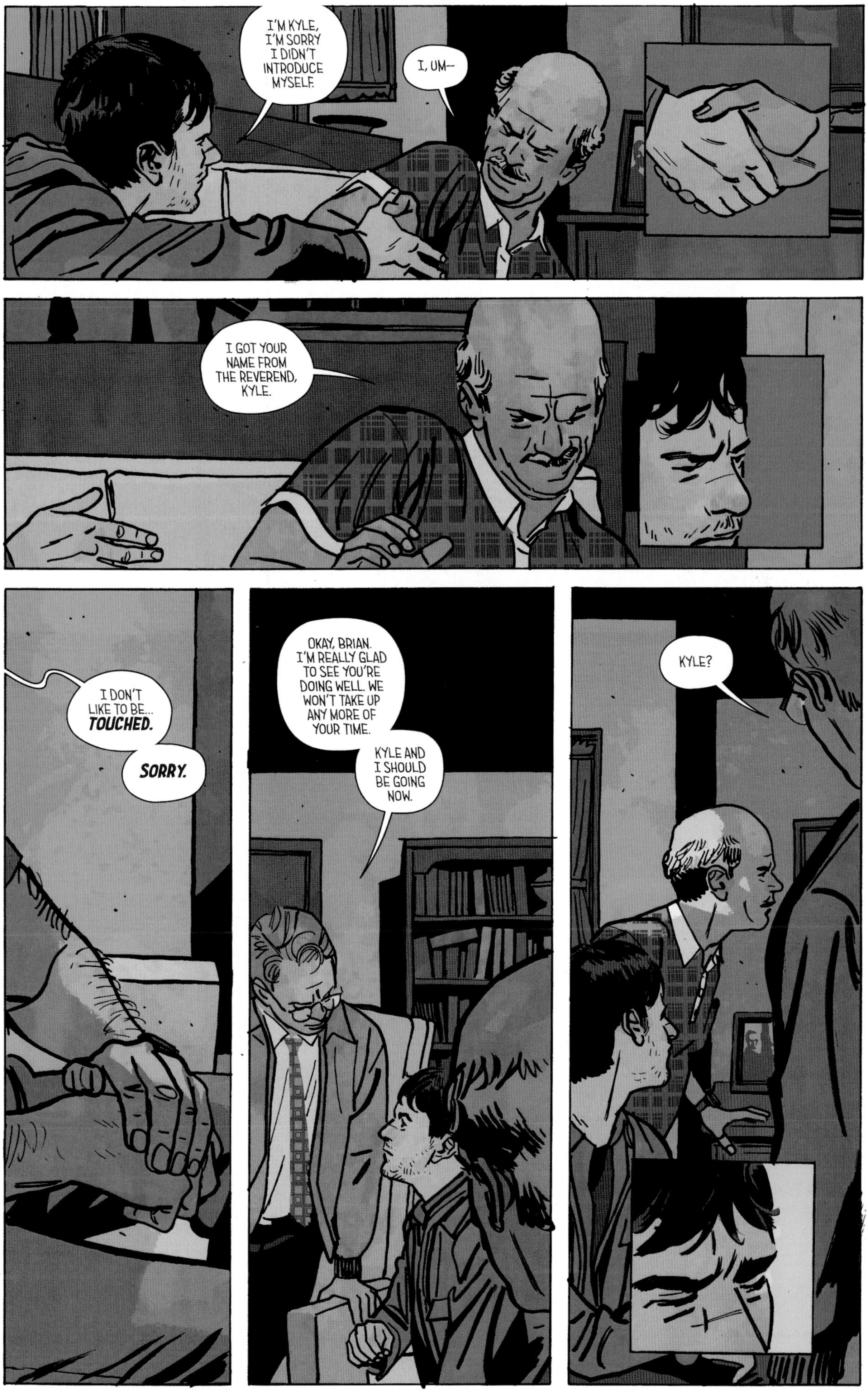
I'M KYLE, I'M SORRY I DIDN'T INTRODUCE MYSELF.
I, UM--
I GOT YOUR NAME FROM THE REVEREND, KYLE.
I DON'T LIKE TO BE... TOUCHED.
SORRY.
OKAY, BRIAN. I'M REALLY GLAD TO SEE YOU'RE DOING WELL. WE WON'T TAKE UP ANY MORE OF YOUR TIME.
KYLE AND I SHOULD BE GOING NOW.
KYLE?

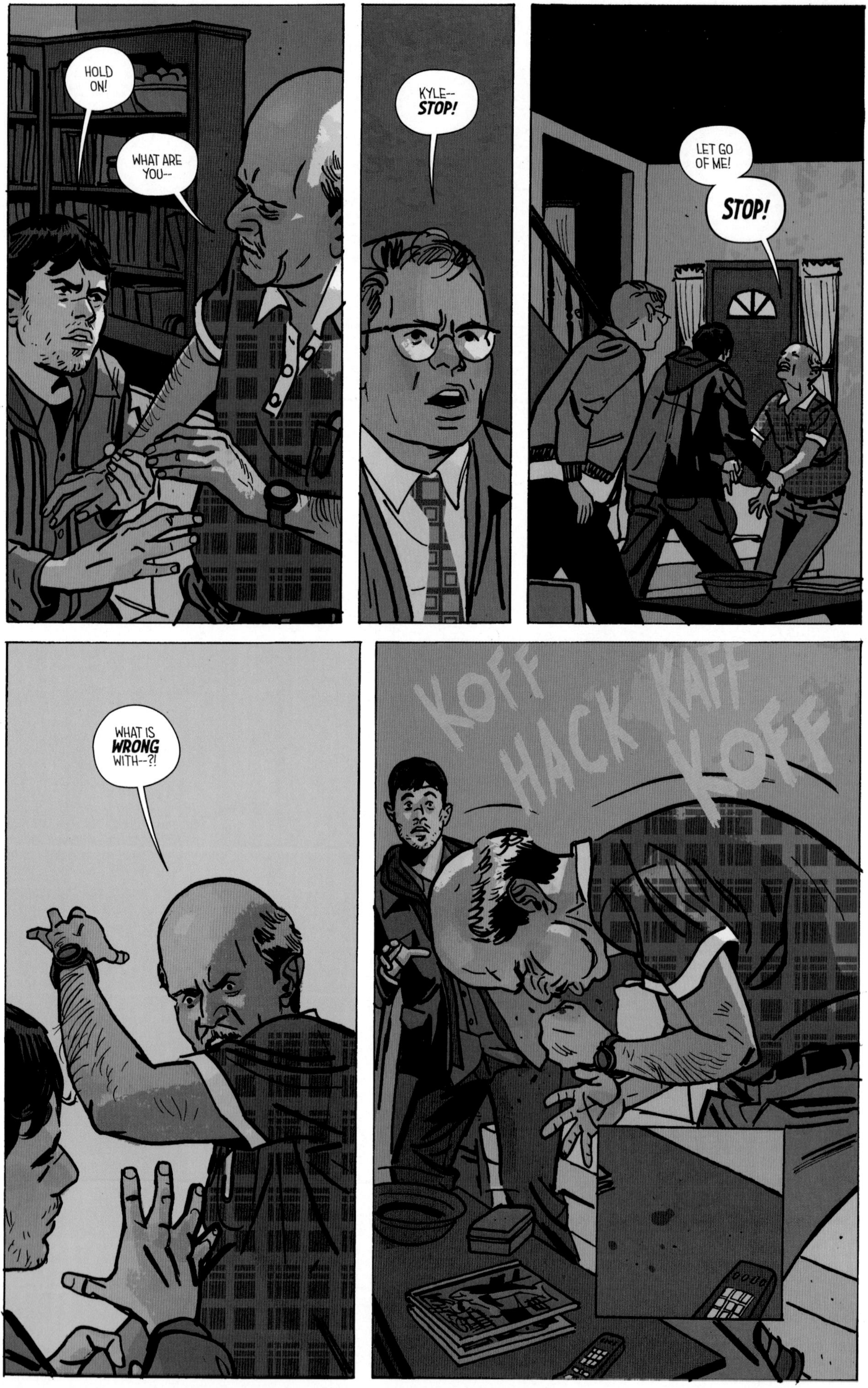
HOLD ON!
WHAT ARE YOU--
KYLE-- STOP!
LET GO OF ME!
STOP!
WHAT IS WRONG WITH--?!
KOFF
HACK
KAFF
KOFF

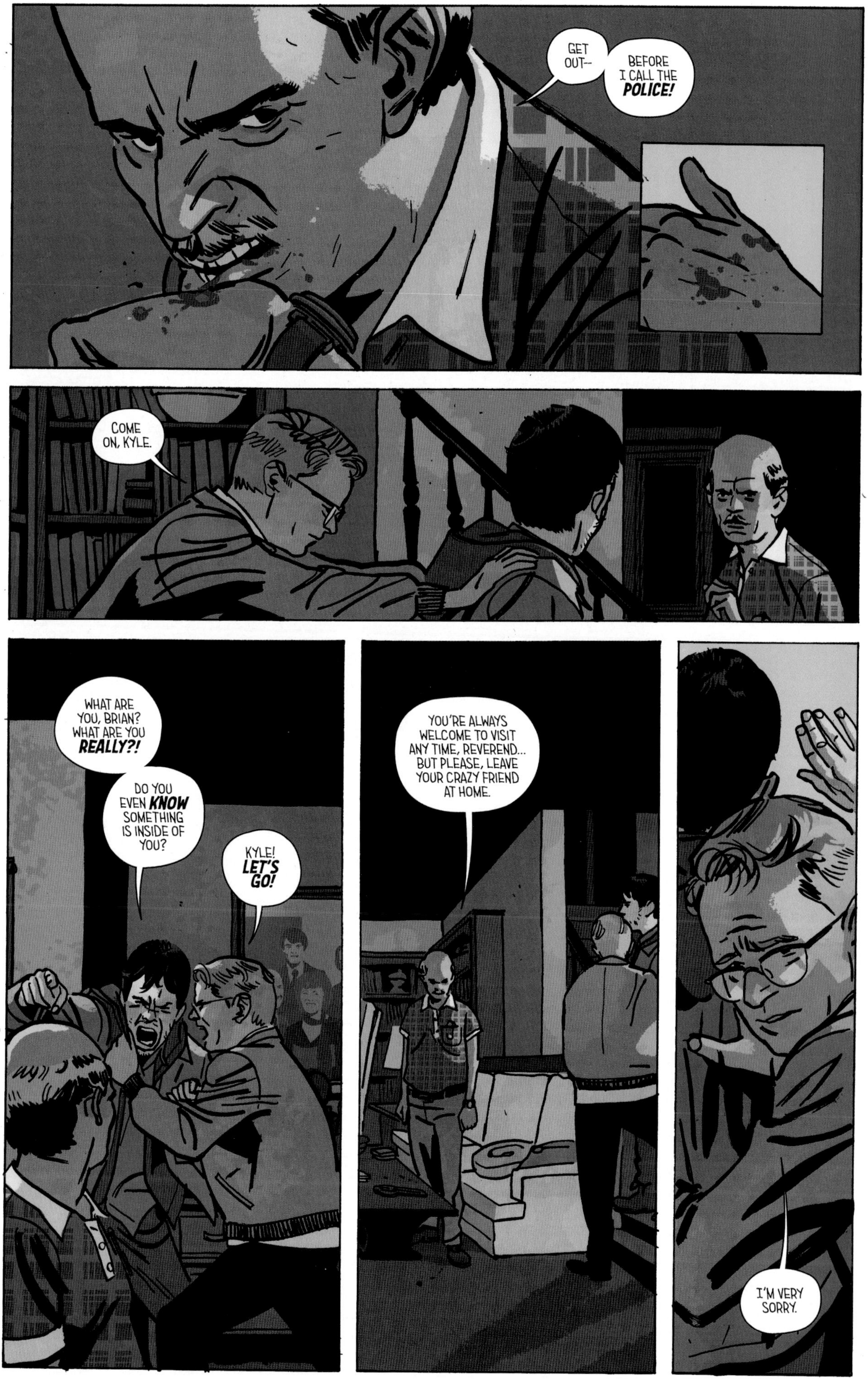
GET OUT--
BEFORE I CALL THE **POLICE!**
COME ON, KYLE.
WHAT ARE YOU, BRIAN? WHAT ARE YOU **REALLY?!**
DO YOU EVEN **KNOW** SOMETHING IS INSIDE OF YOU?
KYLE! **LET'S GO!**
YOU'RE ALWAYS WELCOME TO VISIT ANY TIME, REVEREND... BUT PLEASE, LEAVE YOUR CRAZY FRIEND AT HOME.
I'M VERY SORRY.

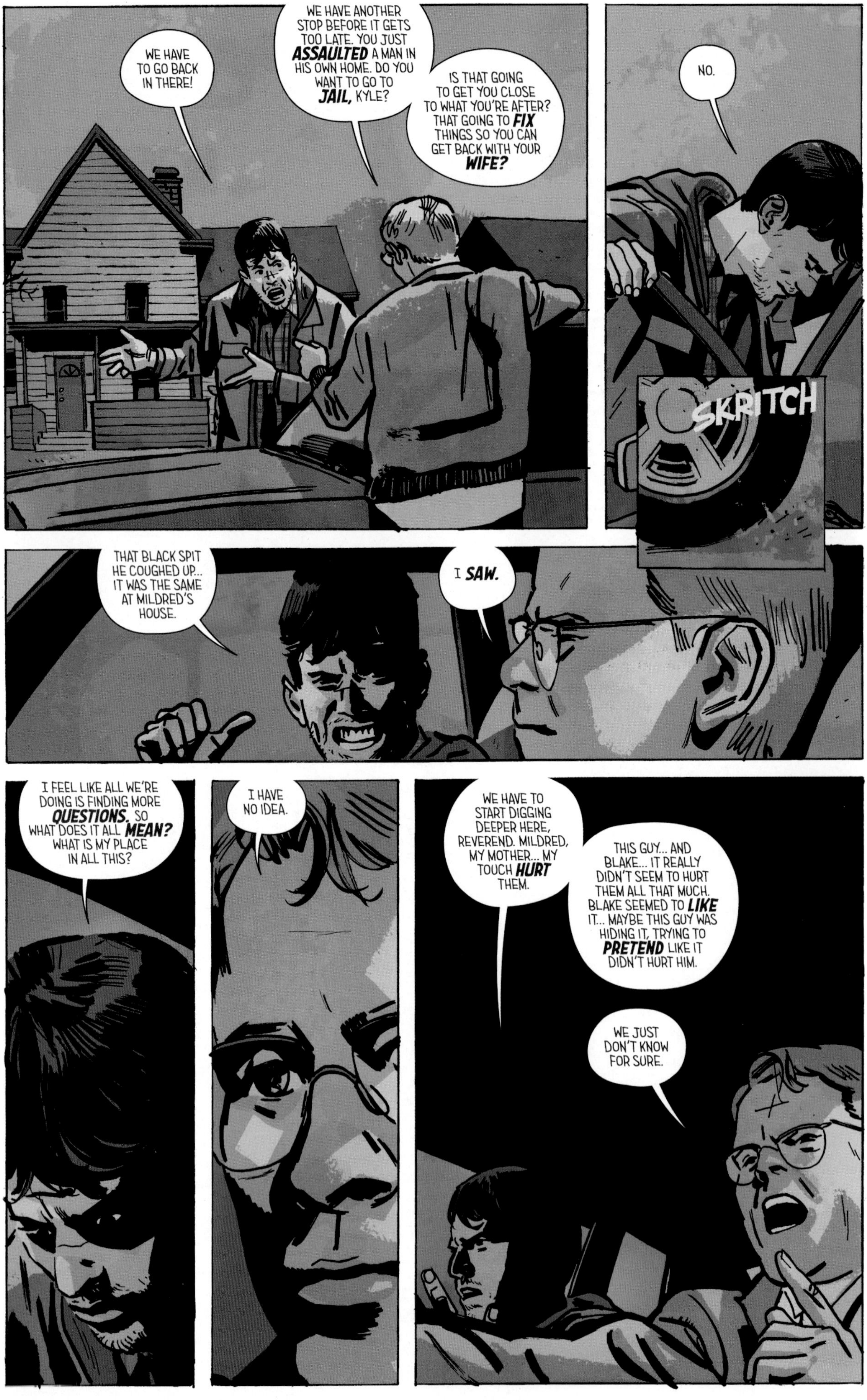
WE HAVE TO GO BACK IN THERE!
WE HAVE ANOTHER STOP BEFORE IT GETS TOO LATE. YOU JUST ASSAULTED A MAN IN HIS OWN HOME. DO YOU WANT TO GO TO JAIL, KYLE?
IS THAT GOING TO GET YOU CLOSE TO WHAT YOU'RE AFTER? THAT GOING TO FIX THINGS SO YOU CAN GET BACK WITH YOUR WIFE?
NO.
SKRITCH
THAT BLACK SPIT HE COUGHED UP... IT WAS THE SAME AT MILDRED'S HOUSE.
I SAW.
I FEEL LIKE ALL WE'RE DOING IS FINDING MORE QUESTIONS. SO WHAT DOES IT ALL MEAN? WHAT IS MY PLACE IN ALL THIS?
I HAVE NO IDEA.
WE HAVE TO START DIGGING DEEPER HERE, REVEREND. MILDRED, MY MOTHER... MY TOUCH HURT THEM.
THIS GUY... AND BLAKE... IT REALLY DIDN'T SEEM TO HURT THEM ALL THAT MUCH. BLAKE SEEMED TO LIKE IT... MAYBE THIS GUY WAS HIDING IT, TRYING TO PRETEND LIKE IT DIDN'T HURT HIM.
WE JUST DON'T KNOW FOR SURE.

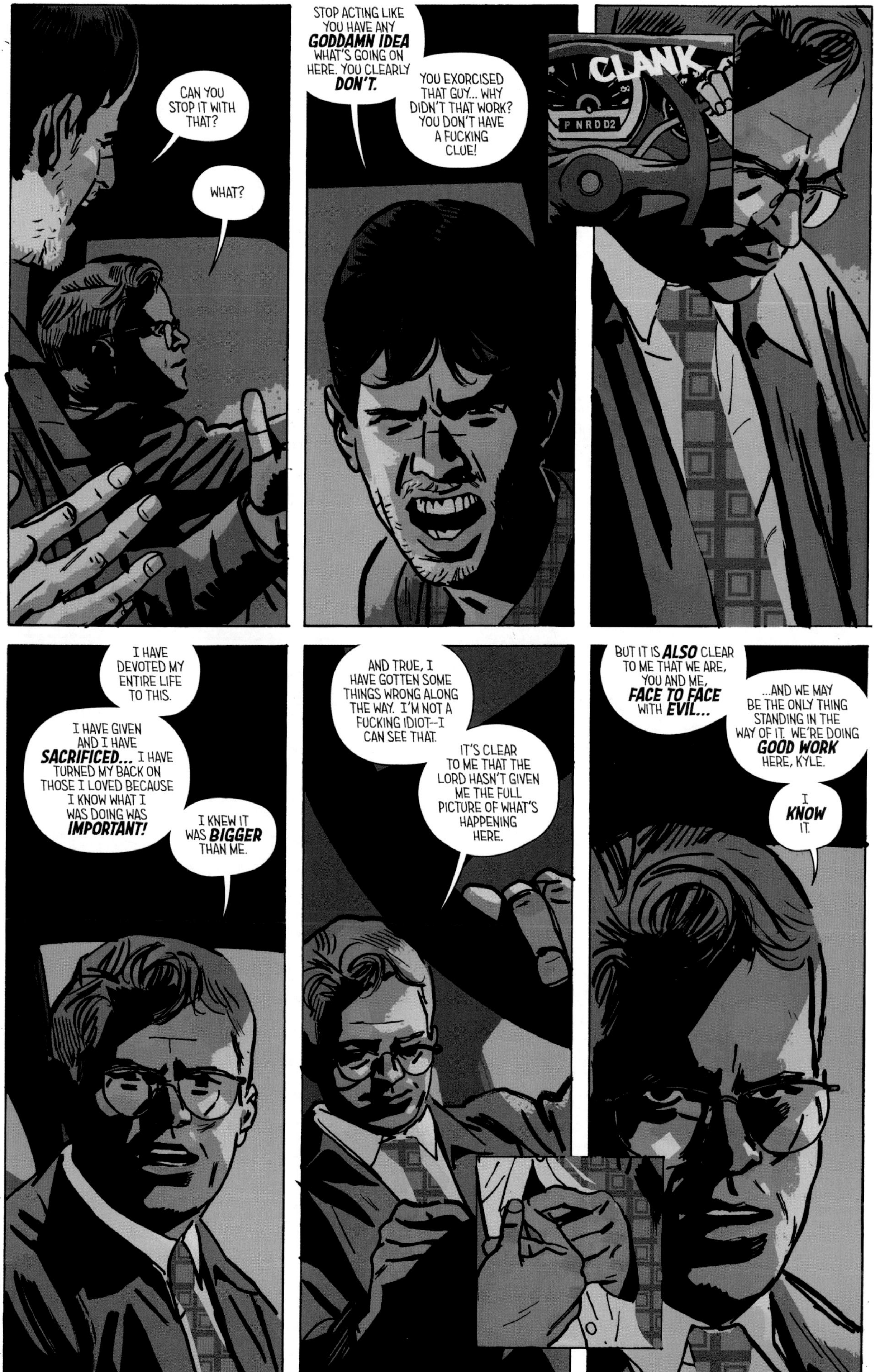
CAN YOU STOP IT WITH THAT?
WHAT?
STOP ACTING LIKE YOU HAVE ANY GODDAMN IDEA WHAT'S GOING ON HERE. YOU CLEARLY DON'T.
YOU EXORCISED THAT GUY... WHY DIDN'T THAT WORK? YOU DON'T HAVE A FUCKING CLUE!
CLANK
P N R D D2
I HAVE DEVOTED MY ENTIRE LIFE TO THIS.
I HAVE GIVEN AND I HAVE SACRIFICED... I HAVE TURNED MY BACK ON THOSE I LOVED BECAUSE I KNOW WHAT I WAS DOING WAS IMPORTANT!
I KNEW IT WAS BIGGER THAN ME.
AND TRUE, I HAVE GOTTEN SOME THINGS WRONG ALONG THE WAY. I'M NOT A FUCKING IDIOT--I CAN SEE THAT.
IT'S CLEAR TO ME THAT THE LORD HASN'T GIVEN ME THE FULL PICTURE OF WHAT'S HAPPENING HERE.
BUT IT IS ALSO CLEAR TO ME THAT WE ARE, YOU AND ME, FACE TO FACE WITH EVIL...
...AND WE MAY BE THE ONLY THING STANDING IN THE WAY OF IT. WE'RE DOING GOOD WORK HERE, KYLE.
I KNOW IT.

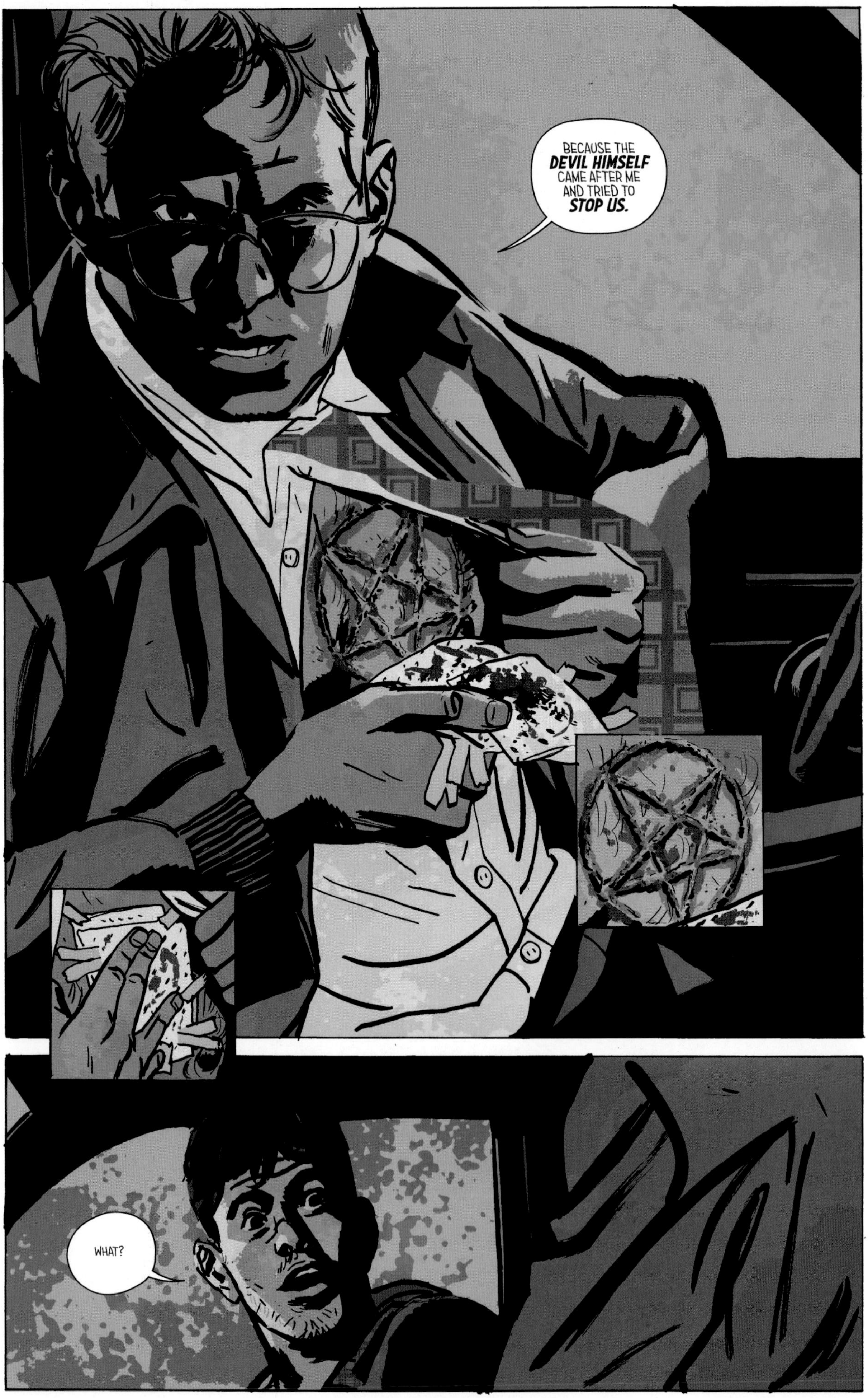
BECAUSE THE **DEVIL HIMSELF** CAME AFTER ME AND TRIED TO **STOP US.**
WHAT?

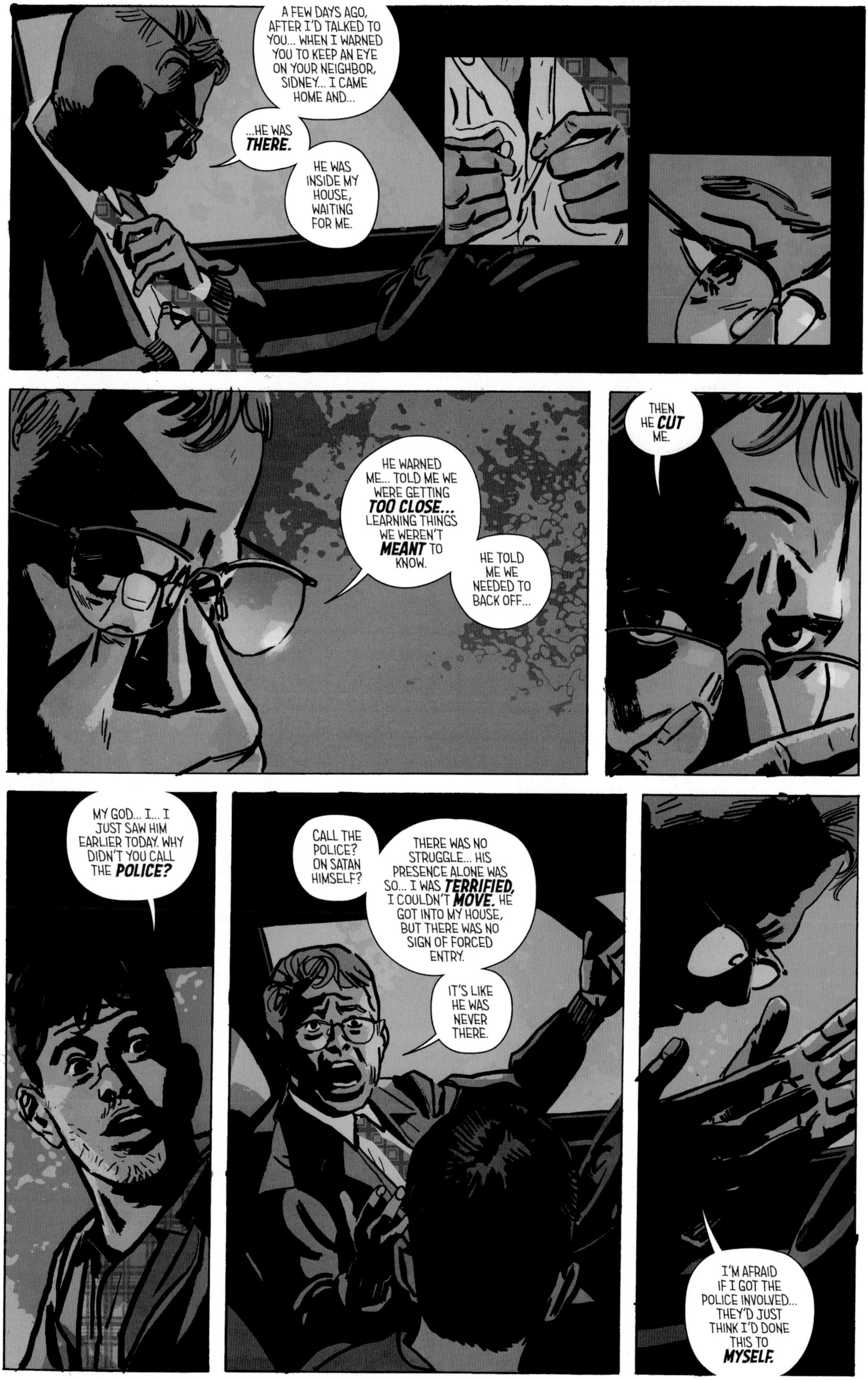
A FEW DAYS AGO, AFTER I'D TALKED TO YOU... WHEN I WARNED YOU TO KEEP AN EYE ON YOUR NEIGHBOR, SIDNEY... I CAME HOME AND...
...HE WAS THERE.
HE WAS INSIDE MY HOUSE, WAITING FOR ME.
HE WARNED ME... TOLD ME WE WERE GETTING TOO CLOSE... LEARNING THINGS WE WEREN'T MEANT TO KNOW.
HE TOLD ME WE NEEDED TO BACK OFF...
THEN HE CUT ME.
MY GOD... I... I JUST SAW HIM EARLIER TODAY. WHY DIDN'T YOU CALL THE POLICE?
CALL THE POLICE? ON SATAN HIMSELF?
THERE WAS NO STRUGGLE... HIS PRESENCE ALONE WAS SO... I WAS TERRIFIED, I COULDN'T MOVE. HE GOT INTO MY HOUSE, BUT THERE WAS NO SIGN OF FORCED ENTRY.
IT'S LIKE HE WAS NEVER THERE.
I'M AFRAID IF I GOT THE POLICE INVOLVED... THEY'D JUST THINK I'D DONE THIS TO MYSELF.

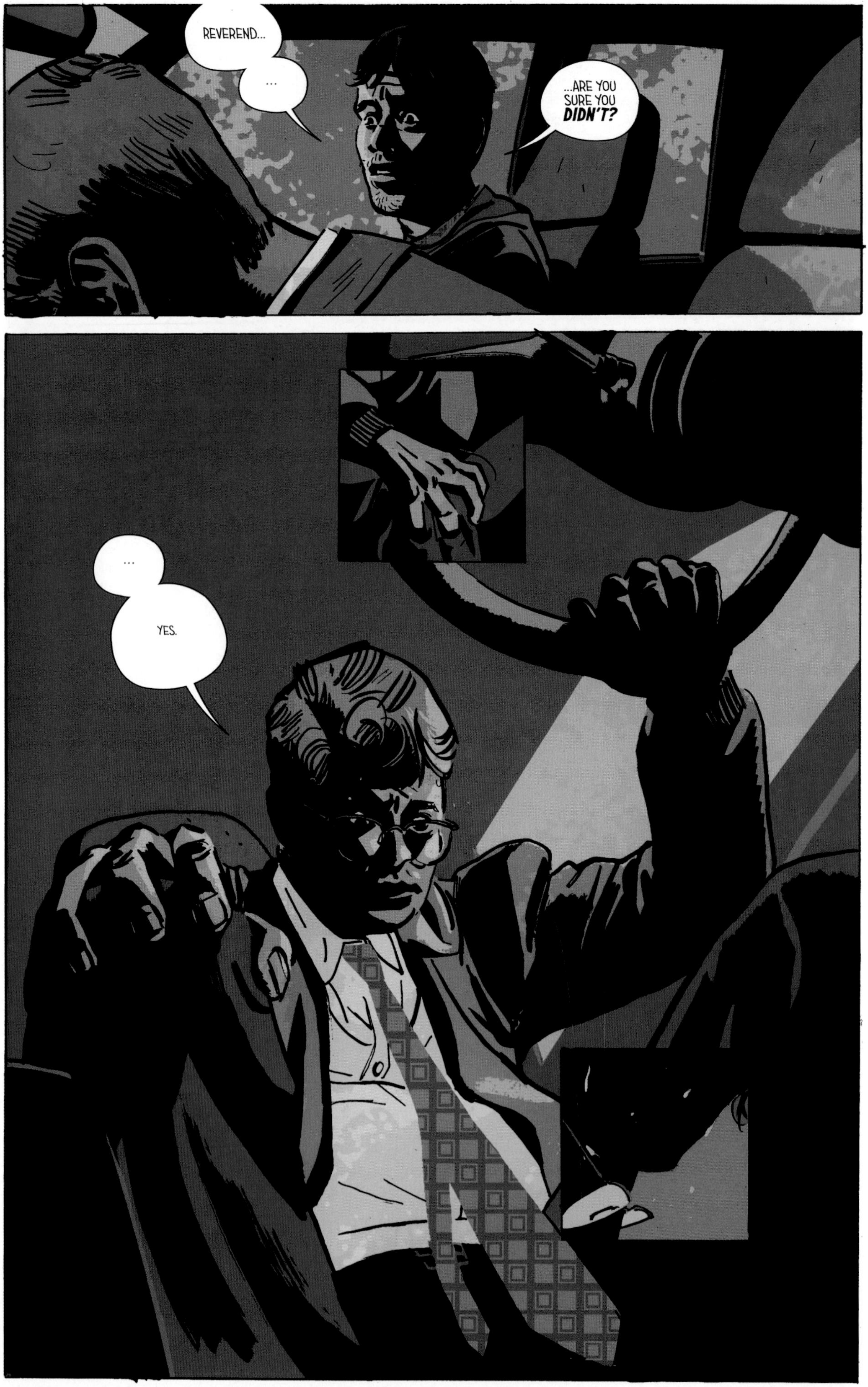
REVEREND...
...
...ARE YOU SURE YOU **DIDN'T?**
...
YES.

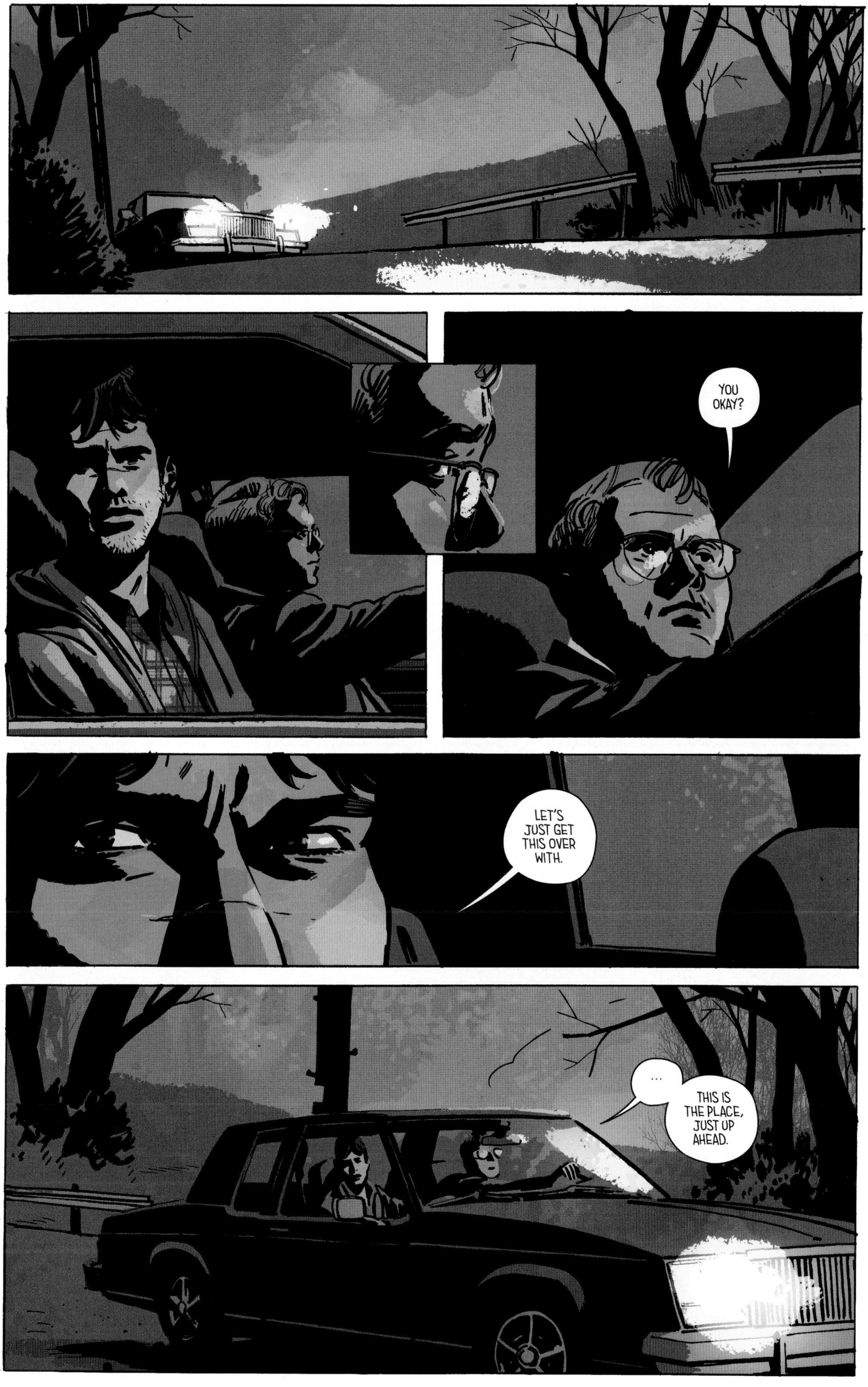
YOU OKAY?
LET'S JUST GET THIS OVER WITH.
...
THIS IS THE PLACE, JUST UP AHEAD.

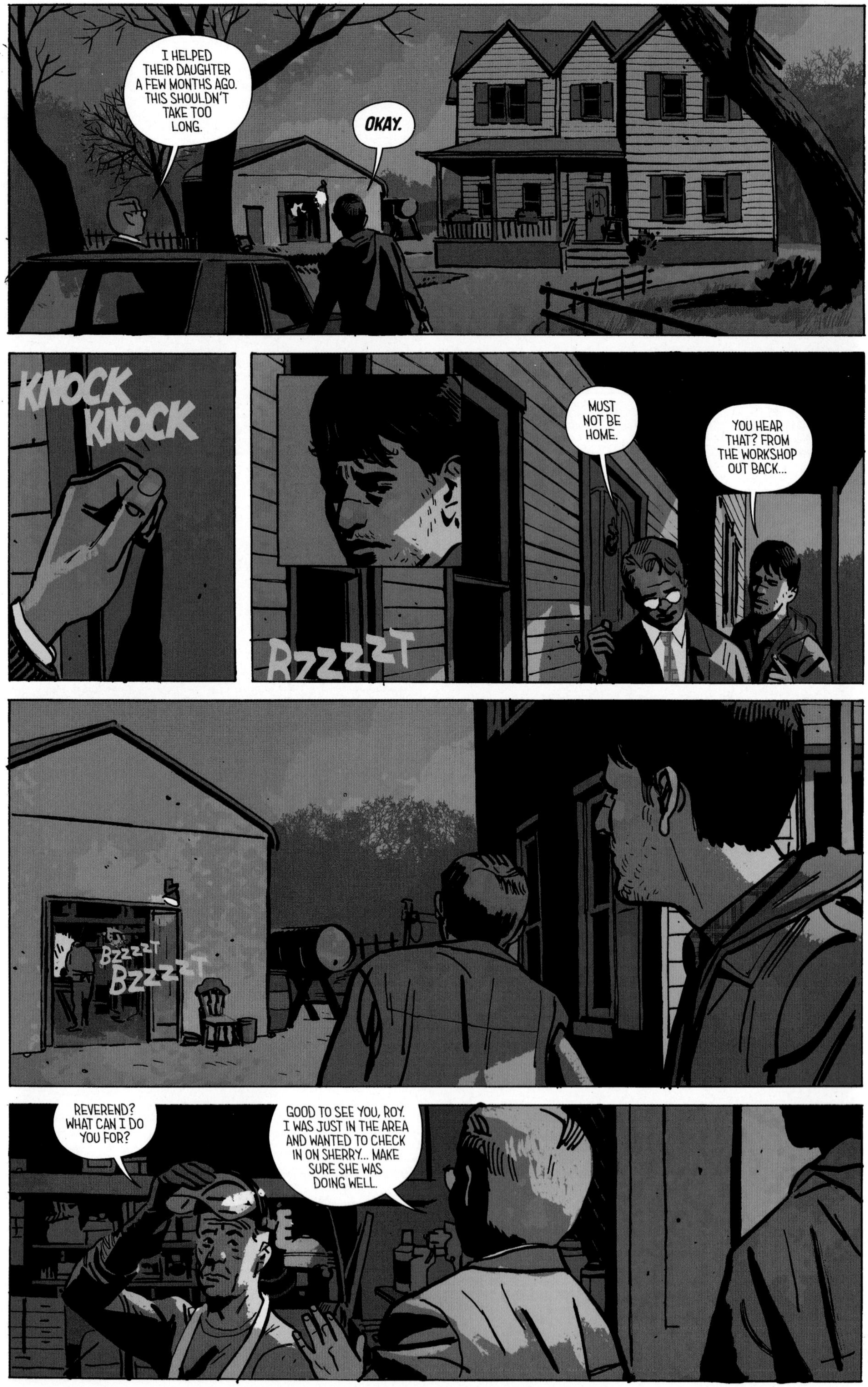
I HELPED THEIR DAUGHTER A FEW MONTHS AGO. THIS SHOULDN'T TAKE TOO LONG.
OKAY.
KNOCK KNOCK
BZZZZT
MUST NOT BE HOME.
YOU HEAR THAT? FROM THE WORKSHOP OUT BACK...
BZZZZT BZZZZT
REVEREND? WHAT CAN I DO YOU FOR?
GOOD TO SEE YOU, ROY. I WAS JUST IN THE AREA AND WANTED TO CHECK IN ON SHERRY... MAKE SURE SHE WAS DOING WELL.

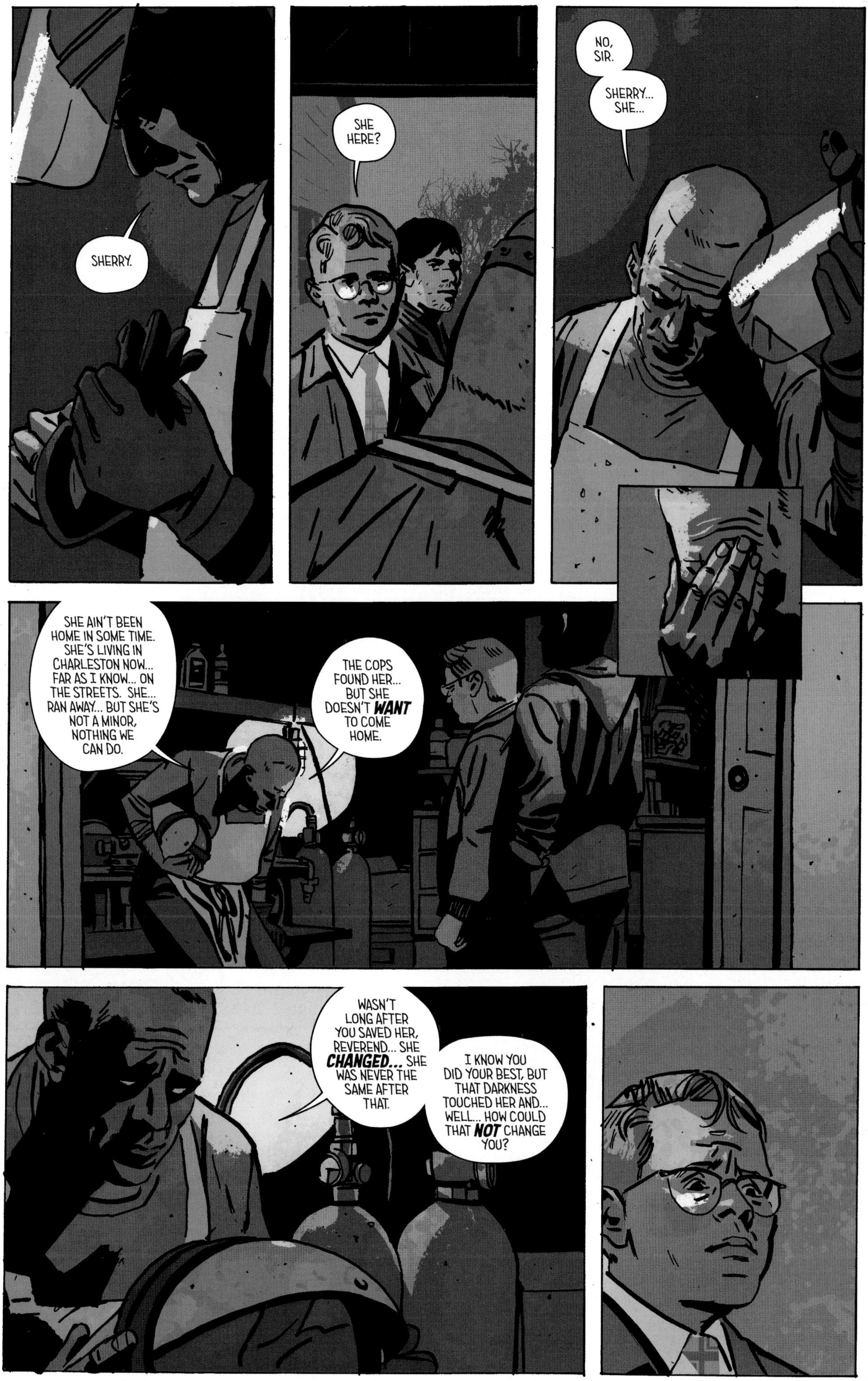
SHERRY.
SHE HERE?
NO, SIR.
SHERRY... SHE...
SHE AIN'T BEEN HOME IN SOME TIME. SHE'S LIVING IN CHARLESTON NOW... FAR AS I KNOW... ON THE STREETS. SHE... RAN AWAY... BUT SHE'S NOT A MINOR, NOTHING WE CAN DO.
THE COPS FOUND HER... BUT SHE DOESN'T WANT TO COME HOME.
WASN'T LONG AFTER YOU SAVED HER, REVEREND... SHE CHANGED... SHE WAS NEVER THE SAME AFTER THAT.
I KNOW YOU DID YOUR BEST, BUT THAT DARKNESS TOUCHED HER AND... WELL... HOW COULD THAT NOT CHANGE YOU?

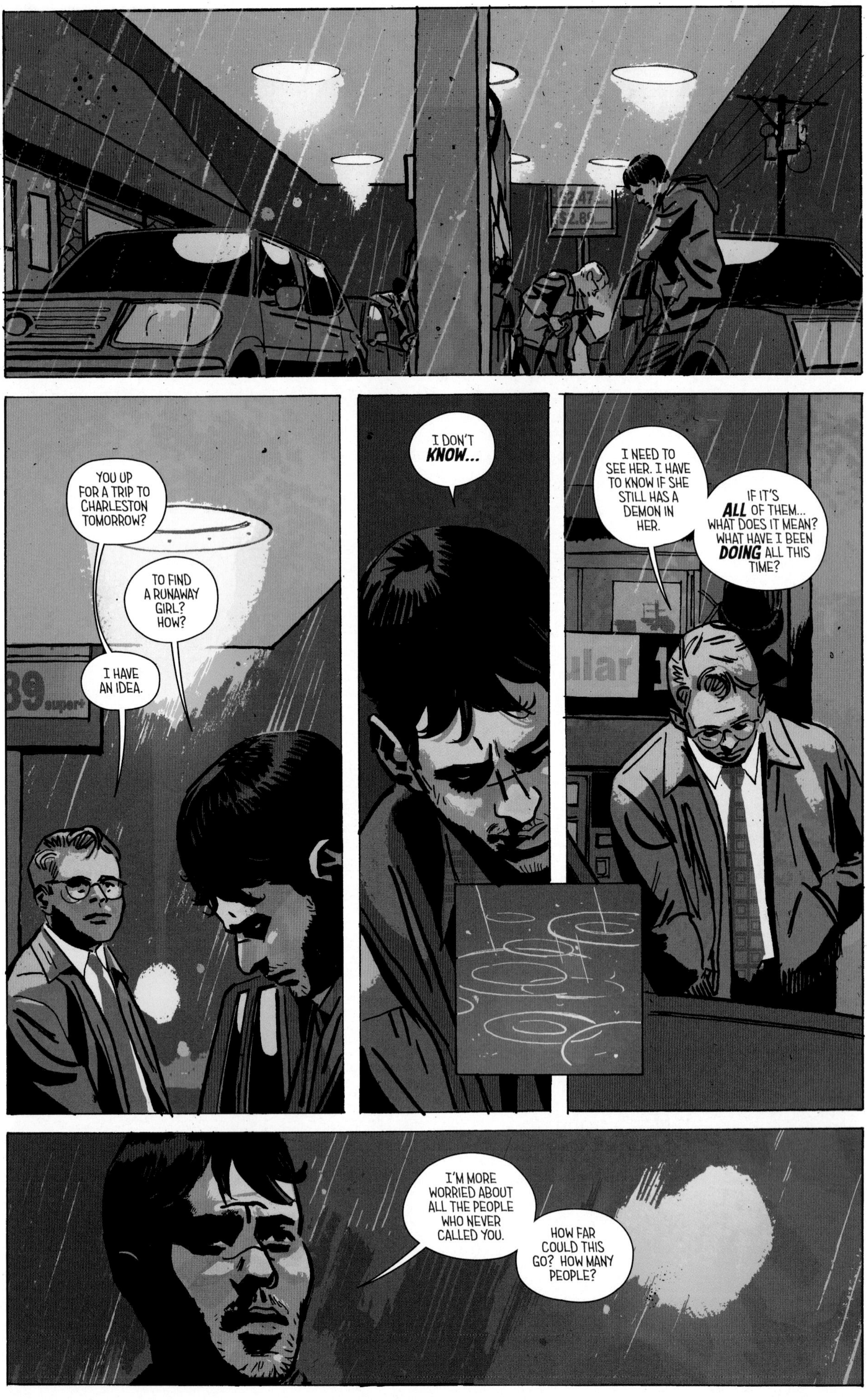
YOU UP FOR A TRIP TO CHARLESTON TOMORROW?
TO FIND A RUNAWAY GIRL? HOW?
I HAVE AN IDEA.
I DON'T **KNOW...**
I NEED TO SEE HER. I HAVE TO KNOW IF SHE STILL HAS A DEMON IN HER.
IF IT'S **ALL** OF THEM... WHAT DOES IT MEAN? WHAT HAVE I BEEN **DOING** ALL THIS TIME?
I'M MORE WORRIED ABOUT ALL THE PEOPLE WHO NEVER CALLED YOU.
HOW FAR COULD THIS GO? HOW MANY PEOPLE?

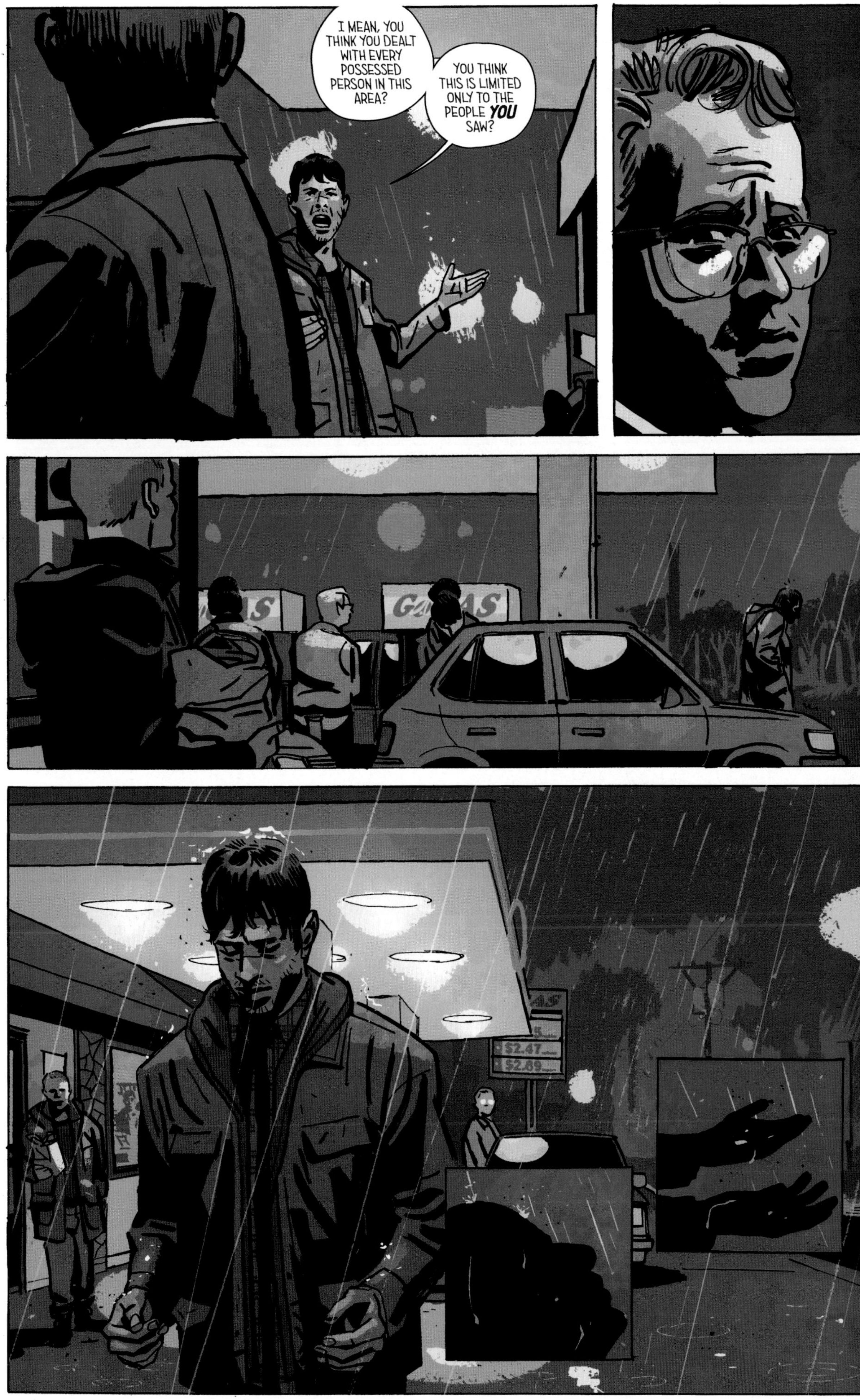
I MEAN, YOU THINK YOU DEALT WITH EVERY POSSESSED PERSON IN THIS AREA?
YOU THINK THIS IS LIMITED ONLY TO THE PEOPLE *YOU* SAW?
GAS
$2.47
$2.89

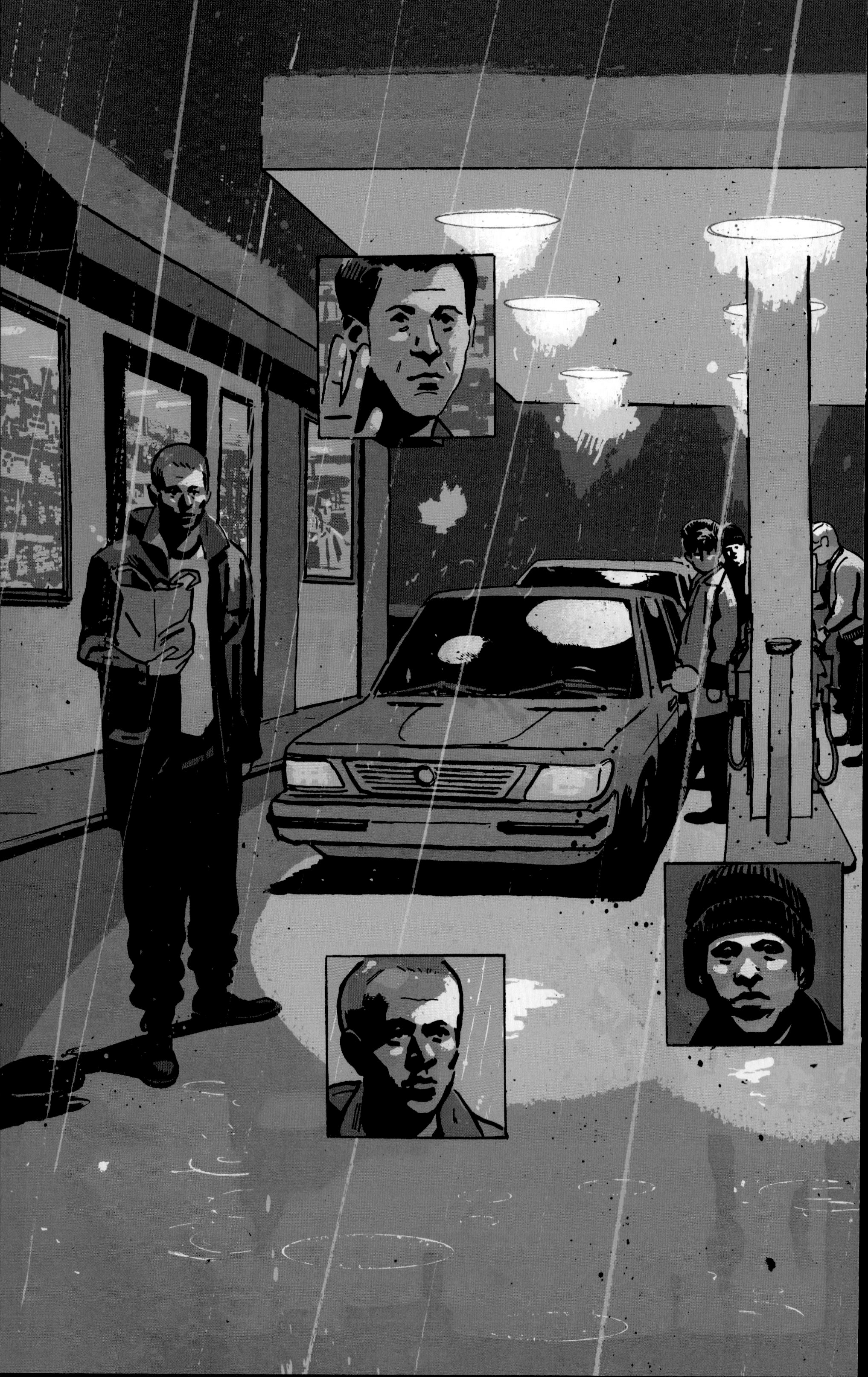

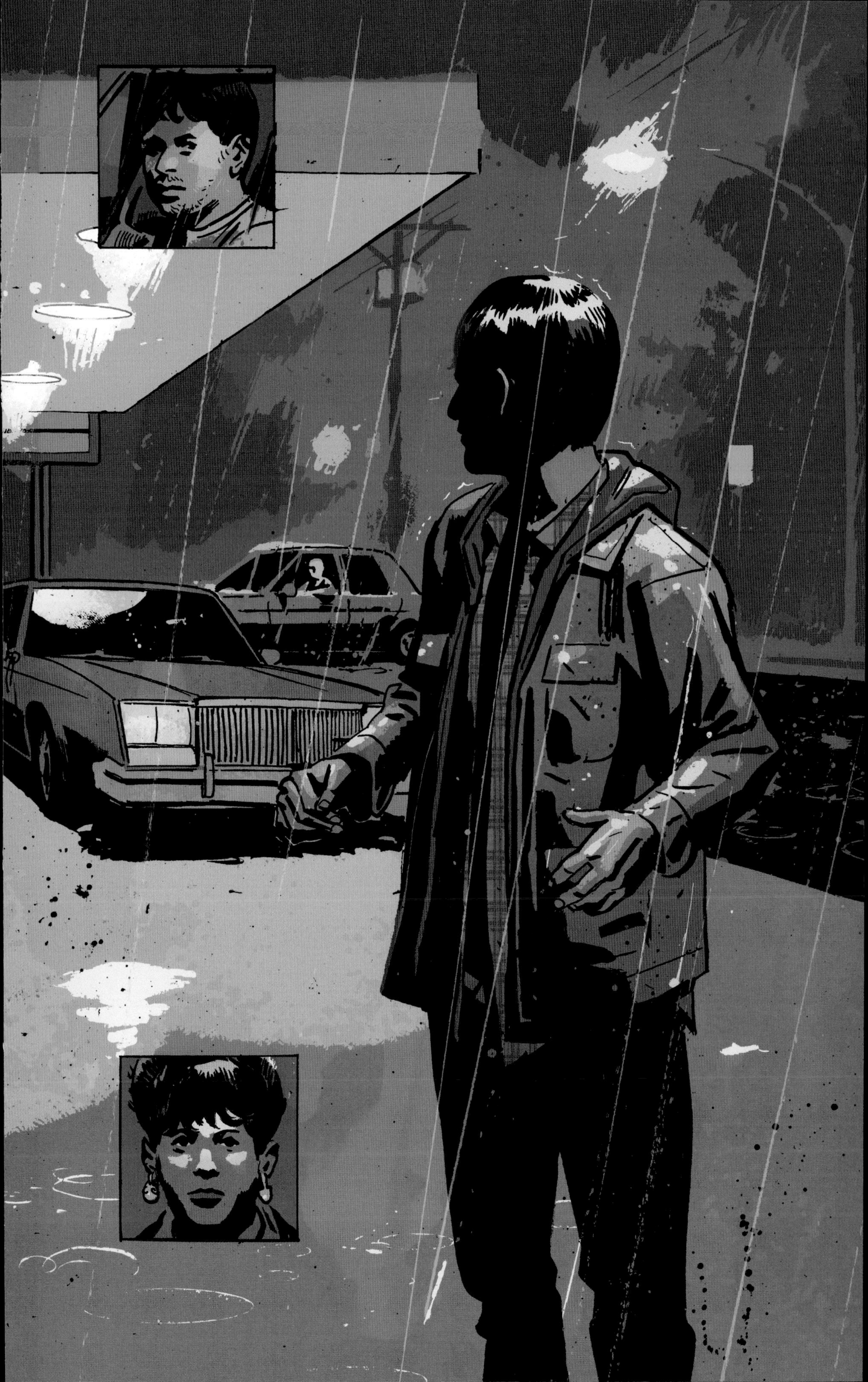

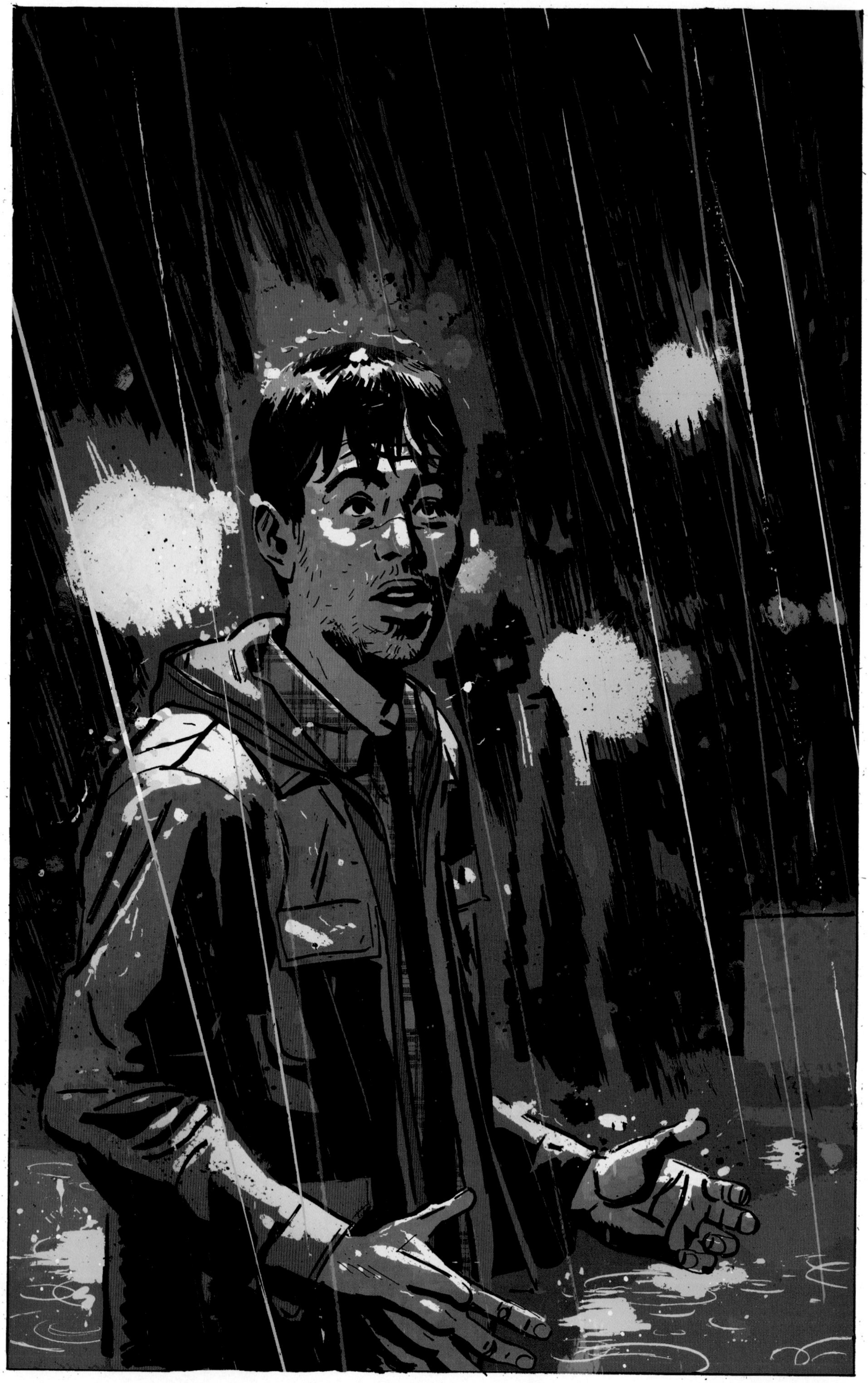

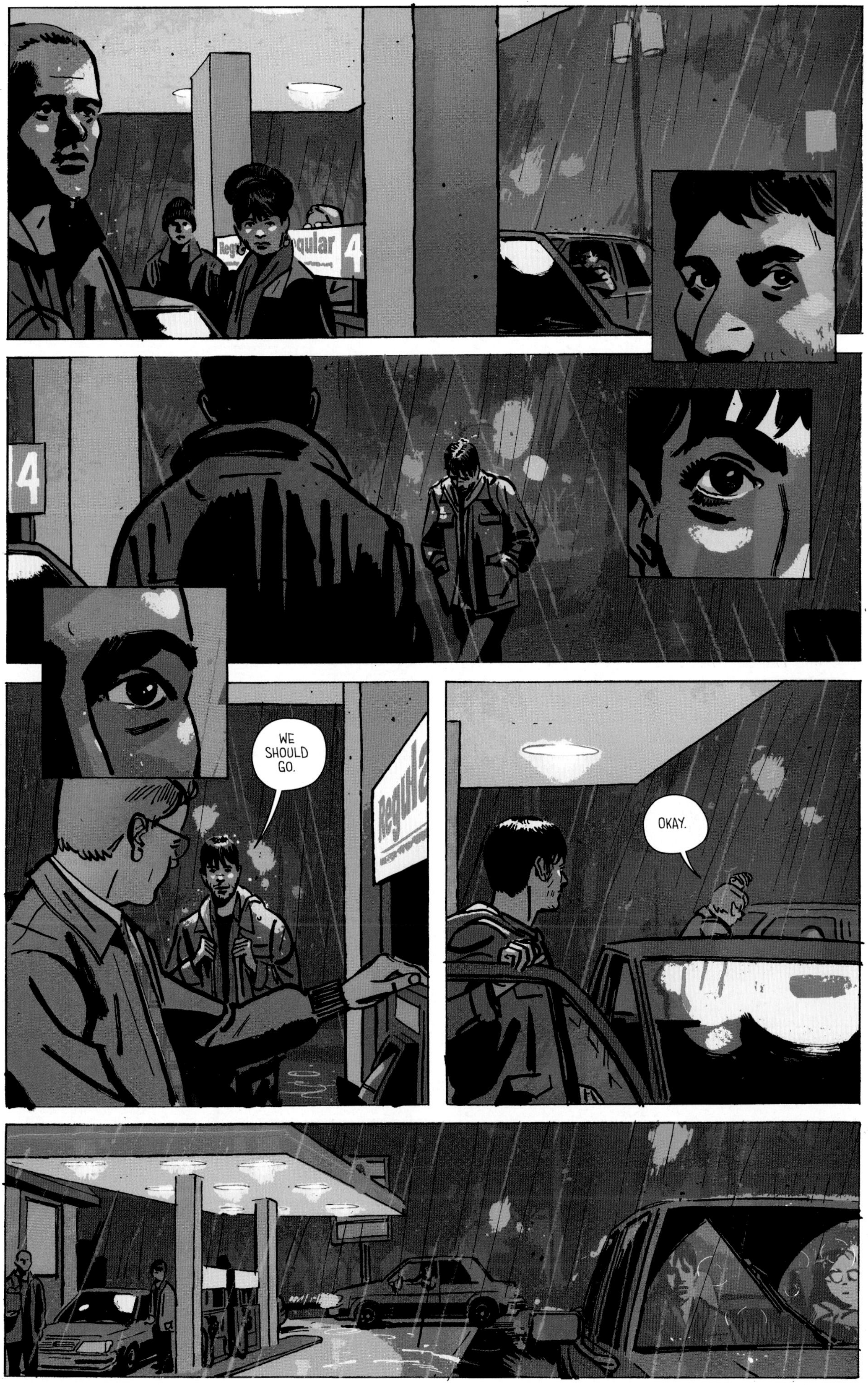
Regular
Regular 4
4
WE SHOULD GO.
Regular
OKAY.

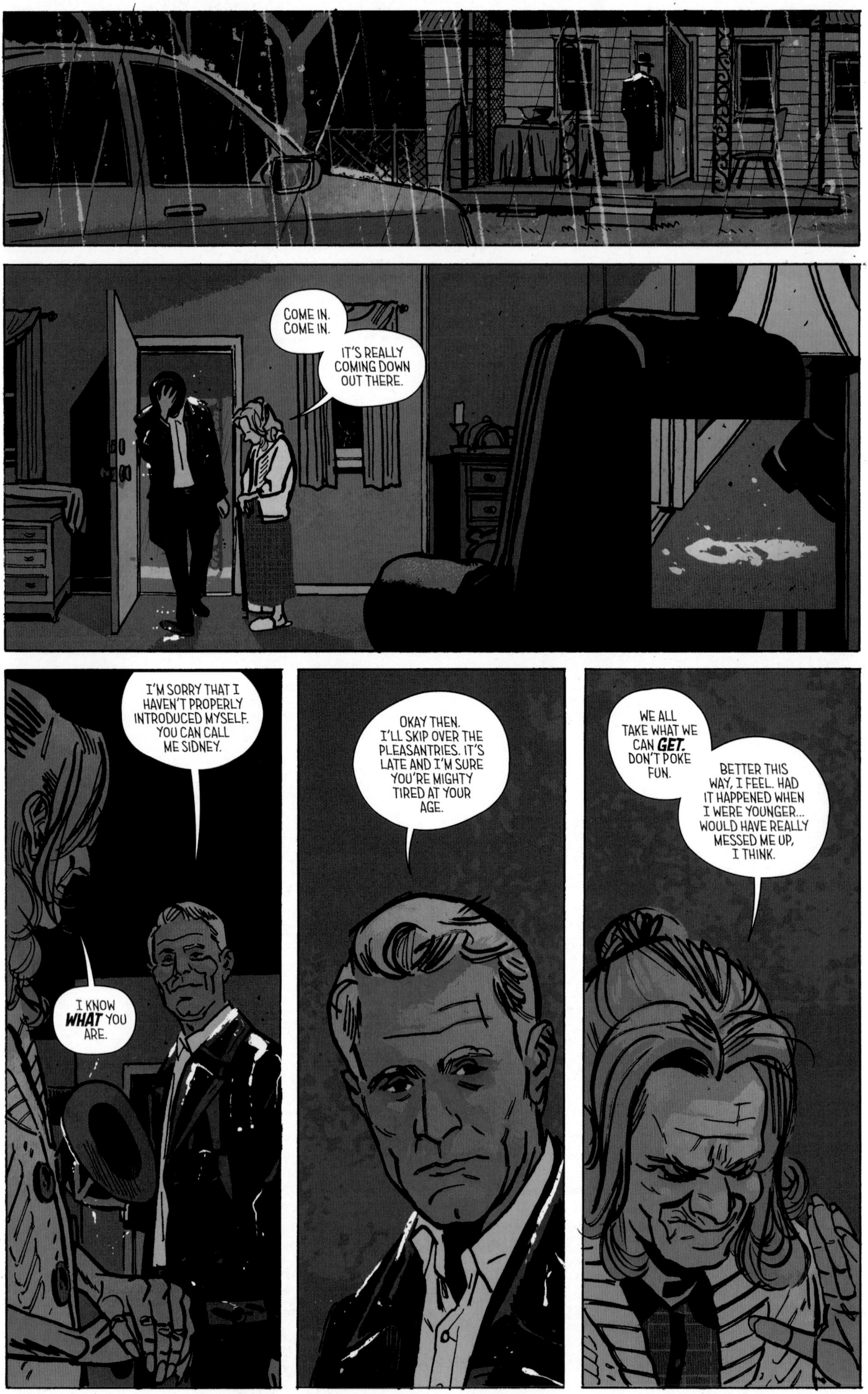
COME IN. COME IN.
IT'S REALLY COMING DOWN OUT THERE.
I'M SORRY THAT I HAVEN'T PROPERLY INTRODUCED MYSELF. YOU CAN CALL ME SIDNEY.
I KNOW **WHAT** YOU ARE.
OKAY THEN. I'LL SKIP OVER THE PLEASANTRIES. IT'S LATE AND I'M SURE YOU'RE MIGHTY TIRED AT YOUR AGE.
WE ALL TAKE WHAT WE CAN **GET.** DON'T POKE FUN.
BETTER THIS WAY, I FEEL. HAD IT HAPPENED WHEN I WERE YOUNGER... WOULD HAVE REALLY MESSED ME UP, I THINK.

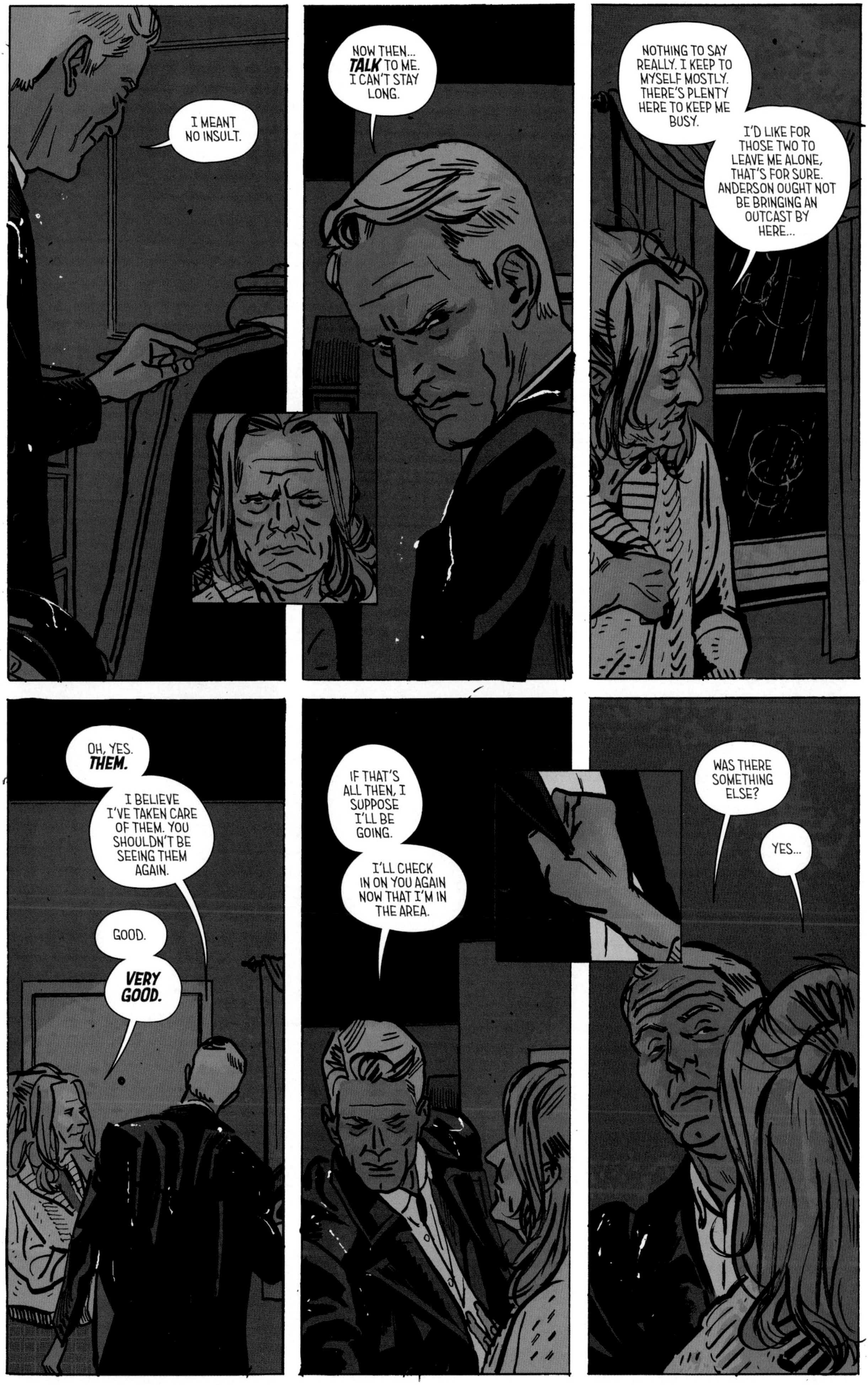
I MEANT NO INSULT.
NOW THEN... TALK TO ME. I CAN'T STAY LONG.
NOTHING TO SAY REALLY. I KEEP TO MYSELF MOSTLY. THERE'S PLENTY HERE TO KEEP ME BUSY.
I'D LIKE FOR THOSE TWO TO LEAVE ME ALONE, THAT'S FOR SURE. ANDERSON OUGHT NOT BE BRINGING AN OUTCAST BY HERE...
OH, YES. THEM.
I BELIEVE I'VE TAKEN CARE OF THEM. YOU SHOULDN'T BE SEEING THEM AGAIN.
GOOD.
VERY GOOD.
IF THAT'S ALL THEN, I SUPPOSE I'LL BE GOING.
I'LL CHECK IN ON YOU AGAIN NOW THAT I'M IN THE AREA.
WAS THERE SOMETHING ELSE?
YES...

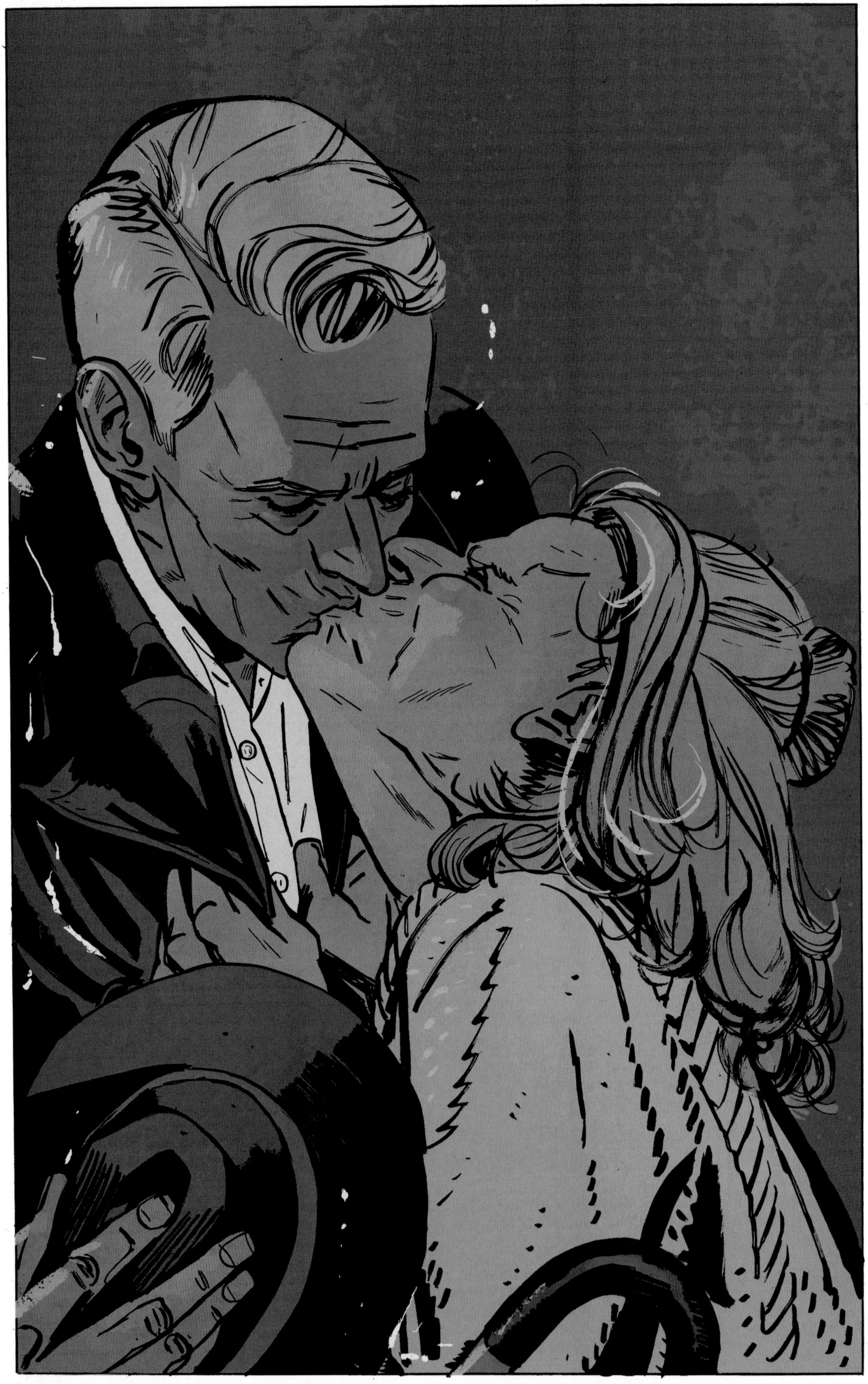

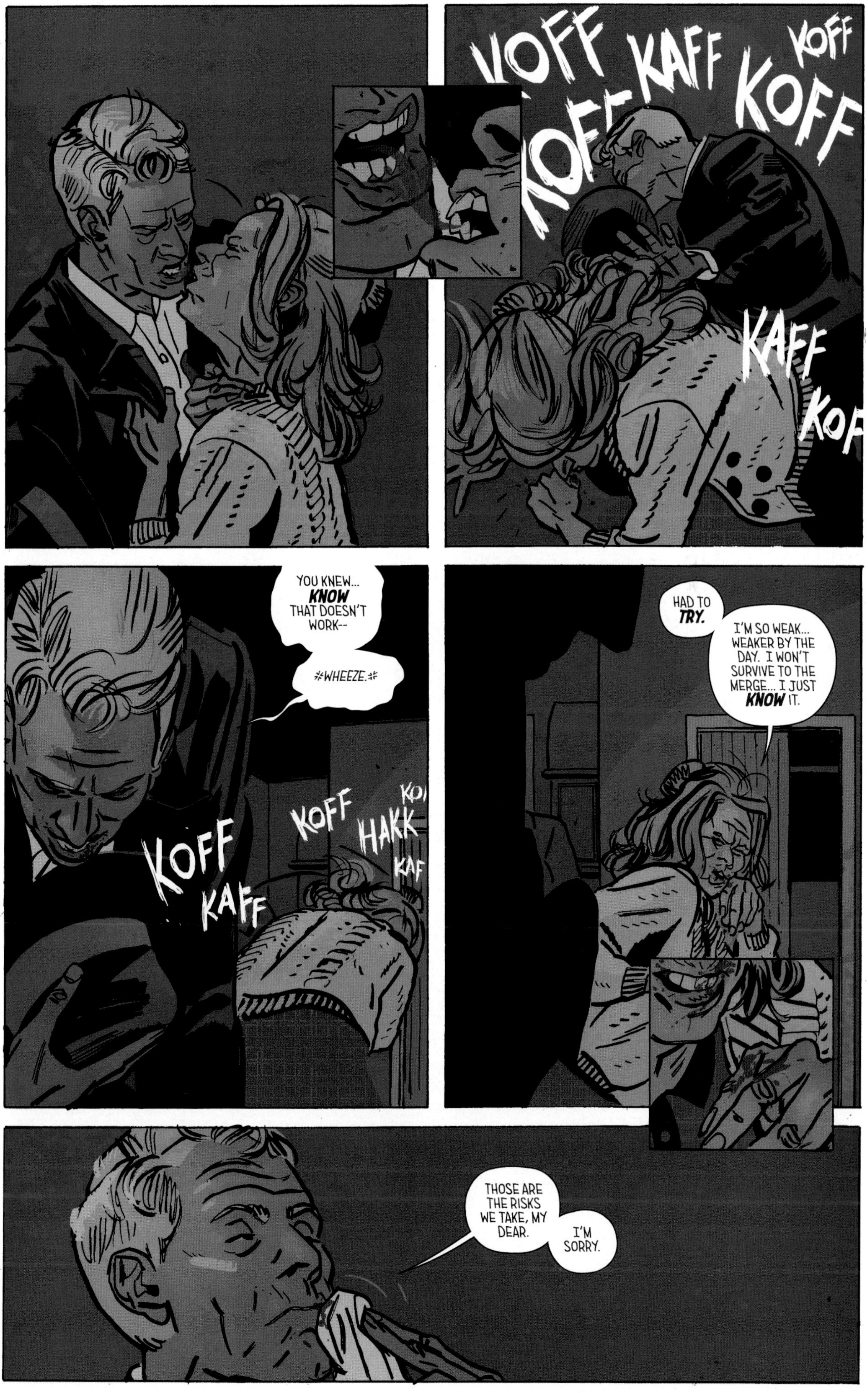
KOFF KOFF-KAFF KOFF KOFF
KAFF
KOF
YOU KNEW... **KNOW** THAT DOESN'T WORK--
#WHEEZE.#
KOFF
KAFF
KOFF
HAKK
KAF
HAD TO **TRY.**
I'M SO WEAK... WEAKER BY THE DAY. I WON'T SURVIVE TO THE MERGE... I JUST **KNOW** IT.
THOSE ARE THE RISKS WE TAKE, MY DEAR.
I'M SORRY.

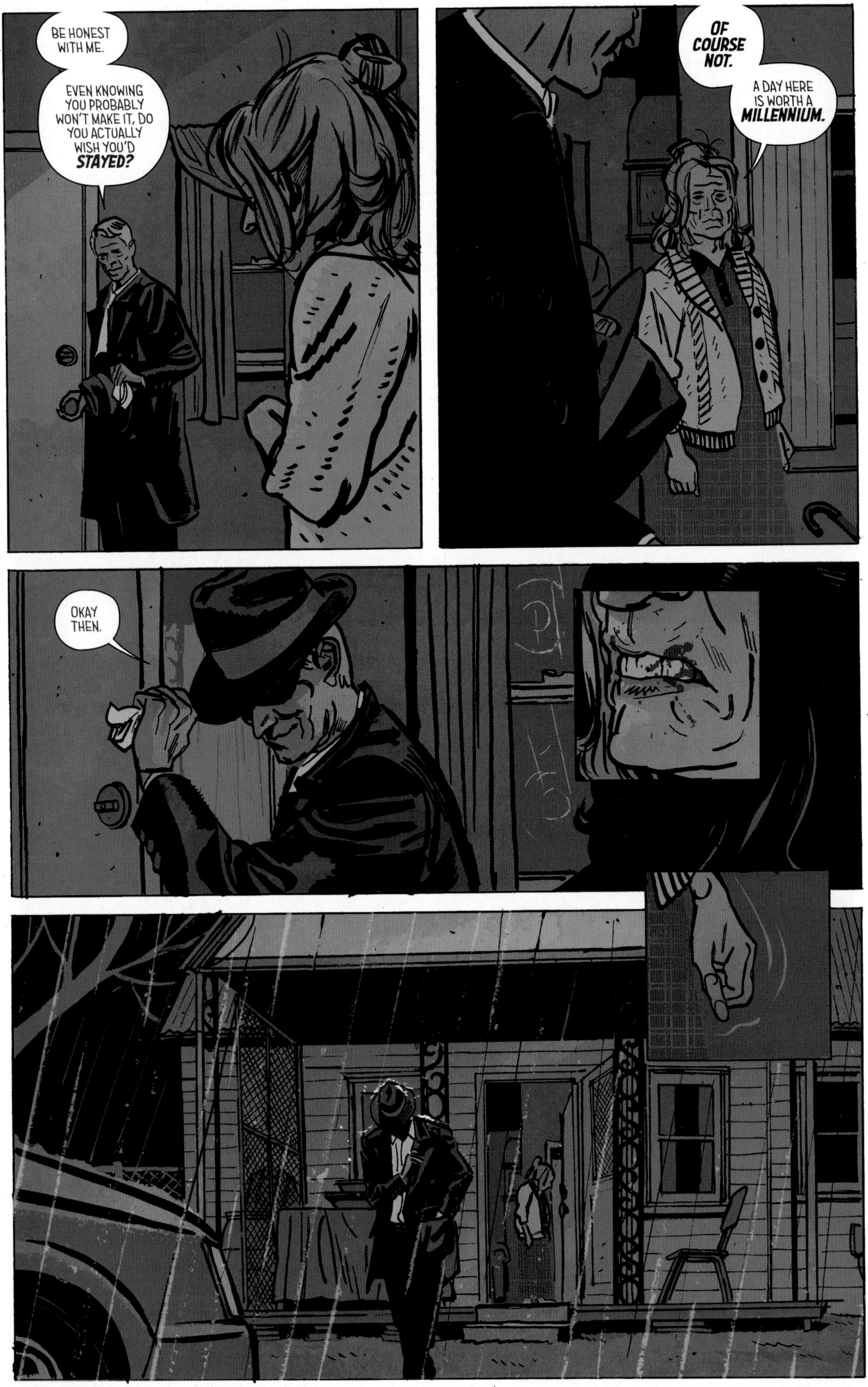
BE HONEST WITH ME.
EVEN KNOWING YOU PROBABLY WON'T MAKE IT, DO YOU ACTUALLY WISH YOU'D STAYED?
OF COURSE NOT.
A DAY HERE IS WORTH A MILLENNIUM.
OKAY THEN.

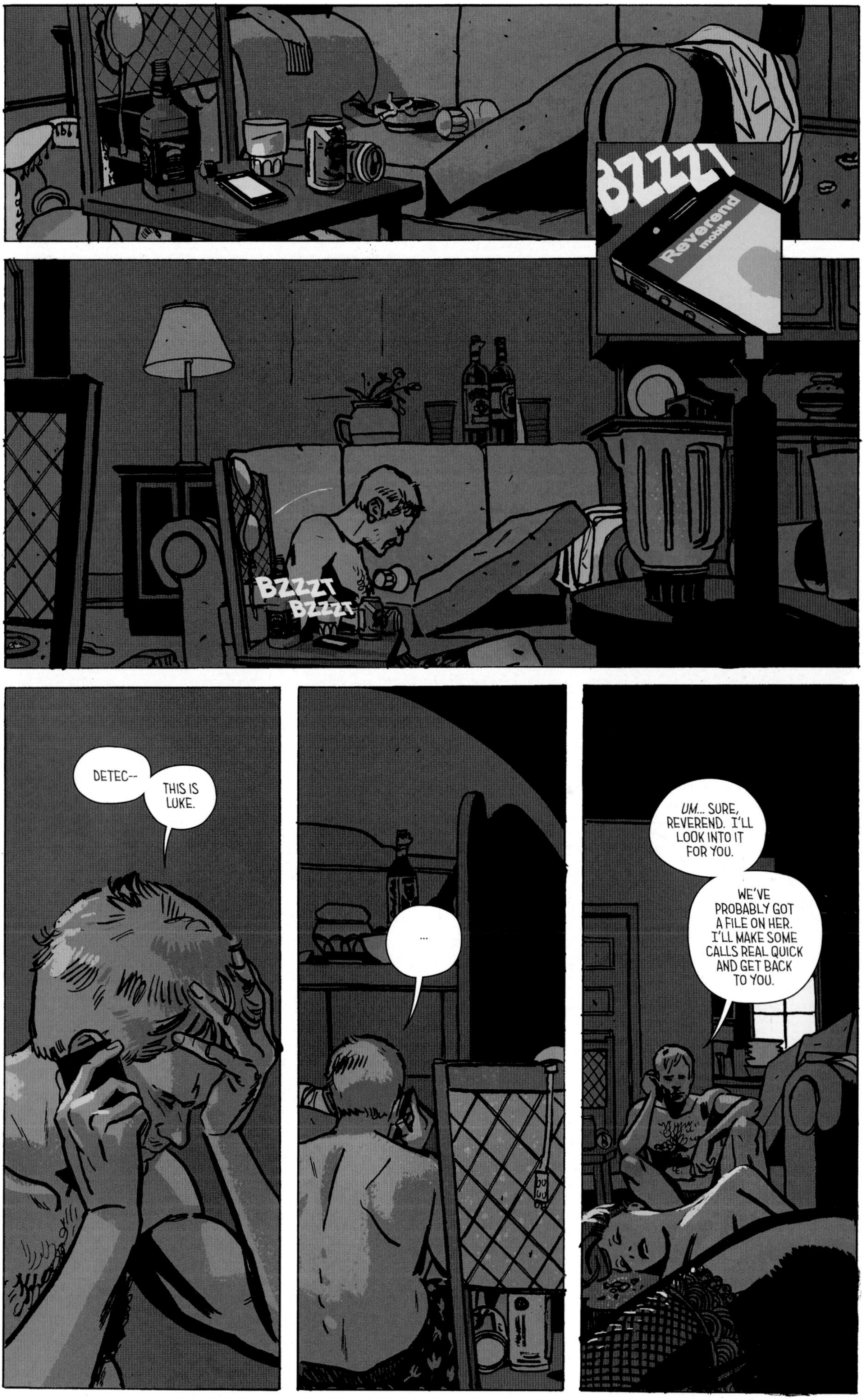
BZZZZT
Reverend mobile
BZZZZT BZZZZT
DETEC--
THIS IS LUKE.
...
UM... SURE, REVEREND. I'LL LOOK INTO IT FOR YOU.
WE'VE PROBABLY GOT A FILE ON HER. I'LL MAKE SOME CALLS REAL QUICK AND GET BACK TO YOU.

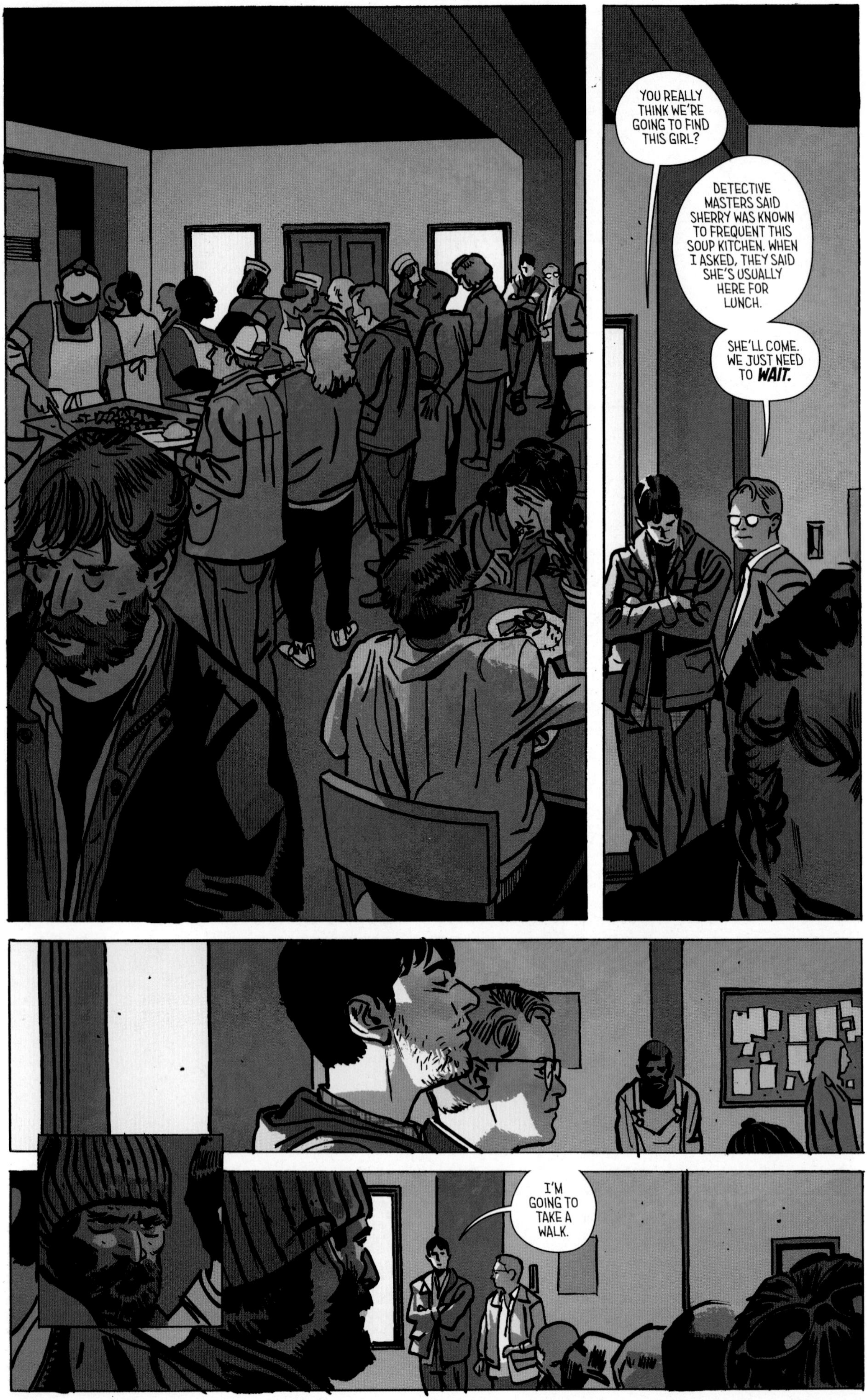
YOU REALLY THINK WE'RE GOING TO FIND THIS GIRL?
DETECTIVE MASTERS SAID SHERRY WAS KNOWN TO FREQUENT THIS SOUP KITCHEN. WHEN I ASKED, THEY SAID SHE'S USUALLY HERE FOR LUNCH.
SHE'LL COME. WE JUST NEED TO ***WAIT.***
I'M GOING TO TAKE A WALK.

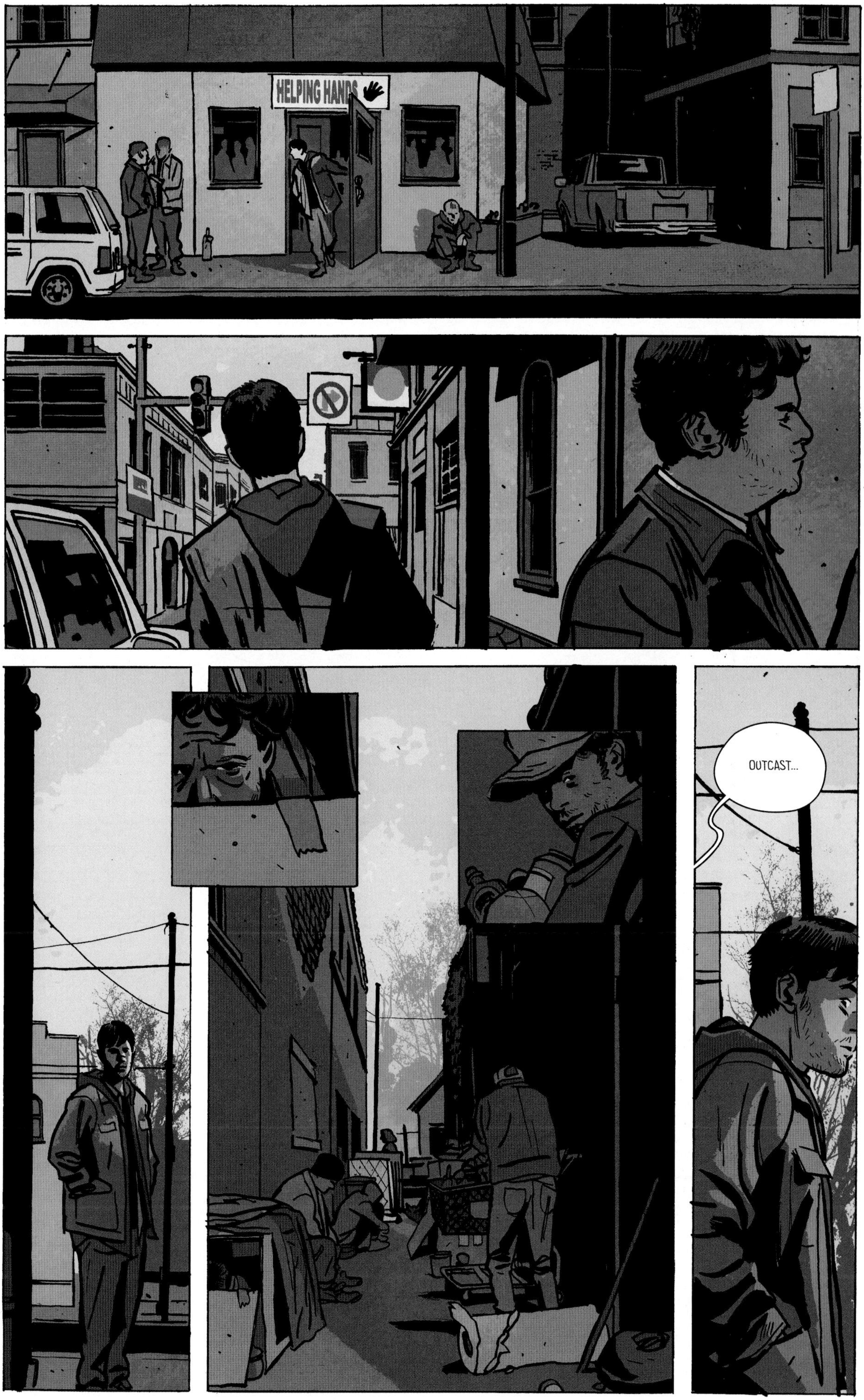
HELPING HANDS
OUTCAST...

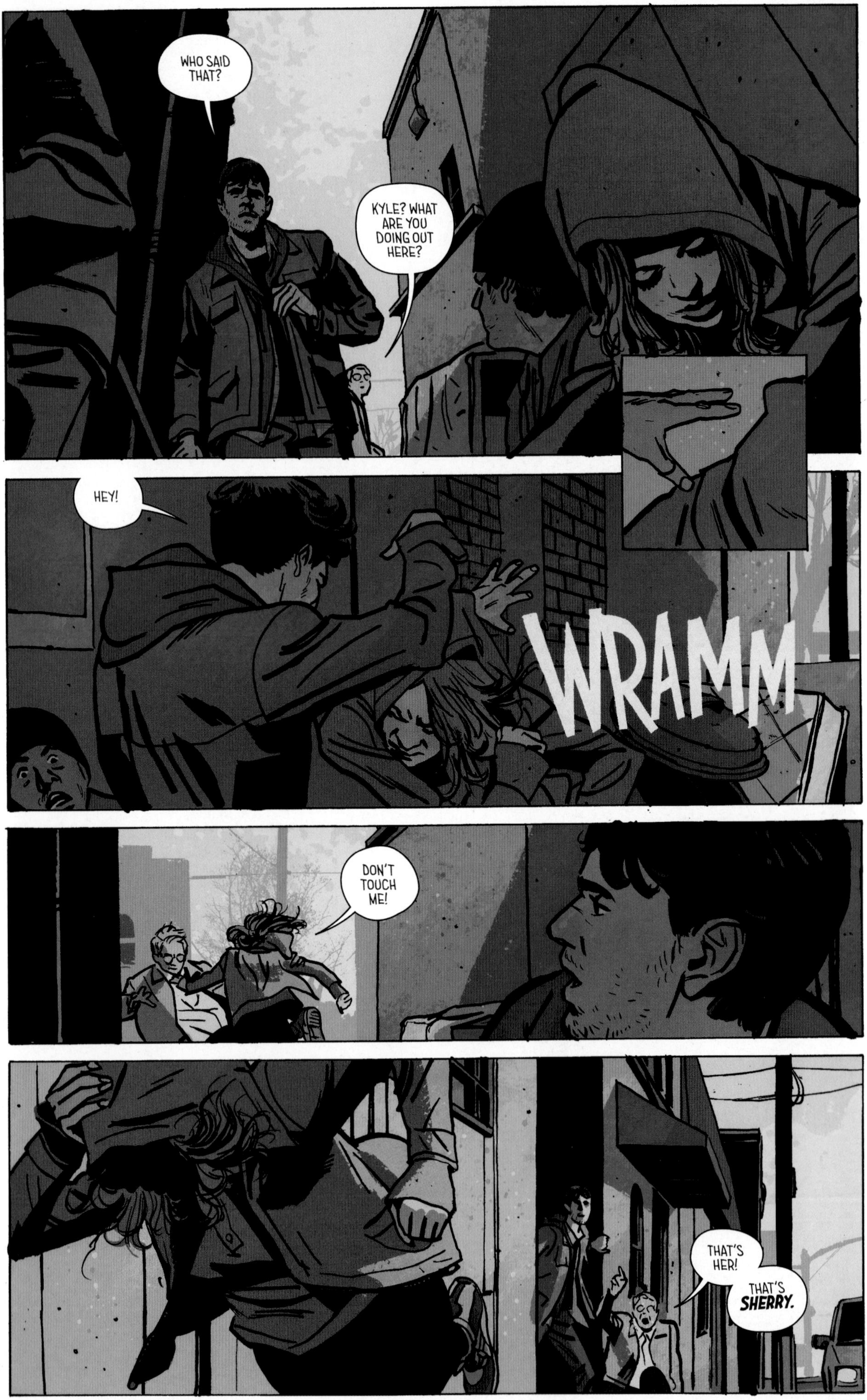
WHO SAID THAT?
KYLE? WHAT ARE YOU DOING OUT HERE?
HEY!
WRAMM
DON'T TOUCH ME!
THAT'S HER!
THAT'S **SHERRY.**

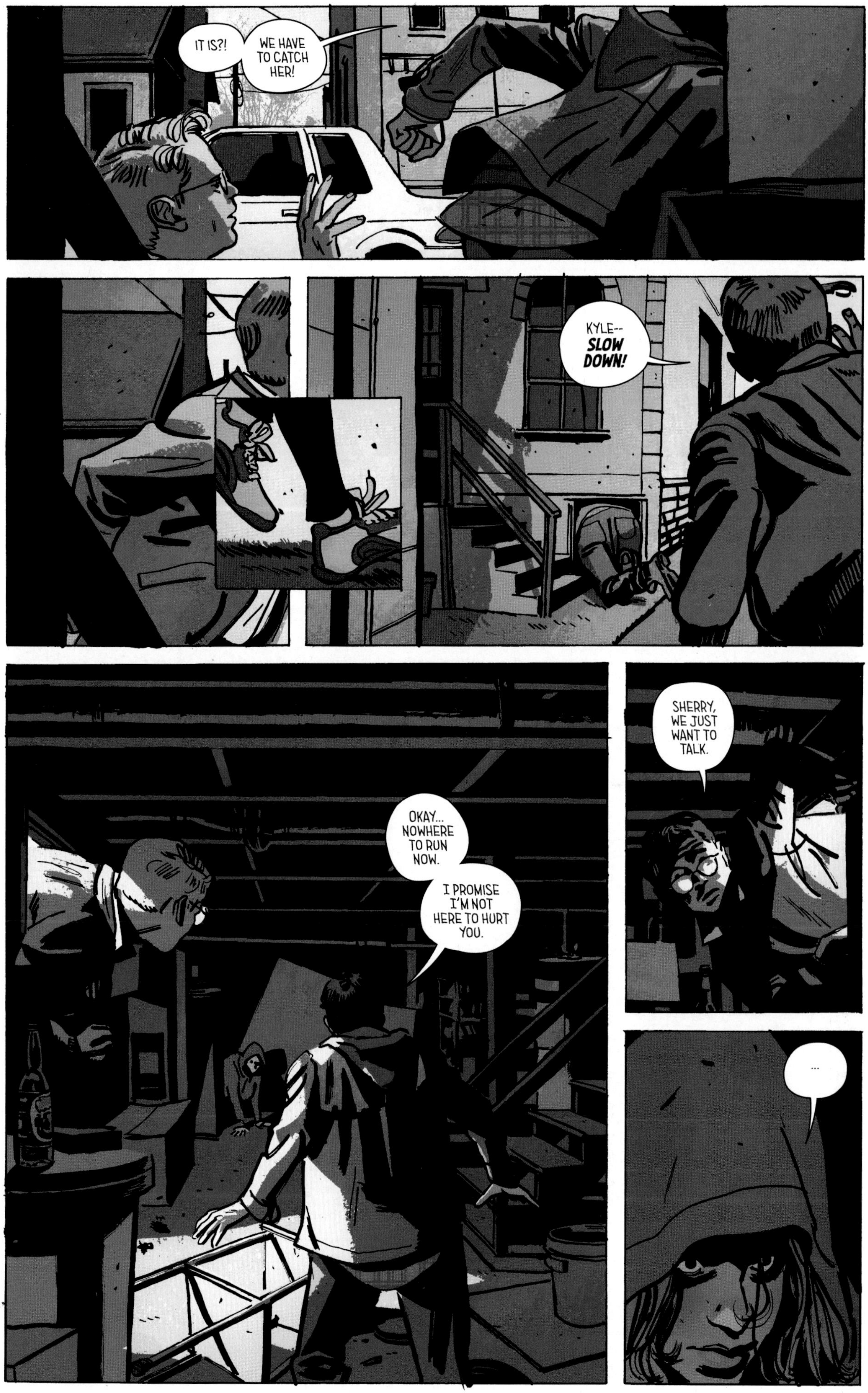
IT IS?!
WE HAVE TO CATCH HER!
KYLE-- **SLOW DOWN!**
OKAY... NOWHERE TO RUN NOW.
I PROMISE I'M NOT HERE TO HURT YOU.
SHERRY, WE JUST WANT TO TALK.
...

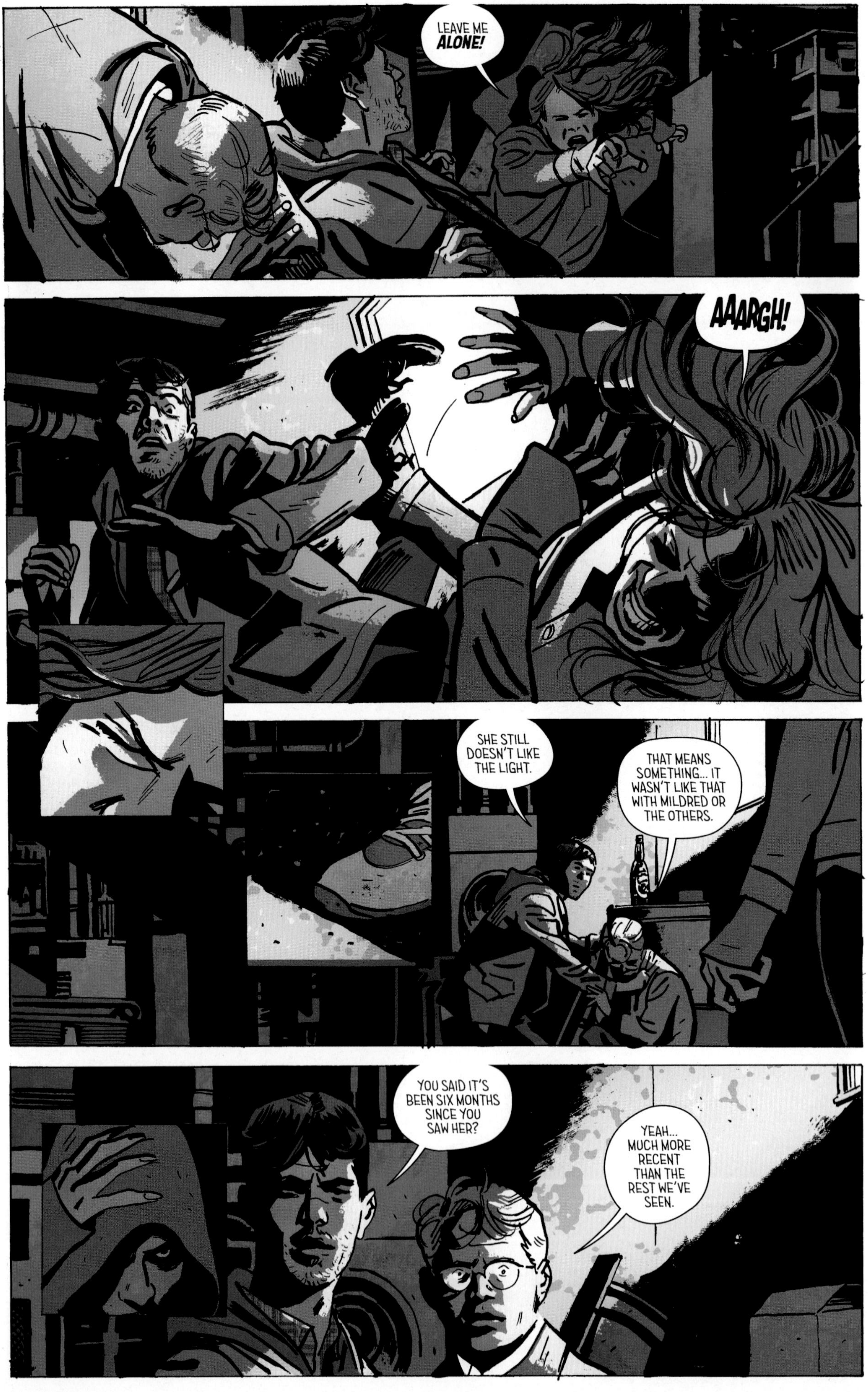

LEAVE ME ALONE!
AAARGH!
SHE STILL DOESN'T LIKE THE LIGHT.
THAT MEANS SOMETHING... IT WASN'T LIKE THAT WITH MILDRED OR THE OTHERS.
YOU SAID IT'S BEEN SIX MONTHS SINCE YOU SAW HER?
YEAH... MUCH MORE RECENT THAN THE REST WE'VE SEEN.

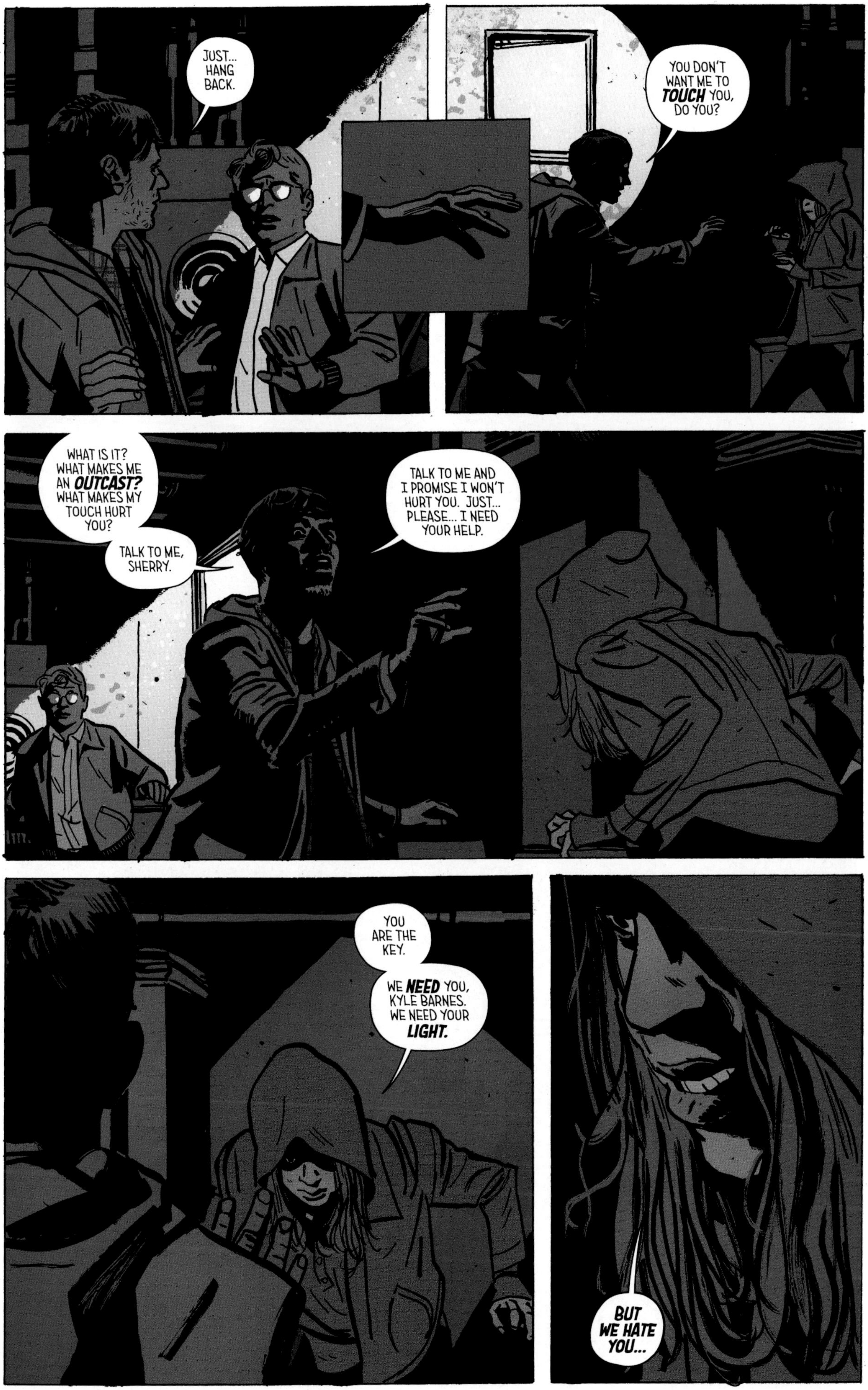

JUST... HANG BACK.
YOU DON'T WANT ME TO TOUCH YOU, DO YOU?
WHAT IS IT? WHAT MAKES ME AN OUTCAST? WHAT MAKES MY TOUCH HURT YOU?
TALK TO ME, SHERRY.
TALK TO ME AND I PROMISE I WON'T HURT YOU. JUST... PLEASE... I NEED YOUR HELP.
YOU ARE THE KEY.
WE NEED YOU, KYLE BARNES. WE NEED YOUR LIGHT.
BUT WE HATE YOU...

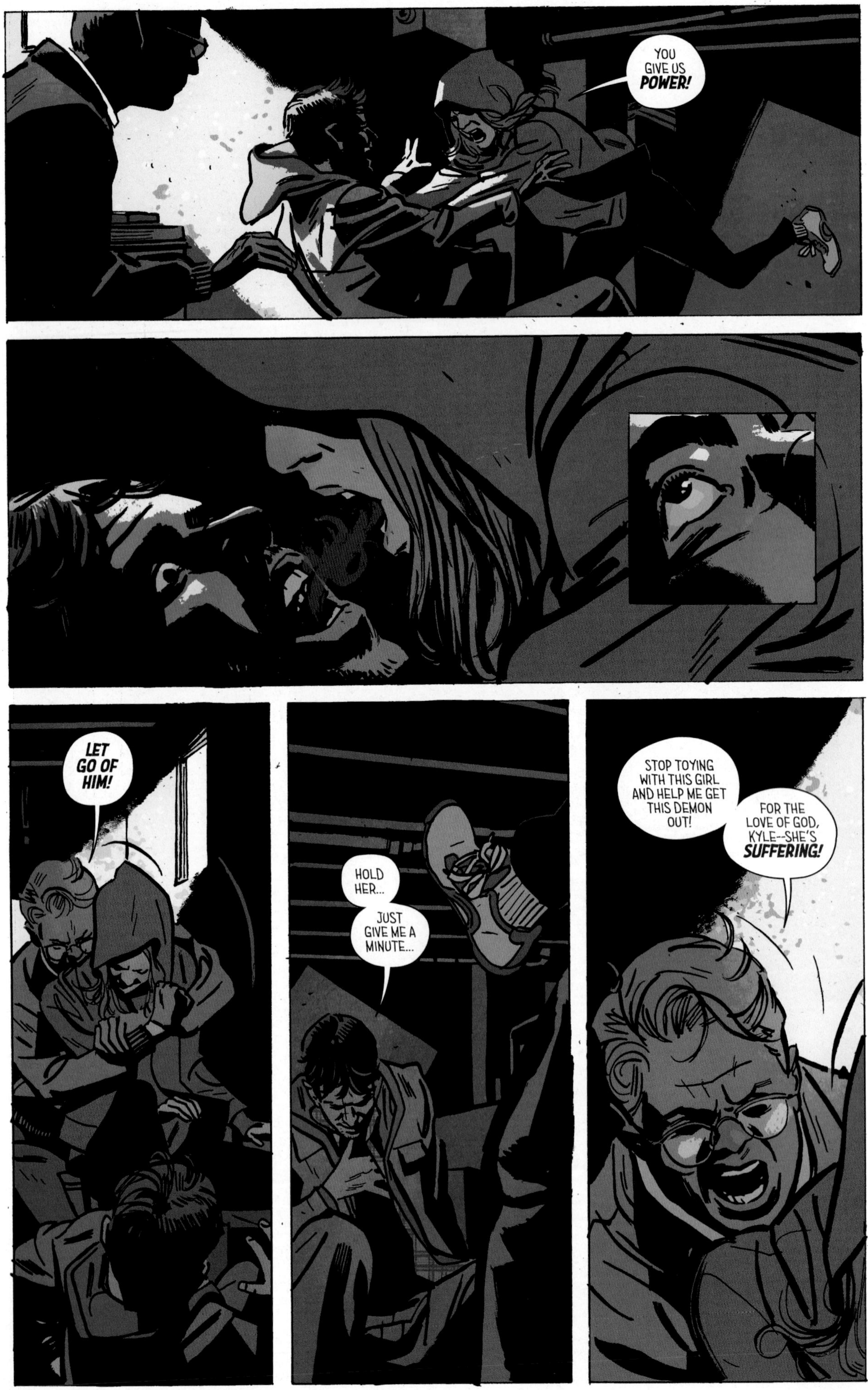
YOU GIVE US **POWER!**
LET GO OF HIM!
HOLD HER...
JUST GIVE ME A MINUTE...
STOP TOYING WITH THIS GIRL AND HELP ME GET THIS DEMON OUT!
FOR THE LOVE OF GOD, KYLE--SHE'S **SUFFERING!**

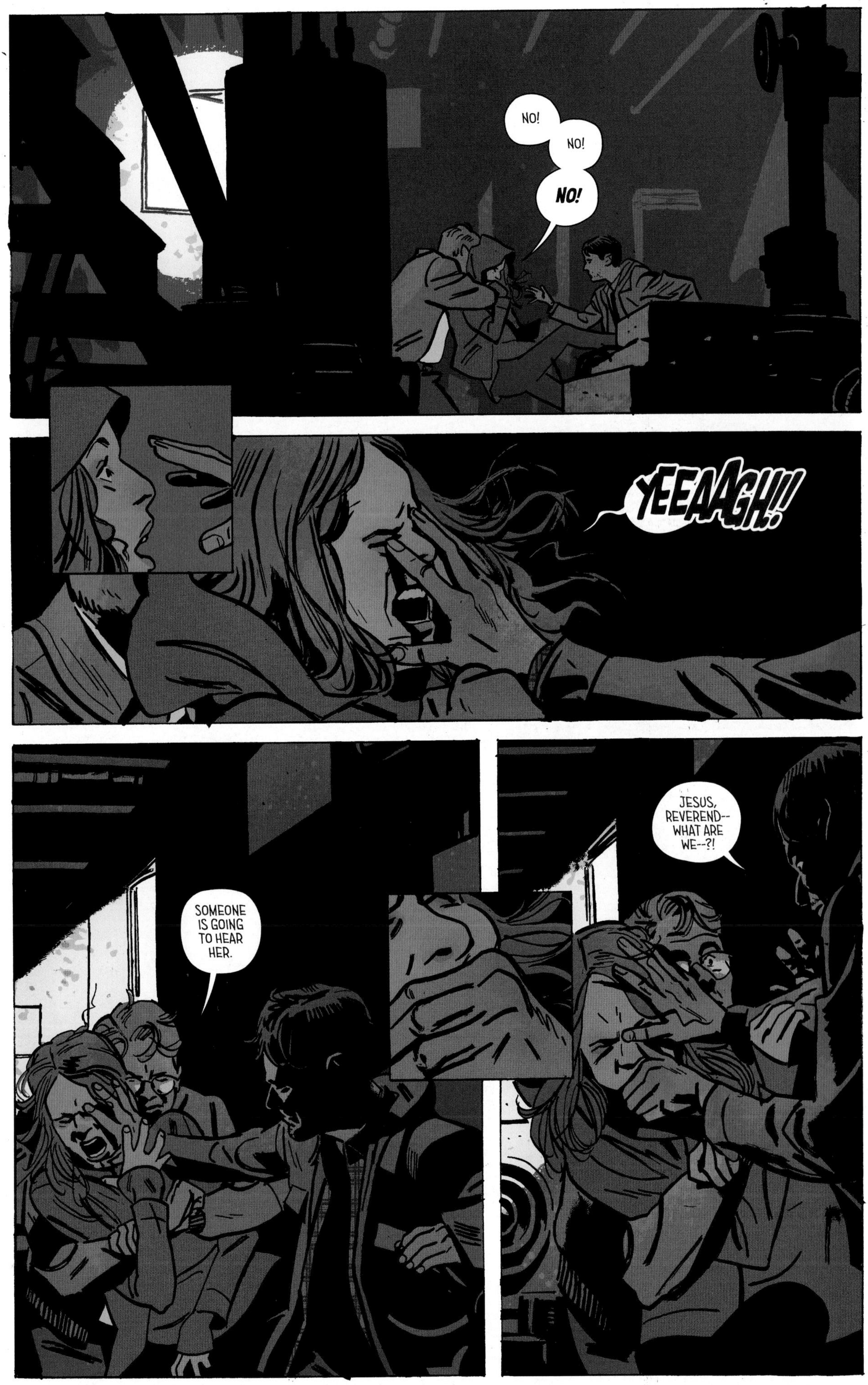
NO!
NO!
NO!
YEEAAGH!!
SOMEONE IS GOING TO HEAR HER.
JESUS, REVEREND-- WHAT ARE WE--?!

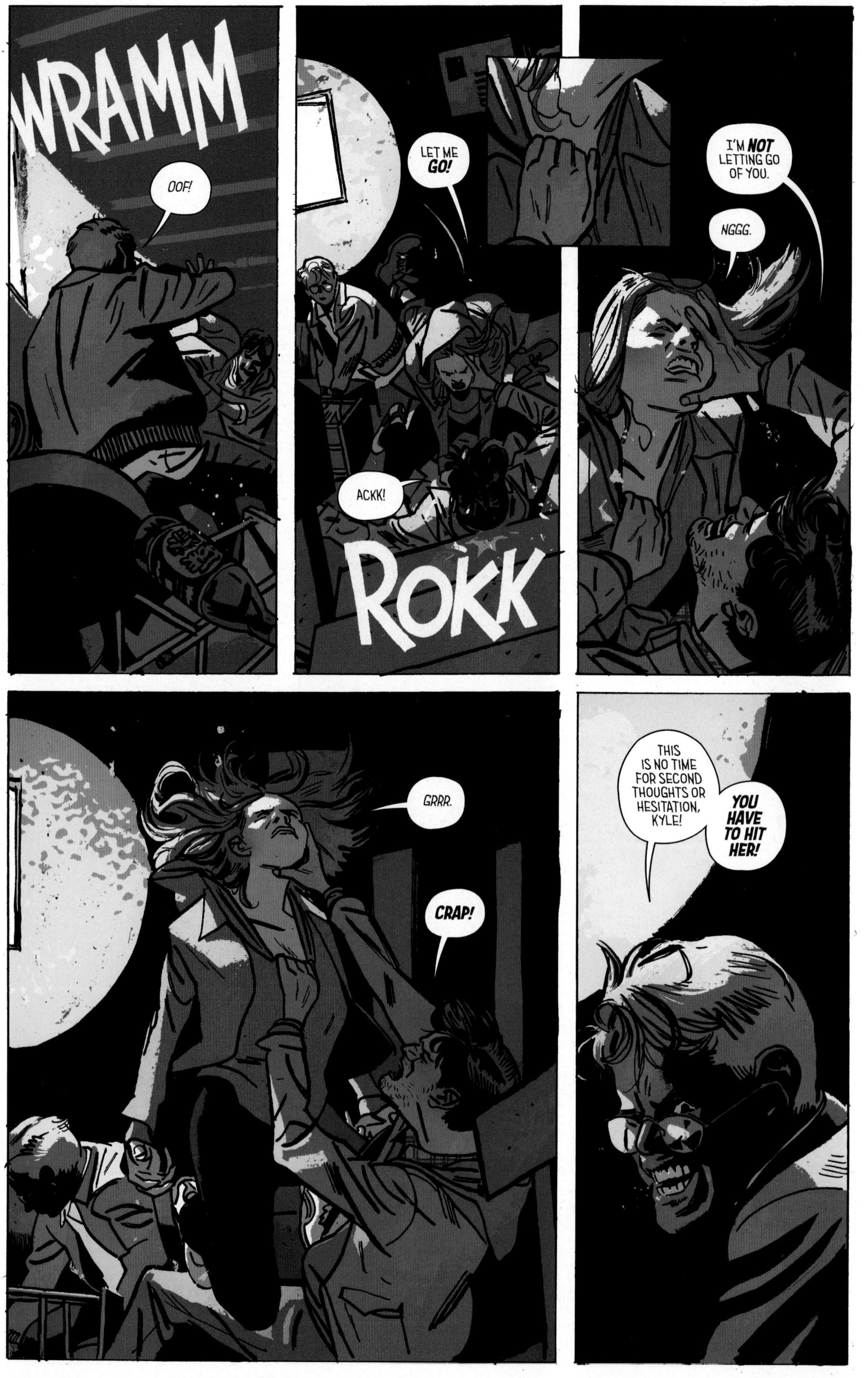
WRAMM
OOF!
LET ME GO!
ACKK!
ROKK
I'M NOT LETTING GO OF YOU.
NGGG.
GRRR.
CRAP!
THIS IS NO TIME FOR SECOND THOUGHTS OR HESITATION, KYLE!
YOU HAVE TO HIT HER!

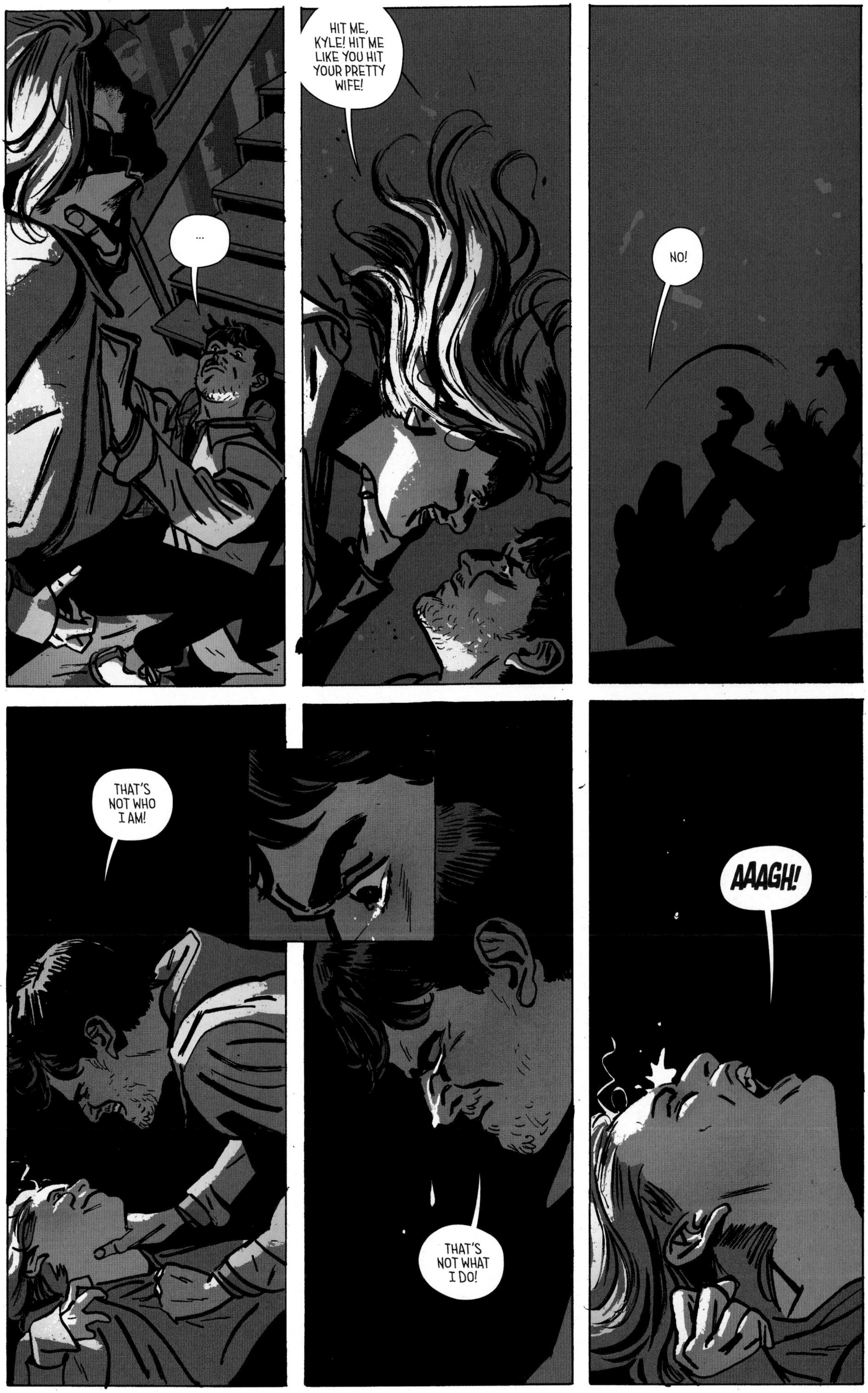
...
HIT ME, KYLE! HIT ME LIKE YOU HIT YOUR PRETTY WIFE!
NO!
THAT'S NOT WHO I AM!
THAT'S NOT WHAT I DO!
AAAGH!

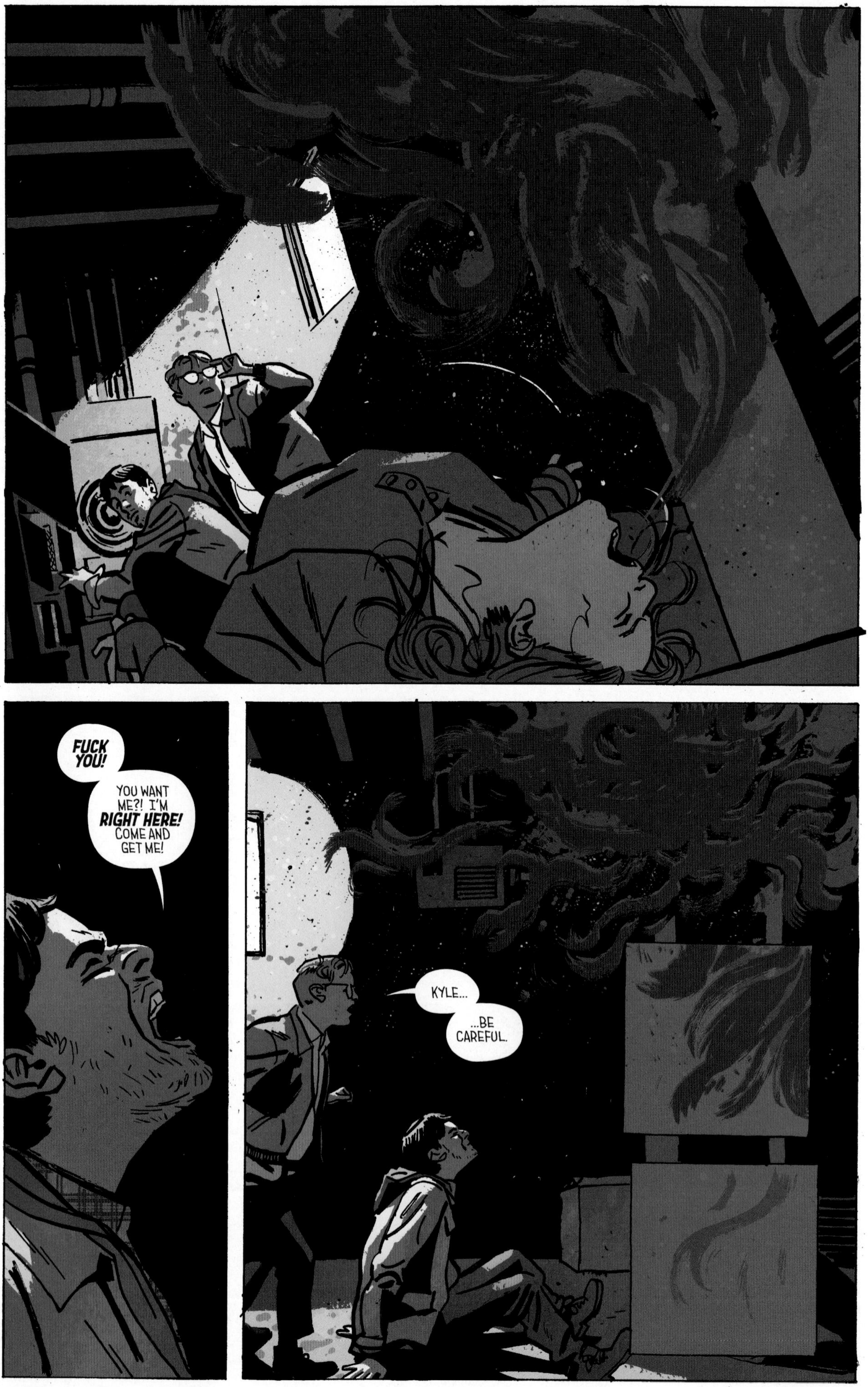
FUCK YOU!
YOU WANT ME?! I'M RIGHT HERE! COME AND GET ME!
KYLE...
...BE CAREFUL.

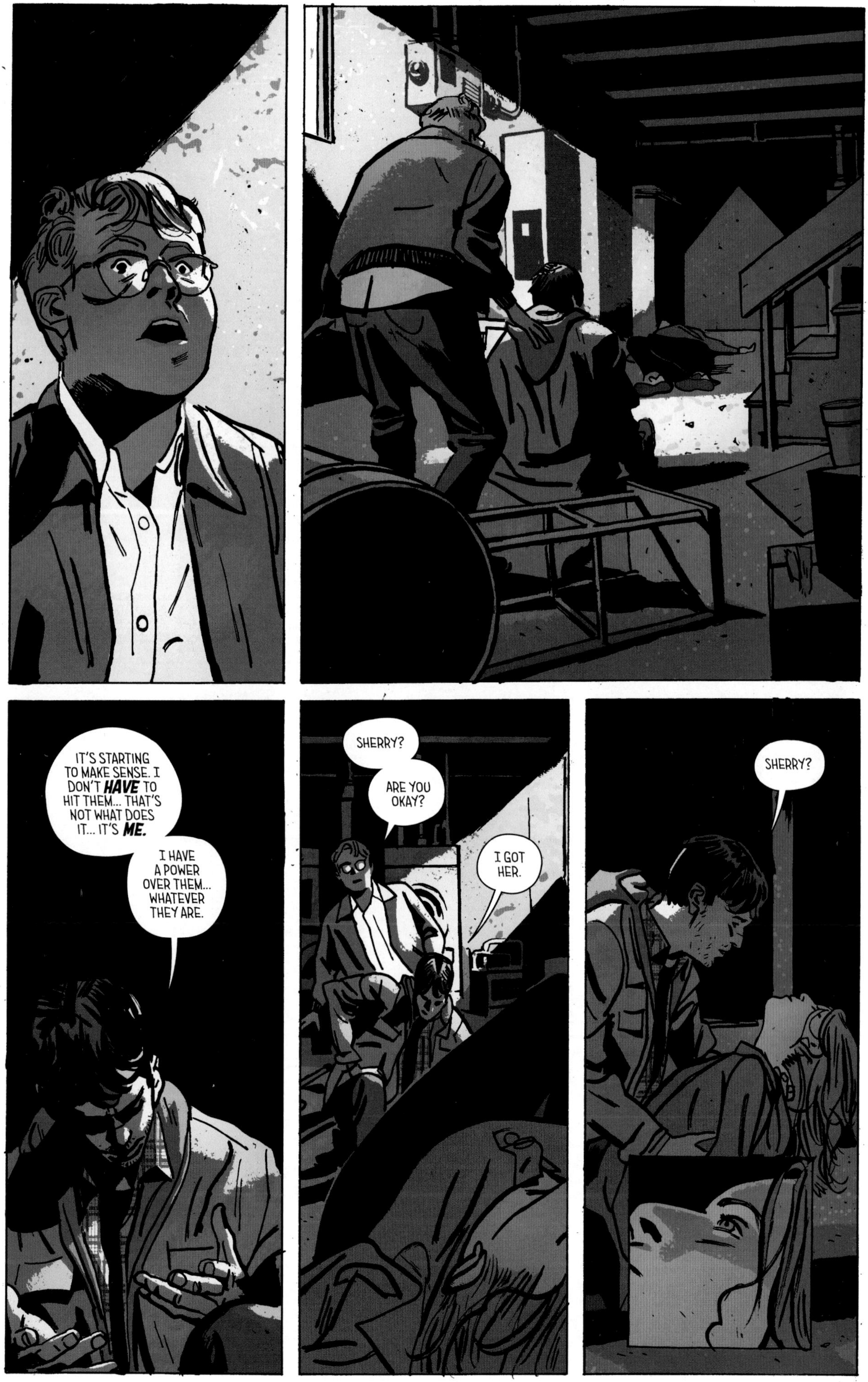
IT'S STARTING TO MAKE SENSE. I DON'T HAVE TO HIT THEM... THAT'S NOT WHAT DOES IT... IT'S ME.
I HAVE A POWER OVER THEM... WHATEVER THEY ARE.
SHERRY?
ARE YOU OKAY?
I GOT HER.
SHERRY?

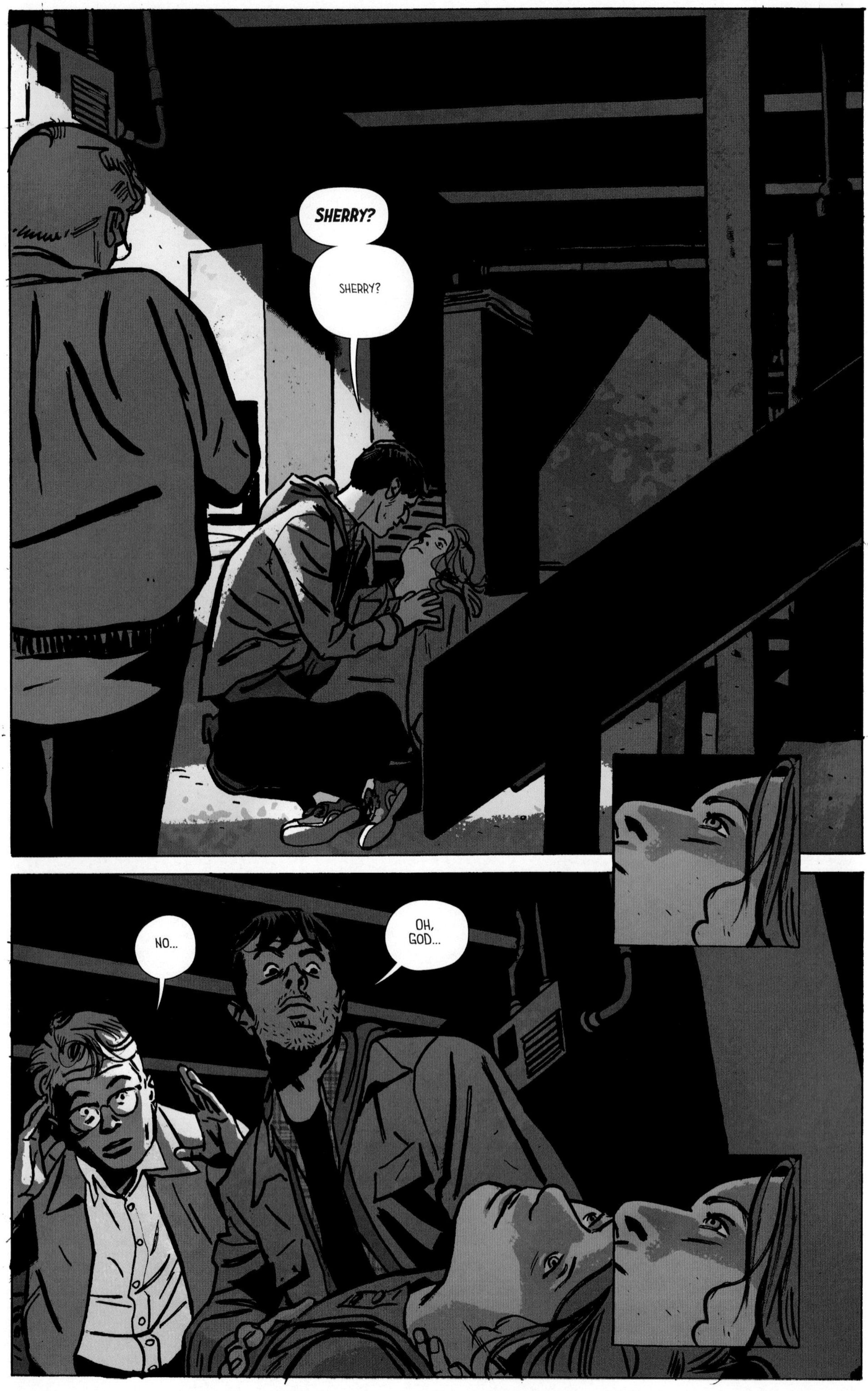
SHERRY?
SHERRY?
NO...
OH, GOD...

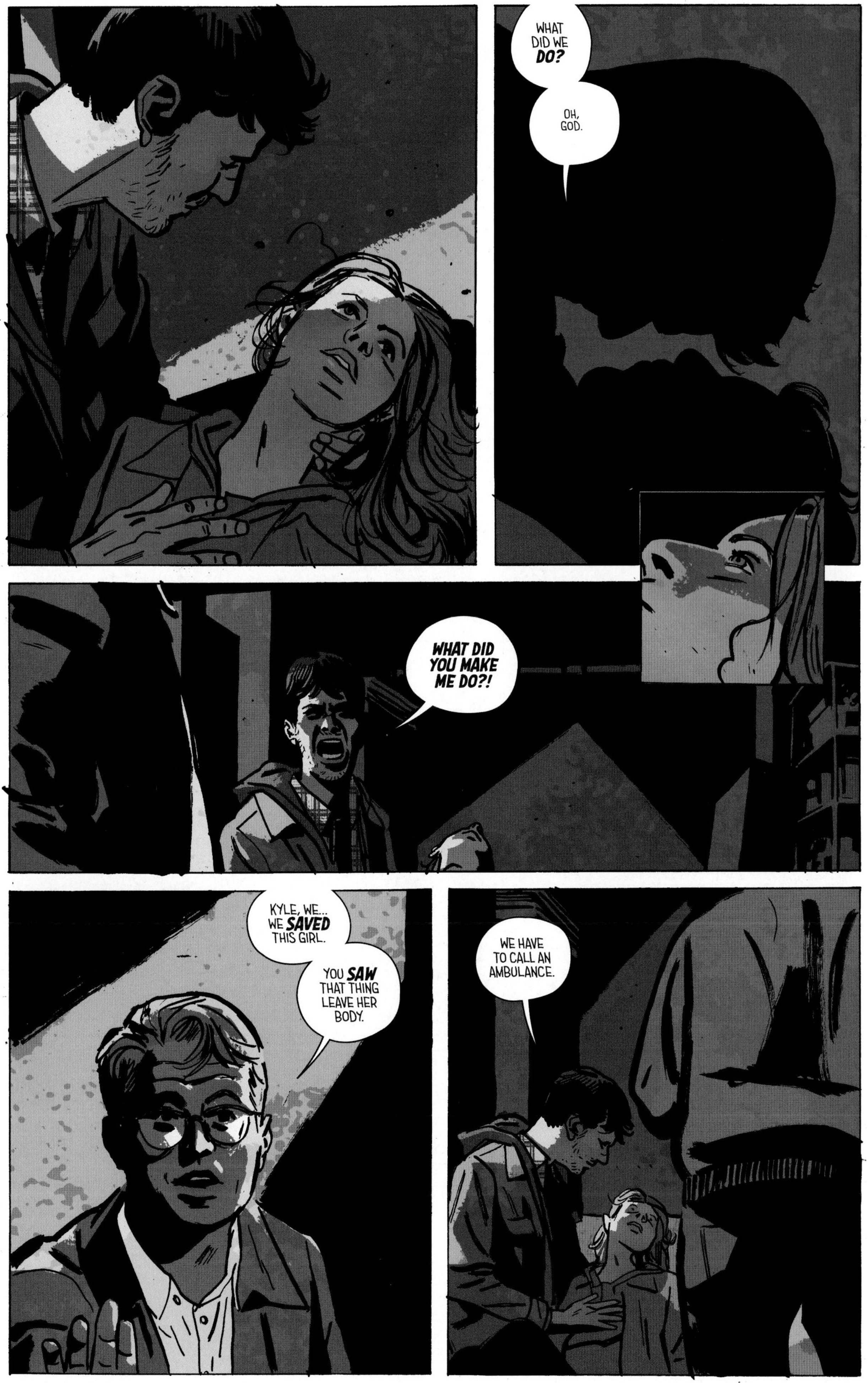
WHAT DID WE ***DO?***
OH, GOD.
WHAT DID YOU MAKE ME DO?!
KYLE, WE... WE ***SAVED*** THIS GIRL.
YOU ***SAW*** THAT THING LEAVE HER BODY.
WE HAVE TO CALL AN AMBULANCE.

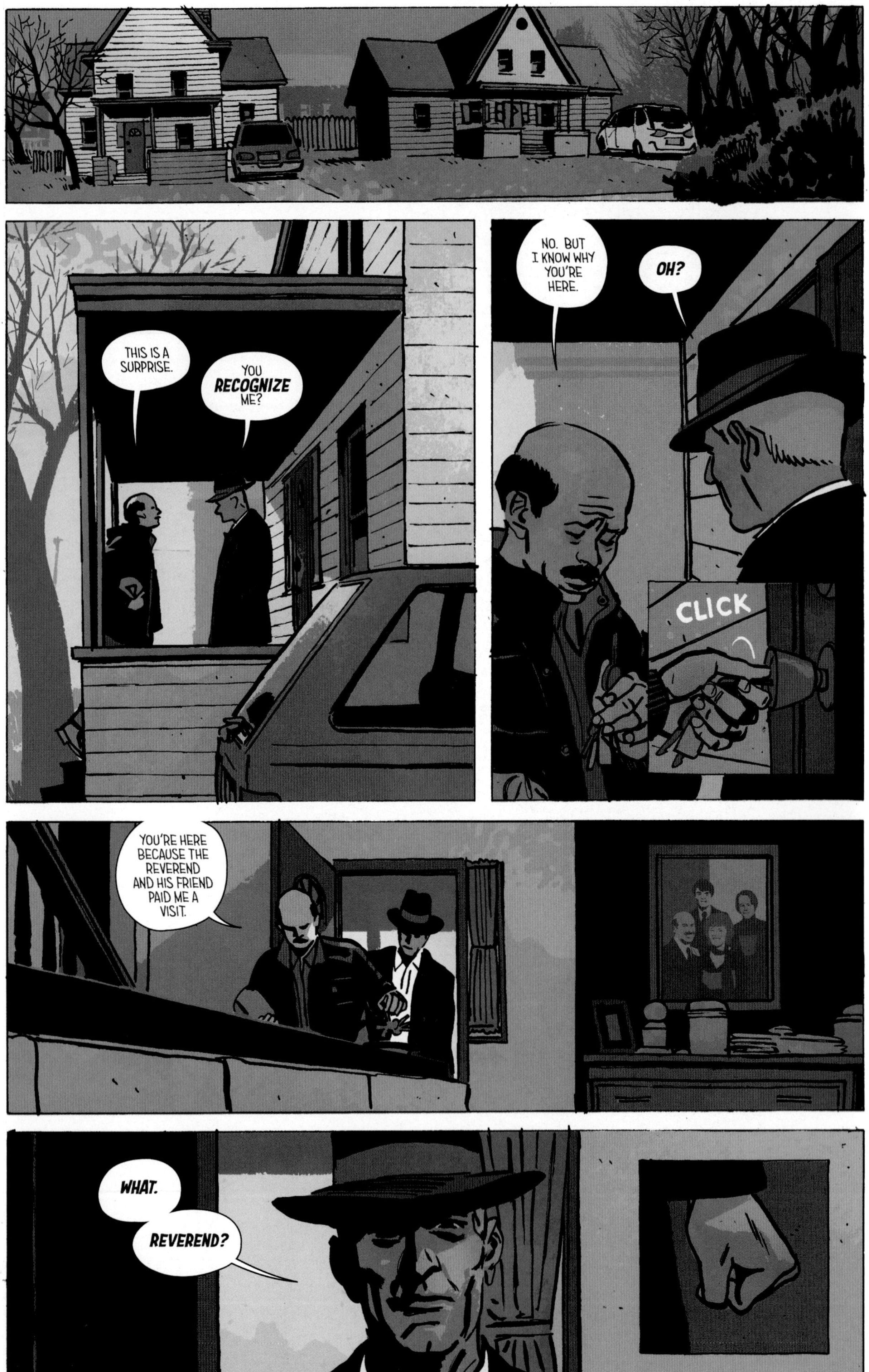
THIS IS A SURPRISE.
YOU **RECOGNIZE** ME?
NO. BUT I KNOW WHY YOU'RE HERE.
OH?
CLICK
YOU'RE HERE BECAUSE THE REVEREND AND HIS FRIEND PAID ME A VISIT.
WHAT.
REVEREND?

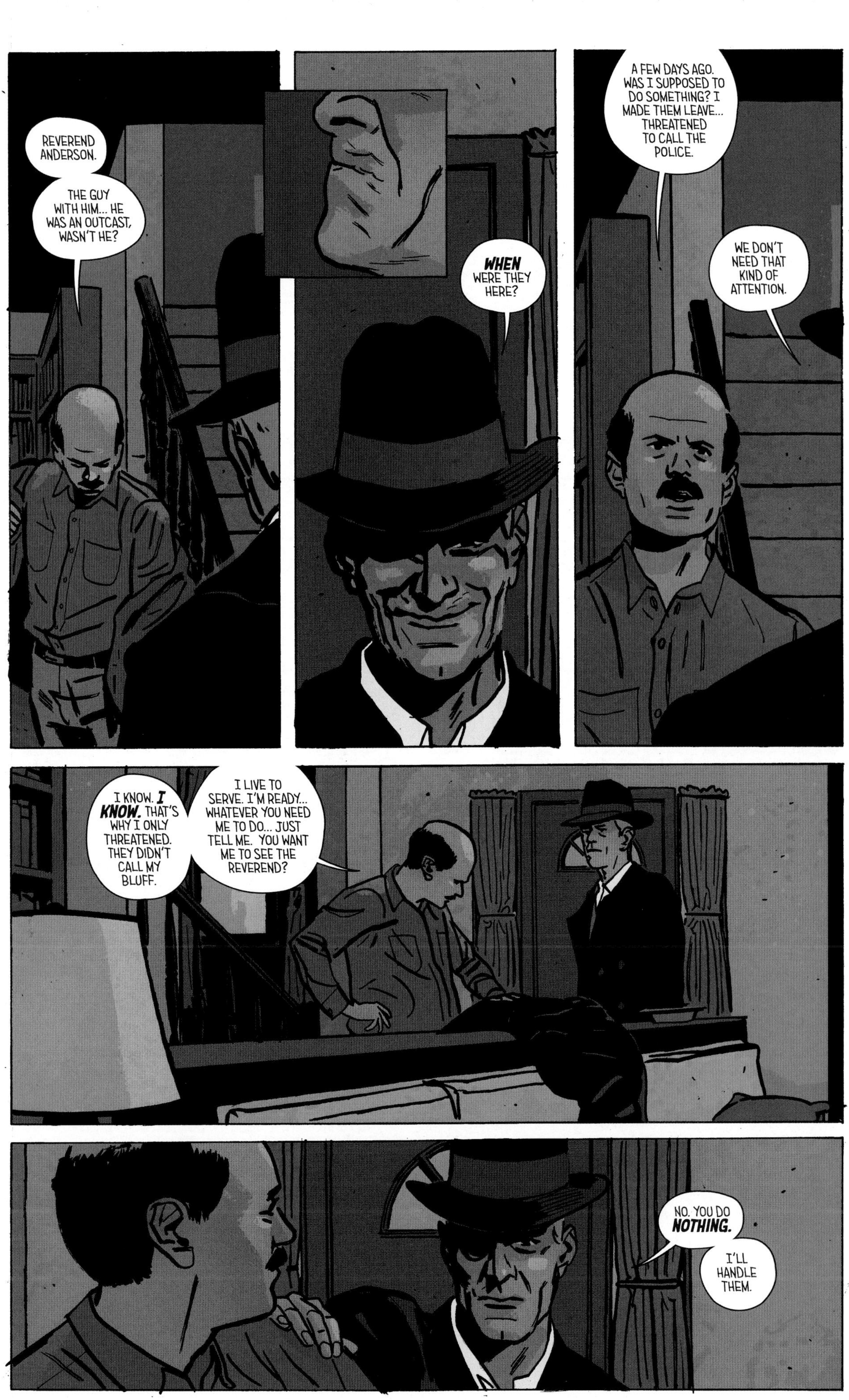
REVEREND ANDERSON.
THE GUY WITH HIM... HE WAS AN OUTCAST, WASN'T HE?
WHEN WERE THEY HERE?
A FEW DAYS AGO. WAS I SUPPOSED TO DO SOMETHING? I MADE THEM LEAVE... THREATENED TO CALL THE POLICE.
WE DON'T NEED THAT KIND OF ATTENTION.
I KNOW. **I KNOW.** THAT'S WHY I ONLY THREATENED. THEY DIDN'T CALL MY BLUFF.
I LIVE TO SERVE. I'M READY... WHATEVER YOU NEED ME TO DO... JUST TELL ME. YOU WANT ME TO SEE THE REVEREND?
NO. YOU DO **NOTHING.**
I'LL HANDLE THEM.

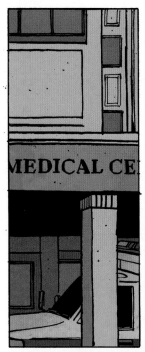

WE WERE LOOKING FOR HER. HER PARENTS SAID SHE DIDN'T WANT TO COME HOME. WE WERE TRYING TO *HELP*.

I KNOW *WHY* YOU WERE THERE... I'M TRYING TO ASCERTAIN WHAT SORT OF ALTERCATION TRANSPIRED BETWEEN YOU AND YOUR FRIEND CHASING THE VICTIM INTO THE ABANDONED BUILDING... AND HER ARRIVING IN HER CURRENT CATATONIC STATE.

SHE WAS VERY UPSET. THAT'S WHY SHE RAN AWAY FROM US IN THE FIRST PLACE. IN HINDSIGHT, FOLLOWING HER INTO THAT BUILDING WAS PROBABLY A MISTAKE, BUT WE WERE CONCERNED FOR HER SAFETY.

ONCE INSIDE, WE... WELL... SHE WAS FINE ONE MINUTE AND THEN THE *NEXT*...

STOP

...SHE WAS LIKE *THIS*.

I HONESTLY HAVE *NO IDEA* WHAT HAPPENED TO HER.

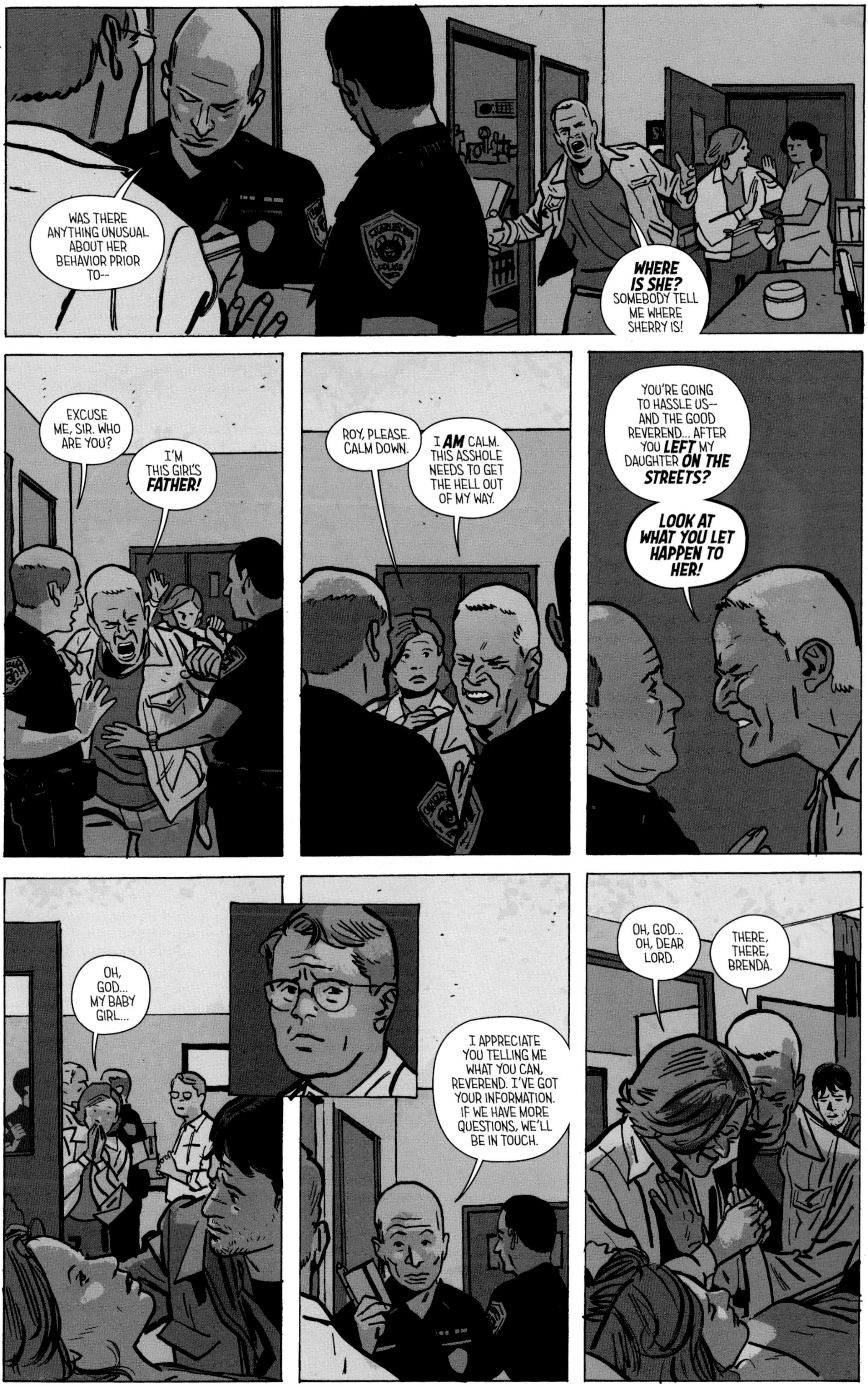
WAS THERE ANYTHING UNUSUAL ABOUT HER BEHAVIOR PRIOR TO--
WHERE IS SHE? SOMEBODY TELL ME WHERE SHERRY IS!
EXCUSE ME, SIR. WHO ARE YOU?
I'M THIS GIRL'S FATHER!
ROY, PLEASE. CALM DOWN.
I AM CALM. THIS ASSHOLE NEEDS TO GET THE HELL OUT OF MY WAY.
YOU'RE GOING TO HASSLE US-- AND THE GOOD REVEREND... AFTER YOU LEFT MY DAUGHTER ON THE STREETS?
LOOK AT WHAT YOU LET HAPPEN TO HER!
OH, GOD... MY BABY GIRL...
I APPRECIATE YOU TELLING ME WHAT YOU CAN, REVEREND. I'VE GOT YOUR INFORMATION. IF WE HAVE MORE QUESTIONS, WE'LL BE IN TOUCH.
OH, GOD... OH, DEAR LORD.
THERE, THERE, BRENDA.

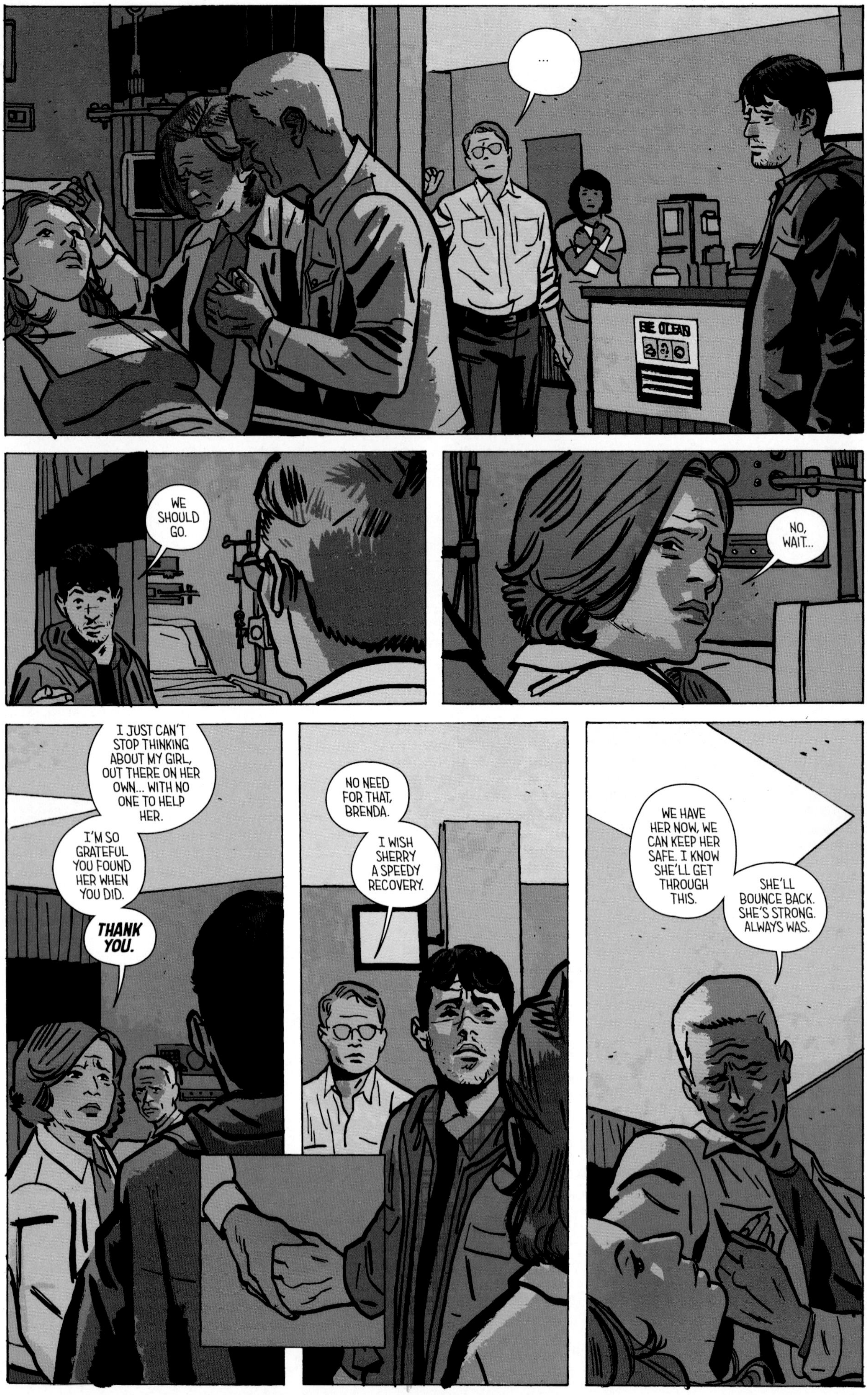
...
WE SHOULD GO.
NO, WAIT...
I JUST CAN'T STOP THINKING ABOUT MY GIRL, OUT THERE ON HER OWN... WITH NO ONE TO HELP HER.
I'M SO GRATEFUL YOU FOUND HER WHEN YOU DID.
THANK YOU.
NO NEED FOR THAT, BRENDA.
I WISH SHERRY A SPEEDY RECOVERY.
WE HAVE HER NOW, WE CAN KEEP HER SAFE. I KNOW SHE'LL GET THROUGH THIS.
SHE'LL BOUNCE BACK. SHE'S STRONG. ALWAYS WAS.

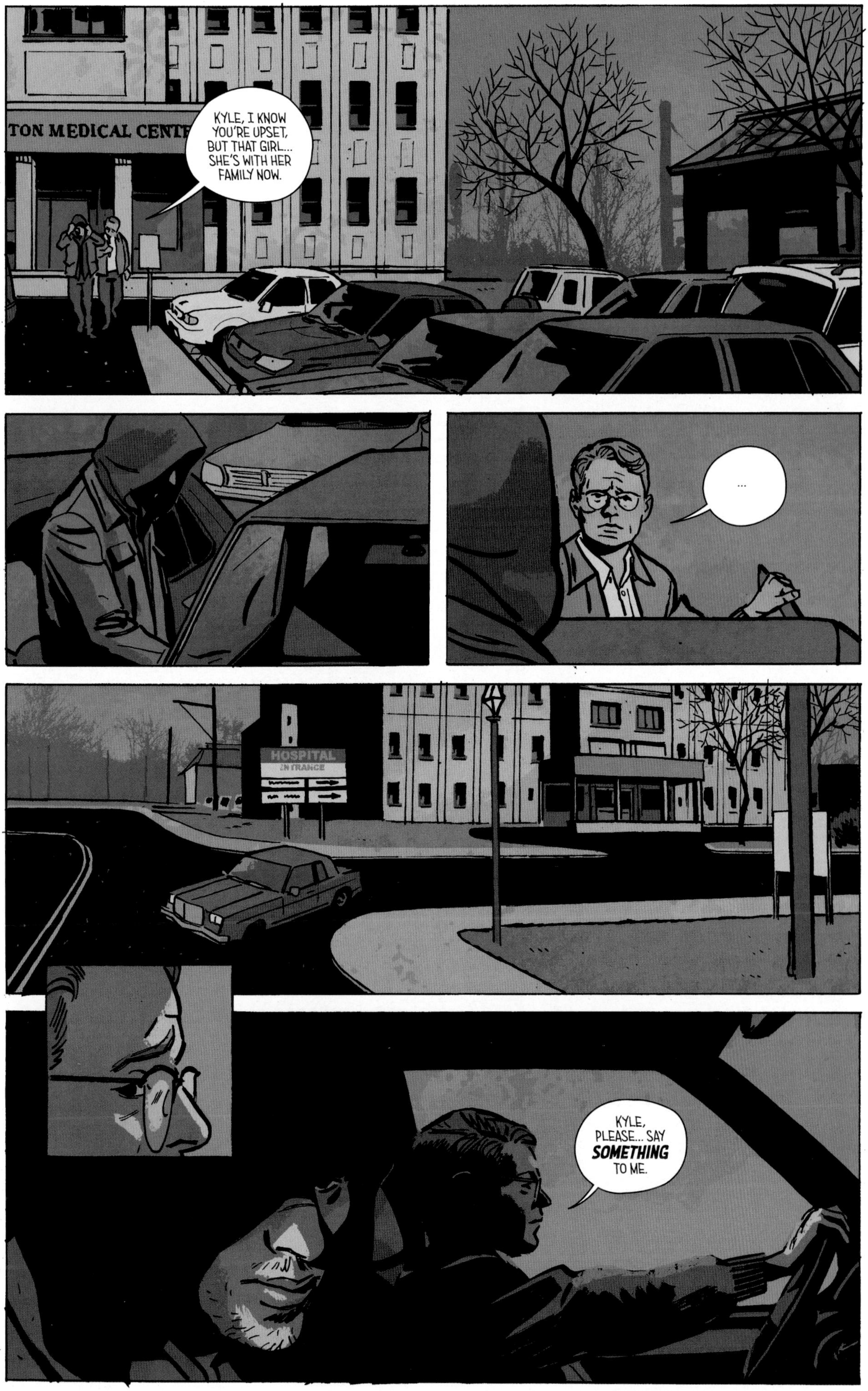
TON MEDICAL CENT
KYLE, I KNOW YOU'RE UPSET, BUT THAT GIRL... SHE'S WITH HER FAMILY NOW.
...
HOSPITAL
ENTRANCE
KYLE, PLEASE... SAY **SOMETHING** TO ME.

WHAT **THE FUCK** DID WE DO TO THAT GIRL?!

CAN YOU TELL ME? DO YOU EVEN FUCKING **KNOW?!**

I KNOW THAT WE **SAVED** HER. I KNOW WE DID THE RIGHT THING.

THE RIGHT--?!

ARE YOU FUCKING KIDDING ME?! WE RUINED THAT POOR GIRL'S LIFE! HER PARENTS ARE IN THAT HOSPITAL RIGHT NOW PRAYING FOR HER TO WAKE UP... AND I HATE TO BREAK IT TO YOU, BUT--

--THAT'S **NEVER** GOING TO HAPPEN!

I KNOW THAT BECAUSE MY MOTHER IS NEVER GOING TO WAKE UP... AND I DID THE SAME THING TO HER. SHE'S BEEN IN A FUCKING BED EVER SINCE.

THAT'S WHAT WE DID TO SHERRY. **THAT'S** THE TRUTH! YOU CAN TELL YOURSELF WE SAVED HER SOUL-- THAT WE HELPED HER IN SOME WAY...

--BUT THAT'S **BULLSHIT!**

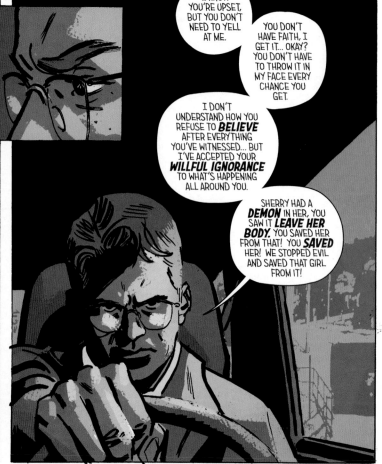
I KNOW YOU'RE UPSET, BUT YOU DON'T NEED TO YELL AT ME.

YOU DON'T HAVE FAITH, I GET IT... OKAY? YOU DON'T HAVE TO THROW IT IN MY FACE EVERY CHANCE YOU GET.

I DON'T UNDERSTAND HOW YOU REFUSE TO **BELIEVE** AFTER EVERYTHING YOU'VE WITNESSED... BUT I'VE ACCEPTED YOUR **WILLFUL IGNORANCE** TO WHAT'S HAPPENING ALL AROUND YOU.

SHERRY HAD A **DEMON** IN HER, YOU SAW IT **LEAVE HER BODY.** YOU SAVED HER FROM THAT! YOU **SAVED** HER! WE STOPPED EVIL AND SAVED THAT GIRL FROM IT!

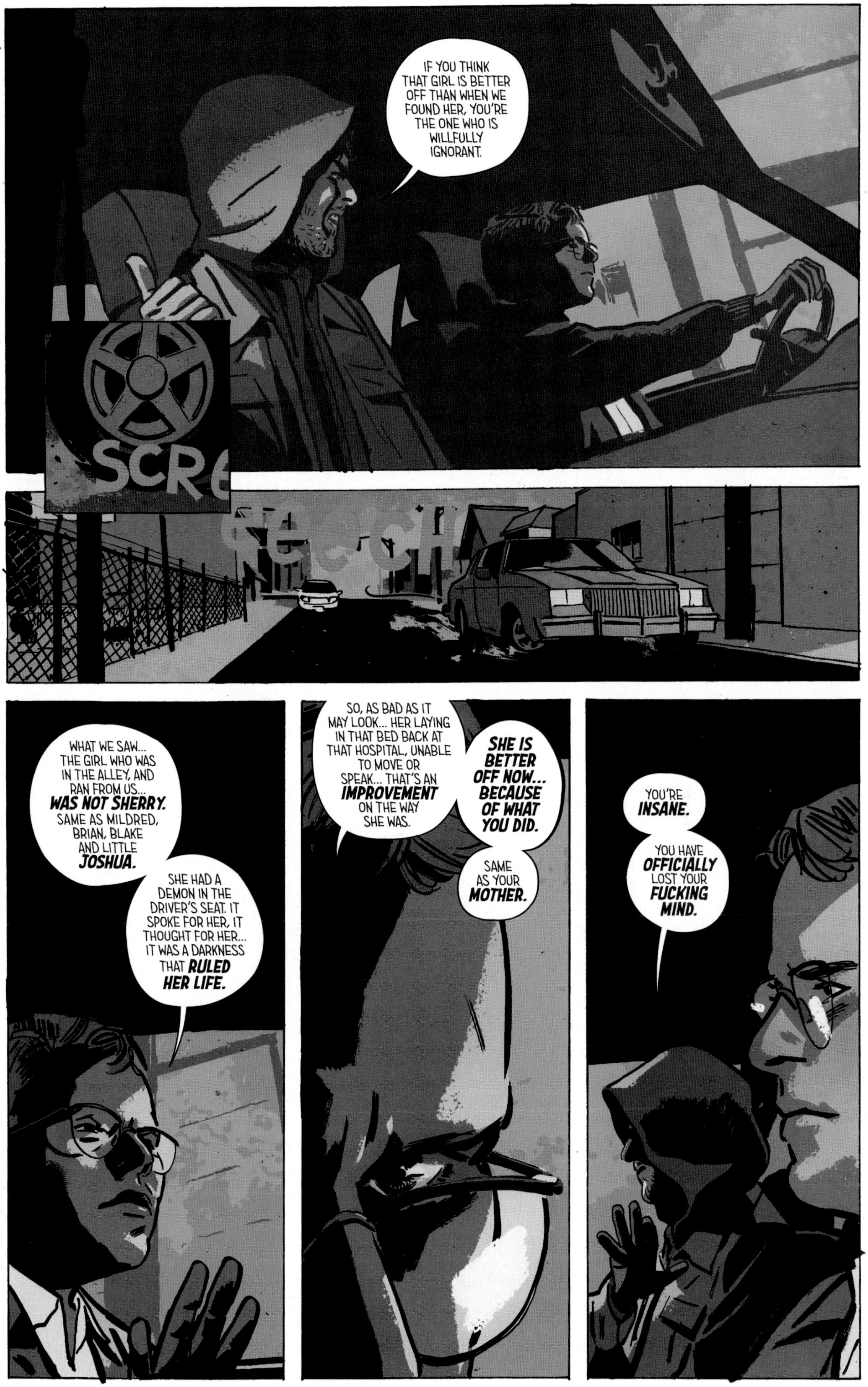
IF YOU THINK THAT GIRL IS BETTER OFF THAN WHEN WE FOUND HER, YOU'RE THE ONE WHO IS WILLFULLY IGNORANT.
SCREEECH
WHAT WE SAW... THE GIRL WHO WAS IN THE ALLEY, AND RAN FROM US... WAS NOT SHERRY. SAME AS MILDRED, BRIAN, BLAKE AND LITTLE JOSHUA.
SHE HAD A DEMON IN THE DRIVER'S SEAT. IT SPOKE FOR HER, IT THOUGHT FOR HER... IT WAS A DARKNESS THAT RULED HER LIFE.
SO, AS BAD AS IT MAY LOOK... HER LAYING IN THAT BED BACK AT THAT HOSPITAL, UNABLE TO MOVE OR SPEAK... THAT'S AN IMPROVEMENT ON THE WAY SHE WAS.
SHE IS BETTER OFF NOW... BECAUSE OF WHAT YOU DID.
SAME AS YOUR MOTHER.
YOU'RE INSANE.
YOU HAVE OFFICIALLY LOST YOUR FUCKING MIND.

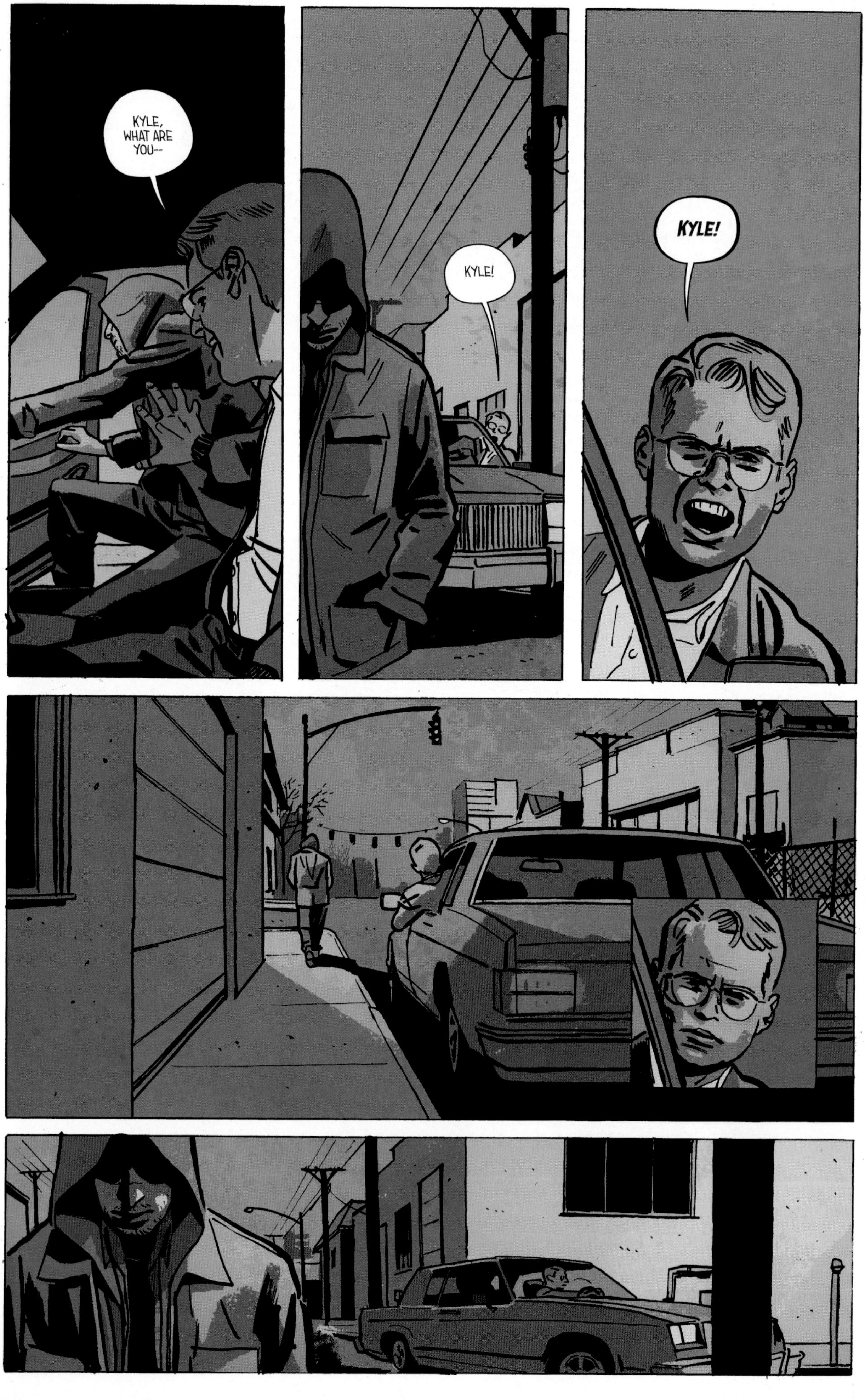
KYLE, WHAT ARE YOU--
KYLE!
KYLE!

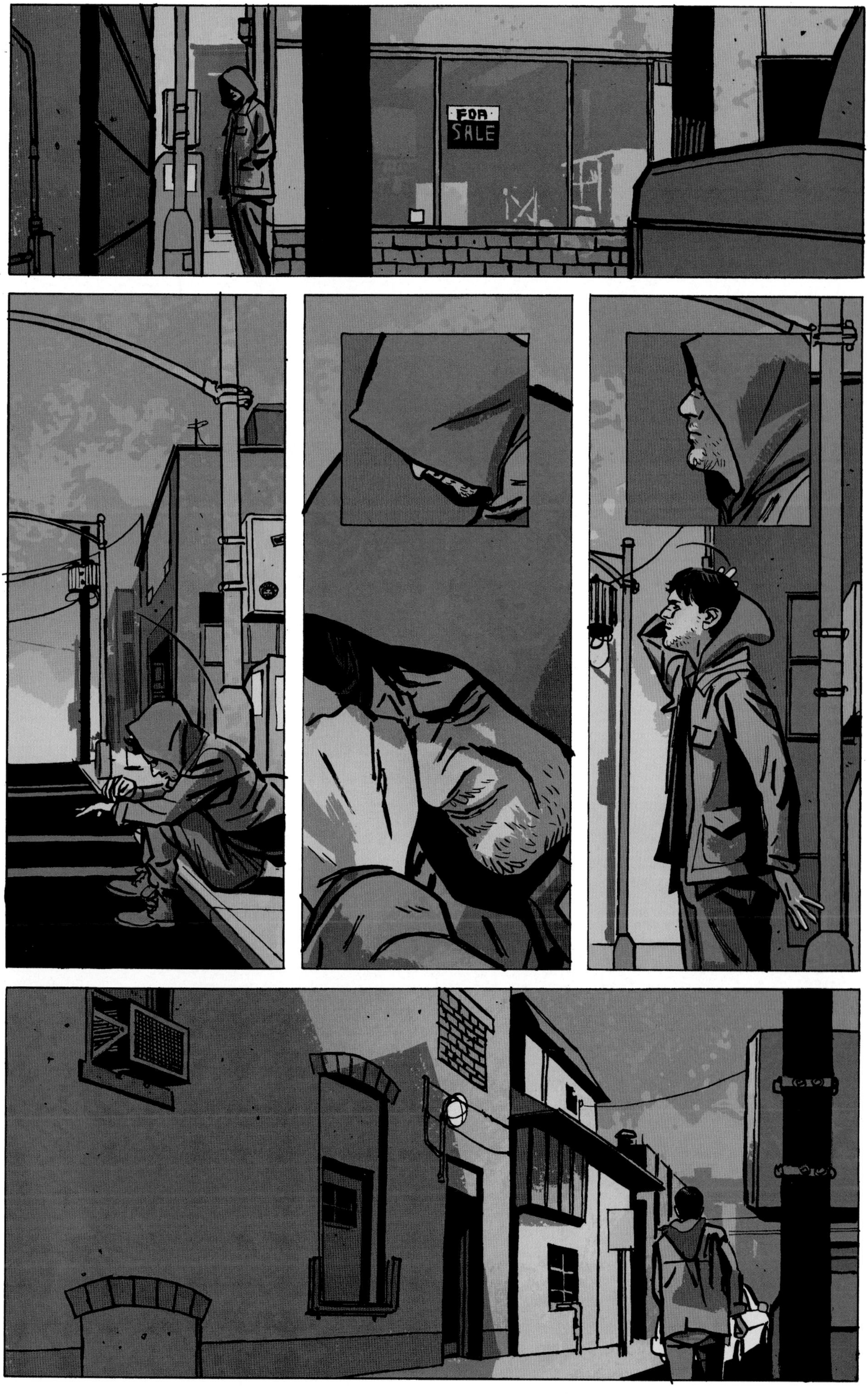
FOR SALE

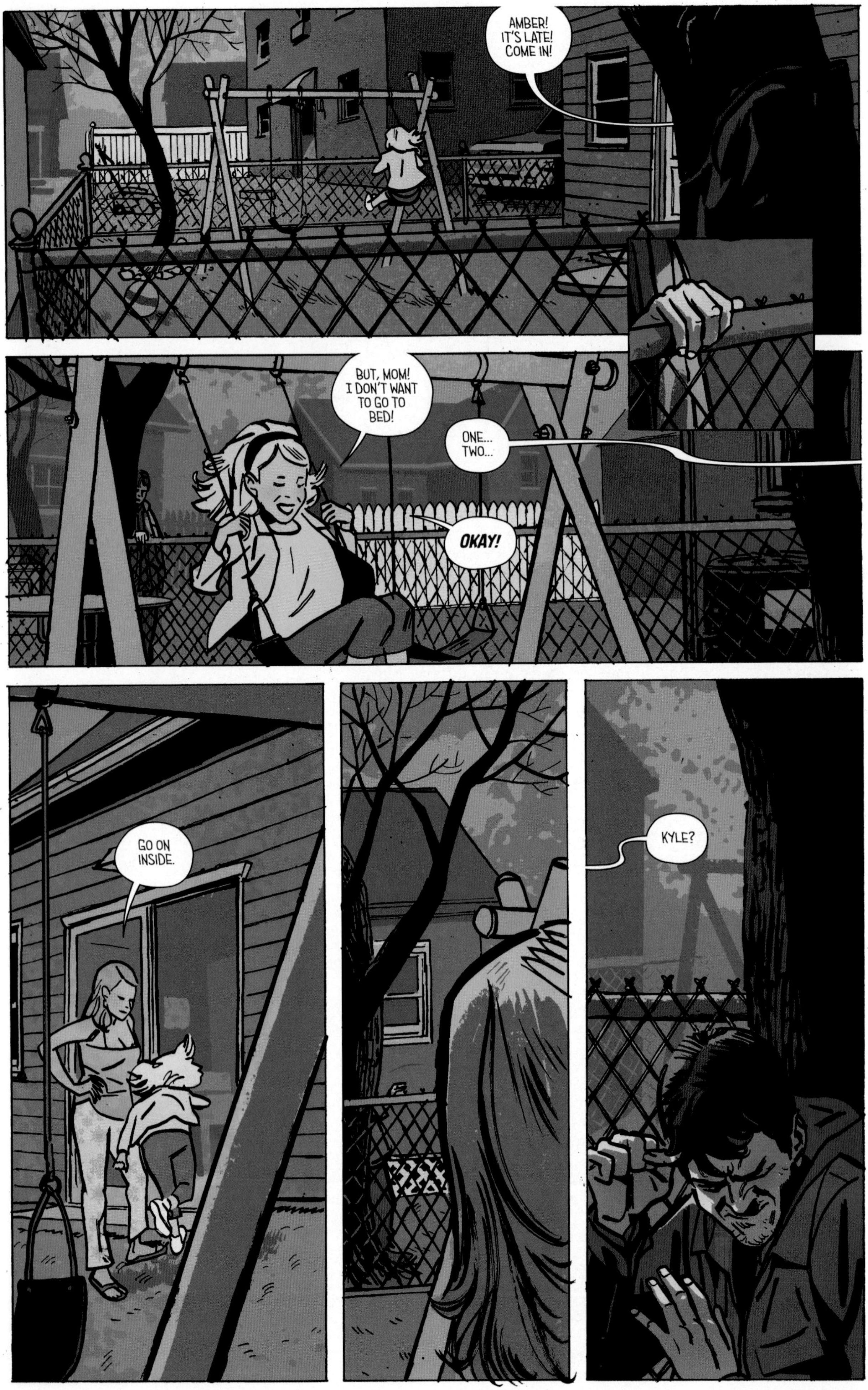
AMBER! IT'S LATE! COME IN!
BUT, MOM! I DON'T WANT TO GO TO BED!
ONE... TWO...
OKAY!
GO ON INSIDE.
KYLE?

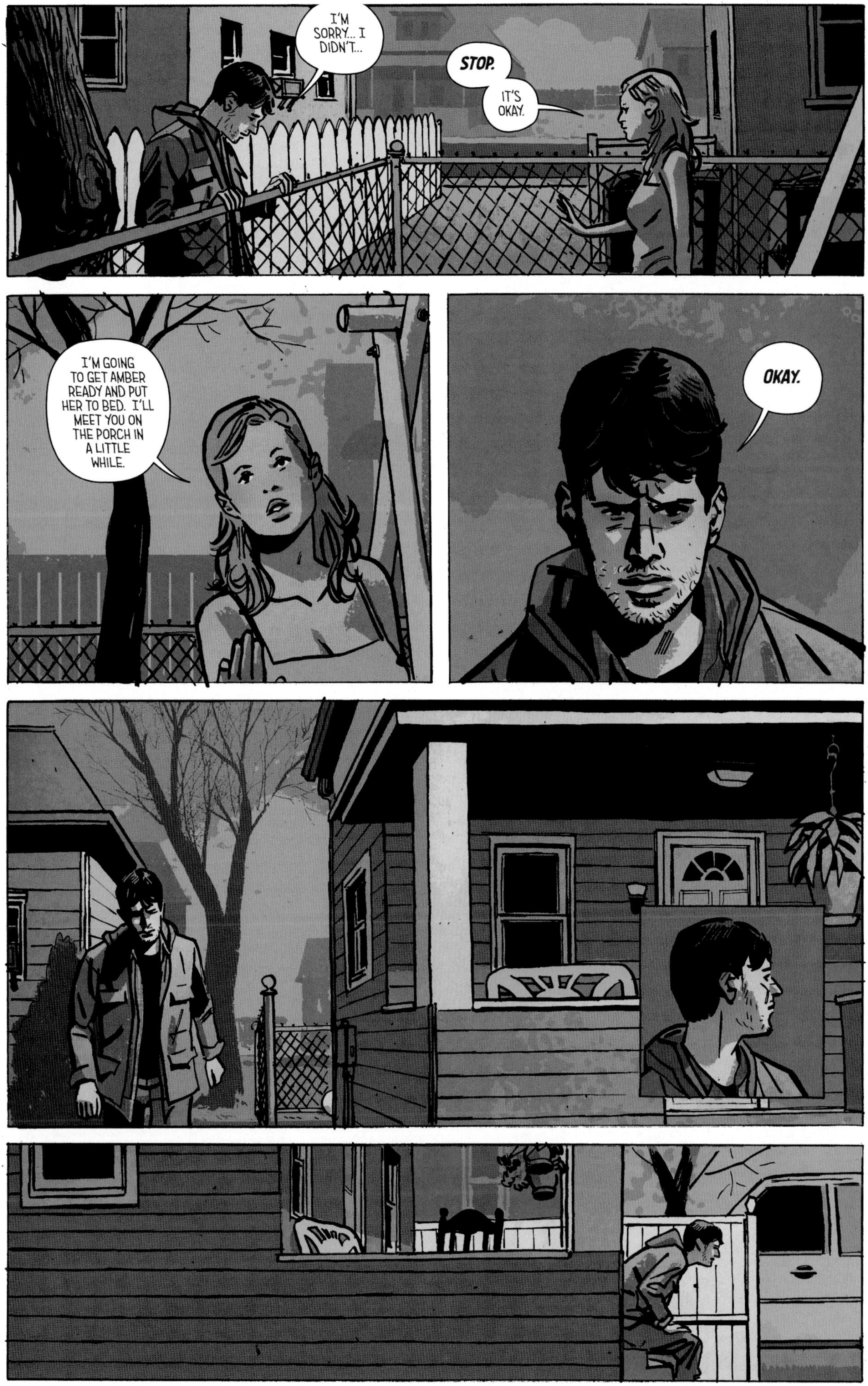
I'M SORRY... I DIDN'T...
STOP.
IT'S OKAY.
I'M GOING TO GET AMBER READY AND PUT HER TO BED. I'LL MEET YOU ON THE PORCH IN A LITTLE WHILE.
OKAY.

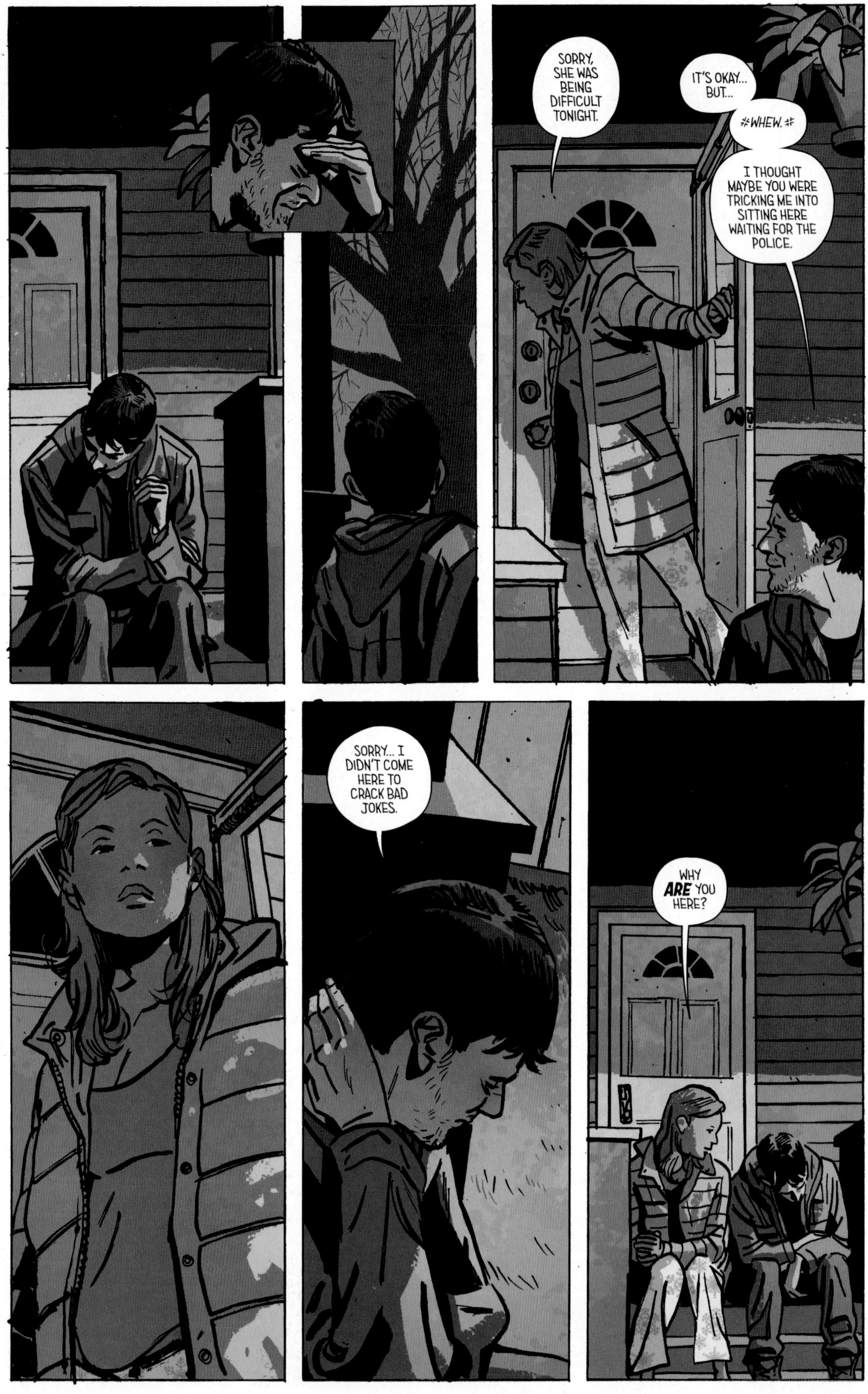

SORRY, SHE WAS BEING DIFFICULT TONIGHT.
IT'S OKAY... BUT...
#WHEW.#
I THOUGHT MAYBE YOU WERE TRICKING ME INTO SITTING HERE WAITING FOR THE POLICE.
SORRY... I DIDN'T COME HERE TO CRACK BAD JOKES.
WHY **ARE** YOU HERE?

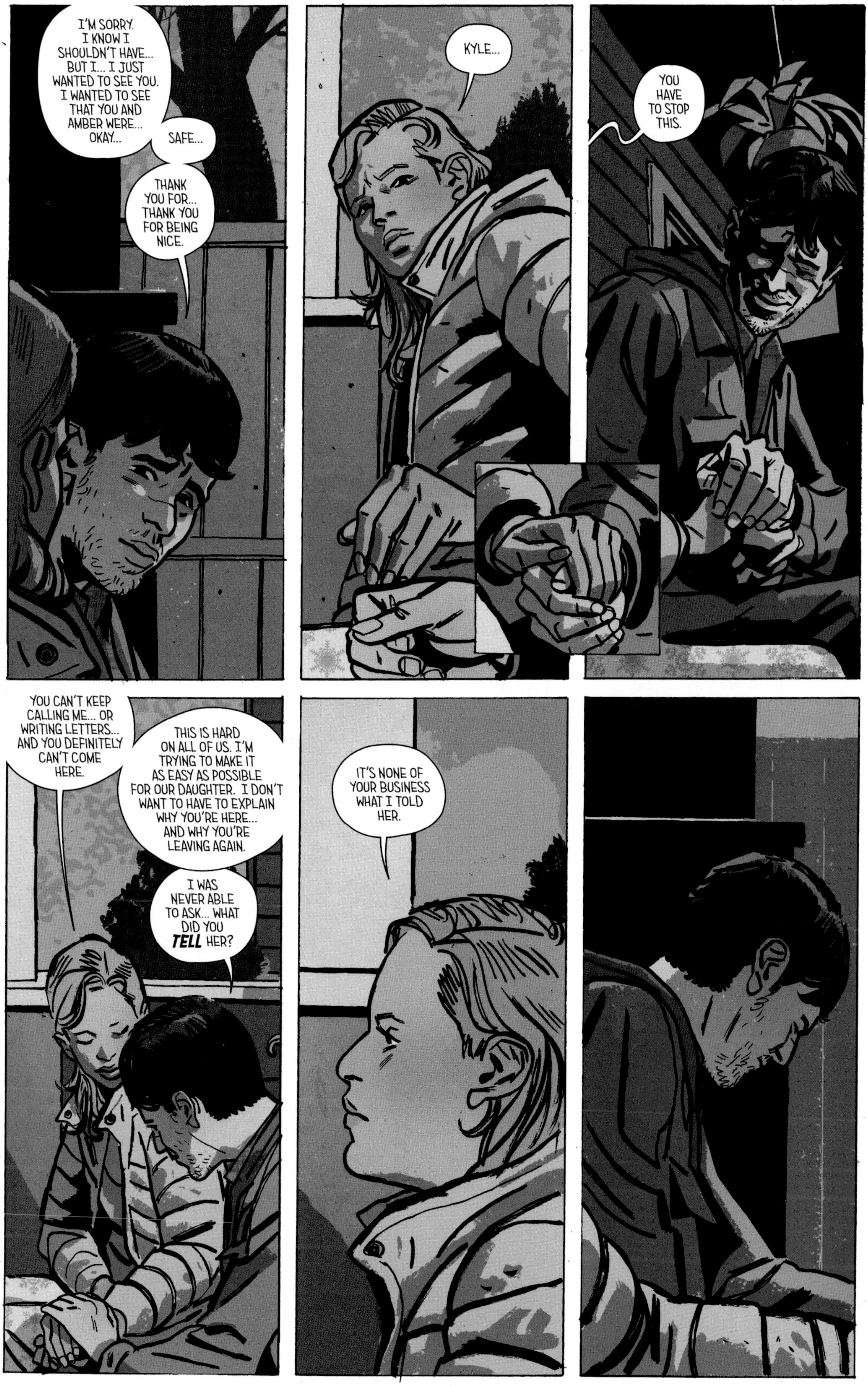

I'M SORRY. I KNOW I SHOULDN'T HAVE... BUT I... I JUST WANTED TO SEE YOU. I WANTED TO SEE THAT YOU AND AMBER WERE... OKAY...
SAFE...
THANK YOU FOR... THANK YOU FOR BEING NICE.
KYLE...
YOU HAVE TO STOP THIS.
YOU CAN'T KEEP CALLING ME... OR WRITING LETTERS... AND YOU DEFINITELY CAN'T COME HERE.
THIS IS HARD ON ALL OF US. I'M TRYING TO MAKE IT AS EASY AS POSSIBLE FOR OUR DAUGHTER. I DON'T WANT TO HAVE TO EXPLAIN WHY YOU'RE HERE... AND WHY YOU'RE LEAVING AGAIN.
I WAS NEVER ABLE TO ASK... WHAT DID YOU **TELL** HER?
IT'S NONE OF YOUR BUSINESS WHAT I TOLD HER.

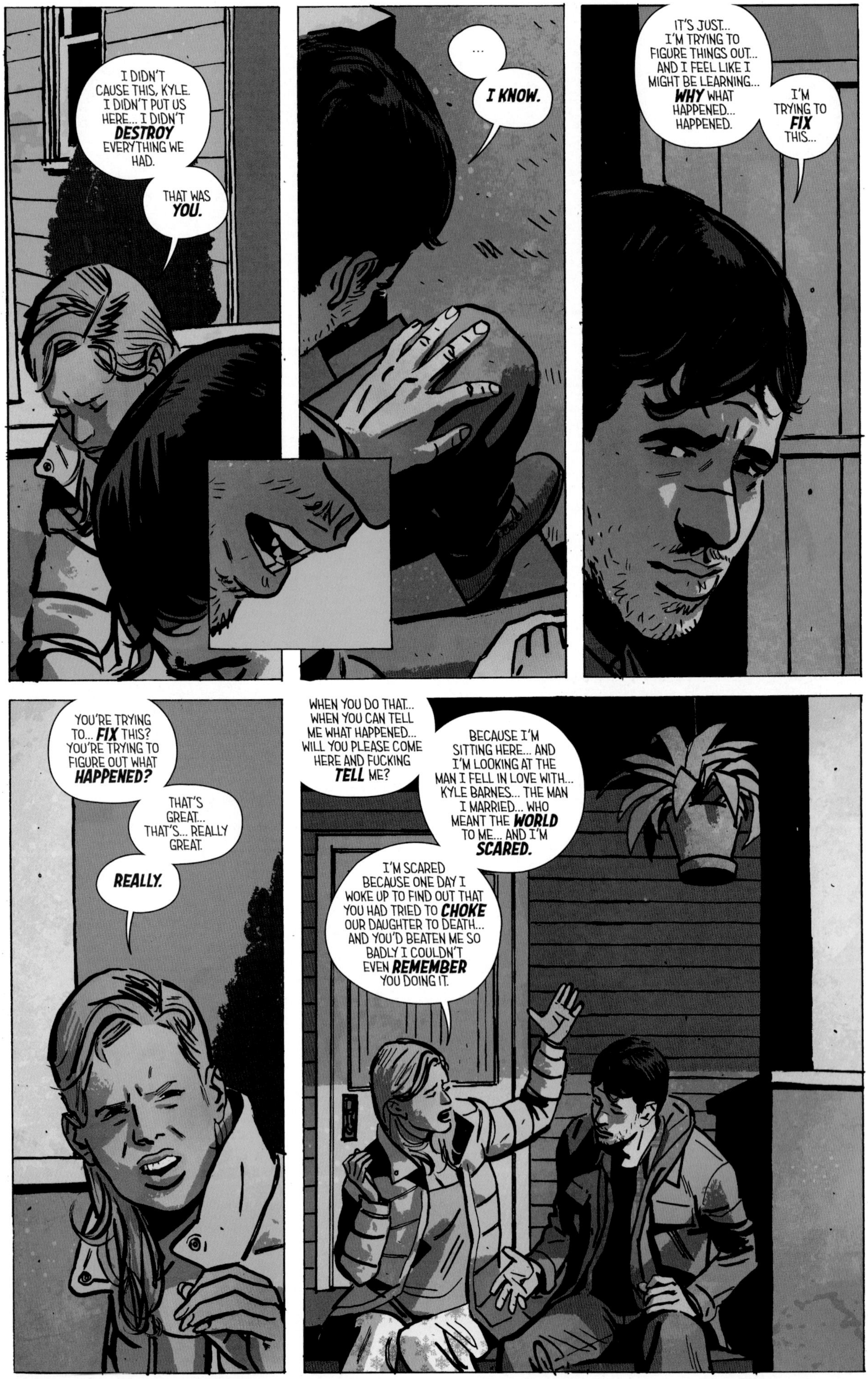
I DIDN'T CAUSE THIS, KYLE. I DIDN'T PUT US HERE... I DIDN'T **DESTROY** EVERYTHING WE HAD.
THAT WAS **YOU.**
...
I KNOW.
IT'S JUST... I'M TRYING TO FIGURE THINGS OUT... AND I FEEL LIKE I MIGHT BE LEARNING... **WHY** WHAT HAPPENED... HAPPENED.
I'M TRYING TO **FIX** THIS...
YOU'RE TRYING TO... **FIX** THIS? YOU'RE TRYING TO FIGURE OUT WHAT **HAPPENED?**
THAT'S GREAT... THAT'S... REALLY GREAT.
REALLY.
WHEN YOU DO THAT... WHEN YOU CAN TELL ME WHAT HAPPENED... WILL YOU PLEASE COME HERE AND FUCKING **TELL** ME?
BECAUSE I'M SITTING HERE... AND I'M LOOKING AT THE MAN I FELL IN LOVE WITH... KYLE BARNES... THE MAN I MARRIED... WHO MEANT THE **WORLD** TO ME... AND I'M **SCARED.**
I'M SCARED BECAUSE ONE DAY I WOKE UP TO FIND OUT THAT YOU HAD TRIED TO **CHOKE** OUR DAUGHTER TO DEATH... AND YOU'D BEATEN ME SO BADLY I COULDN'T EVEN **REMEMBER** YOU DOING IT.

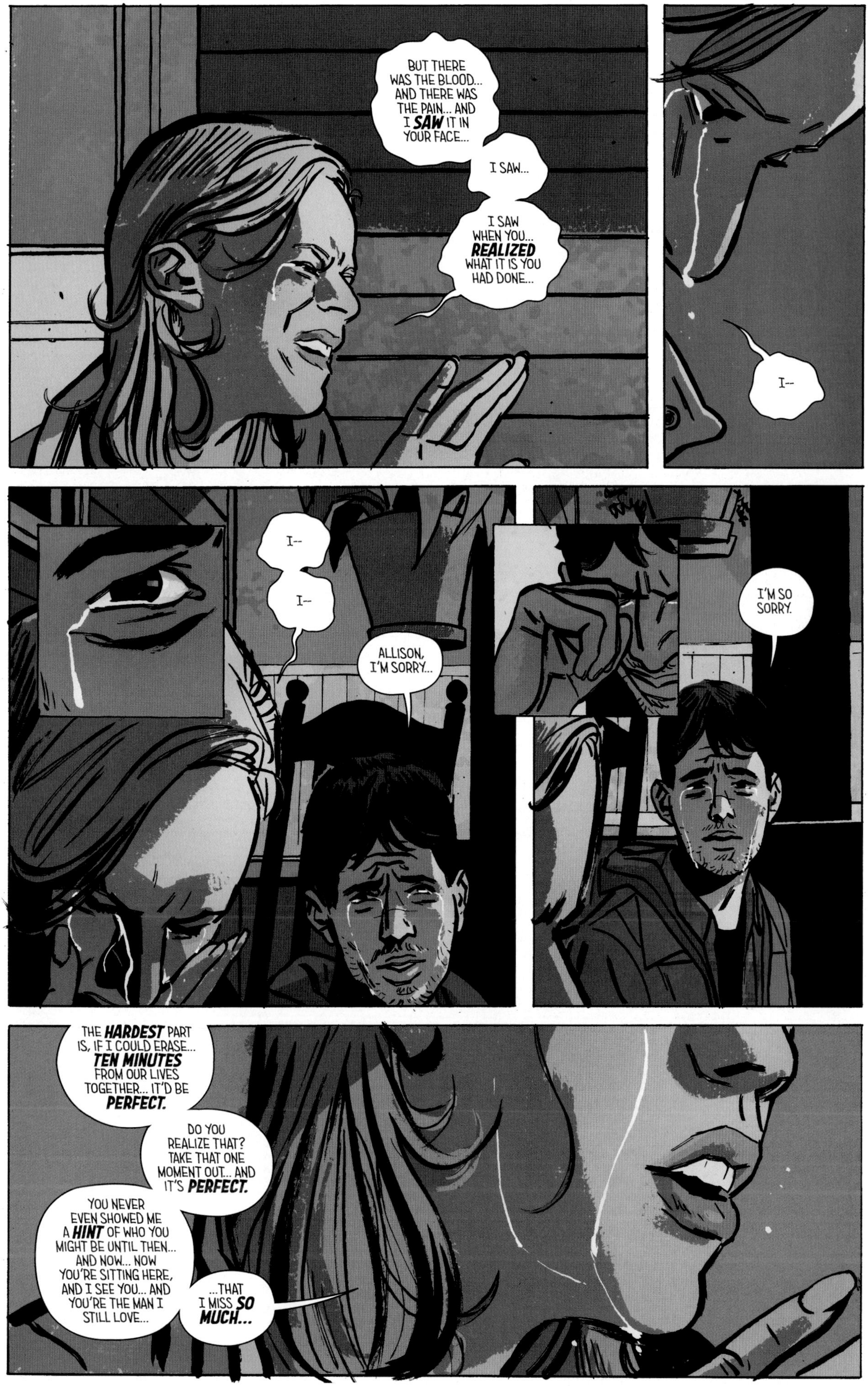

BUT THERE WAS THE BLOOD... AND THERE WAS THE PAIN... AND I SAW IT IN YOUR FACE...
I SAW...
I SAW WHEN YOU... REALIZED WHAT IT IS YOU HAD DONE...
I--
I--
I--
ALLISON, I'M SORRY...
I'M SO SORRY.
THE HARDEST PART IS, IF I COULD ERASE... TEN MINUTES FROM OUR LIVES TOGETHER... IT'D BE PERFECT.
DO YOU REALIZE THAT? TAKE THAT ONE MOMENT OUT... AND IT'S PERFECT.
YOU NEVER EVEN SHOWED ME A HINT OF WHO YOU MIGHT BE UNTIL THEN... AND NOW... NOW YOU'RE SITTING HERE, AND I SEE YOU... AND YOU'RE THE MAN I STILL LOVE...
...THAT I MISS SO MUCH...

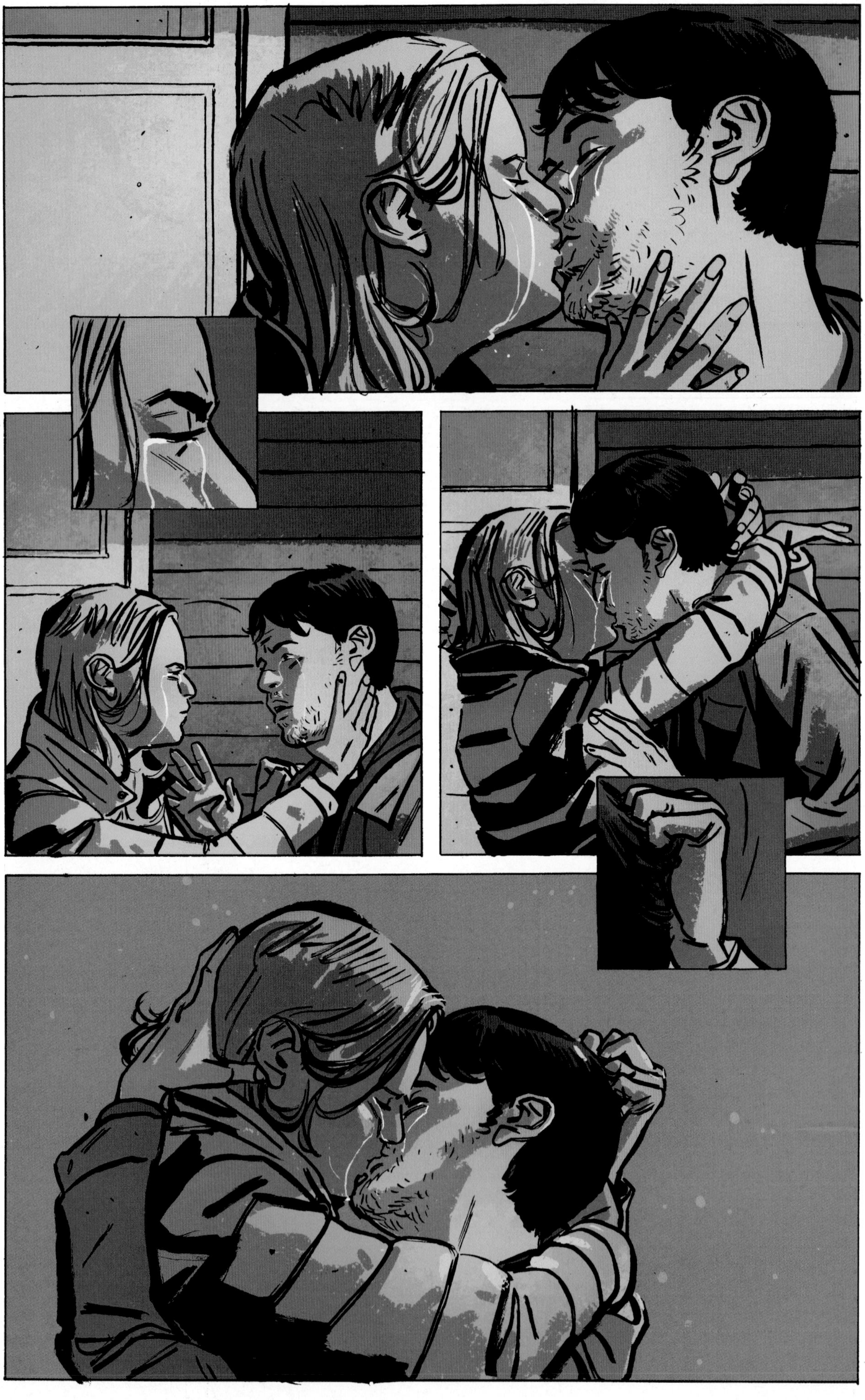

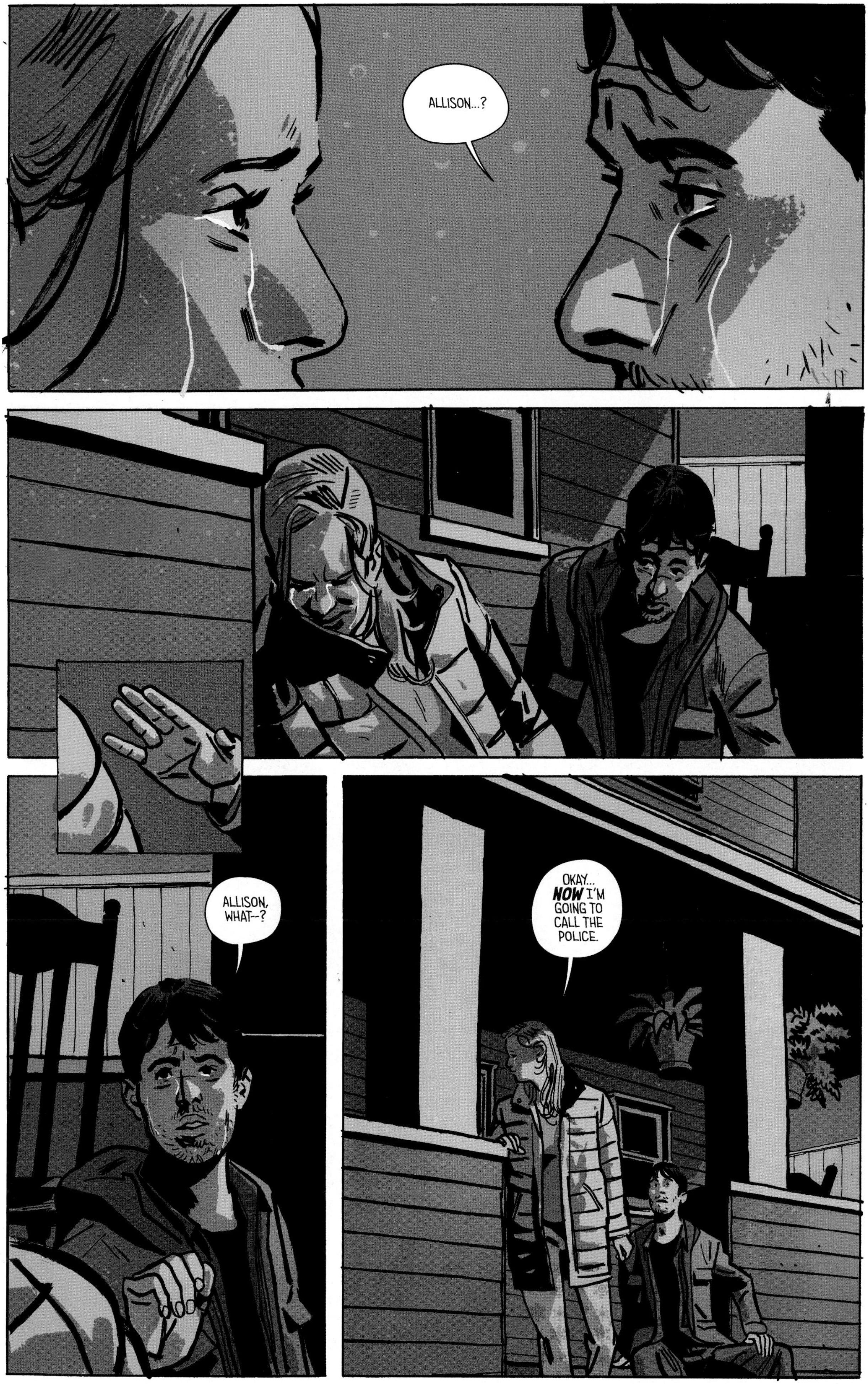
ALLISON...?
ALLISON, WHAT--?
OKAY... NOW I'M GOING TO CALL THE POLICE.

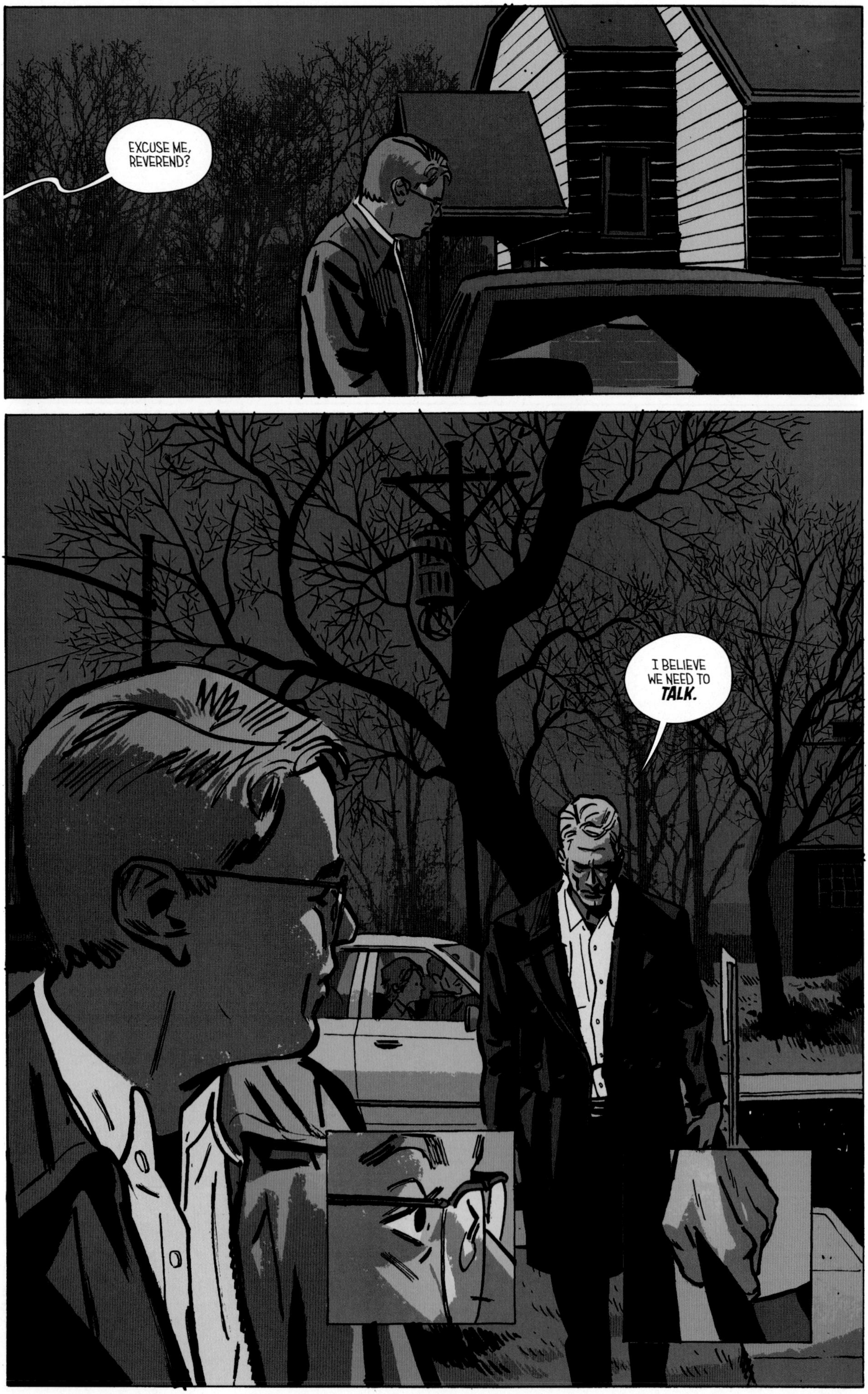
EXCUSE ME, REVEREND?
I BELIEVE WE NEED TO TALK.

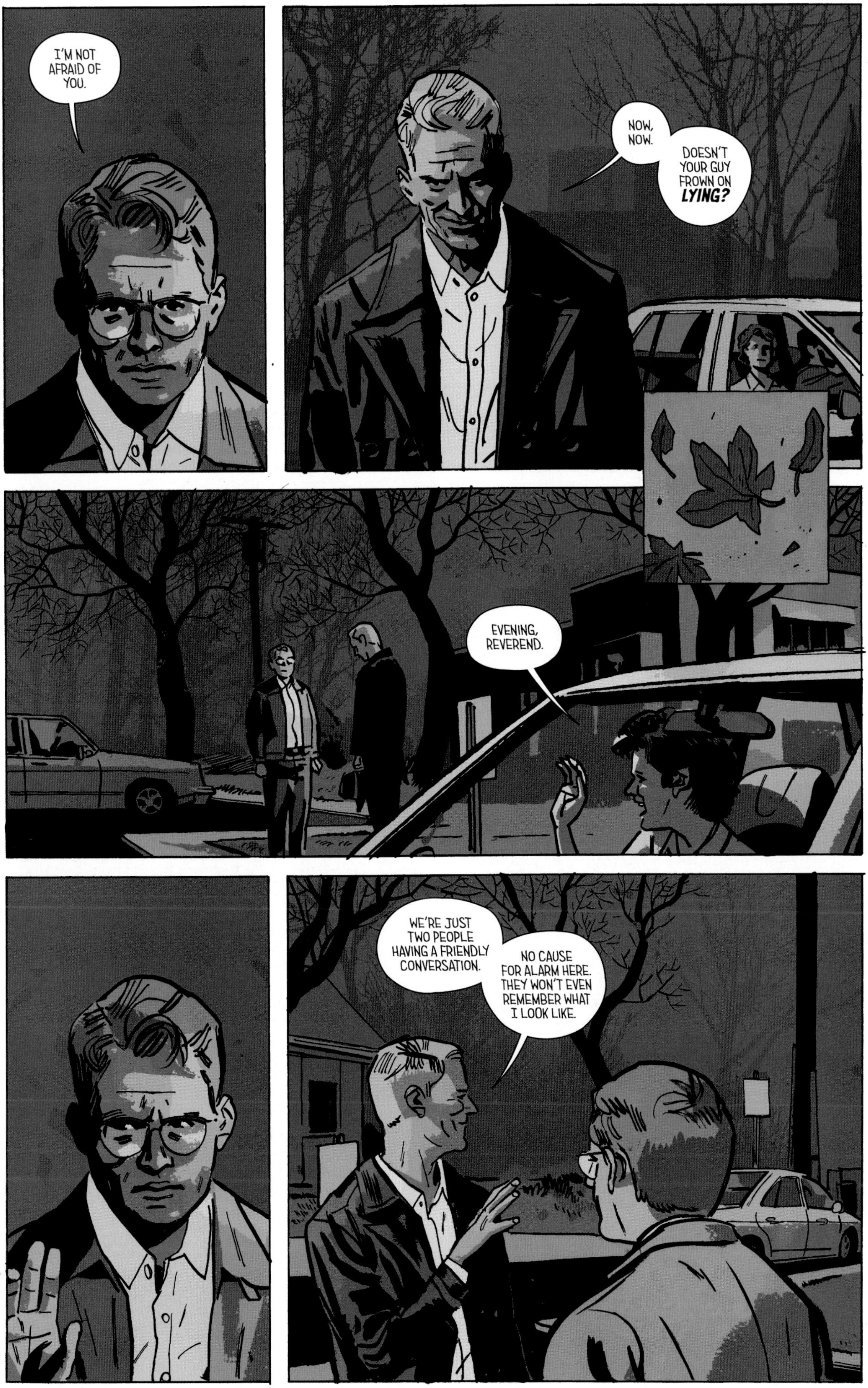
I'M NOT AFRAID OF YOU.
NOW, NOW.
DOESN'T YOUR GUY FROWN ON **LYING?**
EVENING, REVEREND.
WE'RE JUST TWO PEOPLE HAVING A FRIENDLY CONVERSATION.
NO CAUSE FOR ALARM HERE. THEY WON'T EVEN REMEMBER WHAT I LOOK LIKE.

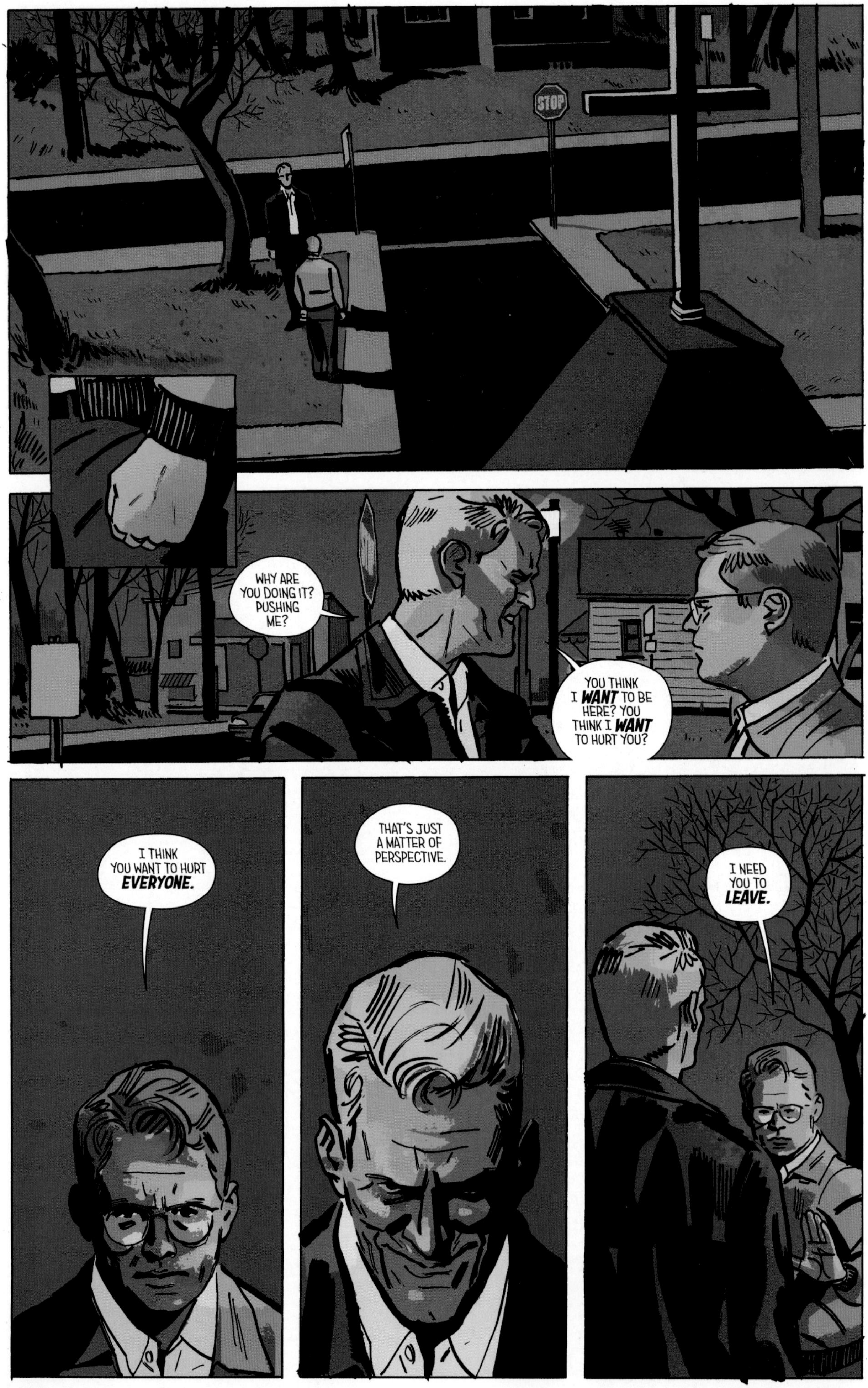
WHY ARE YOU DOING IT? PUSHING ME?
YOU THINK I **WANT** TO BE HERE? YOU THINK I **WANT** TO HURT YOU?
I THINK YOU WANT TO HURT **EVERYONE.**
THAT'S JUST A MATTER OF PERSPECTIVE.
I NEED YOU TO **LEAVE.**

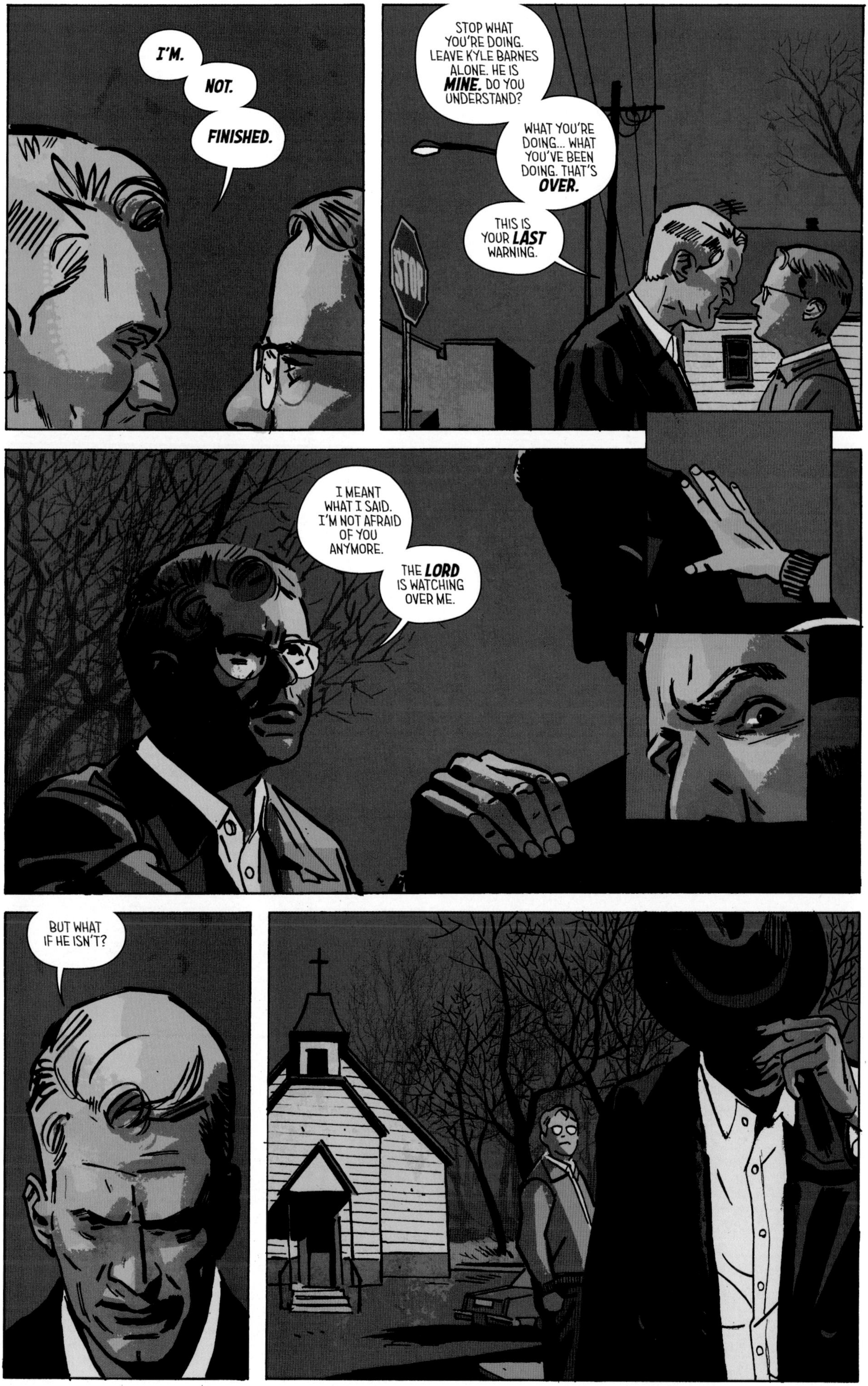
I'M.
NOT.
FINISHED.
STOP WHAT YOU'RE DOING. LEAVE KYLE BARNES ALONE. HE IS MINE. DO YOU UNDERSTAND?
WHAT YOU'RE DOING... WHAT YOU'VE BEEN DOING. THAT'S OVER.
THIS IS YOUR LAST WARNING.
STOP
I MEANT WHAT I SAID. I'M NOT AFRAID OF YOU ANYMORE.
THE LORD IS WATCHING OVER ME.
BUT WHAT IF HE ISN'T?

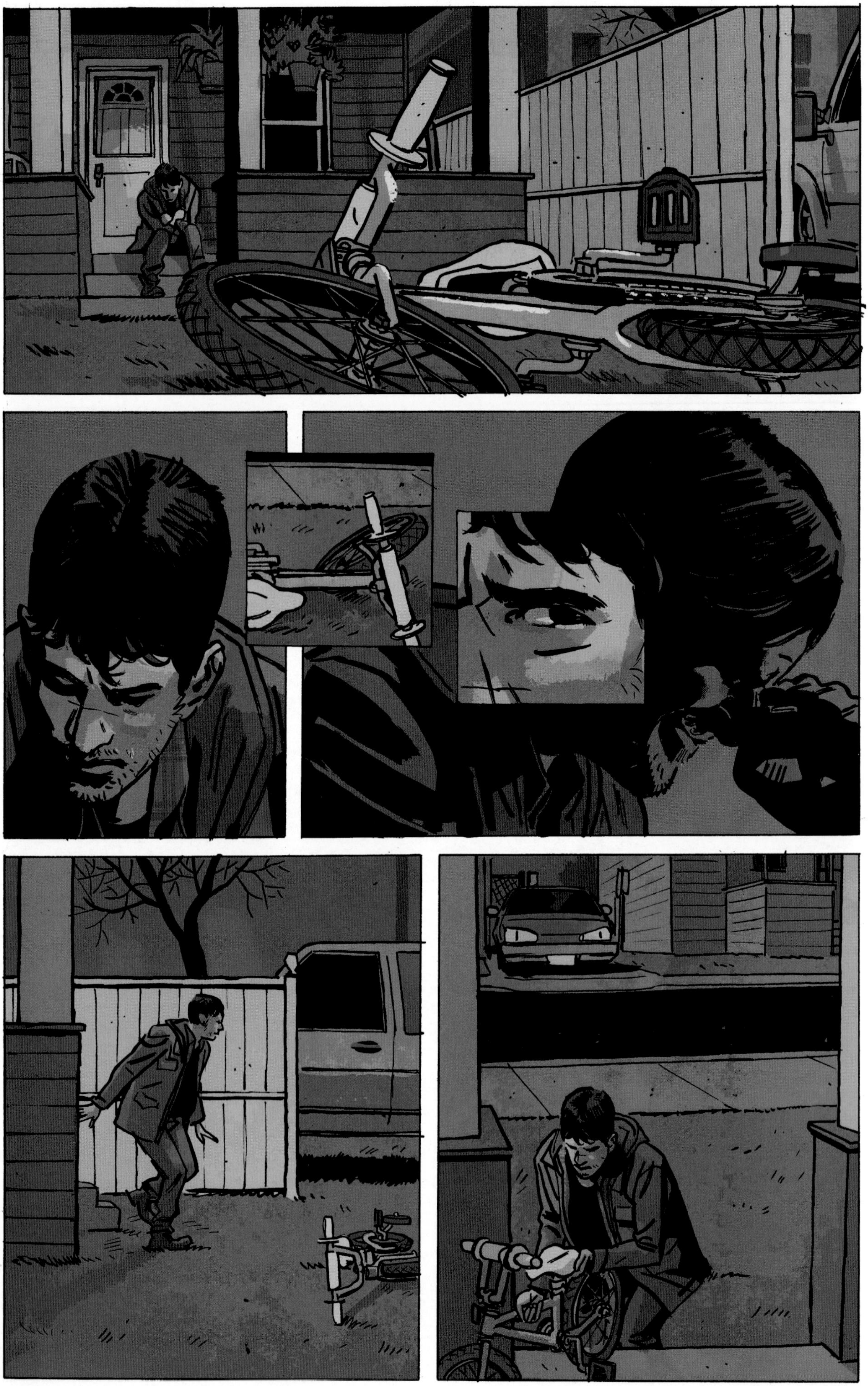

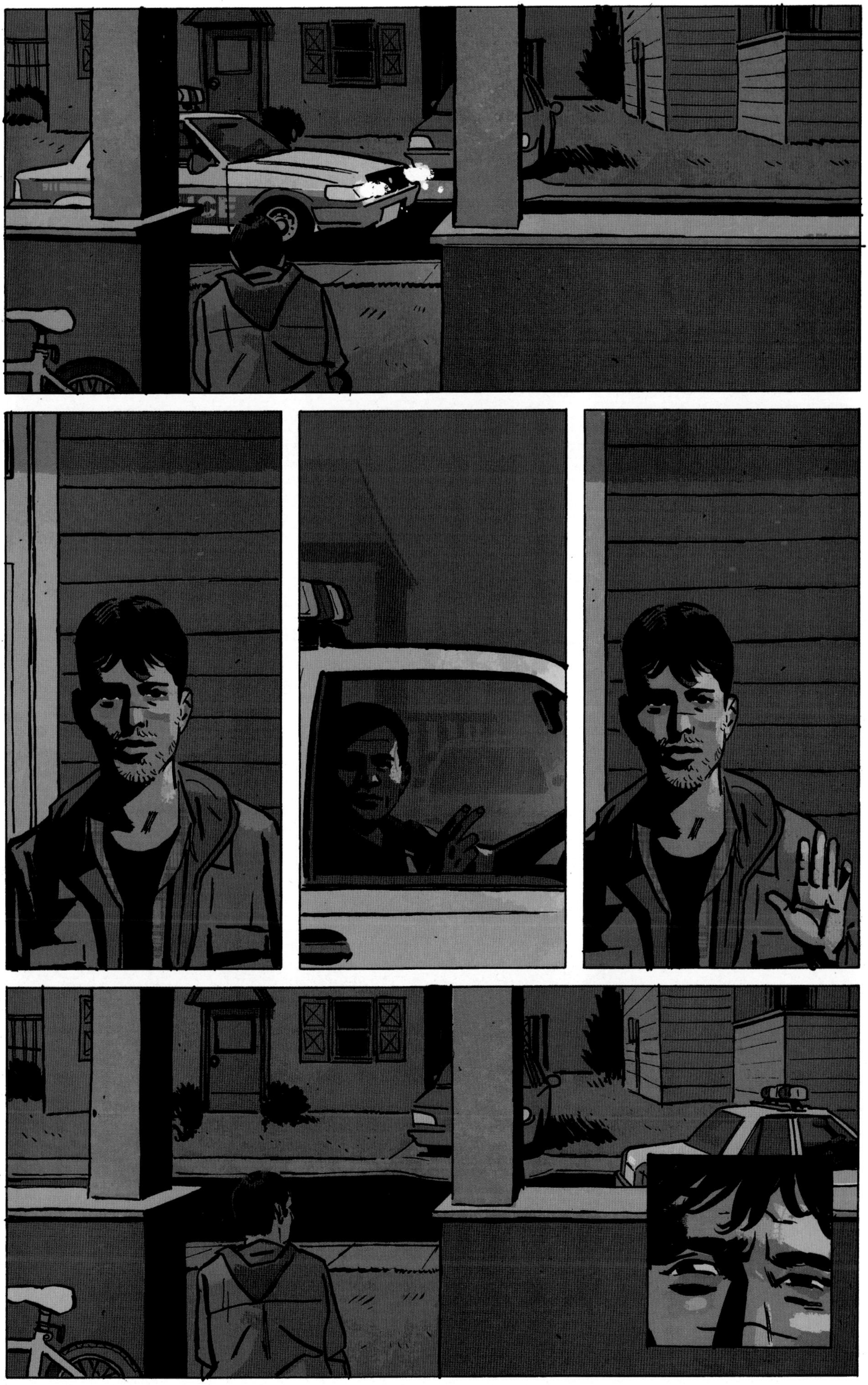

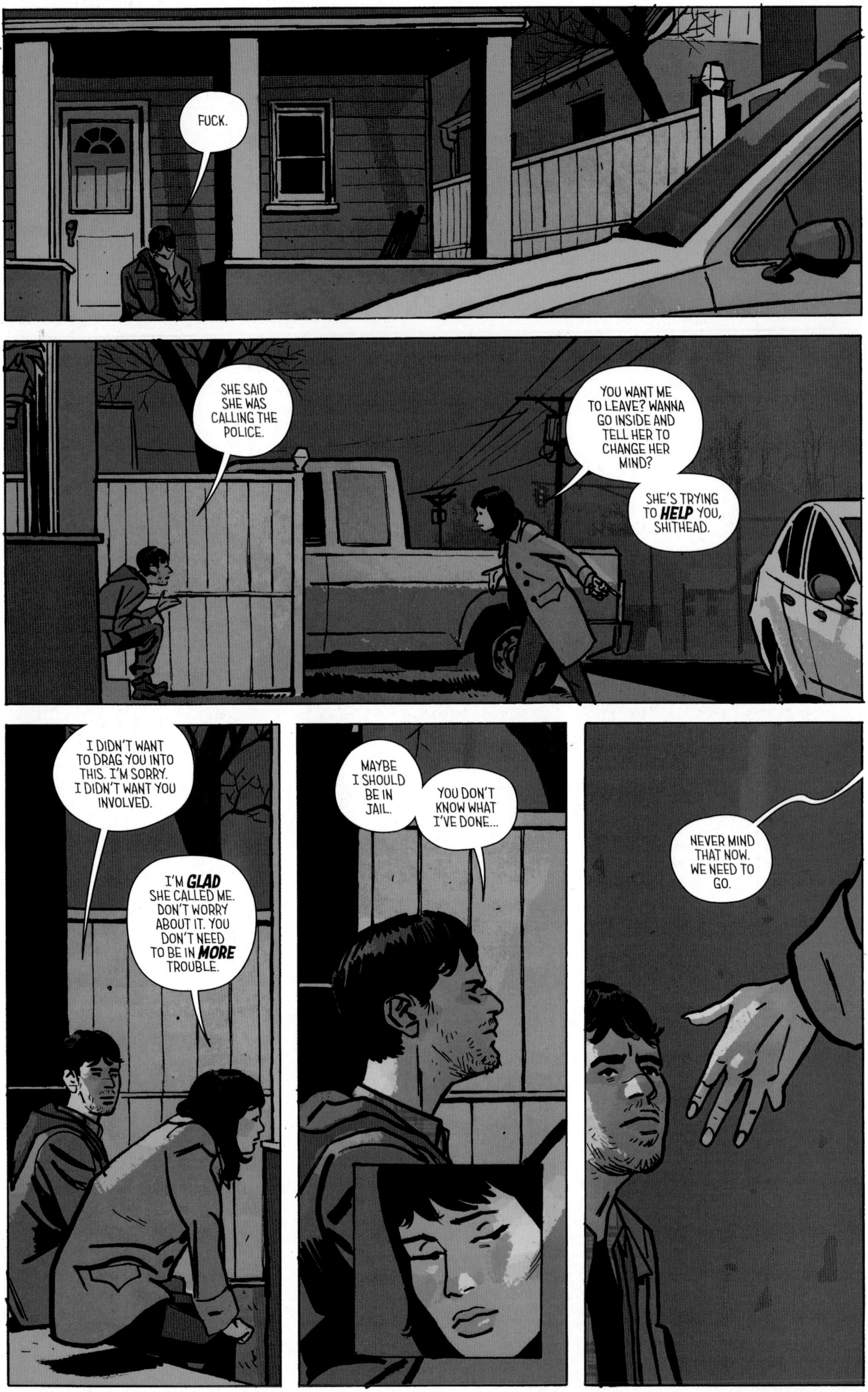
FUCK.
SHE SAID SHE WAS CALLING THE POLICE.
YOU WANT ME TO LEAVE? WANNA GO INSIDE AND TELL HER TO CHANGE HER MIND?
SHE'S TRYING TO **HELP** YOU, SHITHEAD.
I DIDN'T WANT TO DRAG YOU INTO THIS. I'M SORRY. I DIDN'T WANT YOU INVOLVED.
I'M **GLAD** SHE CALLED ME. DON'T WORRY ABOUT IT. YOU DON'T NEED TO BE IN **MORE** TROUBLE.
MAYBE I SHOULD BE IN JAIL.
YOU DON'T KNOW WHAT I'VE DONE...
NEVER MIND THAT NOW. WE NEED TO GO.

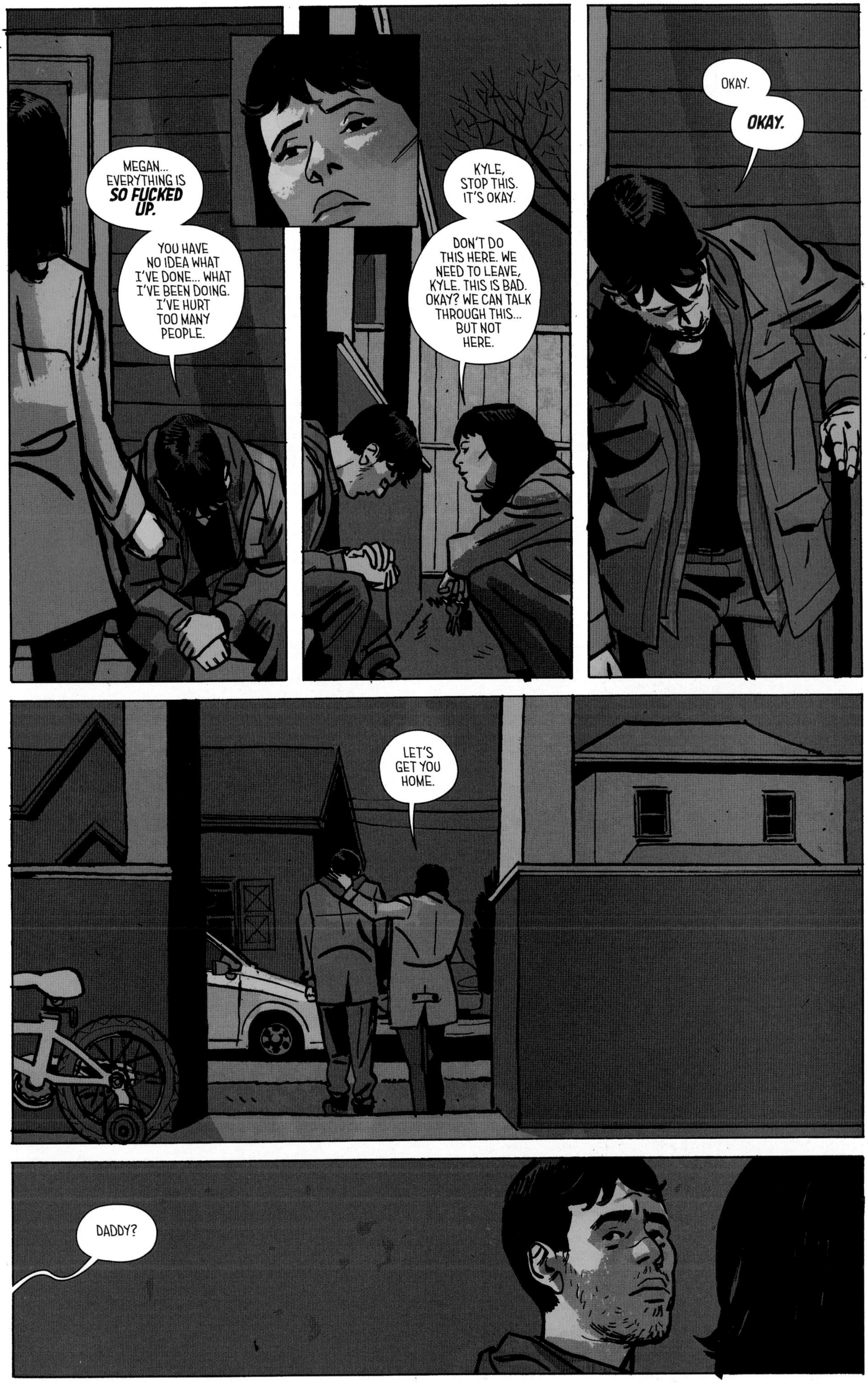
MEGAN... EVERYTHING IS **SO FUCKED UP.**
YOU HAVE NO IDEA WHAT I'VE DONE... WHAT I'VE BEEN DOING. I'VE HURT TOO MANY PEOPLE.
KYLE, STOP THIS. IT'S OKAY.
DON'T DO THIS HERE. WE NEED TO LEAVE, KYLE. THIS IS BAD. OKAY? WE CAN TALK THROUGH THIS... BUT NOT HERE.
OKAY.
OKAY.
LET'S GET YOU HOME.
DADDY?

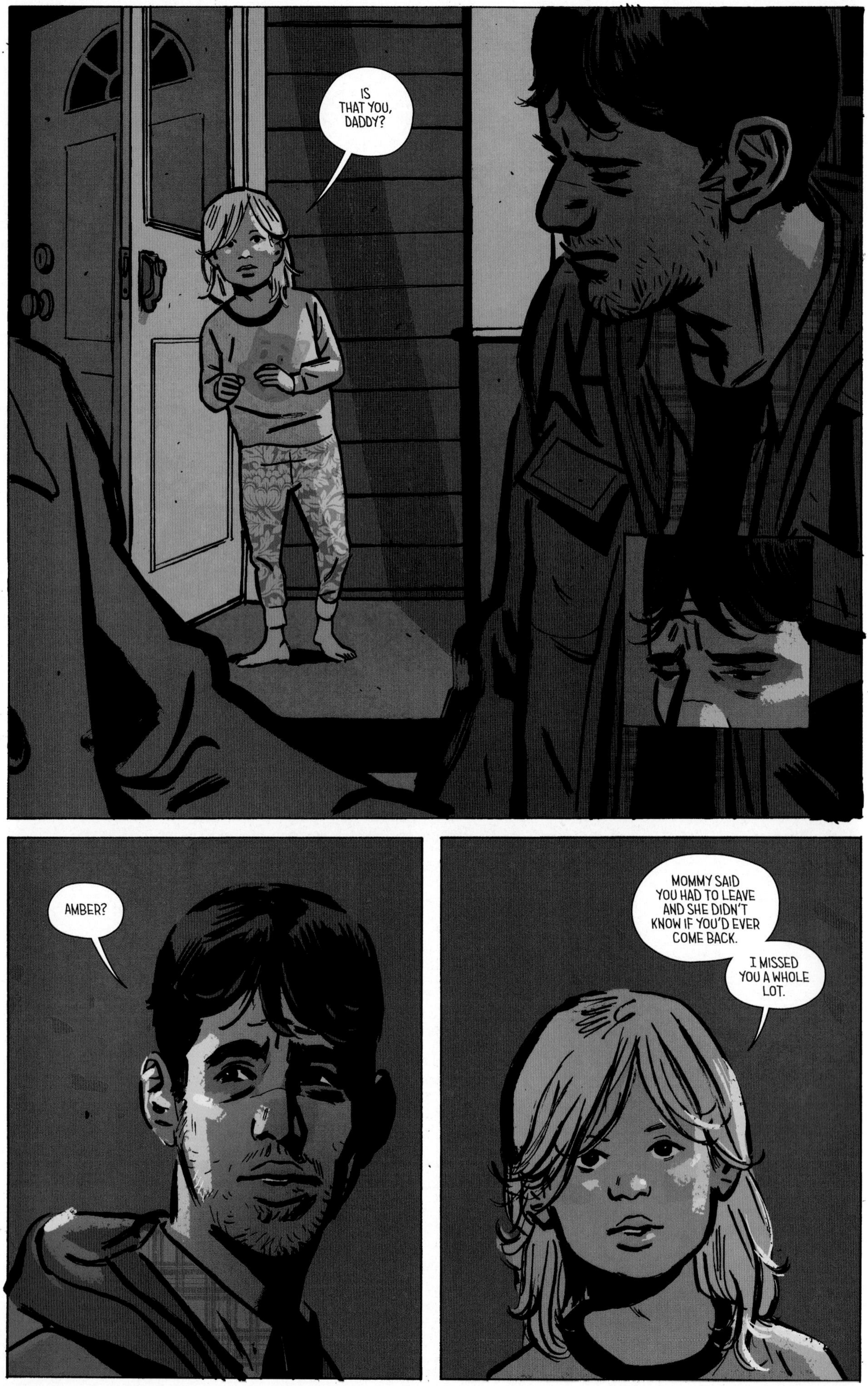
IS THAT YOU, DADDY?
AMBER?
MOMMY SAID YOU HAD TO LEAVE AND SHE DIDN'T KNOW IF YOU'D EVER COME BACK.
I MISSED YOU A WHOLE LOT.

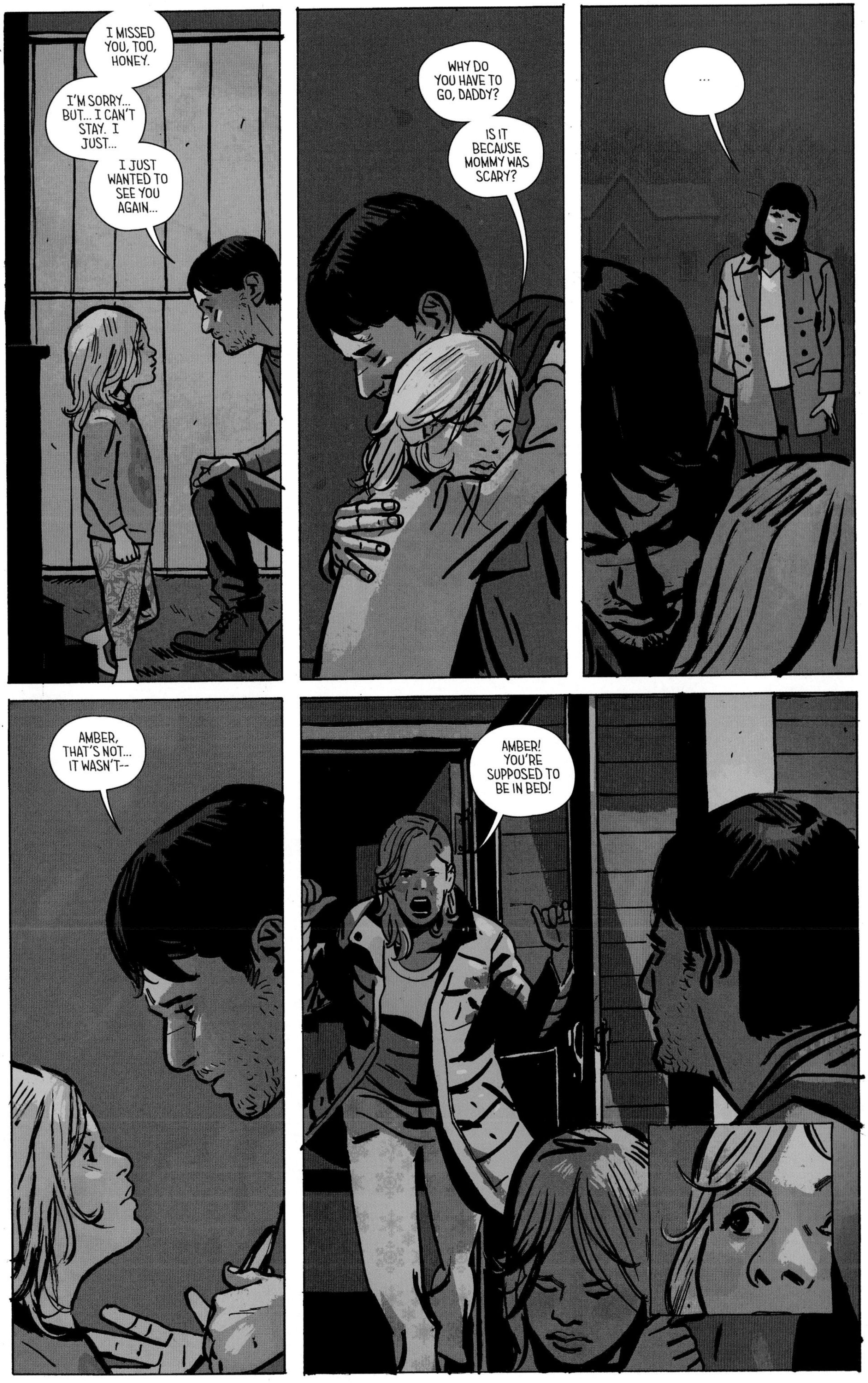

I MISSED YOU, TOO, HONEY.
I'M SORRY... BUT... I CAN'T STAY. I JUST...
I JUST WANTED TO SEE YOU AGAIN...
WHY DO YOU HAVE TO GO, DADDY?
IS IT BECAUSE MOMMY WAS SCARY?
...
AMBER, THAT'S NOT... IT WASN'T--
AMBER! YOU'RE SUPPOSED TO BE IN BED!

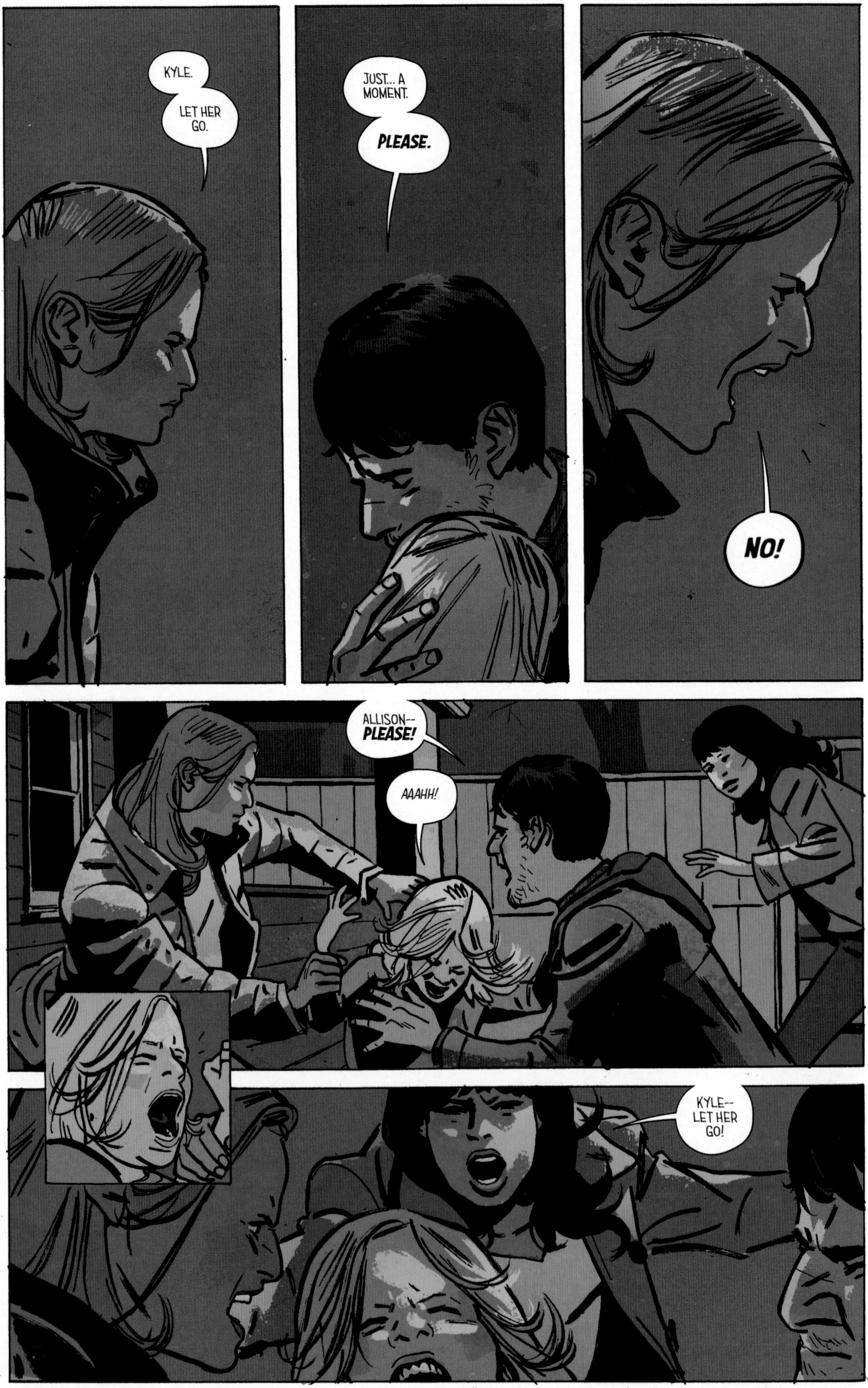
KYLE.
LET HER GO.
JUST... A MOMENT.
PLEASE.
NO!
ALLISON-- PLEASE!
AAAHH!
KYLE-- LET HER GO!

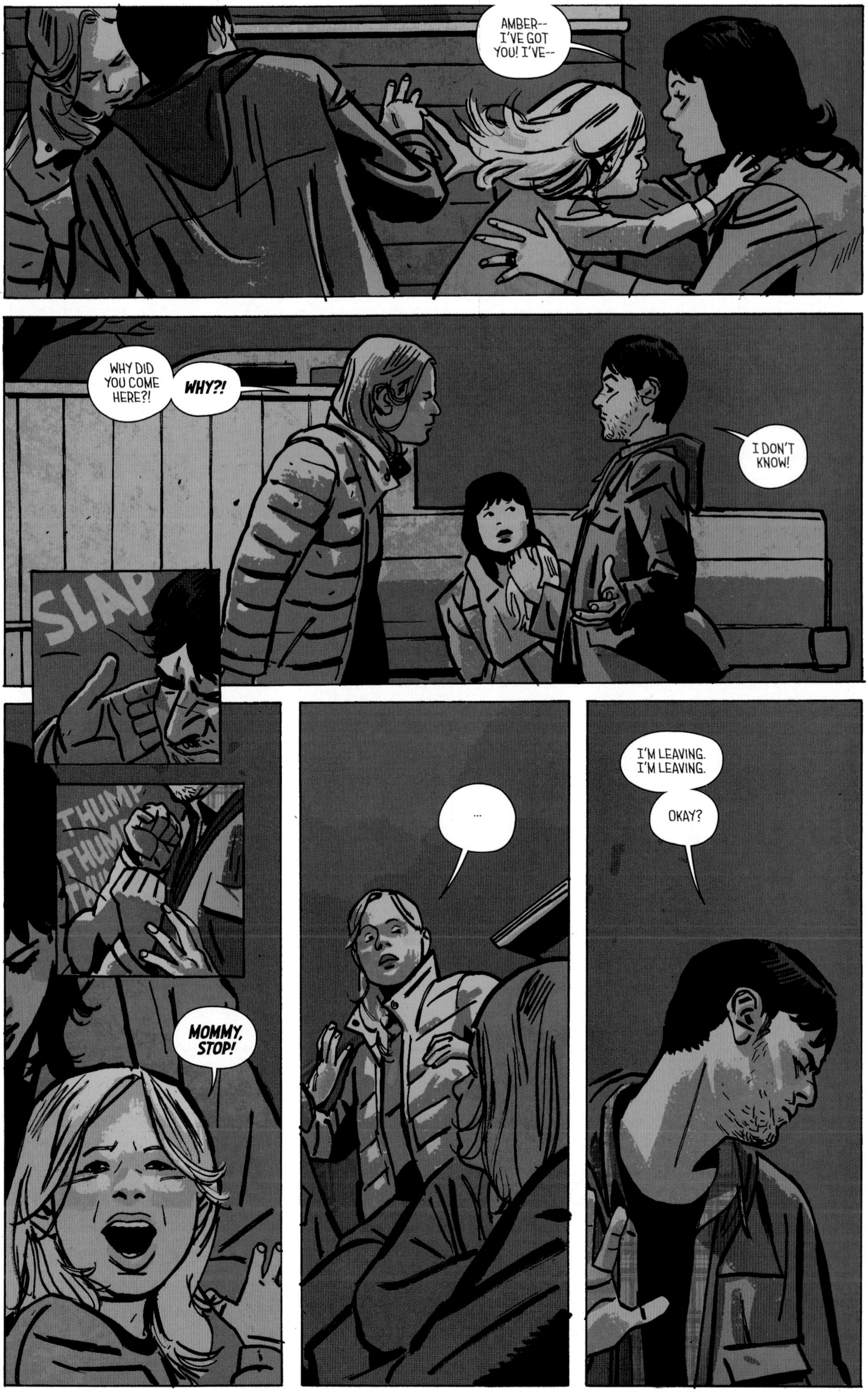
AMBER-- I'VE GOT YOU! I'VE--
WHY DID YOU COME HERE?!
WHY?!
I DON'T KNOW!
SLAP
MOMMY, STOP!
...
I'M LEAVING. I'M LEAVING.
OKAY?

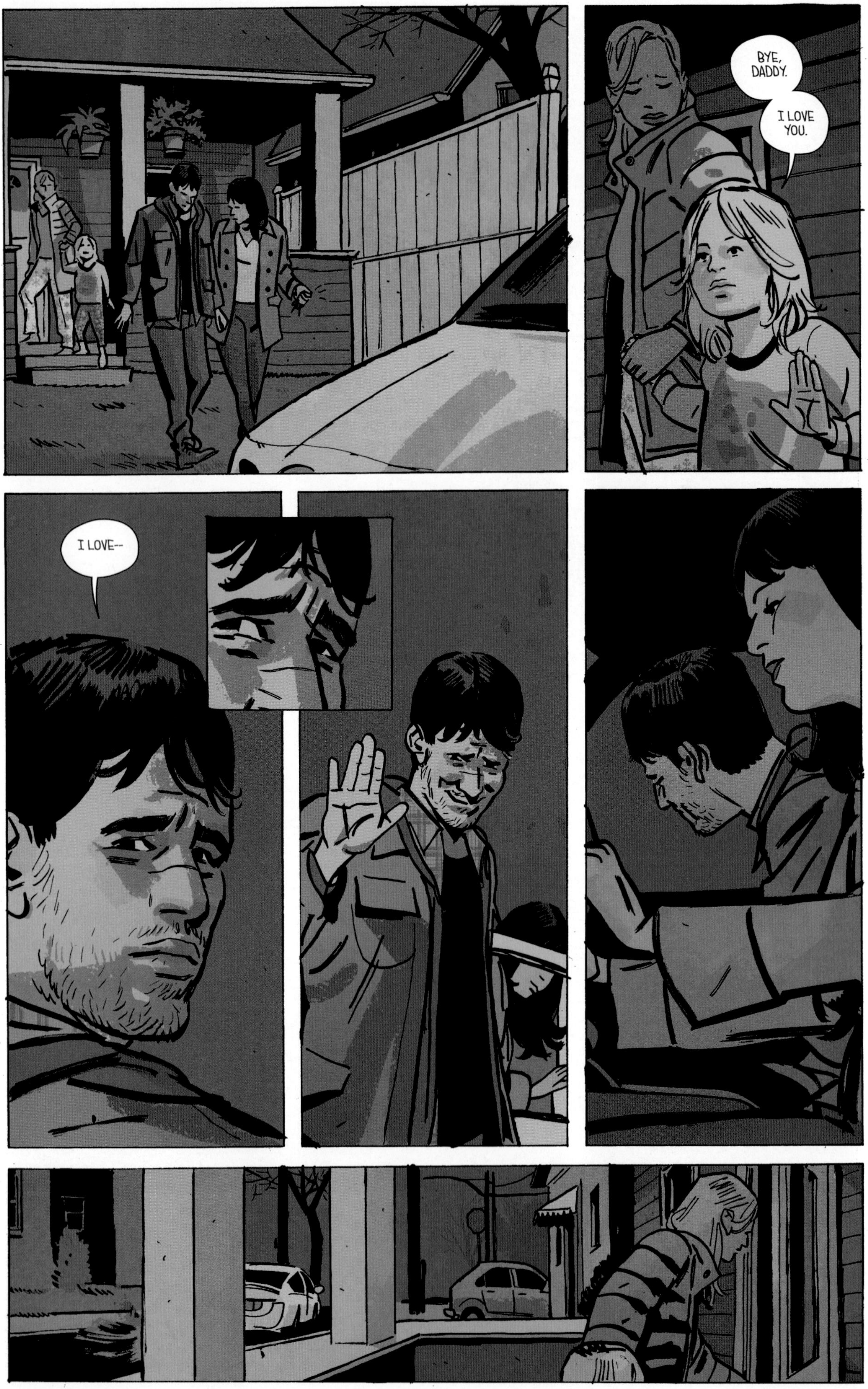
BYE, DADDY.
I LOVE YOU.
I LOVE--

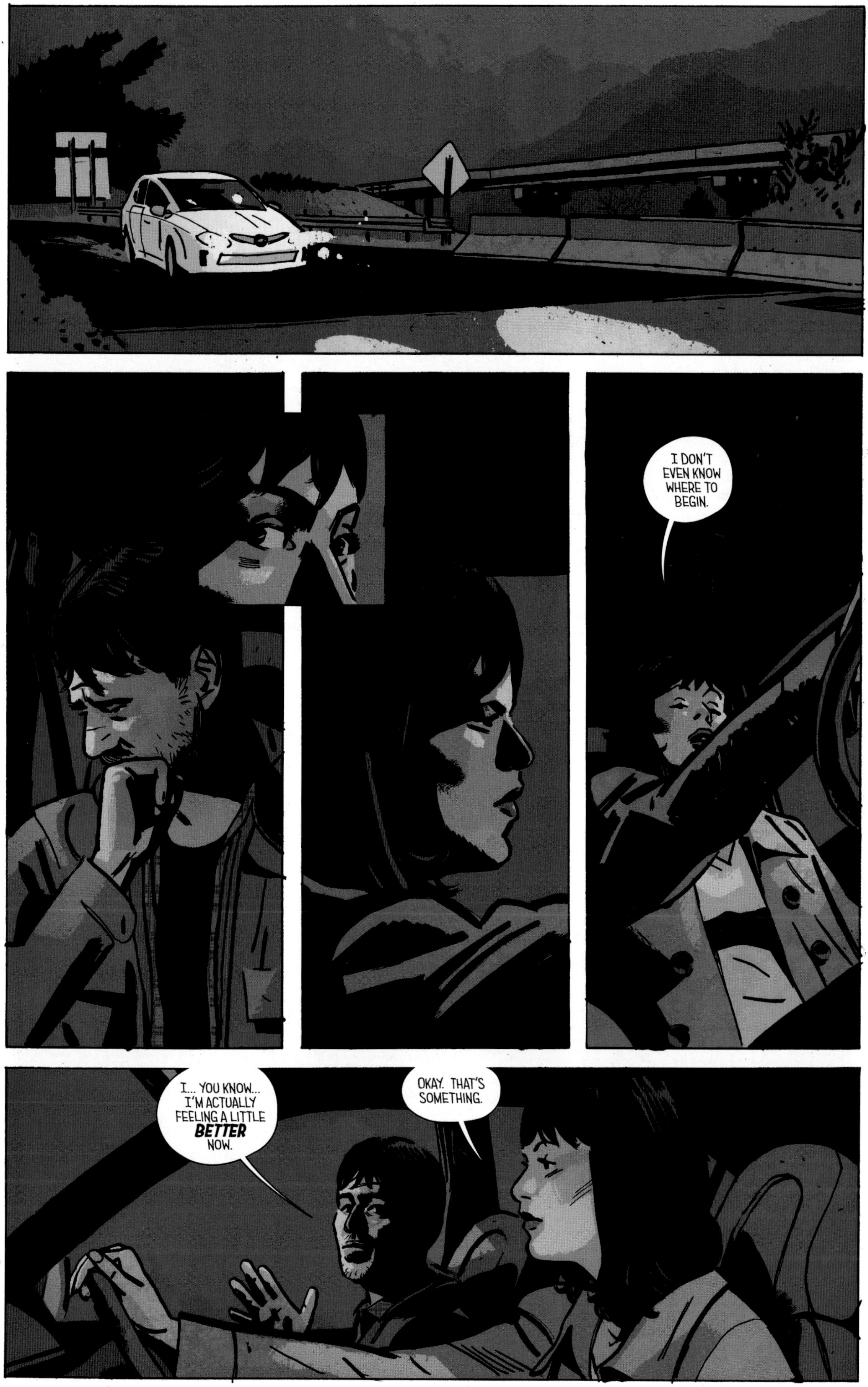
I DON'T EVEN KNOW WHERE TO BEGIN.
I... YOU KNOW... I'M ACTUALLY FEELING A LITTLE **BETTER** NOW.
OKAY. THAT'S SOMETHING.

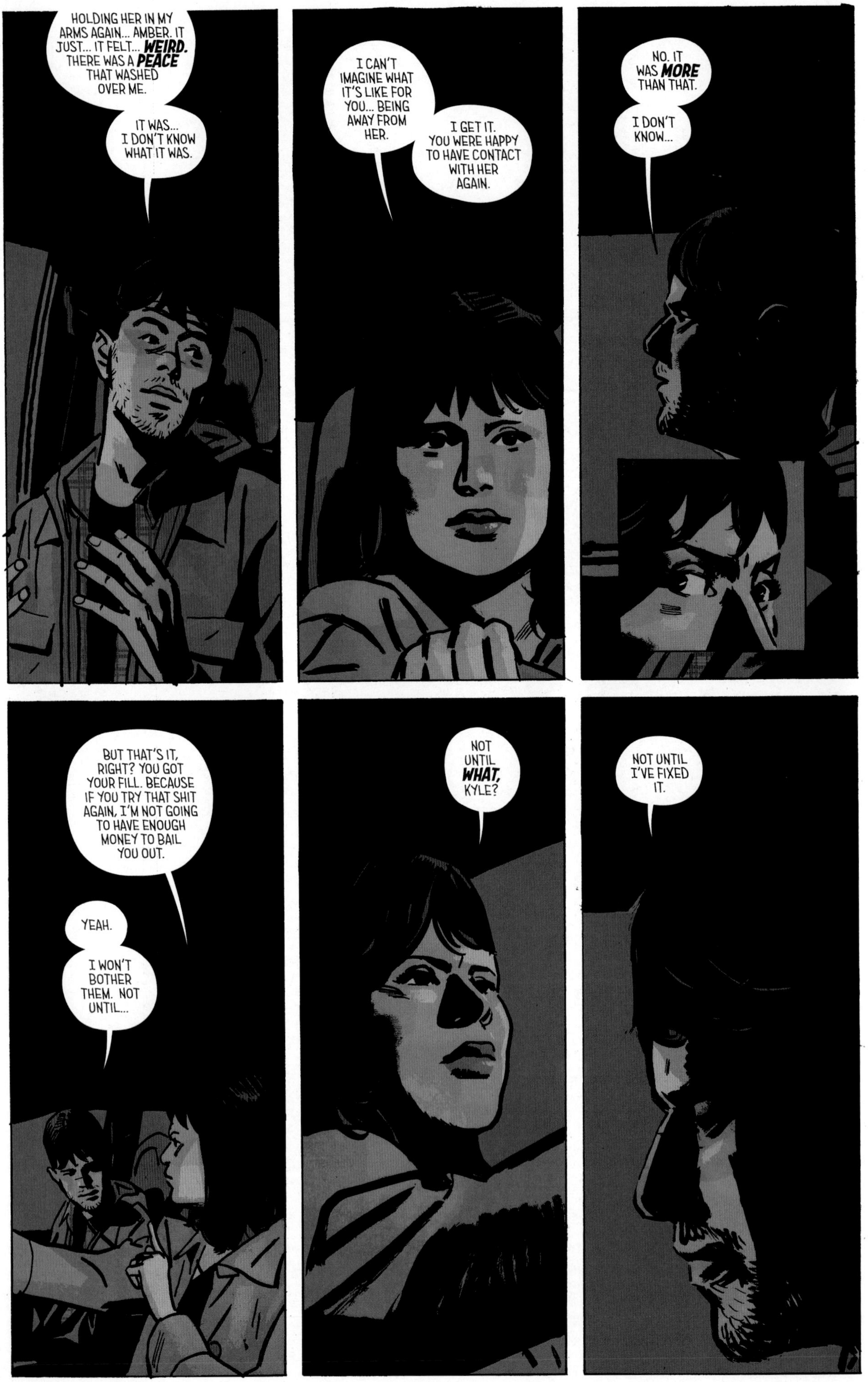
HOLDING HER IN MY ARMS AGAIN... AMBER. IT JUST... IT FELT... **WEIRD.** THERE WAS A **PEACE** THAT WASHED OVER ME.
IT WAS... I DON'T KNOW WHAT IT WAS.
I CAN'T IMAGINE WHAT IT'S LIKE FOR YOU... BEING AWAY FROM HER.
I GET IT. YOU WERE HAPPY TO HAVE CONTACT WITH HER AGAIN.
NO. IT WAS **MORE** THAN THAT.
I DON'T KNOW...
BUT THAT'S IT, RIGHT? YOU GOT YOUR FILL. BECAUSE IF YOU TRY THAT SHIT AGAIN, I'M NOT GOING TO HAVE ENOUGH MONEY TO BAIL YOU OUT.
YEAH.
I WON'T BOTHER THEM. NOT UNTIL...
NOT UNTIL **WHAT,** KYLE?
NOT UNTIL I'VE FIXED IT.

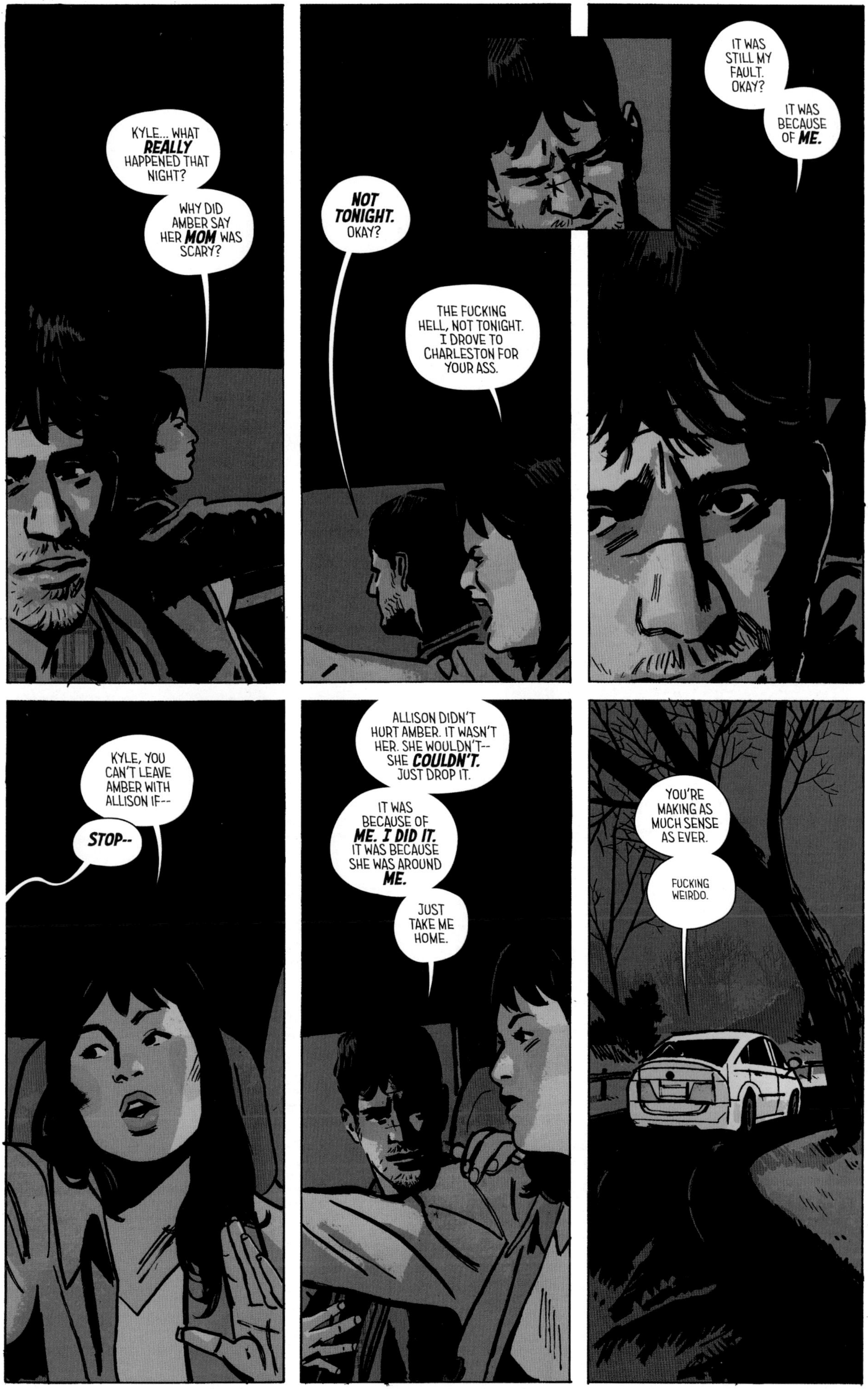

KYLE... WHAT **REALLY** HAPPENED THAT NIGHT?
WHY DID AMBER SAY HER **MOM** WAS SCARY?
NOT TONIGHT. OKAY?
THE FUCKING HELL, NOT TONIGHT. I DROVE TO CHARLESTON FOR YOUR ASS.
IT WAS STILL MY FAULT. OKAY?
IT WAS BECAUSE OF **ME.**
KYLE, YOU CAN'T LEAVE AMBER WITH ALLISON IF--
STOP--
ALLISON DIDN'T HURT AMBER. IT WASN'T HER. SHE WOULDN'T-- SHE **COULDN'T.** JUST DROP IT.
IT WAS BECAUSE OF **ME. I DID IT.** IT WAS BECAUSE SHE WAS AROUND **ME.**
JUST TAKE ME HOME.
YOU'RE MAKING AS MUCH SENSE AS EVER.
FUCKING WEIRDO.

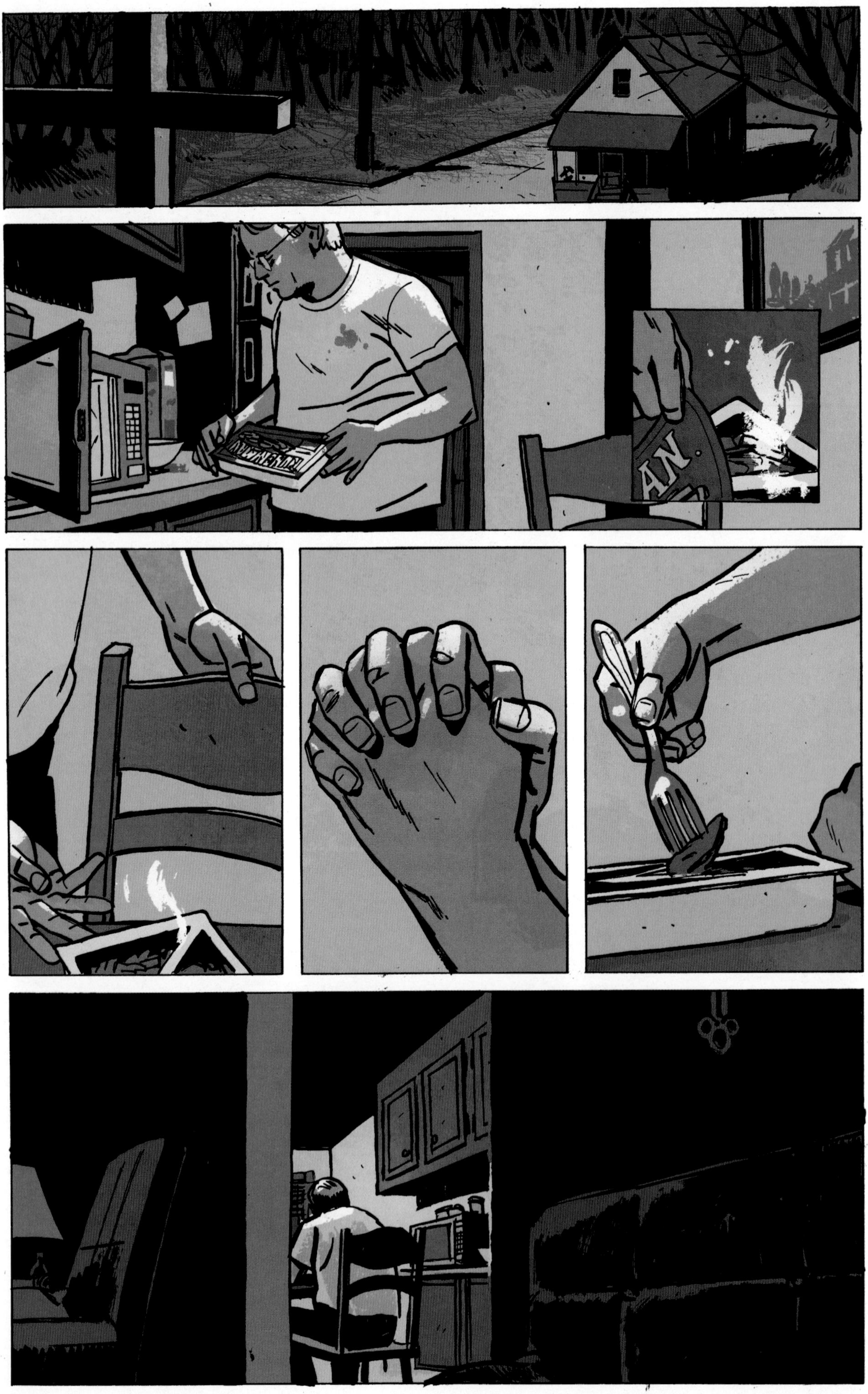

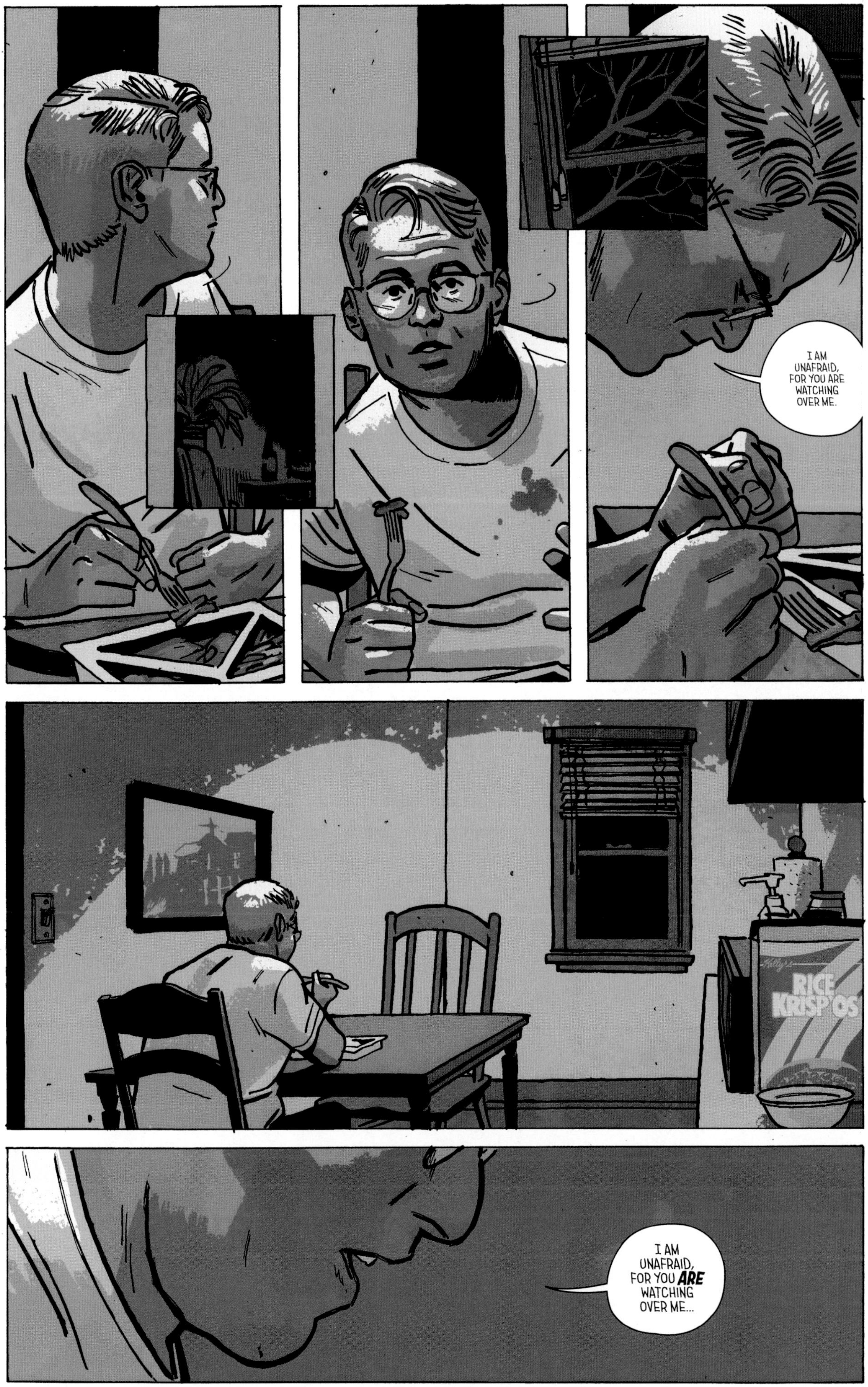
I AM UNAFRAID, FOR YOU ARE WATCHING OVER ME.
Kelly's RICE KRISP'OS
I AM UNAFRAID, FOR YOU **ARE** WATCHING OVER ME...

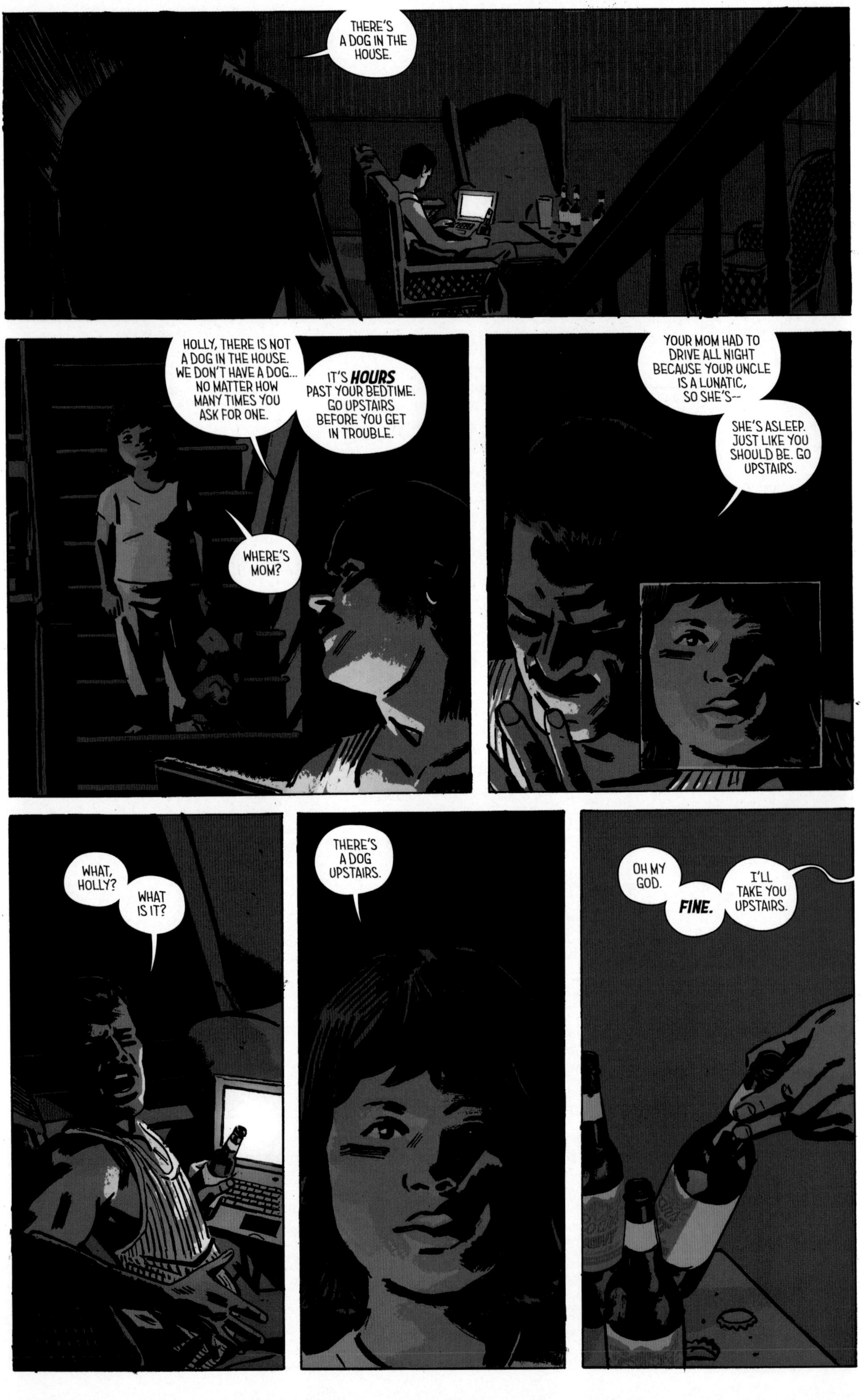
THERE'S A DOG IN THE HOUSE.
HOLLY, THERE IS NOT A DOG IN THE HOUSE. WE DON'T HAVE A DOG... NO MATTER HOW MANY TIMES YOU ASK FOR ONE.
IT'S HOURS PAST YOUR BEDTIME. GO UPSTAIRS BEFORE YOU GET IN TROUBLE.
WHERE'S MOM?
YOUR MOM HAD TO DRIVE ALL NIGHT BECAUSE YOUR UNCLE IS A LUNATIC, SO SHE'S--
SHE'S ASLEEP. JUST LIKE YOU SHOULD BE. GO UPSTAIRS.
WHAT, HOLLY?
WHAT IS IT?
THERE'S A DOG UPSTAIRS.
OH MY GOD.
FINE.
I'LL TAKE YOU UPSTAIRS.

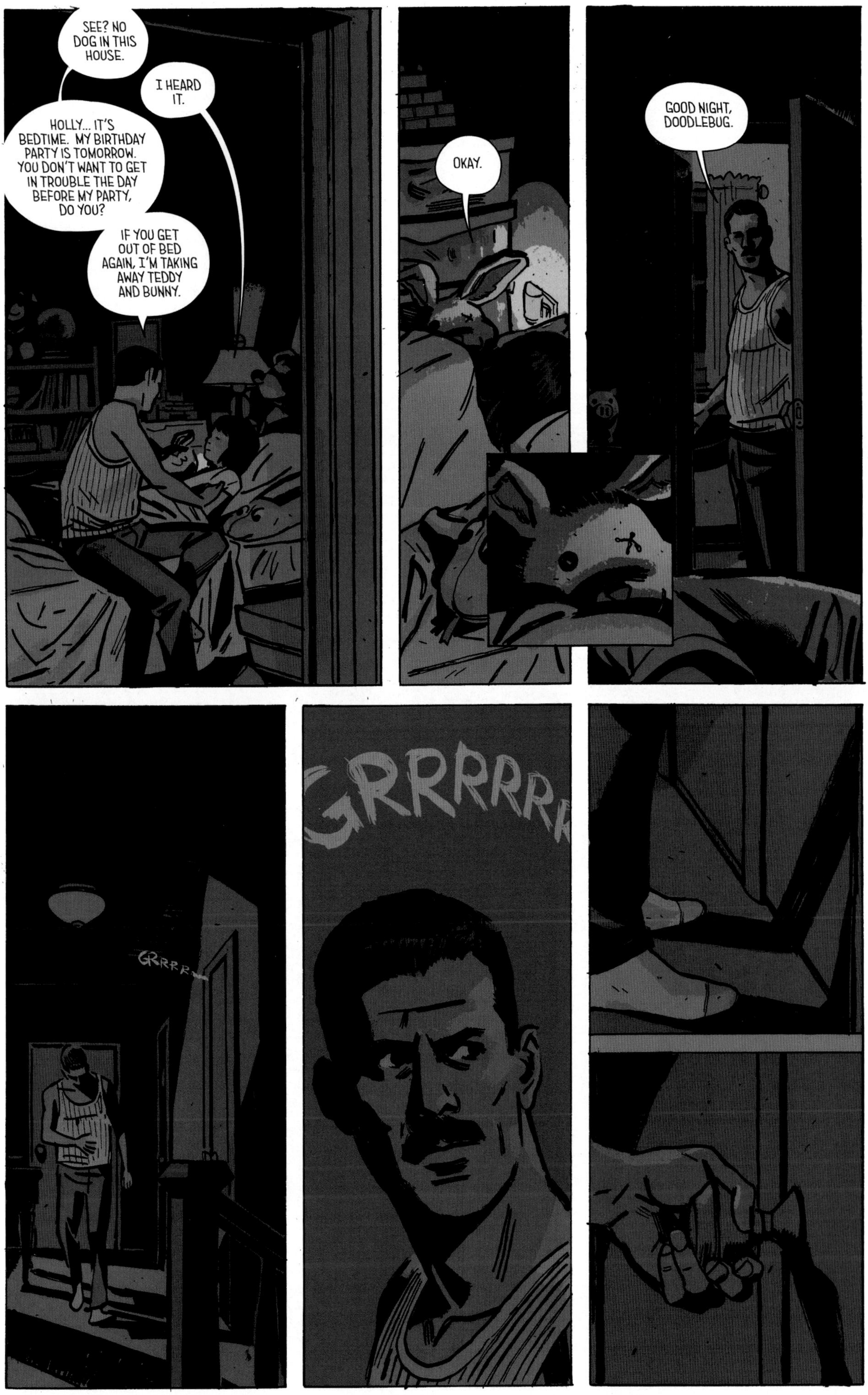
SEE? NO DOG IN THIS HOUSE.
I HEARD IT.
HOLLY... IT'S BEDTIME. MY BIRTHDAY PARTY IS TOMORROW. YOU DON'T WANT TO GET IN TROUBLE THE DAY BEFORE MY PARTY, DO YOU?
IF YOU GET OUT OF BED AGAIN, I'M TAKING AWAY TEDDY AND BUNNY.
OKAY.
GOOD NIGHT, DOODLEBUG.
GRRRR
GRRRRRR

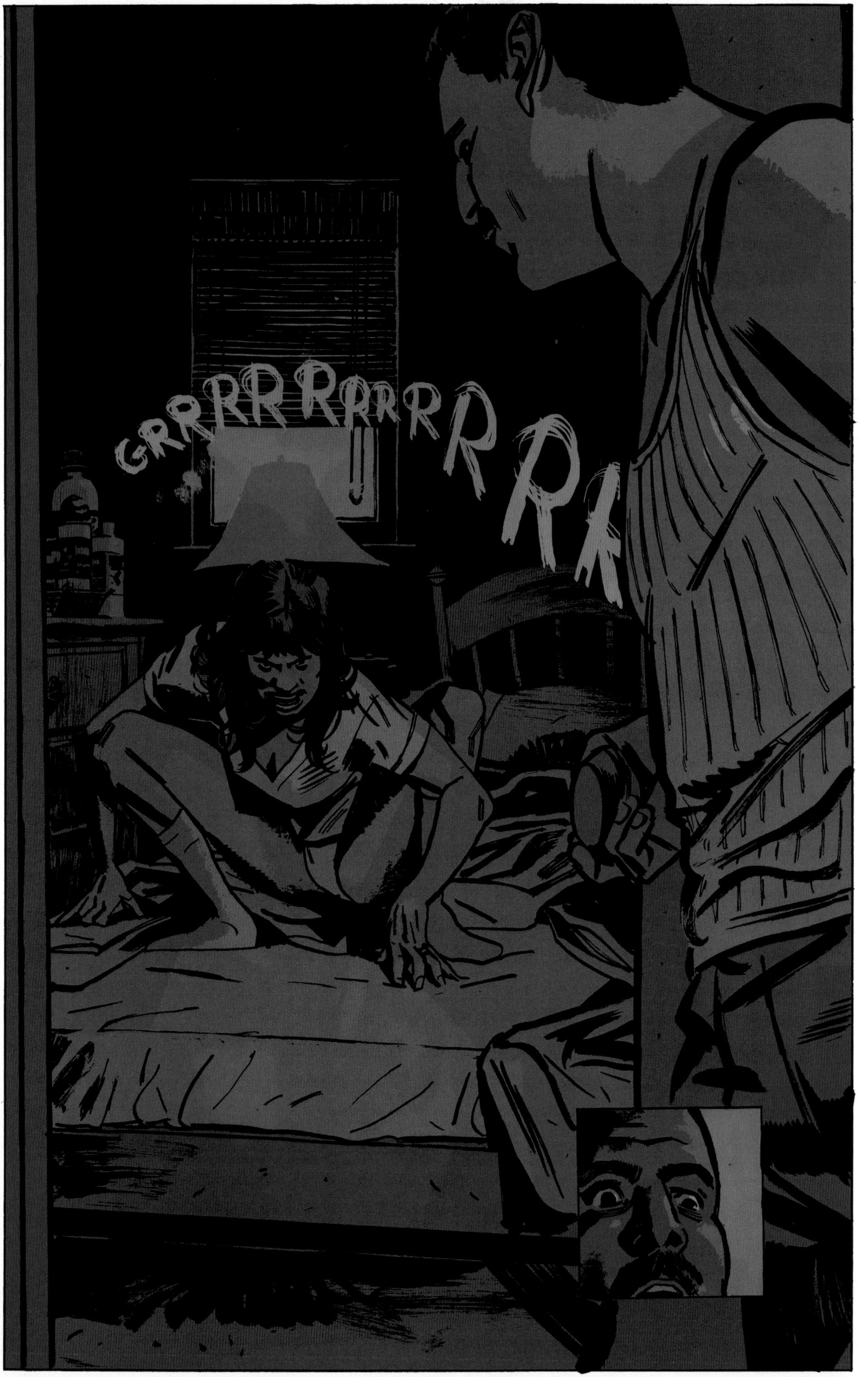
GRRRRRRRRRRRRRA

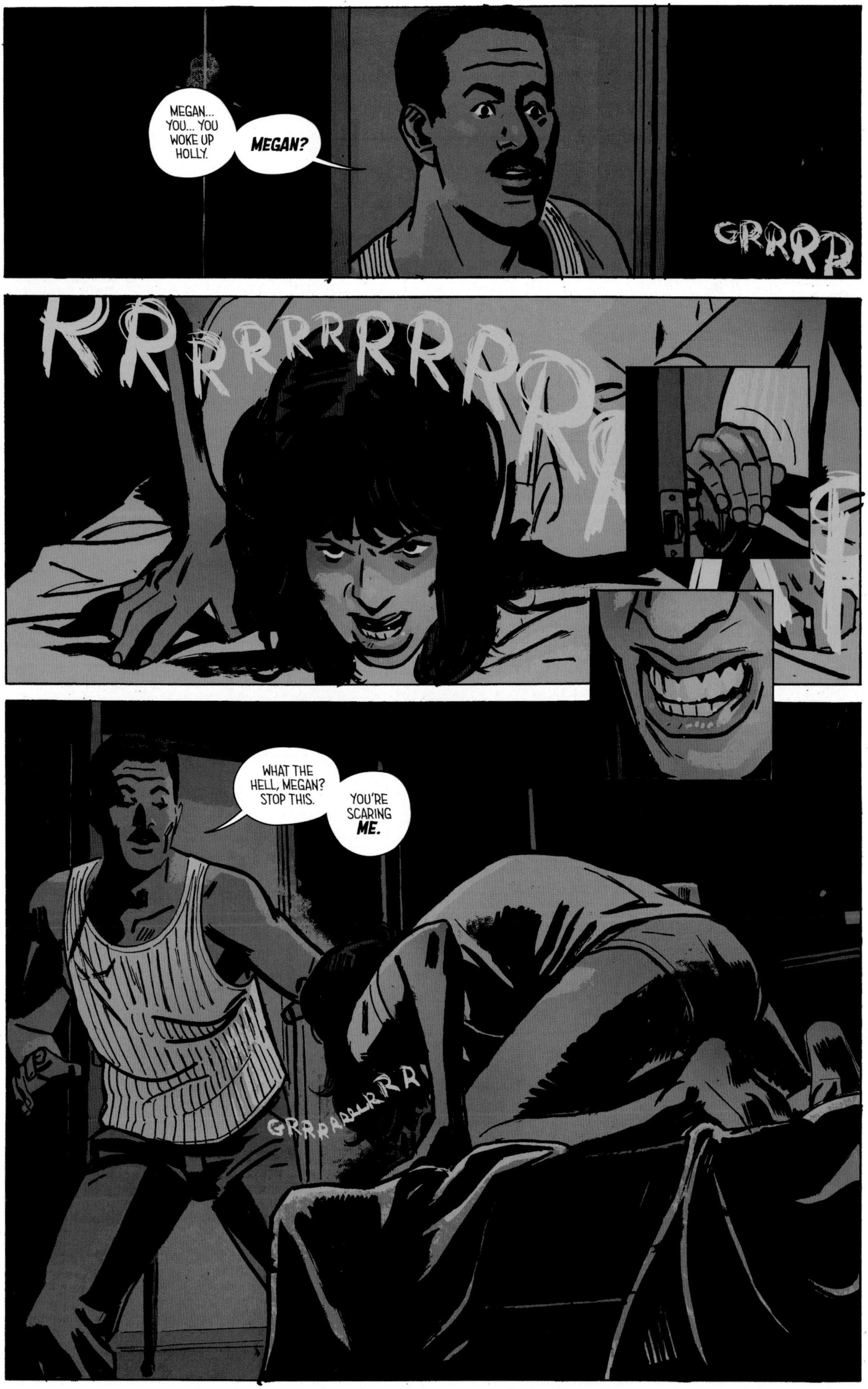

MEGAN... YOU... YOU WOKE UP HOLLY.
MEGAN?
GRRRRR
RRRRRRRRRRR
WHAT THE HELL, MEGAN? STOP THIS.
YOU'RE SCARING ME.
GRRRRRRRR

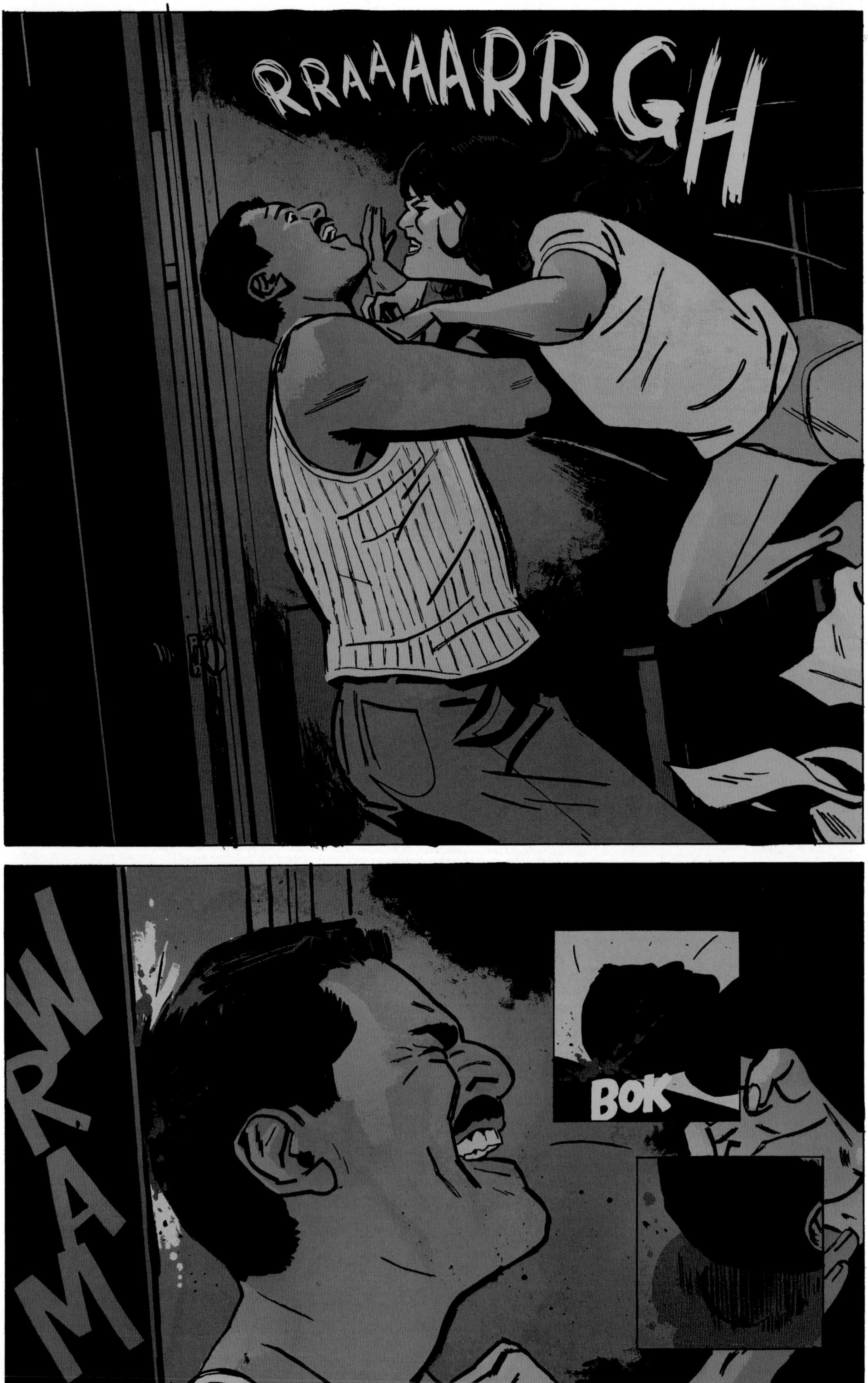
RRAAAARRRGH
WRAM
BOK

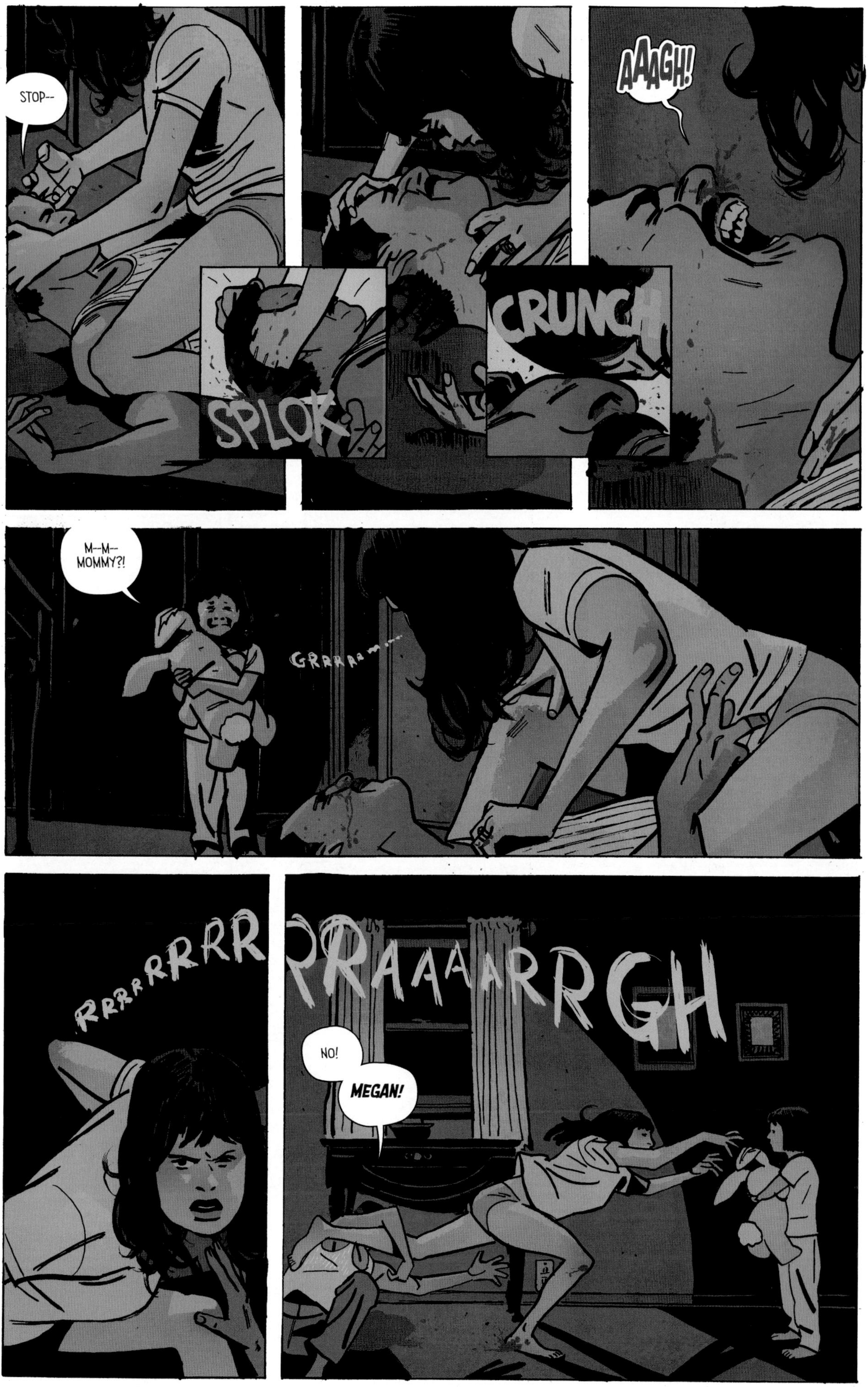
STOP--
SPLOK
CRUNCH
AAAGH!
M--M--
MOMMY?!
GRRRAAM---
RRRRRRRR
RRAAAARRGH
NO!
MEGAN!

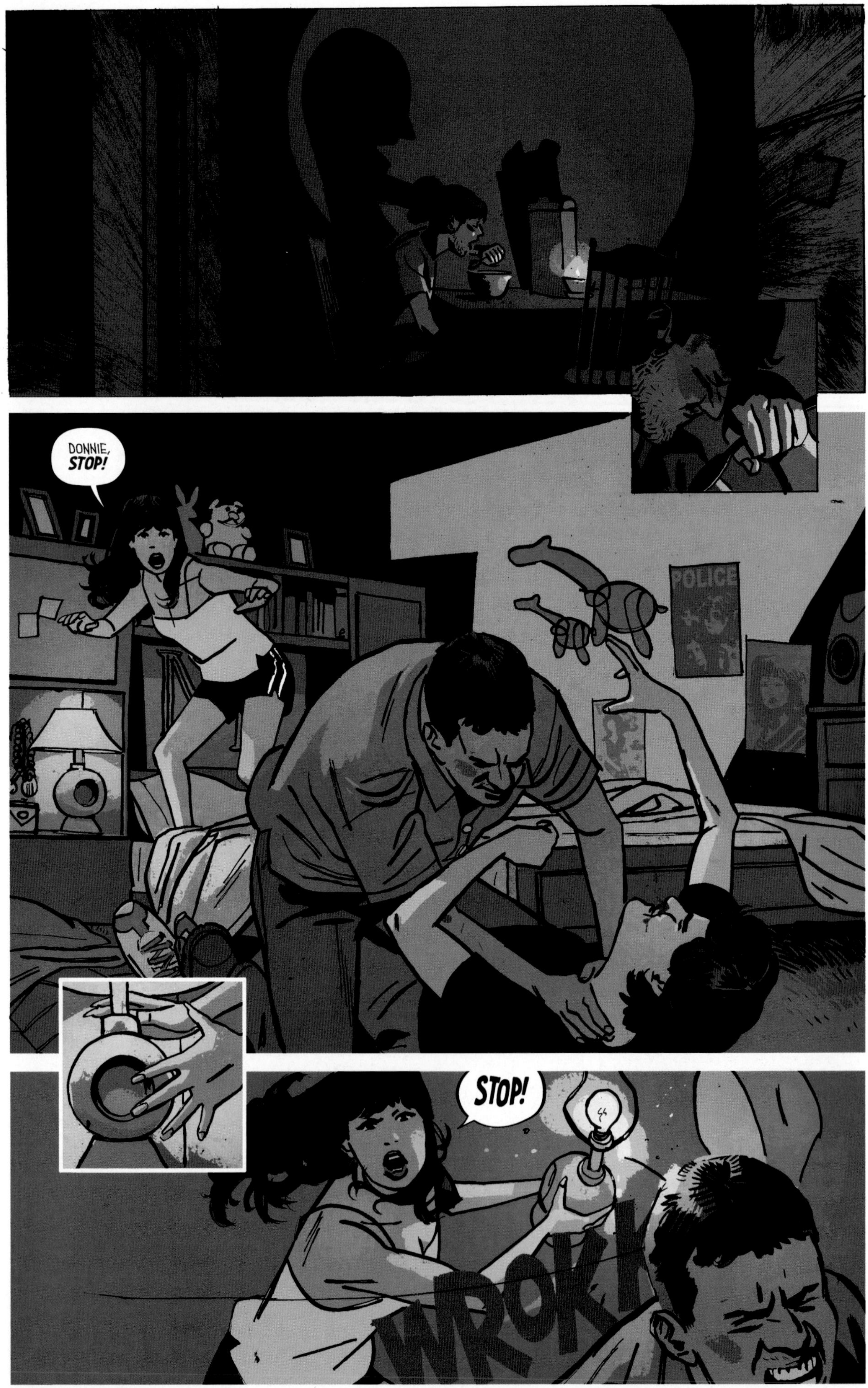
POLICE
DONNIE, STOP!
STOP!
WROK!

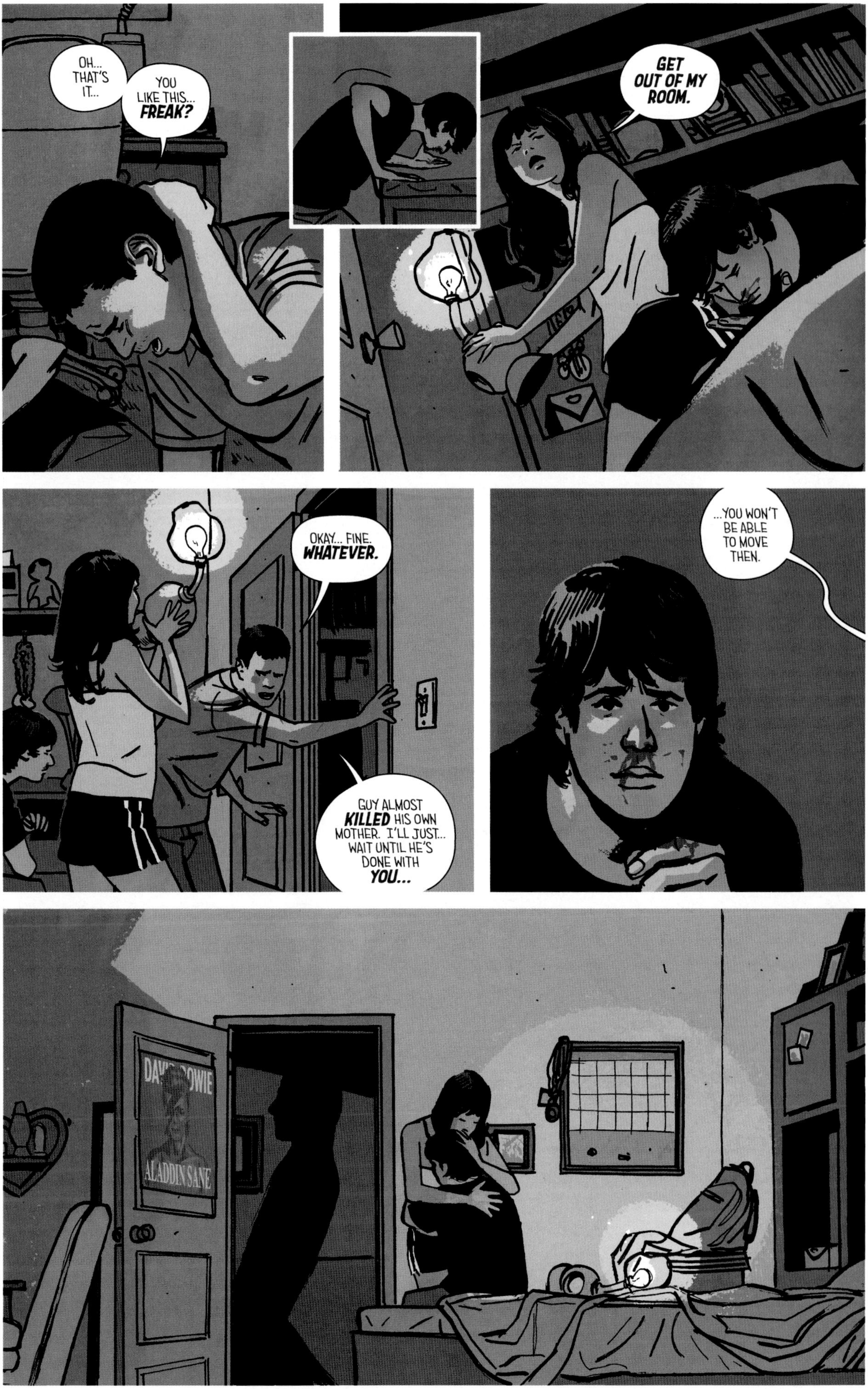
OH... THAT'S IT...
YOU LIKE THIS... **FREAK?**
GET OUT OF MY ROOM.
OKAY... FINE. **WHATEVER.**
GUY ALMOST **KILLED** HIS OWN MOTHER. I'LL JUST... WAIT UNTIL HE'S DONE WITH **YOU...**
...YOU WON'T BE ABLE TO MOVE THEN.
DAVID BOWIE
ALADDIN SANE

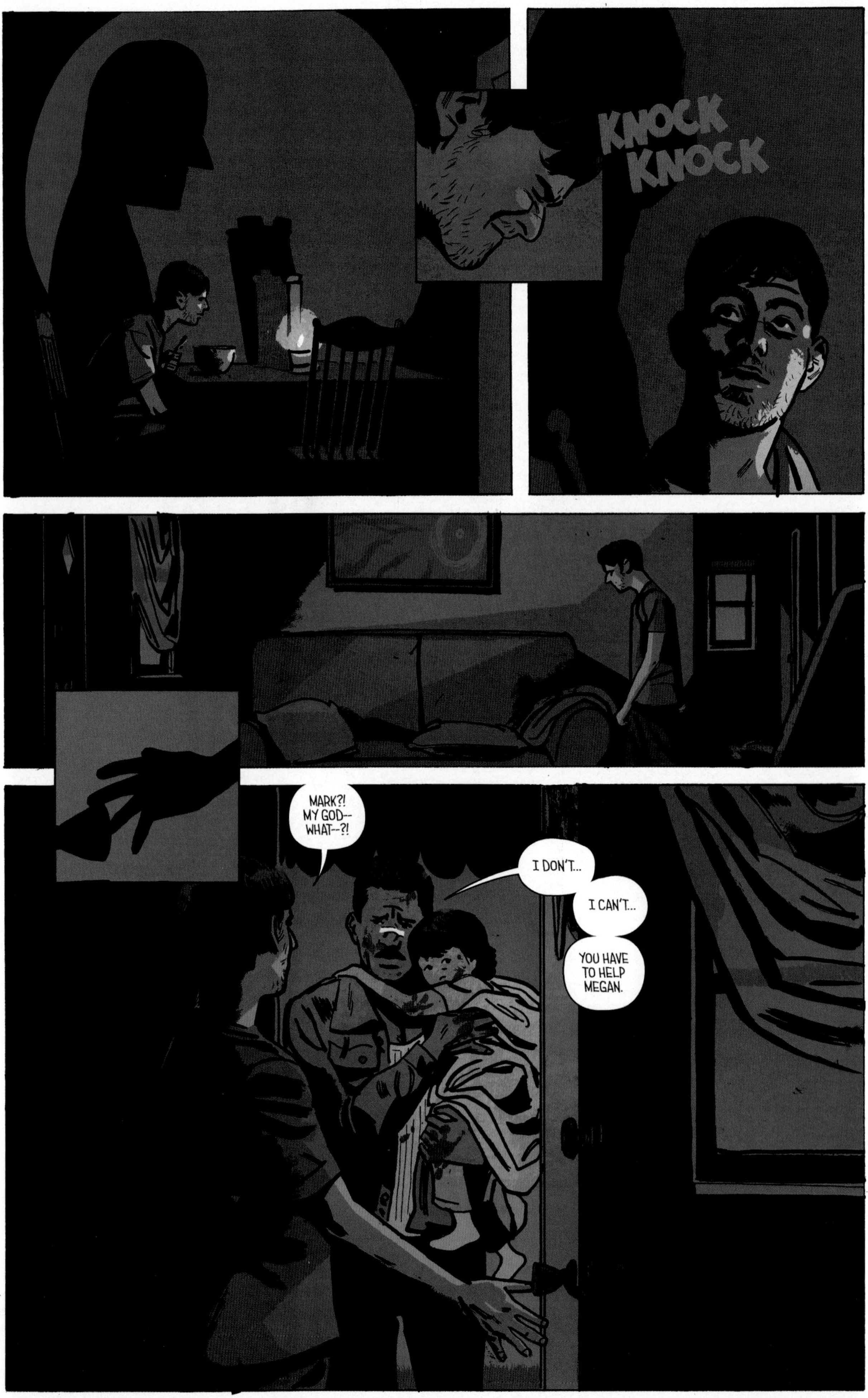
KNOCK KNOCK
MARK?! MY GOD-- WHAT--?!
I DON'T...
I CAN'T...
YOU HAVE TO HELP MEGAN.

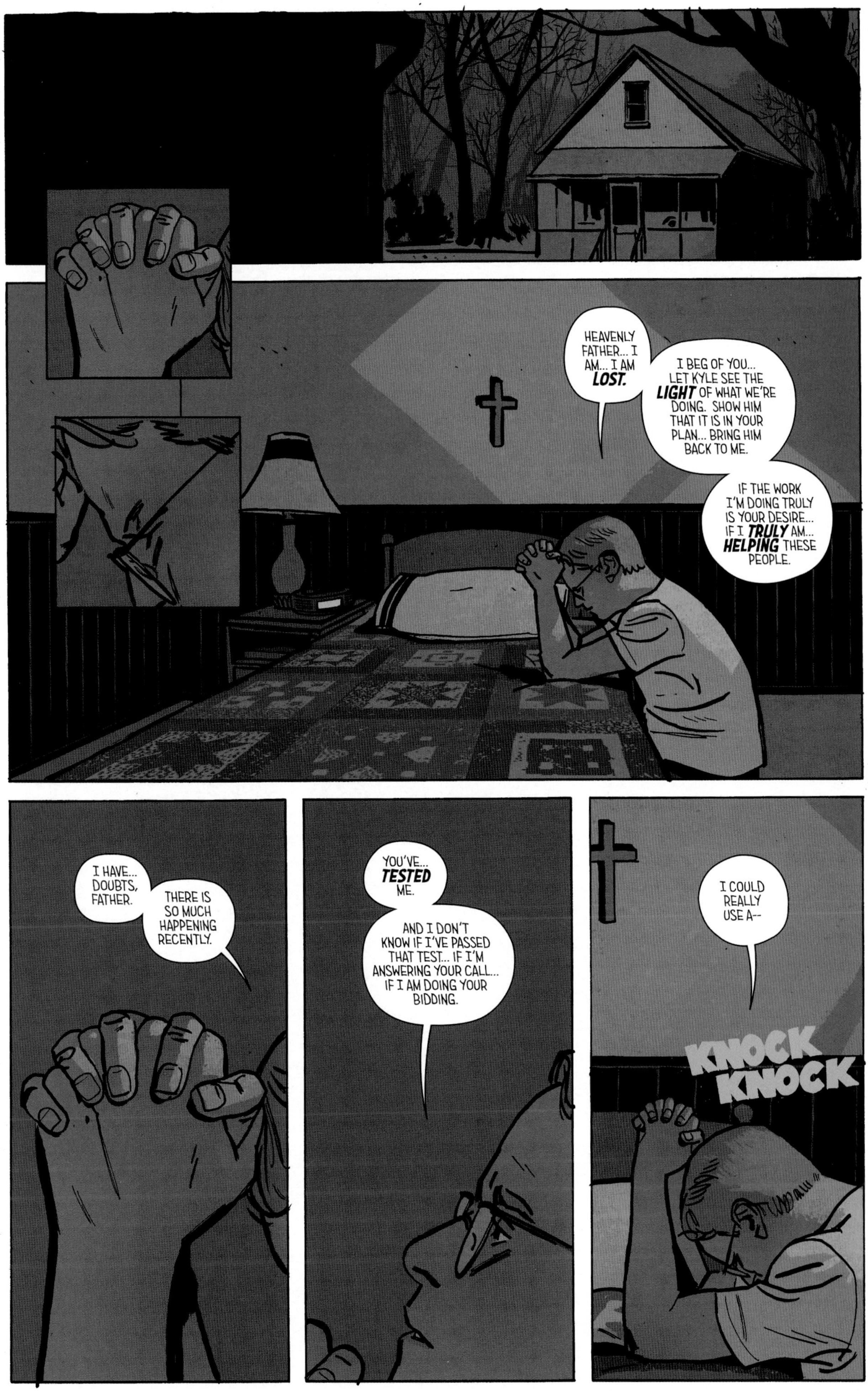
HEAVENLY FATHER... I AM... I AM LOST.
I BEG OF YOU... LET KYLE SEE THE LIGHT OF WHAT WE'RE DOING. SHOW HIM THAT IT IS IN YOUR PLAN... BRING HIM BACK TO ME.
IF THE WORK I'M DOING TRULY IS YOUR DESIRE... IF I TRULY AM... HELPING THESE PEOPLE.
I HAVE... DOUBTS, FATHER.
THERE IS SO MUCH HAPPENING RECENTLY.
YOU'VE... TESTED ME.
AND I DON'T KNOW IF I'VE PASSED THAT TEST... IF I'M ANSWERING YOUR CALL... IF I AM DOING YOUR BIDDING.
I COULD REALLY USE A--
KNOCK KNOCK

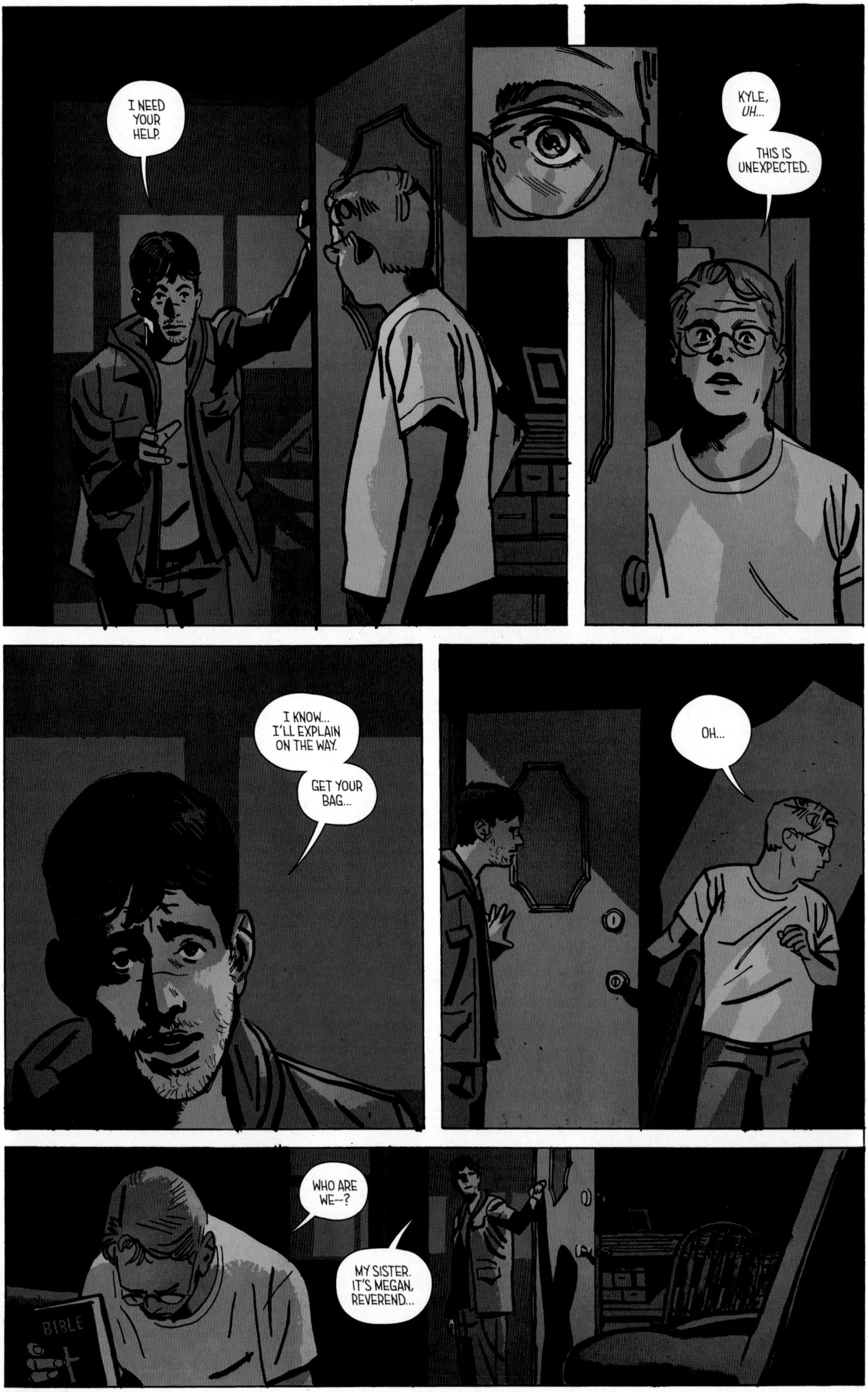
I NEED YOUR HELP.
KYLE, UH...
THIS IS UNEXPECTED.
I KNOW... I'LL EXPLAIN ON THE WAY.
GET YOUR BAG...
OH...
WHO ARE WE--?
MY SISTER. IT'S MEGAN, REVEREND...
BIBLE

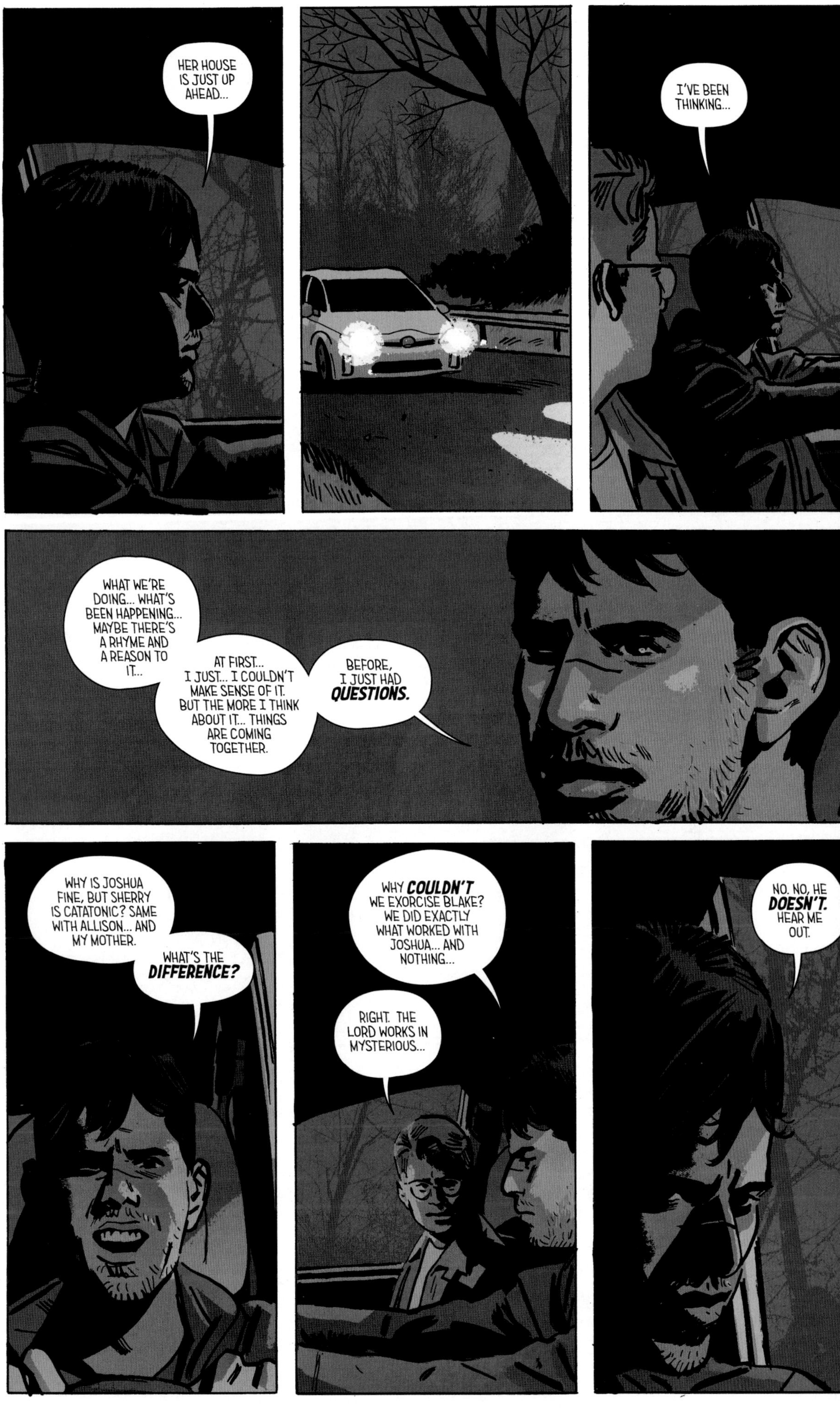
HER HOUSE IS JUST UP AHEAD...
I'VE BEEN THINKING...
WHAT WE'RE DOING... WHAT'S BEEN HAPPENING... MAYBE THERE'S A RHYME AND A REASON TO IT...
AT FIRST... I JUST... I COULDN'T MAKE SENSE OF IT. BUT THE MORE I THINK ABOUT IT... THINGS ARE COMING TOGETHER.
BEFORE, I JUST HAD **QUESTIONS.**
WHY IS JOSHUA FINE, BUT SHERRY IS CATATONIC? SAME WITH ALLISON... AND MY MOTHER.
WHAT'S THE **DIFFERENCE?**
WHY **COULDN'T** WE EXORCISE BLAKE? WE DID EXACTLY WHAT WORKED WITH JOSHUA... AND NOTHING...
RIGHT. THE LORD WORKS IN MYSTERIOUS...
NO. NO, HE **DOESN'T.** HEAR ME OUT.

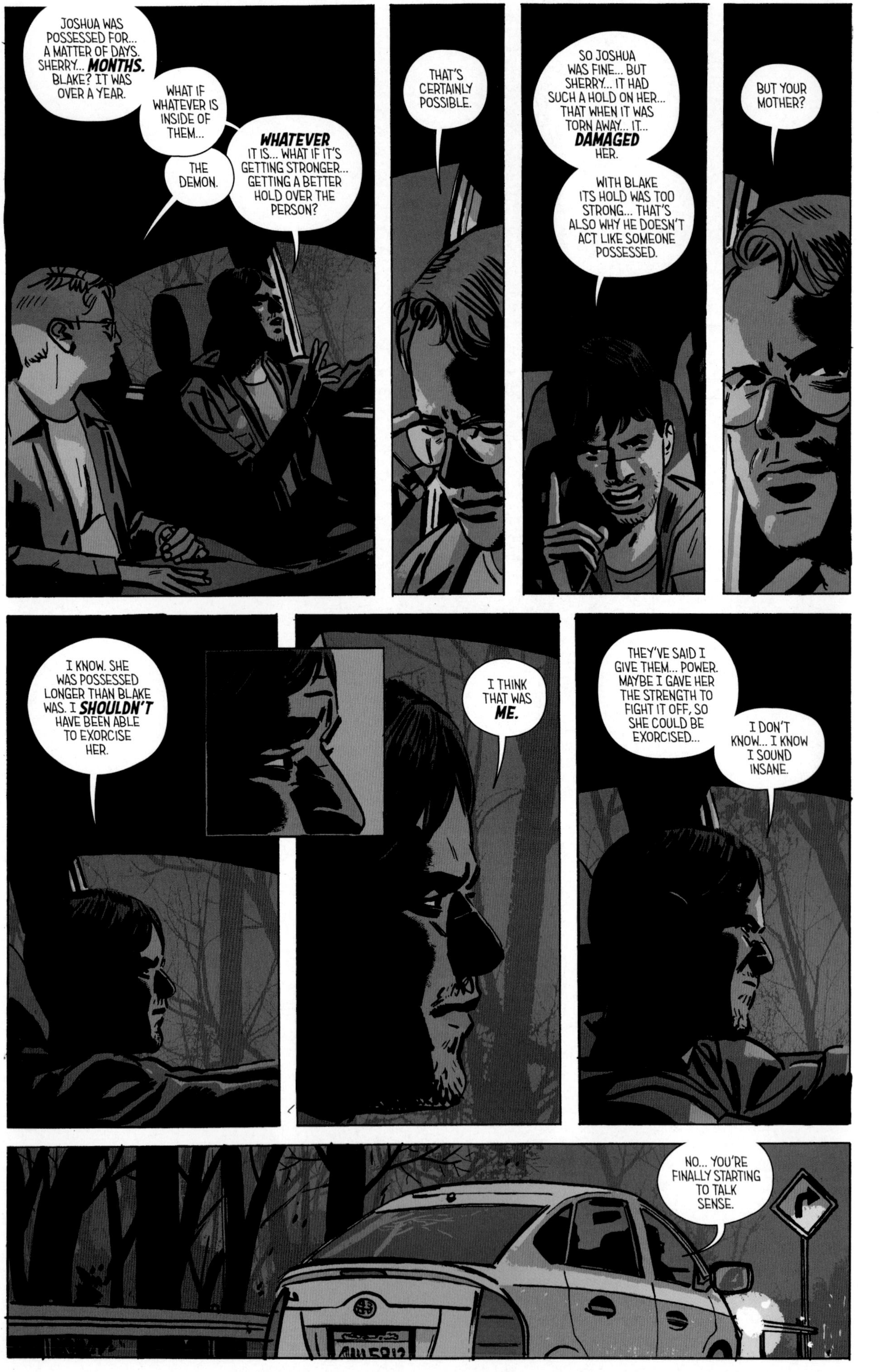
JOSHUA WAS POSSESSED FOR... A MATTER OF DAYS. SHERRY... MONTHS. BLAKE? IT WAS OVER A YEAR.
WHAT IF WHATEVER IS INSIDE OF THEM...
THE DEMON.
WHATEVER IT IS... WHAT IF IT'S GETTING STRONGER... GETTING A BETTER HOLD OVER THE PERSON?
THAT'S CERTAINLY POSSIBLE.
SO JOSHUA WAS FINE... BUT SHERRY... IT HAD SUCH A HOLD ON HER... THAT WHEN IT WAS TORN AWAY... IT... DAMAGED HER.
WITH BLAKE ITS HOLD WAS TOO STRONG... THAT'S ALSO WHY HE DOESN'T ACT LIKE SOMEONE POSSESSED.
BUT YOUR MOTHER?
I KNOW. SHE WAS POSSESSED LONGER THAN BLAKE WAS. I SHOULDN'T HAVE BEEN ABLE TO EXORCISE HER.
I THINK THAT WAS ME.
THEY'VE SAID I GIVE THEM... POWER. MAYBE I GAVE HER THE STRENGTH TO FIGHT IT OFF, SO SHE COULD BE EXORCISED...
I DON'T KNOW... I KNOW I SOUND INSANE.
NO... YOU'RE FINALLY STARTING TO TALK SENSE.

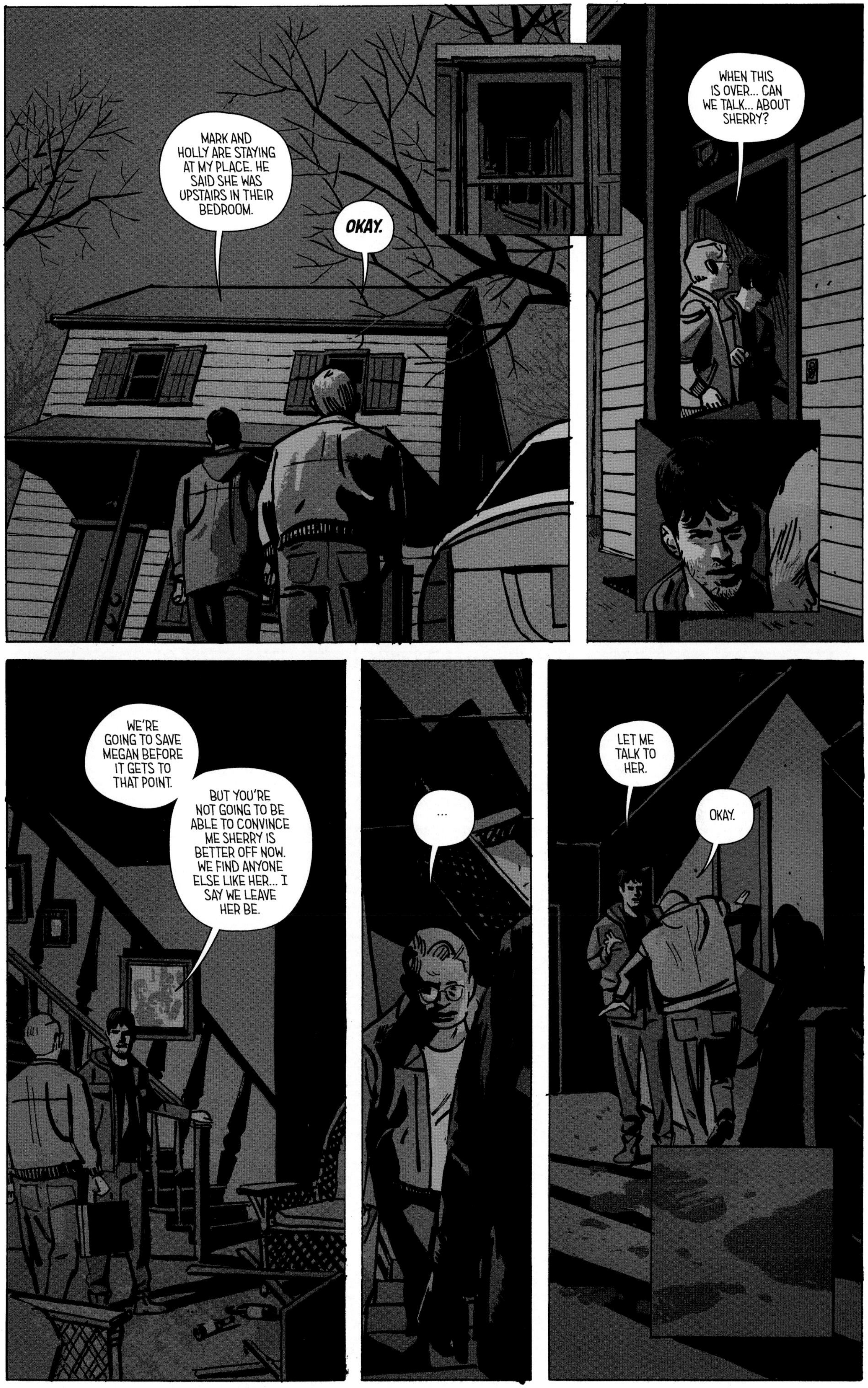
MARK AND HOLLY ARE STAYING AT MY PLACE. HE SAID SHE WAS UPSTAIRS IN THEIR BEDROOM.
OKAY.
WHEN THIS IS OVER... CAN WE TALK... ABOUT SHERRY?
WE'RE GOING TO SAVE MEGAN BEFORE IT GETS TO THAT POINT.
BUT YOU'RE NOT GOING TO BE ABLE TO CONVINCE ME SHERRY IS BETTER OFF NOW. WE FIND ANYONE ELSE LIKE HER... I SAY WE LEAVE HER BE.
...
LET ME TALK TO HER.
OKAY.

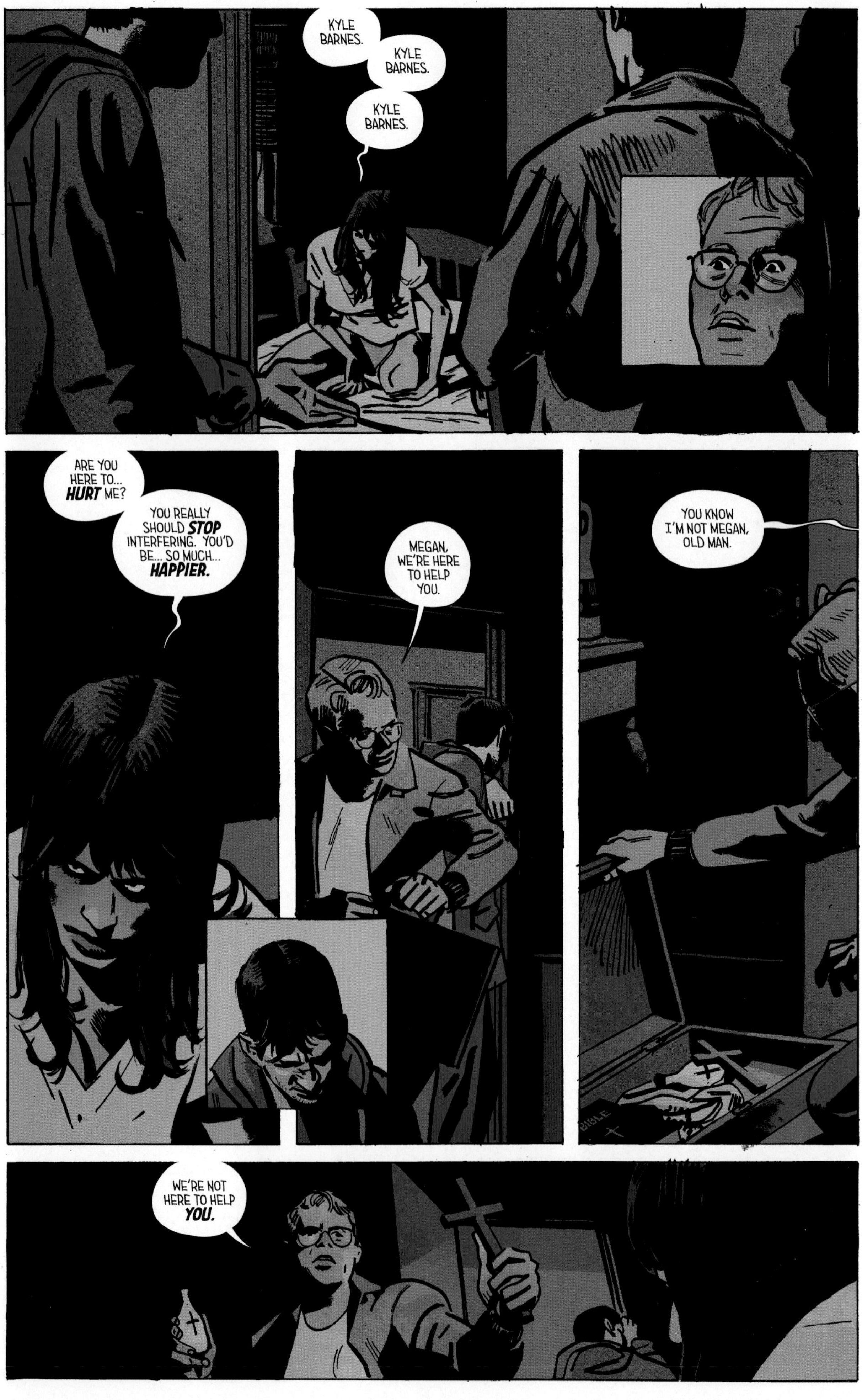
KYLE BARNES.
KYLE BARNES.
KYLE BARNES.
ARE YOU HERE TO... **HURT** ME?
YOU REALLY SHOULD **STOP** INTERFERING. YOU'D BE... SO MUCH... **HAPPIER.**
MEGAN, WE'RE HERE TO HELP YOU.
YOU KNOW I'M NOT MEGAN, OLD MAN.
BIBLE
WE'RE NOT HERE TO HELP **YOU.**

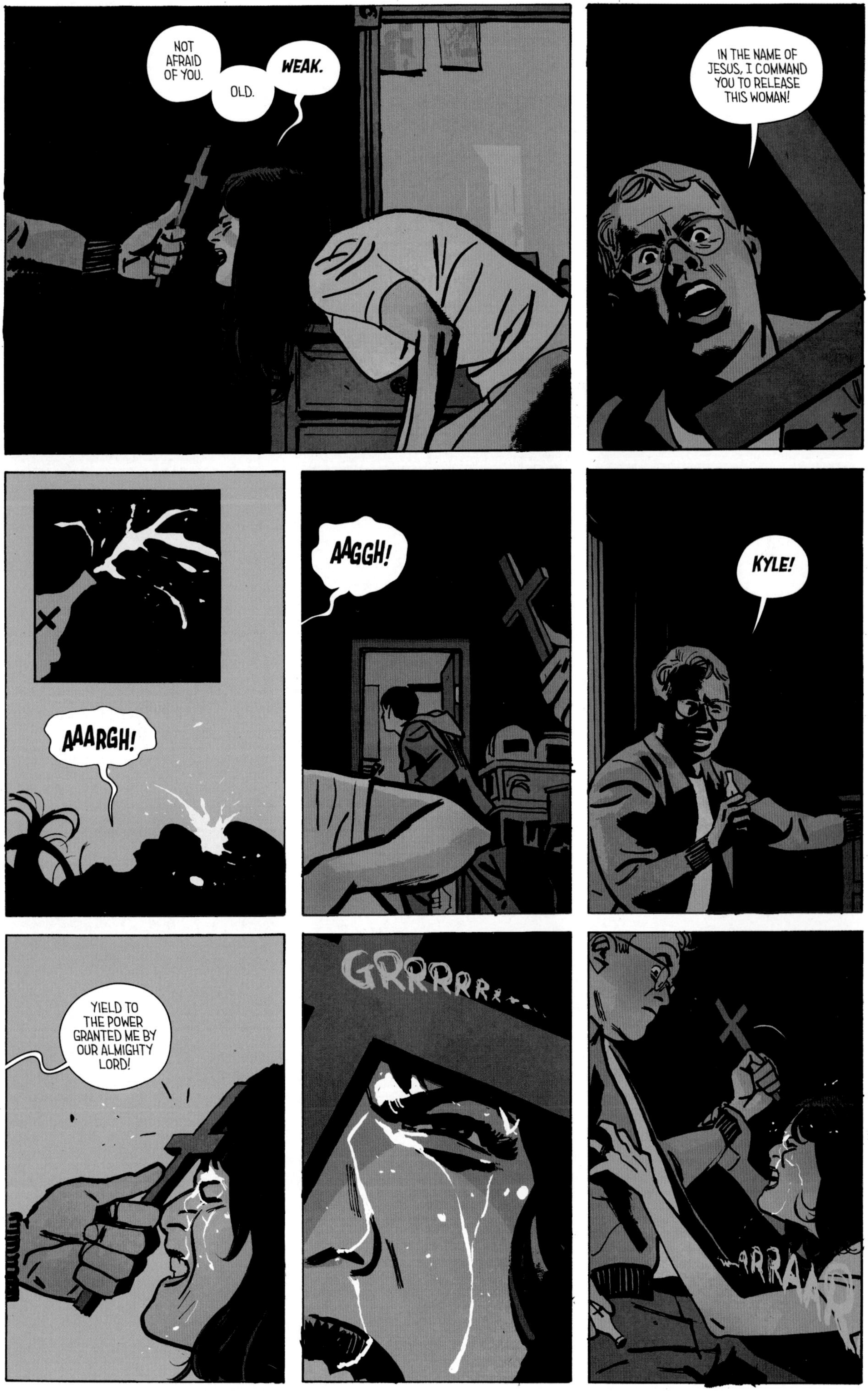
NOT AFRAID OF YOU.
OLD.
WEAK.
IN THE NAME OF JESUS, I COMMAND YOU TO RELEASE THIS WOMAN!
AAARGH!
AAGGH!
KYLE!
YIELD TO THE POWER GRANTED ME BY OUR ALMIGHTY LORD!

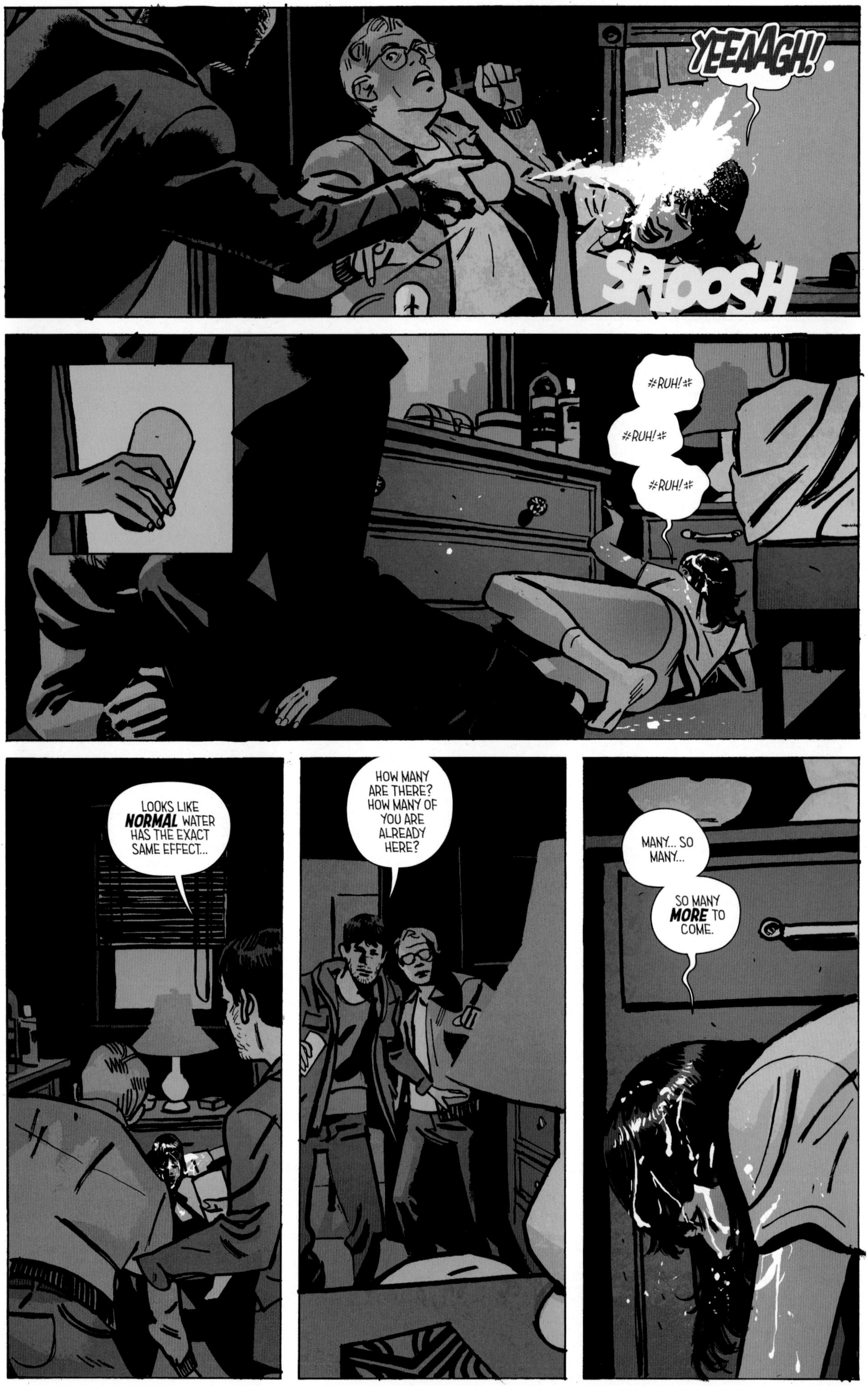
YEEAAGH!
SPLOOSH
RUH!
RUH!
RUH!
LOOKS LIKE NORMAL WATER HAS THE EXACT SAME EFFECT...
HOW MANY ARE THERE? HOW MANY OF YOU ARE ALREADY HERE?
MANY... SO MANY...
SO MANY MORE TO COME.

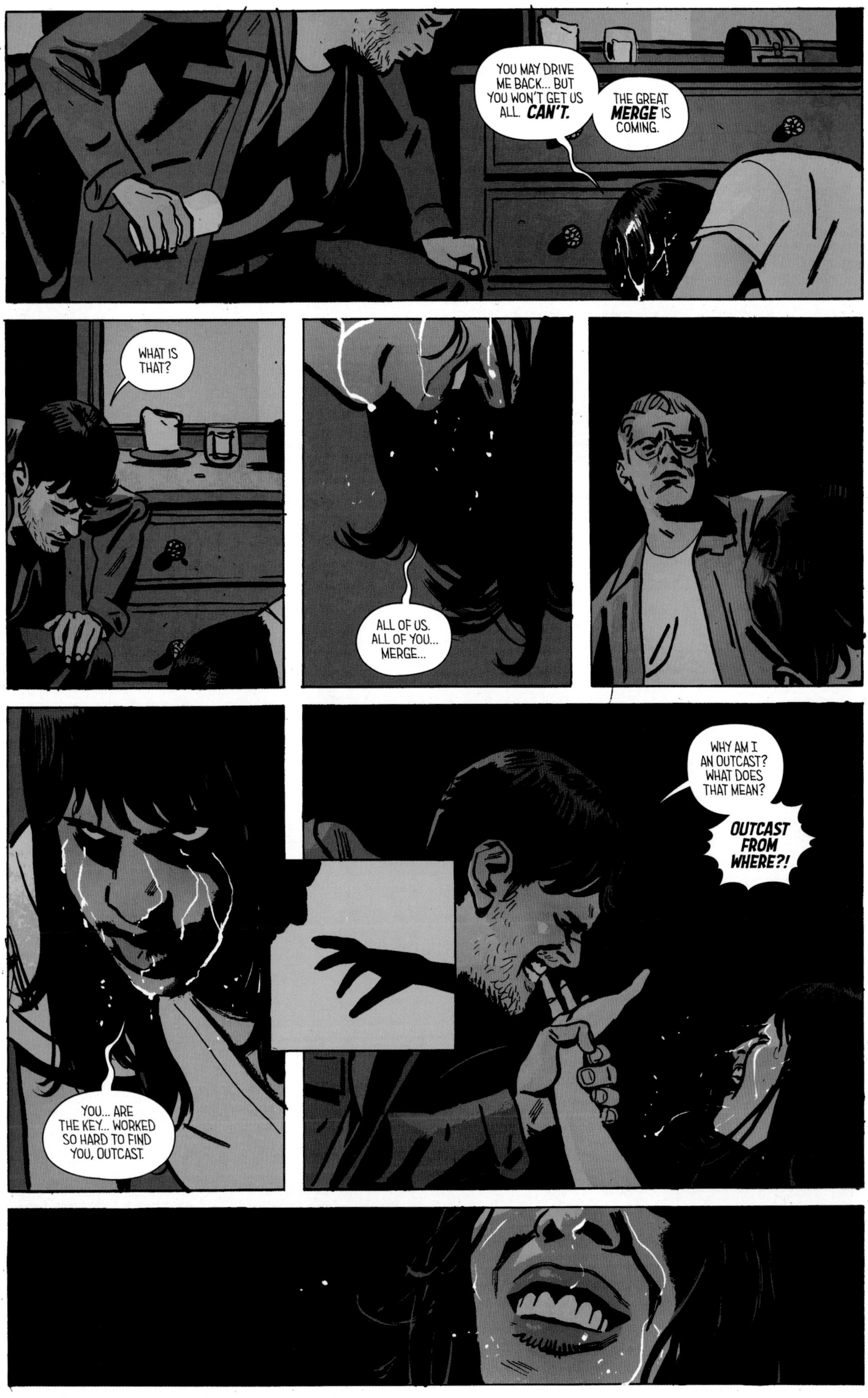
YOU MAY DRIVE ME BACK... BUT YOU WON'T GET US ALL. **CAN'T.**
THE GREAT **MERGE** IS COMING.
WHAT IS THAT?
ALL OF US. ALL OF YOU... MERGE...
YOU... ARE THE KEY... WORKED SO HARD TO FIND YOU, OUTCAST.
WHY AM I AN OUTCAST? WHAT DOES THAT MEAN?
OUTCAST FROM WHERE?!

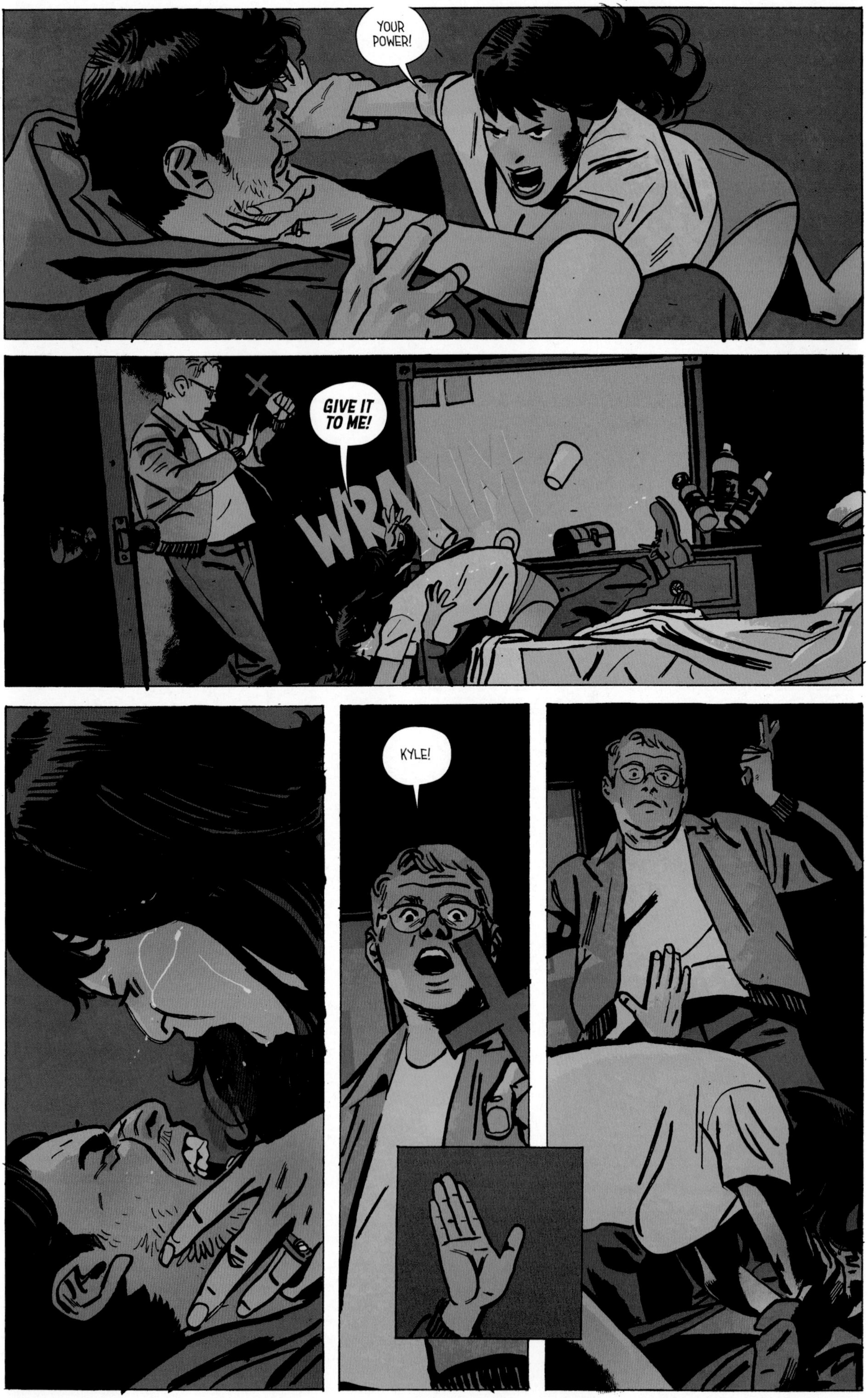
YOUR POWER!
GIVE IT TO ME!
WRAMM
KYLE!

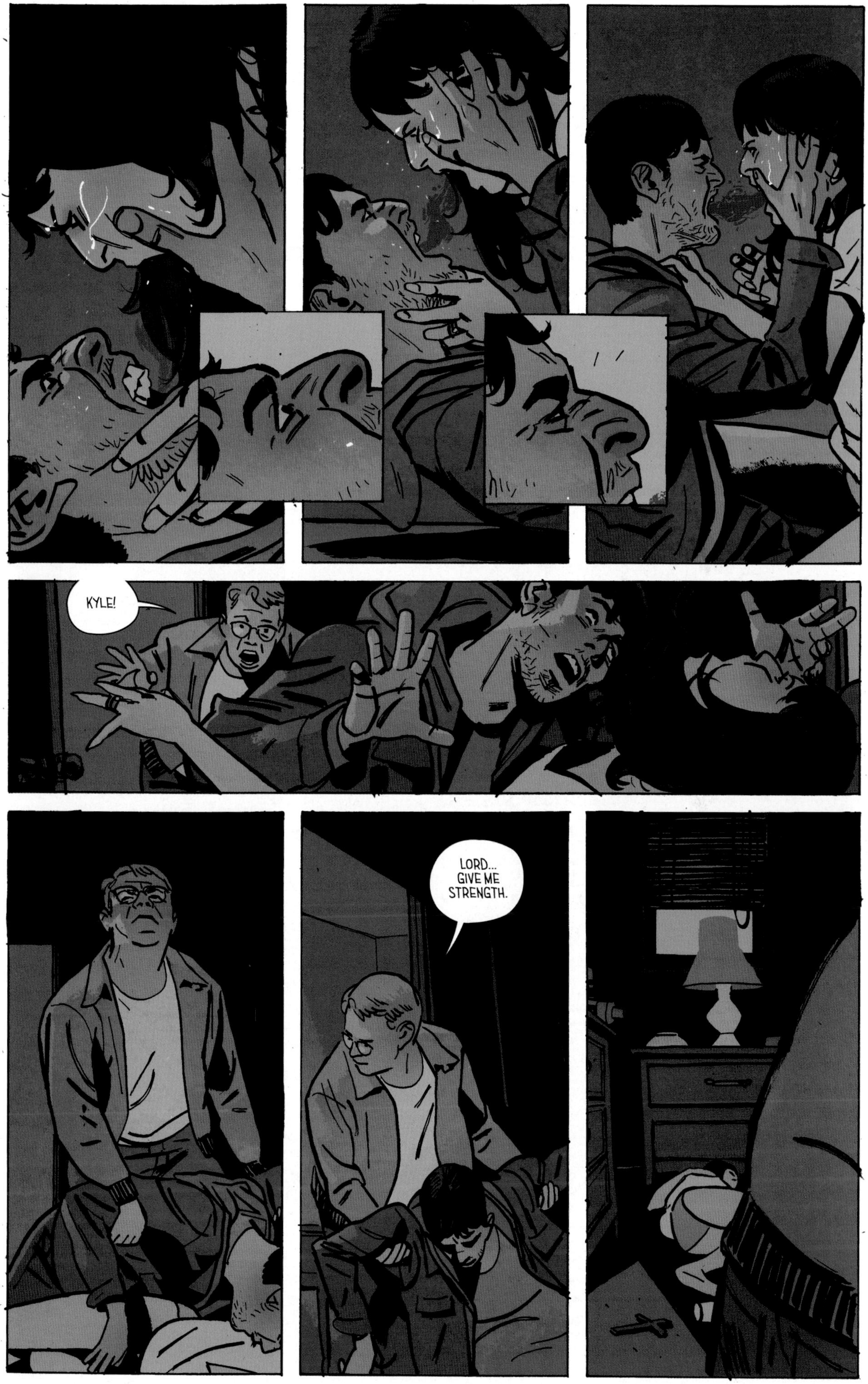
KYLE!
LORD... GIVE ME STRENGTH.

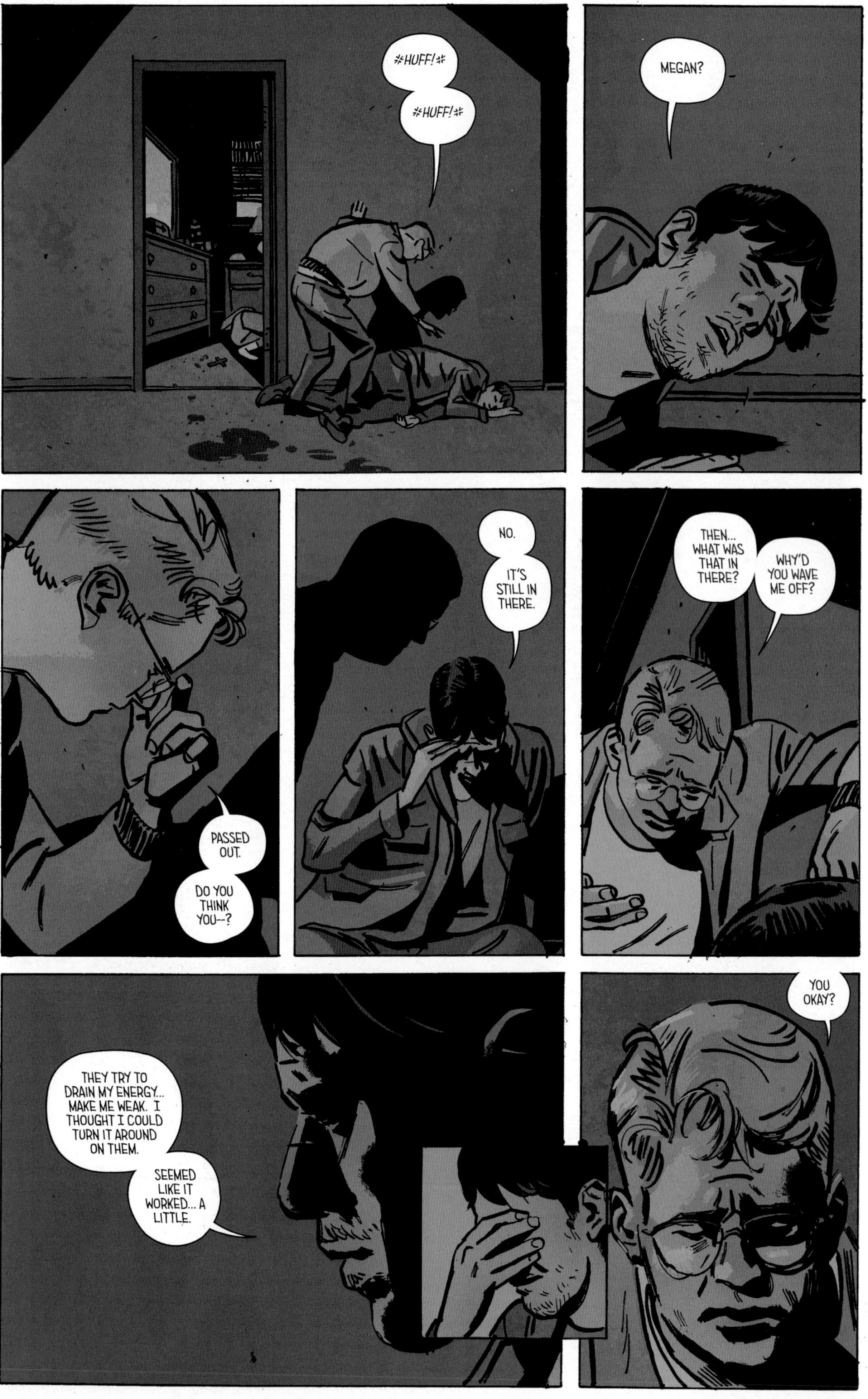
HUFF!
HUFF!
MEGAN?
PASSED OUT.
DO YOU THINK YOU--?
NO.
IT'S STILL IN THERE.
THEN... WHAT WAS THAT IN THERE?
WHY'D YOU WAVE ME OFF?
THEY TRY TO DRAIN MY ENERGY... MAKE ME WEAK. I THOUGHT I COULD TURN IT AROUND ON THEM.
SEEMED LIKE IT WORKED... A LITTLE.
YOU OKAY?

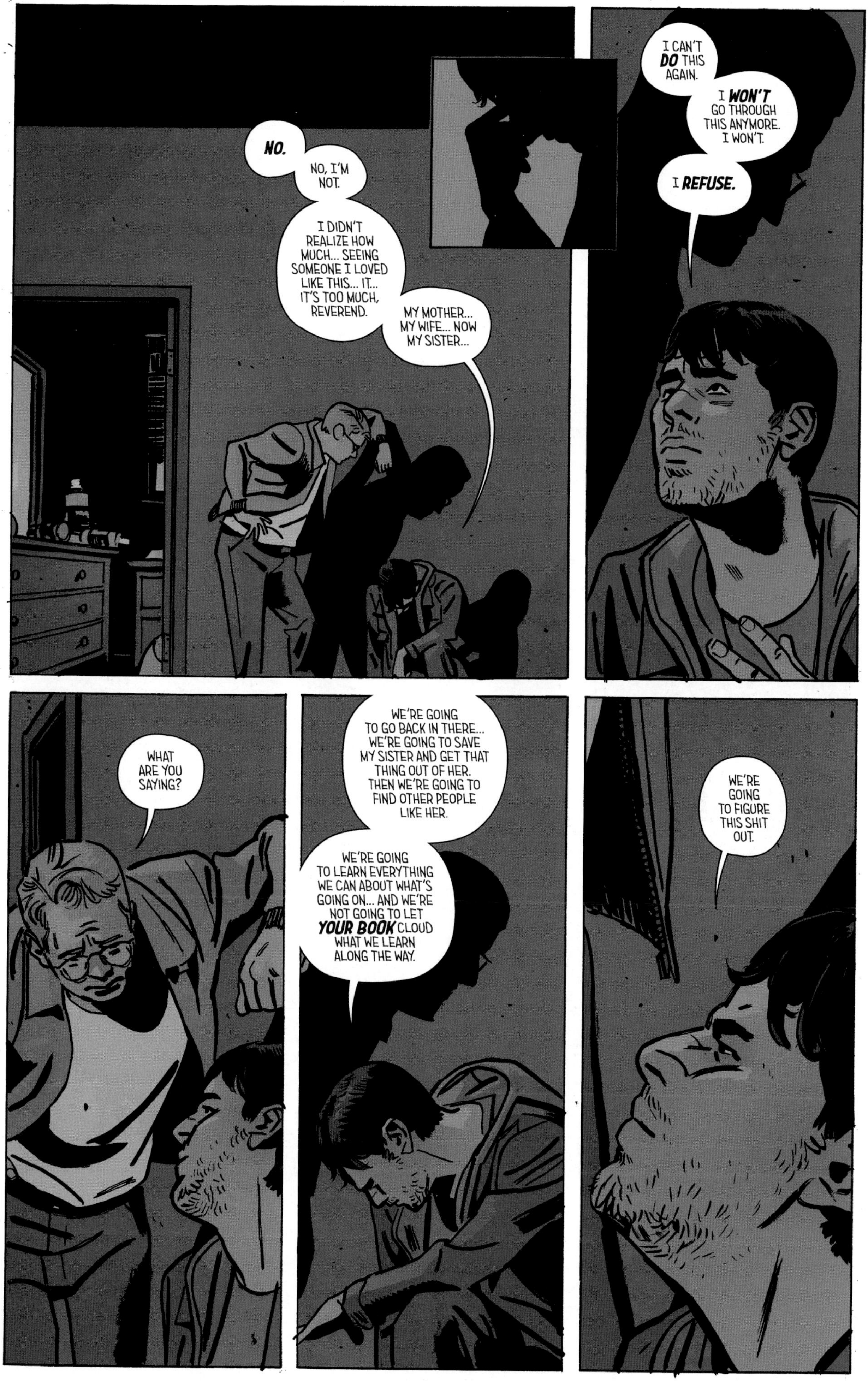
NO.
NO, I'M NOT.
I DIDN'T REALIZE HOW MUCH... SEEING SOMEONE I LOVED LIKE THIS... IT... IT'S TOO MUCH, REVEREND.
MY MOTHER... MY WIFE... NOW MY SISTER...
I CAN'T DO THIS AGAIN.
I WON'T GO THROUGH THIS ANYMORE. I WON'T.
I REFUSE.
WHAT ARE YOU SAYING?
WE'RE GOING TO GO BACK IN THERE... WE'RE GOING TO SAVE MY SISTER AND GET THAT THING OUT OF HER. THEN WE'RE GOING TO FIND OTHER PEOPLE LIKE HER.
WE'RE GOING TO LEARN EVERYTHING WE CAN ABOUT WHAT'S GOING ON... AND WE'RE NOT GOING TO LET YOUR BOOK CLOUD WHAT WE LEARN ALONG THE WAY.
WE'RE GOING TO FIGURE THIS SHIT OUT.

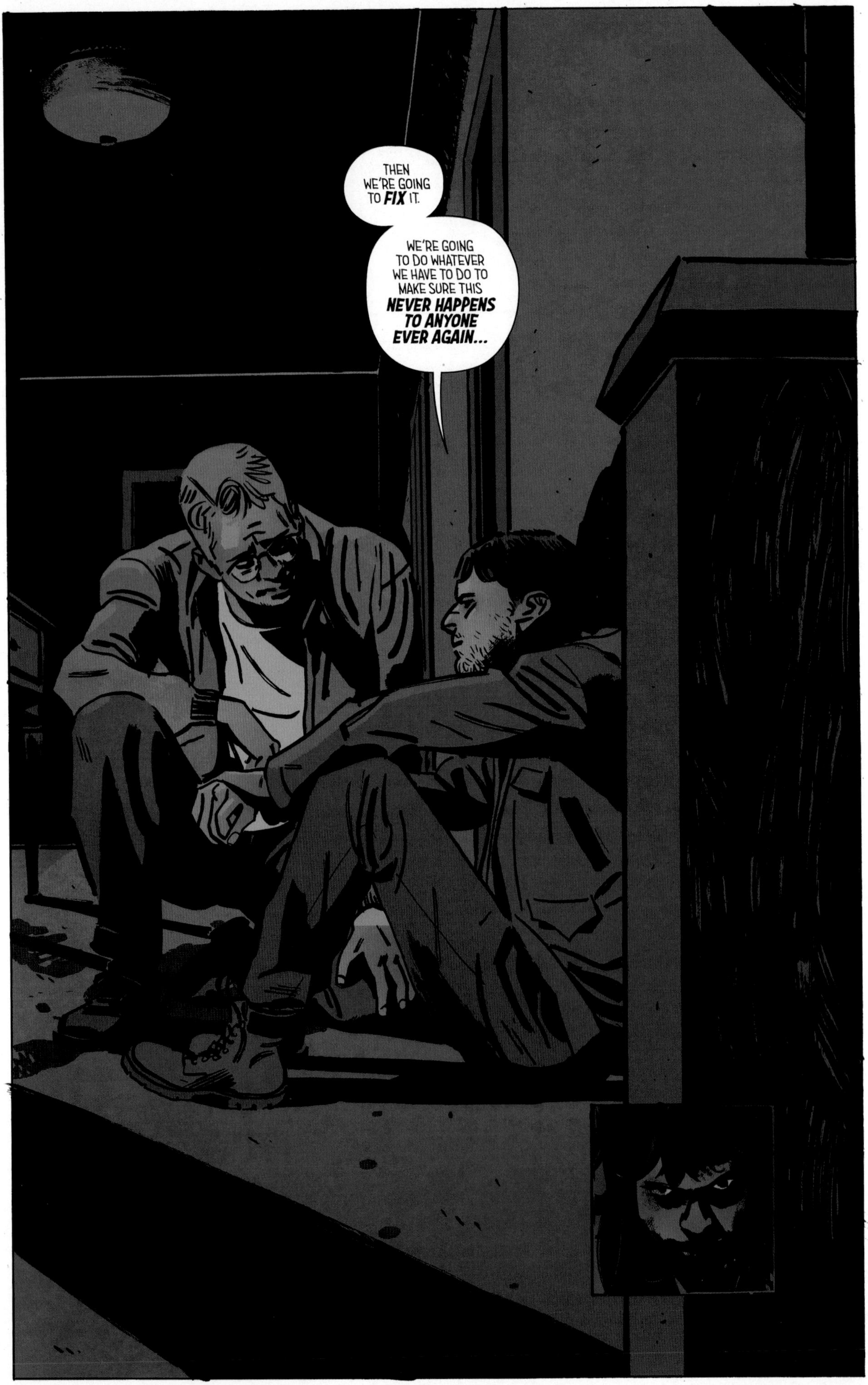
THEN WE'RE GOING TO **FIX** IT.
WE'RE GOING TO DO WHATEVER WE HAVE TO DO TO MAKE SURE THIS **NEVER HAPPENS TO ANYONE EVER AGAIN...**

TO BE CONTINUED

SKETCHBOOK

Robert Kirkman: Welcome to the Book One sketchbook section of this fine series we call OUTCAST! We'll be pulling back the curtain and giving you an exclusive peek at Paul's development work for the look of this series. Take it away, Paul!

Paul Azaceta: The first pass at Kyle was way off. Robert had been talking to me about the series and it was still early on before I had a grasp on what I wanted the book to look like. What the feel and tone of it was. Robert immediately rejected the trilby hat. I don't know what I was thinking.

Robert: Gah! Weird hipster Kyle! Hide it! Burn it! Don't show this to anyone!

Kyle

Kyle

Paul: We later settled on a more modern and layered look. I actually based a lot of Kyle's early look on my older brother, so now whenever I need something new for him to wear I'll just copy whatever my brother was wearing last time I saw him.

Robert: MUUUUCH better.

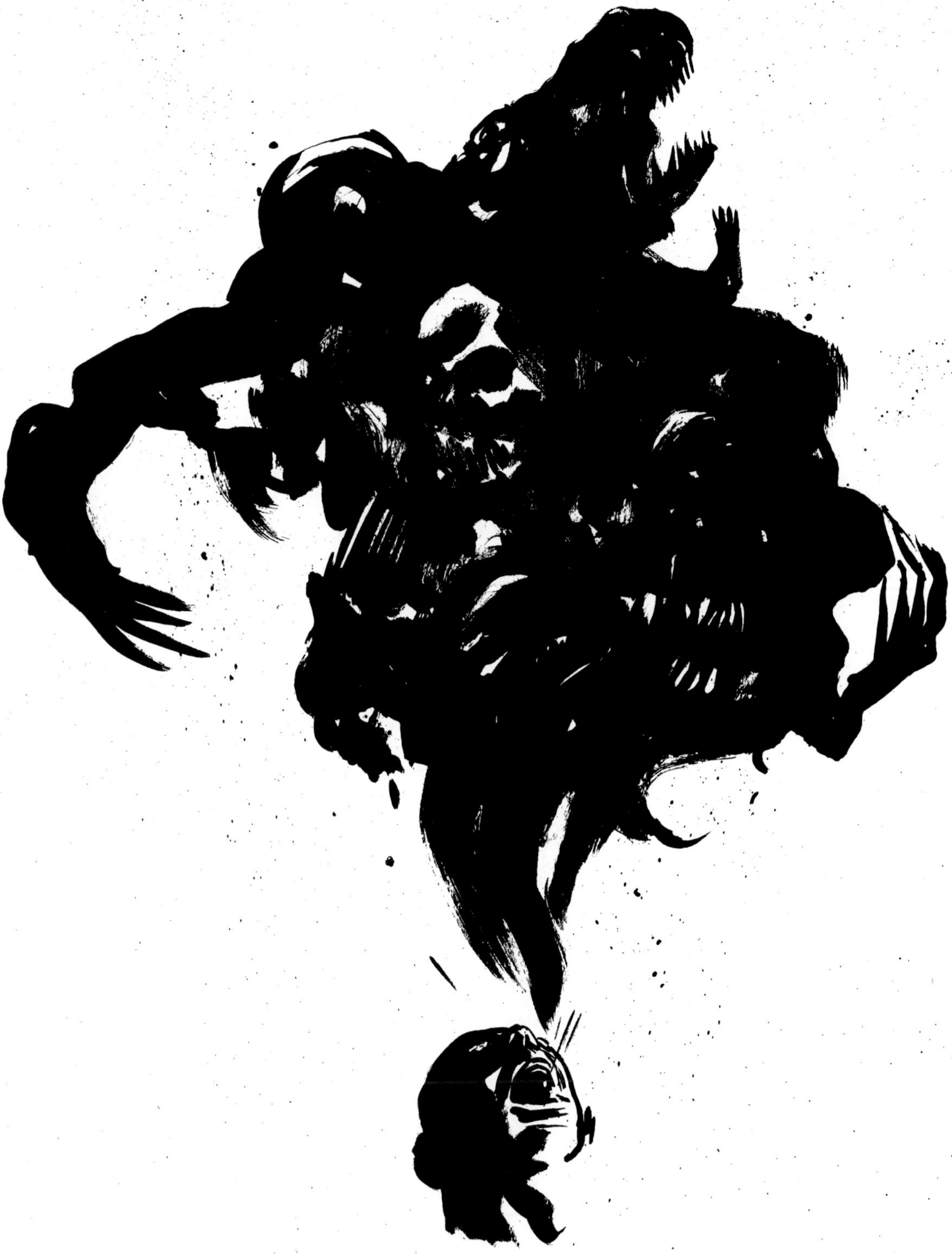

Paul: I remember having a couple of early conversations with Robert about the "demons" in the book. He described them as a formless, thick black cloud. Shapes and teeth and eyes swirling around. Something where two people in the room would see two different things. This was the first quick sketch I did where I think I finally got close.

Robert: Yeah, this was a tough thing to describe and an even harder thing to pull off in a still image. A swirling mass of shapes that you see things in, but they're like clouds... you're projecting your experience on what you see. For instance, is that a T-Rex at the top of that mass? Looks like it to me, maybe you see something different. Paul nailed it!

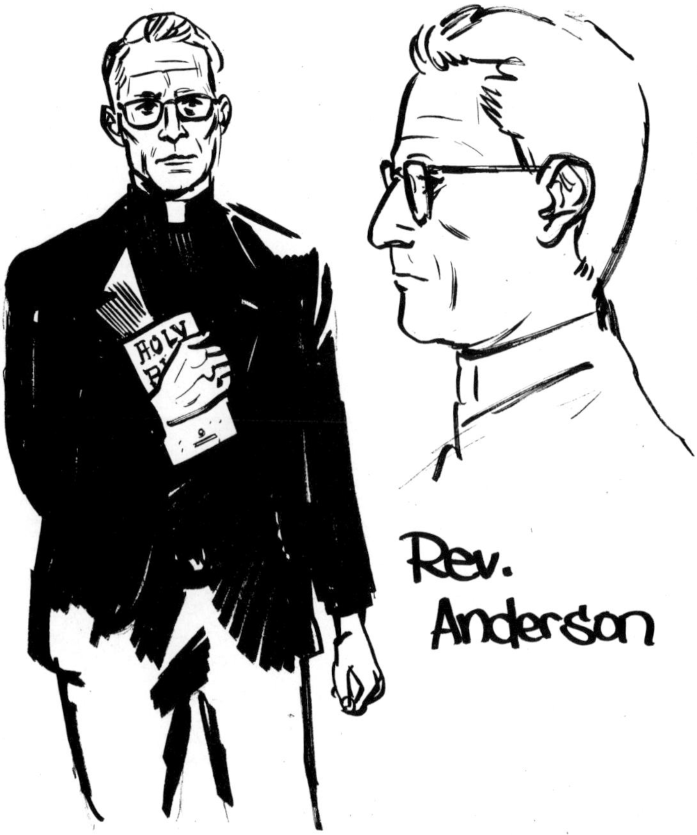
Rev.
Anderson

Paul: The reverend came easier, but Robert initially was thinking of making him look thinner and more like John Slattery. The first sketch was also before I had done any research into West Virginia and I ignorantly made him a Catholic priest. I grew up Catholic, so I guess that's just the image that's burned into my mind when someone says reverend or priest or pastor.

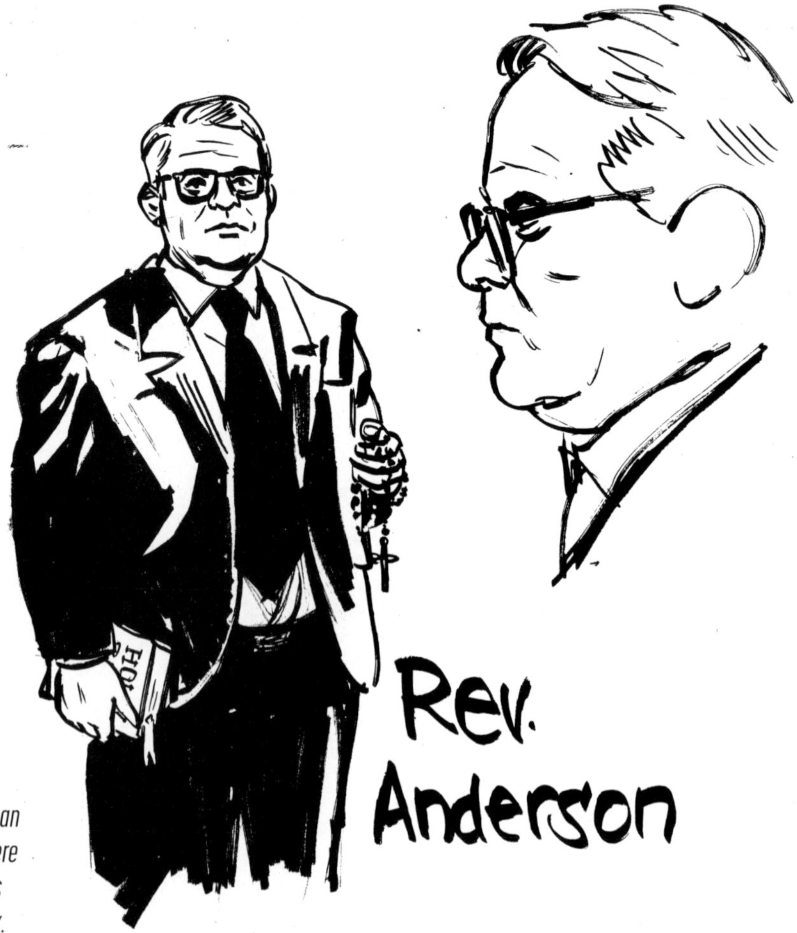
Rev.
Anderson

Paul: We quickly got away from that and went with more of a Philip Seymour Hoffman feel. It lent itself better to the scenes where Anderson is having a rough time of it. He's become my favorite character in the book.

Robert: Yeah, this second take was much closer to what I wanted. We ended up thinning him up a little, but I honestly don't recall why. I think Paul hates fat people.

Alison
Barnes

YOUNG

SARAH
BARNES

OLDER
POSSESSED

Robert: The ladies of OUTCAST ended up being much easier, with Paul coming up with a really great unique look for all of them on the first try. I was especially impressed by how Sarah Barnes looks like she's from twenty years ago without it being really obvious or silly. And I love how confident Megan looked... from the very beginning.

Megan

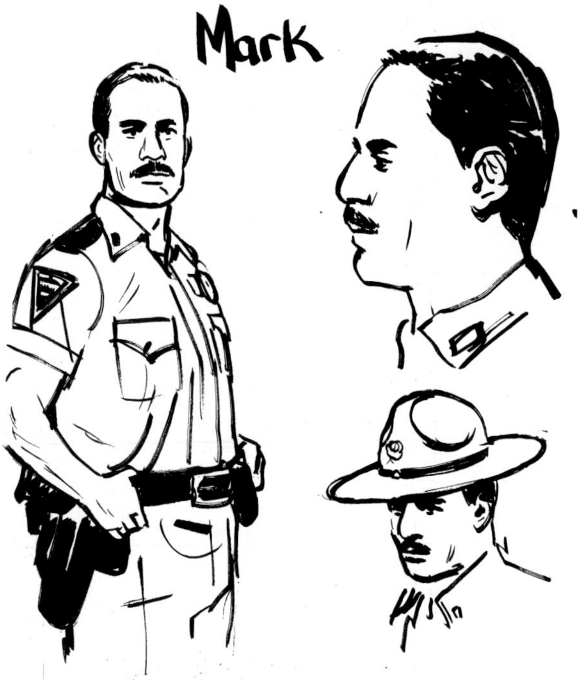
Mark

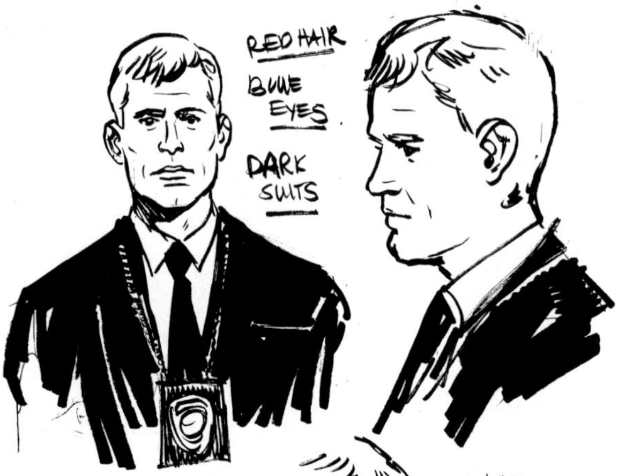
RED HAIR
BLUE EYES
DARK SUITS

Robert: These guys all came together quickly as well. You'd never believe how much conversation went into whether or not Mark would have a mustache in the TV show. It was a lot. The "neighbor", of course, would eventually be named Norville, and he would be killed by Sidney... I'm a huge *Hudsucker Proxy* fan...

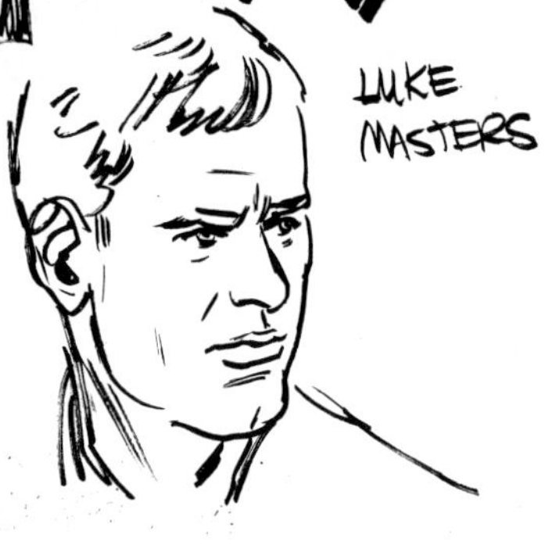
LUKE
MASTERS

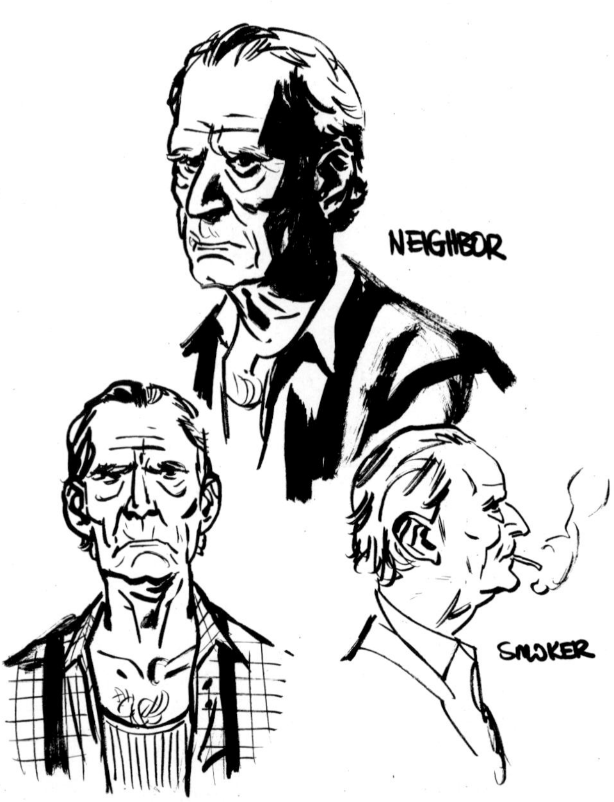
NEIGHBOR
SMOKER

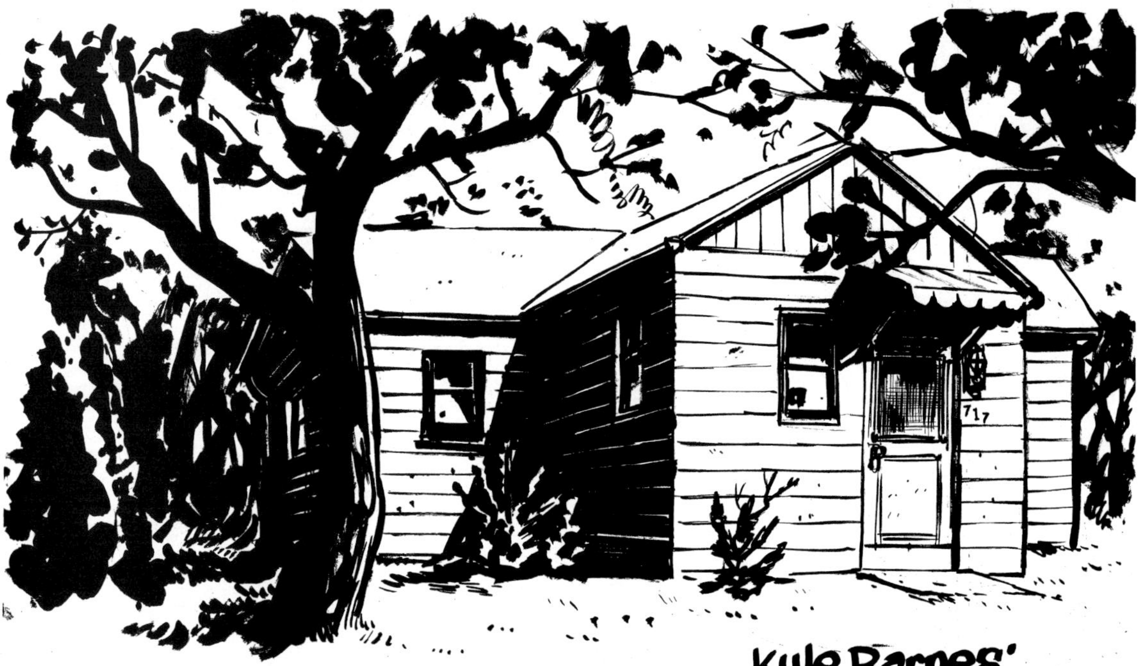
717

Kyle Barnes' House

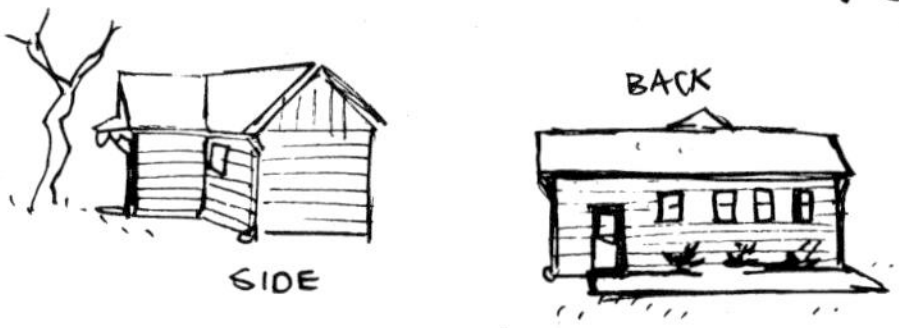
SIDE
BACK

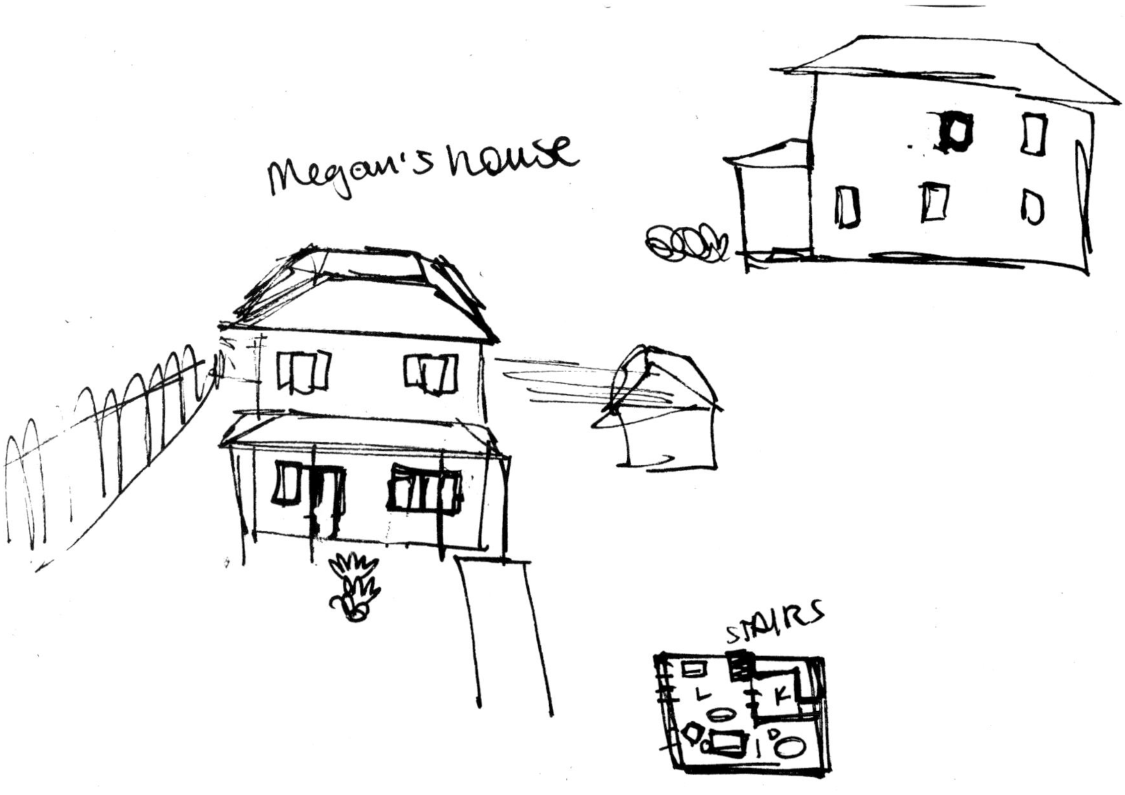
Megan's house
STAIRS
L
K
D

Paul: This was my first time drawing an extended run of a series. I was nervous about keeping everything consistent. So I didn't run into weird logistical problems later, I tried to have a floor plan for each of the main characters' houses. They've really come in handy, and it's one of the few times I saved myself some redrawing.

31
32
SHRIPP!
33
WRAKK
WHUDD
34
WRAKK
WRAKK
35
36
CHOMP
KRAK
WRAK
WROK
WHUMP
37
38
WIDE

39

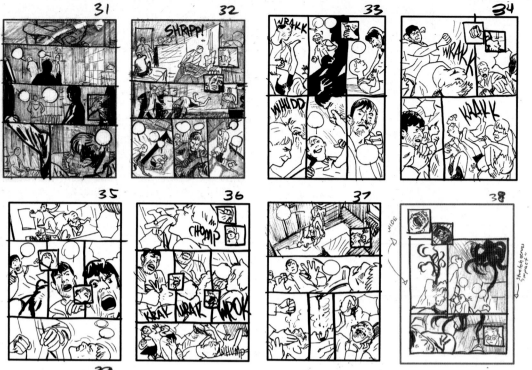

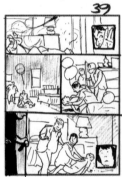

Paul: The first exorcism in the book was going to be a really important scene. It sets the tone for all the exorcisms and evil things that come later. I actually watched a bunch of horror movies before starting my work on OUTCAST to get into the mindset and have a firm grasp on what makes horror work. I tried to bring a lot of that into that scene and I'm pretty proud of how it turned out.

OUTCAST 1
COVER

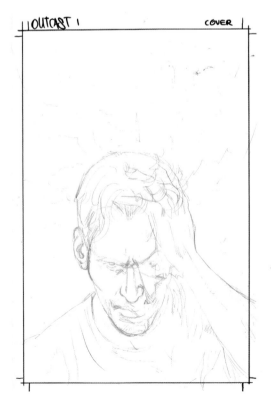

Paul: The first cover was another time when Robert was really adamant that we had to nail it. It's an image we'll have to live with for the length of the series, and if it's a miss we were going to hate having to look at it. I knew it had to be something striking and simple. I tried to capture the feel of being plagued by demons, but Robert didn't want Kyle to come off like a victim. He had to be standing against it all.

Robert: Yeah, thankfully Paul and Elizabeth really knocked it out of the park with this first issue cover. It's just GREAT. I look forward to seeing it hung on the wall behind comic shop counters for many years to come.

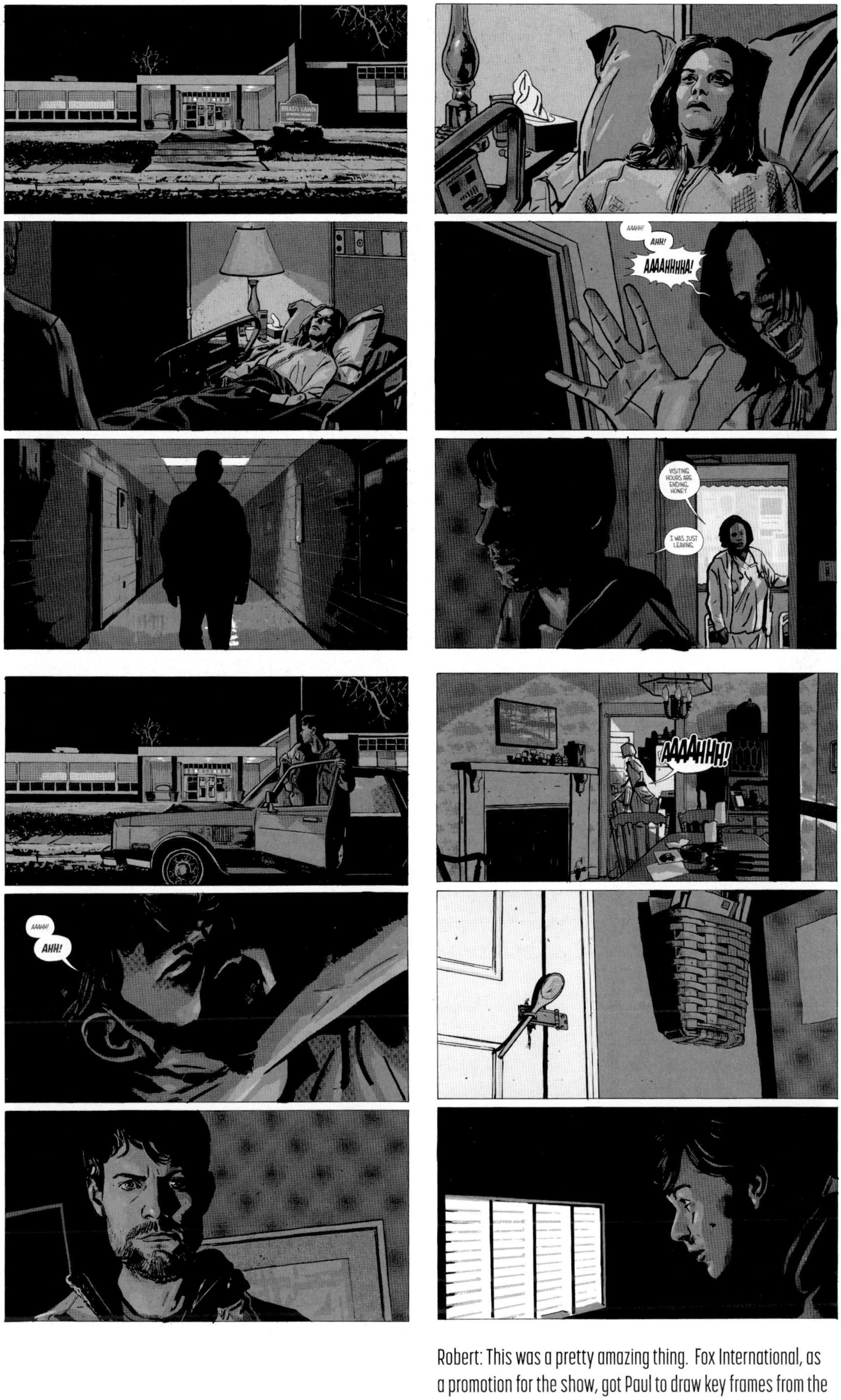
AAAHH!
AHH!
AAAAHHHHA!
VISITING HOURS ARE ENDING, HONEY.
I WAS JUST LEAVING.
AAAAHHH!
AAAHH!
AHH!

Robert: This was a pretty amazing thing. Fox International, as a promotion for the show, got Paul to draw key frames from the show, and then they gave these to artists all around the world to paint onto buildings in cities around the world. So each of these drawings ended up in some form or another on massive buildings, billboard-sized, for all to see.

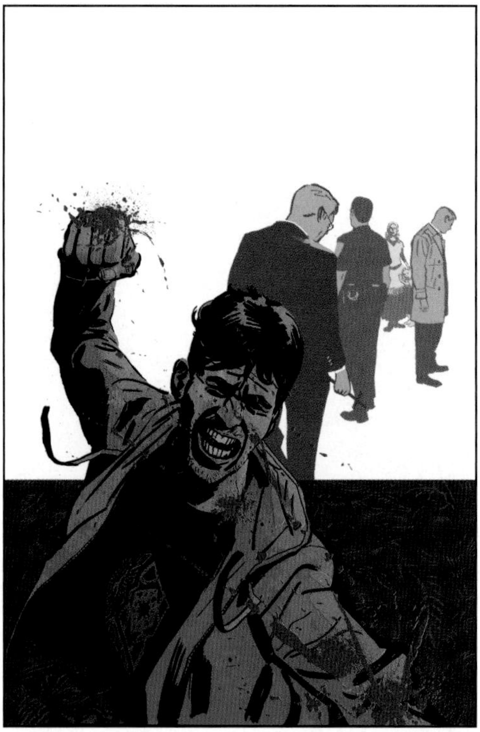

Robert: Sometimes things just don't come together. This image here was the original cover to the volume one trade paperback collection. It's cool... it is, but I just didn't like it after a while. So that's how we ended up with the "sad Kyle, small house" cover... that I think is MUCH better.

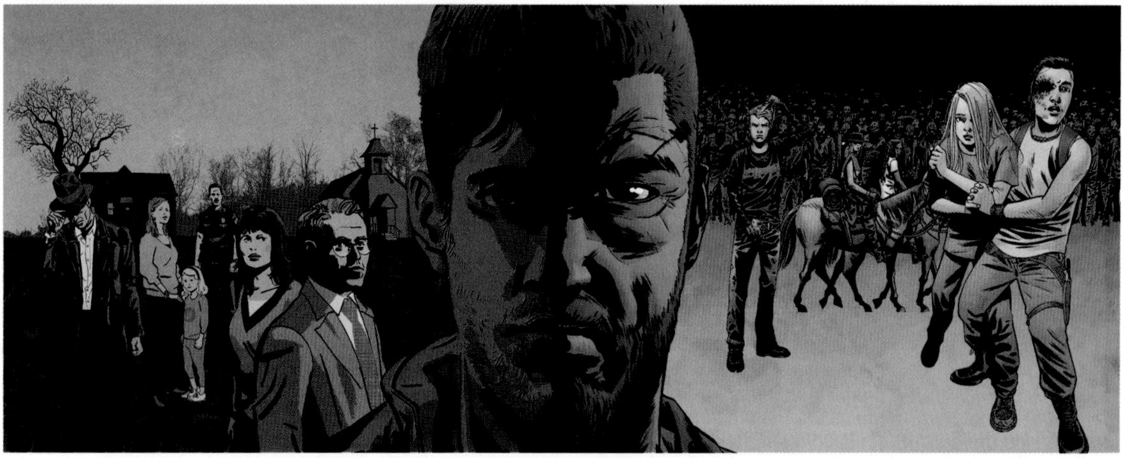

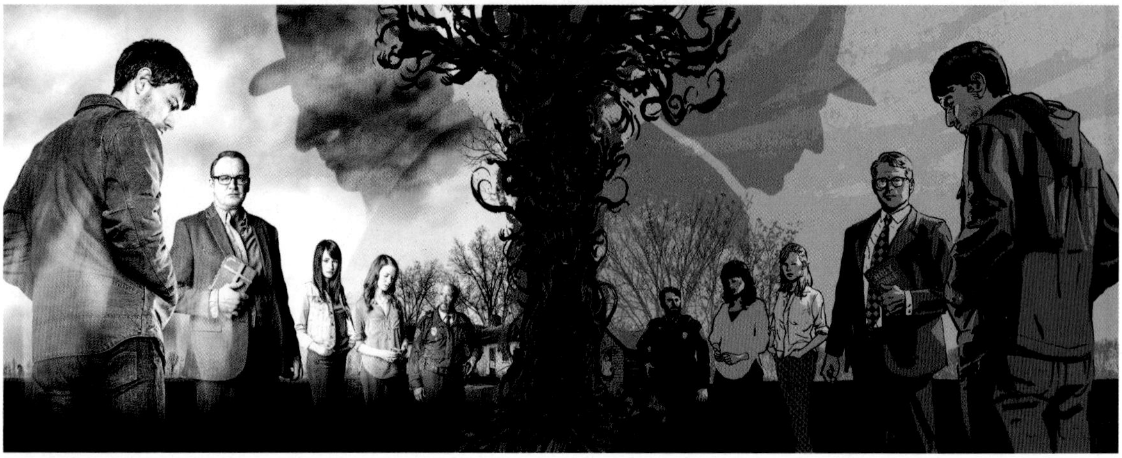

Robert: Comic-Con banners! At the awesome Image/Skybound booth at San Diego Comic-Con International, there's a massive twenty-foot-tall wall that we get to decorate each year. The comic OUTCAST/THE WALKING DEAD banner was used in 2015, and the cool show/comic combo was used in 2016. To me, it's pretty cool because we did a similar show/comic banner for THE WALKING DEAD in 2010, the year that show debuted.

Robert: We are complete sellouts. This is a drawing Paul did for a Scion promotion that featured OUTCAST. They actually made a haunted OUTCAST Scion that was really really really cool and really really really sellouty... if that's a word. You should Google it, it looks really cool.

Robert: This AWESOME thing here was a MASSIVE retailer poster used to launch the series. This poster was the size of traditional 3-sheet movie posters from the olden days of movie posters. Which means it was 40 inches wide and 81 inches tall... HUGE! It was one of the coolest things I've ever done for a series of mine. I love that poster.

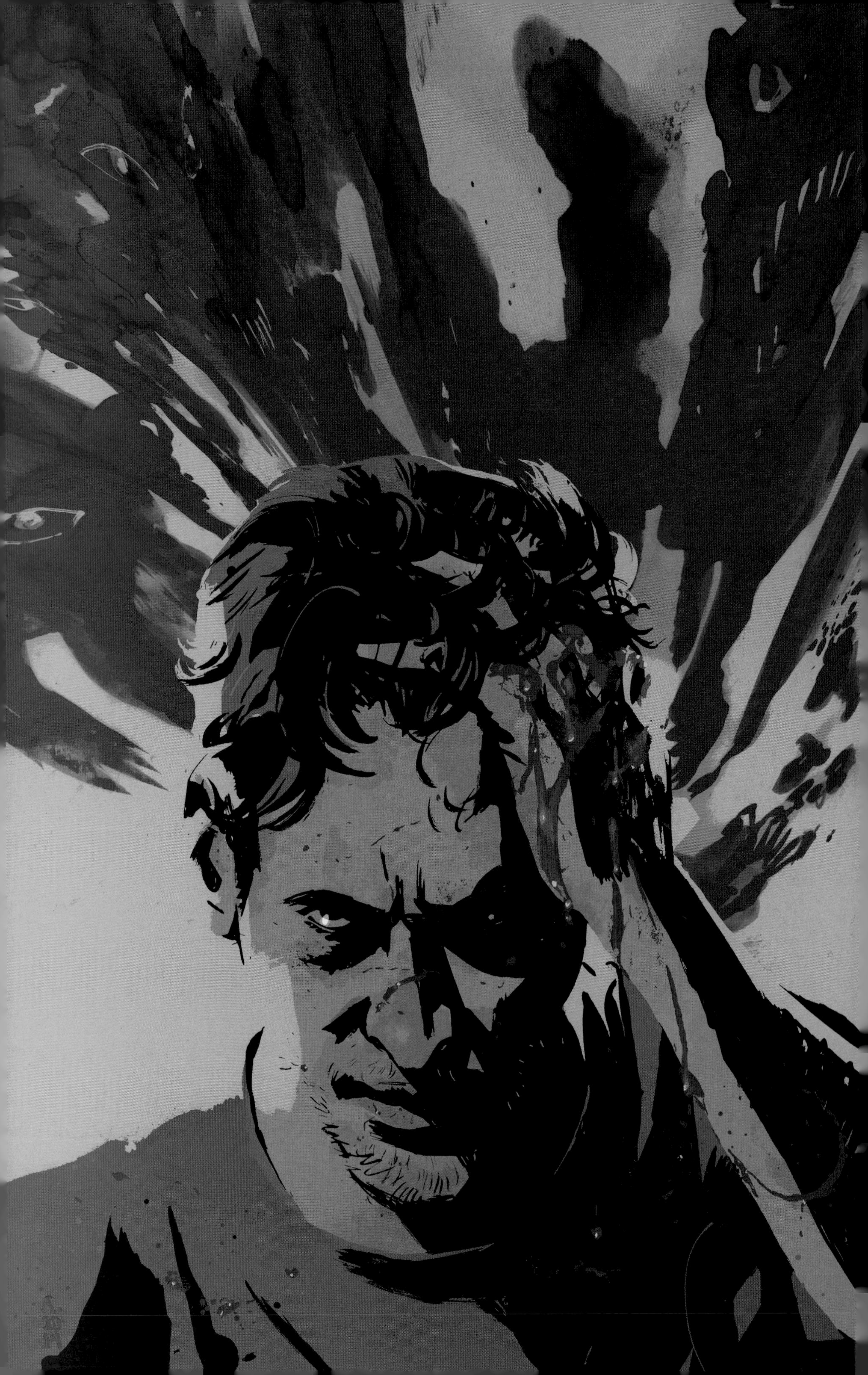

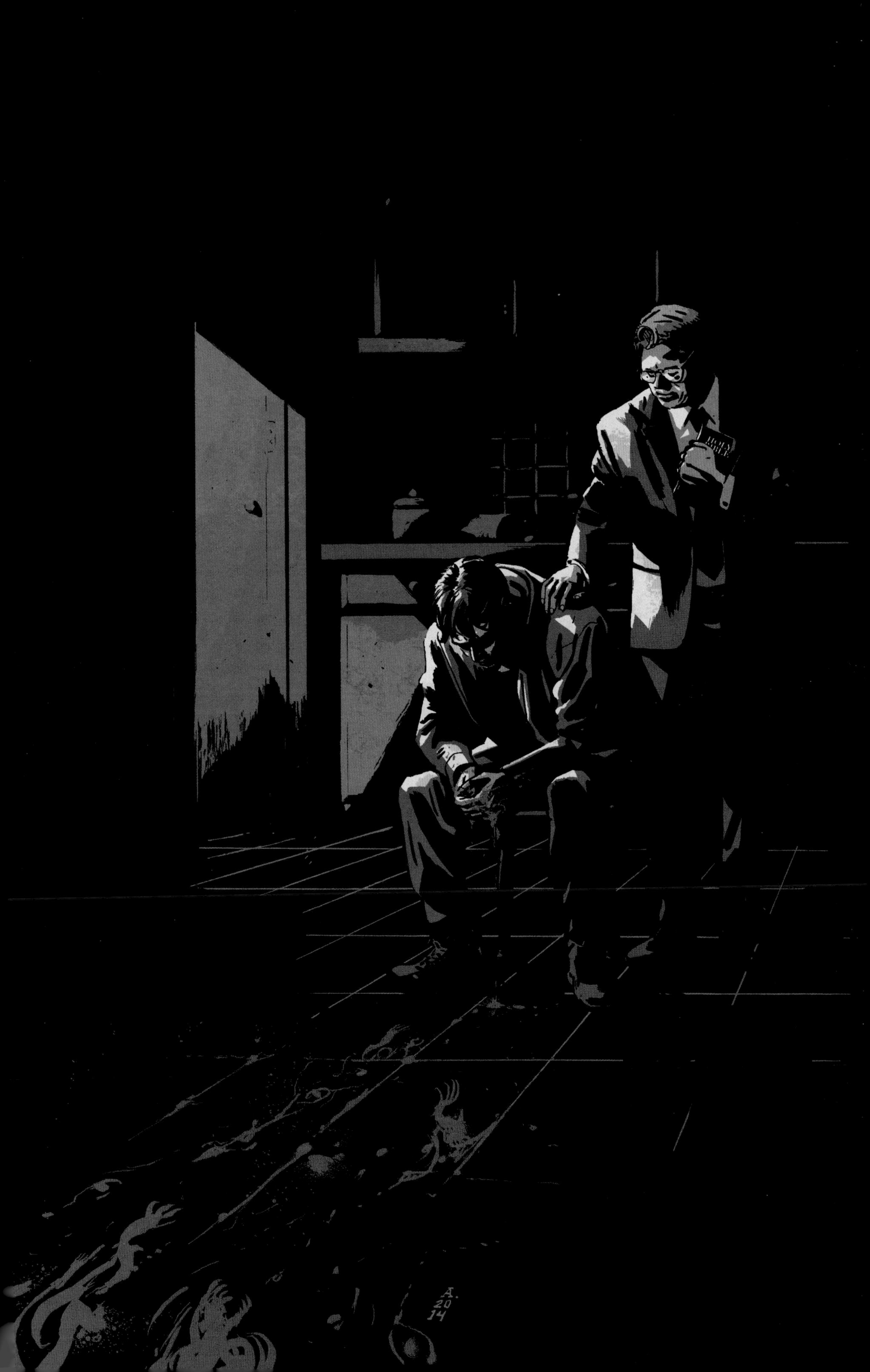
A. 2014

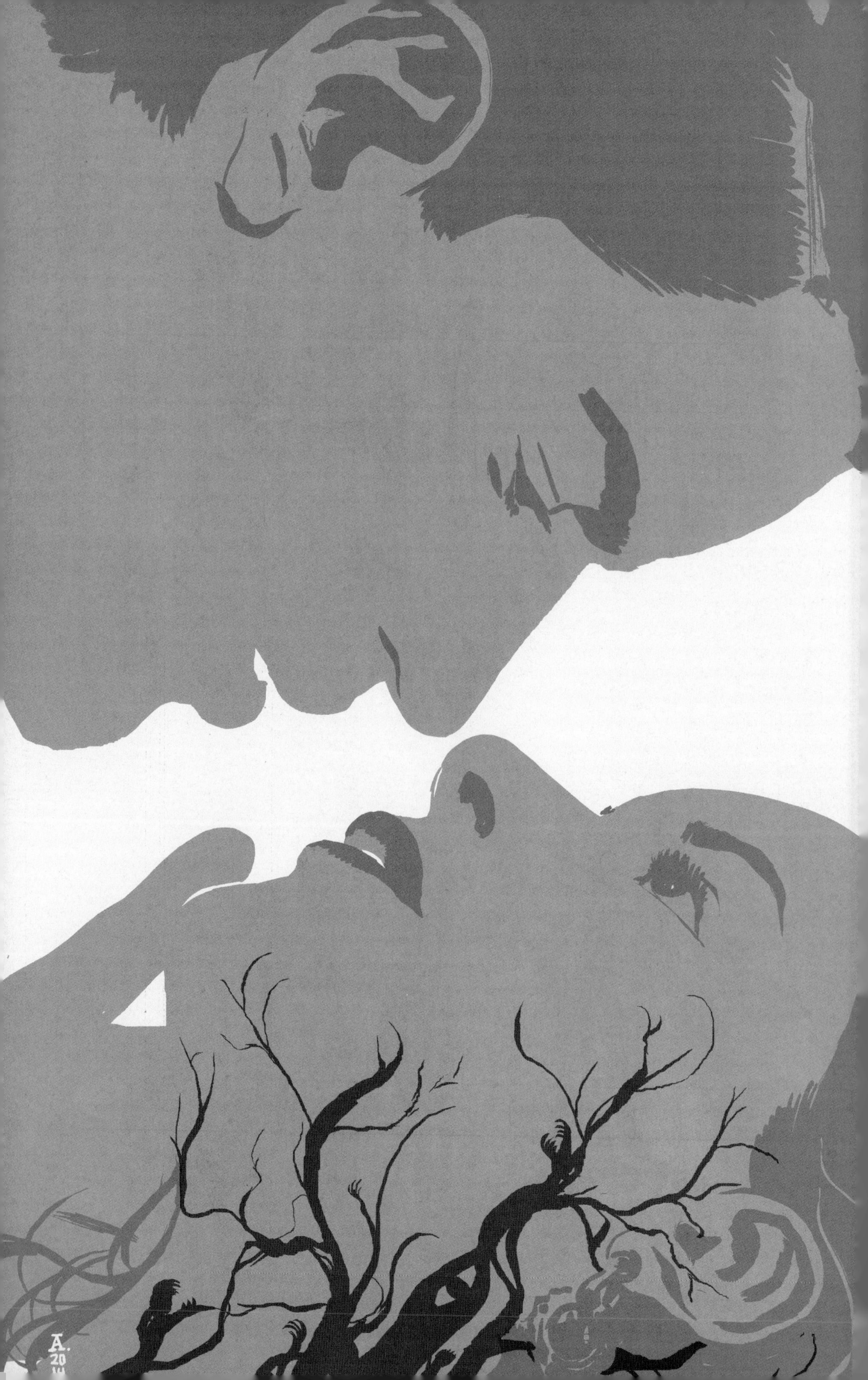

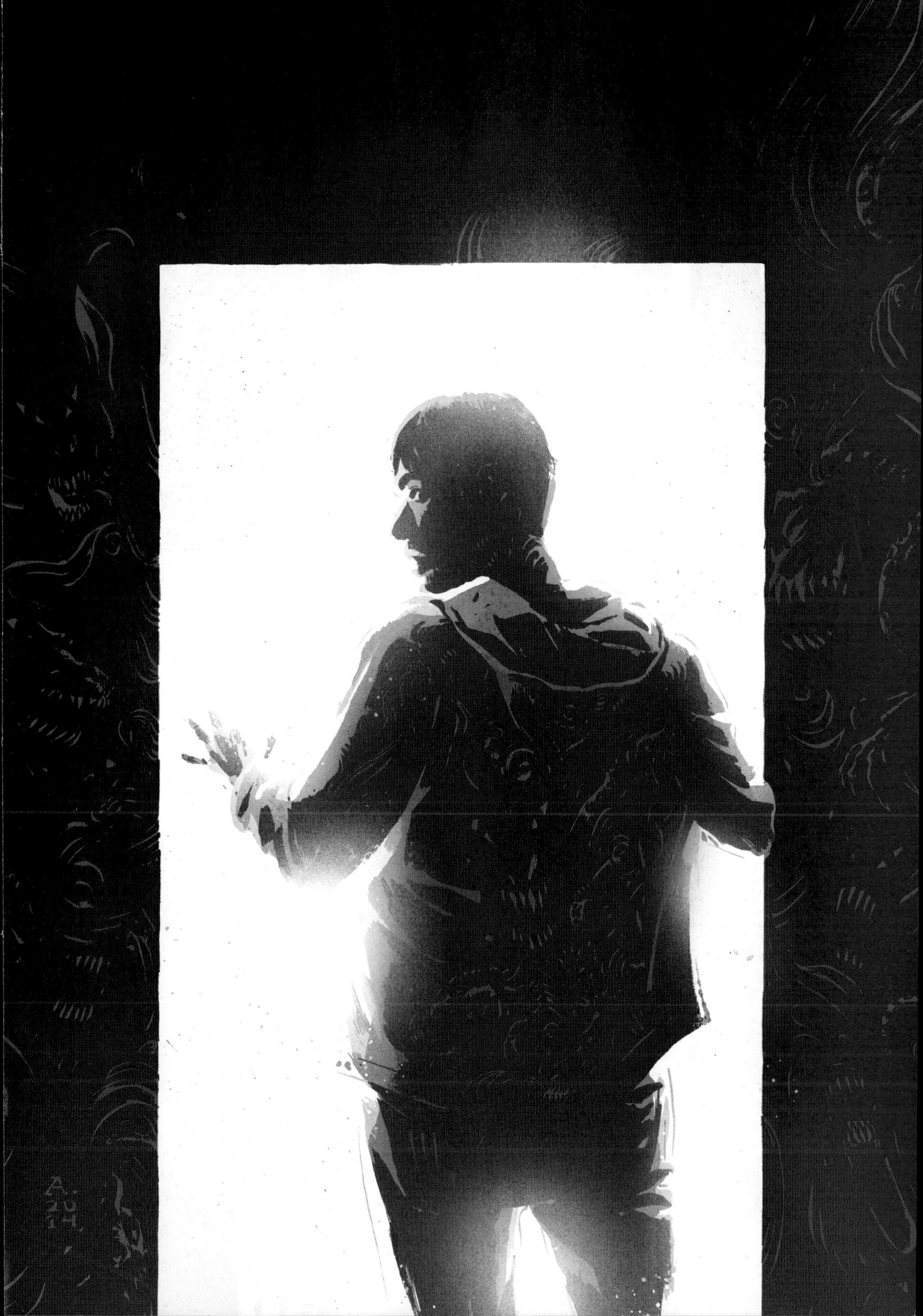

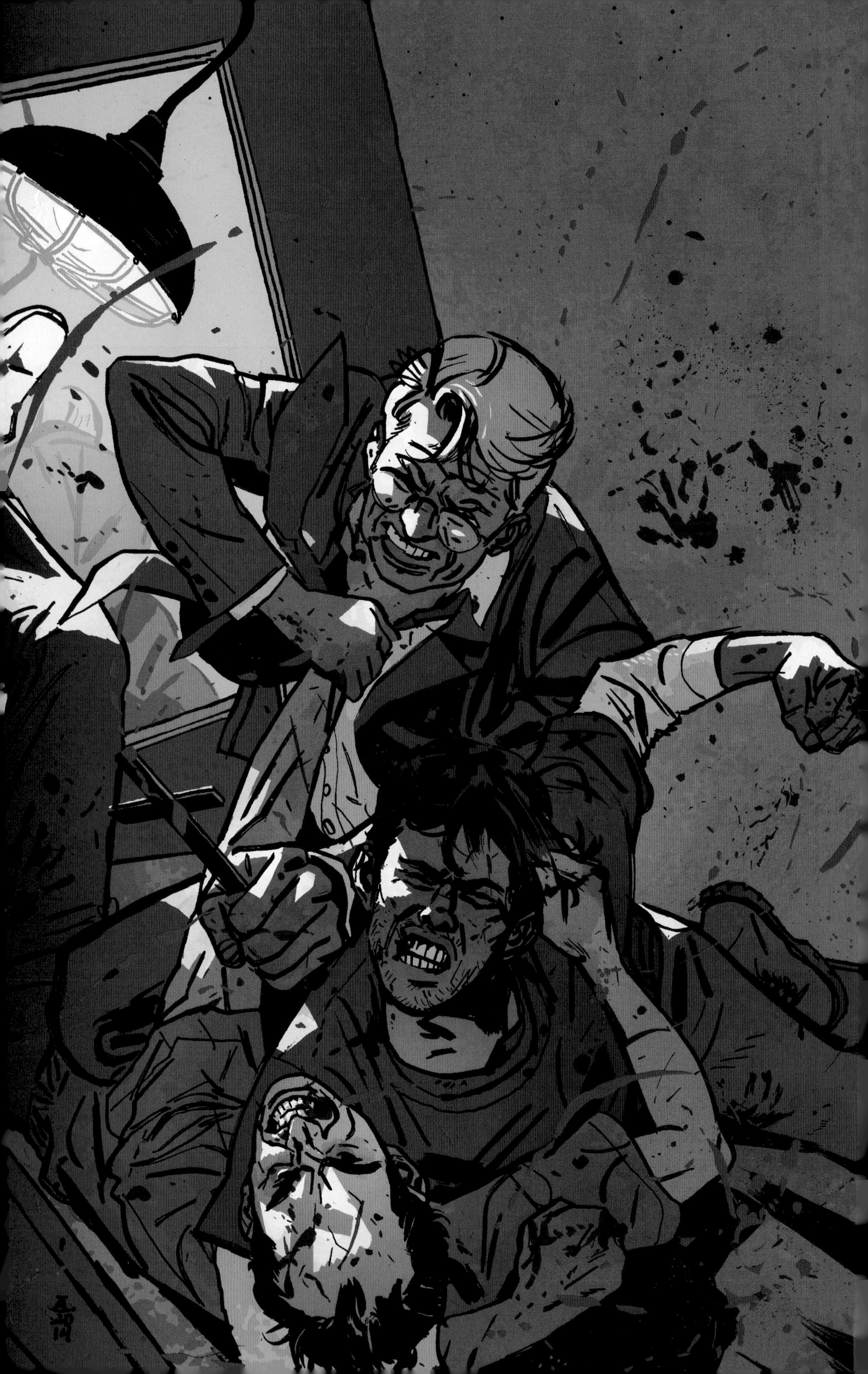

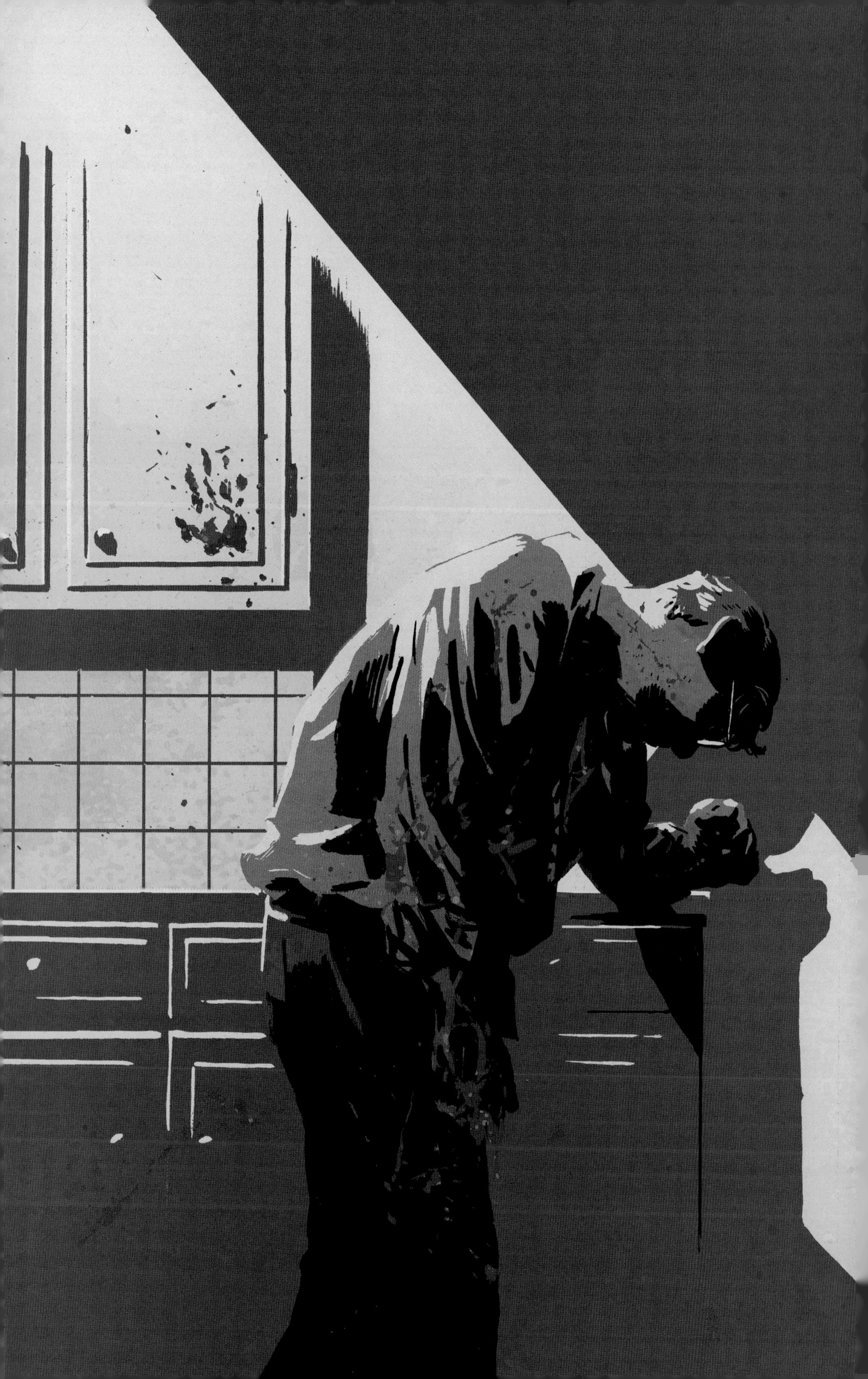

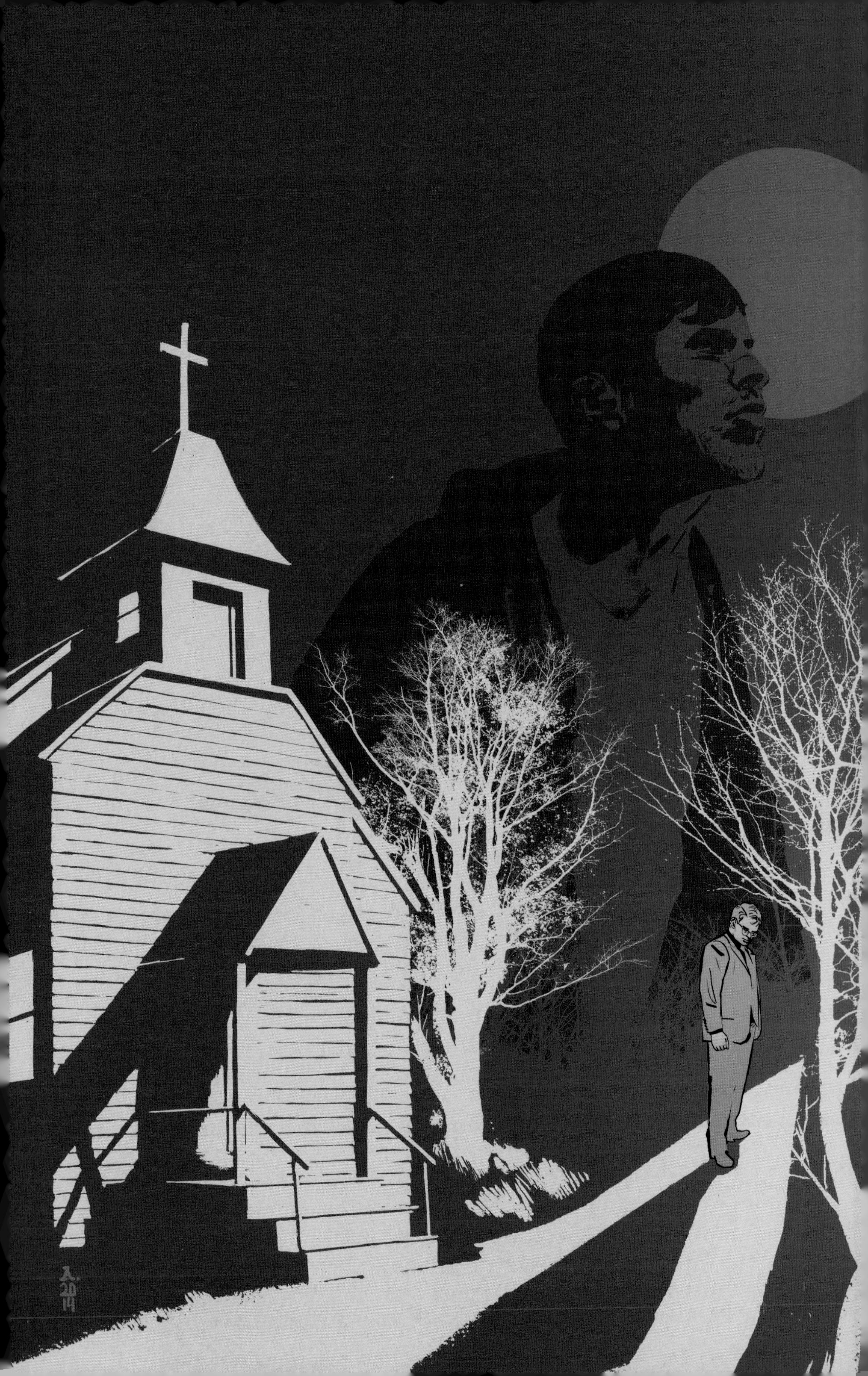

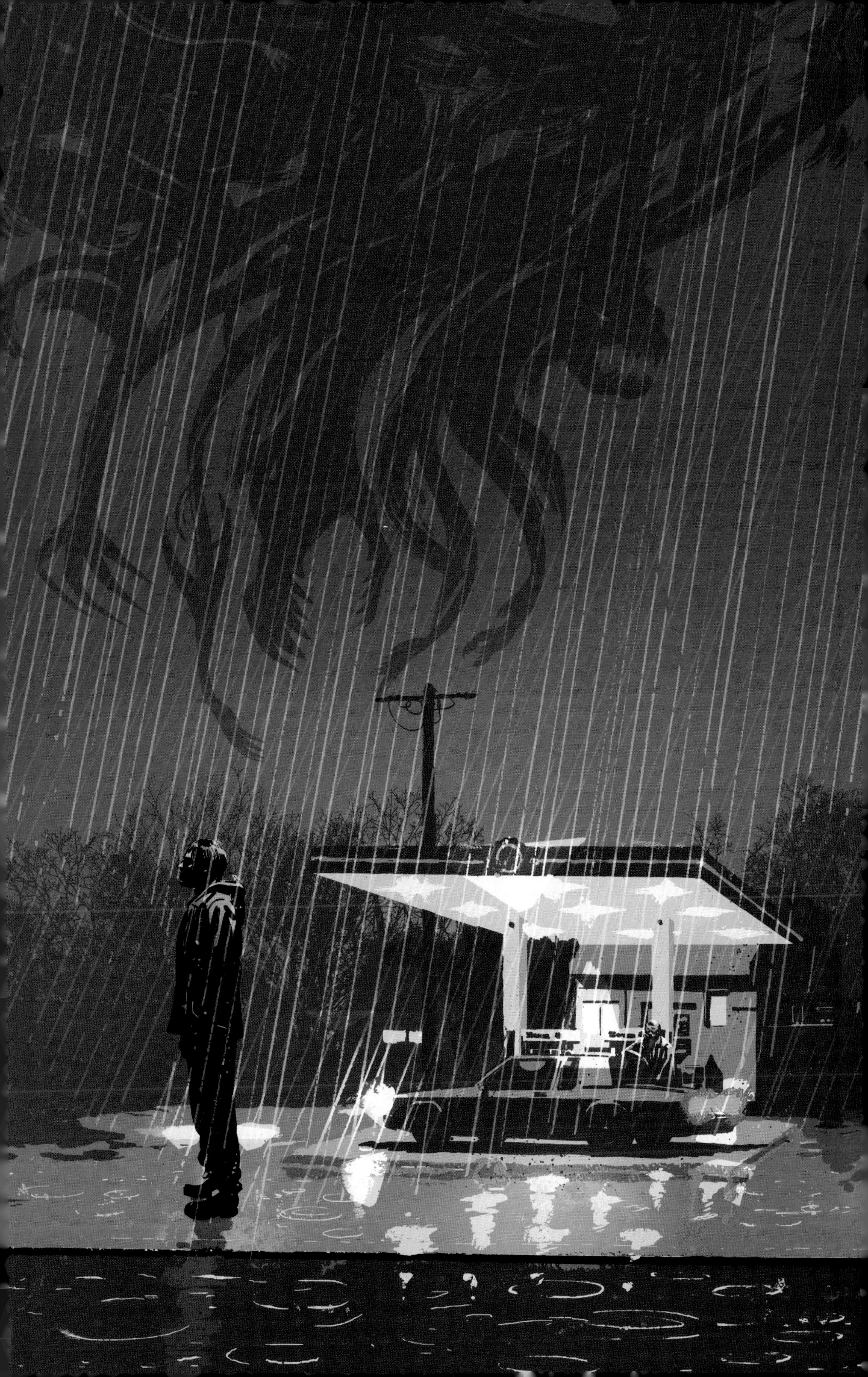

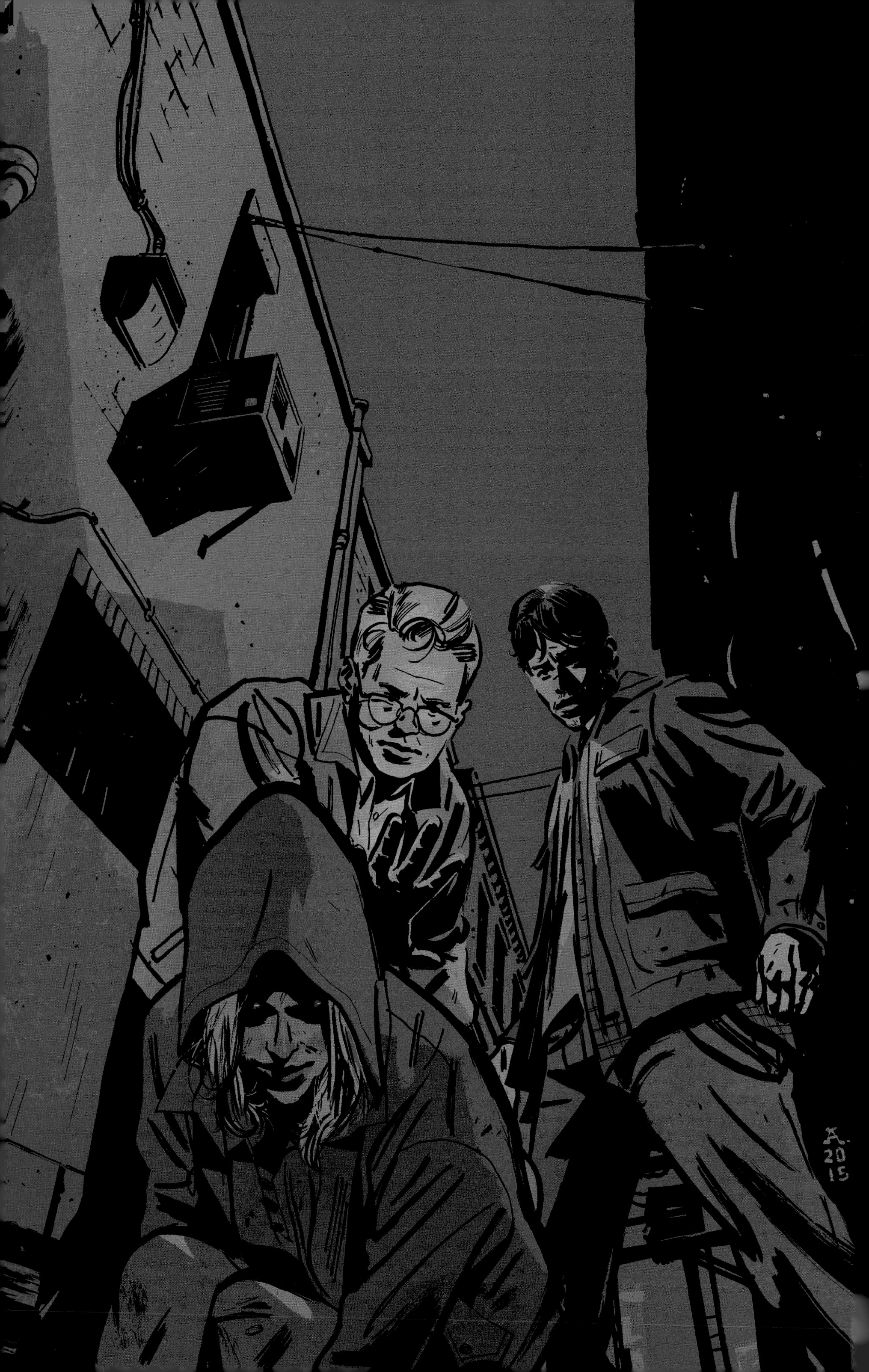
A.
20
15

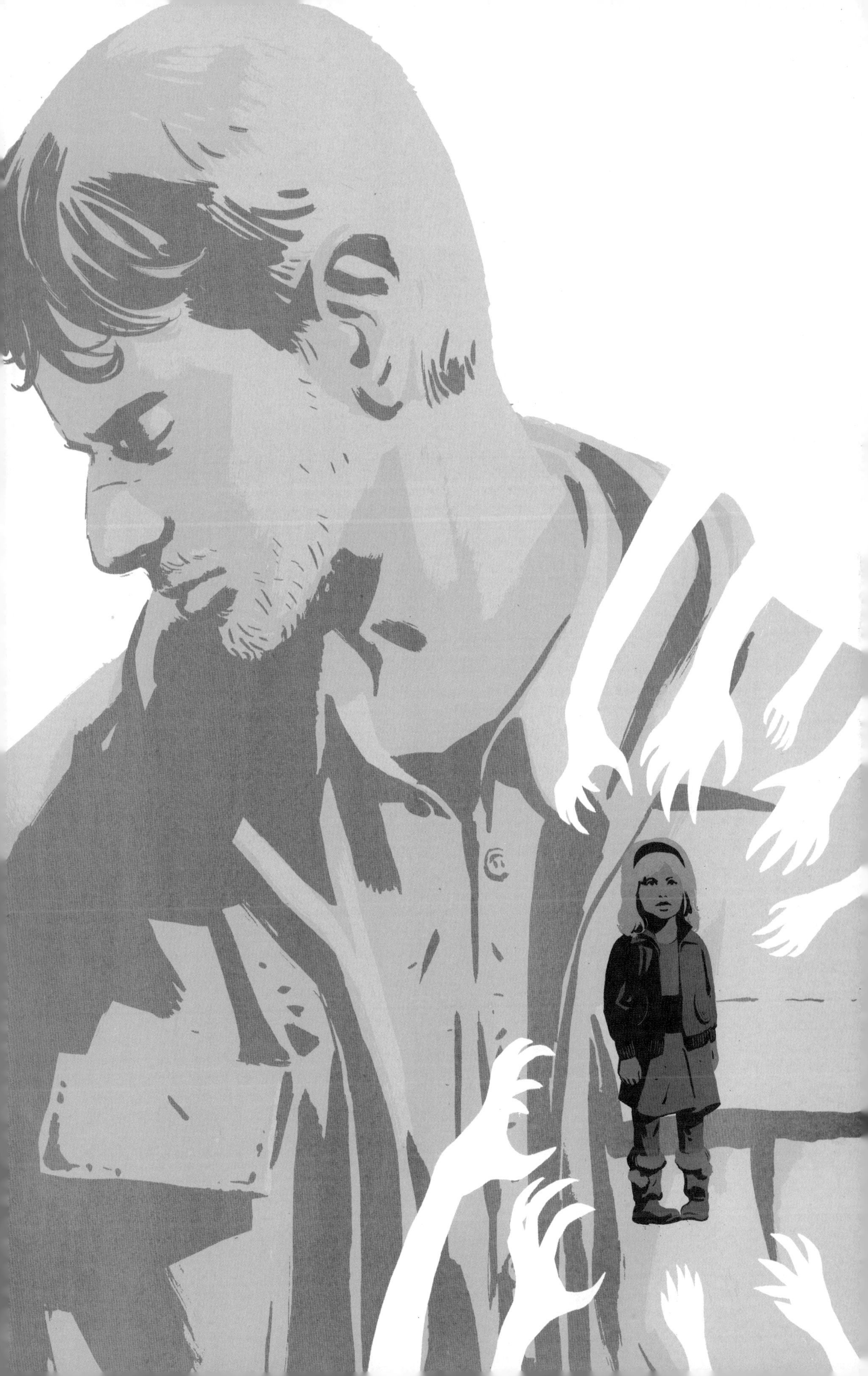

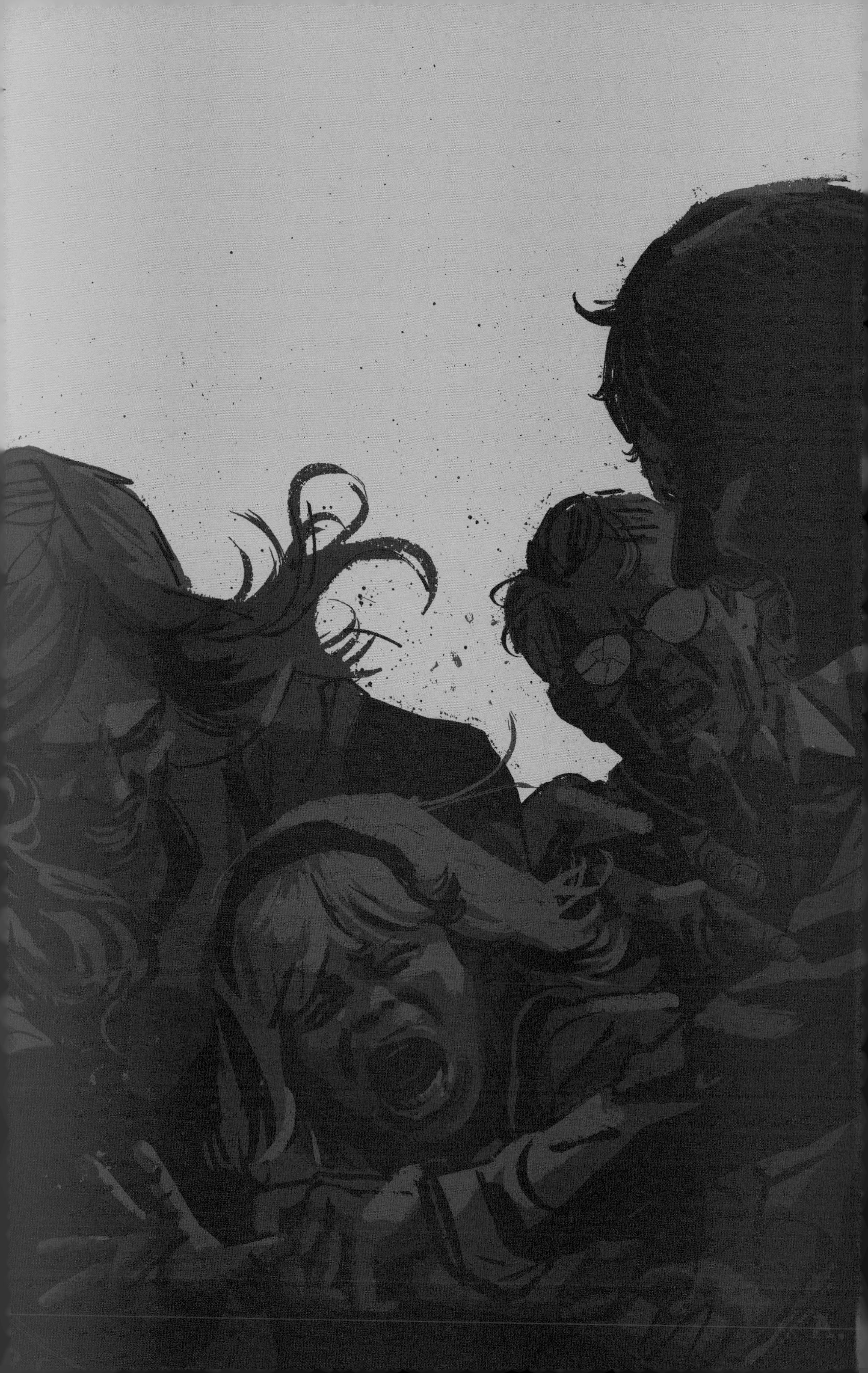

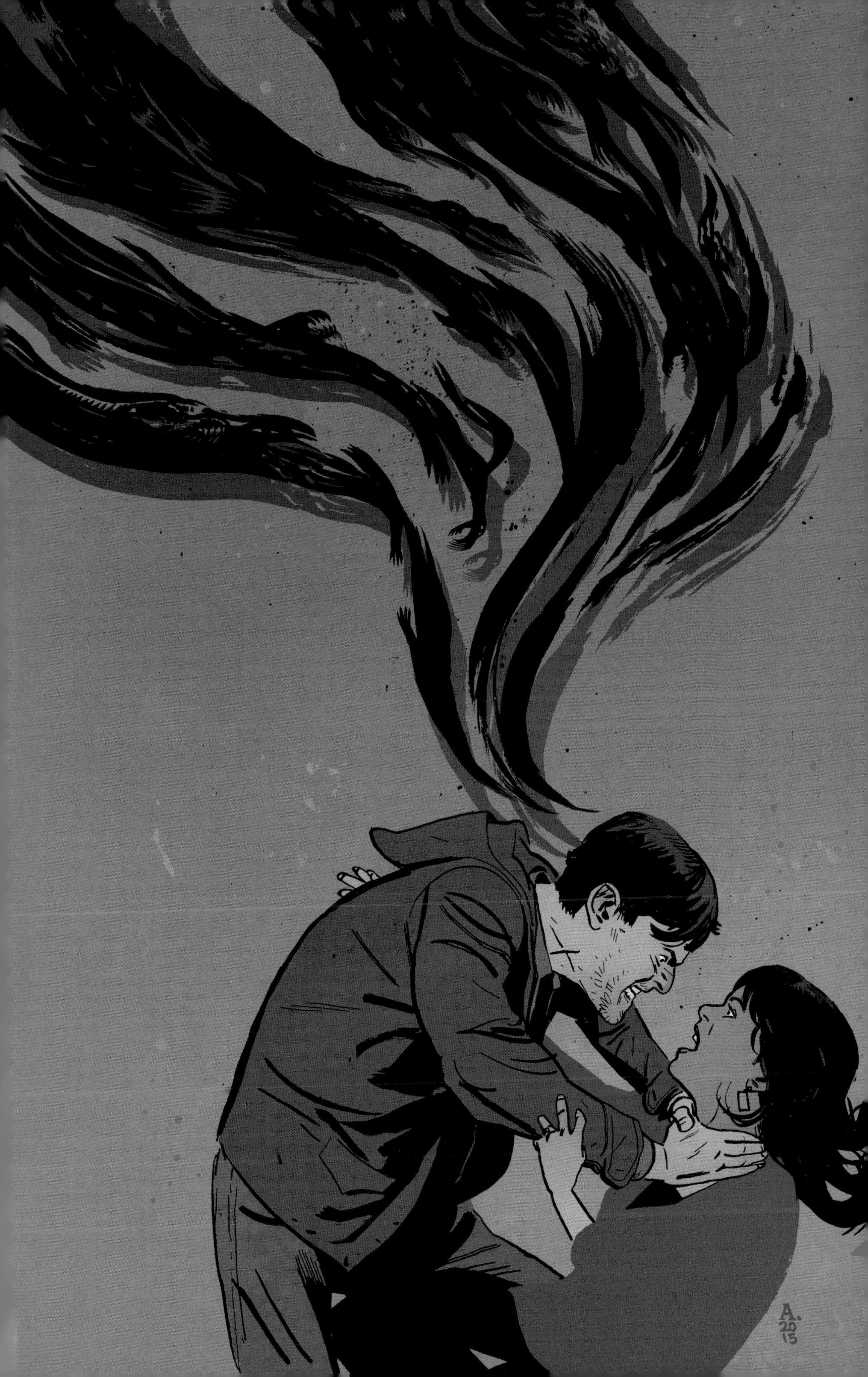
A.
2015

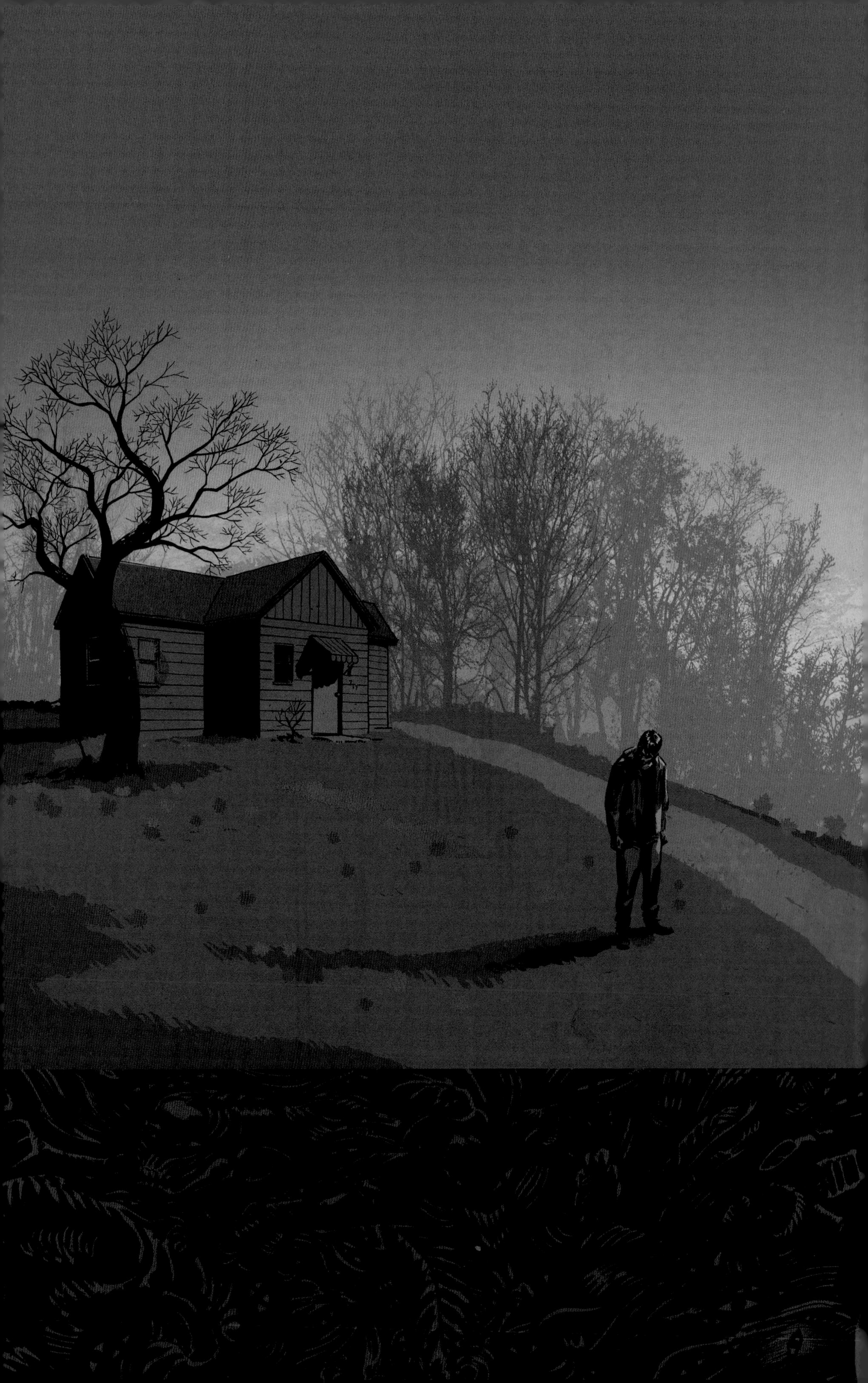

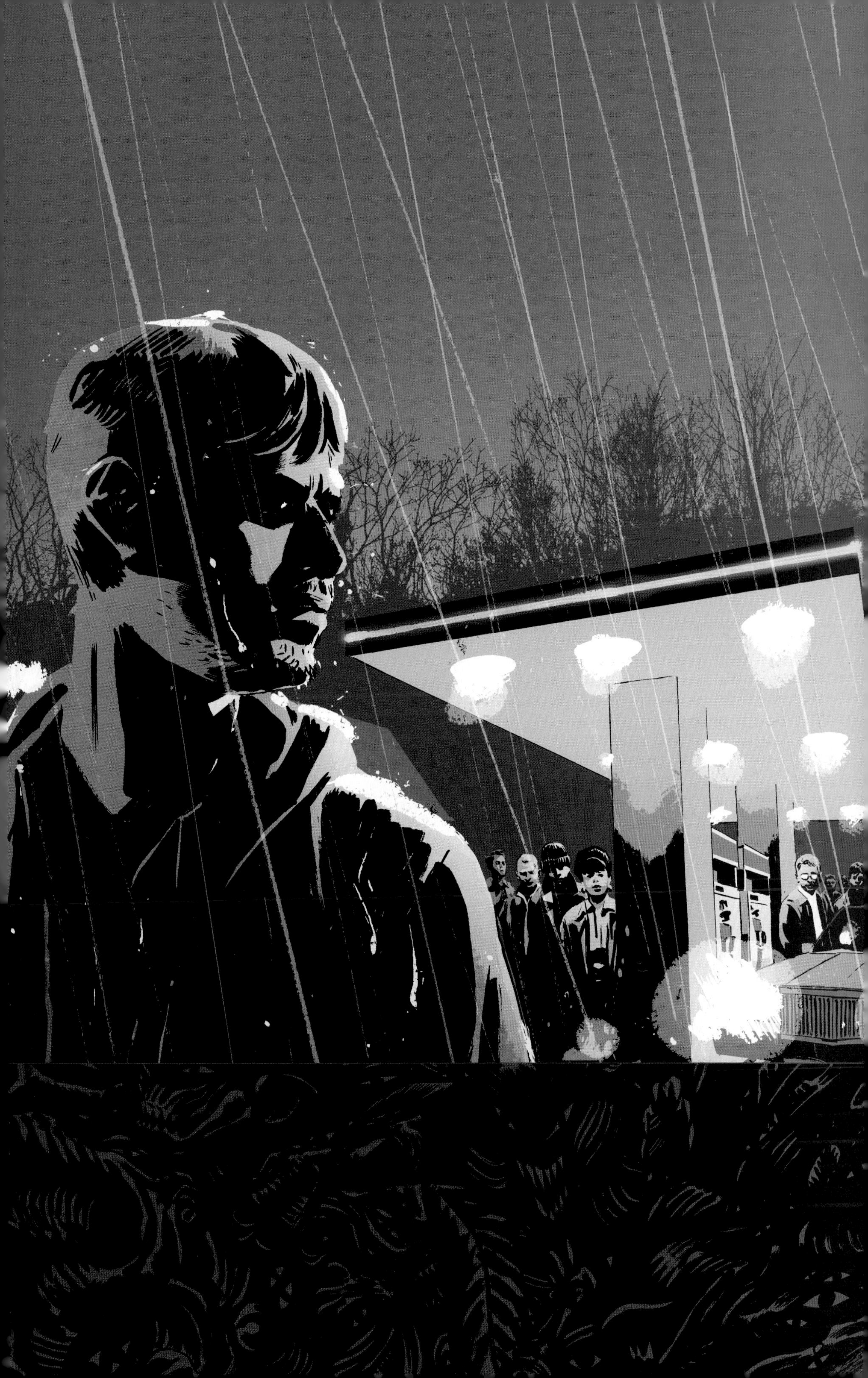

FOR MORE TALES FROM **ROBERT KIRKMAN** AND **SKYBOUND**

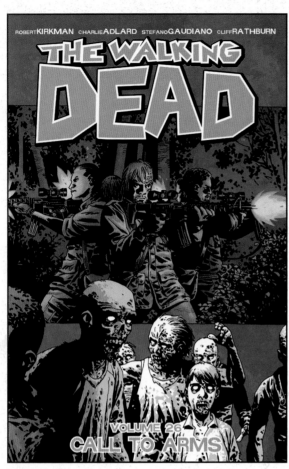

ROBERT KIRKMAN CHARLIE ADLARD STEFANO GAUDIANO CLIFF RATHBURN
THE WALKING DEAD
VOLUME 26
CALL TO ARMS

VOL. 1: DAYS GONE BYE TP
ISBN: 978-1-58240-672-5
$14.99

VOL. 2: MILES BEHIND US TP
ISBN: 978-1-58240-775-3
$14.99

VOL. 3: SAFETY BEHIND BARS TP
ISBN: 978-1-58240-805-7
$14.99

VOL. 4: THE HEART'S DESIRE TP
ISBN: 978-1-58240-530-8
$14.99

VOL. 5: THE BEST DEFENSE TP
ISBN: 978-1-58240-612-1
$14.99

VOL. 6: THIS SORROWFUL LIFE TP
ISBN: 978-1-58240-684-8
$14.99

VOL. 7: THE CALM BEFORE TP
ISBN: 978-1-58240-828-6
$14.99

VOL. 8: MADE TO SUFFER TP
ISBN: 978-1-58240-883-5
$14.99

VOL. 9: HERE WE REMAIN TP
ISBN: 978-1-60706-022-2
$14.99

VOL. 10: WHAT WE BECOME TP
ISBN: 978-1-60706-075-8
$14.99

VOL. 11: FEAR THE HUNTERS TP
ISBN: 978-1-60706-181-6
$14.99

VOL. 12: LIFE AMONG THEM TP
ISBN: 978-1-60706-254-7
$14.99

VOL. 13: TOO FAR GONE TP
ISBN: 978-1-60706-329-2
$14.99

VOL. 14: NO WAY OUT TP
ISBN: 978-1-60706-392-6
$14.99

VOL. 15: WE FIND OURSELVES TP
ISBN: 978-1-60706-440-4
$14.99

VOL. 16: A LARGER WORLD TP
ISBN: 978-1-60706-559-3
$14.99

VOL. 17: SOMETHING TO FEAR TP
ISBN: 978-1-60706-615-6
$14.99

VOL. 18: WHAT COMES AFTER TP
ISBN: 978-1-60706-687-3
$14.99

VOL. 19: MARCH TO WAR TP
ISBN: 978-1-60706-818-1
$14.99

VOL. 20: ALL OUT WAR PART ONE TP
ISBN: 978-1-60706-882-2
$14.99

VOL. 21: ALL OUT WAR PART TWO TP
ISBN: 978-1-63215-030-1
$14.99

VOL. 22: A NEW BEGINNING TP
ISBN: 978-1-63215-041-7
$14.99

VOL. 23: WHISPERS INTO SCREAMS TP
ISBN: 978-1-63215-258-9
$14.99

VOL. 24: LIFE AND DEATH TP
ISBN: 978-1-63215-402-6
$14.99

VOL. 25: NO TURNING BACK TP
ISBN: 978-1-63215-659-4
$14.99

VOL. 26: CALL TO ARMS TP
ISBN: 978-1-63215-917-5
$14.99

VOL. 1: SPANISH EDITION TP
ISBN: 978-1-60706-797-9
$14.99

VOL. 2: SPANISH EDITION TP
ISBN: 978-1-60706-845-7
$14.99

VOL. 3: SPANISH EDITION TP
ISBN: 978-1-60706-883-9
$14.99

VOL. 4: SPANISH EDITION TP
ISBN: 978-1-63215-035-6
$14.99

COMPENDIUM TP, VOL. 1
ISBN: 978-1-60706-076-5
$59.99

COMPENDIUM TP, VOL. 2
ISBN: 978-1-60706-596-8
$59.99

COMPENDIUM TP, VOL. 3
ISBN: 978-1-63215-456-9
$59.99

BOOK ONE HC
ISBN: 978-1-58240-619-0
$34.99

BOOK TWO HC
ISBN: 978-1-58240-698-5
$34.99

BOOK THREE HC
ISBN: 978-1-58240-825-5
$34.99

BOOK FOUR HC
ISBN: 978-1-60706-000-0
$34.99

BOOK FIVE HC
ISBN: 978-1-60706-171-7
$34.99

BOOK SIX HC
ISBN: 978-1-60706-327-8
$34.99

BOOK SEVEN HC
ISBN: 978-1-60706-439-8
$34.99

BOOK EIGHT HC
ISBN: 978-1-60706-593-7
$34.99

BOOK NINE HC
ISBN: 978-1-60706-798-6
$34.99

BOOK TEN HC
ISBN: 978-1-63215-034-9
$34.99

BOOK ELEVEN HC
ISBN: 978-1-63215-271-8
$34.99

BOOK TWELVE HC
ISBN: 978-1-63215-451-4
$34.99

BOOK THIRTEEN HC
ISBN: 978-1-63215-916-8
$34.99

BIRTHRIGHT
WILLIAMSON BRESSAN LUCAS
VOLUME THREE
ALLIES AND ENEMIES

VOL. 1: HOMECOMING TP
ISBN: 978-1-63215-231-2
$9.99

VOL. 2: CALL TO ADVENTURE TP
ISBN: 978-1-63215-446-0
$12.99

VOL. 3: ALLIES AND ENEMIES TP
ISBN: 978-1-63215-683-9
$12.99

WILLIAMSON LACI RYP MRVA
GHOSTED
VOLUME FOUR · GHOST TOWN

VOL. 1: HAUNTED HEIST TP
ISBN: 978-1-60706-836-5
$9.99

VOL. 2: BOOKS OF THE DEAD TP
ISBN: 978-1-63215-046-2
$12.99

VOL. 3: DEATH WISH TP
ISBN: 978-1-63215-051-6
$12.99

VOL. 4: GHOST TOWN TP
ISBN: 978-1-63215-317-3
$12.99

MANIFEST DESTINY
VOLUME 3 · CHIROPTERA & CARNIFORMAVES

VOL. 1: FLORA & FAUNA TP
ISBN: 978-1-60706-982-9
$9.99

VOL. 2: AMPHIBIA & INSECTA TP
ISBN: 978-1-63215-052-3
$14.99

VOL. 3: CHIROPTERA & CARNIFORMAVES TP
ISBN: 978-1-63215-397-5
$14.99

THIEF OF THIEVES
VOLUME 5
"TAKE ME."

VOL. 1: "I QUIT."
ISBN: 978-1-60706-592-0
$14.99

VOL. 2: "HELP ME."
ISBN: 978-1-60706-676-7
$14.99

VOL. 3: "VENICE."
ISBN: 978-1-60706-844-0
$14.99

VOL. 4: "THE HIT LIST."
ISBN: 978-1-63215-037-0
$14.99

VOL. 5: "TAKE ME."
ISBN: 978-1-63215-401-9
$14.99

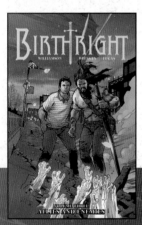

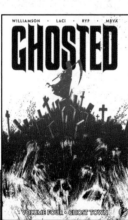

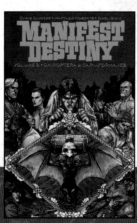

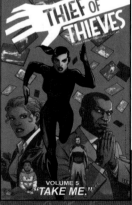